≠9910 41

D1481699

Lineberger Memorial

Library

Lutheran Theological Southern Seminary   Columbia, S. C.

THE LOEB CLASSICAL LIBRARY

FOUNDED BY JAMES LOEB

EDITED BY

G. P. GOOLD

PREVIOUS EDITORS

| T. E. PAGE | E. CAPPS |
| W. H. D. ROUSE | L. A. POST |

E. H. WARMINGTON

TACITUS

III

LCL 249

THE LOEB CLASSICAL LIBRARY

FOUNDED BY JAMES LOEB

EDITED BY

G. P. GOOLD

PREVIOUS EDITORS

T. E. PAGE   E. CAPPS

W. H. D. ROUSE   L. A. POST

E. H. WARMINGTON

TACITUS

III

LCL 249

F9910 41

TACITUS

THE HISTORIES
BOOKS IV–V

WITH AN ENGLISH TRANSLATION BY

CLIFFORD H. MOORE

THE ANNALS
BOOKS I–III

WITH AN ENGLISH TRANSLATION BY

JOHN JACKSON

HARVARD UNIVERSITY PRESS
CAMBRIDGE, MASSACHUSETTS
LONDON, ENGLAND

First published 1931
Reprinted 1943, 1951, 1956, 1962, 1969, 1979, 1992, 1998

LOEB CLASSICAL LIBRARY® is a registered trademark
of the President and Fellows of Harvard College

ISBN 0-674-99274-1

*Printed in Great Britain by St Edmundsbury Press Ltd,
Bury St Edmunds, Suffolk, on acid-free paper.
Bound by Hunter & Foulis Ltd, Edinburgh, Scotland.*

CONTENTS

BIBLIOGRAPHICAL NOTE (1979)

Editions with commentary:

Histories
W. A. Spooner, London 1891
H. Heubner, I (1963); II (1968); III (1972), Heidelberg

Annals
H. Furneaux, I-VI (1896); XI-XVI (rev. Pelham, Fisher 1907), Oxford
Erich Koestermann, 4 vols, Heidelberg 1963–1968
F. R. D. Goodyear, I 1–54, Cambridge (*CTC* 15) 1972

Studies:
B. Walker, *The 'Annals' of Tacitus*, Manchester 1960[2]
Sir Ronald Syme, *Tacitus*, 2 vols, Oxford 1958 (monumental)
Sir Ronald Syme, *Ten Studies in Tacitus*, Oxford 1970

Lexicons:
P. Fabia, *Onomasticon Taciteum*, Paris–Lyons 1900
A. Gerber and A. Greef (compl. C. John), *Lexicon Taciteum*, Leipzig 1903

Surveys of Scholarship:
Classical World (*Weekly*): volumes 48 (1954) 121; 58 (1964) 69; 63 (1970) 253; 71 (1977) 1
F. R. D. Goodyear, *Tacitus: Greece and Rome Surveys 4*, Oxford 1970

THE HISTORIES OF TACITUS

BOOK IV

CORNELII TACITI

HISTORIARUM

LIBER IV

I. Interfecto Vitellio bellum magis desierat quam
pax coeperat. Armati per urbem victores implaca-
bili odio victos consectabantur : plenae caedibus
viae, cruenta fora templaque, passim trucidatis, ut
quemque fors[1] obtulerat. Ac mox augescente licentia
scrutari ac protrahere abditos; si quem procerum
habitu et iuventa conspexerant, obtruncare nullo
militum aut populi discrimine. Quae saevitia recentibus odiis sanguine explebatur, dein verterat in
avaritiam. Nihil usquam secretum aut clausum
sinebant, Vitellianos occultari simulantes. Initium
id perfringendarum domuum, vel si resisteretur,
causa caedis; nec deerat egentissimus quisque e
plebe et pessimi servitiorum prodere ultro ditis
dominos, alii ab amicis monstrabantur. Ubique
lamenta, conclamationes et fortuna[2] captae urbis,
adeo ut Othoniani Vitellianique militis invidiosa

---

[1] fors M^2: sors M.
[2] fortunae M.

THE HISTORIES OF
TACITUS

BOOK IV

I. THE death of Vitellius was rather the end of war than the beginning of peace. The victors ranged through the city in arms, pursuing their defeated foes with implacable hatred: the streets were full of carnage, the fora and temples reeked with blood; they slew right and left everyone whom chance put in their way. Presently, as their licence increased, they began to hunt out and drag into the light those who had concealed themselves; did they espy anyone who was tall and young, they cut him down, regardless whether he was soldier or civilian. Their ferocity, which found satisfaction in bloodshed while their hatred was fresh, turned then afterwards to greed. They let no place remain secret or closed, pretending that Vitellians were in hiding. This led to the forcing of private houses or, if resistance was made, became an excuse for murder. Nor was there any lack of starvelings among the mob or of the vilest slaves ready to betray their rich masters; others were pointed out by their friends. Everywhere were lamentations, cries of anguish, and the misfortunes that befall a captured city; so that the citizens actually longed for the licence of Otho's and Vitellius's

antea petulantia desideraretur. Duces partium accendendo[1] civili bello acres, temperandae victoriae impares, quippe inter[2] turbas et discordias pessimo cuique plurima vis, pax et quies bonis artibus indigent.

II. Nomen sedemque Caesaris Domitianus acceperat, nondum ad curas intentus, sed stupris et adulteriis filium principis agebat. Praefectura praetorii penes Arrium Varum, summa potentiae in Primo Antonio. Is pecuniam familiamque e principis domo quasi Cremonensem praedam rapere: ceteri modestia vel ignobilitate ut in bello obscuri, ita praemiorum expertes. Civitas pavida et servitio parata occupari redeuntem Tarracina L. Vitellium cum cohortibus extinguique reliqua belli postulabat: praemissi Ariciam equites, agmen legionum intra Bovillas stetit. Nec cunctatus est Vitellius seque et cohortis arbitrio victoris permittere, et miles infelicia arma haud minus ira quam metu abiecit. Longus deditorum ordo saeptus armatis per urbem incessit, nemo supplici vultu, sed tristes et truces et adversum plausus ac lasciviam insultantis vulgi immobiles. Paucos erumpere ausos circumiecti oppressere;[3] ceteri in custodiam conditi, nihil quisquam locutus

---

[1] accendo *M.*   [2] inter *Wurm:* in *M.*
[3] oppressere *Faernus:* pressere *M.*

---

[1] Cf. iii. 86.
[2] Bovillae was ten miles from Rome on the Appian Way, Aricia sixteen.

soldiers, which earlier they had detested. The generals of the Flavian party, who had been quick to start the conflagration of civil war, were unequal to the task of controlling their victory, for in times of violence and civil strife the worst men have the greatest power; peace and quiet call for honest arts.

II. Domitian had accepted the name of Caesar and the imperial residence,[1] with no care as yet for his duties; but with debauchery and adulteries he played the part of an emperor's son. The prefecture of the Praetorian watch was held by Arrius Varus, but the supreme authority was exercised by Antonius Primus. He appropriated money and slaves from the emperor's palace as if it were the booty of Cremona; all the other leaders, whom modesty or humble lineage had made obscure in war, had accordingly no share of the rewards. The citizens were in a state of terror and quite ready for slavery; they demanded that Lucius Vitellius, who was on his way back from Tarracina with his cohorts, should be arrested and that the last embers of war should be extinguished: the cavalry was sent forward to Aricia; the infantry rested this side of Bovillae.[2] Vitellius did not hesitate to surrender himself and his legions at the discretion of the victor; his troops threw away their unsuccessful arms no less in anger than in fear. A long line of prisoners, hedged in by armed soldiers, advanced through the city; no man had a suppliant look, but all were gloomy and grim; they faced the cheers, the riot, and the mockery of the crowd unmoved. The few who dared to break out of line were killed by their guards; all the rest were put in ward. No one uttered a word unworthy of him, and even in the midst of misfortune, all

indignum, et quamquam inter adversa, salva virtutis fama. Dein L. Vitellius interficitur, par vitiis fratris, in principatu eius vigilantior, nec perinde prosperis socius quam adversis abstractus.

III. Isdem diebus Lucilius Bassus cum expedito equite ad componendam Campaniam mittitur, discordibus municipiorum animis magis inter semet quam contumacia adversus principem. Viso milite quies et minoribus coloniis impunitas: Capuae legio tertia hiemandi causa locatur et domus inlustres adflictae, cum contra Tarracinenses nulla ope iuvarentur. Tanto proclivius est iniuriae quam beneficio vicem exolvere, quia gratia oneri, ultio in quaestu habetur. Solacio fuit servus Verginii[1] Capitonis, quem proditorem Tarracinensium diximus, patibulo adfixus in isdem anulis quos acceptos a Vitellio gestabat. At Romae senatus cuncta principibus solita Vespasiano decernit, laetus et spei certus, quippe sumpta per Gallias Hispaniasque civilia arma, motis ad bellum Germaniis, mox Illyrico, postquam Aegyptum Iudaeam Syriamque et omnis provincias exercitusque lustraverant, velut expiato terrarum orbe cepisse finem videbantur: addidere alacritatem

[1] Verginii *Puteolanus*: Virgilii *M*.

---

[1] Cf. iii. 12.

[2] Capua was loyal to Vitellius, while Tarracina had favoured Vespasian.

[3] As the insignia of equestrian rank. Cf. i. 13.

[4] The *senatus consultum de imperio Vespasiani* is still extant in part: *C.I.L.* vi. 930; Dessau: *Ins. Lat. Sel.* 244.

[5] Tacitus here thinks of the blood shed in the civil war as an expiation for the sins of the guilty world. In the Roman ceremony of the *lustratio* the sacrificial animals were driven around the people, place, or objects to be purified, their blood

6

maintained their reputation for bravery. Next Lucius Vitellius was put to death. His brother's equal in viciousness, he was more vigilant while that brother was emperor; yet he was not so much associated in his brother's success as dragged to ruin by his adversity.

III. During these same days Lucilius Bassus [1] was sent with a force of light armed cavalry to restore order in Campania, where the people of the towns were rather at variance with one another than rebellious toward the emperor. The sight of the soldiers restored order, and the smaller towns escaped punishment. Capua, however, had the Third legion quartered on it for the winter, and its nobler houses were ruined; [2] while the people of Tarracina, on the other hand, received no assistance: so much easier is it to repay injury than to reward kindness, for gratitude is regarded as a burden, revenge as gain. The Tarracines, however, found comfort in the fact that the slave of Verginius Capito, who had betrayed them, was crucified wearing the very rings that he had received from Vitellius. [3] But at Rome the senators voted to Vespasian all the honours and privileges usually given the emperors. [4] They were filled with joy and confident hope, for it seemed to them that civil warfare, which, breaking out in the Gallic and Spanish provinces, had moved to arms first the Germanies, then Illyricum, and which had traversed Egypt, Judea, Syria, and all provinces and armies, was now at an end, as if the expiation of the whole world had been completed: [5]

thereby becoming a cleansing offering to the gods. In English there is no word exactly equivalent to the Latin *lustrare*, " to go around to purify."

Vespasiani litterae tamquam manente bello scriptae. Ea prima specie forma; ceterum ut princeps loquebatur, civilia de se, et de re publica [1] egregia. Nec senatus obsequium deerat: ipsi consulatus cum Tito filio, praetura Domitiano et consulare imperium decernuntur.

IV. Miserat et Mucianus epistulas ad senatum, quae materiam sermonibus praebuere. Si privatus esset, cur publice loqueretur? Potuisse eadem paucos post dies loco sententiae dici. Ipsa quoque insectatio in Vitellium sera et sine libertate: id vero erga rem publicam superbum, erga principem contumeliosum, quod in manu sua fuisse imperium donatumque Vespasiano iactabat. Ceterum invidia in occulto, adulatio in aperto erant: multo cum honore verborum Muciano triumphalia de bello civium [2] data, sed in Sarmatas expeditio fingebatur. Adduntur Primo Antonio consularia, Cornelio Fusco et Arrio Varo praetoria insignia. Mox deos respexere [3]; restitui Capitolium placuit. Eaque omnia Valerius Asiaticus consul designatus censuit: ceteri vultu manuque, pauci, quibus conspicua dignitas aut ingenium adulatione exercitum, compositis orationibus adsentiebantur. Ubi ad Helvidium Priscum praetorem designatum ventum, prompsit sententiam

---

[1] de re p ⋅b'i⋅a *Muretus*: et RP. *M.*
[2] civium *Walther*: civilium *M.*   [3] re⋅pere *M.*

---

[1] This was done because Vespasian and Titus were still in the East.

their zeal was increased by a letter from Vespasian. written as if war were still going on. That at least was the impression that it made at first; but in reality Vespasian spoke as an emperor, with humility of himself, magnificently of the state. Nor did the senate fail in homage: it elected Vespasian consul with his son Titus, and bestowed a praetorship with consular power on Domitian.[1]

IV. Mucianus also had sent a letter to the senate that gave occasion for comment. "If," they said, "he were a private citizen, why this official language? He might have said the same things a few days later, speaking in the senate." Even his attack on Vitellius came too late and showed no independence. But they thought it a haughty thing toward the state and an act of insolence toward the emperor for him to boast that he had had the empire in his own hand and had presented it to Vespasian. Yet their discontent was concealed; their flattery was open: in magnificent terms the senators gave Mucianus the insignia of a triumph, in reality for civil war, although his expedition against the Sarmatae was made the pretext. They also voted Antonius Primus the insignia of consular rank, Cornelius Fuscus and Arrius Varus of praetorian. Then they took thought for the gods: they voted to restore the Capitol. All these measures were proposed by Valerius Asiaticus,[2] consul elect; the rest of the senators showed their approval by their looks and hands; a few of conspicuous dignity or whose nature was well trained in flattery expressed themselves in formal speeches. When the turn came to Helvidius Priscus, praetor elect, he spoke in terms

[2] Son-in-law of Vitellius.

ut honorificam in bonum principem, . . . falsa
aberant, et studiis senatus attollebatur. Isque
praecipuus illi dies magnae offensae initium et
magnae gloriae fuit.

V. Res poscere videtur, quoniam iterum in mentionem incidimus viri saepius memorandi, ut vitam
studiaque eius, et quali fortuna sit usus, paucis
repetam. Helvidius Priscus [regione Italiae Care-
cina] e municipio Cluviis,[1] patre, qui ordinem primi
pili duxisset, ingenium inlustre altioribus studiis
iuvenis admodum dedit, non, ut plerique, ut nomine
magnifico segne otium velaret, sed quo firmior
adversus fortuita rem publicam capesseret. Doc-
tores sapientiae secutus est, qui sola bona quae
honesta, mala tantum quae turpia, potentiam nobilitatem ceteraque extra animum neque bonis
neque malis adnumerant. Quaestorius adhuc a
Paeto Thrasea gener delectus e moribus soceri nihil
aeque ac libertatem hausit, civis, senator, maritus,
gener, amicus, cunctis vitae officiis aequabilis, opum
contemptor, recti pervicax, constans adversus metus.

VI. Erant quibus adpetentior famae videretur,

---

[1] e Carecinae *Madvig* : Cluviis *Nipperdey* : e municipio
Cluviis *Fisher* : regione italiae carecinae municipio cluvios *M.*

---

[1] How much has been lost from the text here we cannot
now say, nor can we accurately conjecture what Helvidius
said. But clearly his speech lacked warmth and enthusiasm
towards Vespasian, and it apparently contained some plain
advice for the new, but not inexperienced, emperor. Cf.
chap. viii below.

[2] In Samnium.

[3] The Stoic sect, whose stricter members held virtue alone
to be worthy of man's interest : whatever lay beyond the

which, while honourable to a good emperor, . . .[1]
There was no false flattery in his speech, which was
received with enthusiasm by the senate. This was
the day that stood out in his career as marking the
beginning of great disfavour and of great glory.

V. Since I have again had occasion to mention a
man of whom I shall have cause to speak many times,
I think that I ought to give a brief account of his life
and interests, and of the vicissitudes of fortune that
he experienced. Helvidius Priscus was born in the
town of Cluviae [in the district of Caracina[2]]. His
father had been a centurion of the first rank. In his
early youth Helvidius devoted his extraordinary
talents to the higher studies, not as most youths do,
in order to cloak a useless leisure with a pretentious
name, but that he might enter public life better
fortified against the chances of fortune. He followed
those teachers of philosophy who count only those
things " good " which are morally right and only
those things " evil " which are base, and who reckon
power, high birth, and everything else that is beyond
the control of the will as neither good nor bad.[3]
After he had held only the quaestorship, he was
selected by Paetus Thrasea to be his son-in-law;[4]
from the character of his father-in-law he derived
above everything the spirit of freedom; as citizen,
senator, husband, son-in-law, and friend he showed
himself equal to all of life's duties, despising riches,
determined in the right, unmoved by fear.

VI. Some thought that he was rather too eager for

control of the will—health, strength, personal beauty, no
less than " external goods"—was a matter of indifference to
the philosopher.
    [4] Cf. ii. 91.

quando etiam sapientibus cupido gloriae novissima exuitur. Ruina soceri in exilium pulsus, ut Galbae principatu rediit, Marcellum Eprium, delatorem Thraseae, accusare adgreditur. Ea ultio, incertum maior an iustior, senatum in studia diduxerat: nam si caderet Marcellus, agmen reorum sternebatur. Primo minax certamen et egregiis utriusque orationibus testatum; mox dubia voluntate Galbae, multis senatorum deprecantibus, omisit Priscus, variis, ut sunt hominum ingenia, sermonibus moderationem laudantium aut constantiam requirentium.

Ceterum eo senatus die quo de imperio Vespasiani censebant, placuerat mitti ad principem legatos. Hinc inter Helvidium et Eprium acre iurgium: Priscus eligi nominatim a magistratibus iuratis, Marcellus urnam postulabat, quae consulis designati sententia fuerat.

VII. Sed Marcelli studium proprius rubor excitabat ne aliis electis posthabitus crederetur. Paulatimque per altercationem ad continuas et infestas orationes provecti sunt, quaerente Helvidio quid ita Marcellus iudicium magistratuum pavesceret: esse illi pecuniam et eloquentiam, quis multos anteiret, ni memoria flagitiorum urgeretur. Sorte et urna mores non discerni: suffragia et existimationem senatus

---

[1] Cf. ii. 53.

fame, since the passion for glory is that from which even philosophers last divest themselves. Driven into exile by the ruin of his father-in-law, he returned under Galba and brought charges against Marcellus Eprius, who had informed against Thrasea.[1] This attempt to avenge him, at once notable and just, divided the senators: for if Marcellus fell, it was the ruin of a host of the guilty. At first the struggle was threatening, as is proved by the eloquent speeches on both sides; later, since Galba's attitude was uncertain, Priscus yielded to many appeals from his fellow senators and gave up the prosecution. This action called forth varied comments according to the nature of those who made them, some praising his moderation, others regretting his lack of firmness.

However, at the meeting of the senate at which Vespasian was voted the imperial power, the senators decided to send a delegation to the emperor. This gave rise to a sharp difference between Helvidius and Eprius, for Helvidius demanded that the representatives be chosen by the magistrates under oath, Marcellus demanded a selection by lot, as the consul designate had proposed.

VII. The interest that Marcellus felt was prompted by his personal vanity and his fear that others might be chosen and so he might seem neglected. Gradually the disputants were swept on in their wrangling to make long and bitter speeches. Helvidius asked Marcellus why he was so afraid of the decision of the magistrates. "You have," he said, "wealth and eloquence in which you would be superior to many, if you were not burdened with men's memory of your crimes. The lot and urn do not judge character; voting and the judgment of

reperta ut in cuiusque vitam famamque penetrarent.
Pertinere ad utilitatem rei publicae, pertinere ad
Vespasiani honorem, occurrere illi quos innocentissi-
mos senatus habeat, qui honestis sermonibus auris
imperatoris imbuant. Fuisse Vespasiano amicitiam
cum Thrasea, Sorano, Sentio; quorum accusatores
etiam si puniri non oporteat, ostentari non debere.
Hoc senatus iudicio velut admoneri principem quos
probet, quos reformidet. Nullum maius boni imperii
instrumentum quam bonos amicos esse. Satis
Marcello quod Neronem in exitium tot innocentium
impulerit: frueretur praemiis et impunitate, Vespasianum melioribus relinqueret.

VIII. Marcellus non suam sententiam impugnari,
sed consulem designatum censuisse dicebat, secundum vetera exempla quae sortem legationibus
posuissent, ne ambitioni aut inimicitiis locus foret.
Nihil evenisse cur antiquitus instituta exolescerent
aut principis honor in cuiusquam contumeliam
verteretur; sufficere omnis obsequio. Id magis
vitandum ne pervicacia quorundam inritaretur
animus novo principatu suspensus et vultus quoque
ac sermones omnium circumspectans. Se meminisse
temporum quibus natus sit, quam civitatis formam
patres avique instituerint; ulteriora mirari, prae-

---

[1] Marcellus received 5,000,000 sesterces for prosecuting
Thrasea.—*Ann.* xvi. 33.

[2] That is, the establishment of the empire by Augustus.

the senate have been devised as means to penetrate into the life and reputation of the individual. It is for the interests of the state and it touches the honour to be done Vespasian to have the delegation that meets him made up of the men whom the senate considers freest from reproach, that they may fill the emperor's ears with honourable counsels. Vespasian was once the friend of Thrasea, Soranus, and Sentius. Even if it is not well to punish their accusers, we ought not to make a display of them. By its decision in this matter the senate will, in a way, suggest to the emperor whom to approve, whom to fear. For a good government there is no greater instrument at hand than the possession of good friends. You, Marcellus, must be satisfied with the fact that you induced Nero to put to death so many innocent men. Enjoy your rewards [1] and immunity; leave Vespasian to better men."

VIII. Marcellus replied that it was not his proposal, but that of the consul designate that was attacked; and it was a proposal that conformed to the ancient precedents, which prescribed that delegates should be chosen by lot, that there might be no room for self-seeking or for hate. Nothing had occurred to give reason for abandoning long-established customs or for turning the honour due an emperor into an insult to any man: they could all pay homage. What they must try to avoid was allowing the wilfulness of certain individuals to irritate the mind of the emperor, who was as yet unbiassed, being newly come to power and watchful of every look and every word. For his own part he remembered the time in which he was born, the form of government that their fathers and grandfathers had established; [2] he

sentia sequi; bonos imperatores voto expetere, qualiscumque tolerare. Non magis sua oratione Thraseam quam iudicio senatus adflictum; saevitiam Neronis per eius modi imagines inlusisse, nec minus sibi anxiam talem amicitiam quam aliis exilium. Denique constantia fortitudine Catonibus et Brutis aequaretur Helvidius: se unum esse ex illo senatu, qui simul servierit. Suadere etiam Prisco ne supra principem scanderet, ne Vespasianum senem triumphalem, iuvenum liberorum patrem, praeceptis coerceret. Quo modo pessimis imperatoribus sine fine dominationem, ita quamvis egregiis modum libertatis placere. Haec magnis utrimque contentionibus iactata diversis studiis accipiebantur. Vicit pars quae sortiri legatos malebat, etiam mediis patrum adnitentibus retinere morem; et splendidissimus quisque eodem inclinabat metu invidiae, si ipsi eligerentur.

IX. Secutum aliud certamen. Praetores aerarii (nam tum a praetoribus tractabatur aerarium) publicam paupertatem questi modum impensis postulaverant. Eam curam consul designatus ob magnitudinem oneris et remedii difficultatem principi reservabat: Helvidius arbitrio senatus agendum censuit. Cum perrogarent sententias consules, Vul-

---

[1] He was now fifty-nine.

admired the earlier period, but adapted himself to the present; he prayed for good emperors, but endured any sort. It was not by his speech any more than by the judgment of the senate that Thrasea had been brought to ruin; Nero's cruel nature found its delight in such shows of justice, and such a friendship caused him no less anxiety than exile did others. In short, let them set Helvidius on an equality with Cato and Brutus in firmness and courage : for himself, he was only one of a senate which accepted a common servitude. He would also advise Priscus not to exalt himself above an emperor, not to try to check by his precepts a man of ripe age as Vespasian was,[1] a man who had gained the insignia of a triumph, and who had sons grown to man's estate. Just as the worst emperors wish for absolute tyrannical power, even the best desire some limit to the freedom of their subjects. These arguments, which were hurled back and forth with great vehemence, were received with different feelings. The party prevailed that favoured the selection of the envoys by lot, for even the ordinary senators were eager to preserve precedent, and all the most prominent also inclined to the same course, fearing to excite envy if they should be selected themselves.

IX. Another dispute followed. The praetors of the treasury—for at that time the public treasury was managed by praetors—complained of the poverty of the state and asked that expenses should be limited. This problem the consul designate wished to reserve for the emperor in view of the magnitude of the burden and the difficulty of the remedy, but Helvidius held that the decision should rest with the senate. When the consuls began to

cacius Tertullinus tribunus plebis intercessit ne
quid super tanta re principe absente statueretur.
Censuerat Helvidius ut Capitolium publice resti-
tueretur, adiuvaret Vespasianus. Eam sententiam
modestissimus quisque silentio, deinde oblivio transmisit: fuere qui et meminissent.

X. Tum invectus est Musonius Rufus in P. Celerem, a quo Baream Soranum falso testimonio
circumventum arguebat. Ea cognitione renovari
odia accusationum videbantur. Sed vilis et nocens
reus protegi non poterat: quippe Sorani sancta
memoria; Celer professus sapientiam, dein testis in
Baream, proditor corruptorque amicitiae cuius se
magistrum ferebat. Proximus dies causae des-
tinatur; nec tam Musonius aut Publius quam Priscus
et Marcellus ceterique, motis ad ultionem[1] animis,
expectabantur.

XI. Tali rerum statu, cum discordia inter patres,[2]
ira apud victos, nulla in victoribus auctoritas, non
leges, non princeps in civitate essent, Mucianus
urbem ingressus cuncta simul in se traxit. Fracta
Primi Antonii Varique Arrii potentia, male dissimulata in eos Muciani iracundia, quamvis vultu
tegeretur. Sed civitas rimandis offensis sagax
verterat se transtuleratque: ille unus ambiri, coli.

[1] ad ultionem *Lipsius*: adulationibus *M*.
[2] partes *M*.

---

[1] Helvidius was thought to have slighted Vespasian by
inviting him merely to assist in the restoration.
[2] Cf. iii. 81.
[3] Celer was condemned. Cf. chap. xl. below.

ask the senators their views, Vulcacius Tertullinus, tribune of the people, forbade any decision on so important a matter in the absence of the emperor. Helvidius had proposed that the Capitol should be restored at public expense and that Vespasian should assist in the work. This proposal the more prudent senators passed over in silence, and then allowed it to be forgotten. There were some, however, who remembered it.[1]

X. Then Musonius Rufus [2] attacked Publius Celer, charging him with bringing Barea Soranus to ruin by false testimony. This trial seemed to revive the hatred once roused by the informers. But a defendant so base and guilty as Celer could not be protected: the memory of Soranus was revered; Celer had been his teacher in philosophy, then had given testimony against him, thus betraying and profaning friendship, the nature of which he professed to teach. The earliest possible day was set for the case, and men eagerly looked forward to hearing not Musonius or Celer so much as Priscus, Marcellus, and all the rest, for their minds were now set on vengeance.[3]

XI. In this state of affairs, when discord reigned among the senators, when the defeated party was filled with rage, and there was no authority among the victors, neither law nor emperor in the state, Mucianus entered the city and took everything into his own hands. The power of Primus Antonius and of Varus Arrius was broken, for Mucianus poorly concealed his anger toward them, although he did not betray his feelings in his looks. But the city, quick to discover offences, had turned and transferred its devotion to Mucianus: he alone was sought out

THE HISTORIES OF TACITUS

Nec deerat ipse, stipatus [1] armatis domos hortosque
permutans, apparatu incessu excubiis vim principis
amplecti, nomen remittere. Plurimum terroris intulit caedes [2] Calpurnii Galeriani. Is fuit filius Gai
Pisonis, nihil ausus: sed nomen insigne et decora
ipsius [3] iuventa rumore vulgi celebrabantur, erantque
in civitate adhuc turbida et novis sermonibus laeta
qui principatus inanem ei famam circumdarent.
Iussu Muciani custodia militari cinctus, ne in ipsa
urbe conspectior mors foret, ad quadragensimum ab
urbe lapidem Appia via fuso per venas sanguine
extinguitur. Iulius Priscus praetoriarum sub Vitellio
cohortium praefectus se ipse interfecit, pudore
magis quam necessitate. Alfenus Varus ignaviae
infamiaeque suae superfuit. Asiaticus (etenim is [4]
libertus) malam potentiam servili supplicio expiavit.

XII. Isdem diebus crebrescentem cladis Germanicae famam nequaquam maesta civitas exci-
piebat; caesos exercitus, capta legionum hiberna,
descivisse Gallias non ut mala loquebantur. Id
bellum quibus causis ortum, quanto externarum
sociarumque gentium motu flagraverit, altius expediam. Batavi, donec trans Rhenum agebant, pars

---

[1] stipatis *M*.   [2] cedem *M*.   [3] ipsi *M*.
[4] etenim is *Ernesti*: enim is *M*.

---

[1] Gaius Piso conspired against Nero in 65 A.D., and on
the discovery of the conspiracy committed suicide. Cf.
Ann. xv. 59.
[2] Cf. iii. 61.
[3] His elevation to equestrian rank was told in ii. 57. He
was now crucified.

and courted. Nor did he fail in his part: surrounded with armed men, changing his houses and
gardens, by his parade, his gait, his guards, he grasped
at an emperor's power, the title he let pass. The
greatest terror was caused by the execution of Calpurnius Galerianus. He was the son of Gaius Piso,[1]
but he had attempted nothing seditious: yet his
eminent name and his handsome appearance made
him the subject of gossip, and among the citizens,
who were still uneasy and delighted in talk of a
revolution, there were enough ready to bestow on
him the empty honours of the principate. Mucianus
ordered his arrest by a squad of soldiers, and then,
fearing that his execution within the city itself would
attract too much attention, he had him taken to the
fortieth milestone on the Appian Way, where he
was put to death by opening his veins. Julius
Priscus, prefect of the praetorian cohorts under
Vitellius, committed suicide, prompted by shame
rather than necessity. Alfenus Varus survived his
own cowardice and infamy.[2] Asiaticus, being a
freedman, paid for his baneful power by a slave's
punishment.[3]

XII. During these same days the citizens received
increasing rumours of disasters in Germany [4] with
no sign of sorrow: slaughtered armies, the capture
of the legions' winter quarters, a revolt of the
Gallic provinces men spoke of as though they were
not misfortunes. As to that war, I propose to
explain its causes somewhat deeply and the extent
to which foreign and allied tribes were involved in
this conflagration. The Batavians formed part of the

[4] Cf. iii. 46.

Chattorum, seditione domestica pulsi extrema Gallicae orae vacua cultoribus simulque insulam iuxta sitam[1] occupavere, quam mare Oceanus a fronte, Rhenus amnis tergum ac latera circumluit. Nec opibus (rarum[2] in societate validiorum) attritis[3] viros tantum armaque imperio ministrant, diu Germanicis bellis exerciti, mox aucta per Britanniam gloria, transmissis illuc cohortibus, quas vetere instituto nobilissimi popularium regebant. Erat[4] et domi delectus eques, praecipuo nandi studio, arma equosque retinens integris turmis Rhenum perrumpere . . .

XIII. Iulius Paulus et Iulius Civilis[5] regia stirpe multo ceteros anteibant. Paulum Fonteius Capito falso rebellionis crimine interfecit; iniectae Civili catenae, missusque ad Neronem et a Galba absolutus sub Vitellio rursus discrimen adiit,[6] flagitante supplicium eius exercitu: inde causae irarum spesque ex malis nostris. Sed Civilis ultra quam barbaris solitum ingenio sollers et Sertorium se aut Annibalem ferens simili oris dehonestamento, ne ut hosti obviam iretur, si a populo Romano palam descivisset, Ves-

1 iuxta sitam *Walch*: invata sit an *M*.
2 rarum *Tirdke*: romanis *M*.
3 attritis *Tirdke*: adtriti *M*.   4 erant *M*.
5 Iulius Civilis *Ritter*: Claudius Civilis *M*.
6 adit *M*.

---

1 The Chatti. one of the most warlike of the German tribes, lived in the districts known to-day as Hessen-Nassau and Waldeck. For a description of this tribe, see *Germania* 29–31.
2 This *insula Batavorum*, about sixty miles in length, is formed by the Rhine and the Waal. The name is preserved in the modern Beturve.   3 That is, they were not taxed.
4 What has been lost here cannot now be accurately determined.

Chatti[1] so long as they lived across the Rhine; then, being expelled by a civil war, they occupied the edge of the Gallic bank which was uninhabited, and likewise an island close by, which is washed by the ocean in front but by the Rhine on its rear and sides.[2] Without having their wealth exhausted[3]—a thing which is rare in alliance with a stronger people— they furnished our empire only men and arms. They had long training in our wars with the Germans; then later they increased their renown by service in Britain, whither some cohorts were sent, led according to their ancient custom by the noblest among them. They had also at home a select body of cavalry which excelled in swimming; keeping their arms and horses they crossed the Rhine without breaking their formation. . . .[4]

XIII. Julius Paulus and Julius Civilis were by far the most distinguished among the Batavians, being both of royal stock. On a false charge of revolt, Paulus was executed by Fonteius Capito;[5] Civilis was put in chains and sent to Nero, and although acquitted by Galba, he was again exposed to danger under Vitellius owing to the clamour of the army for his punishment:[6] these were the causes of his anger, his hopes sprang from our misfortunes. Civilis, however, who was cunning beyond the average barbarian, bore himself also like a Sertorius or a Hannibal, since his face was disfigured like theirs;[7] in order to avoid being attacked as an enemy, as he would have been if he had openly revolted from the Romans, he pretended to be a friend of Vespasian

[5] Apparently in connection with the revolt of Vindex. Cf. i. 6.
[6] Cf. i. 59.   [7] That is, he had lost an eye.

pasiani amicitiam studiumque partium praetendit, missis sane ad eum Primi Antonii litteris, quibus avertere accita *a*[1] Vitellio auxilia et tumultus Germanici specie retentare legiones iubebatur. Eadem Hordeonius Flaccus praesens monuerat, inclinato in Vespasianum animo et rei publicae cura, cui excidium adventabat, si redintegratum bellum et tot armatorum milia Italiam inrupissent.

XIV. Igitur Civilis desciscendi certus, occultato interim altiore consilio, cetera ex eventu iudicaturus, novare res hoc modo coepit. Iussu Vitellii Batavorum iuventus ad dilectum vocabatur, quem suapte natura gravem onerabant ministri avaritia ac luxu, senes aut invalidos conquirendo, quos pretio dimitterent : rursus impubes et[2] forma conspicui (et est plerisque procera pueritia) ad stuprum trahebantur. Hinc invidia, et compositae[3] seditionis auctores perpulere ut dilectum abnuerent. Civilis primores gentis et promptissimos vulgi specie epularum sacrum in nemus vocatos, ubi nocte ac laetitia incaluisse videt, a laude gloriaque gentis orsus iniurias et raptus et cetera servitii mala enumerat : neque enim societatem, ut olim, sed tamquam mancipia haberi :

[1] a *codd. dett., Halm.*
[2] impubes et *Halm* : impubes sed *M.*
[3] compositae *codd. dett., Halm* : compositi *M.*

---

[1] Governor of Upper Germany.

and enthusiastic for his party; indeed Primus Antonius had actually written to him directing him to divert the auxiliary troops called up by Vitellius and to hold back the legions on the pretext of a German revolt. Hordeonius Flaccus,[1] who was on the ground, had given him the same suggestion, moved by his own partiality toward Vespasian and by his anxiety for the state, whose ruin was sure if war were renewed and all those thousands of armed men burst into Italy.

XIV. So then Civilis, having determined to revolt, concealed for the time his deeper purpose, and being ready to determine his other plans by the event, began to make trouble in the following way. At the orders of Vitellius a levy of the young Batavians was now being made. This burden, which is naturally grievous, was made the heavier by the greed and licence of those in charge of the levy: they hunted out the old and the weak that they might get a price for letting them off; again they dragged away the children to satisfy their lust, choosing the handsomest—and the Batavian children are generally tall beyond their years. These acts aroused resentment, and the leaders in the conspiracy, on which they were now determined, persuaded the people to refuse the levy. Civilis called the leaders of his tribe and the boldest of the common people into a sacred grove under the pretext of giving a banquet, and when he saw that the night and revelry had fired their spirits, he began to speak of the honour and glory of their tribe, then passed on to count over their wrongs, the extortion practised on them, and all the rest of the misfortunes of slavery. "For," he declared, "we are no longer regarded as allies, as once we were, but

quando legatum, gravi quidem comitatu et superbo, cum imperio venire? Tradi se praefectis centurionibusque: quos ubi spoliis et sanguine expleverint, mutari, exquirique novos sinus et varia praedandi vocabula. Instare dilectum quo liberi a parentibus, fratres a fratribus velut supremum dividantur. Numquam magis adflictam rem Romanam nec aliud in hibernis quam praedam et senes: attollerent tantum oculos et inania legionum nomina ne pavescerent. At sibi robur peditum equitumque, consanguineos Germanos, Gallias idem cupientis. Ne Romanis quidem ingratum id bellum, cuius ambiguam fortunam Vespasiano imputaturos: victoriae rationem non reddi.

XV. Magno cum adsensu auditus barbaro ritu et patriis execrationibus universos adigit. Missi ad Canninefatis qui consilia sociarent. Ea gens partem insulae colit, origine lingua virtute par Batavis; numero superantur. Mox occultis nuntiis pellexit Britannica auxilia, Batavorum cohortis missas in Germaniam, ut supra rettulimus, ac tum Mogontiaci agentis. Erat in Canninefatibus stolidae audaciae Brinno, claritate natalium insigni; pater eius multa

---

[1] In the northern part of the island.
[2] ii. 29.
[3] Mayence.

as slaves. When does a governor come to us with full commission, even though his suite would be burdensome and insolent if he came? We are handed over to prefects and centurions: after one band is satisfied with murder and spoils, the troops are shifted, and new purses are looked for to be filled and varied pretexts for plundering are sought. We are threatened with a levy which separates children from parents and brothers from brothers, as if in death. Never has the Roman state been in direr straits than now, and there is nothing in their winter camps but booty and old men. Simply lift your eyes and do not fear the empty name of legions. But on our side are our strong infantry and cavalry, our kinsmen the Germans, the Gallic provinces that cherish the same desires as ourselves. Not even the Romans will regard this war with disfavour; if its outcome is uncertain we shall say that it was undertaken for Vespasian; for victory no account is ever rendered."

XV. His words won great applause, and he bound them all by their national oaths and barbarous rites. Men were despatched to the Canninefates to join them to their plan. The Canninefates live in part of the island; [1] in origin, speech, and courage they are equal to the Batavians, but inferior to them in number. Presently by secret messengers they won over to their cause auxiliary troops from Britain and the Batavian cohorts that had been sent into Germany, as I have stated above,[2] and which were at that time stationed at Mogontiacum.[3] There was among the Canninefates a man of brute courage named Brinno, who was of illustrious descent; his father had dared to commit many hostile acts and

hostilia ausus Gaianarum expeditionum ludibrium impune spreverat. Igitur ipso rebellis familiae nomine placuit impositusque scuto more gentis et sustinentium umeris vibratus dux deligitur. Statimque accitis Frisiis (transrhenana gens est) duarum cohortium hiberna proxima Oceano[1] inrumpit. Nec providerant[2] impetum hostium milites, nec, si providissent, satis virium ad arcendum erat: capta igitur ac direpta castra. Dein vagos et pacis modo effusos lixas negotiatoresque Romanos invadunt. Simul excidiis castellorum imminebant, quae a praefectis cohortium incensa sunt, quia defendi nequibant. Signa vexillaque et quod militum in superiorem insulae partem congregantur, duce Aquilio primipilari, nomen magis exercitus quam robur: quippe viribus cohortium abductis Vitellius e proximis Nerviorum Germanorumque pagis segnem numerum armis oneraverat.

XVI. Civilis dolo grassandum ratus incusavit ultro praefectos quod castella deseruissent: se cum cohorte, cui praeerat, Canninefatem tumultum compressurum, illi sua quisque hiberna repeterent. Subesse fraudem consilio et dispersas cohortis facilius opprimi, nec Brinnonem ducem eius belli, sed

---

[1] proxima (proximo M^1) occupata oceano M: occupata *secl. Urlichs, Novák.*

[2] providerant *ed. Spirensis*: praeviderant M.

---

[1] Cf. Suetonius, *Caligula* 43–47, for Caligula's ridiculous attempts.

[2] Living in modern Friesland.

[3] The Nervii lived chiefly in the modern Belgian districts of Hainaut and Namur, on both banks of the Sambre. The Germans here referred to must be Germanic tribes living in modern Namur and Luxembourg, spoken of by Caesar as the *Germani cisrhenani, B.G.* vi. 2; cf. ii. 4.

had shown his scorn for Gaius' absurd expeditions
without suffering for it.[1] The very name of his
rebellious family therefore made Brinno a favourite;
and in accordance with their tribal custom the Batavians set him on a shield and, lifting him on their
shoulders, chose him as their leader. He at once
called in the Frisians, a tribe living across the Rhine,[2]
and assailed by sea the winter camp of two cohorts
which were nearest to attack. The Roman troops
had not foreseen the assault, and even if they had,
they did not have enough strength to keep off the
enemy: so the camp was captured and plundered.
Then the enemy attacked the Roman foragers and
traders who were scattered about the country as if
it were a time of peace. At the same time they
threatened to destroy the Roman forts, which the
prefects of the cohorts burned, for they could not
defend them. The Roman ensigns and standards
with all the soldiers were concentrated in the upper
part of the island under the leadership of Aquilius,
a centurion of the first rank; but they had rather
the name than the strength of an army: for when
Vitellius had withdrawn the effective cohorts, he had
gathered a useless crowd from the nearest cantons of
the Nervii and Germans and burdened them with
arms.[3]

XVI. Thinking it best to proceed by craft, Civilis
promptly rebuked the prefects for abandoning their
forts, and declared that he would crush the revolt
of the Canninefates with the cohort under his command; they were to return each to his winter quarters. It was clear that treachery lay behind his
advice and that the cohorts when scattered could be
more easily crushed; likewise it was plain that the

Civilem esse [1] patuit, erumpentibus paulatim indiciis quae Germani, laeta bello gens, non diu occulta-verant. Ubi insidiae parum cessere, ad vim trans-gressus Canninefatis, Frisios, Batavos propriis cuneis componit: derecta ex diverso acies haud procul a flumine Rheno et obversis in hostem navibus, quas [2] incensis castellis illuc adpulerant. Nec diu certato Tungrorum cohors signa ad Civilem transtulit, per-culsique milites improvisa proditione a sociis hosti-busque caedebantur. Eadem etiam *in* [3] navibus per-fidia: pars remigum [4] e Batavis tamquam imperitia officia nautarum [5] propugnatorumque impediebant; mox contra tendere et puppis hostili ripae obicere: ad postremum gubernatores centurionesque, nisi eadem volentis, trucidant, donec universa quattuor et viginti navium classis transfugeret aut caperetur.

XVII. Clara ea victoria in praesens, in posterum usui; armaque et navis, quibus indigebant, adepti magna per Germanias Galliasque fama libertatis auctores celebrabantur. Germaniae statim misere legatos auxilia offerentis: Galliarum societatem Civilis arte donisque adfectabat, captos cohortium praefectos suas in civitates remittendo, cohortibus, abire an manere mallent, data potestate. Manen-tibus honorata militia, digredientibus spolia Ro-

---

[1] eius *M*.   [2] quasi *M*.   [3] in *add. Wurm.*
[4] remigium *M*.   [5] nautorum *M*.

real leader in this war was not Brinno but Civilis; the proofs of this gradually appeared, for the Germans, who delight in war, did not long conceal the facts. When treachery did not succeed, Civilis turned to force and organized the Canninefates, the Frisians, and the Batavians, each tribe in a troop by itself: the Roman line was drawn up to oppose them not far from the Rhine, and the vessels which had been brought here after the burning of the forts were turned to front the foe. The battle had not lasted long when a cohort of the Tingri transferred its standards to Civilis, and the Roman soldiers, demoralized by this sudden betrayal, were cut down by allies and foes alike. There was the same treachery also on the part of the fleet: some of the rowers, being Batavians, by pretending a lack of skill interfered with the sailors and combatants; presently they began to row in the opposite direction and bring the sterns to the bank on which the enemy stood; finally, they killed such of the helmsmen and centurions as did not take their view, until the entire fleet of twenty-four vessels either went over to the enemy or was captured.

XVII. This victory was glorious for the enemy at the moment and useful for the future. They gained arms and boats which they needed, and were greatly extolled as liberators throughout the German and Gallic provinces. The Germans at once sent delegations offering assistance; the Gallic provinces Civilis tried to win to an alliance by craft and gifts, sending back the captured prefects to their own states and giving the soldiers of the cohorts permission to go or stay as they pleased. Those who stayed were given honourable service in the army,

manorum offerebantur: simul secretis sermonibus
admonebat malorum, quae tot annis perpessi miseram
servitutem falso pacem vocarent. Batavos, quamquam tributorum expertis, arma contra communis
dominos cepisse; prima acie fusum victumque
Romanum. Quid si Galliae iugum exuant? quantum
in Italia reliquum? provinciarum sanguine provincias
vinci. Ne Vindicis aciem cogitarent: Batavo equite
protritos Aeduos Arvernosque; fuisse inter Verginii
auxilia Belgas, vereque reputantibus Galliam suismet
viribus concidisse. Nunc easdem omnium partis,
addito si quid militaris disciplinae in castris Romanorum viguerit; esse secum veteranas cohortis, quibus
nuper Othonis legiones procubuerint. Servirent
Syria Asiaque et suetus regibus Oriens: multos
adhuc in Gallia vivere ante tributa genitos. Nuper
certe caeso Quintilio Varo pulsam e Germania servitutem, nec Vitellium principem sed Caesarem
Augustum bello provocatum. Libertatem natura
etiam mutis animalibus datam, virtutem proprium
hominum bonum; deos fortioribus adesse: proinde
arriperent vacui occupatos, integri fessos. Dum alii
Vespasianum, alii Vitellium foveant, patere locum
adversus utrumque. XVIII. Sic in Gallias Germa-

---

[1] In 9 A.D.

those who left were offered spoils taken from the Romans. At the same time in private conversation he reminded them of the miseries that they had endured so many years while they falsely called their wretched servitude a peace. "The Batavians," he said, "although free from tribute, have taken up arms against our common masters. In the very first engagement the Romans have been routed and defeated. What if the Gallic provinces should throw off the yoke? What forces are there left in Italy? It is by the blood of the provinces that provinces are won. Do not think of Vindex's battle. It was the Batavian cavalry that crushed the Aedui and Averni; among the auxiliary forces of Virginius were Belgians, and if you consider the matter aright you will see that Gaul owed its fall to its own forces. Now all belong to the same party, and we have gained besides all the strength that military training in Roman camps can give; I have with me veteran cohorts before which Otho's legions lately succumbed. Let Syria, Asia, and the East, which is accustomed to kings, play the slave; there are many still alive in Gaul who were born before tribute was known. Surely it was not long ago that slavery was driven from Germany by the killing of Quintilius Varus,[1] and the emperor whom the Germans then challenged was not a Vitellius but a Caesar Augustus. Liberty is a gift which nature has granted even to dumb animals, but courage is the peculiar blessing of man. The gods favour the braver: on, therefore, carefree against the distressed, fresh against the weary. While some favour Vespasian and others Vitellius, the field is open against both." XVIII. In this way Civilis,

niasque intentus, si destinata provenissent, validissimarum ditissimarumque nationum regno imminebat.

At Flaccus Hordeonius primos Civilis conatus per dissimulationem aluit: ubi expugnata castra, deletas cohortis, pulsum Batavorum insula Romanum nomen trepidi nuntii adferebant, Munium Lupercum legatum (is duarum legionum hibernis praeerat) egredi adversus hostem iubet. Lupercus legionarios e praesentibus, Ubios e proximis, Trevirorum equites haud longe agentis raptim transmisit, addita Batavorum ala, quae iam pridem corrupta fidem simulabat, ut proditis in ipsa acie Romanis maiore pretio fugeret. Civilis captarum cohortium signis circumdatus, ut suo militi recens gloria ante oculos et hostes memoria cladis terrerentur, matrem suam sororesque, simul omnium coniuges parvosque liberos consistere a tergo iubet, hortamenta victoriae vel pulsis pudorem. Ut virorum cantu. feminarum ululatu sonuit acies, nequaquam par a legionibus cohortibusque redditur clamor. Nudaverat sinistrum cornu[1] Batavorum ala transfugiens statimque in nos versa. Sed legionarius

---

[1] cornū *M.*

turning his attention eagerly toward the Germanies and the Gauls, was preparing, should his plans prove successful, to gain the kingship over the strongest and richest nations.

But Hordeonius Flaccus furthered his enterprises at first by affecting to be unaware of them; when, however, terrified messengers brought word of the capture of camps, the destruction of cohorts, and the expulsion of the Roman name from the island of the Batavians, he ordered Munius Lupercus, who commanded the two legions in winter quarters, to take the field against the foe. Lupercus quickly transported to the island all the legionaries that he had, as well as the Ubii from the auxiliaries quartered close by and a body of Treviran cavalry which was not far away. He joined to these forces a squadron of Batavian cavalry, which, although already won over to the other side, still pretended to be faithful, that by betraying the Romans on the very field itself it might win a greater reward for its desertion. Civilis had the standards of the captured cohorts ranged about him that his own troops might have the evidence of their newly-won glory before their eyes and that the enemy might be terrified by the memory of their defeat; he ordered his own mother and his sisters, likewise the wives and little children of all his men, to take their stand behind his troops to encourage them to victory or to shame them if defeated. When the enemy's line re-echoed with the men's singing and the women's cries, the shout with which the legions and cohorts answered was far from equal. Our left had already been exposed by the desertion of the Batavian horse, which at once turned against us. Yet the legionary troops kept

miles, quamquam rebus trepidis, arma ordinesque
retinebat. Ubiorum Trevirorumque auxilia foeda
fuga dispersa totis campis palantur: illuc incubuere
Germani, et fuit interim effugium legionibus in
castra, quibus Veterum nomen est. Praefectus alae
Batavorum Claudius Labeo, oppidano certamine
aemulus Civili, ne interfectus invidiam [1] apud popularis, vel, si retineretur, semina discordiae praeberet,
in Frisios avehitur.

XIX. Isdem diebus Batavorum et Canninefatium
cohortis, cum iussu Vitellii in urbem pergerent,
missus a Civile nuntius adsequitur. Intumuere
statim superbia ferociaque et pretium itineris donativum, duplex stipendium, augeri equitum numerum, promissa sane a Vitellio, postulabant, non
ut adsequerentur, sed causam seditioni. Et Flaccus
multa concedendo nihil aliud effecerat quam ut
acrius exposcerent quae sciebant negaturum. Spreto
Flacco inferiorem Germaniam petivere ut Civili
iungerentur. Hordeonius adhibitis tribunis centurionibusque consultavit num obsequium abnuentis
vi coerceret; mox insita ignavia et trepidis ministris,
quos ambiguus auxiliorum animus et subito dilectu
suppletae legiones angebant, statuit continere intra

---

[1] invidia *M.*

---

[1] Near the modern Xanten.
[2] Cf. i. 59; ii. 97; and iv. 15.
[3] The legionaries received ten asses daily, the auxiliaries
probably somewhat less. The cavalry enjoyed higher pay
than the foot.

their arms and maintained their ranks in spite of the alarming situation. The auxiliary forces made up of the Ubii and Treveri fled disgracefully and wandered in disorder over the country. The Germans made them the object of their attack, and so the legions meanwhile were able to escape to the camp called Vetera.[1] Claudius Labeo, who was in command of the Batavian horse, had been a rival of Civilis in some local matter, and was consequently now removed to the Frisii, that he might not, if killed, excite his fellow-tribesmen to anger, or, if kept with the forces, sow seeds of discord.

XIX. At this time a messenger dispatched by Civilis overtook the cohorts of Batavi and Canninefates which were on their way to Rome in accordance with the orders of Vitellius.[2] They were at once puffed up with pride and insolence: they demanded a gift as a reward for their journey; they insisted on double pay and an increase in the number of cavalry;[3] these things, it is true, had been promised by Vitellius, but the cohorts' real purpose was not to obtain their demands, but to find an excuse for revolt. In fact by granting many of their demands Flaccus accomplished nothing except to make them insist all the more on things which they knew he would refuse. They treated him with scorn and started for lower Germany to join Civilis. Hordeonius summoned the tribunes and centurions and consulted them as to whether he should check the disobedient troops by force; then, moved by his natural timidity and the terrors of his subordinates, who were distressed by the uncertain temper of the auxiliaries and by the fact that the legions had been filled up from a hasty levy, he decided to keep his

castra militem: dein paenitentia et arguentibus ipsis qui suaserant, tamquam secuturus scripsit Herennio Gallo legionis primae legato, qui Bonnam obtinebat, ut arceret transitu Batavos: se cum exercitu tergis eorum haesurum. Et opprimi poterant si hinc Hordeonius, inde Gallus, motis utrimque copiis, medios clausissent. Flaccus omisit inceptum aliisque litteris Gallum monuit ne terreret abeuntis: unde suspicio sponte legatorum excitari bellum cunctaque quae acciderant aut metuebantur non inertia militis neque hostium vi, sed fraude ducum evenire.

XX. Batavi cum castris Bonnensibus propinquarent, praemisere qui Herennio Gallo mandata cohortium exponeret. Nullum sibi bellum adversus Romanos, pro quibus totiens bellassent: longa atque inrita militia fessis patriae atque otii cupidinem esse. Si nemo obsisteret, innoxium iter fore: sin arma occurrant, ferro viam inventuros. Cunctantem legatum milites perpulerant fortunam proelii experiretur. Tria milia legionariorum et tumultuariae Belgarum cohortes, simul paganorum lixarumque ignava sed procax ante periculum manus omnibus

soldiers in camp. Next, repenting of his decision and influenced by the very men who had advised it, he wrote, as though purposing to follow himself, to the commander of the First legion, Herennius Gallus, stationed at Bonn, to keep the Batavi from passing; and added that he would press hard on their rear with his troops. Indeed the Batavi might have been crushed if Hordeonius on one side and Gallus on the other had moved their troops from both directions and caught the foe between them. Flaccus abandoned the undertaking and in a second letter warned Gallus not to alarm the Batavians as they withdrew: this gave rise to the suspicion that war was being begun with the approval of the Roman commanders, and that everything that had happened or that men feared would come to pass was due not to the inactivity of the soldiers or the power of the enemy, but to treachery on the part of the generals.

XX. When the Batavi were approaching the camp at Bonn, they sent a messenger ahead to set forth to Herennius Gallus the demands of the cohorts. This messenger said that they were not making war on the Romans on whose behalf they had often fought, but that they were weary of their long and profitless service and longed for their home and a life of peace. If no one opposed them they would pass without doing any harm; but if armed resistance were offered, they would find a path with the sword. When Gallus hesitated, the soldiers urged him to try the issue of battle. Three thousand legionaries and some cohorts of Belgians, which had been hastily raised, as well as a band of peasants and foragers, unwarlike but bold before they met actual danger,

39

portis prorumpunt[1] ut Batavos numero imparis circumfundant. Illi veteres militiae in cuneos congregantur, densi undique et frontem tergaque ac latus tuti; sic tenuem nostrorum aciem perfringunt. Cedentibus Belgis pellitur legio, et vallum portasque trepidi petebant. Ibi plurimum cladis: cumulatae corporibus fossae, nec caede tantum et vulneribus, sed ruina et suis plerique telis interiere.[2] Victores colonia Agrippinensium vitata, nihil cetero in itinere hostile ausi, Bonnense proelium excusabant, tamquam petita pace, postquam negabatur, sibimet ipsi consuluissent.

XXI. Civilis adventu veteranarum cohortium iusti iam exercitus ductor, sed consilii ambiguus et vim Romanam reputans, cunctos qui aderant in verba Vespasiani adigit mittitque legatos ad duas legiones, quae priore acie pulsae in Vetera castra concesserant, ut idem sacramentum acciperent. Redditur responsum: neque proditoris neque hostium se consiliis uti; esse sibi Vitellium principem, pro quo fidem et arma usque ad supremum spiritum retenturos: proinde perfuga Batavus arbitrium rerum Romanarum[3] ne ageret, sed meritas[4] sceleris poenas expectaret. Quae ubi relata Civili, incensus ira universam Batavorum gentem in arma rapit; iunguntur Bructeri Tencterique et excita nuntiis Germania ad praedam famamque.

XXII. Adversus has concurrentis belli minas legati

---

[1] prorumpunt *Ritter*: rumpunt *M*.   [2] interire *M*.
[3] romanorum *M*.   [4] merita *M*.

---

[1] The Tencteri lived between the Rhine, the Ruhr, and the Lippe; the Bructeri somewhat to the north between the Lippe and the upper Ems.

burst out of all the gates at once to surround the Batavi, who were inferior in numbers. But they, being veterans in service, gathered in solid columns, with their ranks closed on every side, secure on front and flanks and rear; so they broke through our thin line. When the Belgians gave way, the legion was driven back and in terror rushed for the rampart and gates of the camp. At these points there were the greatest losses: the ditches were heaped high with bodies and our men died not only by the sword and from wounds, but also from the crush and very many by their own weapons. The victors avoided Cologne and made no other hostile attempt during the rest of their march; they excused the battle at Bonn on the ground that they had asked for peace, and when this was refused, had consulted their own interests.

XXI. The arrival of these veteran cohorts put Civilis in command of a real army, but being still uncertain what course to adopt and reflecting on the power of the Romans, he had all his forces swear allegiance to Vespasian, and sent a delegation to the two legions which after their recent defeat had retired to the camp called Vetera, bidding them take the same oath. They replied: " We do not follow the advice of a traitor or of enemies. Our emperor is Vitellius, for whom we will keep faith and fight to our last breath: no Batavian deserter therefore shall play the arbiter of Rome's destiny, but rather let him expect the punishment his crime deserves." On receiving this reply Civilis, hot with rage, swept the whole Batavian people into arms; the Bructeri and Tencteri [1] joined, and the Germans, summoned by messengers, hurried to share in booty and glory.

XXII. To meet this threatening war that was rising

legionum Munius Lupercus et Numisius Rufus vallum murosque firmabant. Subversa longae pacis opera, haud procul castris in modum municipii extructa, ne hostibus usui forent. Sed parum provisum ut [1] copiae in castra conveherentur; rapi permisere: ita paucis diebus per licentiam absumpta sunt quae adversus necessitates in longum suffecissent. Civilis medium agmen cum robore Batavorum obtinens utramque Rheni ripam, quo truculentior visu foret, Germanorum catervis complet, adsultante per campos equite; simul naves in adversum amnem agebantur. Hinc veteranarum cohortium signa, inde depromptae silvis lucisque [2] ferarum imagines, ut cuique genti inire proelium mos est, mixta belli civilis [3] externique facie obstupefecerant obsessos. Et spem obpugnantium augebat amplitudo valli, quod duabus legionibus situm vix quinque milia armatorum Romanorum tuebantur; sed lixarum multitudo turbata pace illuc congregata et bello ministra aderat.

XXIII. Pars castrorum in collem leniter exurgens, pars aequo adibatur. Quippe illis hibernis obsideri premique Germanias Augustus crediderat, neque umquam id malorum ut obpugnatum ultro legiones nostras venirent; inde non loco neque munimentis

---

[1] ut *Lipsius*: vi *M*.   [2] luusque *M*.
[3] civili *M*.

---

[1] That is, for about 12,000 men when at full strength.

from many quarters the commanders of the legions, Munius Lupercus and Numisius Rufus, began to strengthen the palisade and rampart of their camp. They tore down the buildings that had been erected during the long peace, and which in fact that grown into a town not far from the camp, for they did not wish them to be of service to the foe. But they did not take sufficient care to have supplies collected; they allowed the troops to pillage: so that in a few days the soldiers' recklessness exhausted what would have met their needs for a long time. Civilis took his post in the centre of his army along with the pick of the Batavi, and to make a more frightful appearance, he filled both banks of the Rhine with bands of Germans, while his cavalry ranged the open plains; and at the same time the ships moved up stream. On one side were the standards of the veteran cohorts, on the other the images of wild beasts taken from the woods and groves, which each tribe carries into battle: these emblems, suggesting at once civil and foreign wars, terrified the besieged troops. In addition the besiegers were encouraged by the extent of the Roman ramparts, which had been built for two legions,[1] but which now had barely five thousand armed Romans to defend them; there was, however, also a crowd of sutlers who had gathered there at the first trouble and who assisted in the struggle.

XXIII. Part of the camp lay on a gentle slope; part could be approached on level ground. Augustus had believed that these winter quarters could keep the Germanies in hand and indeed in subjection, and had never thought of such a disaster as to have the Germans actually assail our legions; therefore nothing had been done to add to the strength of the

labor additus: vis et arma satis placebant. Batavi Transrhenanique, quo discreta virtus manifestius spectaretur, sibi quaeque gens consistunt, eminus lacessentes. Post ubi pleraque telorum turribus pinnisque moenium inrita haerebant et desuper saxis vulnerabantur, clamore atque impetu invasere vallum, adpositis plerique scalis, alii per testudinem suorum; scandebantque iam quidam, cum gladiis et armorum incussu praecipitati sudibus et pilis obruuntur, praeferoces initio et rebus secundis nimii. Sed tum praedae cupidine adversa quoque tolerabant; machinas etiam, insolitum sibi, ausi. Nec ulla ipsis sollertia: perfugae captivique docebant struere materias in modum pontis, mox subiectis rotis propellere, ut alii superstantes tamquam ex aggere proeliarentur, pars intus occulti muros subruerent. Sed excussa ballistis saxa stravere informe opus. Et cratis vineasque parantibus adactae tormentis ardentes hastae, ultroque ipsi obpugnatores ignibus petebantur, donec desperata vi verterent consilium ad moras, haud ignari paucorum dierum inesse alimenta et multum imbellis turbae; simul ex inopia proditio et fluxa servitiorum fides ac fortuita belli sperabantur.

---

[1] The Bructeri, Tencteri, and Frisii (chapters xv, xxi).

position or of the fortifications: the armed force seemed sufficient. The Batavi and the peoples from across the Rhine,[1] to exhibit their individual prowess more clearly, formed each tribe by itself and opened fire first from some distance; but when most of their weapons stuck uselessly in the towers and battlements and they were suffering from the stones shot down on them, with a shout they assailed the ramparts, many raising scaling-ladders, others climbing on a " tortoise " formed by their comrades. Some were already in the act of mounting the walls, when the legionaries threw them down with their swords and shields and buried them under a shower of stakes and javelins. These peoples are always at first too impetuous and easily emboldened by success; but now in their greed for booty they were ready to brave reverses as well, venturing even to use siege machines also, which they are not accustomed to employ. They had no skill in these themselves: deserters and captives taught them how to build of timber a kind of bridge, to put wheels under the structure, and then to push it forward, so that some standing on the top might fight as from a mound and others concealed within might undermine the walls; but stones shot from ballistae broke up the rude structure, and when they began to prepare screens and sheds, the Romans shot blazing darts at these with cross-bows, and threatened the assailants also with fire, until the barbarians, despairing of success by force, changed to a policy of delay, being well aware that the camp had provisions for only a few days and that it contained a great crowd of non-combatants; at the same time they counted on treachery as a result of want, and on the uncertain faith of the slaves and the chances of war.

XXIV. Flaccus interim cognito castrorum obsidio et missis per Gallias qui auxilia concirent, lectos e [1] legionibus Dillio Voculae duoetvicensimae legionis legato tradit, ut quam maximis per ripam itineribus celeraret, ipse navibus *vectus*,[2] invalidus corpore, inter ipsos militibus. Neque enim ambigue fremebant [3] : emissas a Mogontiaco Batavorum cohortis, dissimulatos Civilis conatus adsciri in societatem Germanos. Non Primi Antonii neque Muciani ope Vespasianum magis adolevisse. Aperta odia armaque palam depelli : fraudem et dolum obscura eoque inevitabilia. Civilem stare contra, struere aciem : Hordeonium e cubiculo et lectulo iubere quidquid hosti conducat. Tot armatas fortissimorum virorum manus unius senis valetudine regi : quin potius interfecto traditore fortunam virtutemque suam malo omine exolverent. His inter se vocibus instinctos flammavere insuper adlatae a Vespasiano litterae, quas Flaccus, quia occultari nequibant, pro contione recitavit, vinctosque qui attulerant ad Vitellium misit.

XXV. Sic mitigatis animis Bonnam, hiberna primae legionis, ventum. Infensior illic miles culpam cladis in Hordeonium vertebat : eius iussu derectam [4]

---

[1] e *om. M.*
[2] vectus *add. Haase.*
[3] fremebant *Rhenamus* : p̄mebant *M.*
[4] derecta *M.*

---

[1] At his headquarters at Mayence.
[2] The Twenty-second and the Fourth Macedonian.
[3] At Vetera. Cf. chap. xx.

46

XXIV. Flaccus [1] meanwhile, on hearing that the camp was besieged, sent emissaries through the Gallic provinces to call out auxiliary forces, and entrusted troops picked from his two legions [2] to Dillius Vocula, commander of the Twenty-second legion, with orders to hurry as rapidly as possible along the bank of the Rhine; Flaccus himself went by boat, being in poor health and unpopular with the soldiers; for indeed they murmured against him in no uncertain tone, saying that he had let the Batavian cohorts go from Mogontiacum, had concealed his knowledge of the undertakings of Civilis, and was making allies of the Germans. " Neither Primus Antonius nor Mucianus," they declared, " has contributed more to the strength of Vespasian than Flaccus. Frank hatred and armed action are openly repelled: treachery and deceit are hidden and so cannot be guarded against. Civilis stands before us and forms his battle line: Hordeonius from his chamber and his bed issues orders that are to the enemy's advantage. All these armed companies of the bravest men are dependent on the whim of one sick old man! Rather let us kill the traitor and free our fortune and bravery from this evil omen! " When they had already roused one another by such exhortations, they were further inflamed by a letter from Vespasian, which Flaccus, being unable to conceal it, read aloud before a general assembly, and then sent the men who had brought it in chains to Vitellius.

XXV. In this way the soldiers' anger was appeased and they came to Bonn, the winter quarters of the First legion. There the soldiers were still more threatening and placed the blame for their disaster [3] on Hordeonius: for they declared that it was by his

adversus Batavos aciem, tamquam a Mogontiaco
legiones sequerentur; eiusdem proditione caesos,
nullis supervenientibus auxiliis: ignota haec ceteris
exercitibus neque imperatori suo nuntiari, cum adcursu tot provinciarum extingui repens perfidia
potuerit. Hordeonius exemplaris omnium litterarum,
quibus per Gallias Britanniamque et [1] Hispanias
auxilia orabat, exercitui recitavit instituitque pessi-
mum facinus, ut epistulae aquiliferis legionum tra-
derentur, a quis ante militi quam ducibus legebantur. Tum e seditiosis unum vinciri iubet, magis
usurpandi iuris, quam quia unius culpa foret. Mo-
tusque Bonna exercitus in coloniam Agrippinensem,
adfluentibus auxiliis Gallorum, qui primo rem Romanam enixe iuvabant: mox valescentibus Germanis
pleraeque civitates adversum nos arma *sumpsere* [2]
spe libertatis et, si exuissent servitium, cupidine imperitandi. Gliscebat iracundia legionum, nec terrorem unius militis vincula indiderant: quin idem
ille arguebat ultro conscientiam ducis, tamquam
nuntius inter Civilem Flaccumque falso crimine
testis veri opprimeretur. Conscendit tribunal Vocula mira constantia, prensumque militem ac voci-

---

[1] ex *M*.   [2] sumpsere *add. Agricola.*

orders that they had given battle to the Batavi,
under assurance that the legions were following
from Mogontiacum; that by his treachery their
comrades had been killed, since no help came to
them: that these facts were unknown to the rest
of the armies and were not reported to their emperor,
although this fresh treachery might have been
blocked by a prompt effort on the part of all the
provinces. Hordeonius read to the army copies of
all the letters that he had dispatched throughout
the Gauls, Britain, and the Spains asking for aid.
Moreover, he established the worst kind of precedent
by turning over all letters to the eagle-bearers of the
legions, who read them to the common soldiers before
they were disclosed to the commanders. Then he
ordered a single one of the mutineers to be arrested,
rather to vindicate his authority than because the
fault was that of an individual. The army next
advanced from Bonn to Cologne, while Gallic auxiliary
troops poured in, for the Gauls at first gave vigorous
assistance to the Roman cause: later, as the German
strength increased, many states took up arms against
us, inspired by hope of freedom and by a desire to
have an empire of their own, if they once were rid
of servitude. The angry temper of the legions
increased and the arrest of a single soldier had
brought them no fear: indeed this same soldier
actually charged the general with being privy to
the revolt, claiming that, having been an agent
between Civilis and Flaccus, he was now being
crushed on a false charge because he could bear
witness to the truth. Vocula with admirable courage
mounted the tribunal and ordered the soldier to be
seized, and, in spite of his cries, directed that he be

ferantem duci ad supplicium iussit: et dum mali
pavent, optimus quisque iussis paruere. Exim
consensu ducem Voculam poscentibus, Flaccus
summam rerum ei permisit.

XXVI. Sed discordis animos multa efferabant[1]:
inopia stipendii frumentique et simul dilectum
tributaque Galliae aspernantes, Rhenus incognita
illi caelo siccitate vix navium patiens, arti commeatus,
dispositae per omnem ripam stationes quae Germanos
vado arcerent, eademque de causa minus frugum et
plures qui consumerent. Apud imperitos prodigii
loco accipiebatur ipsa aquarum penuria, tamquam
nos amnes quoque et vetera imperii munimenta
desererent: quod in pace fors seu natura, tunc
fatum et ira deum[2] vocabatur.

Ingressis Novaesium sexta decima legio coniungitur.
Additus Voculae in partem curarum Herennius
Gallus legatus; nec ausi ad hostem pergere . . .[3]
(loco Gelduba nomen est) castra fecere. Ibi struenda
acie, muniendo vallandoque et ceteris belli medita-
mentis militem firmabant. Utque praeda ad virtutem accenderetur, in proximos Cugernorum[4] pagos,
qui societatem Civilis acceperant, ductus a[5] Vocula
exercitus; pars cum Herennio Gallo permansit.

XXVII. Forte navem haud procul castris, fru-

---

[1] efferabant *Beroaldus*: efferebant *M.*
[2] deum *Nipperdey*: dĩ *M.*
[3] *lacunam not. Wurm.*
[4] Cugernorum *Nipperdey*: gugernorum *M.*
[5] a *om. M.*

---

[1] Neuss, near Düsseldorf, but to the west of the Rhine.
[2] Gellep.
[3] Living between the Ubii and the Batavians.

led away to punishment. While the disloyal were cowed, the best obeyed the order. Then, since the troops unanimously demanded Vocula as their general, Flaccus turned over to him the chief command.

XXVI. But there were many things that exasperated their rebellious temper: there was a lack of pay and grain, and at the same time the Gallic provinces scornfully refused a levy and tribute; the Rhine hardly floated boats, owing to a drought unprecedented in that climate; reprovisionment was hampered; detachments were posted all along the bank of the Rhine to keep the Germans from fording it, and for the same reason there was less grain while there were more to eat it. The ignorant regarded even the low water as a prodigy, as if the very rivers, the ancient defences of our empire, were failing us: what they would have called in time of peace an act of chance or nature, they then called fate and the wrath of the gods.

When our troops entered Novaesium [1] the Sixteenth legion joined them. Vocula now had Herennius Gallus associated with him to share his responsibilities; and not daring to move against the enemy, they pitched camp at a place called Gelduba.[2] There they improved the morale of their soldiers by drilling them in battle formation, by having them erect fortifications and a palisade, and by all other forms of military training; and to fire their bravery by giving them a chance to pillage, Vocula led a force into the nearest cantons of the Cugerni,[3] who had allied themselves with Civilis; part of the troops remained with Herennius Gallus.

XXVII. Now it happened that not far from camp

51

mento gravem, cum per vada haesisset, Germani in suam ripam trahebant. Non tulit Gallus misitque subsidio cohortem : auctus et Germanorum numerus, paulatimque adgregantibus se auxiliis acie certatum. Germani multa cum strage nostrorum navem abripiunt. Victi, quod tum in morem verterat, non suam ignaviam, sed perfidiam legati culpabant. Protractum e tentorio, scissa veste, verberato corpore, quo pretio, quibus consciis prodidisset exercitum, dicere iubent. Redit in Hordeonium invidia : illum auctorem sceleris, hunc ministrum vocant, donec exitium minitantibus exterritus proditionem et ipse Hordeonio obiecit; vinctusque adventu demum Voculae exolvitur. Is postera die auctores seditionis morte adfecit : tanta illi exercitui diversitas inerat licentiae patientiaeque. Haud dubie gregarius miles Vitellio fidus, splendidissimus quisque in Vespasianum proni : inde scelerum ac suppliciorum vices et mixtus obsequio furor, ut contineri non possent qui puniri poterant.

XXVIII. At Civilem immensis auctibus universa Germania extollebat, societate nobilissimis obsidum firmata. Ille, ut cuique proximum, vastari Ubios Trevirosque, et aliam manum[1] Mosam amnem transire iubet, ut Menapios et Morinos et extrema Galliarum

---

[1] aliam manum *Freinsheim* : alia manu *M.*

the Germans started to drag to their bank a ship loaded with grain which had grounded on a bar. Gallus did not wish to allow this and sent a cohort to rescue the ship: the Germans also were reinforced, and as assistance gradually gathered, the two sides engaged in a pitched battle. The Germans inflicted heavy losses on our men and got the ship away. The defeated Roman troops, as had then become their fashion, did not blame their own lack of energy, but charged their commander with treachery. They dragged him from his tent, tore his clothing and beat him, bidding him tell what bribe he had received and who his accomplices were in betraying his troops. Their anger toward Hordeonius returned: they called him the author and Gallus the tool, until, frightened by their threats to kill him, he himself actually charged Hordeonius with treachery; and then Hordeonius was put in chains and only released on Vocula's arrival. The following day Vocula had the ringleaders in the mutiny put to death, so great was the contrast in this army between unbridled licence and obedient submission. Undoubtedly the common soldiers were faithful to Vitellius, but all the officers inclined to favour Vespasian: hence that alternation of crimes and punishment and that combination of rage with obedience, so that although the troops could be punished they could not be controlled.

XXVIII. But meanwhile the power of Civilis was being increased by huge reinforcements from all Germany, the alliances being secured by hostages of the highest rank. He ordered the peoples who were nearest to harry the Ubii and Treviri, and directed another force to cross the Meuse to threaten the Menapii and Morini and the borders of the Gallic

quateret. Actae utrobique praedae, infestius in Ubiis, quod gens Germanicae originis eiurata patria [Romanorum nomen][1] Agrippinenses vocarentur. Caesae cohortes eorum in vico Marcoduro incuriosius agentes, quia procul ripa aberant. Nec quievere Ubii quo minus praedas e Germania peterent, primo impune, dein circumventi sunt, per omne id bellum meliore usi fide quam fortuna. Contusis Ubiis gravior et successu rerum ferocior Civilis obsidium legionum urgebat, intentis custodiis ne quis occultus nuntius venientis auxilii penetraret. Machinas molemque operum Batavis delegat: Transrhenanos proelium poscentis ad scindendum vallum ire detrususque redintegrare certamen iubet, superante multitudine et facili damno.

XXIX. Nec finem labori nox attulit: congestis circum lignis accensisque, simul epulantes, ut quisque vino incaluerat, ad pugnam temeritate inani ferebantur. Quippe ipsorum tela per tenebras vana: Romani conspicuam barbarorum aciem, et si quis audacia aut insignibus effulgens,[2] ad ictum destinabant. Intellectum id Civili et restincto igne misceri

---

[1] Romanorum nomen *secl. Gruter.*
[2] et fulgens *M.*

---

[1] The Menapii lived between the Meuse and the Scheldt; the Morini to the south-west of the Menapii on the coast.
[2] Cf. i. 56.   [3] Now Duren.

provinces.[1] Booty was secured from both districts,
but they proceeded with greater severity in the case
of the Ubii, because, though a tribe of Germanic
origin, they had forsworn their native land and
taken the Roman name of Agrippinenses.[2] Some
of their cohorts had been cut to pieces in the district
of Marcodurum,[3] where they were operating care-
lessly, being far from the bank of the Rhine. Yet
the Ubii did not quietly refrain from making plundering raids on Germany, at first with impunity ;
but later they were cut off, and in fact throughout
this entire war their good faith proved superior to
their good fortune. After crushing the Ubii,
Civilis became more threatening, and, being emboldened by his success, pressed on the siege of the
legions, keeping strict guard to see that no secret
messenger should get through to report the approach
of assistance. He charged the Batavi with the duty
of building machines and siege works : the forces
from across the Rhine who demanded battle, he told
to go and tear down the Romans' rampart, and when
they were repulsed, he made them renew the conflict, for their number was more than enough and
the loss easy to bear.

XXIX. Not even night ended the struggle. The
assailants lighted piles of wood about the town, and
while they feasted, as man after man became inflamed with wine, they rushed to battle with unavailing recklessness, for their weapons, thrown into
the darkness, were of no effect : but the Romans
aimed at the barbarians' line, which they could clearly
see, and especially at anyone who was marked by his
courage or decorations. Civilis, grasping the situation, ordered his men to put out their fires and to

cuncta tenebris et armis iubet. Tum vero strepitus dissoni, casus incerti,[1] neque feriendi neque declinandi providentia: unde clamor acciderat, circumagere corpora, tendere artus[2]; nihil prodesse virtus, fors cuncta turbare et ignavorum saepe telis fortissimi cadere. Apud Germanos inconsulta ira: Romanus miles periculorum gnarus[3] ferratas sudis, gravia saxa non forte iaciebat. Ubi sonus molientium aut adpositae scalae hostem in manus dederant, propellere umbone, pilo sequi; multos in moenia egressos pugionibus fodere. Sic exhausta nocte novam aciem dies aperuit.

XXX. Eduxerant Batavi turrim duplici tabulato, quam praetoriae portae (is aequissimus locus) propinquantem promoti contra validi asseres et incussae trabes perfregere multa superstantium pernicie. Pugnatumque in perculsos subita et prospera eruptione; simul a legionariis peritia et arte praestantibus plura struebantur. Praecipuum pavorem intulit suspensum et nutans machinamentum, quo repente demisso praeter suorum ora singuli pluresve hostium sublime rapti verso pondere intra[4] castra effundebantur. Civilis omissa expugnandi[5] spe rursus per

---

[1] casus incerti *codd. dett.*: corsus inceptti *in frustulo membranae adglutinato* M[2].

[2] artus *Lipsius*: arcus *M.*

[3] gnarus b[2], *Rhenanus*: ignarus *M.*   [4] infra *M.*

[5] expugnandi *Ruperti*: obpugnandi *M.*

---

[1] The gate to the camp toward the enemy, so named from its relation to the quarters of the commanding officer, the *praetorium.*

add the confusion of darkness to the combat. Then in truth it was all discordant cries, uncertain chances, no one could see to strike or parry : wherever a shout was raised, there they turned and lunged ; courage was of no avail, chance made utter confusion, and often the bravest fell under the weapons of cowards. The Germans obeyed only blind fury ; the Roman soldiers, being experienced in danger, did not shoot their iron-tipped pikes and heavy stones at random. When the sound showed them that men were climbing up the walls, or the raising of ladders delivered their foes into their hands, they beat them down with the bosses of their shields and followed this action with their javelins ; many who scaled the walls they stabbed with daggers. When the night had been thus spent, the day disclosed a new struggle.

XXX. The Batavi had built a tower with two stories. This they pushed toward the praetorian gate,[1] as the ground was most level there, but the Romans thrust out against it strong poles, and with repeated blows of beams broke it down, inflicting heavy loss on those who were on it. Then, while their foes were in disorder, they made a sudden and successful sally upon them ; and at the same time the legionaries, who were superior in skill and artifices, devised further means against them. The barbarians were most terrified by a well-balanced machine poised above them, which being suddenly dropped caught up one or more of the enemy before the eyes of their comrades and with a shift of the counterweight threw them into camp. Civilis now gave up hope of capturing the camp by storm and again began an inactive siege, trying meanwhile to

otium adsidebat, nuntiis et promissis fidem legionum convellens.

XXXI. Haec in Germania ante Cremonense proelium gesta, cuius eventum litterae Primi Antonii docuere, addito Caecinae edicto; et praefectus cohortis e victis,[1] Alpinius Montanus, fortunam partium praesens fatebatur. Diversi hinc motus animorum: auxilia e Gallia, quis nec amor neque odium in partis, militia[2] sine adfectu, hortantibus praefectis statim a Vitellio desciscunt: vetus miles cunctabatur. Sed adigente Hordeonio Flacco, instantibus tribunis, dixit sacramentum, non vultu neque animo satis adfirmans: et cum cetera iuris iurandi verba conciperent, Vespasiani nomen haesitantes aut levi murmure et plerumque silentio transmittebant.

XXXII. Lectae deinde pro contione epistulae Antonii ad Civilem suspiciones militum inritavere, tamquam ad socium partium scriptae et de Germanico exercitu hostiliter. Mox adlatis Geldubam in castra nuntiis eadem dicta factaque, et missus cum mandatis Montanus ad Civilem ut absisteret[3] bello neve externa armis falsis velaret: si Vespasianum iuvare adgressus foret, satis factum coeptis. Ad ea Civilis primo callide: post ubi videt Montanum praeferocem ingenio paratumque in res novas, orsus

---

[1] victis *Rhenanus*: victus *M*.
[2] militia *Rhenanus*: militiae *M*.　　[3] absistere *M*.

---

[1] That is, before the end of October, 69 A.D.
[2] That is, he pretended to favour Vespasian, but he was actually declaring war on the Roman Empire.

shake the confidence of the legions by messages and promises.

XXXI. These things took place in Germany before the battle of Cremona,[1] the result of which was learned through a letter from Primus Antonius, to which was added a proclamation issued by Caecina; and a prefect of a cohort from the defeated side, one Alpinius Montanus, acknowledged in person the misfortune of his party. This news aroused different emotions: the Gallic auxiliaries, who felt no party attachment or hatred and who served without enthusiasm, at the instigation of their officers immediately abandoned Vitellius; the veteran soldiers hesitated. But at the command of Hordeonius Flaccus and moved by the appeals of their tribunes, they took an oath which neither their looks nor their wills quite confirmed: and while they repeated the greater part of the usual formula, they hesitated at Vespasian's name, some murmuring it faintly, most passing it over in silence.

XXXII. Then some letters of Antonius to Civilis, being read before the assembled troops, roused their suspicions, for they seemed to be addressed to an ally and spoke in hostile fashion of the German army. Presently, when the news reached the Roman camp at Gelduba, it caused the same discussions and the same acts; and Montanus was sent to Civilis with orders bidding him give up the war and cease cloaking hostile acts with a false pretext:[2] he was to say that if Civilis had moved to help Vespasian, his efforts had already been sufficient. To this Civilis at first made a crafty answer: afterwards, when he saw that Montanus was of an impetuous nature and inclined to revolt, he began to complain of the dangers which

a questu periculisque quae per quinque et viginti annos in castris Romanis exhausisset, " egregium " inquit " pretium laborum recepi,[1] necem fratris et vincula mea et saevissimas huius exercitus voces, quibus ad supplicium petitus iure gentium poenas reposco. Vos autem Treviri ceteraeque servientium animae, quod praemium effusi totiens sanguinis expectatis nisi ingratam militiam, inmortalia tributa, virgas, securis et dominorum ingenia? En ego praefectus unius cohortis et Canninefates Batavique, exigua Galliarum portio, vana illa castrorum spatia excidimus vel saepta ferro fameque premimus. Denique ausos aut libertas sequetur aut victi idem erimus." Sic accensum, sed molliora referre iussum dimittit : ille ut inritus legationis redit, cetera dissimulans, quae mox erupere.

XXXIII. Civilis parte copiarum retenta veteranas cohortis et quod e Germanis maxime promptum adversus Voculam exercitumque eius mittit, Iulio Maximo et Claudio Victore, sororis suae filio, ducibus. Rapiunt in transitu hiberna alae Asciburgii sita; adeoque improvisi castra involavere ut non adloqui, non pandere aciem Vocula potuerit : id solum ut in tumultu monuit, subsignano milite media firmare :

[1] recipi *M*.

---

[1] Asberg.
[2] At Gelduba, now Gellep. Cf. chap. xxvi above.

he had passed through for twenty-five years in the camps of the Romans. "A glorious reward indeed," said he, "have I gained for my labours—my brother's murder, my own chains, and the savage cries of this army here, demanding my punishment; the right of nations warrants me in demanding vengeance for these things. You Treviri likewise and all the rest of you who have the spirits of slaves, what return do you expect for the blood you have so often shed save an ungrateful service in arms, endless tribute, floggings, the axes of the executioner, and all that your masters' wits can devise? See how I, prefect of a single cohort, with the Canninefates and Batavi, a trifling part of all the Gauls, have shown their vast camps to be in vain and have destroyed them or am besetting them and pressing them hard with sword and famine. In short, be bold! Either liberty will follow your daring or we shall all be defeated together." With such words Civilis inflamed Montanus, but he sent him away with orders to make a mild report. So Montanus returned, bearing himself as though he had failed in his embassy, but concealing all that later came to light.

XXXIII. Civilis retained part of his troops with him, but dispatched the veteran cohorts and the best of the Germans under the leadership of Julius Maximus and Claudius Victor, his own nephew, to attack Vocula and his army. On their march they plundered the winter quarters of a squadron of cavalry at Asciburgium;[1] and they assailed Vocula's camp[2] so unexpectedly that he could not address his soldiers or form his men in line: the only advice that he could give in the confusion was to strengthen the centre with the legionaries: the auxiliary troops

auxilia passim circumfusa sunt. Eques prorupit, exceptusque compositis hostium ordinibus terga in suos vertit. Caedes inde, non proelium. Et Nerviorum cohortes, metu seu perfidia, latera nostrorum nudavere: sic ad legiones perventum, quae amissis signis intra vallum sternebantur, cum repente novo auxilio fortuna pugnae mutatur. Vasconum lectae a Galba cohortes ac tum accitae, dum castris propinquant, audito proeliantium clamore intentos hostis a tergo invadunt latioremque quam pro numero terrorem faciunt, aliis a Novaesio, aliis a Mogontiaco universas copias advenisse credentibus. Is error Romanis[1] addit animos, et dum alienis viribus confidunt, suas recepere. Fortissimus quisque e Batavis, quantum peditum erat, conciduntur[2]: eques evasit cum signis captivisque, quos prima acie corripuerant. Caesorum eo die in partibus nostris maior numerus set[3] imbellior, e Germanis ipsa robora.

XXXIV. Dux uterque pari culpa meritus adversa prosperis defuere. Nam Civilis si maioribus copiis instruxisset aciem, circumiri a tam paucis cohortibus nequisset castraque perrupta excidisset: Vocula nec adventum hostium exploravit, eoque simul egressus victusque; dein victoriae parum confisus, tritis[4] frustra

[1] is error Romanis: is error *M*.
[2] conciduntur *Halm*: funduntur *M*.
[3] set *Madvig*: et *M*.   [4] triti *M*.

---

[1] The ancestors apparently of the modern Basques, then living in the north-eastern part of Hispania Tarraconensis.

were scattered about everywhere. The cavalry charged, but, being received by the enemy in good order, fled back to their own lines. What followed was a massacre, not a battle. The Nervian cohorts also, prompted by fear or treachery, left our flanks unprotected: thus the burden now fell upon the legionaries, and they, having lost their standards, were already being cut down inside the palisade, when suddenly unexpected aid changed the fortune of the battle. Some cohorts of the Vascones [1] which Galba had levied earlier and which had now been sent for, approaching camp and hearing the sound of the struggle, assailed the enemy in the rear while they were absorbed in the contest, and caused a more widespread panic than their numbers warranted, some imagining that all the troops from Novaesium, others that those from Mogontiacum, had arrived. The enemy's mistake inspired the Romans with courage, and while trusting in the strength of others, they recovered their own. All the best of the Batavian infantry were cut down; their horse escaped with the standards and captives that they had seized at the first onset. The number of the killed on our side that day was larger, but was not made up of the bravest; the Germans lost their very best troops.

XXXIV. The generals on both sides by equal faults deserved their reverses and failed to use their success: had Civilis put more troops in line, he could not have been surrounded by so few cohorts, and after breaking into the Roman camp, he would have destroyed it: Vocula failed to discover the enemy's approach, and therefore the moment that he sallied forth he was beaten; then, lacking confidence in his

diebus castra in hostem movit, quem si statim impellere cursumque rerum sequi maturasset, solvere obsidium legionum eodem impetu potuit. Temptaverat interim Civilis obsessorum animos, tamquam perditae apud Romanos res et suis victoria provenisset : circumferebantur signa vexillaque, ostentati etiam captivi. Ex quibus unus, egregium facinus ausus, clara voce gesta patefecit, confossus ilico[1] a Germanis : unde maior indici fides ; simul vastatione incendiisque flagrantium villarum venire victorem exercitum intellegebatur. In conspectu castrorum constitui signa fossamque et vallum circumdari Vocula iubet : depositis impedimentis sarcinisque expediti certarent. Hinc in ducem clamor pugnam poscentium ; et minari adsueverant. Ne tempore quidem ad ordinandam aciem capto incompositi fessique proelium sumpsere ; nam Civilis aderat, non minus vitiis hostium quam virtute suorum fretus. Varia apud Romanos fortuna et seditiosissimus quisque ignavus : quidam recentis victoriae memores retinere locum, ferire hostem, seque et proximos hortari et redintegrata acie manus ad obsessos tendere ne tempori deessent. Illi cuncta e muris cernentes omnibus portis prorumpunt. Ac forte Civilis lapsu equi pro-

---

[1] illico *Freinsheim* : ilico *Halm* : illic *M.*

victory, he wasted some days before advancing against the foe, whereas if he had been prompt to press him hard and to follow up events, he might have raised the siege of the legions at one blow. Meanwhile Civilis had tested the temper of the besieged by pretending that the Roman cause was lost and that his side was victorious: he paraded the Roman ensigns and standards; he even exhibited captives. One of these had the courage to do an heroic deed, shouting out the truth, for which he was at once run through by the Germans: their act inspired the greater confidence in his statement; and at the same time the harried fields and the fires of the burning farm-houses announced the approach of a victorious army. When in sight of camp Vocula ordered the standards to be set up and a ditch and a palisade to be constructed about them, bidding his troops leave their baggage and kits there that they might fight unencumbered. This caused the troops to cry out against their commander and to demand instant battle; and in fact they had grown accustomed to threaten. Without taking time even to form a line, disordered and weary as they were, they engaged the enemy; for Civilis was ready for them, trusting in his opponents' mistakes no less than in the bravery of his own troops. Fortune varied on the Roman side, and the most mutinous proved cowards: some there were who, remembering their recent victory, kept their places, struck at the enemy, exhorted one another and their neighbours as well; reforming the line, they held out their hands to the besieged, begging them not to lose their opportunity. The latter, who saw everything from the walls, sallied forth from all the gates of their camp. Now at this

stratus, credita per utrumque exercitum fama vulneratum aut interfectum, immane quantum suis pavoris et hostibus alacritatis indidit: sed Vocula omissis fugientium tergis vallum turrisque castrorum augebat, tamquam rursus obsidium immineret, corrupta totiens victoria non falso suspectus bellum malle.

XXXV. Nihil aeque exercitus nostros quam egestas copiarum fatigabat. Impedimenta legionum cum imbelli turba Novaesium missa ut inde terrestri itinere frumentum adveherent; nam flumine hostes potiebantur. Primum agmen securum incessit, nondum satis firmo Civile. Qui ubi rursum missos Novaesium frumentatores datasque in praesidium cohortis velut multa pace ingredi accepit, rarum apud signa militem, arma in vehiculis, cunctos licentia vagos, compositus invadit, praemissis qui pontis et viarum angusta insiderent. Pugnatum longo agmine et incerto Marte, donec proelium nox dirimeret. Cohortes Geldubam perrexere, manentibus, ut fuerant, castris, quae relictorum illic militum praesidio tenebantur. Non erat dubium quantum in regressu discriminis adeundum foret frumentatoribus onustis perculsisque.[1] Addit exercitui suo Vocula mille delectos e quinta et quinta decima legionibus apud

---

[1] perculsisque *Agricola*: periculisque *M*.

moment Civilis's horse happened to slip and throw him; whereupon both sides accepted the report that he had been wounded or killed. It was marvellous how this belief terrified his men and inspired their foes with enthusiasm: yet Vocula, neglecting to pursue his flying foes, proceeded to strengthen the palisade and towers of his camp as if he were again threatened with a siege, thus by his repeated failure to take advantage of victory giving good ground for the suspicion that he preferred war to peace.

XXXV. Nothing distressed our troops so much as the lack of provisions. The legions' baggage train was sent on to Novaesium with the men who were unfit for service to bring provisions from there overland; for the enemy controlled the river. The first convoy went without trouble, since Civilis was not yet strong enough to attack. But when he heard that the sutlers, who had been despatched again to Novaesium, and the cohorts escorting them were proceeding as if in time of peace, that there were few soldiers with the standards, that their arms were being carried in the carts while they all strolled along at will, he drew up his forces and attacked them, sending first some troops to occupy the bridges and narrow parts of the roads. They fought in a long line and indecisively until at last night put an end to the conflict. The cohorts reached Gelduba, where the camp remained in its old condition, being held by a force which had been left there. They had no doubt of the great danger that they would run if they returned with the sutlers heavily loaded and in a state of terror. Vocula reinforced his army with a thousand men picked from the Fifth and Fifteenth legions that had been besieged at Vetera,

Vetera obsessis, indomitum militem et ducibus infensum. Plures quam iussum erat profecti palam in agmine fremebant, non se ultra famem, insidias legatorum toleraturos: at qui remanserant, desertos se[1] abducta parte legionum querebantur. Duplex hinc seditio, aliis revocantibus Voculam, aliis redire in castra abnuentibus.

XXXVI. Interim Civilis Vetera circumsedit: Vocula Geldubam atque inde Novaesium concessit, [Civilis capit Geldubam][2] mox haud procul Novaesio equestri proelio prospere certavit. Sed miles secundis adversisque perinde[3] in exitium ducum accendebatur; et adventu quintanorum quintadecimanorumque auctae legiones donativum exposcunt, comperto pecuniam a Vitellio missam. Nec diu cunctatus Hordeonius nomine Vespasiani dedit, idque praecipuum fuit seditionis alimentum. Effusi in luxum et epulas et nocturnos coetus veterem in Hordeonium iram renovant, nec ullo legatorum tribunorumve obsistere auso (quippe omnem pudorem nox ademerat) protractum e cubili interficiunt. Eadem in Voculam parabantur, nisi servili habitu per tenebras ignoratus evasisset.

XXXVII. Ubi sedato impetu metus rediit, centuriones cum epistulis ad civitates Galliarum misere,

[1] que M.
[2] Civilis capit Geldubam *secl. Urlichs.*
[3] proinde M.

troops untamed and hostile toward their commanders. More men started than had been
ordered to do so, and on the march they began to
murmur openly that they would no longer endure
hunger or the plots of their commanders; but those
who were being left behind complained that they
were being abandoned by the withdrawal of part
of the legions. So a double mutiny began, some
urging Vocula to return, others refusing to go back
to camp.

XXXVI. Meantime Civilis besieged Vetera: Vocula withdrew to Gelduba and then to Novaesium.
Later he was successful in an engagement with the
cavalry not far from Novaesium. But success and
failure alike fired the soldiers with a wish to murder
their leaders; and when the legionaries had been
reinforced by the arrival of the men from the Fifth
and Fifteenth, they began to demand the donative,
for they had learned that Vitellius had sent the
money. Hordeonius did not long delay, but gave
them the gift in Vespasian's name, and this act more
than anything else fostered the mutiny. The
soldiers, abandoning themselves to debauchery,
feasts, and meetings by night, revived their old
hatred for Hordeonius, and without a legate or
tribune daring to oppose them, for the darkness had
taken away all sense of shame, they actually dragged
him from his bed and killed him. They were preparing to treat Vocula in the same way, but he disguised himself in a slave's clothes and escaped in the
darkness.

XXXVII. When this outburst died down, their
fears returned; and the troops sent centurions with
letters to the Gallic communities to ask for auxiliary

auxilia ac stipendia oraturos : ipsi, ut est vulgus sine
rectore praeceps pavidum socors, adventante Civile
raptis temere armis ac statim omissis, in fugam ver-
tuntur. Res adversae discordiam peperere, iis qui
e superiore exercitu erant causam suam dissocianti-
bus ; Vitellii tamen imagines in castris et per proximas Belgarum civitates repositae, cum iam Vitellius
occidisset. Dein mutati in paenitentiam primani
quartanique et duoetvicensimani Voculam sequuntur,
apud quem resumpto Vespasiani sacramento ad
liberandum Mogontiaci obsidium ducebantur. Dis-
cesserant obsessores, mixtus ex Chattis [1] Usipis Mat-
tiacis exercitus, satietate praedae nec incruentati :
quia [2] dispersos [3] et nescios miles noster invaserat.
Quin et loricam vallumque per finis suos Treviri
struxere, magnisque in vicem cladibus cum Germanis
certabant, donec egregia erga populum Romanum
merita mox rebelles foedarent.

XXXVIII. Interea Vespasianus iterum ac Titus
consulatum absentes inierunt, maesta et multiplici
metu suspensa civitate, quae super instantia mala
falsos pavores induerat, descivisse Africam res novas
moliente L. Pisone. Is *pro consule* [4] provinciae nequaquam turbidus ingenio ; sed quia naves saevitia

---

[1] ex Cattis *Rhenanus* : et caitis *M*.
[2] incruentati quia *Heraeus* : incruentati via *dett.* : incruen-
tari via *M*.
[3] adispersos *M*.
[4] pro consule *add*. *I. Gronovius*.

---

[1] Vitellius was killed Dec. 20 or 21. Cf. iii. 85.
[2] For the Chatti, see note on chap. xii. The Usipi lived
south of the Tencteri (chap. xxi) and west of the Chatti,
between the Sieg and the Lahn ; the Mattiaci dwelt between
the Main, the Rhine and the Lahn, around the present
Wiesbaden.

troops and contributions: they themselves, for a mob without a leader is always hasty, timid, and without energy, at the approach of Civilis quickly caught up their arms, then immediately dropped them and fled. Adversity bred discord among them, and the men from the army of upper Germany dissociated their cause from that of the rest; still the images of Vitellius were replaced in camp and in the nearest Belgian communities, although he was already dead.[1] Then, repenting their action, the men of the First, Fourth, and Twenty-second legions followed Vocula, who made them take again the oath of allegiance to Vespasian and led them to break the siege of Mogontiacum. But the besiegers, a motley army made up of Chatti, Usipi, and Mattiaci,[2] had already withdrawn, satisfied with their booty; however, they suffered some loss, for our soldiers had fallen on them while they were scattered and unsuspecting. Moreover, the Treviri built a breastwork and palisade along their borders and fought the Germans with great losses on both sides, until presently by their rebellion they sullied the record of their conspicuous services to the Roman people.

XXXVIII. In the meantime Vespasian entered on his second consulship and Titus on his first, although absent from Rome;[3] the citizens, downcast and anxious from many fears, had added false alarms to the actual evils that threatened them, saying that Lucius Piso had plotted against the government and had led Africa to revolt. Piso, then pro-consul of Africa, was far from being a turbulent spirit; but since the grain ships for Rome were now detained by the

---

[3] This marks the beginning of 70 A.D.

hiemis prohibebantur, vulgus alimenta in dies mercari
solitum, cui una ex re publica annonae cura, clausum
litus, retineri commeatus, dum timet, credebat,
augentibus famam Vitellianis, qui studium partium
nondum posuerant, ne [1] victoribus quidem ingrato
rumore, quorum cupiditates externis quoque bellis
inexplebilis nulla umquam civilis victoria satiavit.

XXXIX. Kalendis Ianuariis in senatu, quem
Iulius Frontinus praetor urbanus vocaverat, legatis
exercitibusque ac regibus laudes gratesque decretae;
et Tettio [2] Iuliano praetura, tamquam transgre-
dientem in partis Vespasiani legionem deseruisset,
ablata ut in Plotium Grypum transferretur; Hormo
dignitas equestris data. Et mox eiurante Frontino
Caesar Domitianus praeturam cepit. Eius nomen
epistulis edictisque praeponebatur, vis penes Mucianum erat, nisi quod pleraque Domitianus insti-
gantibus amicis aut propria libidine audebat. Sed
praecipuus Muciano metus e Primo Antonio Varoque
Arrio, quos recentis clarosque rerum fama ac militum
studiis etiam populus fovebat, quia in neminem ultra
aciem saevierant. Et ferebatur Antonius Scribo-
nianum Crassum, egregiis maioribus et fraterna
imagine fulgentem, ad capessendam rem publicam
hortatus, haud defutura consciorum manu, ni Scri-

---

[1] ne *I. Gronovius*: nec *M*.
[2] Tettio *Orelli*: tito *M*.

---

[1] That is, so rapacious had men become that they cared
less for power than spoils.
[2] Since both consuls were absent.
[3] Cf. ii. 81.
[4] Cf. ii. 85; iii. 52.
[5] Cf. iii. 12, 28.
[6] Brother of Piso, whom Galba had adopted.

severity of the winter, the common people at Rome, being accustomed to buy their food day by day and having no public interests save the grain supply, believed in their fear that the ports were closed and the convoys of grain held back; the partisans of Vitellius who had not yet given up their party zeal fostered the report, nor was, in fact, the rumour ungrateful even to the victorious party, whose greed, for which even foreign wars were insufficient, no civil victory could ever satisfy.[1]

XXXIX. On the first of January the senate, at a session called by the city praetor,[2] Julius Frontinus, passed votes eulogizing and thanking the generals, armies, and allied princes;[3] Tettius Julianus was deprived of his praetorship on the ground that he had left his legion when it went over to Vespasian's side, and the office was given to Plotius Grypus;[4] Hormus received equestrian rank.[5] Soon after, Frontinus having resigned, Caesar Domitian received the praetorship. His name was prefixed to epistles and edicts, but the real power was in the hands of Mucianus, except in so far as Domitian dared to perform many acts at the instigation of his friends or the promptings of his own fancy. But Mucianus chiefly feared Primus Antonius and Varus Arrius, for they had won distinction by their recent victories and were popular with the troops; even the civilians favoured them because they had never drawn the sword against any man save on the battle-field. There was too a rumour that Antonius had urged Scribonianus Crassus,[6] distinguished as he was by his illustrious ancestry and his brother's eminence, to seize the reins of government, with the prospect that there would be no lack of men to support the plot,

bonianus abnuisset, ne paratis quidem corrumpi
facilis, adeo metuens incerta. Igitur Mucianus,
quia propalam opprimi Antonius nequibat, multis in
senatu laudibus cumulatum secretis promissis onerat,
citeriorem Hispaniam ostentans discessu Cluvii
Rufi vacuam; simul amicis eius tribunatus praefectu-
rasque largitur. Dein postquam inanem animum
spe et cupidine impleverat, viris abolet dimissa in
hiberna legione septima, cuius flagrantissimus in
Antonium amor. Et tertia legio, familiaris Arrio
Varo miles, in Syriam remissa; pars exercitus in
Germanias ducebatur. Sic egesto quidquid turbidum rediit[1] urbi sua forma legesque et munia
magistratuum.

XL. Quo die senatum ingressus est Domitianus,
de absentia patris fratrisque ac iuventa sua pauca et
modica disseruit, decorus habitu; et ignotis adhuc
moribus crebra oris confusio pro modestia accipiebatur. Referente Caesare de restituendis Galbae
honoribus, censuit Curtius Montanus ut Pisonis
quoque memoria celebraretur. Patres utrumque
iussere: de Pisone inritum fuit. Tum sorte ducti
per quos redderentur bello rapta, quique aera legum
vetustate delapsa noscerent figerentque, et fastos

---

[1] rediit *Haase*: redit *M*.

---

[1] Cf. ii. 86.
[2] Where their headquarters were.

had not Scribonianus refused the proposal, for he could not be easily corrupted even by a certain prospect of success, still less when he feared an uncertain issue. Therefore Mucianus, being unable to crush Antonius openly, lauded him to the skies in the senate and overwhelmed him with promises in secret, pointing out that the governorship of Hither Spain had been left vacant by the withdrawal of Cluvius Rufus; at the same time he bestowed tribuneships and prefectureships on the friends of Antonius. Then, when he had filled his foolish mind with hope and desire, Mucianus destroyed his strength by sending to its winter quarters the Seventh legion, which was most passionately devoted to him.[1] Furthermore, the Third legion, Arrius Varus's own force, was sent back to Syria;[2] and part of the army was started on its way to the Germanies. Thus the city, freed of turbulent elements, recovered its old appearance; the laws regained their force and the magistrates their functions.

XL. On the day when Domitian entered the senate, he spoke briefly and in moderate terms of his father's and brother's absence and of his own youth; his bearing was becoming; and since his character was as yet unknown, the confusion that frequently covered his face was regarded as a mark of modesty. When Domitian brought up the question of restoring Galba's honours, Curtius Montanus moved that Piso's memory also should be honoured. The senate passed both motions, but the one with regard to Piso was never carried into effect. Then a commission was selected by lot to restore property stolen during the war, to determine and replace the bronze tablets of the laws that had fallen down from

adulatione temporum foedatos exonerarent modumque publicis impensis facerent. Redditur Tettio Iuliano praetura, postquam cognitus est ad Vespasianum confugisse: Grypo honor mansit. Repeti inde cognitionem inter Musonium Rufum et Publium Celerem placuit, damnatusque Publius et Sorani manibus satis factum. Insignis publica severitate dies ne privatim quidem laude caruit. Iustum iudicium explesse Musonius videbatur, diversa fama Demetrio Cynicam sectam professo, quod manifestum reum ambitiosius quam honestius defendisset ; ipsi Publio neque animus in periculis neque oratio suppeditavit. Signo ultionis in accusatores dato, petiit[1] a Caesare Iunius Mauricus[2] ut commentariorum principalium potestatem senatui faceret, per quos nosceret quem quisque accusandum poposcisset. Consulendum tali super re principem respondit.

XLI. Senatus inchoantibus primoribus ius iurandum concepit quo certatim omnes magistratus, ceteri, ut sententiam rogabantur, deos testis advocabant, nihil ope sua factum quo cuiusquam salus laederetur, neque se praemium aut honorem ex calamitate civium cepisse, trepidis et verba iuris iurandi per varias artis mutantibus, quis flagitii conscientia inerat. Probabant religionem patres,

---

[1] petiit *Nipperdey*: petit *M*.
[2] Mauricus *Beroaldus*: maricus *M*.

---

[1] Public festivals and sacrifices had been established in honour of even the worst emperors; and in 65 A.D. the name of the month of April had been changed to Neroneus, May to Claudius, and June to Germanicus. Vid. Tac. *Ann.* xv. 74; xvi. 2. Cf. Suet. *Cal.* 15; *Dom.* 13; and *Hist. Aug. Vit. Com.* 11, 8.

[2] Described above in chap. x.

age, to purge the public records of the additions with
which the flattery of the times had defiled them,[1] and
to check public expenditures. His praetorship was
given back to Tettius Julianus after it became known
that he had fled to Vespasian for protection : Grypus
retained his office. Then the senate decided to take
up again the case between Musonius Rufus and
Publius Celer ; [2] Publius was condemned and the
shades of Soranus were appeased. That day which
was marked by this act of public severity was not
without its private glory also. Musonius was held
to have carried through an act of justice, but public
opinion took a different view of Demetrius the Cynic,
because he had shown more selfish interest than
honourable purpose in defending Publius, who was
manifestly guilty : Publius himself in the hour of
danger had neither the courage nor the eloquence
to meet it. Now that the signal had been given for
vengeance on the informers, Junius Mauricus asked
Caesar to give the senate power to examine the
imperial records that they might know who the
informers were that had brought each accusation.
Domitian replied that on a matter of such importance
he must consult the emperor.

XLI. Under the lead of its principal members the
senate drew up a form of oath, wherein all the
magistrates and the other senators, in the order in
which they were called, eagerly invoked the gods
to witness that they had supported no act by which
any man's safety could be imperilled, and that
they had never received reward or office for any
man's misfortune. Those who were conscious of
guilt repeated it timidly and changed its words in
various ways. The senate approved their scruples,

periurium arguebant; eaque velut censura in Sariolenum Voculam et Nonium Attianum et Cestium Severum acerrime incubuit, crebris apud Neronem delationibus famosos. Sariolenum et recens crimen urgebat, quod apud Vitellium molitus eadem foret: nec destitit senatus manus intentare Voculae, donec curia excederet. Ad Paccium Africanum transgressi eum quoque proturbant, tamquam Neroni Scribonios fratres concordia opibusque insignis ad exitium monstravisset. Africanus neque fateri audebat neque abnuere poterat: in Vibium Crispum, cuius interrogationibus fatigabatur, ultro conversus, miscendo quae defendere nequibat, societate culpae invidiam declinavit.

XLII. Magnam eo die pietatis eloquentiaeque famam Vipstanus [1] Messala adeptus est, nondum senatoria aetate, ausus pro fratre Aquilio Regulo deprecari. Regulum subversa Crassorum et Orfiti domus in summum odium extulerat: sponte [e xsc] [2] accusationem subisse iuvenis admodum, nec depellendi periculi sed in spem potentiae videbatur; et Sulpicia [3] Praetextata Crassi uxor quattuorque liberi, si cognosceret senatus, ultores aderant. Igitur Messala non causam neque reum tueri, sed periculis fratris semet opponens flexerat quosdam. Occurrit

---

[1] Vipstanus *Ruperti*: viptanus *M*.
[2] e xsc *secl. Colerus aliique*: Caesaris *Müller, Halm*.
[3] Sulpicia *Puteolanus*: supplicia *M*.

---

[1] Rufus and Proculus Scribonius, devoted brothers, had been governors of Upper and Lower Germany respectively. During his tour of Greece in 67 A.D., Nero, wishing to seize their wealth, sent for them and basely forced them to commit suicide. See Dio Cass. lxiii. 17.
[2] Cf. ii. 10.   [3] Cf. iii. 9.

but disapproved their perjuries; this kind of censure fell heaviest on Sariolenus Vocula, Nonius Attianus, and Cestius Severus, who were notorious for their many delations under Nero. Sariolenus was also under the burden of recent charges, for he had tried the same course under Vitellius; nor did the senate cease threatening him with personal violence until he left the senate house. They then turned on Paccius Africanus and drove him out also, because he had suggested to Nero the ruin of the brothers Scribonii, who were eminent for their fraternal concord and their wealth.[1] Africanus did not dare to confess his crime nor could he deny it : but turning upon Vibius Crispus,[2] who was harassing him with questions, he implicated him in acts that he could not deny, and so by making Vibius a partner in his guilt he diverted the indignation of the senate.

XLII. On that day Vipstanus Messala[3] gained great reputation for his fraternal affection and his eloquence, for although he was not yet old enough to enter the senate,[4] he dared to appeal for his brother Aquilius Regulus.[5] Regulus had made himself most bitterly hated for causing the downfall of the houses of the Crassi and of Orfitus : he seemed voluntarily to have taken the accusation on himself though quite a youth, not to ward off danger from himself, but because he hoped thereby to gain power; and Sulpicia Pratextata, the wife of Crassus, and her four children were also there to ask vengeance, if the senate took up the case. So Messala had offered no defence on the case or for the accused, but by facing himself the dangers that threatened his brother, had succeeded in moving some of the sena-

---

[4] That is, he was not yet twenty-five.   [5] Cf. i. 48.

truci oratione Curtius Montanus, eo usque progressus
ut post caedem Galbae datam interfectori Pisonis
pecuniam a Regulo adpetitumque morsu Pisonis
caput obiectaret. " Hoc certe " inquit " Nero non
coegit, nec dignitatem aut salutem [1] illa saevitia
redemisti. Sane toleremus istorum defensiones qui
perdere alios quam periclitari ipsi maluerunt: te
securum reliquerat exul pater et divisa inter creditores bona, nondum honorum capax aetas, nihil quod
ex te concupisceret Nero, nihil quod timeret. Libidine sanguinis et hiatu praemiorum ignotum adhuc
ingenium et nullis defensionibus expertum caede
nobili imbuisti, cum ex funere rei publicae raptis
consularibus spoliis, septuagiens sestertio [2] saginatus [3]
et sacerdotio fulgens innoxios pueros, inlustris senes,
conspicuas feminas eadem ruina prosterneres, cum
segnitiam Neronis incusares, quod per singulas
domos seque et delatores fatigaret: posse universum
senatum una voce subverti. Retinete, patres conscripti, et reservate hominem tam expediti consilii
ut omnis aetas instructa sit, et quo modo senes nostri
Marcellum, Crispum, iuvenes Regulum imitentur.
Invenit aemulos etiam [4] infelix nequitia: quid si
floreat vigeatque? Et quem adhuc quaestorium
offendere non audemus, praetorium et consularem
ausuri [5] sumus? An Neronem extremum dominorum

---

[1] aut salutem *Lipsius*: austa lutem *M.*
[2] septuagenses tertio *M.*
[3] saginatus *b, Faernus*: signatus *M.*
[4] aemulos etiam *Acidalius*: etiam emulos *M.*
[5] ausuri *Lipsius*: visuri *M.*

tors. But Curtius Montanus opposed him with a
bitter speech, and went so far as to charge that after
the murder of Galba, Regulus had given money to
Piso's assassin and had torn Piso's head with his
teeth. " That surely," said he, " is something which
Nero did not compel you to do, and you did not buy
immunity for your position or your life by that
savage act. Let us, to be sure, put up with the
defence of such folk as have preferred to ruin others
rather than run risks themselves : in your case the
exile of your father and the division of his property
among his creditors left you in security ; you were
not yet old enough to hold office, you had nothing
that Nero could covet, nothing that he could fear.
Through lust for slaughter and greed for rewards you
gave your talents, till then undiscovered and inexperienced in defence, their first taste for noble blood,
when in the ruin of the state you seized the spoils
of a consular, battened on seven million sesterces, and
enjoyed the splendour of a priesthood, involving in
the same ruin innocent children, eminent old men,
and noble women ; you reproved Nero for his lack
of energy in wearying himself and his informers over
single houses ; you declared that the whole senate
could be overthrown with a word. Keep and preserve, gentlemen of the senate, this man of such
ready counsel, that every age may learn of him and
that our young men may imitate Regulus, as our old
men did a Marcellus, a Crispus. Wickedness, even
if unlucky, finds rivals. What would be the case if
it should flourish and be strong ? And if we do not
dare to offend this man while he is only an ex-
quaestor, shall we dare to oppose him when he has
been praetor and consul ? Do you think that Nero

putatis? Idem crediderant qui Tiberio, qui Gaio superstites fuerunt, cum interim intestabilior et saevior exortus est. Non timemus Vespasianum; ea principis aetas, ea moderatio: sed diutius durant exempla quam mores. Elanguimus, patres conscripti, nec iam ille senatus sumus qui occiso Nerone delatores et ministros more maiorum puniendos flagitabat. Optimus est post malum principem dies primus."

XLIII. Tanto cum adsensu senatus auditus est Montanus ut spem caperet Helvidius posse etiam Marcellum prosterni. Igitur a laude Cluvii Rufi orsus, qui perinde dives et eloquentia clarus nulli umquam sub Nerone periculum facessisset, crimine simul exemploque Eprium urgebat, ardentibus patrum animis. Quod ubi sensit Marcellus, velut excedens curia " imus " inquit, " Prisce, et relinquimus tibi senatum tuum: regna praesente Caesare." Sequebatur Vibius Crispus, ambo infensi, vultu diverso, Marcellus minacibus oculis, Crispus renidens, donec adcursu amicorum retraherentur. Cum glisceret certamen, hinc multi bonique, inde pauci et validi pertinacibus odiis tenderent, consumptus per discordiam dies.

XLIV. Proximo senatu, inchoante Caesare de abolendo dolore iraque et priorum temporum ne-

was the last tyrant? That same belief was held by those who survived Tiberius and Gaius; yet meantime Nero arose more implacable and more cruel. We do not fear Vespasian, such are his years and his moderation; but examples last longer than men's characters. We are growing weak, fellow-senators, and are no longer that senate which after Nero had been cut down demanded that his informers and tools should be punished according to the custom of our forefathers. The fairest day after a bad emperor is the first."

XLIII. The senate listened to Montanus with such approval that Helvidius began to hope that even Marcellus could be overthrown. So beginning with a panegyric of Cluvius Rufus, who, though equally wealthy and eminent for eloquence, had put no man in danger under Nero, by thus combining his own charge with that great example, he overwhelmed Marcellus and fired the enthusiasm of the senators. When Marcellus perceived this, he said as he apparently started to leave the senate house, " I go, Priscus, and leave you your senate: play the king in the presence of Caesar." Vibius Crispus started to follow him; they both were angry but did not have the same looks, for Marcellus's eyes were flashing threateningly, while Crispus affected to smile; but finally they were drawn back by their friends who ran up to them. As the quarrel grew, the larger number and the more honourable senators ranged themselves on one side, while on the other were a few strong men, all contending with obstinate hate; so the day was spent in discord.

XLIV. At the next meeting of the senate, Caesar took the lead in recommending that the wrongs, the

cessitatibus, censuit Mucianus prolixe pro accusatoribus; simul eos qui coeptam, deinde omissam actionem repeterent, monuit sermone molli et tamquam rogaret. Patres coeptatam libertatem, postquam obviam itum, omisere. Mucianus, ne sperni senatus iudicium et cunctis sub Nerone admissis data impunitas videretur, Octavium Sagittam [1] et Antistium Sosianum senatorii ordinis egressos exilium in easdem insulas redegit. Octavius Pontiam Postuminam,[2] stupro cognitam et nuptias suas abnuentem, impotens amoris interfecerat, Sosianus pravitate morum multis exitiosus. Ambo gravi senatus consulto damnati pulsique, quamvis concesso aliis reditu, in eadem poena retenti sunt. Nec ideo lenita erga Mucianum invidia: quippe Sosianus ac Sagitta viles, etiam si reverterentur: accusatorum ingenia et opes et exercita malis artibus potentia timebantur.

XLV. Reconciliavit paulisper studia patrum habita in senatu cognitio secundum veterem morem. Manlius Patruitus senator pulsatum se in colonia Seniensi coetu multitudinis et iussu magistratuum querebatur; nec finem iniuriae hic stetisse: planctum et lamenta et supremorum imaginem praesenti sibi circumdata cum contumeliis ac probris, quae in

[1] sagittam *Rhenanus*: sabinum sagittam *M*.
[2] Postuminam *Urlichs*: Postumiam *vulgo*: positū inästu procognitā *M*.

---

[1] The modern Siena.

resentments, and the unavoidable necessities of the past be forgotten; Mucianus then spoke at great length in behalf of the informers; yet at the same time, addressing those who were now reviving indictments which they once brought and then dropped, he admonished them in mild terms and almost in a tone of appeal. The senators now that they were opposed gave up the liberty that they had begun to enjoy. Mucianus, to avoid seeming to treat lightly the senate's judgment or to grant impunity to all the misdeeds committed under Nero, sent back to their islands Octavius Sagitta and Antistius Sosianus, two men of the senatorial class, who had broken their exile. Octavius had debauched Pontia Postumina, and when she refused to marry him, in a frenzy of jealousy he had killed her; Sosianus had ruined many by his depravity. Both had been condemned and driven into exile by a severe vote of the senate; while others were allowed to return, they were kept under the same punishment. Yet the unpopularity of Mucianus was not diminished by this action: for Sosianus and Sagitta were insignificant, even if they did return; the informers' abilities, wrath, and power, which they used to evil ends, were what men feared.

XLV. The senators' discordant sentiments were reconciled for a time by an investigation which was held according to ancient custom. A senator, Manlius Patruitus, complained that he had been beaten by a mob in the colony of Sena,[1] and that too by the orders of the local magistrates; moreover, he said that the injury had not stopped there: the mob had surrounded him and before his face had wailed, lamented, and conducted a mock funeral, accompanying it with insults and outrageous expressions

senatum universum iacerentur. Vocati qui arguebantur, et cognita causa in convictos vindicatum,
additumque senatus consultum quo Seniensium
plebes modestiae admoneretur. Isdem diebus Antonius Flamma *accusantibus*[1] Cyrenensibus damnatur
lege repetundarum et exilio ob saevitiam.

XLVI. Inter quae militaris seditio prope exarsit.
Praetorianam militiam repetebant a Vitellio dimissi,
pro Vespasiano congregati; et lectus in eandem spem
e legionibus miles promissa stipendia flagitabat.
Ne Vitelliani quidem sine multa caede pelli poterant:
sed immensa pecunia[2] tanta vis hominum retinenda
erat. Ingressus castra Mucianus, quo rectius stipendia singulorum spectaret, suis cum insignibus
armisque victores constituit, modicis inter se spatiis
discretos. Tum Vitelliani, quos apud Bovillas in
deditionem acceptos memoravimus, ceterique per
urbem et urbi vicina conquisiti producuntur prope
intecto corpore. Eos Mucianus diduci et Germanicum Britannicumque militem, ac si qui aliorum
exercituum, separatim adsistere iubet. Illos primus
statim aspectus obstupefecerat, cum ex diverso velut
aciem telis et armis trucem, semet clausos nudosque

[1] *accusantibus hic add. Wurm*: C. *accusantibus Heraeus.*

[2] *post* pecunia *ordo verborum in cod. Med. sic turbatus*: (pecunia) ferunt ne criminantium (C. lii.) . . . defuisse crede (C.
liii.); *deinde* tanta vis hominum (C. xlvi.) . . . multo apud
patrem sermone orasse (C. lii.); *deinde* dicebatur audita interim
(C. liv.), *verbum ultimum* (C. liii.) *in duas partes discerptum
erat* crede batur: *foliis transpositis librarius quidam syllabas*
batur *in* dicebatur *explevit. Verum ordinem restituit Agricola.*

---

[1] Cf. ii. 67.
[2] The praetorians received two denarii a day, twice the pay
of the legionaries.
[3] Probably those who surrendered at Narnia and Bovillae.
Cf. iii. 63; iv. 2.

directed against the whole senate. The accused
were summoned, and after the case had been heard,
those convicted were punished, and the senate also
passed a vote warning the populace of Sena to be
more orderly. At the same time Antonius Flamma
was condemned under the law against extortion on
charges brought by the people of Cyrene, and was
exiled for his cruelty.

XLVI. Meanwhile a mutiny almost broke out
among the troops. Those who had been dismissed
by Vitellius [1] and had then banded together to
support Vespasian now asked to be restored to
service in the praetorian cohorts; and the legionaries
selected with the same prospect demanded the pay
promised them.[2] Even the Vitellians [3] could not be
removed without much bloodshed; but it would cost
an enormous sum to keep such a great force of men
under arms. Mucianus entered the camp to examine
more closely the length of each man's service; he drew
up the victors with their proper insignia and arms,
leaving a moderate space between the companies.
Then the Vitellians who had surrendered at Bovillae,
as we have said above, and all the other soldiers
attached to the same cause who had been hunted
out in the city and suburbs, were brought out almost
without clothes or arms. Mucianus ordered them
to march to one side, and directed that the soldiers
from Germany and Britain and all the troops there
were among them from other armies should take
positions by themselves. They were paralyzed by
the first sight of their situation, when they beheld
opposite them what seemed to them like an enemy's
line, threatening them with weapons and defensive
arms, while they were themselves hemmed in,

87

et inluvie deformis aspicerent: ut vero huc illuc distrahi coepere, metus per omnis et praecipua Germanici militis formido, tamquam ea separatione ad caedem destinaretur. Prensare commanipularium pectora, cervicibus innecti, suprema oscula petere, ne desererentur soli neu pari causa disparem fortunam paterentur; modo Mucianum, modo absentem principem, postremum caelum ac deos obtestari, donec Mucianus cunctos eiusdem sacramenti, eiusdem imperatoris milites appellans, falso timori obviam iret; namque et victor exercitus clamore lacrimas eorum iuvabat. Isque finis illa die. Paucis post diebus adloquentem Domitianum firmati iam excepere: spernunt oblatos agros, militiam et stipendia orant. Preces erant, sed quibus contra dici non posset; igitur in praetorium accepti. Dein quibus aetas et iusta stipendia, dimissi cum honore, alii ob culpam, sed carptim ac singuli, quo tutissimo remedio consensus multitudinis extenuatur.

XLVII. Ceterum verane pauperie an uti videretur, actum in senatu ut sescentiens sestertium a privatis mutuum acciperetur, praepositusque ei curae Pompeius Silvanus. Nec multo post necessitas abiit

---

[1] A soldier might be discharged at the age of fifty, or after sixteen years service in the praetorian guard or twenty with the legionaries.

unprotected, squalid and filthy; then, when they
began to be divided and marched in different directions, all were smitten with horror; the soldiers from
Germany were the most terrified, for they thought
that by this division they were being marked for
slaughter. They began to throw themselves on the
breasts of their fellow-soldiers, to hang on their
necks, to beg for a farewell kiss, praying them not
to desert them or allow them to suffer a different fate
when their cause had been the same; they kept
appealing now to Mucianus, now to the absent
emperor, finally to heaven and the gods, until Mucianus stopped their needless panic by calling them
all " soldiers bound by the same oath " and " soldiers
of the same emperor." He was the readier to do
this as the victorious troops by their cheers seconded
the tears of the others. Thus this day ended. But
a few days later, when Domitian addressed them,
they received him with recovered confidence: they
treated with scorn the offers of lands but asked for
service in the army and pay. They resorted to
appeals, it is true, but to appeals that admitted no
denial; accordingly they were received into the
praetorian camp. Then those whose age and length
of service warranted it were honourably discharged; [1]
others were dismissed for some fault or other, but
gradually and one at a time—the safe remedy for
breaking up a united mob.

XLVII. However, whether the treasury was really
poor or the senate wished it to appear so, the
senators voted to accept a loan of sixty million
sesterces from private individuals and put Pompeius
Silvanus in charge of the matter. Not long after,
either the necessity passed or the pretence of such

sive omissa simulatio. Abrogati inde legem ferente
Domitiano consulatus quos Vitellius dederat, funus-
que censorium Flavio Sabino ductum, magna documenta instabilis fortunae summaque et ima miscentis.

XLVIII. Sub idem tempus L. Piso pro consule
interficitur. Ea de caede quam verissime expediam,
si pauca supra repetiero ab initio causisque talium
facinorum non absurda. Legio in Africa auxiliaque
tutandis imperii finibus sub divo Augusto Tiberioque
principibus proconsuli parebant. Mox C. Caesar,
turbidus animi ac[1] Marcum Silanum obtinentem Africam metuens, ablatam proconsuli legionem misso in
eam rem legato tradidit. Aequatus inter duos
beneficiorum numerus, et mixtis utriusque mandatis
discordia quaesita auctaque pravo certamine. Legatorum ius adolevit diuturnitate officii, vel quia
minoribus maior aemulandi cura, proconsulum
splendidissimus quisque securitati magis quam
potentiae consulebant.

XLIX. Sed tum legionem in Africa regebat
Valerius Festus, sumptuosae adulescentiae neque
modica cupiens et adfinitate Vitellii anxius. Is
crebris sermonibus temptaveritne Pisonem ad res

<hr>

[1] ad *M*.

[1] Cf. chap. xxxviii above.

necessity was dropped. Then on the motion of Domitian the consulships which Vitellius had conferred were cancelled; and the honours of a censor's funeral were given Flavius Sabinus—signal proof of the fickleness of fortune, ever confounding honours with humiliations.

XLVIII. At about the same time the proconsul Lucius Piso was put to death.[1] I shall give the most faithful account I can of his murder, after having reviewed a few earlier matters which are not unrelated to the source and causes of such crimes. The legion and the auxiliary troops employed in Africa to protect the borders of the empire were commanded by a proconsul during the reigns of the deified Augustus and of Tiberius. Afterwards Gaius Caesar, who was confused in mind and afraid of Marcus Silanus, then governor of Africa, took the legion away from the proconsul and gave it to a legate sent out for that purpose. Patronage was now equally divided between the two officials; and a source of discord was sought in the conflict of authority between the two, while this discord was increased by their unseemly strife. The power of the legates increased, owing to their long terms of office or else because in lesser posts men are more eager to play the rival, while the most distinguished of the proconsuls cared more for security than power.

XLIX. At that time the legion in Africa was commanded by Valerius Festus, a young man of extravagant habits, whose ambitions were by no means moderate, and who was made uneasy by his relationship to Vitellius. Whether he, in their many interviews, tempted Piso to revolt or whether he resisted

91

novas an temptanti restiterit, incertum, quoniam secreto eorum nemo adfuit, et occiso Pisone plerique ad gratiam interfectoris inclinavere. Nec ambigitur provinciam et militem alienato erga Vespasianum animo fuisse; et quidam e Vitellianis urbe profugi ostentabant Pisoni nutantis Gallias, paratam Germaniam, pericula ipsius et in pace suspecto[1] tutius bellum. Inter quae Claudius Sagitta, praefectus alae Petrianae,[2] prospera navigatione praevenit Papirium centurionem a Muciano missum, adseveravitque mandata interficiendi Pisonis centurioni data: cecidisse[3] Galerianum consobrinum eius generumque; unam in audacia spem salutis, sed duo itinera audendi,[4] seu mallet statim arma, seu petita navibus Gallia ducem se Vitellianis exercitibus ostenderet. Nihil ad ea moto Pisone, centurio a Muciano missus, ut portum Carthaginis attigit, magna voce laeta Pisoni omnia tamquam principi continuare, obvios et subitae rei miraculo attonitos ut eadem adstreperent hortari. Vulgus credulum ruere in forum, praesentiam Pisonis exposcere; gaudio clamoribusque cuncta miscebant, indiligentia veri[5] et adulandi libidine. Piso indicio Sagittae vel insita modestia non in publicum egressus est neque se studiis vulgi permisit: centurionemque

---

[1] suspecto *Victorius*: suscepto *M*.
[2] Petrianae *Böcking*: petrinae *M*.   [3] cedisse *M*.
[4] audiendi *M*.   [5] veri *Rhenanus*: viri *M*.

---

[1] Named from a certain Petra who had organised the troop. Cf. I, 70.

Piso's proposals, we do not know, for no one was present at their private conversations, and after Piso's assassination the majority tried to win favour with the murderer. There is no question that the province and the troops were unfavourably disposed toward Vespasian; moreover, some of the Vitellians who fled from Rome pointed out to Piso that the Gallic provinces were hesitating and that Germany was ready to revolt, that he was himself in danger, and that war is the safer course for a man who is suspected in time of peace. Meantime Claudius Sagitta, prefect of Petra's horse,[1] by a fortunate voyage, arrived before the centurion Papirius who had been dispatched by Mucianus; Sagitta declared that the centurion had been ordered to kill Piso, and that Galerianus, his cousin and son-in-law, had been put to death. He urged that the only hope of safety was in some bold step, but that there were two ways open for such action: Piso might prefer war at once or he might sail to Gaul and offer himself as a leader to the Vitellian troops. Although Piso was not at all inclined to such courses, the moment that the centurion whom Mucianus sent arrived in the harbour of Carthage, he raised his voice and kept repeating prayers and vows for Piso as if he were emperor, and he urged those who met him and were amazed at this strange proceeding to utter the same acclamations. The credulous crowd, rushing into the forum, demanded Piso's presence, and raised an uproar with their joyful shouts, caring nothing for the truth and only eager to flatter. Piso, moved by Sagitta's information or prompted by his native modesty, did not appear in public or trust himself to the enthu siastic mob: and when, on questioning the cen-

percontatus, postquam quaesitum sibi crimen caedem-
que comperit, animadverti in eum iussit, haud perinde
spe vitae quam ira in percussorem, quod idem ex
interfectoribus Clodii Macri cruentas legati sanguine
manus ad caedem proconsulis rettulisset. Anxio
deinde edicto Carthaginiensibus increpitis, ne solita
quidem munia usurpabat, clausus intra domum, ne
qua motus novi causa vel forte oreretur.

L. Sed ubi Festo consternatio vulgi, centurionis
supplicium veraque et falsa more famae in maius
innotuere, equites in necem Pisonis mittit. Illi
raptim vecti obscuro adhuc coeptae lucis domum
proconsulis inrumpunt destrictis gladiis, et magna
pars Pisonis ignari, quod Poenos auxiliaris Maurosque in eam caedem delegerat. Haud procul
cubiculo obvium forte servum quisnam et ubi esset
Piso interrogavere. Servus egregio mendacio se
Pisonem esse respondit ac statim obtruncatur. Nec
multo post Piso interficitur; namque aderat qui
nosceret, Baebius Massa e procuratoribus Africae,
iam tunc optimo cuique exitiosus et inter [1] causas
malorum quae mox tulimus saepius rediturus.
Festus Adrumeto, ubi speculabundus substiterat, ad
legionem contendit praefectumque castrorum Cae-

----

[1] inter *Wex*: in *M*.

----

[1] Cf. i. 7.
[2] Massa became a notorious informer under Domitian, but
the books of Tacitus's *Histories* dealing with that period are
unfortunately lost.
[3] To-day Susa; south of ancient Carthage.

turion, he learned that this officer had sought an opportunity to bring a charge against him and to kill him, he ordered him to be put to death, moved not so much by hope of saving his own life as by anger against the assassin, for this centurion had been one of the murderers of Clodius Macer [1] and then had come with his hands dripping with the blood of the legate to kill a proconsul. Next he reproved the Carthaginians in a proclamation that betrayed his anxiety, and abandoned even his usual duties, remaining shut up in his residence that no excuse for a new outbreak might arise even by chance.

L. When report of the popular excitement reached Festus, as well as the news of the centurion's execution and of other matters, both true and false, with the usual exaggerations, he sent horsemen to kill Piso. They rode so rapidly that they broke into the proconsul's residence in the half-light of the early dawn with drawn swords. The majority of them were unacquainted with Piso, for Festus had selected Carthaginian auxiliaries and Moors to accomplish this murder. Not far from Piso's bedroom a slave happened to meet them. The soldiers asked him who and where Piso was. The slave answered with an heroic falsehood that he was Piso, and was at once cut down. Yet soon after Piso was murdered; for there was present a man who recognized him, Baebius Massa, one of the imperial agents in Africa— a man, even at that time, ruinous to the best citizens, and his name will reappear only too often among the causes of the evils that we later endured.[2] From Adrumetum,[3] where he had waited to watch the course of events, Festus hurried to the legion and

tronium Pisanum vinciri iussit proprias ob simultates,
sed Pisonis satellitem vocabat, militesque et centuriones quosdam puniit, alios praemiis adfecit,
neutrum ex merito, sed ut oppressisse bellum crederetur. Mox Oeensium [1] Leptitanorumque discordias componit, quae raptu frugum et pecorum
inter agrestis modicis principiis, iam per arma atque
acies exercebantur; nam populus Oeensis [1] multitudine inferior Garamantas exciverat, gentem indo-
mitam et inter accolas latrociniis fecundam. Unde
artae Leptitanis res, lateque vastatis agris intra
moenia trepidabant, donec interventu cohortium
alarumque fusi Garamantes et recepta omnis praeda,
nisi quam vagi per inaccessa mapalium ulterioribus
vendiderant.

LI. At Vespasiano post Cremonensem pugnam et
prosperos undique nuntios cecidisse Vitellium multi
cuiusque ordinis, pari audacia fortunaque hibernum
mare adgressi, nuntiavere. Aderant legati regis
Vologaesi [2] quadraginta milia [3] Parthorum equitum
offerentes. Magnificum laetumque tantis sociorum
auxiliis ambiri neque indigere: gratiae Vologaeso [2]
actae mandatumque ut legatos ad senatum mitteret
et pacem esse sciret. Vespasianus in Italiam resque

[1] Oeensium, Oeensis *infra*, *Lipsius*: offensium, offensis *M*.
[2] Vologaesi, Vologaeso *infra*, *Nipperdey*: vologesi, vologeso
M.
[3] milia *hic add. b, post* equitum *alii: om. M*.

---

[1] Tripoli and Lebda.
[2] Living in the modern Fezzan.
[3] Still at Alexandria. Cf. ii. 82; iii. 48; iv. 38.
[4] Cf. ii. 82.

ordered the arrest of the prefect of the camp,
Caetronius Pisanus, to satisfy personal hatred,
but he called him Piso's tool; and he also punished
some soldiers and centurions, others he rewarded;
neither course of action was prompted by merit but
by his desire to appear to have crushed a war.
Later he settled the differences between the people
of Oea and Leptis,[1] which, though small at first,
beginning among these peasants with the stealing
of crops and cattle, had now increased to the point
of armed contests and regular battles; for the people
of Oea, being fewer than their opponents, had called
in the Garamantes,[2] an ungovernable tribe and one
always engaged in practising brigandage on their
neighbours. This had reduced the fortunes of the
Leptitani to a low ebb; their lands had been ravaged
far and wide and they lay in terror within their walls,
until, by the arrival of the auxiliary foot and horse,
the Garamantes were routed and the entire booty
was recovered except that which the robbers as they
wandered through inaccessible native villages had
sold to remote tribes.

LI. But Vespasian,[3] after learning of the battle of
Cremona and receiving favourable news from every
quarter, now heard of the fall of Vitellius from many
of every class who with equal courage and good
fortune braved the wintry sea. Envoys also came
from King Vologaesus with an offer of forty thousand
Parthian horse.[4] It was glorious and delightful to
be courted with such offers of assistance from the
allies and not to need them: he thanked Vologaesus
and instructed him to send his envoys to the senate
and to be assured that the empire was at peace.
While Vespasian was absorbed with thoughts of

urbis intentus adversam de Domitiano famam accipit, tamquam terminos aetatis et concessa filio egrederetur: igitur validissimam exercitus partem Tito tradit ad reliqua Iudaici belli perpetranda.

LII. Titum, antequam digrederetur, multo apud patrem sermone orasse ferunt[1] ne criminantium nuntiis temere accenderetur integrumque se ac placabilem filio praestaret. Non legiones, non classis proinde firma imperii munimenta quam numerum liberorum; nam amicos tempore, fortuna, cupidinibus aliquando aut erroribus imminui, transferri, desinere: suum cuique sanguinem indiscretum, sed maxime principibus, quorum prosperis et alii fruantur, adversa ad iunctissimos pertineant. Ne fratribus quidem mansuram concordiam, ni parens exemplum praebuisset. Vespasianus haud aeque Domitiano mitigatus quam Titi pietate gaudens, bono esse animo iubet belloque et armis rem publicam attollere: sibi pacem domumque curae fore. Tum celerrimas navium frumento onustas saevo adhuc mari committit: quippe tanto discrimine urbs nutabat ut decem haud amplius dierum frumentum in horreis fuerit, cum a Vespasiano commeatus subvenere.

LIII. Curam restituendi Capitolii in Lucium Vestinum confert, equestris ordinis virum, sed auctoritate

---

[1] *Vid. ad cap.* xlvi.

Cf. iii. 48.

Italy and conditions in Rome, he heard an unfavourable report concerning Domitian, to the effect that he was transgressing the bounds set by his youth and what might be permissible in a son : accordingly he turned over to Titus the main force of his army to complete the war with the Jews.

LII. It is said that Titus, before leaving, in a long interview with his father begged him not to be easily excited by the reports of those who calumniated Domitian, and urged him to show himself impartial and forgiving toward his son. " Neither armies nor fleets," he argued, " are so strong a defence of the imperial power as a number of children ; for friends are chilled, changed, and lost by time, fortune, and sometimes by inordinate desires or by mistakes : the ties of blood cannot be severed by any man, least of all by princes, whose success others also enjoy, but whose misfortunes touch only their nearest kin. Not even brothers will always agree unless the father sets the example." Not so much reconciled toward Domitian as delighted with Titus's show of brotherly affection, Vespasian bade him be of good cheer and to magnify the state by war and arms ; he would himself care for peace and his house. Then he had some of the swiftest ships laden with grain and entrusted to the sea, although it was still dangerous : for, in fact, Rome was in such a critical condition that she did not have more than ten days' supplies in her granaries when the supplies from Vespasian came to her relief.[1]

LIII. The charge of restoring the Capitol was given by Vespasian to Lucius Vestinus, a member of the equestrian order, but one whose influence and reputation put him on an equality with the nobility.

famaque inter proceres. Ab eo contracti haruspices
monuere ut reliquiae prioris delubri in paludes
aveherentur, templum isdem vestigiis sisteretur:
nolle deos mutari veterem formam. XI kalendas
Iulias serena luce spatium omne quod templo dicaba-
tur evinctum vittis coronisque[1]; ingressi milites, quis
fausta nomina, felicibus ramis; dein virgines Vestales
cum pueris puellisque patrimis matrimisque aqua[2] e
fontibus amnibusque[3] hausta perluere.[4] Tum Helvidius Priscus praetor, praeeunte Plautio[5] Aeliano
pontifice, lustrata[6] suovetaurilibus[7] area et super
caespitem redditis extis, Iovem, Iunonem, Minervam
praesidesque imperii deos precatus uti coepta
prosperarent sedisque suas pietate hominum in-
choatas divina ope attollerent, vittas, quis ligatus
lapis innexique funes erant, contigit; simul ceteri
magistratus et sacerdotes et senatus et eques et
magna pars populi, studio laetitiaque conixi, saxum
ingens traxere. Passimque iniectae fundamentis
argenti aurique stipes et metallorum primitiae, nullis
fornacibus victae, sed ut gignuntur[8]: praedixere
haruspices ne temeraretur opus saxo aurove in aliud
destinato. Altitudo aedibus adiecta: id solum

---

[1] victis cornisque M: coronisque M^2.
[2] aqua *Baiter*: aquatrimis M.   [3] omnibusque M.
[4] perluere *Rhenanus*: pluere M.
[5] Plautio *Ursinus*: plauto M.   [6] lustratas M.
[7] suovetaurilibus *Lipsius*: bove taurilibus M.
[8] gignuntur *dett.*: signuntur M.

---

[1] The sacrifice of a boar, a ram, and a bull.

The haruspices when assembled by him directed
that the ruins of the old shrine should be carried
away to the marshes and that a new temple should
be erected on exactly the same site as the old: the
gods were unwilling to have the old plan changed.
On the twenty-first of June, under a cloudless sky,
the area that was dedicated to the temple was surrounded with fillets and garlands; soldiers, who had
auspicious names, entered the enclosure carrying
boughs of good omen; then the Vestals, accompanied
by boys and girls whose fathers and mothers were
living, sprinkled the area with water drawn from
fountains and streams. Next Helvidius Priscus, the
praetor, guided by the pontifex Plautius Aelianus,
purified the area with the sacrifice of the suove-
taurilia,[1] and placed the vitals of the victims on an
altar of turf; and then, after he had prayed to
Jupiter, Juno, Minerva, and to the gods who protect
the empire to prosper this undertaking and by their
divine assistance to raise again their home which
man's piety had begun, he touched the fillets with
which the foundation stone was wound and the ropes
entwined; at the same time the rest of the magistrates, the priests, senators, knights, and a great
part of the people, putting forth their strength
together in one enthusiastic and joyful effort, dragged
the huge stone to its place. A shower of gold and
silver and of virgin ores, never smelted in any furnace,
but in their natural state, was thrown everywhere
into the foundations: the haruspices had warned
against the profanation of the work by the use of
stone or gold intended for any other purpose. The
temple was given greater height than the old: this
was the only change that religious scruples allowed,

religio adnuere et prioris templi magnificentiae defuisse credebatur.[1]

LIV. Audita interim per Gallias Germaniasque mors Vitellii duplicaverat bellum. Nam Civilis omissa dissimulatione in populum Romanum ruere, Vitellianae legiones vel externum servitium quam imperatorem Vespasianum malle. Galli sustulerant animos, eandem ubique exercituum nostrorum fortunam rati, vulgato rumore a Sarmatis Dacisque Moesica ac Pannonica hiberna circumsederi; paria de Britannia fingebantur. Sed nihil aeque quam incendium Capitolii, ut finem imperio adesse crederent, impulerat. Captam olim a Gallis urbem, sed integra Iovis sede mansisse imperium: fatali nunc igne signum caelestis irae datum et possessionem rerum humanarum Transalpinis gentibus portendi superstitione vana Druidae canebant. Incesseratque fama primores Galliarum ab Othone adversus Vitellium missos, antequam digrederentur, pepigisse ne deessent libertati, si populum Romanum continua civilium bellorum series et interna mala fregissent.

LV. Ante Flacci Hordeonii caedem nihil prorupit quo coniuratio intellegeretur: interfecto Hordeonio commeavere nuntii inter Civilem Classicumque

___

[1] credebatur *Döderlein*: crede *M*. *Vid. ad cap.* xlvi.

___

[1] Tacitus resumes from chap. xxxvii, at January 70 A.D.

and the only feature that was thought wanting in the magnificence of the old structure.

LIV. In the meantime [1] the news of the death of Vitellius, spreading through the Gallic and German provinces, had started a second war; for Civilis, now dropping all pretence, openly attacked the Roman people, and the legions of Vitellius preferred to be subject even to foreign domination rather than to obey Vespasian as emperor. The Gauls had plucked up fresh courage, believing that all our armies were everywhere in the same case, for the rumour had spread that our winter quarters in Moesia and Pannonia were being besieged by the Sarmatae and Dacians; similar stories were invented about Britain. But nothing had encouraged them to believe that the end of our rule was at hand so much as the burning of the Capitol. " Once long ago Rome was captured by the Gauls, but since Jove's home was unharmed, the Roman power stood firm: now this fatal conflagration has given a proof from heaven of the divine wrath and presages the passage of the sovereignty of the world to the peoples beyond the Alps." Such were the vain and superstitious prophecies of the Druids. Moreover, the report had gone abroad that the Gallic chiefs, when sent by Otho to oppose Vitellius, had pledged themselves before their departure not to fail the cause of freedom in case an unbroken series of civil wars and internal troubles destroyed the power of the Roman people.

LV. Before the murder of Hordeonius Flaccus nothing came to the surface to make the conspiracy known: but after Hordeonius had been killed, messengers passed between Civilis and Classicus.

praefectum alae Trevirorum. Classicus nobilitate opibusque ante alios: regium illi genus et pace belloque clara origo, ipse e maioribus suis hostis populi Romani quam socios[1] iactabat. Miscuere sese Iulius Tutor et Iulius Sabinus, hic Trevir, hic Lingonus, Tutor ripae Rheni a Vitellio praefectus; Sabinum super insitam vanitatem falsae stirpis gloria incendebat: proaviam suam divo Iulio per Gallias bellanti corpore atque adulterio placuisse. Hi secretis sermonibus animos ceterorum scrutati,[2] ubi quos idoneos rebantur conscientia obstrinxere, in colonia Agrippinensi in domum privatam conveniunt; nam publice civitas talibus inceptis abhorrebat; ac tamen interfuere quidam Ubiorum Tungrorumque. Sed plurima vis penes Treviros ac Lingonas, nec tulere moras consultandi. Certatim proclamant furere discordiis populum Romanum, caesas legiones, vastatam Italiam, capi cum maxime urbem, omnis exercitus suis quemque bellis distineri: si Alpes praesidiis firmentur, coalita libertate disceptaturas[3] Gallias quem virium suarum terminum velint.

LVI. Haec dicta pariter probataque: de reliquiis Vitelliani exercitus dubitavere. Plerique inter-

[1] socios *Mercerus*: socius *M.*
[2] scrutati *Pichena*: scrutari *M.*
[3] disceptaturas *Victorius*: discepras *M.*

---

[1] The prefect of the bank of the Rhine was apparently in command of the troops that policed the border. Cf. chap. xxvi above: *dispositae per ripam stationes,* and chap. lxiv below.
[2] This statement refers to the capture of Rome by the Flavian forces in December, 69 *Vid.* III, 82–85.

prefect of the Treviran cavalry. Classicus was superior to the others in birth and wealth; he was of royal family and his line had been famous in both peace and war, and he himself boasted that more of his ancestors had been enemies than allies of the Romans. Julius Tutor and Julius Sabinus joined the conspirators: Tutor was of the tribe of the Treviri, Sabinus one of the Lingones. Tutor had been made prefect of the bank of the Rhine by Vitellius[1]; Sabinus was fired by his native vanity, and especially by his pride in his imaginary descent, for it was said that his great-grandmother by her charms and complaisance had found favour in the eyes of the deified Julius when he was carrying on his campaigns in Gaul. These chiefs by private interviews first tested the sentiments of all their associates; then, when they had secured the participation of those whom they thought suitable, they met at Cologne in a private house, for the state in its public capacity shrank from such an undertaking; and yet some of the Ubii and Tungri were present. But the Treviri and the Lingones, who had the dominant power in the matter, permitted no delay in deliberation. They rivalled one another in declaring that the Roman people were wild with discord, that the legions were cut to pieces, Italy laid waste, Rome at that moment was being captured,[2] and that all the Roman armies were occupied each with its own wars: if they but held the Alps with armed forces, the Gallic lands, once sure of their freedom, would have only to decide what limits they wished to set to their power.

LVI. These statements were approved as soon as made: with regard to the survivors of the army of Vitellius they were in doubt. The majority were

ficiendos censebant, turbidos, infidos, sanguine
ducum pollutos: vicit ratio parcendi, ne sublata
spe veniae pertinaciam accenderent: adliciendos
potius in societatem. Legatis tantum legionum
interfectis, ceterum vulgus conscientia scelerum et
spe impunitatis facile accessurum. Ea primi con-
cilii forma missique per Gallias concitores belli;
simulatum ipsis obsequium quo incautiorem Voculam
opprimerent. Nec defuere qui Voculae nuntiarent,
sed vires ad coercendum deerant, infrequentibus
infidisque legionibus. Inter ambiguos milites et
occultos hostis optimum e praesentibus ratus mutua
dissimulatione et isdem quibus petebatur grassari, in
coloniam Agrippinensem descendit. Illuc Claudius[1]
Labeo, quem captum et [extra commentum][2] aman-
datum[3] in Frisios diximus, corruptis custodibus per-
fugit; pollicitusque, si praesidium daretur, iturum
in Batavos et potiorem civitatis partem ad societatem
Romanam retracturum, accepta peditum equitumque
modica manu nihil apud Batavos ausus quosdam Nerviorum Baetasiorumque in arma traxit, et furtim
magis quam bello Canninefatis Marsacosque in-
cursabat.

[1] Claudius *Puteolanus*: Gladius *M.*
[2] extra commentum *secl. Nipperdey.*
[3] amendatum *M.*

---

[1] Chap. xviii.
[2] Living between the Meuse and the Scheldt.
[3] About the mouth of the Scheldt.

for putting them to death on the ground that they were mutinous, untrustworthy, and defiled with the blood of their commanders: the proposal to spare them, however, prevailed since the conspirators feared to provoke an obstinate resistance if they deprived the troops of all hope of mercy: it was argued that these soldiers should rather be won over to alliance. "If we execute only the commanders of the legions," they said, "the general mass of the soldiers will be easily led to join us by their consciousness of guilt and by their hope of escaping punishment." This was in brief the result of their first deliberation; and they sent emissaries through the Gallic provinces to stir up war; the ringleaders feigned submission in order to take Vocula the more off his guard. Yet there was no lack of people to carry the story to Vocula; he, however, did not have force enough to check the conspiracy, for the legions were incomplete and not to be trusted. Between his soldiers whom he suspected and his secret foes, he thought it best for the time to dissemble in his turn and to employ the same methods of attack that were being used against him, and accordingly went down to Cologne. There Claudius Labeo, of whose capture and banishment among the Frisians I have spoken above,[1] fled for refuge, having bribed his guards to let him escape; and now he promised, if he were given a force of men, that he would go among the Batavians and bring the majority of that people back to alliance with Rome. He got a small force of foot and horse, but he did not dare to undertake anything among the Batavians; however, he did induce some of the Nervii and Baetasii[2] to take up arms, and he continuously harried the Canninefates and Marsaci[3] rather by stealth than in open war.

LVII. Vocula Gallorum fraude inlectus ad hostem contendit; nec procul Veteribus aberat, cum Classicus ac Tutor per speciem explorandi praegressi cum ducibus Germanorum pacta firmavere. Tumque primum discreti a legionibus proprio vallo castra sua circumdant, obtestante Vocula non adeo turbatam civilibus armis rem Romanam ut Treviris etiam Lingonibusque despectui sit. Superesse fidas provincias, victores exercitus, fortunam imperii et ultores deos. Sic olim Sacrovirum et Aeduos, nuper Vindicem Galliasque singulis proeliis concidisse. Eadem rursus numina,[1] eadem fata ruptores foederum expectarent. Melius divo Iulio divoque Augusto notos eorum animos: Galbam et infracta tributa hostilis spiritus induisse. Nunc hostis, quia molle servitium; cum spoliati exutique fuerint, amicos fore. Haec ferociter locutus, postquam perstare in perfidia Classicum Tutoremque videt, verso itinere Novaesium concedit: Galli duum milium spatio distantibus campis consedere. Illuc commeantium centurionum militumque emebantur animi, ut (flagitium incognitum) Romanus exercitus in externa verba iurarent pignusque tanti sceleris nece aut vinculis legatorum daretur. Vocula, quamquam

---

[1] numina *Rhenanus*: nomina *M*.

LVII. Vocula, lured on by the artifices of the Gauls, hurried against the enemy; and he was not far from Vetera when Classicus and Tutor, advancing from the main force under the pretext of reconnoitring, concluded their agreement with the German chiefs, and it was then that they first withdrew apart from the legions and fortified their own camp with a separate rampart, although Vocula protested that the Roman state had not yet been so broken by civil war as to be an object of contempt in the eyes of even the Treviri and Lingones. "There are still left faithful provinces," he said; "there still remain victorious armies, the fortune of the empire, and the avenging gods. Thus in former times Sacrovir and the Aeduans, more recently Vindex and all the Gallic provinces, have been crushed in a single battle. Those who break treaties must still face the same divinities, the same fates as before. The deified Julius and the deified Augustus better understood the spirit of the Gauls: Galba's acts and the reduction of the tribute have inspired them with a hostile spirit. Now they are enemies because the burden of their servitude is light; when we have despoiled and stripped them they will be friends." After speaking thus in anger, seeing that Classicus and Tutor persisted in their treachery, Vocula turned and withdrew to Novaesium: the Gauls occupied a position two miles away. There the centurions and soldiers frequently visited them, and attempts were made so to tamper with their loyalty, that, by an unheard-of crime, a Roman army should swear allegiance to foreigners and pledge themselves to this awful sin by killing or arresting their chief officers. Although many advised Vocula to escape, he thought

plerique fugam suadebant, audendum ratus vocata contione in hunc modum disseruit:

LVIII. " Numquam apud vos verba feci aut pro vobis sollicitior aut pro me securior. Nam mihi exitium parari libens audio mortemque in tot malis [hostium][1] ut finem miseriarum expecto: vestri me pudet miseretque, adversus quos non proelium et acies parantur; id enim fas armorum et ius hostium est: bellum cum populo Romano vestris se manibus gesturum Classicus sperat imperiumque et sacramentum Galliarum ostentat. Adeo nos, si fortuna in praesens virtusque deseruit, etiam vetera exempla deficiunt, quotiens Romanae legiones perire praeoptaverint ne loco pellerentur? Socii saepe nostri excindi urbis suas seque cum coniugibus ac liberis cremari pertulerunt, neque aliud pretium exitus quam fides famaque. Tolerant cum maxime inopiam obsidiumque apud Vetera legiones nec terrore aut promissis demoventur: nobis super arma et viros et egregia castrorum munimenta frumentum et commeatus quamvis longo bello pares. Pecunia nuper etiam donativo suffecit,[2] quod sive a Vespasiano sive a Vitellio datum interpretari mavultis, ab imperatore certe Romano accepistis. Tot bellorum victores, apud Geldubam, apud Vetera, fuso totiens hoste, si

---

[1] hostium *secl. Acidalius.*   [2] suffecit *Lipsius:* sufficit *M.*

it wise to act boldly, called an assembly, and spoke to this effect.

LVIII. " Never have I spoken to you with greater anxiety on your account or with less on my own. For I am glad to hear that my death is determined on, and in the midst of my present misfortunes I await my fate as the end of my sufferings. It is for you that I feel shame and pity,—for you against whom no battle is arrayed, no lines are marshalled. That would be only the law of arms and the just right of enemies. No! It is with your hands that Classicus hopes to fight against the Roman people : it is a Gallic empire and an allegiance to the Gauls that he holds out to you. Even if fortune and courage fail us at the moment, have we completely lost the memories of the past, forgotten how many times Roman legions have preferred to die rather than be driven from their positions ? How often have our allies endured the destruction of their cities and allowed themselves to be burned with their wives and children, when the only reward that they could gain in their death was the glory of having kept their faith ? At this very moment the legions at Vetera are bearing the hardships of famine and siege unmoved by threats or promises : we have not only our arms, our men, and the splendid fortifications of our camp, but we have grain and supplies sufficient for a war regardless of its length. We had money enough lately even for a donative ; and whether you prefer to regard this as given by Vespasian or by Vitellius, it was certainly a Roman emperor from whom you received it. If you, the victors in so many wars, if you who have so often put the enemy to flight at Gelduba and Vetera, fear an open battle, that is

pavetis aciem, indignum id quidem, sed est vallum murique et trahendi artes, donec e proximis provinciis auxilia exercitusque concurrant. Sane ego displiceam : sunt alii legati, tribuni, centurio denique aut miles ; ne hoc prodigium toto terrarum orbe vulgetur, vobis satellitibus Civilem et Classicum Italiam invasuros. An, si ad moenia urbis Germani Gallique duxerint, arma patriae inferetis ? Horret animus tanti flagitii imagine. Tutorine[1] Treviro agentur excubiae ? Signum belli Batavus dabit ? Et Germanorum catervas supplebitis ? Quis deinde sceleris exitus, cum Romanae legiones se contra[2] derexerint ? Transfugae e transfugis et proditores e proditoribus inter recens et vetus sacramentum invisi deis errabitis ? Te, Iuppiter optime maxime, quem per octingentos viginti annos tot triumphis coluimus, te, Quirine Romanae parens urbis, precor venerorque ut, si vobis non fuit cordi me duce haec castra incorrupta et intemerata servari, at certe pollui foedarique a Tutore et Classico ne sinatis, militibus Romanis aut innocentiam detis aut maturam et sine noxa paenitentiam."

LIX. Varie excepta oratio inter spem metumque ac pudorem. Digressum Voculam et de supremis agitantem liberti servique prohibuere foedissimam

---

[1] Tutorine *I. Gronovius* : tutor in *M.*
[2] se contra *Madvig.*

indeed a disgrace; but still you have fortifications, ramparts, and ways of delaying the crisis until troops hurry to your aid from the neighbouring provinces. What if I do not please you! There are other commanders, tribunes, or even some centurion or common soldier on whom you can fall back, that the monstrous news may not spread over the whole world that you are to follow in the train of Civilis and Classicus and support them in their invasion of Italy. When the Germans and Gauls have led you to the walls of Rome, will you then raise your arms against your native land? My soul revolts at the thought of such a crime. Will you mount guard for Tutor, a Treveran? Shall a Batavian give the signal for battle? Will you recruit the ranks of the Germans? What will be the result of your crime when the Roman legions have ranged themselves against you? Will you become deserters for a second time, a second time traitors, and waver back and forth between your new and old allegiance, hated by the gods? I pray and beseech thee, Jupiter, most good and great, to whom we have rendered the honour of so many triumphs during eight hundred and twenty years, and thee, Quirinus, father of Rome, that, if it has not been your pleasure that this camp be kept pure and inviolate under my leadership, at least you will not allow it to be defiled and polluted by a Tutor and a Classicus; give to Roman soldiers either innocence or repentance, prompt and without disaster."

LIX. The troops received this speech with varied feelings of hope, fear, and shame. Vocula had withdrawn and was preparing to end his life, but his freedmen and slaves prevented him from voluntarily

mortem sponte praevenire. Et Classicus misso
Aemilio Longino, desertore primae legionis, caedem
eius maturavit; Herennium et Numisium legatos
vinciri satis visum. Dein sumptis Romani imperii
insignibus in castra venit. Nec illi, quamquam ad
omne facinus durato, verba ultra suppeditavere
quam ut sacramentum recitaret: iuravere qui
aderant pro imperio Galliarum. Interfectorem Voculae altis ordinibus, ceteros, ut quisque flagitium
navaverat, praemiis attollit.

Divisae inde inter Tutorem et Classicum curae.
Tutor valida manu circumdatos Agrippinensis quantumque militum apud superiorem Rheni ripam in
eadem verba adigit, occisis[1] Mogontiaci tribunis,
pulso castrorum praefecto, qui detractaverant:
Classicus corruptissimum quemque e deditis pergere
ad obsessos iubet, veniam ostentantis, si praesentia
sequerentur: aliter nihil spei, famem ferrumque
et extrema passuros. Adiecere qui missi erant
exemplum suum.

LX. Obsessos hinc fides, inde egestas inter decus
ac flagitium distrahebant. Cunctantibus solita insoli-
taque alimenta deerant, absumptis iumentis equisque
et ceteris animalibus, quae profana foedaque in
usum necessitas vertit. Virgulta postremo et stirpis
et internatas saxis herbas vellentes miseriarum

[1] occisi M.

anticipating the most hideous of deaths. Classicus
sent Aemilius Longinus, a deserter from the First
legion, and so had Vocula quickly despatched; as
for the legates, Herennius and Numisius, he was satisfied with putting them into chains. Then he assumed
the insignia of a Roman general and entered the
camp. Hardened as he was to every crime, he found
not a word to utter beyond stating the oath: those
who were present swore allegiance to the "Empire
of the Gauls." Vocula's assassin he honoured with
promotion to a high rank; on the others he bestowed
rewards proportionate to their crimes.

Then Tutor and Classicus divided the conduct of
the war between them. Tutor besieged Cologne
with a strong force and compelled its inhabitants
and all the soldiers on the upper Rhine to take the
same oath of allegiance; at Mayence he killed the
tribunes and expelled the prefect of the camp when
they refused to swear: Classicus ordered the worst
of the men who had surrendered to go to the besieged, and offer them pardon if they would accept
the actual situation: otherwise there was no hope;
they would suffer famine, sword, and the worst
extremities. His messengers emphasized their words
by citing their own example.

LX. Loyalty on the one hand, famine on the
other, kept the besieged hesitating between honour
and disgrace. As they thus wavered, their sources
of food, both usual and even unusual, failed them,
for they had consumed their beasts of burden, their
horses, and all other animals, which, even though
unclean and disgusting, necessity forced them to
use. Finally, they tore up even shrubs and roots
and grasses growing in the crevices of the rocks,

patientiaeque documentum fuere, donec egregiam
laudem fine turpi macularent, missis ad Civilem
legatis vitam orantes. Neque ante preces admissae
quam in verba Galliarum iurarent: tum pactus
praedam castrorum dat custodes qui pecuniam calones
sarcinas retentarent atque [1] ipsos levis abeuntis
prosequerentur. Ad quintum ferme [2] lapidem coorti
Germani incautum agmen adgrediuntur. Pugna-
cissimus quisque in vestigio, multi palantes occu-
buere: ceteri retro in castra perfugiunt, querente
sane Civile et increpante Germanos tamquam fidem
per scelus abrumperent. Simulata ea fuerint an
retinere saevientis nequiverit, parum adfirmatur.
Direptis castris faces iniciunt, cunctosque qui proelio
superfuerant incendium hausit.

LXI. Civilis barbaro voto post coepta adversus
Romanos arma propexum rutilatumque crinem
patrata demum caede legionum deposuit; et ferebatur parvulo filio quosdam captivorum sagittis
iaculisque puerilibus figendos obtulisse. Ceterum
neque se neque quemquam Batavum in verba
Galliarum adegit, fisus Germanorum opibus et, si
certandum adversus Gallos de possessione rerum

---

[1] atque *Pichena*: atqui *M*.   [2] ferme *Wölfflin*: fere *M*.

[1] Cf. Pliny, *N.H.* xxviii. 191, and Martial, viii. 33, 20.
[2] Cf. Tac. *Germ.* 31.

giving thereby a proof at once of their miseries and
of their endurance, until at last they shamefully
stained what might have been a splendid reputation
by sending a delegation to Civilis and begging for
their lives. He refused to hear their appeals until
they swore allegiance to the empire of Gaul: then
he stipulated for the booty of their camp and sent
guards to secure the treasure, the camp followers,
and the baggage, and to escort the soldiers as they
left their camp empty-handed. When they had
proceeded about five miles the German troops
suddenly attacked and beset them as they advanced
unsuspicious of any danger. The bravest were cut
down where they stood, many were slain as they
scattered; the rest escaped back to camp. Civilis,
it is true, complained of the Germans' action and
reproached them for breaking faith shamefully.
But whether this was mere pretence on his part or
whether he was unable to hold their fury in check
is not certainly proved. His troops plundered the
camp and then set it on fire; the flames consumed
all who had survived the battle.

LXI. Civilis, in accordance with a vow such as
these barbarians frequently make, had dyed his
hair red [1] and let it grow long from the time he first
took up arms against the Romans, but now that the
massacre of the legions was finally accomplished, he
cut it short; [2] it was also said that he presented his
little son with some captives to be targets for the
child's arrows and darts. However, he did not bind
himself or any Batavian by an oath of allegiance to
Gaul, for he relied on the resources of the Germans,
and he felt that, if it became necessary to dispute
the empire with the Gauls, he would have the

foret, inclutus fama et potior. Munius Lupercus legatus legionis inter dona missus Veledae.[1] Ea virgo nationis Bructerae late imperitabat, vetere apud Germanos more, quo plerasque feminarum fatidicas et augescente superstitione arbitrantur[2] deas. Tuncque Veledae auctoritas adolevit; nam prosperas Germanis res et excidium legionum praedixerat. Sed Lupercus in itinere interfectus. Pauci centurionum tribunorumque in Gallia geniti reservantur pignus societati. Cohortium alarum legionum hiberna subversa cremataque, iis tantum relictis quae Mogontiaci ac Vindonissae sita sunt.

LXII. Legio sexta decima cum auxiliis simul deditis a Novaesio in coloniam Trevirorum transgredi iubetur, praefinita die intra quam castris excederet. Medium omne tempus per varias curas egere, ignavissimus quisque caesorum apud Vetera exemplo paventes, melior pars rubore et infamia: quale illud iter? Quis dux viae? Et omnia in arbitrio eorum quos vitae necisque dominos fecissent. Alii nulla dedecoris cura pecuniam aut carissima sibimet ipsi circumdare, quidam expedire arma telisque tamquam in aciem accingi. Haec meditantibus advenit proficiscendi hora expectatione tristior.

---

[1] Veledae *Ryckius*: velaedae *M.*
[2] arbitrantur *ed. Spirensis*: arbitrentur *M.*

---

[1] Later Veleda was captured and brought to Rome. Cf. Tac. *Germ.* 8; and Statius, *Silvae* i. 4, 90.
[2] Windisch.

advantage of his reputation and his superior power. Munius Lupercus, commander of a legion, was sent, among other gifts, to Veleda. This maiden of the tribe of the Bructeri enjoyed extensive authority, according to the ancient German custom, which regards many women as endowed with prophetic powers and, as the superstition grows, attributes divinity to them. At this time Veleda's influence was at its height, since she had foretold the German success and the destruction of the legions.[1] But Lupercus was killed on the road. A few of the centurions and tribunes of Gallic birth were reserved as hostages to assure the alliance. The winter quarters of the auxiliary infantry and cavalry and of the legions were pulled down and burned, with the sole exception of those at Mayence and Vindonissa.[2]

LXII. The Sixteenth legion, with the auxiliary troops that had submitted to Civilis at the same time, was ordered to move from Novaesium to the colony of the Treviri, and the day was fixed before which it was to leave camp. All the intervening time the soldiers spent amid many anxieties: the cowards were terrified by the fate of those who had been massacred at Vetera, the better troops were distressed by a sense of shame and disgrace. They asked themselves: "What kind of a march will this be? Who will lead us? Everything will be at the mercy of those whom we have made masters of life and death." Others had no sense of disgrace and stowed about their persons their money and dearest possessions; some made ready their arms and girded on their weapons as if for battle. While they were thus occupied, the hour for departure arrived; but this proved sadder than their period

Quippe intra vallum deformitas haud perinde nota-
bilis: detexit ignominiam campus et dies. Revulsae
imperatorum imagines, indecora[1] signa, fulgentibus
hinc inde Gallorum vexillis; silens agmen et velut
longae exequiae; dux Claudius Sanctus effosso oculo
dirus ore, ingenio debilior. Duplicatur flagitium,
postquam desertis Bonnensibus castris altera se legio
miscuerat. Et vulgata captarum legionum fama
cuncti qui paulo ante Romanorum nomen horrebant,
procurrentes ex agris tectisque et undique effusi
insolito spectaculo nimium fruebantur. Non tulit
ala Picentina gaudium insultantis vulgi, spretisque
Sancti promissis aut minis Mogontiacum abeunt;
ac forte obvio interfectore Voculae Longino, coniectis
in eum telis initium exolvendae in posterum culpae
fecere: legiones nihil mutato itinere ante moenia
Trevirorum considunt.

LXIII. Civilis et Classicus rebus secundis sublati,
an coloniam Agrippinensem diripiendam exercitibus
suis permitterent dubitavere. Saevitia ingenii[2] et
cupidine praedae ad excidium civitatis trahebantur:
obstabat ratio belli et novum imperium inchoantibus
utilis clementiae fama; Civilem etiam beneficii

---

[1] indecora *Madvig*: inhora *M*.
[2] ingenii *Agricola*: ingenti *M*.

---

[1] Portrait medallions of the emperors were regularly
attached to the shafts of the standards and eagles. Cf. i. 41.
[2] At the modern Trèves.

of anticipation; for within the walls their humiliating condition had not been so noticeable: the open ground and the light of day disclosed their shame. The portraits of the emperors had been torn down; their standards were unadorned,[1] while the Gauls' ensigns glittered on every side; their line moved in silence, like a long funeral train, led by Claudius Sanctus, who was repulsive in appearance, having had one eye gouged out, and was even weaker in intellect. Their shame was doubled when another legion deserting the camp at Bonn joined their line. Moreover, now that the report that the legions had been captured was spread abroad, all who but yesterday were shuddering at the name of Rome, running from their fields and houses and pouring in from every side, displayed extravagant delight in this unusual spectacle. The squadron of Picentine horse could not endure the joy exhibited by the insulting mob, but, scorning the promises and threats of Sanctus, rode away to Mayence; on the way they happened to meet Longinus, the assassin of Vocula, whom they buried under a shower of weapons and so began the future expiation of their guilt: the legions, without changing their course, pitched camp before the walls of the Treviri.[2]

LXIII. Civilis and Classicus, elated by their success, debated whether they should not turn Cologne over to their armies to plunder. Their natural cruelty and their greed for booty inclined them to favour the destruction of the city: in opposition were the interests of the war and the advantage of a reputation for clemency at this time when they were establishing a new empire; Civilis, moreover, was influenced also by the memory of

memoria flexit, quod filium eius primo rerum motu in colonia Agrippinensi deprehensum honorata custodia habuerant.[1] Sed Transrhenanis gentibus invisa civitas opulentia auctuque; neque alium finem belli rebantur quam si promisca ea sedes omnibus Germanis foret aut disiecta Ubios quoque dispersisset.

LXIV. Igitur Tencteri, Rheno discreta gens, missis legatis mandata apud concilium Agrippinensium edi iubent,[2] quae ferocissimus e legatis in hunc modum protulit: " redisse vos in corpus nomenque Germaniae communibus deis et praecipuo deorum Marti grates agimus, vobisque gratulamur quod tandem liberi inter liberos eritis; nam ad hunc diem flumina ac terras et caelum quodam modo ipsum clauserant Romani ut conloquia congressusque nostros arcerent, vel, quod contumeliosius est viris ad arma natis, inermes ac prope nudi sub custode et pretio coiremus. Sed ut amicitia societasque nostra in aeternum rata sint, postulamus a vobis muros coloniae, munimenta servitii, detrahatis (etiam fera animalia, si clausa teneas, virtutis obliviscuntur), Romanos omnis in finibus vestris trucidetis (haud facile libertas et domini miscentur): bona inter-

---

[1] custodia habuerant *Wurm*: custodiae erant *M*.
[2] iuberent *M*.

---

[1] The Ubii were naturally suspected by their neighbours in Germany, for, although of German origin, they had long since adopted Roman customs, developed a prosperous urban life, and grown wealthy and great. Cf. chap. xxviii above.
[2] Cf. chap. xxi.

the service done him, when at the beginning of the
revolt his son had been arrested in Cologne, but had
been treated with honour while in custody. Yet
the tribes across the Rhine hated the city for its
wealth and rapid growth; and they believed that
there could be no end to the war unless this place
should be a common home for all the Germans without distinction, or else the city destroyed and the
Ubii scattered like the other peoples.[1]

LXIV. So the Tencteri, a tribe separated from
the colony by the Rhine,[2] sent an embassy with
orders to present their demands in an assembly of
the people of Cologne. These demands the most
violent of the delegates set forth thus: " We give
thanks to our common gods and to Mars before all
others that you have returned to the body of the
German peoples and to the German name, and we
congratulate you that at last you are going to be
free men among free men; for until to-day the
Romans have closed rivers and lands, and in a
fashion heaven itself, to keep us from meeting and
conferring together, or else—and this is a severer
insult to men born to arms—to make us meet unarmed and almost naked, under guard and paying
a price for the privilege.[3] But to secure for ever
our friendship and alliance, we demand that you
take down the walls of your colony, the bulwarks
of your slavery, for even wild animals forget their
courage if you keep them shut up; we demand that
you kill all the Romans in your territories. Liberty
and masters are not easily combined together. The

[3] The colony being defended by a wall, admission to the
town was subject to police regulations and a tax. Cf. the
following chapter.

fectorum in medium cedant, ne quis occulere quicquam aut segregare causam suam possit. Liceat
nobis vobisque utramque ripam colere, ut olim
maioribus nostris : quo modo lucem diemque omnibus
hominibus, ita omnis terras fortibus viris natura
aperuit. Instituta cultumque patrium resumite,
abruptis voluptatibus, quibus Romani plus adversus
subiectos quam armis valent. Sincerus et integer
et servitutis oblitus populus aut ex aequo agetis aut
aliis[1] imperitabitis."

LXV. Agrippinenses sumpto consultandi spatio,
quando neque subire condiciones metus futuri neque
palam aspernari condicio praesens sinebat, in hunc
modum respondent : " quae prima libertatis facultas
data est, avidius quam cautius sumpsimus, ut vobis
ceterisque Germanis, consanguineis nostris, iungere-
mur. Muros civitatis, congregantibus se cum maxime
Romanorum exercitibus, augere nobis quam diruere
tutius est. Si qui ex Italia aut provinciis alienigenae
in finibus nostris fuerant, eos bellum absumpsit vel
in suas quisque sedis refugerunt. Deductis olim et
nobiscum per conubium sociatis quique mox pro-
venerunt haec patria est; nec vos adeo iniquos
existimamus ut interfici a nobis parentes fratres
liberos nostros velitis. Vectigal et onera commer-
ciorum resolvimus : sint transitus incustoditi sed
diurni et inermes, donec nova et recentia iura

---

[1] avis *M*.

---

[1] The veterans settled here in 50 A.D. Cf. *Ann.* xii. 27.

property of those killed is to be put into the common stock that no one may be able to hide anything or separate his own interest. Both we and you are to have the right to live on both banks, as our fathers once did. Even as Nature has always made the light of day free to all mankind, so she has made all lands open to the brave. Resume the manners and customs of your fathers, cutting off those pleasures which give the Romans more power over their subjects than their arms bestow. A people pure, untainted, forgetting your servitude, you will live the equals of any or will rule others."

LXV. The people of Cologne first took some time to consider the matter, and then, since fear for the future did not allow them to submit to the terms proposed and present circumstances made it impossible to reject them openly, they made the following reply: " The first opportunity of freedom we seized with more eagerness than caution that we might join ourselves with you and the other Germans who are of our own blood. But it is safer to build the walls of the town higher rather than to pull them down at the moment when the Roman armies are concentrating. All the foreigners of Italian or provincial origin within our lands have been destroyed by war or have fled each to his own home. The first settlers,[1] established here long ago, have become allied with us by marriage, and to them as well as to their children this is their native city; nor can we think that you are so unjust as to wish us to kill our own parents, brothers, and children. We now suppress the duties and all charges that are burdens on trade: let there be free intercourse between us, but by day and without arms until by

vetustate in consuetudinem[1] vertantur. Arbitrum
habebimus Civilem et Veledam, apud quos pacta
sancientur." Sic lenitis Tencteris legati ad Civilem
ac Veledam missi cum donis cuncta ex voluntate
Agrippinensium perpetravere; sed coram adire
adloquique Veledam negatum: arcebantur aspectu
quo venerationis plus inesset. Ipsa edita in turre;
delectus e propinquis consulta responsaque ut inter-
nuntius numinis portabat.

LXVI. Civilis societate Agrippinensium auctus
proximas civitates adfectare aut adversantibus bellum inferre statuit. Occupatisque Sunucis et iuventute eorum per cohortis composita, quo minus ultra
pergeret, Claudius Labeo Baetasiorum Tungrorumque et Nerviorum tumultuaria manu restitit,
fretus loco, quia pontem Mosae fluminis anteceperat.
Pugnabaturque in angustiis ambigue donec Germani
transnatantes terga Labeonis invasere; simul Civilis,
ausus an ex composito, intulit se agmini Tungrorum,
et clara voce "non ideo[2]" inquit " bellum sumpsimus,
ut Batavi et Treviri gentibus imperent: procul haec
a nobis adrogantia. Accipite societatem: trans-

---

[1] vetustate in consuetudinem *Madvig*: in vetustatem
consuetudine *M.*
[2] non dō *M.*

---

[1] Neighbours of the Ubii, to the west between the Meuse
and the Roer.
[2] Cf. chap. lvi.

lapse of time we shall become accustomed to our
new and unfamiliar rights. We will have as arbiters
Civilis and Veleda, before whom all our agreements
shall be ratified." With these proposals they first
calmed the Tencteri and then sent a delegation to
Civilis and Veleda with gifts which obtained from
them everything that the people of Cologne desired;
yet the embassy was not allowed to approach Veleda
herself and address her directly: they were kept
from seeing her to inspire them with more respect.
She herself lived in a high tower; one of her relatives,
chosen for the purpose, carried to her the questions
and brought back her answers, as if he were the
messenger of a god.

LXVI. Now that the power of Civilis was increased by alliance with the people of Cologne, he
decided to try to win over the neighbouring peoples,
or, if they refused, to attack them. He had already
gained the Sunuci [1] and had organized their young
men into companies of infantry, when Claudius
Labeo offered resistance with a force of the Baetasii,
Tungri, and Nervii that he had hastily assembled,[2]
but he had confidence in his position because he
had seized the bridge over the Meuse. The forces
engaged in this narrow space without a decisive issue
until the Germans swam across the river and attacked
Labeo's rear; at the same time Civilis, acting under
a bold impulse or in accord with a previous arrangement, rushed to the line of the Tungri and cried
in a loud voice: "We did not begin the war with
the purpose of making the Batavians and the Treviri
lords over the other peoples: such arrogance is far
from our minds. Accept alliance with us: I am
joining you, whether you wish me to be your leader

127

gredior ad vos, seu me ducem seu militem mavultis."
Movebatur vulgus condebantque gladios, cum Campanus ac Iuvenalis e primoribus Tungrorum universam
ei gentem dedidere; Labeo antequam circumveniretur profugit. Civilis Baetasios quoque ac Nervios
in fidem acceptos copiis suis adiunxit, ingens rerum,
perculsis civitatum animis vel sponte inclinantibus.

LXVII. Interea Iulius Sabinus proiectis foederis
Romani monumentis Caesarem se salutari iubet
magnamque et inconditam popularium turbam in
Sequanos rapit, conterminam civitatem et nobis
fidam; nec Sequani detractavere certamen. Fortuna
melioribus adfuit: fusi Lingones. Sabinus festinatum temere proelium pari formidine deseruit;
utque famam exitii sui faceret, villam, in quam
perfugerat, cremavit, illic voluntaria morte interisse
creditus. Sed quibus artibus latebrisque vitam per
novem mox annos traduxerit, simul amicorum eius
constantiam et insigne Epponinae uxoris exemplum
suo loco reddemus. Sequanorum prospera acie belli
impetus stetit. Resipiscere paulatim civitates fasque
et foedera respicere, principibus Remis, qui per

---

¹ Cf. chap. lv.
² That is, the bronze records recording the terms of alliance.
³ Living around the modern Besançon.
⁴ The portion of the *Histories* in which Tacitus must have
related the story is now lost, but the tale is given by Dio
Cassius, lxvi. 16, and Plutarch, *Amat.* 25. Sabinus and his
wife lived for nine years in a cave where two sons were born.
Later they were discovered and put to death.

or prefer me to be a common soldier." The mass
of the Tungri were moved by this appeal and were
in the act of sheathing their swords when Companus
and Juvenalis, two of their chief men, surrendered
the whole people to him; Labeo escaped before he
could be surrounded. Civilis received the submission of the Baetasii and the Nervii as well, and
added them to his forces: his power was now great,
for the peoples were either terrified or inclined
voluntarily to his cause.

LXVII. In the meantime Julius Sabinus[1] had
destroyed all memorials of the alliance with Rome[2]
and directed that he should be saluted as Caesar;
then he hurried a great and unorganized mob of his
countrymen against the Sequani,[3] a people that
touched the boundaries of the Lingones and were
faithful to us. The Sequani did not refuse battle;
fortune favoured the better cause: the Lingones were
routed. Sabinus was as prompt to flee in terror
from the battle as he had been over-ready to begin
it; and to spread a report of his own death he
burned the country house to which he had fled for
refuge, and it was generally believed that he had
perished there by suicide. But I shall later tell in
the proper place by what means and in what hiding-
places he prolonged his life for nine years, and I
shall also describe the fidelity of his friends and the
noble example set by his wife Epponina.[4] The
success of the Sequani brought the impulse for war
to a halt. Gradually the communities came to
their senses and began to regard their duty under
their treaties; in this movement the Remi took the
lead by sending word through the Gallic provinces
that envoys should be despatched to debate in their

Gallias edixere ut missis legatis in commune consultarent, libertas an pax placeret.

LXVIII. At Romae cuncta in deterius audita Mucianum angebant, ne quamquam[1] egregii duces (iam enim Gallum Annium et Petilium Cerialem delegerat) summam belli parum tolerarent.[2] Nec relinquenda urbs sine rectore; et Domitiani indomitae libidines timebantur, suspectis, uti diximus, Primo Antonio Varoque Arrio. Varus praetorianis praepositus vim atque arma retinebat: eum Mucianus pulsum loco, ne sine solacio ageret, annonae praefecit. utque Domitiani animum Varo haud alienum deleniret, Arrecinum Clementem, domui Vespasiani per adfinitatem innexum et gratissimum Domitiano, praetorianis praeposuit, patrem eius sub C. Caesare egregie functum ea cura dictitans, laetum militibus idem nomen, atque ipsum, quamquam senatorii ordinis, ad utraque munia sufficere. Adsumuntur e civitate clarissimus quisque et alii per ambitionem. simul Domitianus Mucianusque accingebantur, dispari animo, ille spe ac iuventa properus, hic moras nectens quis flagrantem retineret, ne ferocia aetatis et pravis impulsoribus, si exercitum invasisset, paci

----

[1] ne quamquam *Mercerus*: nequaquam *M*.
[2] tolerarent *Mercerus*: tolerare *M*.

----

[1] Mucianus had good reason to be anxious: Domitian was unstable and ambitious, and there was cause to doubt the fidelity of Primus Antonius and Varus Arrius (Cf. III, lii f. lxxviii; IV, xxxix). By making Arrecinus Clemens prefect of the praetorians, Mucianus disarmed Domitian and his possible supporter Varus, and at the same time he secured the fidelity of the praetorian guard to Vespasian.

[2] Vespasian's first wife had been a sister of Clemens.

common interest whether the Gallic peoples preferred liberty or peace.

LXVIII. But at Rome all the news from Gaul was exaggerated for the worse and caused Mucianus anxiety lest even distinguished generals—for he had already selected Gallus Annius and Petilius Cerealis —should not be able to support the whole burden of this great war. He could not leave the city without a head; and he looked with anxiety on the unbridled passions of Domitian, while he suspected, as I have said, Primus Antonius and Varus Arrius.[1] Varus, at the head of the praetorian guard, still had control of an armed force: Mucianus removed him, but, to avoid leaving him with no solace, placed him in charge of the supply of grain. And to pacify Domitian's feelings, which were not unfavourable to Varus, he put in command of the praetorians Arrecinus Clemens, who was connected with Vespasian's house by marriage[2] and beloved by Domitian, dwelling on the fact that Clemens's father had held the same office with distinction under Gaius Caesar, that his name was popular with the soldiers, and that Clemens himself, although of senatorial rank, was equal to the duties of prefect as well as to those of his own class.[3] All the most eminent citizens were enrolled for the expedition, others at their own solicitation. So Domitian and Mucianus were making ready to set out, but with different feelings; Domitian being eager with youthful hope, Mucianus contriving delays to check the other's ardour for fear that, if he once got control of the army, his youthful impetuosity and his evil counsellors would

[3] From Augustus's day, the prefect of the praetorian guard had regularly been of equestrian rank.

belloque male consuleret. Legiones victrices, octava, undecima, decima tertia,[1] Vitellianarum unaetvicensima, e recens conscriptis secunda Poeninis Cottianisque Alpibus, pars monte Graio traducuntur; quarta decima legio a Britannia, sexta ac prima ex Hispania accitae.

Igitur venientis exercitus fama et suopte ingenio ad mitiora inclinantes Galliarum civitates in Remos convenere. Trevirorum legatio illic opperiebatur, acerrimo instinctore belli Iulio Valentino. Is meditata oratione cuncta magnis imperiis obiectari solita contumeliasque et invidiam in populum Romanum effudit, turbidus miscendis seditionibus et plerisque gratus vaecordi facundia.

LXIX. At Iulius Auspex a primoribus Remorum, vim Romanam pacisque bona dissertans et sumi bellum etiam ab ignavis, strenuissimi cuiusque periculo geri, iamque super caput legiones, sapientissimum quemque reverentia fideque, iuniores periculo ac metu continuit: et Valentini animum laudabant, consilium Auspicis sequebantur. Constat obstitisse Treviris Lingonibusque apud Gallias, quod Vindicis motu cum Verginio steterant. Deterruit plerosque provinciarum aemulatio: quod bello caput? Unde

---

[1] octava, undecima, decima tertia *Mommsen*: vim. xj viij *M*.

make him a peril to peace and war alike. The
victorious legions, the Eighth, Eleventh, Thirteenth,
and the Twenty-first, which had been of the Vitellian
party, as well as the Second, lately enlisted, were
led into Gaul, part over the Pennine and Cottian
Alps, part over the Graian; the Fourteenth legion
was called from Britain, the Sixth and First were
summoned from Spain.

So when the news of the approaching army got
abroad, the Gallic states that naturally inclined to
milder courses assembled among the Remi. A
delegation of the Treviri was waiting for them
there, led by Julius Valentinus, the most fiery
advocate of war. In a studied speech he poured
forth all the common charges against great empires,
and heaped insults and invectives on the Roman
people, being a speaker well fitted to stir up trouble
and revolt, and popular with the mass of his hearers
for his mad eloquence.

LXIX. But Julius Auspex, a noble of the Remi,
dwelt on the power of Rome and the blessings of
peace; he pointed out that even cowards can begin
war, but that it can be prosecuted only at the risk
of the bravest, and, moreover, the legions were
already upon them; thus he restrained the most
prudent of his people by considerations of reverence
and loyalty, the younger men by pointing out the
danger and arousing their fears: the people praised
the spirit of Valentinus, but they followed the advice
of Auspex. It is beyond question that the fact that
the Treviri and Lingones had stood with Verginius
at the time of the revolt of Vindex injured them in
the eyes of the Gauls. Many were deterred by the
rivalry between the Gallic provinces. "Where,"

ius auspiciumque peteretur? Quam, si cuncta provenissent, sedem imperio legerent? Nondum victoria, iam discordia erat, aliis foedera, quibusdam opes virisque aut vetustatem originis per iurgia[1] iactantibus: taedio futurorum praesentia placuere. Scribuntur ad Treviros epistulae nomine Galliarum ut abstinerent armis, impetrabili venia et paratis deprecatoribus, si paeniteret: restitit idem Valentinus obstruxitque civitatis suae auris, haud perinde instruendo bello intentus quam frequens contionibus.

LXX. Igitur non Treviri neque Lingones ceteraeve rebellium civitates pro magnitudine suscepti discriminis agere; ne duces quidem in unum consulere, sed Civilis avia Belgarum circumibat, dum Claudium Labeonem capere aut exturbare nititur; Classicus segne plerumque otium trahens velut parto imperio fruebatur; ne Tutor quidem maturavit superiorem Germaniae ripam et ardua Alpium praesidiis claudere. Atque interim unaetvicensima legio Vindonissa, Sextilius Felix cum auxiliariis cohortibus per Raetiam inrupere; accessit ala Singularium excita olim a Vitellio, deinde in partis Vespasiani transgressa.

---

[1] iurgia *Manitius*: Iuria *M*.

---

[1] Cf. iii. 5.

they asked, " are we to find a leader for the war? Where look for orders and the auspices? What shall we choose for our capital if all goes well?" They had not yet gained the victory, but discord already prevailed; some boasted in insulting fashion of their treaties, some of their wealth and strength or of their ancient origin: in disgust at the prospects of the future, they finally chose their present state. Letters were sent to the Treviri in the name of the Gallic provinces, bidding them to refrain from armed action, and saying pardon could be obtained and that men were ready to intercede for them, if they repented: Valentinus opposed again and succeeded in closing the ears of his fellow tribesmen to these proposals; he was not, however, so active in making actual provision for war as he was assiduous in haranguing the people.

LXX. The result was that neither the Treviri nor the Lingones nor the other rebellious people made efforts at all proportionate to the gravity of the crisis; not even the leaders consulted together, but Civilis ranged the pathless wilds of Belgium in his efforts to capture Claudius Labeo or to drive him out of the country, while Classicus spent most of his time in indolent ease, enjoying his supreme power as if it were already secured; even Tutor made no haste to occupy with troops the Upper Rhine and the passes of the Alps. In the meantime the Twenty-first legion penetrated by way of Vindonissa and Sextilius Felix entered through Raetia with some auxiliary infantry [1]; these troops were joined by the squadron of picked horse that had originally been formed by Vitellius but which had later gone over to Vespasian's side. These were commanded

Praeerat Iulius Briganticus sorore Civilis genitus,
ut ferme acerrima proximorum odia sunt, invisus
avunculo infensusque. Tutor Trevirorum copias,
recenti Vangionum, Caeracatium, Tribocorum dilectu
auctas, veterano pedite atque equite firmavit, corruptis spe aut metu subactis legionariis; qui primo
cohortem praemissam a Sextilio Felice interficiunt,
mox ubi duces exercitusque Romanus propinquabant,
honesto transfugio rediere, secutis Tribocis Van-
gionibusque et Caeracatibus. Tutor Treviris comi-
tantibus, vitato Mogontiaco, Bingium concessit,
fidens loco, quia pontem Navae[1] fluminis abruperat,
sed incursu cohortium, quas Sextilius ducebat, et
reperto vado proditus fususque. Ea clade perculsi
Treviri, et plebes omissis armis per agros palatur:
quidam principum, ut primi posuisse bellum viderentur, in civitates quae societatem Romanam non
exuerant, perfugere. Legiones a Novaesio Bonnaque
in Treviros, ut supra memoravimus, traductae se
ipsae[2] in verba Vespasiani adigunt. Haec Valentino
absente gesta; qui ubi adventabat furens cunctaque
rursus in turbas et exitium conversurus, legiones in
Mediomatricos, sociam civitatem, abscessere: Valentinus ac Tutor in arma Treviros retrahunt, occisis

---

[1] Navae *Rhenanus*: navas *M*.
[2] ipsae *Ernesti*: ipsas *M*.

---

[1] Cf. ii. 22.
[2] The Vangiones lived in the district of Worms; the Triboci
in Lower Alsace; while the Caeracates are otherwise unknown.
[3] Bingen.   [4] The Nahe.   [5] Living about Metz.

by Julius Briganticus, the son of a sister of Civilis,[1]
who was hated by his uncle and who hated his uncle
in turn with all the bitter hatred that frequently
exists between the closest relatives. Tutor first
added to the Treviran troops a fresh levy of Vangiones, Caeracates, and Triboci,[2] and then reinforced
these with veteran foot and horse, drawn from the
legionaries whom he had either corrupted by hope
or overcome with fear; these forces first massacred
a cohort despatched in advance by Sextilius Felix;
then, when the Roman generals and armies began to
draw near, they returned to their allegiance by an
honourable desertion, followed by the Triboci, Vangiones, and Caeracates. Tutor, accompanied by the
Treviri, avoided Mayence and withdrew to Bingium.[3]
He had confidence in this position, for he had destroyed the bridge across the Nava,[4] but he was
assailed by some cohorts under Sextilius, whose
discovery of a ford exposed him and forced him
to flee. This defeat terrified the Treviri, and the
common people abandoned their arms and dispersed among their fields: some of the chiefs, in
their desire to seem the first to give up war, took
refuge in those states that had not abandoned their
alliance with Rome. The legions that had been
moved from Novaesium and Bonn to the Treviri, as
I have stated above, now voluntarily took the oath
of allegiance to Vespasian. All this happened during
the absence of Valentinus; when he returned, however, he was beside himself and wished to throw
everything again into confusion and ruin; whereupon the legions withdrew among the Mediomatrici,
an allied people [5]: Valentinus and Tutor swept the
Treviri again into arms, and murdered the two

Herennio ac Numisio legatis quo minore spe veniae
cresceret vinculum sceleris.

LXXI. Hic belli status erat cum Petilius Cerialis
Mogontiacum venit. Eius adventu erectae spes;
ipse pugnae avidus et contemnendis quam cavendis
hostibus melior, ferocia verborum militem incendebat, ubi primum congredi licuisset, nullam proelio
moram facturus. Dilectus per Galliam habitos in
civitates remittit ac nuntiare iubet sufficere imperio
legiones: socii ad munia pacis redirent securi velut
confecto bello quod Romanae manus excepissent.
Auxit ea res Gallorum obsequium: nam recepta
iuventute facilius tributa toleravere, proniores ad
officia quod spernebantur. At Civilis et Classicus
ubi pulsum Tutorem, caesos Treviros, cuncta hostibus prospera accepere, trepidi ac properantes, dum
dispersas suorum copias conducunt, crebris interim
nuntiis Valentinum monuere ne summae rei periculum faceret. Eo rapidius Cerialis, missis in Mediomatricos qui breviore itinere legiones in hostem
verterent, contracto quod erat militum Mogontiaci
quantumque secum transvexerat, tertiis castris
Rigodulum venit, quem locum magna Trevirorum

---

[1] Riol.

commanders Herennius and Numisius to strengthen the bond of their common crime by diminishing their hope of pardon.

LXXI. This was the state of war when Petilius Cerialis reached Mayence. His arrival aroused great hopes; Cerialis was himself eager for battle and better fitted by nature to despise a foe than to guard against him; he fired his soldiers by his fierce words, declaring that he would not delay a moment when he had a chance to engage the enemy. The troops that had been levied throughout Gaul he sent back to their several states, and told them to report that the legions were sufficient to sustain the empire: the allies were to return to their peaceful duties without any anxiety, since, when the Roman arms once undertook a war, that war was virtually ended. This act increased the ready submission of the Gauls; for now that they had recovered their young men they bore the burdens of the tribute more easily, and they were more ready to be obedient when they saw that they were despised. But when Civilis and Classicus heard that Tutor had been defeated, the Treviri cut to pieces, and that their foes were everywhere successful, they became alarmed and hastened to collect their scattered forces; in the meantime they sent many messages to warn Valentinus not to risk a decisive engagement. These circumstances moved Cerialis to prompter action: he despatched some officers to the Mediomatrici to direct the legions against the enemy by a more direct route, while he united the troops at Mayence with all the forces that he had brought with him; after a three days' march he came to Rigodulum,[1] which Valentinus had occupied

manu Valentinus insederat, montibus aut Mosella
amne saeptum; et addiderat fossas obicesque saxo-
rum. Nec deterruere ea munimenta Romanum
ducem quo minus peditem perrumpere iuberet,
equitum aciem in collem erigeret,[1] spreto hoste,
quem temere collectum haud ita loco iuvari ut non
plus suis in virtute foret. Paulum morae in adscensu,
dum missilia hostium praevehuntur: ut ventum in
manus, deturbati ruinae modo praecipitantur. Et
pars equitum aequioribus iugis circumvecta nobilis-
simos Belgarum, in quis ducem Valentinum, cepit.

LXXII. Cerialis postero die coloniam Trevirorum
ingressus est, avido milite eruendae civitatis. Hanc
esse Classici, hanc Tutoris patriam; horum scelere
clausas caesasque legiones. Quid tantum Cremonam
meruisse? Quam e gremio Italiae raptam quia unius
noctis moram victoribus attulerit. Stare in confinio
Germaniae integram sedem spoliis exercituum et
ducum caedibus ovantem. Redigeretur praeda in
fiscum: ipsis sufficere ignis et rebellis coloniae ruinas,
quibus tot castrorum excidia pensarentur. Cerialis
metu[2] infamiae, si licentia saevitiaque imbuere mili-

---

[1] erigeret b: frigeret M.
[2] ametu M.

---

[1] They had in mind Hordeonius, Vocula, Herennius, and
Numisius.

with a large force of Treviri. The town was naturally protected by hills or by the Moselle; in addition Valentinus had constructed ditches and stone ramparts. But these fortifications did not deter the Roman general from ordering his infantry to assault or from sending his cavalry up the hill, since he despised his foe, believing that his own men would have more advantage from their courage than the enemy's hastily collected forces could gain from their position. The Roman troops were delayed a little in their ascent while they were exposed to the enemy's missiles: when they came to close quarters, the Treviri were hurled down headlong like a falling building. Moreover, some of the cavalry rode round along the lower hills and captured the noblest of the Belgians, among them their leader Valentinus.

LXXII. On the next day Cerialis entered the colony of the Treviri. His soldiers were eager to plunder the town and said: " This is Classicus's native city, and Tutor's as well; they are the men whose treason has caused our legions to be besieged and massacred. What monstrous crime had Cremona committed? Yet Cremona was torn from the very bosom of Italy because she delayed the victors one single night. This colony stands on the boundaries of Germany, unharmed, and rejoices in the spoils taken from our armies and in the murder of our commanders.[1] The booty may go to the imperial treasury: it is enough for us to set fire to this rebellious colony and to destroy it, for in that way we can compensate for the destruction of so many of our camps." Cerialis feared the disgrace that he would suffer if men were to believe that he imbued his troops with a spirit of licence and cruelty,

tem crederetur, pressit iras: et paruere, posito civium bello ad externa modestiores. Convertit inde animos accitarum e Mediomatricis legionum miserabilis aspectus. Stabant conscientia flagitii maestae, fixis in terram oculis: nulla inter coeuntis exercitus consalutatio[1]; neque solantibus hortantibusve responsa dabant, abditi per tentoria et lucem ipsam vitantes. Nec proinde periculum aut metus quam pudor ac dedecus obstupefecerat, attonitis etiam victoribus, qui vocem precesque adhibere non ausi lacrimis ac silentio veniam poscebant, donec Cerialis mulceret animos, fato acta dictitans quae militum ducumque discordia vel fraude hostium evenissent. Primum illum stipendiorum et sacramenti diem haberent: priorum facinorum neque imperatorem neque se meminisse. Tunc recepti in eadem castra, et edictum per manipulos ne quis in certamine iurgiove seditionem aut cladem commilitoni obiectaret.

LXXIII. Mox Treviros ac Lingonas ad contionem vocatos ita adloquitur: " neque ego umquam facundiam exercui, et populus Romanus[2] virtutem armis adfirmavit: sed quoniam[3] apud vos verba plurimum

---

[1] consalutatio *dett.*: consultatio *M.*
[2] populus Romanus *Nipperdey*: populi Romani *M.*
[3] quoniam: q̄ *M.*

---

[1] These legions were the First and the Sixteenth. Cf. chaps. xxv, xxxvii, lix, lxii, and lxx above.

and he therefore checked their passionate anger:
and they obeyed him, for now that they had given
up civil war, they were more moderate with reference to foreign foes. Their attention was then
attracted by the sad aspect which the legions summoned from among the Mediomatrici presented.[1]
These troops stood there, downcast by the consciousness of their own guilt, their eyes fixed on the
ground: when the armies met, there was no exchange
of greetings; the soldiers made no answer to those
who tried to console or to encourage them; they
remained hidden in their tents and avoided the very
light of day. It was not so much danger and fear
as a sense of their shame and disgrace that paralyzed
them, while even the victors were struck dumb.
The latter did not dare to speak or make entreaty,
but by their tears and silence they continued to ask
forgiveness for their fellows, until Cerialis at last
quieted them by saying that fate was responsible for
all that had resulted from the differences between
the soldiers and their commanders or from the
treachery of their enemies. He urged them to consider this as the first day of their service and of
their allegiance, and he declared that neither the
emperor nor he remembered their former misdeeds.
Then they were taken into the same camp with the
rest, and a proclamation was read in each company
forbidding any soldier in quarrel or dispute to taunt
a comrade with treason or murder.

LXXIII. Presently Cerialis called an assembly of
the Treviri and Lingones and addressed them
thus: " I have never practised oratory and the
Roman people has ever asserted its merits by arms:
but since words have the greatest weight with you

valent bonaque ac mala non sua natura, sed vocibus
seditiosorum aestimantur, statui pauca disserere
quae profligato bello utilius sit vobis audisse quam
nobis dixisse. Terram vestram ceterorumque Gallorum ingressi sunt duces imperatoresque Romani
nulla cupidine, sed maioribus vestris invocantibus,
quos discordiae usque ad exitium fatigabant, et
acciti auxilio Germani sociis pariter atque hostibus
servitutem imposuerant. Quot proeliis adversus
Cimbros Teutonosque, quantis exercituum nostrorum laboribus quove eventu Germanica bella tracta-
verimus, satis clarum. Nec ideo Rhenum insedimus
ut Italiam tueremur, sed ne quis alius Ariovistus¹
regno Galliarum potiretur. An vos cariores Civili
Batavisque et transrhenanis gentibus creditis quam
maioribus eorum patres avique vestri fuerunt?
Eadem semper causa Germanis transcendendi in
Gallias, libido atque avaritia et mutandae sedis
amor, ut relictis paludibus et solitudinibus suis
fecundissimum hoc solum vosque ipsos possiderent:
ceterum libertas et speciosa nomina praetexuntur;
nec quisquam alienum servitium et dominationem
sibi concupivit ut non eadem ista vocabula usurparet.

LXXIV. "Regna bellaque per Gallias semper
fuere donec in nostrum ius concederetis. Nos, quamquam totiens lacessiti, iure victoriae id solum vobis

¹ The ambition of Ariovistus had been checked by Julius
Caesar during his first campaign in Gaul, 58 B.C.

and you do not reckon good and evil according to
their own nature, but estimate them by the talk of
seditious men, I have decided to say a few things
which now that the war is over are more useful for
you to hear than for me to say. Roman commanders
and generals entered your land and the lands of the
other Gauls from no desire for gain but because they
were invited by your forefathers, who were wearied
to death by internal quarrels, while the Germans
whom they had invited to help them had enslaved
them all, allies and enemies alike. How many
battles we have fought against the Cimbri and
Teutoni, with what hardships on the part of our
armies and with what result we have conducted our
wars against the Germans, is perfectly well known.
We have occupied the banks of the Rhine not to
protect Italy but to prevent a second Ariovistus
from gaining the throne of Gaul.[1] Do you believe
that you are dearer to Civilis and his Batavians or
to the peoples across the Rhine than your grandfathers and fathers were to their ancestors? The
Germans always have the same reasons for crossing
into the Gallic provinces—lust, avarice, and their
longing to change their homes, that they may leave
behind their swamps and deserts, and become
masters of this most fertile soil and of you yourselves: freedom, however, and specious names are
their pretexts; but no man has ever been ambitious
to enslave another or to win dominion for himself
without using those very same words.

LXXIV. "There were always kings and wars
throughout Gaul until you submitted to our laws.
Although often provoked by you, the only use we
have made of our rights as victors has been to

addidimus, quo pacem tueremur; nam neque quies gentium sine armis neque arma sine stipendiis neque stipendia sine tributis haberi queunt: cetera in communi sita sunt. Ipsi plerumque legionibus nostris praesidetis, ipsi has aliasque provincias regitis; nihil separatum clausumve. Et laudatorum principum usus ex aequo quamvis procul agentibus: saevi proximis ingruunt. Quo modo sterilitatem aut nimios imbris et cetera naturae mala, ita luxum vel avaritiam dominantium tolerate. Vitia erunt, donec homines, sed neque haec continua et meliorum interventu pensantur: nisi forte Tutore et Classico regnantibus moderatius imperium speratis, aut minoribus quam nunc tributis parabuntur exercitus quibus Germani Britannique arceantur. Nam pulsis, quod di prohibeant, Romanis quid aliud quam bella omnium inter se gentium existent? Octingentorum annorum fortuna disciplinaque compages haec coaluit, quae convelli sine exitio convellentium non potest: sed vobis maximum discrimen, penes quos aurum et opes, praecipuae bellorum causae. Proinde pacem et urbem, quam victi victoresque eodem iure obtinemus, amate colite: moneant vos utriusque fortunae documenta ne contumaciam cum pernicie quam obsequium cum securitate malitis." Tali oratione graviora metuentis composuit erexitque.

LXXV. Tenebantur victore exercitu Treviri, cum

impose on you the necessary costs of maintaining peace; for you cannot secure tranquillity among nations without armies, nor maintain armies without pay, nor provide pay without taxes: everything else we have in common. You often command our legions; you rule these and other provinces; we claim no privileges, you suffer no exclusion. You enjoy the advantage of the good emperors equally with us, although you dwell far from the capital: the cruel emperors assail those nearest them. You endure barren years, excessive rains, and all other natural evils; in like manner endure the extravagance or greed of your rulers. There will be vices so long as there are men, but these vices are not perpetual and they are compensated for by the coming of better times: unless perchance you hope that you will enjoy a milder rule if Tutor and Classicus reign over you, or that the taxes required to provide armies to keep out the Germans and Britons will be less than now. For, if the Romans are driven out—which Heaven forbid—what will follow except universal war among all peoples? The good fortune and order of eight hundred years have built up this mighty fabric which cannot be destroyed without overwhelming its destroyers: moreover, you are in the greatest danger, for you possess gold and wealth, which are the chief causes of war. Therefore love and cherish peace and the city wherein we, conquerors and conquered alike, enjoy an equal right: be warned by the lessons of fortune both good and bad not to prefer defiance and ruin to obedience and security." With such words Cerialis quieted and encouraged his hearers, who feared severer measures.

LXXV. The Treviri were now being held in sub-

Civilis et Classicus misere ad Cerialem epistulas, quarum haec sententia fuit: Vespasianum, quamquam nuntios occultarent, excessisse vita, urbem atque Italiam interno bello consumptam, Muciani ac Domitiani vana et sine viribus nomina: si Cerialis imperium Galliarum velit, ipsos finibus civitatium suarum contentos; si proelium malit,[1] ne id quidem abnuere. Ad ea Cerialis Civili et Classico nihil: eum qui attulerat *et* ipsas[2] epistulas ad Domitianum misit.

Hostes divisis copiis advenere undique. Plerique culpabant Cerialem passum iungi quos discretos intercipere licuisset. Romanus exercitus castra fossa valloque circumdedit, quis temere antea intutis consederat.

LXXVI. Apud Germanos diversis sententiis certabatur. Civilis opperiendas Transrhenanorum gentis, quarum terrore fractae populi Romani vires obtererentur: Gallos quid aliud quam praedam victoribus? Et tamen, quod roboris sit, Belgas secum palam aut voto stare. Tutor cunctatione crescere rem Romanam adfirmabat, coeuntibus undique exercitibus: transvectam e Britannia legionem, accitas ex Hispania, adventare ex Italia; nec subitum militem, sed veterem expertumque belli. Nam Germanos,

---

[1] malit *Ernesti*: mallet *M*.
[2] et ipsas *Ruperti*: ipsas *M*.

mission by the victorious army when Civilis and Classicus wrote to Cerialis to this effect: " Vespasian is dead, although the news of his death is held back; Rome and Italy have been exhausted by internal wars; the names of Mucianus and Domitian are empty and carry no weight: if you wish the empire of the Gauls, we are satisfied with the boundaries of our own states; if you prefer to fight, we do not refuse you that alternative either." Cerialis made no reply to Civilis and Classicus; but he sent the messenger who had brought the letter and the letter itself to Domitian.

The enemy, whose forces were divided, now approached from every quarter. Many blamed Cerialis for having allowed this concentration of troops when he might have cut them off in detail. The Roman army constructed a ditch and palisade around their camp, which they had rashly occupied up to this time in spite of its unprotected condition.

LXXVI. Among the Germans there was a clash of diverse opinions. Civilis urged that they should wait for the peoples from beyond the Rhine, who would so terrify the Romans that their strength would break and collapse. " As for the Gauls," said he, " what are they but booty for the victors? And yet the Belgians, their only real strength, are openly on our side or wish our success." Tutor maintained that delay improved the condition of the Romans, for their armies were coming from every quarter. " One legion," he said, " has been brought from Britain; others have been summoned from Spain, or are coming from Italy; these are no hastily levied troops, but a veteran and seasoned army. The Germans, on whom we place our hopes, are

qui ab ipsis sperentur, non iuberi, non regi, sed
cuncta ex libidine agere; pecuniamque ac dona,
quis solis corrumpantur, maiora apud Romanos, et
neminem adeo in arma pronum ut non idem pretium
quietis quam periculi malit. Quod si statim congre-
diantur, nullas esse Ceriali nisi e reliquiis Germanici[1]
exercitus legiones, foederibus Galliarum obstrictas.
Idque ipsum quod inconditam nuper Valentini
manum contra spem suam fuderint, alimentum illis
ducique temeritatis: ausuros rursus venturosque in
manus non imperiti adulescentuli,[2] verba et contiones
quam ferrum et arma meditantis, sed Civilis et
Classici; quos ubi aspexerint, reditura in animos
formidinem, fugam famemque ac totiens captis precariam vitam. Neque Treviros aut Lingonas benevo-
lentia contineri: resumpturos arma, ubi metus
abscesserit. Diremit consiliorum diversitatem adprobata Tutoris sententia Classicus, statimque exequuntur.

LXXVII. Media acies Ubiis Lingonibusque data;
dextro cornu cohortes Batavorum, sinistro Bructeri
Tencterique. Pars montibus, alii viam inter Mosel-
lamque flumen tam improvisi[3] adsiluere ut in cubiculo ac lectulo Cerialis (neque enim noctem in castris
egerat) pugnari simul vincique suos audierit, incre-

---

[1] reliquis germanicis *M.*
[2] inperitia d . . . . adulescentuli *M.*
[3] inprovisi *Agricola*: inprovisa *M.*

never obedient to orders and directions, but always act according to their own caprice; as for money and gifts, the only things by which they can be won, the Romans have more than we, and no man is so bent on war as not to prefer quiet to danger, if he get the same reward. Whereas if we engage at once, Cerialis has no legions except those made up of the remnants of the army in Germany, and these have been bound by treaties to the Gallic states. As for the mere fact that, contrary to their own expectations, they lately routed the undisciplined force of Valentinus, that only feeds the rash spirit of troops and general alike : they will dare a second time and will fall into the hands not of an inexperienced youth, more concerned with words and speeches than with steel and arms, but into the power of a Civilis and a Classicus. When our enemies see these leaders, their souls will be once more possessed with terror and with the memories of their flight, hunger, and the many times that they have been captured when their lives were at our mercy. Nor are the Treviri or Lingones restrained by any affection : they will resume their arms as soon as their fright has left them." Classicus ended these differences of opinion by approving Tutor's views, on which they at once acted.

LXXVII. The centre of their line was assigned to the Ubii and Lingones; on the right wing were the Batavian cohorts, on the left the Bructeri and the Tencteri. These rushed forward, some by the hills, others between the road and the Moselle, so rapidly that Cerialis was in his chamber and bed— for he had not passed the night in camp—when at the same moment he received the report that his

pans pavorem nuntiantium, donec universa clades
in oculis fuit: perrupta legionum castra, fusi equites,
medius Mosellae pons, qui ulteriora coloniae adnectit,
ab hostibus insessus. Cerialis turbidis rebus intre-
pidus et fugientis manu retrahens, intecto corpore
promptus inter tela, felici temeritate et fortissimi
cuiusque adcursu reciperatum pontem electa manu
firmavit. Mox in castra reversus palantis captarum
apud Novaesium Bonnamque legionum manipulos
et rarum apud signa militem ac prope circumventas
aquilas videt. Incensus ira "non Flaccum" inquit,
"non Voculam deseritis: nulla hic proditio; neque
aliud excusandum habeo quam quod vos Gallici
foederis oblitos redisse in[1] memoriam Romani sacramenti temere credidi. Adnumerabor Numisiis et
Herenniis, ut omnes legati vestri aut militum manibus aut hostium ceciderint. Ite, nuntiate Vespasiano
vel, quod propius est, Civili et Classico, relictum a
vobis in acie ducem: venient legiones quae neque
me inultum neque vos impunitos patiantur."

LXXVIII. Vera erant, et a tribunis praefectisque
eadem ingerebantur. Consistunt per cohortis et

---

[1] redisse in *Lipsius*: praedixerim *M*.

troops were engaged and were being beaten. He kept on abusing the messengers for their alarm until the whole disaster was before his eyes: the enemy had broken into the legions' camp, had routed the cavalry, and had occupied the middle of the bridge over the Moselle, which connects the remoter quarters with the colony. Undismayed in this crisis, Cerialis stopped the fugitives with his own hand, and, although quite unprotected, exposed himself to the enemy's fire; then by his good fortune and rash courage, aided by the bravest of his troops who rushed to his assistance, he recovered the bridge and held it with a picked force. Afterwards he returned to the camp, where he saw the companies of those legions that had been captured at Novaesium and Bonn wandering aimlessly about, with few soldiers supporting the standards, and the eagles almost surrounded by the enemy. Flaming with indignation he cried: "It is not Flaccus or Vocula that you are now deserting: there is no treachery here; nor have I need for excuse save that I rashly believed that, forgetting your pledge to the Gauls, you had remembered your oath of allegiance to Rome. I shall be numbered with the Numisii and Herennii, so that all your commanders may have perished by the hands of their soldiers or of the enemy. Go, report to Vespasian or, since they are nearer, to Civilis and Classicus that you have abandoned your general on the field of battle: yet there will come legions that will not suffer me to be unavenged or you unpunished."

LXXVIII. All this was true, and the same reproofs were heaped on them by the tribunes and the prefects. The troops drew up in cohorts

manipulos; neque enim poterat patescere acies effuso hoste et impedientibus tentoriis sarcinisque, cum intra vallum pugnaretur. Tutor et Classicus et Civilis suis quisque locis pugnam ciebant, Gallos pro libertate, Batavos pro gloria, Germanos ad praedam instigantes. Et cuncta pro hostibus erant, donec legio unaetvicensima patentiore quam ceterae spatio conglobata sustinuit ruentis, mox impulit. Nec sine ope divina mutatis repente animis terga victores vertere. Ipsi territos se cohortium aspectu ferebant, quae primo impetu disiectae summis rursus iugis congregabantur ac speciem novi auxilii fecerant. Sed obstitit vincentibus pravum inter ipsos certamen omisso hoste spolia consectandi. Cerialis ut incuria prope rem adflixit, ita constantia restituit; secutusque fortunam castra hostium eodem die capit excinditque.

LXXIX. Nec in longum quies militi data. Orabant auxilium Agrippinenses offerebantque uxorem ac sororem Civilis et filiam Classici, relicta sibi pignora societatis. Atque interim dispersos in domibus Germanos trucidaverant; unde metus et iustae preces invocantium, antequam hostes reparatis viri-

and maniples, for indeed they could not form an extended line since their foes were everywhere, and as the battle was being fought within their ramparts they were also hindered by their tents and baggage. Tutor and Classicus and Civilis, each at his post, spurred on their followers to battle, urging the Gauls to fight for liberty, the Batavians for glory, and the Germans for booty. Everything favoured the enemy until the Twenty-first legion, having more room than the rest, concentrated its entire strength and so resisted the enemy's attack and presently drove him back. Yet it was not without divine aid that with a sudden change of spirit the victorious enemy took to flight. They said themselves that they were smitten with terror by the sight of those cohorts which, though dislodged by their first assault, formed again on the ridges and seemed to them to be fresh reinforcements. But the fact is that the victorious barbarians were checked by a disgraceful struggle to secure booty which began among them so that they forgot their foes. Thus Cerialis, having almost ruined the situation by his carelessness, restored it by his resolution; and, following up his success, he captured and destroyed the enemy's camp on that same day.

LXXIX. The troops, however, were not allowed long repose. The people of Cologne begged for aid and offered to give up the wife and sister of Civilis and the daughter of Classicus, who had been left as pledges of fidelity to the alliance. In the meantime they had killed the Germans who were scattered among their homes. This gave them cause to fear and made reasonable their appeals for help before the enemy recovered his strength and

155

bus ad spem vel ad ultionem accingerentur. Namque et Civilis illuc intenderat, non invalidus, flagrantissima cohortium suarum integra, quae e Chaucis[1] Frisiisque composita Tolbiaci in finibus Agrippinensium agebat: sed tristis nuntius avertit, deletam cohortem dolo Agrippinensium, qui largis epulis vinoque sopitos Germanos, clausis foribus, igne iniecto cremavere; simul Cerialis propero agmine subvenit. Circumsteterat Civilem et alius metus, ne quarta decima legio adiuncta Britannica classe adflictaret Batavos, qua Oceano ambiuntur. Sed legionem terrestri itinere Fabius Priscus legatus in Nervios Tungrosque duxit, eaeque civitates in deditionem acceptae: classem ultro Canninefates adgressi sunt maiorque pars navium depressa aut capta. Et Nerviorum multitudinem, sponte commotam ut pro Romanis bellum capesseret, idem Canninefates fudere. Classicus quoque adversus equites Novaesium a Ceriale praemissos secundum proelium fecit: quae modica sed crebra damna famam victoriae nuper partae lacerabant.

LXXX. Isdem diebus Mucianus Vitellii filium interfici iubet, mansuram discordiam obtendens, ni[2] semina belli restinxisset. Neque Antonium Primum adsciri inter comites a[3] Domitiano passus est, favore

---

[1] integra quae e Chaucis *Pichena*: integraque et e cauchis *M*.
[2] ne *M*.   [3] ad *M*.

---

[1] Zülpich.
[2] The account of this revolt is resumed at v. 14.
[3] Cf. ii. 59.

armed for some new venture or for revenge. For in fact Civilis had marched in the direction of Cologne; he was yet formidable since the most warlike of his cohorts was still unharmed, which, made up of Chauci and Frisii, was stationed at Tolbiacum [1] on the borders of the territory of the people of Cologne: he was, however, turned aside by the depressing news that this cohort had been destroyed by a stratagem of the inhabitants of Cologne, who, after stupefying the Germans with an elaborate dinner and abundant wine, had closed the doors, set fire to the building, and burned them all; at the same moment Cerialis hurried up by forced marches. Civilis had been beset also by another fear: he was anxious lest the Fourteenth legion, supported by the fleet from Britain, might injure the Batavians along their coast. But Fabius Priscus, leading his legion inland, directed it against the Nervii and Tungri, and accepted the surrender of these two states: as for the fleet, it was actually attacked by the Canninefates and most of the ships were sunk or captured. The same Canninefates routed a great force of the Nervii who had voluntarily risen to fight for the Romans. Classicus also engaged successfully with some cavalry which Cerialis had despatched to Novaesium: and these reverses, though small, were frequent enough to injure the prestige of the Romans' recent victory.[2]

LXXX. During these same days Mucianus had Vitellius's son put to death,[3] for he maintained that discord would continue if he did not destroy the seeds of war. Nor did he allow Domitian to invite Antonius Primus to become a member of his suite since he was disturbed by his popularity with the

militum anxius et superbia viri aequalium quoque, adeo superiorum intolerantis. Profectus ad[1] Vespasianum Antonius ut non pro spe sua excipitur, ita neque averso[2] imperatoris animo. Trahebatur in diversa, hinc meritis Antonii, cuius ductu confectum haud dubie bellum erat, inde Muciani epistulis: simul ceteri ut infestum tumidumque insectabantur, adiunctis prioris vitae criminibus. Neque ipse deerat adrogantia vocare offensas, nimius commemorandis quae meruisset: alios ut imbellis, Caecinam ut captivum ac dediticium increpat. Unde paulatim levior viliorque haberi, manente tamen in speciem amicitia.

LXXXI. Per eos mensis quibus Vespasianus Alexandriae statos aestivis flatibus dies et certa maris opperiebatur, multa miracula evenere, quis caelestis[3] favor et quaedam in Vespasianum inclinatio numinum ostenderetur. E plebe Alexandrina quidam oculorum tabe notus genua eius advolvitur, remedium caecitatis exposcens gemitu, monitu Serapidis dei, quem dedita superstitionibus gens ante alios colit; precabaturque principem ut genas et oculorum orbis dignaretur respergere oris excremento. Alius manum aeger eodem deo auctore ut pede ac vestigio Caesaris calcaretur orabat. Vespasianus primo inridere, aspernari; atque illis

---

[1] a _M._   [2] adverso _M._
[3] caelestis _Rhenanus_: celis ē _M._

---

[1] Cf. ii. 86.   [2] _Vid._ III, 13 f.
[3] Such as he would have in June and July.

soldiers as well as by the haughty temper of a man who could not endure even his equals, to say nothing of his superiors. Antonius left Rome to join Vespasian, who received him, not as he had hoped, but yet with no unfriendly feelings. Vespasian was drawn in two directions: in one by the services of Antonius, under whose leadership the war had unquestionably been finished,[1] in the other by letters of Mucianus; while at the same time everyone else attacked Antonius, as hostile and swollen with conceit, and brought charges against his former life. And Antonius himself did not fail to arouse hostility by his arrogance and by dwelling too constantly on his own achievements: he charged some with cowardice and taunted Caecina with having been a captive and a voluntary prisoner.[2] The result was that he was gradually regarded as of less weight and importance, although his friendship with Vespasian apparently remained the same.

LXXXI. During the months while Vespasian was waiting at Alexandria for the regular season of the summer winds and a settled sea,[3] many marvels occurred to mark the favour of heaven and a certain partiality of the gods toward him. One of the common people of Alexandria, well known for his loss of sight, threw himself before Vespasian's knees, praying him with groans to cure his blindness, being so directed by the god Serapis, whom this most superstitious of nations worships before all others; and he besought the emperor to deign to moisten his cheeks and eyes with his spittle. Another, whose hand was useless, prompted by the same god, begged Caesar to step and trample on it. Vespasian at first ridiculed these appeals and treated them with

instantibus modo famam vanitatis metuere, modo
obsecratione ipsorum et vocibus adulantium in spem
induci: postremo aestimari a medicis iubet an talis
caecitas ac debilitas ope humana superabiles forent.
Medici varie disserere: huic non exesam vim luminis
et redituram si pellerentur obstantia; illi elapsos
in pravum artus, si salubris vis adhibeatur, posse
integrari. Id fortasse cordi deis et divino ministerio
principem electum; denique patrati remedii gloriam
penes Caesarem, inriti ludibrium penes miseros fore.
Igitur Vespasianus cuncta fortunae suae patere ratus
nec quicquam ultra incredibile, laeto ipse vultu,
erecta quae adstabat multitudine, iussa exequitur.
Statim conversa ad usum manus, ac caeco reluxit
dies. Utrumque qui interfuere nunc quoque memorant, postquam nullum mendacio pretium.

LXXXII. Altior inde Vespasiano cupido adeundi
sacram sedem ut super rebus imperii consuleret:
arceri templo cunctos iubet. Atque ingressus in-
tentusque numini respexit pone tergum e primoribus
Aegyptiorum nomine Basiliden, quem procul Alexandria plurium dierum itinere et aegro corpore

---

[1] That is, " King's son."

scorn; then, when the men persisted, he began at one moment to fear the discredit of failure, at another to be inspired with hopes of success by the appeals of the suppliants and the flattery of his courtiers: finally, he directed the physicians to give their opinion as to whether such blindness and infirmity could be overcome by human aid. Their reply treated the two cases differently: they said that in the first the power of sight had not been completely eaten away and it would return if the obstacles were removed; in the other, the joints had slipped and become displaced, but they could be restored if a healing pressure were applied to them. Such perhaps was the wish of the gods, and it might be that the emperor had been chosen for this divine service; in any case, if a cure were obtained, the glory would be Caesar's, but in the event of failure, ridicule would fall only on the poor suppliants. So Vespasian, believing that his good fortune was capable of anything and that nothing was any longer incredible, with a smiling countenance, and amid intense excitement on the part of the bystanders, did as he was asked to do. The hand was instantly restored to use, and the day again shone for the blind man. Both facts are told by eye-witnesses even now when falsehood brings no reward.

LXXXII. These events gave Vespasian a deeper desire to visit the sanctuary of the god to consult him with regard to his imperial fortune: he ordered all to be excluded from the temple. Then after he had entered the temple and was absorbed in contemplation of the god, he saw behind him one of the leading men of Egypt, named Basilides,[1] who he knew was detained by sickness in a place many

detineri haud ignorabat. Percontatur sacerdotes num illo die Basilides templum inisset, percontatur obvios num in urbe visus sit; denique missis equitibus explorat illo temporis momento octoginta milibus passuum afuisse: tunc divinam speciem et vim responsi ex nomine Basilidis interpretatus est.

LXXXIII. Origo dei nondum nostris auctoribus celebrata: Aegyptiorum antistites sic memorant, Ptolemaeo regi, qui Macedonum primus Aegypti opes firmavit, cum Alexandriae recens conditae moenia templaque et religiones adderet, oblatum per quietem decore eximio et maiore quam humana specie iuvenem, qui moneret ut fidissimis amicorum in Pontum missis effigiem suam acciret; laetum id regno magnamque et inclutam sedem fore quae excepisset: simul visum eundem iuvenem in caelum igne plurimo attolli. Ptolemaeus omine et miraculo excitus sacerdotibus Aegyptiorum, quibus mos talia intellegere, nocturnos visus aperit. Atque illis Ponti et externorum parum gnaris, Timotheum Atheniensem e gente Eumolpidarum, quem ut antistitem caerimoniarum Eleusine[1] exciverat, quaenam illa superstitio, quod numen, interrogat. Timotheus quaesitis in Pontum meassent, cognoscit urbem illic Sinopen, nec procul templum vetere inter accolas

---

[1] Eleusine *I. F. Gronovius*: eleusim *M*.

---

[1] Ptolemy Soter, 306–283 B.C.
[2] In whose family the more important offices of the mysteries at Eleusis in Attica were hereditary.
[3] Lord of the Lower World. Cf. Clem. Alex. *Protrep.* iv. 48.

days' journey distant from Alexandria. He asked
the priests whether Basilides had entered the temple
on that day; he questioned the passers-by whether
he had been seen in the city; finally, he sent some
cavalry and found that at that moment he had been
eighty miles away: then he concluded that this
was a supernatural vision and drew a prophecy from
the name Basilides.

LXXXIII. The origin of this god has not yet
been generally treated by our authors: the Egyptian
priests tell the following story, that when King
Ptolemy,[1] the first of the Macedonians to put the
power of Egypt on a firm foundation, was giving the
new city of Alexandria walls, temples, and religious
rites, there appeared to him in his sleep a vision of
a young man of extraordinary beauty and of more
than human stature, who warned him to send his
most faithful friends to Pontus and bring his statue
hither; the vision said that this act would be a
happy thing for the kingdom and that the city that
received the god would be great and famous: after
these words the youth seemed to be carried to
heaven in a blaze of fire. Ptolemy, moved by this
miraculous omen, disclosed this nocturnal vision to
the Egyptian priests, whose business it is to interpret
such things. When they proved to know little of
Pontus and foreign countries, he questioned Timotheus, an Athenian of the clan of the Eumolpidae,[2]
whom he had called from Eleusis to preside over the
sacred rites, and asked him what this religion was
and what the divinity meant. Timotheus learned
by questioning men who had travelled to Pontus
that there was a city there called Sinope, and that
not far from it there was a temple of Jupiter Dis,[3]

fama Iovis Ditis: namque et muliebrem effigiem
adsistere quam plerique Proserpinam vocent. Sed
Ptolemaeus, ut sunt ingenia regum, pronus ad formidinem, ubi securitas rediit, voluptatum quam
religionum adpetens neglegere paulatim aliasque ad
curas animum vertere, donec eadem [1] species terri-
bilior iam et instantior exitium ipsi regnoque
denuntiaret ni iussa patrarentur.[2] Tum legatos et
dona Scydrothemidi regi (is tunc Sinopensibus imperitabat) expediri iubet praecipitque[3] navigaturis
ut Pythicum Apollinem adeant. Illis mare secundum, sors oraculi haud ambigua: irent simulacrum-
que patris sui reveherent, sororis relinquerent.

LXXXIV. Ut Sinopen venere, munera preces
mandata regis sui Scydrothemidi adlegant. qui
diversus[4] animi modo numen pavescere, modo minis
adversantis populi terreri; saepe donis promissisque
legatorum flectebatur. Atque interim triennio exacto
Ptolemaeus non studium, non preces omittere:
dignitatem legatorum, numerum navium, auri pondus
augebat. Tum minax facies Scydrothemidi offertur
ne destinata deo ultra moraretur: cunctantem varia
pernicies morbique et manifesta caelestium ira
graviorque in dies fatigabat. Advocata contione

[1] caedem M.   [2] paterentur M.
[3] praecepitque M.
[4] diversus *Puteolanus*: versus M.

---

[1] Jupiter of the Lower World is not here distinguished
from Jupiter of the Heavens, whose son Apollo was. Apollo's
sister then is Proserpina.

long famous among the natives : for there sits beside
the god a female figure which most call Proserpina.
But Ptolemy, although prone to superstitious fears
after the nature of kings, when he once more felt
secure, being more eager for pleasures than religious
rites, began gradually to neglect the matter and to
turn his attention to other things, until the same
vision, now more terrible and insistent, threatened
ruin upon the king himself and his kingdom unless
his orders were carried out. Then Ptolemy directed
that ambassadors and gifts should be despatched to
King Scydrothemis—he ruled over the people of
Sinope at that time—and when the embassy was
about to sail he instructed them to visit Pythian
Apollo. The ambassadors found the sea favourable ; and the answer of the oracle was not uncertain : Apollo bade them go on and bring back the
image of his father, but leave that of his sister.[1]

LXXXIV. When the ambassadors reached Sinope,
they delivered the gifts, requests, and messages of
their king to Scydrothemis. He was all uncertainty,
now fearing the god and again being terrified by
the threats and opposition of his people ; often he
was tempted by the gifts and promises of the ambassadors. In the meantime three years passed during
which Ptolemy did not lessen his zeal or his appeals :
he increased the dignity of his ambassadors, the
number of his ships, and the quantity of gold offered.
Then a terrifying vision appeared to Scydrothemis,
warning him not to hinder longer the purposes of
the god : as he still hesitated, various disasters,
diseases, and the evident anger of the gods, growing
heavier from day to day, beset the king. He called
an assembly of his people and made known to them

iussa numinis, suos Ptolemaeique visus, ingruentia
mala exponit: vulgus aversari[1] regem, invidere
Aegypto, sibi metuere templumque circumsedere.
Maior hinc fama tradidit deum ipsum adpulsas litori
navis sponte conscendisse: mirum inde dictu, tertio
die tantum maris emensi Alexandriam adpelluntur.
Templum pro magnitudine urbis extructum loco cui
nomen Rhacotis; fuerat illic sacellum Serapidi atque
Isidi antiquitus sacratum. Haec de origine et ad-
vectu dei celeberrima. Nec sum ignarus esse quosdam qui Seleucia urbe Syriae accitum regnante
Ptolemaeo, quem tertia aetas tulit; alii auctorem
eundem Ptolemaeum, sedem, ex qua transierit,
Memphim perhibent, inclutam olim et veteris
Aegypti columen. Deum ipsum multi Aesculapium,
quod medeatur aegris corporibus, quidam Osirin,
antiquissimum illis gentibus numen, plerique Iovem
ut rerum omnium potentem, plurimi Ditem patrem
insignibus, quae[2] in ipso manifesta, aut per ambages
coniectant.

LXXXV. At Domitianus Mucianusque antequam
Alpibus propinquarent, prosperos rerum in Treviris
gestarum nuntios accepere. Praecipua victoriae fides
dux hostium Valentinus nequaquam abiecto animo,

---

[1] aversari *Muretus*: adversari *M*.
[2] quae *Puteolanus*: queque *M*.

---

[1] Ptolemy Euergetes, 247–222 B.C.
[2] Tacitus seems to have drawn his account from Manetho,
who apparently played an important part in the reorganiza-
tion of the cult of Serapis-Osiris. Cf. Plutarch, *De Iside* 28.

the god's orders, the visions that had appeared to
him and to Ptolemy, and the misfortunes that were
multiplying upon them: the people opposed their
king; they were jealous of Egypt, afraid for themselves, and so gathered about the temple of the god.
At this point the tale becomes stranger, for tradition says that the god himself, voluntarily embark-
ing on the fleet that was lying on the shore, miracu-
ously crossed the wide stretch of sea and reached
Alexandria in two days. A temple, befitting the
size of the city, was erected in the quarter called
Rhacotis; there had previously been on that spot
an ancient shrine dedicated to Serapis and Isis.
Such is the most popular account of the origin and
arrival of the god. Yet I am not unaware that
there are some who maintain that the god was
brought from Seleucia in Syria in the reign of
Ptolemy III[1]; still others claim that the same
Ptolemy introduced the god, but that the place
from which he came was Memphis, once a famous
city and the bulwark of ancient Egypt. Many
regard the god himself as identical with Aesculapius,
because he cures the sick; some as Osiris, the oldest
god among these peoples; still more identify him
with Jupiter as the supreme lord of all things; the
majority, however, arguing from the attributes of
the god that are seen on his statue or from their
own conjectures, hold him to be Father Dis.[2]

LXXXV. But before Domitian and Mucianus
reached the Alps, they received news of the success
among the Treviri. The chief proof of their victory
was given by the presence of the enemy's leader,
Valentinus, who, never losing courage, continued
to show by his looks the same spirit that he had

quos spiritus gessisset, vultu ferebat. Auditus ideo
antum ut nosceretur ingenium eius, damnatusque
nter ipsum supplicium exprobranti cuidam patriam
us captam accipere se solacium mortis respondit. Sed
ucianus quod diu occultaverat, ut recens expromp-
: quoniam benignitate deum fractae hostium vires
forent, parum decore Domitianum confecto prope
bello alienae gloriae interventurum. Si status imperii
aut salus Galliarum in discrimine verteretur, debuisse
Caesarem in acie stare, Canninefatis Batavosque
minoribus ducibus delegandos: ipse Luguduni vim
fortunamque principatus e proximo ostentaret,[1] nec
parvis periculis immixtus et maioribus non defuturus.

LXXXVI. Intellegebantur artes, sed pars obsequii
in eo ne deprehenderentur: ita Lugudunum ventum.
Unde creditur Domitianus occultis ad Cerialem
nuntiis fidem eius temptavisse an praesenti sibi
exercitum imperiumque traditurus foret. Qua cogi-
tatione bellum adversus patrem agitaverit an opes
virisque adversus fratrem, in incerto fuit: nam
Cerialis salubri temperamento elusit ut vana pueriliter
cupientem. Domitianus sperni a senioribus iuventam

---

[1] ostentaret *Rhenanus*: ostentare *M*.

---

[1] Domitian was now playing the part of a very modest
"obsequious" youth.

always maintained. He was given an opportunity to speak, but solely that his questioners might judge of his nature; and he was condemned. While being executed, someone taunted him with the fact that his native country had been subdued, to which he replied that he found therein consolation for his own death. Mucianus now brought forward a proposal, as if he had just thought of it, but which in reality he had long concealed. He urged that since, thanks to the gods' kindness, the enemy's strength has been broken, it would little become Domitian, now that the war is almost over, to interfere in the glory of others. If the stability of the empire or the safety of Gaul were imperilled, then Caesar ought to take his place in the battle-line; but the Canninefates and the Batavi he should assign to inferior commanders. "You should," he added, "personally display the power and majesty of the imperial throne from close quarters at Lyons, not mixing yourself up with trifling risks, but ready to deal with graver ones."

LXXXVI. His artifice was understood, but Domitian's obsequious rôle required that he should let it pass unnoticed: thus they came to Lyons. Men believe that from this city Domitian sent secret messages to Cerialis and tempted his loyalty by asking whether, if he came in person, Cerialis would turn over the command of his army to him. Whether in this plan Domitian was thinking of war against his father or whether he wished to get control of resources and troops in order to oppose his brother was uncertain; for Cerialis wisely temporized and avoided the request, treating it as a boy's foolish wish. When Domitian realized that

suam cernens modica quoque et usurpata antea munia imperii omittebat, simplicitatis ac modestiae imagine in altitudinem conditus studiumque litterarum et amorem carminum simulans, quo velaret animum et fratris *se*[1] aemulationi subduceret, cuius disparem mitioremque naturam contra interpretabatur.[2]

[1] se *add. Halm.*
[2] *post* interpretabatur *add. in M* neque vos inpunitos patiantur. *quae falso ex c.* LXXVII *ex. repetita sunt.*

his youth was treated contemptuously by his elders, he abandoned the exercise of all imperial duties, even those of a trifling character and duties which he had exercised before; then, under the cloak of simplicity and moderation, he gave himself up to profound dissimulation, pretending a devotion to literature and a love of poetry to conceal his real character and to withdraw before the rivalry of his brother, on whose milder nature, wholly unlike his own, he put a bad construction.

BOOK V

LIBER V

I. Eiusdem anni principio Caesar Titus, perdomandae Iudaeae delectus a patre et privatis[1] utriusque rebus militia clarus, maiore tum vi famaque agebat, certantibus provinciarum et exercituum studiis. Atque ipse, ut super fortunam[2] crederetur, decorum se promptumque in armis ostendebat, comitate et adloquiis officia provocans ac plerumque in opere, in agmine gregario militi mixtus, incorrupto ducis honore. Tres eum in Iudaea legiones, quinta et decima et quinta decima, vetus Vespasiani miles, excepere. Addidit e Syria duodecimam et adductos Alexandria duoetvicensimanos tertianosque; comitabantur viginti sociae cohortes, octo equitum alae, simul Agrippa Sohaemusque reges et auxilia regis Antiochi validaque et solito inter accolas odio infensa Iudaeis Arabum manus, multi quos urbe atque Italia sua quemque spes acciverat occupandi principem adhuc vacuum. His cum copiis finis hostium

---

[1] privatis *Rhenanus*: platis *M.*
[2] super fortunam *Lipsius*: superiori unam *M.*

---

[1] 70 A.D.
[2] Cf. ii. 4; iv. 51.
[3] Agrippa was prince of Trachonitis and Galilee; Sohaemus, king of Sophene and prince of Emesa in Syria; while Antiochus was king of Commagene and of a part of Cilicia. Cf. ii. 81.

BOOK V

I. At the beginning of this same year[1] Titus
Caesar, who had been selected by his father to complete the subjugation of Judea,[2] and who had already
won distinction as a soldier while both were still
private citizens, began to enjoy greater power and
reputation, for provinces and armies now vied with
one another in enthusiasm for him. Moreover, in
his own conduct, wishing to be thought greater than
his fortune, he always showed himself dignified and
energetic in the field; by his affable address he called
forth devotion, and he often mingled with the common
soldiers both at work or on the march without im-
pairing his position as general. He found awaiting
him in Judea three legions, Vespasian's old troops,
the Fifth, the Tenth, and the Fifteenth. He reinforced these with the Twelfth from Syria and with
some soldiers from the Twenty-second and the Third
which he brought from Alexandria; these troops
were accompanied by twenty cohorts of allied
infantry, eight squadrons of cavalry, as well as by the
princes Agrippa and Sohaemus, the auxiliaries sent
by King Antiochus,[3] and by a strong contingent of
Arabs, who hated the Jews with all that hatred that
is common among neighbours; there were besides
many Romans who had been prompted to leave the
capital and Italy by the hope that each entertained
of securing the prince's favour while he was yet free
from engagements. With these forces Titus entered

ingressus composito agmine, cuncta explorans paratusque decernere, haud procul Hierosolymis castra facit.

II. Sed quoniam famosae urbis supremum diem tradituri sumus, congruens videtur primordia eius aperire.

Iudaeos Creta insula profugos novissima Libyae insedisse memorant, qua tempestate Saturnus vi Iovis pulsus cesserit regnis. Argumentum e nomine petitur: inclutum in Creta Idam montem, accolas Idaeos[1] aucto in barbarum cognomento Iudaeos vocitari. Quidam regnante Iside exundantem per Aegyptum multitudinem ducibus Hierosolymo ac Iuda proximas in terras exoneratam; plerique Aethiopum prolem, quos rege Cepheo metus atque odium mutare sedis perpulerit. Sunt qui tradant Assyrios convenas, indigum agrorum populum, parte Aegypti potitos, mox proprias urbis Hebraeasque terras et propiora Syriae coluisse. Clara alii Iudaeorum initia, Solymos, carminibus Homeri celebratam gentem, conditae urbi Hierosolyma nomen e suo fecisse.

III. Plurimi auctores consentiunt orta per Aegyptum tabe quae corpora foedaret, regem Bocchorim adito Hammonis oraculo remedium petentem pur-

[1] Indeos *M.*

---

[1] Tacitus in this brief and somewhat confused account of the Jews apparently followed the Alexandrian historians, Chaeremon and Lysimachus.

[2] *Il.* vi. 184; *Od.* v. 282.

[3] King Bocchoris reigned in the eighth century B.C., whereas the exodus seems to have taken place about five centuries earlier. But the account of the exodus as given in the Old Testament requires much revision in the light of modern historical scholarship. *Vid. Cambridge Ancient History*, II, 352 ff.

the enemy's land: his troops advanced in strict order, he reconnoitred at every step and was always ready for battle; not far from Jerusalem he pitched camp.

II. However, as I am about to describe the last days of a famous city, it seems proper for me to give some account of its origin.[1]

It is said that the Jews were originally exiles from the island of Crete who settled in the farthest parts of Libya at the time when Saturn had been deposed and expelled by Jove. An argument in favour of this is derived from the name: there is a famous mountain in Crete called Ida, and hence the inhabitants were called the Idaei, which was later lengthened into the barbarous form Iudaei. Some hold that in the reign of Isis the superfluous population of Egypt, under the leadership of Hierosolymus and Iuda, discharged itself on the neighbouring lands; many others think that they were an Egyptian stock, which in the reign of Cepheus was forced to migrate by fear and hatred. Still others report that they were Assyrian refugees, a landless people, who first got control of a part of Egypt, then later they had their own cities and lived in the Hebrew territory and the nearer parts of Syria. Still others say that the Jews are of illustrious origin, being the Solymi, a people celebrated in Homer's poems,[2] who founded a city and gave it the name Hierosolyma, formed from their own.

III. Most authors agree that once during a plague in Egypt which caused bodily disfigurement, King Bocchoris[3] approached the oracle of Ammon[4] and

[4] The famous Egyptian oracle in the oasis Siwah, in the Libyan desert.

gare regnum et id genus hominum ut invisum deis
alias in terras avehere iussum. Sic conquisitum
collectumque vulgus, postquam vastis locis relictum
sit, ceteris per lacrimas torpentibus, Moysen unum
exulum monuisse ne quam deorum hominumve opem
expectarent utrisque deserti, sed[1] sibimet duce
caelesti crederent, primo cuius auxilio praesentis[2]
miserias pepulissent. Adsensere atque omnium
ignari fortuitum iter incipiunt. Sed nihil aeque
quam inopia aquae fatigabat, iamque haud procul
exitio totis campis procubuerant, cum grex asinorum
agrestium e pastu in rupem nemore opacam concessit.
Secutus Moyses coniectura herbidi soli largas aquarum
venas aperit. Id levamen; et continuum sex dierum
iter emensi septimo pulsis cultoribus obtinuere terras,
in quis urbs et templum dicata.

IV. Moyses quo sibi in posterum gentem firmaret,
novos ritus contrariosque ceteris mortalibus indidit.
Profana illic omnia quae apud nos sacra, rursum
concessa apud illos quae nobis incesta. Effigiem
animalis, quo monstrante errorem sitimque depul-
erant, penetrali sacravere, caeso ariete velut in
contumeliam Hammonis; bos quoque immolatur,
quoniam[3] Aegyptii Apin colunt. Sue abstinent

---

[1] sed *dett.*, *Orosius*: et *M.*
[2] praesentes *Orosius*: credentes p̄sentes *M.*
[3] quoniam *Orellius*: q̄ *M.*

---

[1] Cf. the story in *Genesis* with this fantastic account, which
Tacitus took chiefly from Lysimachus.
[2] That is, an ass. The same charge of worshipping an ass
was frequently made against the Christians later.
[3] The Egyptian god was represented in art with a ram's
horns.

asked for a remedy, whereupon he was told to purge his kingdom and to transport this race into other lands, since it was hateful to the gods. So the Hebrews were searched out and gathered together; then, being abandoned in the desert, while all others lay idle and weeping, one only of the exiles, Moses by name, warned them not to hope for help from gods or men, for they were deserted by both, but to trust to themselves, regarding as a guide sent from heaven the one whose assistance should first give them escape from their present distress. They agreed, and then set out on their journey in utter ignorance, but trusting to chance. Nothing caused them so much distress as scarcity of water, and in fact they had already fallen exhausted over the plain nigh unto death, when a herd of wild asses moved from their pasturage to a rock that was shaded by a grove of trees. Moses followed them, and, conjecturing the truth from the grassy ground, discovered abundant streams of water. This relieved them, and they then marched six days continuously, and on the seventh seized a country, expelling the former inhabitants; there they founded a city and dedicated a temple.[1]

IV. To establish his influence over this people for all time, Moses introduced new religious practices, quite opposed to those of all other religions. The Jews regard as profane all that we hold sacred; on the other hand, they permit all that we abhor. They dedicated, in a shrine, a statue of that creature whose guidance enabled them to put an end to their wandering and thirst,[2] sacrificing a ram, apparently in derision of Ammon.[3] They likewise offer the ox, because the Egyptians worship Apis. They abstain

179

memoria cladis, quod ipsos scabies quondam turpaverat, cui id animal obnoxium. Longam olim famem crebris adhuc ieiuniis fatentur, et raptarum frugum argumentum panis Iudaicus nullo fermento detinetur. Septimo die otium placuisse ferunt, quia is finem laborum tulerit; dein blandiente inertia septimum quoque annum ignaviae datum. Alii honorem eum Saturno haberi, seu principia religionis tradentibus Idaeis,[1] quos cum Saturno pulsos et conditores gentis accepimus, seu quod de septem sideribus, quis mortales reguntur, altissimo orbe et praecipua potentia stella Saturni feratur, ac pleraque caelestium viam[2] suam et cursus septenos[3] per numeros commeent.[4]

V. Hi[5] ritus quoquo modo inducti antiquitate defenduntur: cetera instituta, sinistra foeda, pravitate valuere. Nam pessimus quisque spretis religionibus patriis tributa et stipes illuc congerebant,[6] unde auctae Iudaeorum res, et quia apud ipsos fides obstinata, misericordia in promptu, sed adversus

---

[1] Idaeis *Lipsius*: iudaeis *M*.
[2] viam *Bezzenberger*: vim *M*.
[3] septenos *Halm*: septimos *M*.
[4] commeent *Wölfflin*: commearent *M*.
[5] hi *ed. Spirensis*: is *M*.
[6] congerebant *Puteolanus*: gerebant *M*.

---

[1] Cf. *Exod.* xii. 15–20, 34–39.
[2] Cf. *Deut.* v. 15; *Levit.* xxv. 4.
[3] The seventh day being Saturn's day.
[4] Cf. Dio Cass. xxxvii. 18 f.

from pork, in recollection of a plague, for the scab
to which this animal is subject once afflicted them.
By frequent fasts even now they bear witness to
the long hunger with which they were once distressed, and the unleavened Jewish bread is still
employed in memory of the haste with which they
seized the grain.[1] They say that they first chose
to rest on the seventh day because that day ended
their toils; but after a time they were led by
the charms of indolence to give over the seventh
year as well to inactivity.[2] Others say that this
is done in honour of Saturn,[3] whether it be that
the primitive elements of their religion were given
by the Idaeans, who, according to tradition, were
expelled with Saturn and became the founders of
the Jewish race, or is due to the fact that, of the
seven planets that rule the fortunes of mankind,
Saturn moves in the highest orbit and has the
greatest potency; and that many of the heavenly
bodies traverse their paths and courses in multiples
of seven.[4]

V. Whatever their origin, these rites are maintained by their antiquity: the other customs of the
Jews are base and abominable, and owe their per-
sistence to their depravity. For the worst rascals
among other peoples,[5] renouncing their ancestral
religions, always kept sending tribute and contributions to Jerusalem, thereby increasing the wealth
of the Jews; again, the Jews are extremely loyal
toward one another, and always ready to show
compassion, but toward every other people they

[5] The proselytes, whose contributions were important.
The tribute amounted to two drachmae a head each year,
according to Josephus, *Bell. Iud.* vii. 218 (Niese).

omnis alios hostile odium. Separati epulis, discreti
cubilibus, proiectissima ad libidinem gens, alienarum
concubitu abstinent; inter se nihil inlicitum. Cir-
cumcidere genitalia instituerunt ut diversitate nos-
cantur. Transgressi in morem eorum idem usurpant,
nec quicquam prius imbuuntur quam contemnere
deos, exuere patriam, parentes liberos fratres vilia
habere. Augendae tamen multitudini consulitur;
nam et necare quemquam ex agnatis nefas, animosque
proelio aut suppliciis peremptorum aeternos putant:
hinc generandi amor et moriendi contemptus.
Corpora condere quam cremare e more Aegyptio,
eademque cura et de infernis persuasio, caelestium
contra. Aegyptii pleraque animalia effigiesque com-
positas venerantur, Iudaei mente sola unumque
numen intellegunt: profanos qui deum imagines
mortalibus materiis in species hominum effingant;
summum illud et aeternum neque imitabile neque
interiturum. Igitur nulla simulacra urbibus suis,
nedum templis sistunt[1]; non regibus haec adulatio,
non Caesaribus honor. Sed quia sacerdotes eorum
tibia tympanisque concinebant, hedera vinciebantur
vitisque aurea in templo[2] reperta, Liberum patrem

[1] sistunt *Döderlein*: sunt *M*.
[2] in templo *Ritter*: templo *M*.

---

[1] The word here used, "agnatus," means a child born after
the father had made his will, or one that was not desired.
Cf. *Germ.* 19.

feel only hate and enmity. They sit apart at meals, and they sleep apart, and although as a race, they are prone to lust, they abstain from intercourse with foreign women; yet among themselves nothing is unlawful. They adopted circumcision to distinguish themselves from other peoples by this difference. Those who are converted to their ways follow the same practice, and the earliest lesson they receive is to despise the gods, to disown their country, and to regard their parents, children, and brothers as of little account. However, they take thought to increase their numbers; for they regard it as a crime to kill any late-born child,[1] and they believe that the souls of those who are killed in battle or by the executioner are immortal: hence comes their passion for begetting children, and their scorn of death. They bury the body rather than burn it, thus following the Egyptians' custom; they likewise bestow the same care on the dead, and hold the same belief about the world below; but their ideas of heavenly things are quite the opposite. The Egyptians worship many animals and monstrous images; the Jews conceive of one god only, and that with the mind alone: they regard as impious those who make from perishable materials representations of gods in man's image; that supreme and eternal being is to them incapable of representation and without end. Therefore they set up no statues in their cities, still less in their temples; this flattery is not paid their kings, nor this honour given to the Caesars. But since their priests used to chant to the accompaniment of pipes and cymbals and to wear garlands of ivy, and because a golden vine was found in their temple, some have thought that they were devotees

THE HISTORIES OF TACITUS

coli, domitorem Orientis, quidam arbitrati sunt, nequaquam congruentibus institutis. Quippe Liber festos laetosque ritus posuit, Iudaeorum mos absurdus sordidusque.

VI. Terra finesque qua ad Orientem vergunt Arabia terminantur, a meridie Aegyptus obiacet, ab occasu Phoenices et mare, septentrionem e latere Syriae longe prospectant. Corpora hominum salubria et ferentia laborum. Rari imbres, uber solum : [exuberant]¹ fruges nostrum ad morem praeterque eas balsamum et palmae. Palmetis proceritas et decor, balsamum modica arbor : ut quisque ramus intumuit, si vim ferri adhibeas, pavent venae ; fragmine lapidis aut testa aperiuntur ; umor in usu medentium est. Praecipuum montium Libanum erigit, mirum dictu, tantos inter ardores opacum fidumque nivibus ; idem amnem Iordanen alit funditque. Nec Iordanes pelago accipitur, sed unum atque alterum lacum integer perfluit, tertio retinetur. Lacus immenso ambitu, specie maris, sapore corruptior, gravitate odoris accolis pestifer, neque vento impellitur neque piscis aut suetas aquis volucris patitur. Inertes undae superiacta ut solido ferunt ; periti imperitique nandi perinde attolluntur. Certo anni bitumen egerit, cuius legendi usum, ut ceteras artis, experientia docuit.

---

¹ exuberant *secl. Lipsius.*

---

¹ Looking from Lebanon, over Coele-Syria.
² Famed for its medicinal qualities and fragrance. Strabo xvi. 763 ; Pliny xii. 111.
³ The source of the Jordan is on Mt. Hermon, which Tacitus apparently identifies with Lebanon.

of Father Liber, the conqueror of the East, in spite of the incongruity of their customs. For Liber established festive rites of a joyous nature, while the ways of the Jews are preposterous and mean.

VI. Their land is bounded by Arabia on the east, Egypt lies on the south, on the west are Phoenicia and the sea, and toward the north the people enjoy a wide prospect over Syria.[1] The inhabitants are healthy and hardy. Rains are rare; the soil is fertile: its products are like ours, save that the balsam and the palm also grow there. The palm is a tall and handsome tree; the balsam [2] a mere shrub: if a branch, when swollen with sap, is pierced with steel, the veins shrivel up; so a piece of stone or a potsherd is used to open them; the juice is employed by physicians. Of the mountains, Lebanon rises to the greatest height, and is in fact a marvel, for in the midst of the excessive heat its summit is shaded by trees and covered with snow; it likewise is the source and supply of the river Jordan.[3] This river does not empty into the sea, but after flowing with volume undiminished through two lakes is lost in the third.[4] The last is a lake of great size: it is like the sea, but its water has a nauseous taste, and its offensive odour is injurious to those who live near it. Its waters are not moved by the wind, and neither fish nor water-fowl can live there. Its lifeless waves bear up whatever is thrown upon them as on a solid surface; all swimmers, whether skilled or not, are buoyed up by them. At a certain season of the year the sea throws up bitumen, and experience has taught the natives how to collect this, as she teaches

[4] The marshy Lake Merom, then Gennesareth, and finally the Dead Sea.

Ater suapte natura liquor et sparso aceto concretus innatat; hunc manu captum, quibus ea cura, in summa navis trahunt: inde nullo iuvante influit oneratque, donec abscindas. Nec abscindere aere ferrove possis: fugit cruorem vestemque infectam sanguine, quo feminae per mensis exolvuntur. Sic veteres auctores, sed gnari locorum tradunt undantis bitumine moles pelli manuque trahi ad litus, mox, ubi vapore terrae, vi solis inaruerint, securibus cuneisque ut trabes aut saxa discindi.

VII. Haud[1] procul inde campi quos ferunt olim uberes magnisque urbibus habitatos fulminum iactu arsisse; et[2] manere vestigia, terramque ipsam, specie torridam,[3] vim frugiferam perdidisse. Nam cuncta sponte edita aut manu sata, sive herba tenus aut flore[4] seu solitam in speciem adolevere, atra et inania velut in cinerem vanescunt. Ego sicut inclitas[5] quondam urbis igne caelesti flagrasse concesserim, ita halitu lacus infici terram, corrumpi superfusum spiritum, eoque fetus segetum et autumni putrescere reor,[6] solo caeloque iuxta gravi. At[7] Belus[8] amnis

---

[1] Haud . . . perdidisse *et* ego . . . reor *citat* Orosius I. 5.
[2] sed *Orosius.*
[3] torrida *M* : solidam *Orosius.*
[4] herba tenus aut flore *Rhenanus* : herbas tenues aut flores *M.*
[5] inclutas *codd. dett., Orosius* : Indicas *M.*
[6] terram et corrumpi reor *Orosius.*
[7] at *Ritter* : et *M.*
[8] Belus *Rhenanus* : bel Ius *M.*

all arts. Bitumen is by nature a dark fluid which coagulates when sprinkled with vinegar, and swims on the surface. Those whose business it is, catch hold of it with their hands and haul it on shipboard: then with no artificial aid the bitumen flows in and loads the ship until the stream is cut off. Yet you cannot use bronze or iron to cut the bituminous stream; it shrinks from blood or from a cloth stained with a woman's menses. Such is the story told by ancient writers, but those who are acquainted with the country aver that the floating masses of bitumen are driven by the winds or drawn by hand to shore, where later, after they have been dried by vapours from the earth or by the heat of the sun, they are split like timber or stone with axes and wedges.

VII. Not far from this lake is a plain which, according to report, was once fertile and the site of great cities, but which was later devastated by lightning; and it is said that traces of this disaster still exist there, and that the very ground looks burnt and has lost its fertility. In fact, all the plants there, whether wild or cultivated, turn black, become sterile, and seem to wither into dust, either in leaf or in flower or after they have reached their usual mature form. Now for my part, although I should grant that famous cities were once destroyed by fire from heaven, I still think that it is the exhalations from the lake that infect the ground and poison the atmosphere about this district, and that this is the reason that crops and fruits decay, since both soil and climate are deleterious.[1] The river Belus also

[1] With this description compare that of Josephus, *Bell. Jud.* iv. 8, 4; Strabo xvi. 763 f.; and Pliny, *N.H.* v. 71 f., vii. 65.

Iudaico mari inlabitur, circa cuius os lectae harenae admixto nitro [1] in vitrum excoquuntur. Modicum id litus et egerentibus inexhaustum.

VIII. Magna pars Iudaeae vicis dispergitur, habent et oppida; Hierosolyma genti caput. Illic immensae opulentiae templum, et primis munimentis urbs, dein regia,[2] templum intimis clausum. Ad fores tantum Iudaeo aditus, limine praeter sacerdotes arcebantur. Dum Assyrios penes Medosque et Persas [3] Oriens fuit, despectissima pars servientium: postquam Macedones praepolluere,[4] rex Antiochus demere superstitionem et mores Graecorum dare adnisus, quo minus taeterrimam gentem in melius mutaret, Parthorum bello prohibitus est; nam ea tempestate Arsaces desciverat. Tum Iudaei Macedonibus invalidis, Parthis nondum adultis (et Romani procul erant), sibi ipsi reges imposuere; qui mobilitate vulgi expulsi,[5] resumpta per arma dominatione fugas civium, urbium eversiones, fratrum coniugum parentum neces aliaque solita regibus ausi

---

[1] vitro *in rasura* M.   [2] dein regia *Mercerus*: de Ingia M.
[3] persaxas M.   [4] praepolluere *Halm*: praepotuere M.
[5] volgis epulsi M.

---

[1] Cf. Pliny, *N.H.* xxxvi. 190 ff.   The river Belus (Naaman), which rises in the highlands of Galilee and empties in the Mediterranean near St. Jean d'Acre, really belongs to Phoenicia.

[2] It will be observed that Tacitus is writing after the destruction of the temple.

[3] Tacitus is somewhat inexact here, for the walls were not concentric.

[4] The Seleucid dynasty is meant.

[5] It was under Antiochus II (260–245 B.C.) that Arsaces revolted; but Tacitus may be confusing the revolt of Arsaces with the Maccabean war of 167–164 B.C.

empties into the Jewish Sea; around its mouth a kind of sand is gathered, which when mixed with soda is fused into glass. The beach is of moderate size, but it furnishes an inexhaustible supply.[1]

VIII. A great part of Judea is covered with scattered villages, but there are some towns also; Jerusalem is the capital of the Jews. In it was a temple possessing enormous riches.[2] The first line of fortifications protected the city, the next the palace, and the innermost wall the temple.[3] Only a Jew might approach its doors, and all save the priests were forbidden to cross the threshold. While the East was under the dominion of the Assyrians, Medes, and Persians, the Jews were regarded as the meanest of their subjects: but after the Macedonians gained supremacy,[4] King Antiochus endeavoured to abolish Jewish superstition and to introduce Greek civilization; the war with the Parthians, however, prevented his improving this basest of peoples; for it was exactly at that time that Arsaces had revolted.[5] Later on, since the power of Macedon had waned, the Parthians were not yet come to their strength, and the Romans were far away, the Jews selected their own kings[6] These in turn were expelled by the fickle mob; but recovering their throne by force of arms,[7] they banished citizens, destroyed towns, killed brothers, wives, and parents, and dared essay every other kind of royal crime without hesitation; but they fostered the national super-

---

[6] The Hasmonean line.

[7] This may refer to the war between King Alexander and the Pharisees that began in 92 B.C. and lasted for six years; or to the struggle for the throne that followed on the death of Alexander's widow, Salome, in 70 B.C.

superstitionem fovebant, quia honor sacerdotii
firmamentum potentiae adsumebatur.

IX. Romanorum primus Cn. Pompeius Iudaeos
domuit templumque iure victoriae ingressus est:
inde vulgatum nulla intus deum effigie vacuam sedem
et inania arcana. Muri Hierosolymorum diruti,
delubrum mansit. Mox civili inter nos[1] bello,
postquam in dicionem M. Antonii provinciae cesserant, rex Parthorum Pacorus Iudaea potitus inter-
fectusque a P. Ventidio, et Parthi trans Euphraten
redacti: Iudaeos C. Sosius subegit. Regnum ab
Antonio Herodi datum victor Augustus auxit. Post
mortem Herodis, nihil expectato Caesare, Simo
quidam regium nomen invaserat. Is a Quintilio
Varo obtinente Syriam punitus, et gentem coercitam
liberi Herodis tripertito rexere. Sub Tiberio quies.
Dein iussi a C. Caesare effigiem eius in templo locare
arma potius sumpsere, quem motum Caesaris mors
diremit. Claudius, defunctis regibus aut ad modicum redactis, Iudaeam provinciam equitibus Romanis
aut libertis permisit, e quibus Antonius Felix per

---

[1] inter nos *Agricola*: Interno *M*.

---

[1] In 63 B.C.

[2] Pacorus advanced on Judea in 40 B.C., but two years later
he was killed.

[3] Both Ventidius and Sosius were lieutenants of Antony.
Aided by Sosius, Herod defeated the last of the Maccabees in
37 B.C., and thenceforth the throne of Judea was held by
princes friendly to Rome.

[4] One of Herod's former slaves.

stition, for they had assumed the priesthood to support their civil authority.

IX. The first Roman to subdue the Jews and set foot in their temple by right of conquest was Gnaeus Pompey : [1] thereafter it was a matter of common knowledge that there were no representations of the gods within, but that the place was empty and the secret shrine contained nothing. The walls of Jerusalem were razed, but the temple remained standing. Later, in the time of our civil wars, when these eastern provinces had fallen into the hands of Mark Antony, the Parthian prince, Pacorus, seized Judea, but he was slain by Publius Ventidius, and the Parthians were thrown back across the Euphrates : [2] the Jews were subdued by Gaius Sosius. [3] Antony gave the throne to Herod, and Augustus, after his victory, increased his power. After Herod's death, a certain Simon [4] assumed the name of king without waiting for Caesar's decision. He, however, was put to death by Quintilius Varus, governor of Syria ; the Jews were repressed ; and the kingdom was divided into three parts and given to Herod's sons. [5] Under Tiberius all was quiet. Then, when Caligula ordered the Jews to set up his statue in their temple, they chose rather to resort to arms, but the emperor's death put an end to their uprising. The princes now being dead or reduced to insignificance, Claudius made Judea a province and entrusted it to Roman knights or to freedmen ; one of the latter, Antonius Felix, practised every kind of cruelty and

[5] Archilaus, as Ethnarch, ruled Judea, southern Idumea and northern Samaria ; Herod Antipas, as Tetrarch, had Galilee and Perea ; while Philip, as Tetrarch, received the district east of the Jordan.

omnem saevitiam ac libidinem ius regium servili ingenio exercuit, Drusilla Cleopatrae et Antonii nepte in matrimonium accepta, ut eiusdem Antonii Felix progener, Claudius nepos esset.

X. Duravit tamen patientia Iudaeis usque ad Gessium Florum procuratorem : sub eo bellum ortum. Et comprimere coeptantem Cestium Gallum Syriae legatum varia proelia ac saepius adversa excepere. Qui ubi fato aut taedio occidit, missu Neronis Vespasianus fortuna famaque et egregiis ministris intra [1] duas aestates cuncta camporum omnisque praeter Hierosolyma urbis victore exercitu tenebat. Proximus annus civili bello intentus quantum ad Iudaeos per otium transiit. Pace per Italiam parta [2] et externae curae rediere : [3] augebat iras quod soli Iudaei non cessissent; simul manere apud exercitus Titum ad omnis principatus novi eventus casusve utile [4] videbatur.

XI. Igitur castris, uti diximus, ante moenia Hierosolymorum positis instructas legiones ostentavit : Iudaei sub ipsos muros struxere aciem, rebus secundis longius ausuri et, si pellerentur, parato perfugio. Missus in eos eques cum expeditis cohortibus ambigue certavit; mox cessere hostes et sequentibus diebus crebra pro portis proelia serebant, donec

---

[1] intra *Rhenanus*: inter *M*.
[2] parta *codd. dett.*; parata *M*.
[3] redire *M*.
[4] utili *M*, utilis *corr. M*[1].

---

[1] Antonius Felix, the brother of Claudius's notorious favourite Pallas, was procurator of Judea 52–60 according to Josephus, *Ant.* xx. 7, 1, but seems to have governed the southern half before 52. Cf. Tacitus, *Ann.* xii. 54.
[2] Procurator 64–66 A.D.

lust, wielding the power of king with all the instincts of a slave;[1] he had married Drusilla, the grand-daughter of Cleopatra and Antony, and so was Antony's grandson-in-law, while Claudius was Antony's grandson.

X. Still the Jews' patience lasted until Gessius Florus became procurator:[2] in his time war began. When Cestius Gallus, governor of Syria, tried to stop it, he suffered varied fortunes and met defeat more often than he gained victory. On his death, whether in the course of nature or from vexation, Nero sent out Vespasian, who, aided by his good fortune and reputation as well as by his excellent subordinates, within two summers occupied with his victorious army the whole of the level country and all the cities except Jerusalem. The next year was taken up with civil war, and thus was passed in inactivity so far as the Jews were concerned. When peace had been secured throughout Italy, foreign troubles began again; and the fact that the Jews alone had failed to surrender increased our resentment; at the same time, having regard to all the possibilities and hazards of a new reign, it seemed expedient for Titus to remain with the army.

XI. Therefore, as I have said above,[3] Titus pitched his camp before the walls of Jerusalem and displayed his legions in battle array: the Jews formed their line close beneath their walls, being thus ready to advance if successful, and having a refuge at hand in case they were driven back. Some horse and light-armed foot were sent against them, but fought indecisively; later the enemy retired, and during the following days they engaged in many skirmishes

[3] In chap. i.

adsiduis damnis intra moenia pellerentur. Romani ad obpugnandum versi; neque enim dignum videbatur famem hostium opperiri, poscebantque pericula, pars virtute, multi ferocia et cupidine praemiorum. Ipsi Tito Roma et opes voluptatesque ante oculos; ac ni statim Hierosolyma conciderent, morari videbantur. Sed urbem arduam situ opera molesque firmaverant, quis vel plana satis munirentur. Nam duos collis in immensum editos claudebant muri per artem obliqui aut introrsus sinuati, ut latera obpugnantium ad ictus patescerent. Extrema rupis abrupta, et turres, ubi mons iuvisset, in sexagenos[1] pedes, inter devexa in centenos vicenosque attollebantur, mira specie ac procul intuentibus pares. Alia intus moenia regiae circumiecta, conspicuoque fastigio turris Antonia, in honorem M. Antonii ab Herode appellata.

XII. Templum in modum arcis propriique muri, labore et opere ante alios; ipsae porticus, quis templum ambibatur, egregium propugnaculum. Fons perennis aquae, cavati sub terra montes et piscinae cisternaeque servandis imbribus. Providerant conditores ex diversitate morum crebra bella: inde cuncta quamvis adversus longum obsidium; et a

---

[1] sexagenos *Bekker* : sexaginta *M.*

---

[1] The two hills here meant are apparently Acra and Bezetha, which were included within Herod's wall.

[2] The outer circuit of fortifications had 90 towers; there were in all 164, according to Josephus, *Bell. Iud.* v. 4, 3.

[3] The palace stood on Zion, the temple on Moriah. At the north-west corner of the temple enclosure Herod built Antony's Tower.

[4] It is possible, but not probable, that Tacitus means the Pool of Siloam; for the context seems to show that he is thinking of the temple.

before their gates until at last their continual defeats drove them within their walls. The Romans now turned to preparations for an assault; for the soldiers thought it beneath their dignity to wait for the enemy to be starved out, and so they began to clamour for danger, part being prompted by bravery, but many were moved by their savage natures and their desire for booty. Titus himself had before his eyes a vision of Rome, its wealth and its pleasures, and he felt that if Jerusalem did not fall at once, his enjoyment of them was delayed. But the city stands on an eminence, and the Jews had defended it with works and fortifications sufficient to protect even level ground; for the two hills that rise to a great height had been included within walls that had been skilfully built, projecting out or bending in so as to put the flanks of an assailing body under fire.[1] The rocks terminated in sheer cliffs, and towers rose to a height of sixty feet where the hill assisted the fortifications, and in the valleys they reached one hundred and twenty; they presented a wonderful sight, and appeared of equal height when viewed from a distance.[2] An inner line of walls had been built around the palace, and on a conspicuous height stands Antony's Tower, so named by Herod in honour of Mark Antony.[3]

XII. The temple was built like a citadel, with walls of its own, which were constructed with more care and effort than any of the rest; the very colonnades about the temple made a splendid defence. Within the enclosure is an ever-flowing spring;[4] in the hills are subterraneous excavations, with pools and cisterns for holding rain-water. The founders of the city had foreseen that there would be many wars because the ways of their people differed so from those

Pompeio expugnatis metus atque usus pleraque monstravere. Atque per avaritiam Claudianorum temporum empto iure muniendi struxere muros in pace tamquam ad bellum, magna conluvie et ceterarum urbium clade aucti; nam pervicacissimus quisque illuc perfugerat eoque seditiosius agebant. Tres duces, totidem exercitus: extrema et latissima moenium Simo, mediam urbem Ioannes [quem et Bargioram[1] vocabant],[2] templum Eleazarus[3] firmaverat. Multitudine et armis Ioannes ac Simo, Eleazarus loco pollebat: sed proelia dolus incendia inter ipsos, et magna vis frumenti ambusta. Mox Ioannes, missis per speciem sacrificandi qui Eleazarum manumque eius obtruncarent, templo potitur. Ita in duas factiones civitas discessit, donec propinquantibus Romanis bellum externum concordiam pareret.

XIII. Evenerant prodigia, quae neque hostiis neque votis piare fas habet gens superstitioni obnoxia, religionibus adversa. Visae per caelum concurrere acies, rutilantia arma et subito nubium igne conlucere templum. Apertae repente delubri fores et audita maior humana vox excedere deos; simul ingens

---

[1] Bargioram *Rhenanus*: barbagiorem *M.*
[2] quem . . . vocabant *secl.* Bipontini.
[3] alazarus *M*; *sic infra.*

---

[1] *i.e.* taken by Vespasian and Titus in 67 and 68 A.D.
[2] Simon had carried on guerilla warfare east of the Jordan, but had been called in by the Idumean party in 68 A.D., when he was greeted as a saviour by the people; John of Gischala headed the Galilean zealots; and Eleazar led the patriotic war party.
[3] Cf. *Jerem.* x. 2: Thus saith the Lord, learn not the way of the heathen, and be not dismayed at the signs of heaven; for the heathen are dismayed at them.

The word *religiones* probably refers to the formal ceremonies

of the neighbours: therefore they had built at every point as if they expected a long siege; and after the city had been stormed by Pompey, their fears and experience taught them much. Moreover, profiting by the greed displayed during the reign of Claudius, they had bought the privilege of fortifying their city, and in time of peace had built walls as if for war. The population at this time had been increased by streams of rabble that flowed in from the other captured cities,[1] for the most desperate rebels had taken refuge here, and consequently sedition was the more rife. There were three generals, three armies: the outermost and largest circuit of the walls was held by Simon, the middle of the city by John, and the temple was guarded by Eleazar.[2] John and Simon were strong in numbers and equipment, Eleazar had the advantage of position: between these three there was constant fighting, treachery, and arson, and a great store of grain was consumed. Then John got possession of the temple by sending a party, under pretence of offering sacrifice, to slay Eleazar and his troops. So the citizens were divided into two factions until, at the approach of the Romans, foreign war produced concord.

XIII. Prodigies had indeed occurred, but to avert them either by victims or by vows is held unlawful by a people which, though prone to superstition, is opposed to all propitiatory rites.[3] Contending hosts were seen meeting in the skies, arms flashed, and suddenly the temple was illumined with fire from the clouds. Of a sudden the doors of the shrine opened and a superhuman voice cried: "The gods are departing": at the same moment the

by which the Romans warded off (*procurare*) the evil effect of prodigies; but it may have a wider connotation here.

motus excedentium. Quae pauci in metum trahebant: pluribus persuasio inerat antiquis sacerdotum litteris contineri eo ipso tempore fore ut valesceret Oriens profectique Iudaea rerum potirentur. Quae ambages Vespasianum ac Titum praedixerat, sed vulgus more humanae cupidinis sibi tantam fatorum magnitudinem interpretati ne adversis quidem ad vera mutabantur. Multitudinem obsessorum omnis[1] aetatis, virile ac muliebre secus, sescenta milia fuisse accepimus: arma cunctis, qui ferre possent, et plures quam pro numero audebant. Obstinatio viris feminisque par; ac si transferre sedis cogerentur, maior vitae metus quam mortis. Hanc adversus urbem gentemque Caesar Titus, quando impetus et subita belli locus abnueret, aggeribus vineisque certare statuit: dividuntur legionibus munia et quies proeliorum fuit, donec cuncta expugnandis urbibus reperta apud veteres aut novis ingeniis struerentur.

XIV. At Civilis post malam in Treviris pugnam reparato per Germaniam exercitu apud Vetera castra consedit, tutus loco, et ut memoria prosperarum illic rerum augescerent barbarorum animi. Secutus est

[1] hominis *M.*

---

[1] Cf. Verg. *Aen.* ii. 351 f.; excessere omnes adytis arisque relictis / di quibus imperium hoc steterat; and the remarks by Macrob., *Sat.* iii. 9 on these verses. Josephus, *Bell. Iud.* vi. 299 (Niese) relates that at Pentecost the priests heard repeatedly a cry from the innermost part of the temple: μεταβαίνουεν ἐντεῦθεν.

[2] Cf. *Dan.* ii. 44; Suet. *Vesp.* 4.

[3] Tacitus here resumes the story of the revolt of Civilis which he dropped at iv. 79.

mighty stir of their going was heard.[1] Few interpreted these omens as fearful; the majority firmly
believed that their ancient priestly writings contained
the prophecy that this was the very time when the
East should grow strong and that men starting from
Judea should possess the world.[2] This mysterious
prophecy had in reality pointed to Vespasian and
Titus, but the common people, as is the way of
human ambition, interpreted these great destinies
in their own favour, and could not be turned to
the truth even by adversity. We have heard that
the total number of the besieged of every age and
both sexes was six hundred thousand: there were
arms for all who could use them, and the number
ready to fight was larger than could have been
anticipated from the total population. Both men
and women showed the same determination; and
if they were to be forced to change their home, they
feared life more than death.

Such was the city and people against which Titus
Caesar now proceeded; since the nature of the ground
did not allow him to assault or employ any sudden
operations, he decided to use earthworks and mant-
lets: the legions were assigned to their several tasks,
and there was a respite of fighting until they made
ready every device for storming a town that the
ancients had ever employed or modern ingenuity
invented.

XIV. But meantime Civilis,[3] after his reverse
among the Treviri, recruited his army in Germany
and encamped at Vetera, where he was protected by
his position, and he also wished to inspire his barbarian troops with new courage from the memory
of their former successes there. Cerialis followed

eodem Cerialis, duplicatis copiis adventu secundae et tertiae decimae [1] et quartae decimae legionum; cohortesque et alae iam pridem accitae post victoriam properaverant. Neuter ducum cunctator, sed arcebat latitudo camporum suopte ingenio umentium; addiderat Civilis obliquam in Rhenum molem, cuius obiectu revolutus amnis adiacentibus superfunderetur. Ea loci forma, incertis vadis subdola et nobis adversa: quippe miles Romanus armis gravis et nandi pavidus, Germanos fluminibus suetos levitas armorum et proceritas corporum attollit.

XV. Igitur lacessentibus Batavis ferocissimo cuique nostrorum coeptum certamen, deinde orta trepidatio, cum praealtis paludibus arma equi haurirentur.[2] Germani notis vadis persultabant, omissa plerumque fronte latera ac terga circumvenientes. Neque ut in pedestri acie comminus certabatur, sed tamquam navali pugna vagi inter undas aut, si quid stabile occurrebat, totis illic corporibus nitentes, vulnerati[3] cum integris, periti nandi cum ignaris in mutuam perniciem implicabantur. Minor tamen quam pro tumultu caedes,[4] quia non ausi egredi paludem Germani in castra rediere. Eius proelii eventus utrumque ducem diversis animi motibus ad maturandum

---

[1] xiij *M*.
[2] armae qui aurirentur *M*, h superscr. *M*[1].
[3] volneratis *M*.   [4] ceres *M*.

after him, having had his forces doubled by the
arrival of the Second, Sixth, and Fourteenth legions;
moreover, the auxiliary foot and horse that he had
ordered up long before had hurried to join him after
his victory. Neither general was given to delay,
but they were separated by a wide plain that was
naturally marshy; moreover, Civilis had built a dam
obliquely into the Rhine, so that the river, thrown
from its course by this obstacle, flooded the adjacent
fields. Such was the nature of the ground, which
was treacherous for our men because the shallows
were uncertain and therefore dangerous: for the
Roman soldier is heavily weighted with arms and
afraid of swimming, but the Germans are accustomed
to streams, are lightly armed, and their great stature
keeps their heads above water.

XV. Therefore when the Batavians attacked our
men, the bravest of our troops engaged; but a panic
soon followed as arms and horses were swallowed up
in the deep marshes. The Germans, knowing the
shallows, leaped through the waters, and frequently,
leaving our front, surrounded our men on the flanks
and rear; there was no fighting at close quarters, as
is usual in an engagement between infantry, but the
struggle was rather like a naval fight, for the men
floundered about in the water, or, if they found firm
ground, they exerted all their strength to secure it;
so the wounded and the uninjured, those who could
swim and those who could not, struggled together to
their common destruction. Yet our loss was not in
proportion to the confusion, because the Germans,
not daring to come out of the marshes on to firm
ground, returned to their camp. The outcome of
this engagement encouraged both leaders from

summae rei discrimen erexit. Civilis instare fortunae, Cerialis abolere ignominiam : Germani prosperis feroces, Romanos pudor excitaverat. Nox apud barbaros cantu aut clamore, nostris per iram et minas acta.

XVI. Postera luce Cerialis equite et auxiliariis cohortibus frontem explet, in secunda acie legiones locatae, dux sibi delectos retinuerat ad improvisa. Civilis haud porrecto agmine, sed cuneis adstitit : Batavi Cugernique in dextro, laeva ac propiora flumini[1] Transrhenani tenuere. Exhortatio ducum non more contionis apud universos, sed ut quosque suorum advehebantur. Cerialis veterem Romani nominis gloriam, antiquas recentisque victorias; ut perfidum ignavum victum hostem in aeternum exciderent, ultione magis[2] quam proelio opus esse. Pauciores nuper cum pluribus certasse, ac tamen fusos Germanos, quod roboris fuerit : superesse qui fugam animis, qui vulnera tergo ferant. Proprios inde stimulos legionibus admovebat, domitores Britanniae quartadecimanos appellans ; principem Galbam sextae legionis auctoritate factum; illa primum acie secundanos nova signa novamque aquilam dicaturos. Hinc praevectus ad Germanicum exercitum manus tendebat, ut suam ripam, sua

---

[1] flumini *Nipperdey*: fluminis *M*.
[2] *a verbo* magis *usque ad* sagulis versicoloribus *c. xxiii scripturam evanidam renovavit* M^2.

---

[1] Cf. ii. 11.   [2] Cf. iii. 44.
[3] The Second had been recently enrolled. See iv. 68.
[4] The legions (i, xvi, and xxi) that had gone over to the Gauls and returned again to Roman allegiance. Cf. iv. 72.

different motives to hasten the final struggle. Civilis wished to follow up his good fortune ; Cerialis to wipe out his disgrace : the Germans were emboldened by their success ; the Romans were stirred by shame. The barbarians spent the night in singing or shouting ; our men in rage and threats of vengeance.

XVI. The next day Cerialis stationed his cavalry and auxiliary infantry in his front line and placed his legions in the second, while he reserved some picked troops under his own leadership to meet emergencies. Civilis did not oppose him with an extended front, but ranged his troops in columns : the Batavi and Cugerni were on his right ; the left wing, nearer the river, was held by tribes from across the Rhine. The generals did not encourage their troops in formal appeals to the whole body, but they addressed each division as they rode along the line. Cerialis recalled the ancient glories of the Roman name, their victories old and new ; he urged them to destroy for ever these treacherous and cowardly foes whom they had already beaten ; it was vengeance rather than battle that was needed. "You have recently fought against superior numbers, and yet you routed the Germans, and their picked troops at that : those who survive carry terror in their hearts and wounds on their backs." He applied the proper spur to each of the legions, calling the Fourteenth the "Conquerors of Britain,"[1] reminding the Sixth that it was by their influence that Galba had been made emperor,[2] and telling the Second that in the battle that day they would dedicate their new standards, and their new eagle.[3] Then he rode toward the German army,[4] and stretching out his hands begged these troops to recover their own river-bank and

castra sanguine hostium reciperarent. Alacrior omnium clamor, quis vel ex longa pace proelii cupido vel fessis bello pacis amor, praemiaque et quies in posterum sperabantur.

XVII. Nec Civilis silens[1] instruxit aciem, locum pugnae testem virtutis ciens: stare Germanos Batavosque super vestigia gloriae, cineres ossaque legionum calcantis. Quocumque oculos Romanus intenderet, captivitatem clademque et dira omnia obversari. Ne terrerentur vario Trevirici proelii eventu: suam illic victoriam Germanis obstitisse, dum omissis telis praeda manus impediunt: sed cuncta mox prospera et hosti contraria evenisse. Quae provideri[2] astu ducis oportuerit, providisse, campos madentis et ipsis gnaros, paludes hostibus noxias. Rhenum et Germaniae deos in aspectu: quorum numine capesserent pugnam, coniugum parentum patriae memores: illum diem aut gloriosissimum inter maiores aut ignominiosum apud posteros fore. Ubi sono armorum tripudiisque (ita illis mos) adprobata sunt dicta, saxis glandibusque et ceteris missilibus proelium incipitur, neque nostro milite paludem ingrediente et Germanis, ut elicerent, lacessentibus.

XVIII. Absumptis quae iaciuntur et ardescente pugna procursum ab hoste infestius: immensis corporibus et praelongis hastis fluitantem labantem-

---

[1] silens *Pichena*: silentem *M*.
[2] previse *in rasura* M^2, p̄vise *in margine* M^2.

---

[1] Vetera.   [2] Cf. iv. 77 ff.

their camp[1] at the expense of the enemy's blood. An enthusiastic shout arose from all, for some after their long peace were eager for battle, others weary of war desired peace; and they all hoped for rewards and rest thereafter.

XVII. Nor did Civilis form his lines in silence, but called on the place of battle to bear witness to his soldiers' bravery: he reminded the Germans and Batavians that they were standing on the field of glory, that they were trampling underfoot the bones and ashes of Roman legions. " Wherever the Roman turns his eyes," he cried, " captivity, disaster, and dire omens confront him. You must not be alarmed by the adverse result of your battle with the Treviri:[2] there their very victory hampered the Germans, for they dropped their arms and filled their hands with booty: but everything since has gone favourably for us and against the Romans. Every provision has been made that a wise general should make: the fields are flooded, but we know them well; the marshes are fatal to our foes. Before you are the Rhine and the gods of Germany: engage under their divine favour, remembering your wives, parents, and fatherland: this day shall crown the glories of our sires or be counted the deepest disgrace by our descendants!" When the Germans had applauded these words with clashing arms and wild dancing according to their custom, they opened battle with a volley of stones, leaden balls, and other missiles, and since our soldiers did not enter the marsh, the foe tried to provoke them and so lure them on.

XVIII. When they had spent their missiles, as the battle grew hotter, the enemy charged fiercely: their huge stature and their extremely long spears allowed

que militem eminus fodiebant; simul e mole, quam eductam in Rhenum rettulimus, Bructerorum cuneus transnatavit. Turbata ibi res et pellebatur sociarum cohortium acies, cum legiones pugnam excipiunt suppressaque hostium ferocia proelium aequatur. Inter quae perfuga Batavus adiit Cerialem, terga hostium promittens, si extremo paludis eques mitteretur: solidum illa et Cugernos, quibus custodia obvenisset, parum intentos. Duae alae cum perfuga missae incauto hosti circumfunduntur. Quod ubi clamore cognitum, legiones a fronte incubuere, pulsique Germani Rhenum fuga petebant. Debellatum eo die foret, si Romana classis sequi maturasset: ne eques quidem institit, repente fusis imbribus et propinqua nocte.

XIX. Postera die quartadecima legio in superiorem provinciam Gallo Annio [1] missa: Cerialis exercitum decima ex Hispania legio supplevit: Civili Chaucorum auxilia venere. Non tamen ausus oppidum Batavorum armis tueri, raptis quae ferri poterant, ceteris iniecto igni, in insulam concessit, gnarus deesse navis efficiendo ponti, neque exercitum Romanum aliter transmissurum: quin et diruit [2] molem a Druso Germanico factam Rhenumque prono alveo

---

[1] Annio *Puteolanus*: animo M^2.
[2] diluit M^2.

them to wound our men from a distance as they slipped and floundered in the water; at the same time a column of the Bructeri swam across from the dam that, as I have said, had been built out into the Rhine. This caused some confusion and the line of allied infantry was being driven back, when the legions took up the fight, checked the enemy's savage advance, and so equalised the contest. Meantime a Batavian deserter approached Cerialis, promising him a chance to attack the enemy's rear if he would send some cavalry along the edge of the marsh; for there, he said, was solid ground and the Cugerni, who guarded at that spot, were careless. Two troops of horse were despatched with the deserter and succeeded in outflanking the unsuspecting enemy. When this was made evident by a shout, the legions charged in front, and the Germans were routed and fled towards the Rhine. The war would have been ended on that day if the Roman fleet had hurried to follow after them: as it was, not even the cavalry pressed forward, for rain suddenly began to fall and night was close at hand.

XIX. The next day the Fourteenth legion was sent to Gallus Annius in the upper province: the Tenth, coming from Spain, took its place in the army of Cerialis: Civilis was reinforced by some auxiliaries from the Chauci. Yet he did not dare to defend the capital of the Batavians, but seizing everything that was portable, he burned the rest and retired into the island, for he knew that Cerialis did not have the boats to build a bridge, and that the Roman army could not be got across the river in any other way; moreover, he destroyed the dike that Drusus Germanicus had built, and so by demolishing the barriers

in Galliam ruentem, disiectis quae morabantur, effudit. Sic velut abacto amne tenuis alveus insulam inter Germanosque continentium terrarum speciem fecerat. Transiere Rhenum Tutor quoque et Classicus et centum tredecim Trevirorum senatores, in quis fuit Alpinius Montanus, quem a Primo Antonio missum in Gallias superius memoravimus. Comitabatur eum frater D. Alpinius: simul ceteri miseratione ac donis auxilia concibant inter gentis periculorum avidas.

XX. Tantumque belli superfuit ut praesidia cohortium alarum legionum uno die[1] Civilis quadripertito[2] invaserit, decimam legionem Arenaci, secundam Batavoduri et Grinnes Vadamque, cohortium alarumque castra, ita divisis copiis ut ipse et Verax, sorore eius genitus, Classicusque ac Tutor suam quisque manum traherent, nec omnia patrandi fiducia, sed multa ausis aliqua in parte fortunam adfore: simul Cerialem neque satis cautum et pluribus nuntiis huc illuc cursantem posse medio intercipi. Quibus obvenerant castra decimanorum, obpugnationem legionis arduam rati egressum militem et caedendis materiis operatum turbavere, occiso praefecto castrorum et quinque primoribus centurionum paucisque militibus: ceteri se munimentis[3]

[1] legionem modie M^2.
[2] quadripertito *Ernesti*: quadripertita M^2.
[3] ceteris eminentis M^2.

---

[1] This dike or rampart had been begun by Drusus in 9 B.C. and completed by Pompeius Paulinus in 55 A.D. (*Ann.* xiii. 53). By breaking it down Civilis let the water sweep into the Waal, the southernmost arm of the Rhine.
[2] Cf. iii. 35.
[3] The identity of these towns is uncertain.

that checked it, he let the Rhine pour in full flow into Gaul along an unencumbered channel.[1] Thus the Rhine was virtually drawn off, and the shallow channel that was left between the island and Germany made the lands seem uninterrupted. Tutor also and Classicus crossed the Rhine, with one hundred and thirteen Treviran senators, among whom was Alpinius Montanus, who had been sent into Gaul by Primus Antonius, as we stated above.[2] He was accompanied by his brother, Decimus Alpinius; at the same time the others also were trying to raise reinforcements among these bold and adventurous tribes by appeals to their pity and by gifts.

XX. In fact the war was so far from being over that in a single day Civilis attacked the standing camps of the auxiliary foot and horse and of the regular legions as well, at four several points, assailing the Tenth legion at Arenacum, the Second at Batavodurum, and the camp of the auxiliary foot and horse at Grinnes and Vada;[3] he so divided his troops that he and Verax, his nephew, Classicus and Tutor, each led his own force; they did not expect to be successful everywhere, but they trusted that by making many ventures they would be successful in some one point; besides, they thought that Cerialis was not very cautious and that, as he hurried from place to place on receiving various reports, he might be cut off. The force that was to assail the camp of the Tenth legion, thinking that it was a difficult task to storm a legion, cut off some troops that had left their fortifications and were busy felling timber, and succeeded in killing the prefect of the camp, five centurions of the first rank, and a few common soldiers; the rest defended themselves in the fortifi-

defendere. Interim Germanorum manus Batavoduri interrumpere [1] inchoatum pontem nitebantur: ambiguum proelium nox diremit.

XXI. Plus discriminis apud Grinnes Vadamque. Vadam Civilis, Grinnes Classicus obpugnabant: nec sisti poterant interfecto fortissimo quoque, in quis Briganticus praefectus alae ceciderat, quem fidum Romanis et Civili avunculo infensum diximus. Sed ubi Cerialis cum delecta equitum manu subvenit, versa fortuna praecipites Germani in amnem aguntur. Civilis dum fugientis retentat, agnitus petitusque telis relicto equo transnatavit [2]; idem Veraci [3] effugium: Tutorem Classicumque adpulsae lintres transvexere. [4] Ne tum quidem Romana classis pugnae adfuit, et iussum erat, sed obstitit formido et remiges per alia militiae munia dispersi. Sane Cerialis parum temporis ad exequenda imperia dabat, subitus consiliis set eventu clarus: aderat fortuna, etiam ubi artes defuissent: hinc ipsi exercituique minor cura disciplinae. Et paucos post dies, quamquam periculum captivitatis evasisset, infamiam non vitavit. [5]

XXII. Profectus Novaesium Bonnamque ad visenda castra, quae hiematuris legionibus erigebantur, navibus remeabat disiecto agmine, incuriosis vigiliis.

[1] interrumpere *Kiessling*: inrumpere M^2.
[2] tnataum M^2.   [3] Veraci *Ritter*: germani M^2.
[4] transvexere *Halm*: vexere M^2.
[5] mutavit M^2.

[1] Cf. iv. 70.

cations. Meanwhile a force of Germans at Batavodurum tried to destroy a bridge that had been begun there; the indecisive struggle was ended by the coming of night.

XXI. There was greater danger at Grinnes and Vada. Civilis tried to capture Vada by assault, Classicus, Grinnes; and they could not be checked, for the bravest of our men had fallen, among them Briganticus, captain of a squadron of cavalry, who, as we have said,[1] was loyal to the Romans and hostile to his uncle Civilis. But the arrival of Cerialis with a picked body of horse changed the fortunes of the day and the Germans were driven headlong into the river. As Civilis was trying to rally the fugitives he was recognized and made a target for our weapons, but he abandoned his horse and swam across the river; Verax escaped in the same way; Tutor and Classicus were carried over by some boats that were brought up for the purpose. Not even on this occasion was the Roman fleet at hand; the order had indeed been given, but fear and also the dispersal of the rowers among other military duties prevented its execution. Indeed, Cerialis commonly gave insufficient time for the execution of his orders, being hasty in planning, but brilliant in his successes: good fortune attended him even when he had lacked skill; and the result was that both he and his troops paid too little regard to discipline. A few days later he narrowly avoided being taken prisoner, but he did not escape the attendant disgrace.

XXII. He had gone to Novaesium and Bonn to inspect the camps that were being built for the legions' winter quarters, and was now returning with the fleet, while his escort straggled and his sentries

Animadversum id Germanis et insidias composuere:
electa nox atra nubibus, et prono amne rapti nullo
prohibente vallum ineunt. Prima caedes astu
adiuta: incisis tabernaculorum funibus suismet
tentoriis coopertos trucidabant. Aliud agmen turbare
classem, inicere vincla, trahere puppis; utque
ad fallendum silentio, ita coepta caede, quo plus
terroris adderent, cuncta clamoribus miscebant.
Romani vulneribus exciti quaerunt arma, ruunt
per vias, pauci ornatu militari, plerique circum
brachia torta veste et strictis mucronibus. Dux
semisomnus ac prope intectus errore hostium servatur;
namque praetoriam navem vexillo insignem,
illic ducem rati, abripiunt. Cerialis alibi noctem[1]
egerat, ut plerique credidere, ob stuprum Claudiae
Sacratae mulieris Ubiae.[2] Vigiles flagitium suum
ducis dedecore excusabant, tamquam iussi silere ne
quietem eius turbarent; ita intermisso signo et
vocibus se quoque in somnum lapsos. Multa luce
revecti hostes captivis navibus, praetoriam triremem
flumine Lupia donum Veledae traxere.

XXIII. Civilem cupido incessit[3] navalem aciem
ostentandi: complet quod biremium quaeque sim-

---

[1] nave M^2.   [2] Ubiae *Rhenanus*: ubie M^2.
[3] invasi incessit M^2.

---

[1] Cf. iv. 61.

were careless. The Germans noticed this and planned an ambuscade; they selected a night black with clouds, and slipping down-stream got within the camp without opposition. Their onslaught was helped at first by cunning, for they cut the tent ropes and massacred the soldiers as they lay buried beneath their own shelters. Another force put the fleet into confusion, throwing grappling-irons on board and dragging the boats away; while they acted in silence at first to avoid attracting attention, after the slaughter had begun they endeavoured to increase the panic by their shouts. Roused by their wounds the Romans looked for their arms and ran up and down the streets of the camp; few were properly equipped, most with their garments wrapped around their arms and their swords drawn. Their general, half-asleep and almost naked, was saved only by the enemy's mistake; for the Germans dragged away his flagship, which was distinguished by a standard, thinking that he was there. But Cerialis had spent the night elsewhere, as many believe, on account of an intrigue with Claudia Sacrata, a Ubian woman. The sentries tried to use the scandalous behaviour of their general to shield their own fault, claiming that they had been ordered to keep quiet that his rest might not be disturbed; that was the reason that the trumpet-call and the challenges had been omitted, and so they had dropped to sleep themselves. The enemy sailed off in broad daylight on the ships that they had captured; the flagship they took up the Lippe as a gift to Veleda.[1]

XXIII. Civilis was now seized with a desire to make a naval demonstration; he therefore manned all the biremes and all the ships that had but a single

plici ordine agebantur; adiecta ingens lintrium vis,
tricenos quadragenosque . . .[1] armamenta Libur-
nicis solita; et simul captae lintres sagulis versicoloribus haud indecore[2] pro velis iuvabantur.
Spatium velut aequoris electum quo Mosae fluminis
os amnem Rhenum Oceano adfundit. Causa in-
struendae classis super insitam genti vanitatem ut
eo terrore commeatus Gallia adventantes inter-
ciperentur. Cerialis miraculo magis quam metu
derexit classem, numero imparem, usu remigum,[3]
gubernatorum arte, navium magnitudine potiorem.
His flumen secundum, illi vento agebantur: sic
praevecti temptato levium telorum iactu dirimuntur.
Civilis nihil ultra ausus trans Rhenum concessit:
Cerialis insulam Batavorum hostiliter populatus
agros villasque Civilis intactas nota arte ducum
sinebat, cum interim flexu autumni et crebris per
aequinoctium[4] imbribus superfusus amnis palustrem
humilemque insulam in faciem stagni opplevit. Nec
classis aut commeatus aderant, castraque in plano
sita vi fluminis differebantur.

XXIV. Potuisse tunc opprimi legiones et volu-
isse Germanos, sed dolo a se flexos imputavit
Civilis; neque abhorret vero, quando paucis post

[1] *lacunam notavit Ritter.*
[2] *ab* haud indecore *usque ad* concussa transrhenanorum
fide inter *c. xxv* scripturam evanidam superscripsit *M²*.
[3] remigium *M*.
[4] aequinoctium *Orellius* : equin . . tium *in rasura M*.

[1] In the confused condition of the text at the beginning of
this chapter, we cannot do more than give the probable sense
of what Tacitus wrote.
[2] That Civilis might be suspected by his supporters of
collusion with the Romans.

bank of oars; to this fleet he added a vast number of
boats, [putting in each] thirty or forty men, the
ordinary complement of a Liburnian cruiser; and at
the same time the boats that he had captured were
fitted with particoloured plaids for sails, which made
a fine show and helped their movement.[1] The place
chosen for the display was a small sea, so to speak,
formed at the point where the mouth of the Maas
discharges the water of the Rhine into the ocean.
Now his purpose in marshalling this fleet, apart from
the native vanity of a Batavian, was to frighten away
the convoys of supplies that were coming from Gaul.
Cerialis, more surprised than frightened by this
action of Civilis, drew up his fleet, which, although
inferior in numbers, was superior in having more
experienced rowers, more skilful pilots, and larger
ships. His vessels were helped by the current, his
opponents enjoyed a favourable wind; so they sailed
past each other and separated, after trying some shots
with light missiles. Civilis dared attempt nothing
further, but withdrew across the Rhine; Cerialis
devastated the island of the Batavians in relentless
fashion, but, adopting a familiar device of generals,
he left untouched the farms and buildings of Civilis.[2]
In the meantime the turn of autumn and the frequent
equinoctial rains that followed caused the river to
overflow and made the low marshy island look like a
swamp. Neither fleet nor supplies were on hand,
and the Roman camp, being situated on flat ground,
began to be washed away by the current.

XXIV. That the legions could then have been
crushed, and that the Germans wished to do so but
were craftily dissuaded by him, were claims afterwards made by Civilis; and in fact his claim seems

diebus deditio insecuta est. Nam Cerialis per occultos nuntios Batavis pacem, Civili veniam ostentans, Veledam propinquosque monebat fortunam belli, tot cladibus adversam, opportuno erga populum Romanum merito mutare : caesos Treviros, receptos Ubios, ereptam Batavis patriam ; neque aliud Civilis amicitia partum[1] quam vulnera fugas luctus. Exulem eum et extorrem recipientibus oneri, et satis peccavisse quod totiens Rhenum transcenderint. Si quid ultra moliantur, inde iniuriam et culpam, hinc ultionem et deos fore.

XXV. Miscebantur minis promissa; et concussa Transrhenanorum fide inter Batavos quoque sermones orti : non prorogandam ultra ruinam, nec posse ab una natione totius orbis servitium depelli. Quid profectum caede et incendiis legionum nisi ut plures[2] validioresque accirentur? Si Vespasiano bellum navaverint, Vespasianum rerum potiri : sin populum Romanum armis vocent, quotam partem generis humani Batavos esse? Respicerent Raetos Noricosque et ceterorum onera sociorum : sibi non tributa, sed virtutem et viros indici. Proximum id libertati;

1 partum Ritter : paratum *M*.
2 fures *M*.

not far from the truth, since his surrender followed a few days later. For while Cerialis by secret messengers was holding out to the Batavians the prospect of peace and to Civilis of pardon, he was also advising Veleda and her relatives to change the fortunes of a war, which repeated disasters had shown to be adverse to them, by rendering a timely service to the Roman people : he reminded them that the Treviri had been cut to pieces, the Ubii had returned to their allegiance, and the Batavians had lost their native land; they had gained nothing from their friendship with Civilis but wounds, banishment, and grief. An exile and homeless he would be only a burden to any who harboured him, and they had already done wrong enough in crossing the Rhine so many times. If they transgressed further, the wrong and guilt would be theirs, but vengeance and the favour of heaven would belong to the Romans.

XXV. These promises were mingled with threats ; and when the fidelity of the tribes across the Rhine had been shaken, debates began among the Batavians as well : " We must not extend our ruin further ; no single nation can avert the enslavement of the whole world. What have we accomplished by destroying legions with fire and sword except to cause more legions and stronger forces to be brought up ? If we have fought for Vespasian, Vespasian is now master of the world; if we are challenging the whole Roman people in arms, we must recognize what a trifling part of mankind we Batavians are. Look at the Raetians, the Noricans, and consider the burdens Rome's other allies bear: we are not required to pay tribute, but only to furnish valour and men. This is a condition next to freedom ; and

et si dominorum electio sit, honestius principes
Romanorum quam Germanorum feminas tolerari.
Haec vulgus, proceres atrociora : Civilis rabie semet
in arma trusos; illum domesticis malis excidium
gentis opposuisse. Tunc infensos Batavis deos, cum
obsiderentur legiones, interficerentur legati, bellum
uni necessarium, ferale ipsis sumeretur. Ventum
ad extrema, ni resipiscere incipiant et noxii capitis
poena paenitentiam fateantur.

XXVI. Non fefellit Civilem ea inclinatio et praevenire statuit, super taedium malorum etiam spe [1]
vitae, quae plerumque magnos animos infringit.
Petito conloquio scinditur Nabaliae fluminis pons,
in cuius abrupta progressi duces, et Civilis ita coepit :
" si apud Vitellii [2] legatum defenderer, neque facto
meo venia neque dictis fides debebatur; cuncta
inter nos inimica : hostilia ab illo coepta, a me aucta
erant : erga Vespasianum vetus mihi observantia, et
cum privatus esset, amici vocabamur. Hoc Primo
Antonio notum, cuius epistulis ad bellum actus sum,
ne Germanicae legiones et Gallica iuventus Alpis
transcenderent. Quae Antonius epistulis, Hordeonius
Flaccus praesens monebat : arma in Germania movi, [3]
quae Mucianus in Syria, Aponius in Moesia, Flavianus
in Pannonia [4] * * * *

[1] spem M.	[2] vitel'ium M.
[3] movit M.	[4] pannia M.

---

[1] At this point the *Histories* break off. Of the fate of
Civilis we know nothing. That the Batavians were treated
favourably seems clear from *Germ.* 29 : manet honos et
antiquae societatis insigne; nam nec tributis contemnuntur
nec publicanus atterit; exempti oneribus et collationibus
et tantum in usum proeliorum sepositi, velut tela atque arma,
bellis reservantur.

if we are to choose our masters, we can more honourably bear the rule of Roman emperors than of German women." So the common people; the chiefs spoke more violently: "We have been drawn into arms by the madness of Civilis; he wished to avert his own misfortunes by the ruin of his country. The gods were hostile to the Batavians on the day when we besieged the legions, murdered their commanders, and began this war that was a necessity only to Civilis, but to us fatal. There is nothing left us, unless we begin to come to our senses and show our repentance by punishing the guilty individual."

XXVI. Civilis was not unaware of this change of feeling and he decided to anticipate it, not only because he was weary of suffering, but also for the hope of life, which often breaks down high courage. When he asked for a conference, the bridge over the Nabalia was cut in two and the leaders advanced to the broken ends; then Civilis began thus: "If I were defending myself before a legate of Vitellius, my acts would deserve no pardon nor my words any credence; there was nothing but hatred between him and me—he began the quarrel, I increased it; toward Vespasian my respect is of long standing, and when he was still a private citizen we were called friends. Primus Antonius knew this when he sent me a letter calling me to arms to keep the legions of Germany and the young men of Gaul from crossing the Alps. What Antonius advised by letter, Hordeonius urged in person; I have begun the same war in Germany that Mucianus began in Syria, Aponius in Moesia, Flavianus in Pannonia." . . .[1]

FRAGMENTA HISTORIARUM

1. Iudaei obsidione clausi, quia nulla neque pacis neque deditionis copia dabatur, ad extremum fame interibant, passimque viae oppleri cadaveribus coepere, victo iam officio humandi : quin omnia nefanda esca super ausi ne humanis quidem corporibus pepercerunt, nisi quae eiusmodi alimentis tabes praeripuerat.—Sulpicius Severus, *Chron.* ii. 30. 3.

2. Fertur Titus adhibito [1] consilio prius deliberasse **an** templum tanti operis everteret. Etenim nonnullis videbatur aedem sacratam ultra omnia mortalia inlustrem non oportere deleri, quae servata modestiae Romanae testimonium, diruta perennem crudelitatis notam praeberet. At contra alii et Titus ipse evertendum in primis templum censebant quo plenius Iudaeorum et Christianorum religio tolleretur : quippe has religiones, licet contrarias sibi, isdem tamen ab auctoribus profectas ; Christianos ex Iudaeis extitisse : radice sublata stirpem facile perituram.—Sulpicius Severus, *Chron.* ii. 30. 6.

3. Sescenta milia Iudaeorum eo bello interfecta Cornelius et Suetonius referunt.—Orosius vii. 9. 7.

---

[1] Tacitus actually says (v. 13) that six hundred thousand was the number of the besieged. Suetonius, in his extant works, says nothing of the number of those killed.

FRAGMENTS OF THE HISTORIES

1. The Jews, being closely besieged and given no opportunity to make peace or to surrender, were finally dying of starvation, and the streets began to be filled with corpses everywhere, for they were now unequal to the duty of burying their dead; moreover, made bold to resort to every kind of horrible food, they did not spare even human bodies—save those of which they had been robbed by the wasting that such food had caused.

2. It is said that Titus first called a council and deliberated whether he should destroy such a mighty temple. For some thought that a consecrated shrine, which was famous beyond all other works of men, ought not to be razed, arguing that its preservation would bear witness to the moderation of Rome, while its destruction would for ever brand her cruelty. Yet others, including Titus himself, opposed, holding the destruction of this temple to be a prime necessity in order to wipe out more completely the religion of the Jews and the Christians; for they urged that these religions, although hostile to each other, nevertheless sprang from the same sources; the Christians had grown out of the Jews: if the root were destroyed, the stock would easily perish.

3. That six hundred thousand Jews were killed in that war is stated by Cornelius and Suetonius.[1]

4. Deinde, ut verbis Cornelii Taciti loquar, sene Augusto Ianus patefactus, dum apud extremos terrarum terminos novae gentes saepe ex usu et aliquando cum damno quaeruntur, usque ad Vespasiani duravit imperium. Hucusque Cornelius.—Orosius vii. 3. 7.

5. Gordianus . . . Iani portas aperuit: quas utrum post Vespasianum et Titum aliquis clauserit, neminem scripsisse memini, cum tamen eas ab ipso Vespasiano post annum apertas Cornelius Tacitus prodat.—Orosius vii. 19. 4.

6. Nam quanta fuerint Diurpanei, Dacorum regis, cum Fusco duce proelia quantaeque Romanorum clades, longo textu evolverem, nisi Cornelius Tacitus, qui hanc historiam diligentissime contexuit, de reticendo interfectorum numero et Sallustium Crispum et alios auctores quam plurimos sanxisse et se ipsum idem potissimum elegisse dixisset.—Orosius vii. 10. 4.

7. Theodosius . . . maximas illas Scythicas gentis formidatasque cunctis maioribus, Alexandro quoque illi Magno, sicut Pompeius Corneliusque testati sunt, evitatis . . ., hoc est Alanos Hunos et Gothos, incunctanter adgressus magnis multisque proeliis vicit.—Orosius vii. 34. 5.

8. Hi vero (Locri), qui iuxta Delphos colunt, Ozolae nuncupantur . . . qui autem Libyam delati sunt, Nasamones appellantur, ut Cornelius Tacitus refert, oriundi a Naryciis etc. Servii *Comment. in Verg. Aen.* iii. 399 = I. p. 413, Thilo.

---

[1] A.D. 242.

[2] Cornelius Fuscus (*vid. index*), who under Domitian suffered a serious defeat at the hands of the Dacians. Cf. Suet., *Domit.* 6: Martial, *Epig.* vi. 76; Dio Cass. lxvii. 6.

[3] Pompeius Trogus, whose history is preserved in the abridgment by Justin.

FRAGMENTS OF THE HISTORIES

4. Next, to quote the words of Cornelius Tacitus, " the gate of Janus, that had been opened when Augustus was old, remained so while on the very boundaries of the world new peoples were being attacked, often to our profit and sometimes to our loss, even down to the reign of Vespasian." Thus far Cornelius.

5. Gordianus . . . opened the gates of Janus : [1] as to the question whether anyone closed them after Vespasian and Titus, I can recall no statement by any historian; yet Cornelius Tacitus reports that they were opened after a year by Vespasian himself.

6. For the mighty battles of Diurpaneus, king of the Dacians, with the Roman general Fuscus,[2] and the mighty losses of the Romans I should now set forth at length, if Cornelius Tacitus, who composed the history of these times with the greatest care, had not said that Sallustius Crispus and very many other historians had approved of passing over in silence the number of our losses, and that he for his own part had chosen the same course before all others.

7. Those vast Scythian peoples whom all our ancestors and even the famous Alexander the Great had feared and avoided according to the testimony of Pompeius [3] and Cornelius . . . I mean the Alans, the Huns, and the Goths, Theodosius attacked without hesitation and defeated in many great battles.

8. But these (Locrians) who live near Delphi are called the Ozolians . . .; however, those who moved to Libya have the name of Nasomones, as Cornelius Tacitus reports, being sprung from the Narycii.

THE ANNALS OF TACITUS

BOOK I

INTRODUCTION

Since the life of Tacitus has already been sketched in Mr. Moore's introduction to the Histories, a brief account may suffice here. Brevity, indeed, is a necessity; for the ancient evidence might almost be compressed into a dozen lines, nor has even the industry or imagination of modern scholars been able to add much that is of value to this exiguous material.

For the parentage of the greatest of Roman historians no witness can be called, nor was the famous name *Cornelius*, vulgarized by Sulla's numerous emancipations, a patent of nobility in the first century of the Christian era. The elder Pliny, however, was acquainted with a Roman knight, Cornelius Tacitus, who held a procuratorship in Belgic Gaul,[1] and

---

[1] *H.N.* VII. 16, 76. The passage is characteristic enough to deserve transcribing :—*Invenimus in monumentis Salamine Euthymenis filium in tria cubita triennio adolevisse, incessu tardum, sensu hebetem, puberem etiam factum voce robusta, absumptum contractione membrorum subita triennio circumacto. Ipsi non pridem vidimus eadem fere omnia praeter pubertatem in filio Corneli Taciti, equitis Romani, Belgicae Galliae rationes procurantis.*—The fact that the emperor M. Claudius Tacitus (276 A.D.) claimed kinship with the historian may well be the sole reason that his works have survived. See Vopisc. *Tac.* 10 :—*Cornelium Tacitum, scriptorem historiae Augustae, quod parentem suum eundem diceret, in omnibus bibliothecis conlocari iussit, et ne lectorum incuria deperiret, librum per annos singulos deciens scribi publicitus in cunctis archiis iussit et in bibliothecis poni.*

obviously there is a faint possibility that this may have
been the father or an uncle of the historian. Be that
as it may, a certain standard of inherited wealth and
consequence is presupposed alike by his career and by
his prejudices. The exact date of his birth is equally
unknown, but he was senior by a few years to his
intimate friend and correspondent, the younger
Pliny; who states in a letter to him that he was in
his eighteenth year at the time of the great eruption
of Vesuvius which destroyed Pompeii, Herculaneum,
and his uncle, in the late summer of 79 A.D. Certainty is out of the question, yet the provisional
date of 55 A.D., which harmonizes with the ascertainable facts of his life, can hardly be far wide of the
mark.

Of his early youth nothing can be gathered but
that he studied rhetoric " with surprising avidity
and a certain juvenile fervour "; his principal heroes
and instructors being Marcus Aper and Julius
Secundus, two of the characters in the *Dialogus de
Oratoribus*.[1] We have Pliny's testimony to his
mastery of the spoken word,[2] and throughout his
works, quite apart from the " Dialogue," his unabated
interest in the art is noticeable.[3]

The first certain date is 77 A.D., the consulate of
Cn. Julius Agricola; who was sufficiently impressed
by the character and prospects of the young Tacitus
to select him for the husband of his daughter, the
marriage taking place on the expiry of his term of

---

[1] *Dial.* 2.

[2] E.g., *Ep.* II. 11, 17, *respondit Cornelius Tacitus eloquen-
tissime et, quod eximium orationi eius inest, σεμνῶς*.

[3] For instance, in his scattered obituary notices of famous
orators.

INTRODUCTION

office (78 A.D.).[1]   Matters are less clear when we come
to his official career, which he describes as " owing
its inception to Vespasian, its promotion to Titus, and
its further advancement to Domitian." [2]   The question is whether the first step mentioned was the
quaestorship or a minor office, but the balance of
probability seems to be that he was *tribunus militum
laticlavius* under Vespasian, and quaestor under
Titus : [3] under Domitian, by his own statement, he
took part in the celebration of the Secular Games
(88 A.D.), in the double capacity of praetor and
quindecimvir.[4]   Between the quaestorship and the
praetorship, however, must have lain—still in the
principate of Domitian—either a tribunate or an
aedileship, which may be assigned roughly to 84 A.D.

Some two years after the praetorship, Tacitus
with his wife left Rome, and in 93 A.D., when Agricola
passed away—*felix opportunitate mortis*—they were
still absent. Service abroad is a natural explanation :
that the service consisted in the governorship of a
minor imperial province, a highly plausible conjecture.
In any case, the return to the capital followed shortly :
for the striking references to the three last and most
terrible years of Domitian are too clearly those of an
eye-witness. He emerged from the Terror with life,
also with the indelible memories of the few who " had
outlived both others and themselves." [5]   In the

---

[1] *Agr.* 9 fin.   [2] *Hist.* I. 1.
[3] A curious statement is made by Petrarch's friend Gugli-
elmo da Pastrengo, *de orig. rerum*, fol. 18 :—*Cornelius Tacitus,
quem Titus imperator suae praefecit bibliothecae, Augusti gesta
descripsit atque Domitiani* (Voigt, *Wiederbelebung d. class.
Altertums,* I. 249).
[4] *Ann.* XI. 11.   [5] *Agr.* 2–3.

happier age of Nerva and Trajan, all—or virtually all
—of his literary work was accomplished. His public
life was crowned by the consulate in 97 or 98 A.D.,[1]
when he pronounced the funeral panegyric on Verginius Rufus, who some thirty years before had
crushed Vindex and refused the throne proffered by
his legions. In 100 A.D. he conducted with Pliny
the prosecution of the extortionate governor of
Africa, Marius Priscus.[2] This constituted the last
recorded fact of his biography until it was revealed
by an inscription from the Carian town of Mylasa[3]
that he had attained the chief prize of the senatorial
career by holding the proconsulate of Asia (probably
between 113 and 116 A.D.). The year of his death is
unknown, but it is improbable that he long survived
the publication of the Annals in 116 A.D.

So much for the man : as to the author, little space
can be given here to the three minor works—the
Dialogus de Oratoribus, the *Agricola*, and the *Germania*.
The first of these ostensibly reproduces a conversation
held in the house of Curiatius Maternus in the sixth
year of Vespasian (74–75 A.D.), the discussion turning
on the relative merits of the republican and imperial
types of oratory : the author himself—described as
admodum adulescens—is assumed to be present. The
work, written in the neo-Ciceronian style, offers so
sharp a contrast to the later manner of Tacitus that
its authenticity was early called into question, first

[1] Plin. Ep. II. 1, 6. He was *consul suffectus*, and the year
depends on the question whether the senator, who had been
three times consul when Trajan refused a third consulate
(Plin. *Pan.* 58), was or was not Verginius Rufus.

[2] See Mayor on Juv. I. 49.

[3] Published in the *Bulletin de correspondance hellénique*, 1890.

INTRODUCTION

by Beatus Rhenanus, then by Justus Lipsius, with
the full weight of his great name. Only in 1811 were
the doubts dispelled by Lange's discovery that a
letter from Pliny to Tacitus alludes unmistakably to
the Dialogue.[1] The date of composition presents one
of those tempting, though ultimately insoluble
problems, which hold so great a fascination for many
scholars: the years proposed range from 81 A.D.
(Gudeman) to 98 A.D. (Schanz), with Norden's 91 A.D.
as a middle term.

For the fifteen years of Domitian historical composition had ranked as a dangerous trade,[2] but in
98 A.D., in the early days of Trajan, Tacitus broke
silence with the biography, or panegyric, of his
father-in-law, Agricola. Ample justice, to say the
least, is measured out to the virtues of the hero; and
since he was numbered with those who declined to
" challenge fame and fate " under Domitian,[3] the
light is naturally enough centred upon his administrative and military achievements in Britain. The
brilliant, though perhaps too highly coloured, style
shows already the influence of Sallust; and the work
is described by its author as the precursor of one
which " in artless and rough-hewn language shall
chronicle the slavery of the past and attest the felicity
of the present." [4]

But before this undertaking was at least partially
fulfilled, the *Agricola* was followed, still in 98 A.D., by

[1] Plin. *Ep.* IX. 10: *itaque poemata quiescunt, quae tu inter
nemora et lucos commodissime perfici putas,* as compared with
Dial. 9: *adice quod poetis . . . in nemora et lucos . . .
secedendum est* (also *ib.* 12: *nemora vero et luci e.q.s.*).
[2] *Agr.* 2; Suet. *Dom.* 10; D. Cass. LXVII. 13.
[3] *Agr.* 42. [4] *Agr.* 3.

the *Germania*, a monograph whose fate has been, in Gibbon's words, " to exercise the diligence of innumerable antiquarians, and to excite the genius and penetration of the philosophic historians of our own times." Its more immediate *raison d'être* is probably to be sought in the fact that the German question was, at the time, pressing enough to keep Trajan from the capital during the whole of the period between the death of Nerva and 99 A.D. Judged from the standpoint of the geographer and the ethnologist, the *Germania* must be pronounced guilty of most of the sins of omission and commission to be expected in a work published before the dawn of the second century; but the materials, written and verbal, at the disposal of the writer must have been considerable, and the book is of equal interest and value as the first extant study of early Teutonic society.

The foundation, however, on which the fame of Tacitus rests, is his history of the principate from the accession of Tiberius to the murder of Domitian. It falls into two halves, the *Annals* and the *Histories* (neither of which has descended to us intact), and the chronological order is reversed in the order of composition.[1] To follow the latter, the Histories— as the name, perhaps, indicates [2]—comprise a chronicle of the author's own time: they are, in fact, the redemption of the promise made in the Agricola; though the *incondita ac rudis vox* may be sought in

---

[1] The fact, obvious in itself, is explicitly stated in *Ann.* XI. 11.
[2] Gell. V. 18.—That *Historiae* was the author's title may be fairly inferred from Tertull. *Apol.* 16 : *Annales*, on the other hand, has no authority.

vain, and the period there announced for treatment is in part expanded, in part contracted. For the *praesentia bona*, the golden years of Nerva and Trajan, are now reserved by the writer to be the " theme of his age," [1] while the proposed account of Domitian's tyranny swells into the history, first, of the earthquake that upheaved and engulfed Galba, Otho, and Vitellius; then, of the three princes of the Flavian dynasty. Between what years the work was written, when it was published, and whether by instalments or as a whole, the evidence is as inadequate to determine as it is to resolve the endlessly debated question of the relationship between the narrative of Tacitus and that of Plutarch in the Lives of Galba and Otho.[2] Pliny, writing perhaps in 106 A.D., answers the request of his friend for details of the eruption of Vesuvius in 79 A.D.; [3] and elsewhere, on his own initiative, suggests for inclusion in the book an incident of the year 93 A.D.[4] The exact number of books into which the Histories were divided is not certain, but is more likely to have been twelve than fourteen: [5] the first four survive in entirety, together with twenty-six chapters of the fifth; the rest are known only by a few citations, chiefly from Orosius. The events embraced in the extant part are those of the twenty crowded months from January, 69 A.D., to August, 70 A.D.: we have lost, therefore, virtually the principate of Vespasian, that of Titus, and that of Domitian. The language is now completely " Tacitean."

---

[1] *Hist.* I. 1.

[2] The fullest English account (though supporting a thesis) is that in E. G. Hardy's edition of the *Lives* in question (*Introd.* ix-lx).

[3] *Ep.* VI. 16 and 20. [4] *Ep.* VII. 33. [5] See later.

INTRODUCTION

The Histories were followed in 116 A.D.[1] by the Annals (*libri ab excessu divi Augusti*); which, after a short introduction, open with the death of Augustus in 14 A.D., and closed in 68 A.D., not, however, at the dramatically appropriate date of Nero's suicide (June 8), but, in accordance with the annalistic scheme, at the year's end. The probable distribution of the books was hexadic, Tiberius claiming I–VI, Caligula and Claudius VII–XII, and Nero (with Galba) XIII–XVIII.[2] Of these there remain I–IV complete,

---

[1] Between the extension of the Empire to the Persian Gulf, under Trajan (115 A.D.), and the retrocession under Hadrian (117 A.D.).

[2] It is known from Jerome (*Comm. in Zach.* iii. 4 : *Cornelius Tacitus, qui post Augustum usque ad mortem Domitiani vitas Caesarum XXX voluminibus exaravit*) that the combined books of the Annals and Histories amounted to thirty. The manuscript tradition of the former breaks short rather less than half-way through the sixteenth book, which it is still usual to reckon as the last—fourteen books being thus assigned to the Histories. On this assumption, the last book as a whole contained the events of 65 A.D. in part and 66–68 A.D. in full; the lost portion (about fifty chapters at most), those of 66 A.D. in part and 67–68 A.D. in full. But it is beyond all question that, upon the scale observed in the surviving part of the book, fifty chapters are a totally inadequate allowance for the dramatic and momentous period still to be dealt with. Hence the probability of the symmetrical arrangement (Annals, 6 + 6 + 6; Histories, 6 + 6) advocated by Ritter, Hirschfeld, and Wölfflin. The objection, that even more than three and a half years have elsewhere been compressed by Tacitus into a single book, rests on the naïve assumption that to the historian all years are periods of twelve months apiece. Indeed, to be convinced of the untenability of the traditional view, a man has only to read XVI. 21–35, and then to reflect that the self-same pen has yet to record the insurrection in Judaea with the rise of Vespasian and Titus, the imperial tour in Greece, the execution of Corbulo, the rebellion of Vindex, the victory and great refusal of Verginius Rufus, the *pronunci-*

the first chapters of V, VI without the beginning,
and XI–XVI. 35. Thus our losses, though not so
disastrous as in the case of the Histories, include
none the less, about two years of Tiberius' reign, the
whole of that of Caligula, the earliest and best days
of Claudius, and the latter end of Nero. Fate might
perhaps have been blinder; yet posterity might well
renounce something of its knowledge of Corbulo's
operations, could it view in return the colouring of
two or three of those perished canvases—Sejanus
forlorn in the Senate, hope rising and falling with
every complex period of the interminable epistle
from Capreae—Cassius Chaerea, with his sword and
his *hoc age* in the vaulted corridor—Sporus, Epaphro-
ditus, and the last heir of the Julian blood, in the
villa at the fourth milestone. Still, what has been
spared—how narrowly spared may be read in Voigt—
constitutes, upon the whole, a clear title to immor-
tality: an amazing chronicle of an amazing era,
brilliant, unfair, and unforgettable. The Annals
are not as Galba was—*magis extra vitia quam cum
virtutibus*. But the virtues are virtues for all time;
the vices, those of an age. Exactitude, according to
Pindar, dwelt in the town of the Zephyrian Locrians,
but few of the ancients worshipped steadfastly at
her shrine: they wrote history as a form of literature,
and with an undissembled ambition to be read. It
would have been convenient, doubtless, had the
Annals been equipped with a preliminary dissertation

---

amiento of Galba, those scenes of Nero's fall and death which
fire even the frigid pages of Suetonius, the leisurely progress
of Galba's litter to the capital, the massacre of the marines,
and the gathering of the clouds in November and December,
68 A.D.

on the sources, a select bibliography, footnotes with
references to the roll of Aufidius Bassus or the month
and day of the Acta Publica: but the era of those
blessings is not reckoned *Ab Vrbe Condita*; and, with
rare exceptions, we must acquiesce in the vague
warranty of a *plerique tradidere* or a *sunt qui ferant*, or,
if here and there belief is difficult, then suspend our
judgment.   In the main, however, it is not the facts
of Tacitus, but his interpretations, that awaken mis-
giving.   " I know of no other historian," said a
latter-day consul and emperor, " who has so calumniated and belittled mankind as he.   In the simplest
transactions he seeks for criminal motives: out of
every emperor he fashions a complete villain, and
so depicts him that we admire the spirit of evil
permeating him, and nothing more.   It has been said
with justice that his Annals are a history, not of the
Empire, but of the Roman criminal tribunals—
nothing save accusations and men accused, persecu-
tions and the persecuted, and people opening veins in
baths.   He speaks continually of denunciations, and
the greatest denouncer is himself." [1]   That a streak
of truth runs through the wild exaggerations can
hardly be denied.   Tacitus had not, and could not
have, a charity that thinks no evil: Seneca, in words

[1] Schanz cites the passage in German (from Fröhlich's
Napoleon I, und seine Beziehungen zum klassischen Altertum,
1882), and I am unable to refer to the French.—It may be
noted in passing, however, that in this case, too, the uncle's
views were piously adopted by the nephew : for during his
imprisonment at Ham, the future Napoleon III, " speaking
low " (to Louis Blanc) " lest the wind should carry the words
to the gaoler," took the part of the " tyrants branded on the
shoulders for ever by Tacitus."   See Simpson, *Rise of Louis-
Napoleon,* p. 218.

prophetic of his style, spoke of *abruptae sententiae et supiciosae, in quibus plus intelligendum est quam audiendum*; and never, perhaps, has that poisoned weapon been used more ruthlessly. Yet, of conscious disingenuity a dispassionate reader finds no trace: the man, simply, has overpowered the historian. To write *sine ira et studio* even of the earlier principate, was a rash vow to be made by one who had passed his childhood under Nero and the flower of his manhood under Domitian. Nor, in any case, is it given to many historians—to none, perhaps, of the greatest—to comply with the precept of Lucian (repeated almost to the letter by Ranke):—Τοῦ συγγραφέως ἔργον ἕν, ὡς ἐπράχθη εἰπεῖν. For not the most stubborn of facts can pass through the brain of a man of genius, and issue such as they entered.—One charge, it is noticeable, Napoleon does not make: it was reserved for Mommsen to style Tacitus " the most unmilitary of historians "—a verdict to which Furneaux could only object that it was unjust to Livy. Both, it is true enough, lack the martial touch, and betray all too clearly that βυβλιακὴ ἕξις which Polybius abhorred. Yet even here they have one merit, generally withheld from the authentic military historian, that, when they describe a battle, the reader is somehow conscious that a battle is being described. *Mox infensius praetorianis " Vos " inquit, " nisi vincitis, pagani, quis alius imperator, quae castra alia excipient? Illic signa armaque vestra sunt, et mors victis: nam ignominiam consumpsistis." Vndique clamor, et orientem solem (ita in Syria mos est) tertiani salutavere*—the hues are not the wear, but it is possible to find them striking.

It is usual to enumerate a few of the peculiarities

of Tacitus and his diction: on the one hand, for example, his trend to fatalism, his disdain of the multitude, his Platonic affection for the commonwealth, his Roman ethics, and his pessimism; on the other, his brachylogy, his poetical and rhetorical effects, his dislike of the common speech of men, his readiness to tax to the uttermost every resource of Latin in the cause of antithesis or innuendo. Here no such catalogue can be attempted; nor, if it could, would the utility be wholly beyond dispute. The personality of the author and his style must be felt as unities; and it is a testimony to the greatness of both that they can so be felt after the lapse of eighteen centuries. How long they will continue to be felt, one must at whiles wonder. There was a time when, as Victor Hugo sang of another Empire,

" *On se mit à fouiller dans ces grandes années,*
  Et vous applaudissiez, nations inclinées,
  Chaque fois qu'on tirait de ce sol souverain
  Ou le consul de marbre ou l'empereur d'airain."

That fervour of the pioneers is no more; the sovereign soil has rendered up its more glittering treasures, and the labourers, and their rewards, are already fewer. Yet, so long as Europe retains the consciousness of her origins, so long—by some at least —must the history of Rome be read in the Roman tongue, and not the least momentous part of it in the pages of Tacitus.

The text of the first six books of the Annals depends entirely on the *Mediceus primus* (*saec.* IX); for the remainder, the authority is the *Mediceus*

secundus (*saec.* XI); both are now in the Laurentian Library. For the details of their discovery the reader may be referred to Voigt (*Wiederbelebung u.s.w.* I. p. 249 sqq.). The text of this edition is eclectic. In the first book the variations from the manuscript are recorded with some fulness; afterwards, in order to economize space, obvious and undisputed corrections, especially of the older scholars, are seldom noticed.

STEMMA OF THE JULIO-CLAUDIAN FAMILY

A

C. Iulius Caesar = Aurelia

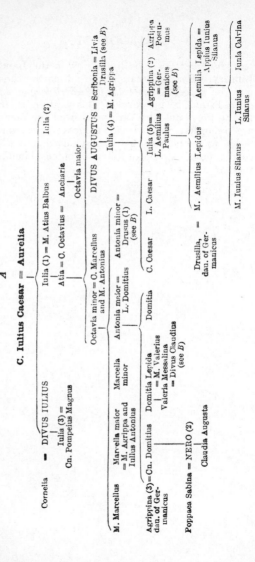

B

Divus Augustus = Livia Drusilla = Tib. Claudius Nero

(Tib. iv. 3)

Agrippina* (1) = TIBERIUS

Livilla = Drusus (2)

Tiberius

Iulia (6) = Nero (1)
and G. Rubellius
Blandus

Rubellius Plautus

Agrippina (2) = Germanicus

Nero (1) = Iulia (6)

Drusus = Aemilia Lepida

C. CAESAR CALIGULA

Agrippina (3) = Cn. Domitius

NERO (2)

Drusilla = L. Cassius Longinus and
M. Aemilius Lepidus

Iulia Livilla = M. Vinicius

Drusus (1) = Antonia minor

DIVUS CLAUDIUS

Livilla
= Drusus (2)

* Vipsania Agrippina, daughter of M. Agrippa
by his first wife Pomponia: divorced by Tiberius at
the order of Augustus, who desired him to marry
Julia.

AB EXCESSU DIVI AUGUSTI

P. CORNELII TACITI

LIBER I

I. Vrbem Romam a principio reges habuere:
libertatem et consulatum L. Brutus instituit. Dic-
taturae ad tempus sumebantur; neque decemviralis
potestas ultra biennium, neque tribunorum militum consulare ius diu valuit. Non Cinnae, non Sullae
longa dominatio; et Pompei Crassique potentia
cito in Caesarem, Lepidi atque Antonii arma in
Augustum cessere, qui cuncta discordiis civilibus
fessa nomine principis sub imperium accepit. Sed
veteris populi Romani prospera vel adversa claris
scriptoribus memorata sunt; temporibusque Augusti dicendis non defuere decora ingenia, donec
gliscente adulatione deterrerentur. Tiberii Gaique
et Claudii ac Neronis res florentibus ipsis ob metum

---

[1] This rendering is generally so convenient as to be inevitable, but the English reader should be careful to strip the
word of its monarchical connotation.

[2] The principal dates for the opening sentences are :—
B.C. 753 Foundation of Rome ; 509 Consulate of L. Brutus;
451–450 (with part of 449) Decemvirate ; 445 Institution of
Tribuni militum consulari potestate (found with little inter-
ruption from 408 to 367) ; 87–84 Four Consulates of Cinna ;

THE ANNALS OF
TACITUS

BOOK I

I. ROME at the outset was a city state under the government of kings : liberty and the consulate were institutions of Lucius Brutus. Dictatorships were always a temporary expedient: the decemviral office was dead within two years, nor was the consular authority of the military tribunes long-lived. Neither Cinna nor Sulla created a lasting despotism : Pompey and Crassus quickly forfeited their power to Caesar, and Lepidus and Antony their swords to Augustus. who, under the style of " Prince,"[1] gathered beneath his empire a world outworn by civil broils.[2] But, while the glories and disasters of the old Roman commonwealth have been chronicled by famous pens, and intellects of distinction were not lacking to tell the tale of the Augustan age, until the rising tide of sycophancy deterred them, the histories of Tiberius and Caligula, of Claudius and Nero, were falsified

82–79 Dictatorship of Sulla ; 53 Battle of Carrhae and death of Crassus ; 48 Battle of Pharsalia and death of Pompey (in Egypt) ; 36 Lepidus divested of his powers by Octavian ; 31 Defeat of Antony at Actium ; 27 Octavian receives the title of Augustus.

falsae, postquam occiderant recentibus odiis compositae sunt. Inde consilium mihi pauca de Augusto et extrema tradere, mox Tiberii principatum et cetera, sine ira et studio, quorum causas procul habeo.

II. Postquam Bruto et Cassio caesis nulla iam publica arma, Pompeius apud Siciliam oppressus, exutoque Lepido, interfecto Antonio, ne Iulianis quidem partibus nisi Caesar dux reliquus, posito triumviri nomine, consulem se ferens et ad tuendam plebem tribunicio iure contentum, ubi militem donis, populum annona, cunctos dulcedine otii pellexit, insurgere paulatim, munia senatus, magistratuum, legum in se trahere, nullo adversante, cum ferocissimi per acies aut proscriptione cecidissent, ceteri nobilium, quanto quis servitio promptior, opibus et honoribus extollerentur ac novis ex rebus aucti, tuta et praesentia quam vetera et periculosa mallent. Neque provinciae illum rerum statum abnuebant, suspecto senatus populique imperio ob certamina potentium et avaritiam magistratuum, invalido legum auxilio, quae vi, ambitu, postremo pecunia turbabantur.

III. Ceterum Augustus subsidia dominationi Claudium Marcellum, sororis filium, admodum adu-

---

[1] Sextus Pompeius, defeated by Agrippa off Pelorum (*C. di Faro*) in 36 B.C.
[2] For this and the other names in the chapter see the table on p. 240.

through cowardice while they flourished, and composed, when they fell, under the influence of still rankling hatreds. Hence my design, to treat a small part (the concluding one) of Augustus' reign, then the principate of Tiberius and its sequel, without anger and without partiality, from the motives of which I stand sufficiently removed.

II. When the killing of Brutus and Cassius had disarmed the Republic; when Pompey had been crushed in Sicily,[1] and, with Lepidus thrown aside and Antony slain, even the Julian party was leaderless but for the Caesar; after laying down his triumviral title and proclaiming himself a simple consul content with tribunician authority to safeguard the commons, he first conciliated the army by gratuities, the populace by cheapened corn, the world by the amenities of peace, then step by step began to make his ascent and to unite in his own person the functions of the senate, the magistracy, and the legislature. Opposition there was none: the boldest spirits had succumbed on stricken fields or by proscription-lists; while the rest of the nobility found a cheerful acceptance of slavery the smoothest road to wealth and office, and, as they had thriven on revolution, stood now for the new order and safety in preference to the old order and adventure. Nor was the state of affairs unpopular in the provinces, where administration by the Senate and People had been discredited by the feuds of the magnates and the greed of the officials, against which there was but frail protection in a legal system for ever deranged by force, by favouritism, or (in the last resort) by gold.

III. Meanwhile, to consolidate his power, Augustus raised Claudius Marcellus,[2] his sister's son and a mere

lescentem pontificatu et curuli aedilitate, M. Agrippam, ignobilem loco, bonum militia et victoriae
socium, geminatis consulatibus extulit, mox defuncto Marcello generum sumpsit; Tiberium Neronem
et Claudium Drusum privignos imperatoriis nominibus auxit, integra etiam tum [1] domo sua. Nam
genitos Agrippa Gaium ac Lucium in familiam Caesarum induxerat, necdum posita puerili praetexta
principes iuventutis appellari, destinari [2] consules
specie recusantis flagrantissime cupiverat. Vt Agrippa vita concessit, Lucium Caesarem euntem ad His-
paniensis exercitus, Gaium remeantem Armenia
et vulnere invalidum mors fato propera vel nover-
cae Liviae dolus abstulit, Drusoque pridem exstincto,
Nero solus e privignis erat, illuc cuncta vergere:
filius, collega imperii, consors tribuniciae potestatis adsumitur omnisque per exercitus ostentatur,
non obscuris, ut antea, matris artibus, sed palam
hortatu. Nam senem Augustum devinxerat adeo,
uti nepotem unicum, Agrippam Postumum, in
insulam Planasiam proiecerit,[3] rudem sane bonarum
artium et robore corporis stolide ferocem, nullius
tamen flagitii conpertum. At hercule Germanicum.
Druso ortum, octo apud Rhenum legionibus inposuit
adscirique per adoptionem a Tiberio iussit, quamquam esset in domo Tiberii filius iuvenis, sed quo
pluribus munimentis [4] insisteret. Bellum ea tem-

---

[1] tum *Wolf*: dum.
[2] destinari *Acidalius*: destinare.
[3] proiecerit *Ritter*: proieceret.
[4] munimentis *Lipsius*: monimentis.

---

[1] Now Pianosa, pretty nearly midway between Corsica and
the coast of Tuscany.

stripling, to the pontificate and curule aedileship:
Marcus Agrippa, no aristocrat, but a good soldier
and his partner in victory, he honoured with two
successive consulates, and a little later, on the death
of Marcellus, selected him as a son-in-law. Each of
his step-children, Tiberius Nero and Claudius Drusus,
was given the title of Imperator, though his family
proper was still intact: for he had admitted Agrippa's
children, Gaius and Lucius, to the Caesarian hearth,
and even during their minority had shown, under a
veil of reluctance, a consuming desire to see them
consuls designate with the title Princes of the
Youth. When Agrippa gave up the ghost, untimely
fate, or the treachery of their stepmother Livia, cut
off both Lucius and Gaius Caesar, Lucius on his road
to the Spanish armies, Gaius—wounded and sick—
on his return from Armenia. Drusus had long been
dead, and of the stepsons Nero survived alone. On
him all centred. Adopted as son, as colleague in the
empire, as consort of the tribunician power, he was
paraded through all the armies, not as before by the
secret diplomacy of his mother, but openly at her
injunction. For so firmly had she riveted her chains
upon the aged Augustus that he banished to the isle
of Planasia[1] his one remaining grandson, Agrippa
Postumus, who, though guiltless of a virtue, and
confident brute-like in his physical strength, had been
convicted of no open scandal. Yet, curiously
enough, he placed Drusus' son Germanicus at the
head of eight legions on the Rhine, and ordered
Tiberius to adopt him: it was one safeguard the
more, even though Tiberius had already an adult son
under his roof.

War at the time was none, except an outstanding

pestate nullum nisi adversus Germanos supererat, abolendae magis infamiae ob amissum cum Quintilio Varo exercitum quam cupidine proferendi imperii aut dignum ob praemium. Domi res tranquillae, eadem magistratuum vocabula; iuniores post Actiacam victoriam, etiam senes plerique inter bella civium nati: quotus quisque reliquus, qui rem publicam vidisset?

IV. Igitur verso civitatis statu nihil usquam prisci et integri moris: omnes, exuta aequalitate, iussa principis aspectare, nulla in praesens formidine, dum Augustus aetate validus seque et domum et pacem sustentavit. Postquam provecta iam senectus aegro et corpore fatigabatur aderatque finis et spes novae, pauci bona libertatis in cassum disserere, plures bellum pavescere, alii cupere. Pars multo maxima imminentis dominos variis rumoribus differebant: trucem Agrippam et ignominia accensum, non aetate neque rerum experientia tantae moli parem; Tiberium Neronem maturum annis, spectatum bello, sed vetere atque insita Claudiae familiae superbia; multaque indicia saevitiae, quamquam premantur, erumpere. Hunc et prima ab infantia eductum in domo regnatrice; congestos iuveni consulatus, triumphos; ne iis quidem annis quibus Rhodi specie secessus exul[1] egerit aliud[2] quam iram et simulationem et secretas lubidines meditatum. Accedere matrem muliebri inpotentia:

[1] exul *Muretus* : exulem.
[2] aliud *Nipperdey* : aliquid.

[1] Husband of a great-niece of Augustus, destroyed, with three legions (XVII–XIX), by Arminius in the forests of Westphalia (9 A.D.).

campaign against the Germans, waged more to redeem the prestige lost with Quintilius Varus[1] and his army than from any wish to extend the empire or with any prospect of an adequate recompense. At home all was calm. The officials carried the old names; the younger men had been born after the victory of Actium; most even of the elder generation, during the civil wars; few indeed were left who had seen the Republic.

IV. It was thus an altered world, and of the old, unspoilt Roman character not a trace lingered. Equality was an outworn creed, and all eyes looked to the mandate of the sovereign—with no immediate misgivings, so long as Augustus in the full vigour of his prime upheld himself, his house, and peace. But when the wearing effects of bodily sickness added themselves to advancing years, and the end was coming and new hopes dawning, a few voices began idly to discuss the blessings of freedom; more were apprehensive of war; others desired it; the great majority merely exchanged gossip derogatory to their future masters:—"Agrippa, fierce-tempered, and hot from his humiliation, was unfitted by age and experience for so heavy a burden. Tiberius Nero was mature in years and tried in war, but had the old, inbred arrogance of the Claudian family, and hints of cruelty, strive as he would to repress them, kept breaking out. He had been reared from the cradle in a regnant house; consulates and triumphs had been heaped on his youthful head: even during the years when he lived at Rhodes in ostensible retirement and actual exile, he had studied nothing save anger, hypocrisy, and secret lasciviousness. Add to the tale his mother with her feminine

serviendum feminae duobusque insuper adulescentibus qui rem publicam interim premant quandoque distrahant.

V. Haec atque talia agitantibus gravescere valetudo Augusti et quidam scelus uxoris suspectabant. Quippe rumor incesserat paucos ante mensis Augustum, electis consciis et comite uno Fabio Maximo, Planasiam vectum ad visendum Agrippam; multas illic utrimque lacrimas et signa caritatis spemque ex eo fore ut iuvenis penatibus avi redderetur: quod Maximum uxori Marciae aperuisse, illam Liviae. Gnarum[1] id Caesari; neque multo post extincto Maximo, dubium an quaesita morte, auditos in funere eius Marciae gemitus semet incusantis quod causa exitii marito fuisset. Vtcumque se ea res habuit, vixdum ingressus Illyricum Tiberius properis matris litteris accitur; neque satis conpertum est, spirantem adhuc Augustum apud urbem Nolam an exanimem reppererit. Acribus namque custodiis domum et vias saepserat Livia, laetique interdum nuntii vulgabantur, donec provisis quae tempus monebat simul excessisse Augustum et rerum potiri Neronem fama eadem tulit.

VI. Primum facinus novi principatus fuit Postumi Agrippae caedes, quem ignarum inermumque

---

[1] gnarum *Lipsius* : gnavum (*primitus* cnavum).

---

[1] August 19, 14 A.D.

caprice: they must be slaves, it appeared, to the distaff, and to a pair of striplings as well, who in the interval would oppress the state and in the upshot rend it asunder!"

V. While these topics and the like were under discussion, the malady of Augustus began to take a graver turn; and some suspected foul play on the part of his wife. For a rumour had gone the round that, a few months earlier, the emperor, confiding in a chosen few, and attended only by Fabius Maximus, had sailed for Planasia on a visit to Agrippa. "There tears and signs of affection on both sides had been plentiful enough to raise a hope that the youth might yet be restored to the house of his grandfather. Maximus had disclosed the incident to his wife Marcia; Marcia, to Livia. It had come to the Caesar's knowledge; and after the death of Maximus, which followed shortly, possibly by his own hand, Marcia had been heard at the funeral, sobbing and reproaching herself as the cause of her husband's destruction." Whatever the truth of the affair, Tiberius had hardly set foot in Illyricum, when he was recalled by an urgent letter from his mother; and it is not certainly known whether on reaching the town of Nola, he found Augustus still breathing or lifeless. For house and street were jealously guarded by Livia's ring of pickets, while sanguine notices were issued at intervals, until the measures dictated by the crisis had been taken: then one report announced simultaneously that Augustus had passed away and that Nero was master of the empire.[1]

VI. The opening crime of the new principate was the murder of Agrippa Postumus; who, though off his guard and without weapons, was with difficulty dis-

quamvis firmatus animo centurio aegre confecit. Nihil de ea re [1] Tiberius apud senatum disseruit: patris iussa simulabat, quibus praescripsisset tribuno custodiae adposito ne cunctaretur Agrippam morte adficere quandoque ipse supremum diem explevisset. Multa sine dubio saevaque Augustus de moribus adulescentis questus, ut exilium eius senatus consulto sanciretur, perfecerat; ceterum in nullius umquam suorum necem duravit, neque mortem nepoti pro securitate privigni inlatam credibile erat. Propius vero Tiberium ac Liviam, illum metu, hanc novercalibus odiis, suspecti et invisi iuvenis caedem festinavisse. Nuntianti centurioni, ut mos militiae, factum esse quod imperasset, neque imperasse sese et rationem facti reddendam apud senatum respondit. Quod postquam Sallustius Crispus particeps secretorum (is ad tribunum miserat codicillos) comperit, metuens ne reus subderetur, iuxta periculoso ficta seu vera promeret, monuit Liviam ne arcana domus, ne consilia amicorum, ministeria militum vulgarentur, neve Tiberius vim principatus resolveret cuncta ad senatum vocando: eam condicionem esse imperandi, ut non aliter ratio constet quam si uni reddatur.

VII. At Romae ruere in servitium consules,

[1] ea re *Beroaldus* : aere.

---

[1] See the sketch of him in III. 30.
[2] "Weil vieles geschehen muss, was nur der, zu dessen Vorteil es geschieht, billigen kann" (Nipperdey). The verbal point of Crispus' apophthegm lies in the double sense of *rationem reddere* (see just above).

patched by a resolute centurion. In the senate
Tiberius made no reference to the subject: his pretence was an order from his father, instructing the
tribune in charge to lose no time in making away with
his prisoner, once he himself should have looked his
last on the world. It was beyond question that by
his frequent and bitter strictures on the youth's
character Augustus had procured the senatorial
decree for his exile: on the other hand, at no time
did he harden his heart to the killing of a relative, and
it remained incredible that he should have sacrificed
the life of a grandchild in order to diminish the
anxieties of a stepson. More probably, Tiberius
and Livia, actuated in the one case by fear, and in
the other by stepmotherly dislike, hurriedly procured
the murder of a youth whom they suspected and
detested. To the centurion who brought the usual
military report, that his instructions had been
carried out, the emperor rejoined that he had given
no instructions and the deed would have to be
accounted for in the senate. The remark came to
the ears of Sallustius Crispus.[1] A partner in the
imperial secrets—it was he who had forwarded the
note to the tribune—he feared the charge might be
fastened on himself, with the risks equally great
whether he spoke the truth or lied. He therefore
advised Livia not to publish the mysteries of the
palace, the counsels of her friends, the services of the
soldiery; and also to watch that Tiberius did not
weaken the powers of the throne by referring everything and all things to the senate:—" It was a condition of sovereignty that the account balanced only
if rendered to a single auditor."[2]

VII. At Rome, however, consuls, senators, and

patres, eques. Quanto quis inlustrior, tanto magis falsi ac festinantes, vultuque composito, ne laeti excessu principis neu tristiores[1] primordio, lacrimas, gaudium, questus, adulationem[2] miscebant. Sex. Pompeius et Sex. Appuleius consules primi in verba Tiberii Caesaris iuravere, apudque eos Seius Strabo et C. Turranius, ille praetoriarum cohortium praefectus, hic annonae; mox senatus milesque et populus. Nam Tiberius cuncta per consules incipiebat, tamquam vetere re publica et ambiguus imperandi: ne edictum quidem, quo patres in curiam vocabat, nisi tribuniciae potestatis praescriptione posuit sub Augusto acceptae. Verba edicti fuere pauca et sensu permodesto: de honoribus parentis consulturum, neque abscedere a corpore, idque unum ex publicis muneribus usurpare. Sed, defuncto Augusto, signum praetoriis cohortibus ut imperator dederat; excubiae, arma, cetera aulae; miles in forum, miles in curiam comitabatur. Litteras ad exercitus tamquam adepto principatu misit, nusquam cunctabundus nisi cum in senatu loqueretur. Causa praecipua ex formidine, ne Germanicus, in cuius manu tot legiones, immensa sociorum auxilia, mirus apud populum favor, habere imperium quam exspectare

---

[1] tristiores *Beroaldus* : tristior.
[2] adulationem *Heinsius* : adulatione.

knights were rushing into slavery. The more exalted the personage, the grosser his hypocrisy and his haste,—his lineaments adjusted so as to betray neither cheerfulness at the exit nor undue depression at the entry of a prince; his tears blent with joy, his regrets with adulation. The consuls, Sextus Pompeius and Sextus Appuleius, first took the oath of allegiance to Tiberius Caesar. It was taken in their presence by Seius Strabo and Caius Turranius, chiefs respectively of the praetorian cohorts and the corn department. The senators, the soldiers, and the populace followed. For in every action of Tiberius the first step had to be taken by the consuls, as though the old republic were in being, and himself undecided whether to reign or no. Even his edict, convening the Fathers to the senate-house was issued simply beneath the tribunician title which he had received under Augustus. It was a laconic document of very modest purport:—" He intended to provide for the last honours to his father, whose body he could not leave—it was the one function of the state which he made bold to exercise." Yet, on the passing of Augustus he had given the watchword to the praetorian cohorts as Imperator; he had the sentries, the men-at-arms, and the other appurtenances of a court; soldiers conducted him to the forum, soldiers to the curia; he dispatched letters to the armies as if the principate was already in his grasp; and nowhere manifested the least hesitation, except when speaking in the senate. The chief reason was his fear that Germanicus—backed by so many legions, the vast reserves of the provinces, and a wonderful popularity with the nation—might prefer the ownership to the reversion of a throne.

mallet. Dabat et famae, ut vocatus electusque potius a re publica videretur quam per uxorium ambitum et senili adoptione inrepsisse. Postea cognitum est ad introspiciendas etiam procerum voluntates indutam [1] dubitationem: nam verba, vultus in crimen detorquens recondebat.

VIII. Nihil primo senatus die agi passus est [2] nisi de supremis Augusti, cuius testamentum inlatum per virgines Vestae Tiberium et Liviam heredes habuit. Livia in familiam Iuliam nomenque Augustum adsumebatur; in spem secundam nepotes pronepotesque, tertio gradu primores civitatis scripserat, plerosque invisos sibi, sed iactantia gloriaque ad posteros. Legata non ultra civilem modum, nisi quod populo et plebi quadringenties tricies quinquies, praetoriarum cohortium militibus singula nummum milia, urbanis quingenos,[3] legionariis aut cohortibus civium Romanorum trecenos nummos viritim dedit. Tum consultatum de honoribus; ex quis qui [4] maxime insignes visi, ut porta triumphali duceretur funus Gallus Asinius, ut legum latarum tituli, victarum ab eo gentium vocabula anteferrentur, L. Arruntius censuere. Addebat Messala Valerius renovandum per annos sacramentum in

----

[1] indutam *J. F. Gronovius* : inductam.
[2] passus est *Nipperdey* : passus.
[3] urbanis quingenos *Sauppe* : om.
[4] quis qui *Bezzenberger* : quis.

----

[1] Cohorts (normally of Italian volunteers—*ingenuorum, voluntariorum*) attached to no particular legion, but otherwise on a parity with the legionaries. Over thirty of them have been traced in the imperial age.

He paid public opinion, too, the compliment of wishing to be regarded as the called and chosen of the state, rather than as the interloper who had wormed his way to power with the help of connubial intrigues and a senile act of adoption. It was realized later that his coyness had been assumed with the further object of gaining an insight into the feelings of the aristocracy : for all the while he was distorting words and looks into crimes and storing them in his memory.

VIII. The only business which he allowed to be discussed at the first meeting of the senate was the funeral of Augustus. The will, brought in by the Vestal Virgins, specified Tiberius and Livia as heirs, Livia to be adopted into the Julian family and the Augustan name. As legatees in the second degree he mentioned his grandchildren and great-grandchildren ; in the third place, the prominent nobles— an ostentatious bid for the applause of posterity, as he detested most of them. His bequests were not above the ordinary civic scale, except that he left 43,500,000 sesterces to the nation and the populace, a thousand to every man in the praetorian guards, five hundred to each in the urban troops, and three hundred to all legionaries or members of the Roman cohorts.[1]

The question of the last honours was then debated. The two regarded as the most striking were due to Asinius Gallus and Lucius Arruntius— the former proposing that the funeral train should pass under a triumphal gateway ; the latter, that the dead should be preceded by the titles of all laws which he had carried and the names of all peoples whom he had subdued. In addition, Valerius Messalla suggested that the oath of allegiance to

nomen Tiberii; interrogatusque a Tiberio num se
mandante eam sententiam prompsisset, sponte
dixisse respondit, neque in iis quae ad rem publicam pertinerent consilio nisi suo usurum, vel cum
periculo offensionis: ea sola species adulandi supererat. Conclamant patres corpus ad rogum umeris
senatorum ferendum. Remisit Caesar adroganti
moderatione, populumque edicto monuit ne, ut
quondam nimiis studiis funus divi Iulii turbassent,
ita Augustum in foro potius quam in campo Martis,
sede destinata, cremari vellent. Die funeris milites
velut praesidio stetere, multum inridentibus qui
ipsi viderant quique a parentibus acceperant diem
illum crudi adhuc servitii et libertatis inprospere
repetitae,[1] cum occisus dictator Caesar aliis pes-
simum, aliis pulcherrimum facinus videretur: nunc
senem principem, longa potentia, provisis etiam
heredum in rem publicam opibus, auxilio scilicet
militari tuendum, ut sepultura eius quieta foret.

IX. Multus hinc ipso de Augusto sermo, plerisque vana mirantibus quod idem dies accepti
quondam imperii princeps et vitae supremus, quod
Nolae in domo et cubiculo in quo pater eius Octavius vitam finivisset. Numerus etiam consulatuum
celebrabatur, quo Valerium Corvum et C. Marium

---

[1] inprospere repetitae *Lipsius*: inprospera repetita.

---

[1] The Mausoleum. which he had built in his sixth consulate
(28 B.C.) in the northern part of the Campus Martius, between
the Flaminian Road and the Tiber.

Tiberius should be renewed annually. To a query from Tiberius, whether that expression of opinion came at *his* dictation, he retorted—it was the one form of flattery still left—that he had spoken of his own accord, and, when public interests were in question, he would (even at the risk of giving offence) use no man's judgment but his own. The senate clamoured for the body to be carried to the pyre on the shoulders of the Fathers. The Caesar, with haughty moderation, excused them from that duty, and warned the people by edict not to repeat the enthusiastic excesses which on a former day had marred the funeral of the deified Julius, by desiring Augustus to be cremated in the Forum rather than in the Field of Mars, his appointed resting-place.[1]

On the day of the ceremony, the troops were drawn up as though on guard, amid the jeers of those who had seen with their eyes, or whose fathers had declared to them, that day of still novel servitude and freedom disastrously re-wooed, when the killing of the dictator Caesar to some had seemed the worst, and to others the fairest, of high exploits:—" And now an aged prince, a veteran potentate, who had seen to it that not even his heirs should lack for means to coerce their country, must needs have military protection to ensure a peaceable burial!"

IX. Then tongues became busy with Augustus himself. Most men were struck by trivial points— that one day should have been the first of his sovereignty and the last of his life—that he should have ended his days at Nola in the same house and room as his father Octavius. Much, too, was said of the number of his consulates (in which he had equalled the combined totals of Valerius Corvus and Caius

simul aequaverat; continuata per septem et triginta annos tribunicia potestas, nomen imperatoris
semel atque vicies partum aliaque honorum multiplicata aut nova. At apud prudentis vita eius varie
extollebatur arguebaturve. Hi pietate erga parentem et necessitudine rei publicae, in qua nullus tunc
legibus locus, ad arma civilia actum, quae neque
parari possent neque haberi per bonas artis. Multa
Antonio, dum[1] interfectores patris ulcisceretur,[2]
multa Lepido concessisse. Postquam hic socordia
senuerit, ille per libidines pessum datus sit, non aliud
discordantis patriae remedium fuisse quam ut ab[3]
uno regeretur. Non regno tamen neque dictatura,
sed principis nomine constitutam rem publicam; mari
Oceano aut amnibus longinquis saeptum imperium;
legiones, provincias, classis, cuncta inter se conexa;
ius apud civis, modestiam apud socios; urbem ipsam magnifico ornatu; pauca admodum vi tractata
quo ceteris quies esset.

X. Dicebatur contra: pietatem erga parentem
et tempora rei publicae obtentui sumpta; ceterum cupidine dominandi concitos per largitionem
veteranos, paratum ab adulescente privato exercitum, corruptas consulis legiones, simulatam Pompeianarum gratiam partium; mox ubi decreto
patrum fascis et ius praetoris invaserit, caesis Hirtio

---

[1] dum *Muretus* : tunc.
[2] ulcisceretur *Beroaldus* : ulciscerentur.
[3] quam ut *Ferretti* : quam.

---

[1] Thirteen (= 6 + 7).   [2] Of Antony (44 B.C.).

Marius),[1] his tribunician power unbroken for thirty-seven years, his title of Imperator twenty-one times earned, and his other honours, multiplied or new. Among men of intelligence, however, his career was praised or arraigned from varying points of view. According to some, " filial duty and the needs of a country, which at the time had no room for law, had driven him to the weapons of civil strife—weapons which could not be either forged or wielded with clean hands. He had overlooked much in Antony, much in Lepidus, for the sake of bringing to book the assassins of his father. When Lepidus grew old and indolent, and Antony succumbed to his vices, the sole remedy for his distracted country was government by one man. Yet he organized the state, not by instituting a monarchy or a dictatorship, but by creating the title of First Citizen. The empire had been fenced by the ocean or distant rivers. The legions, the provinces, the fleets, the whole administration, had been centralized. There had been law for the Roman citizen, respect for the allied communities; and the capital itself had been embellished with remarkable splendour. Very few situations had been treated by force, and then only in the interests of general tranquillity."

X. On the other side it was argued that " filial duty and the critical position of the state had been used merely as a cloak: come to facts, and it was from the lust of dominion that he excited the veterans by his bounties, levied an army while yet a stripling and a subject, seduced the legions of a consul,[2] and affected a leaning to the Pompeian side. Then, following his usurpation by senatorial decree of the symbols and powers of the praetorship, had come the

et Pansa, sive hostis illos, seu Pansam venenum
vulneri adfusum, sui milites Hirtium et machina-
tor doli Caesar abstulerat, utriusque copias occupa-
visse; extortum invito senatu consulatum, armaque
quae in Antonium acceperit contra rem publicam
versa; proscriptionem civium, divisiones agrorum
ne ipsis quidem qui fecere laudatas. Sane Cassii
et Brutorum exitus paternis inimicitiis datos, quamquam fas sit privata odia publicis utilitatibus remittere: sed Pompeium imagine pacis, sed Lepidum
specie amicitiae deceptos; post Antonium, Taren-
tino Brundisinoque foedere et nuptiis sororis inlectum, subdolae adfinitatis poenas morte exsolvisse.
Pacem sine dubio post haec, verum cruentam:
Lollianas Varianasque cladis, interfectos Romae
Varrones, Egnatios, Iullos.[1] Nec domesticis abs-
tinebatur: abducta Neroni uxor et consulti per
ludibrium pontifices an concepto necdum edito
partu rite nuberet; Vedii [2] Pollionis luxus; postremo Livia gravis [3] in rem publicam mater, gravis

[1] Iullos *Andresen (post Lipsium, ut alibi)*: Iulios.
[2] Vedii *Mommsen*: que tedii et Vedii.
[3] gravis *Beroaldus*: gravius.

---

[1] Mutina (44 B.C.). "The rumour gained currency that
both had perished by his agency; so that with Antony in
flight and the commonwealth bereft of its consuls, he might
as sole victor seize the command of three armies" (Suet.
Aug. 11).
[2] To the soldiery: see Virg. *Ecl.* I. IX.
[3] The treaty of Misenum between Octavian, Antony, and
Sextus Pompeius (39 B.C.); not kept, and followed next year
by war.
[4] Brundisian treaty (practically dividing the Roman world
between Octavian and Antony), 40 B.C.: Tarentine, 37 B.C.

deaths of Hirtius and Pansa,[1]—whether they perished
by the enemy's sword, or Pansa by posion sprinkled
on his wound, and Hirtius by the hands of this own
soldiery, with the Caesar to plan the treason.   At all
events, he had possessed himself of both their
armies, wrung a consulate from the unwilling senate,
and turned against the commonwealth the arms
which he had received for the quelling of Antony.
The proscription of citizens and the assignments of
land [2] had been approved not even by those who
executed them. Grant that Cassius and the Bruti were
sacrificed to inherited enmities—though the moral
law required that private hatreds should give way
to public utility—yet Pompey was betrayed by the
simulacrum of a peace,[3] Lepidus by the shadow of
a friendship: then Antony, lured by the Tarentine
and Brundisian treaties [4] and a marriage with his
sister, had paid with life the penalty of that delusive
connexion.   After that there had been undoubtedly
peace, but peace with bloodshed—the disasters of
Lollius [5] and of Varus, the execution at Rome of a
Varro, an Egnatius, an Iullus."[6] His domestic
adventures were not spared: the abduction of Nero's
wife, and the farcical question to the pontiffs, whether,
with a child conceived but not yet born, she could
legally wed; the debaucheries of Vedius Pollio;[7]
and, lastly, Livia,—as a mother, a curse to the realm;

[5] Defeated with the loss of an eagle in Germany, 16 B.C.

[6] Varro Murena and Egnatius Rufus, executed for conspiracy
in 23 B.C. and 19 B.C. respectively: Iullus Antonius, son of
the triumvir, compelled to suicide in 2 B.C. for adultery with
Julia (see below, chap. 53).

[7] A Roman knight of obscure origin and great wealth, said
to have thrown slaves to his lampreys: a friend of Augustus.
See D. Cass. LIV. 23, with Fabricius' notes *ad loc.*

domui Caesarum noverca. Nihil deorum honoribus relictum, cum se templis et effigie numinum per flamines et sacerdotes coli vellet. Ne Tiberium quidem caritate aut rei publicae cura successorem adscitum, sed, quoniam adrogantiam saevitiamque eius introspexerit, comparatione deterrima sibi gloriam quaesivisse. Etenim Augustus, paucis ante annis, cum Tiberio tribuniciam potestatem a patribus rursum postularet, quamquam honora oratione, quaedam de habitu cultuque et institutis eius iecerat, quae velut excusando exprobraret. Ceterum sepultura more perfecta, templum et caelestes religiones decernuntur.

XI. Versae inde ad Tiberium preces. Et ille varie[1] disserebat de magnitudine imperii, sua modestia. Solam divi Augusti mentem tantae molis capacem : se in partem curarum ab illo vocatum experiendo didicisse quam arduum, quam subiectum fortunae regendi cuncta onus. Proinde, in civitate tot illustribus viris subnixa, non ad unum omnia deferrent : plures facilius munia rei publicae sociatis laboribus exsecuturos. Plus in oratione tali dignitatis quam fidei erat ; Tiberioque, etiam in rebus quas non occuleret, seu natura sive adsuetudine, suspensa semper et obscura verba ; tunc vero nitenti ut sensus

[1] varie *Beroaldus* : variae.

---

[1] Because, in the one capacity, she had borne Tiberius, and, in the other, was credited with procuring the deaths of Gaius and Lucius Caesar.

as a stepmother, a curse to the house of the Caesars.[1]
" He had left small room for the worship of heaven,
when he claimed to be himself adored in temples and
in the image of godhead by flamens and by priests!
Even in the adoption of Tiberius to succeed him, his
motive had been neither personal affection nor regard
for the state: he had read the pride and cruelty of
his heart, and had sought to heighten his own glory by
the vilest of contrasts." For Augustus, a few years
earlier, when requesting the Fathers to renew the
grant of the tribunician power to Tiberius, had in the
course of the speech, complimentary as it was, let
fall a few remarks on his demeanour, dress, and habits
which were offered as an apology and designed for
reproaches.

However, his funeral ran the ordinary course;
and a decree followed, endowing him with a temple
and divine rites.

XI. Then all prayers were directed towards
Tiberius; who delivered a variety of reflections on
the greatness of the empire and his own diffidence :—
" Only the mind of the deified Augustus was equal to
such a burden: he himself had found, when called
by the sovereign to share his anxieties, how arduous,
how dependent upon fortune, was the task of ruling
a world! He thought, then, that, in a state which
had the support of so many eminent men, they ought
not to devolve the entire duties on any one person;
the business of government would be more easily
carried out by the joint efforts of a number." A
speech in this tenor was more dignified than con-
vincing. Besides, the diction of Tiberius, by habit
or by nature, was always indirect and obscure, even
when he had no wish to conceal his thought; and

suos penitus abderet, in incertum et ambiguum magis implicabantur. At patres, quibus unus metus si intellegere viderentur, in questus, lacrimas, vota effundi; ad deos, ad effigiem Augusti, ad genua ipsius manus tendere, cum proferri libellum recitarique iussit. Opes publicae continebantur, quantum civium sociorumque in armis, quot classes, regna, provinciae, tributa aut vectigalia, et necessitates ac largitiones. Quae cuncta sua manu perscripserat Augustus addideratque consilium coercendi intra terminos imperii, incertum metu an per invidiam.

XII. Inter quae senatu ad infimas obtestationes procumbente dixit forte Tiberius se ut non toti rei publicae parem, ita quaecumque pars sibi mandaretur, eius tutelam suscepturum. Tum Asinius Gallus "Interrogo," inquit, "Caesar, quam partem rei publicae mandari tibi velis." Perculsus inprovisa interrogatione paulum reticuit; dein, collecto animo, respondit nequaquam decorum pudori suo legere aliquid aut evitare ex eo, cui in universum excusari mallet. Rursum Gallus (etenim vultu offensionem coniectaverat) non idcirco interrogatum, ait, ut divideret quae separari nequirent, sed ut[1] sua confessione argueretur unum esse rei publicae corpus atque unius animo regendum. Addidit laudem

[1] ut *Lipsius* : et.

---

[1] One of three left by Augustus; the first dealing with his own funeral arrangements; the second (known in part from the *Monumentum Ancyranum*), a record of his achievements; the third (here meant), a *breviarium totius imperii* (Suet. *Aug.* 101).

now, in the effort to bury every trace of his sentiments, it became more intricate, uncertain, and
equivocal than ever. But the Fathers, whose one
dread was that they might seem to comprehend him,
melted in plaints, tears, and prayers. They were
stretching their hands to heaven, to the effigy of
Augustus, to his own knees, when he gave orders for
a document[1] to be produced and read. It contained
a statement of the national resources—the strength
of the burghers and allies under arms; the number
of the fleets, protectorates, and provinces; the taxes
direct and indirect; the needful disbursements and
customary bounties: all catalogued by Augustus in
his own hand, with a final clause (due to fear or
jealousy?) advising the restriction of the empire
within its present frontiers.

XII. The senate, meanwhile, was descending to
the most abject supplications, when Tiberius casually
observed that, unequal as he felt himself to the whole
weight of government, he would still undertake the
charge of any one department that might be assigned
to him. Asinius Gallus then said:—" I ask you,
Caesar, what department you wish to be assigned
you." This unforeseen inquiry threw him off his
balance. He was silent for a few moments; then
recovered himself, and answered that it would not
at all become his diffidence to select or shun any part
of a burden from which he would prefer to be wholly
excused. Gallus, who had conjectured anger from
his look, resumed:—" The question had been put to
him, not with the hope that he would divide the
inseparable, but to gain from his own lips an admission
that the body politic was a single organism needing
to be governed by a single intelligence." He added

de Augusto Tiberiumque ipsum victoriarum suarum,
quaeque in toga per tot annos egregie fecisset ad-
monuit. Nec ideo iram eius lenivit, pridem invisus,
tamquam ducta in matrimonium Vipsania, M. Agrippae filia, quae quondam Tiberii uxor fuerat, plus
quam civilia agitaret Pollionisque Asinii patris
ferociam retineret.

XIII. Post quae L. Arruntius haud multum dis-
crepans a Galli oratione perinde offendit, quamquam [1] Tiberio nulla vetus in Arruntium ira: sed
divitem, promptum, artibus egregiis et pari fama
publice, suspectabat. Quippe Augustus supremis
sermonibus, cum tractaret quinam adipisci principem locum suffecturi abnuerent, aut inpares vellent,
vel idem possent cuperentque, M'.[2] Lepidum dixerat
capacem, sed aspernantem, Gallum Asinium avidum
et minorem, L. Arruntium non indignum et, si casus
daretur, ausurum. De prioribus consentitur, pro
Arruntio quidam Cn. Pisonem tradidere; omnesque
praeter Lepidum variis mox criminibus struente
Tiberio circumventi sunt. Etiam Q. Haterius et
Mamercus Scaurus suspicacem animum perstrin-
xere, Haterius cum dixisset: "Quo usque patieris,
Caesar, non adesse caput [3] rei publicae?" Scaurus
quia dixerat spem esse ex eo non inritas fore senatus
preces, quod relationi consulum iure tribuniciae
potestatis non intercessisset. In Haterium statim

---

[1] quamquam *Beroaldus*: quam.
[2] M'. *Lipsius*: M.   [3] caput *Rhenanus*: aput te.

---

[1] This assertion is hardly borne out by Tacitus himself.
In the case of Piso, it runs counter to his whole narrative; in
that of Arruntius, he half acquits Tiberius at VI. 47; while
thirteen years were to elapse before the arrest of Gallus, and
sixteen before his execution.

a panegyric on Augustus, and urged Tiberius to
remember his own victories and the brilliant work
which he had done year after year in the garb of
peace. He failed, however, to soothe the imperial
anger: he had been a hated man ever since his
marriage to Vipsania (daughter of Marcus Agrippa,
and once the wife of Tiberius), which had given the
impression that he had ambitions denied to a subject
and retained the temerity of his father Asinius
Pollio.

XIII. Lucius Arruntius, who followed in a vein not
much unlike that of Gallus, gave equal offence,
although Tiberius had no standing animosity against
him: he was, however, rich, enterprising, greatly
gifted, correspondingly popular, and so suspect.
For Augustus, in his last conversations, when discussing possible holders of the principate—those
who were competent and disinclined, who were
inadequate and willing, or who were at once able and
desirous—had described Manius Lepidus as capable
but disdainful, Asinius Gallus as eager and unfit,
Lucius Arruntius as not undeserving and bold
enough to venture, should the opportunity arise.
The first two names are not disputed; in some
versions Arruntius is replaced by Gnaeus Piso: all
concerned, apart from Lepidus, were soon entrapped
on one charge or another, promoted by Tiberius.[1]
Quintus Haterius and Mamercus Scaurus also jarred
that suspicious breast—Haterius, by the sentence,
" How long, Caesar, will you permit the state to lack
a head? " and Scaurus, by remarking that, as he had
not used his tribunician power to veto the motion of
the consuls, there was room for hope that the prayers
of the senate would not be in vain. Haterius he

invectus est; Scaurum, cui inplacabilius irascebatur, silentio tramisit. Fessusque clamore omnium, expostulatione singulorum flexit paulatim, non ut fateretur suscipi a se imperium, sed ut negare et rogari desineret. Constat Haterium, cum deprecandi causa Palatium introisset ambulantisque Tiberii genua advolveretur, prope a militibus interfectum, quia Tiberius casu an manibus eius inpeditus prociderat. Neque tamen periculo talis viri mitigatus est, donec Haterius Augustam oraret eiusque [1] curatissimis precibus protegeretur.

XIV. Multa patrum et in Augustam adulatio: alii parentem, alii matrem patriae appellandam, plerique ut nomini Caesaris adscriberetur "Iuliae filius" censebant. Ille moderandos feminarum honores dictitans eademque se temperantia usurum in iis [2] quae sibi tribuerentur, ceterum anxius invidia et muliebre fastigium in deminutionem sui accipiens, ne lictorem quidem ei decerni passus est, aramque adoptionis et alia huiusce modi prohibuit. At Germanico Caesari proconsulare imperium petivit, missique legati qui deferrent, simul maestitiam eius ob excessum Augusti solarentur. Quo minus idem pro Druso postularetur, ea causa

---

[1] eiusque *Lipsius* : et usque.
[2] iis *Muretus* : his.

---

[1] *i.e.*, of her adoption *in familiam Iuliam nomenque Augustum* (chap. 8).
[2] Not the ordinary proconsular *imperium* of the governor of a senatorial province, but a renewal of the *imperium maius* in Gaul and Germany, which he had held for three years.

favoured with an immediate invective: against
Scaurus his anger was less placable, and he passed
him over in silence. Wearied at last by the universal
outcry and by individual appeals, he gradually gave
ground, up to the point, *not* of acknowledging that he
assumed the sovereignty, but of ceasing to refuse
and to be entreated. Haterius, it is well known, on
entering the palace to make his excuses, found
Tiberius walking, threw himself down at his knees,
and was all but dispatched by the guards, because
the prince, either from accident or through being
hampered by the suppliant's hands, had fallen flat
on his face. The danger of a great citizen failed
however, to soften him, until Haterius appealed to
Augusta, and was saved by the urgency of her
prayers.

XIV. Augusta herself enjoyed a full share of
senatorial adulation. One party proposed to give
her the title " Parent of her Country "; some preferred, " Mother of her Country ": a majority
thought the qualification " Son of Julia " ought to
be appended to the name of the Caesar. Declaring
that official compliments to women must be kept
within bounds, and that he would use the same
forbearance in the case of those paid to himself
(in fact he was fretted by jealousy, and regarded
the elevation of a woman as a degradation of himself),
he declined to allow her even the grant of a lictor,
and banned both an Altar of Adoption [1] and other
proposed honours of a similar nature. But he asked
proconsular powers [2] for Germanicus Caesar, and a
commission was sent out to confer them, and, at the
same time, to console his grief at the death of
Augustus. That the same demand was not preferred

271

quod designatus consul Drusus praesensque erat.
Candidatos praeturae duodecim nominavit, numerum ab Augusto traditum; et hortante senatu ut
augeret, iure iurando obstrinxit se non excessu-
rum.

XV. Tum primum e campo comitia ad patres
translata sunt; nam ad eam diem, etsi potissima
arbitrio principis, quaedam tamen studiis tribuum
fiebant. Neque populus ademptum ius questus est
nisi inani rumore, et senatus, largitionibus ac precibus sordidis exsolutus, libens tenuit, moderante
Tiberio ne plures quam quattuor candidatos com-
mendaret sine repulsa et ambitu designandos.
Inter quae tribuni plebei petivere ut proprio sump-
tu ederent ludos, qui de nomine Augusti, fastis additi,
Augustales vocarentur. Sed decreta pecunia ex
aerario, utque per circum triumphali veste uteren-
tur: curru vehi haud permissum. Mox celebratio
ad[1] praetorem translata, cui inter civis et peregrinos
iurisdictio evenisset.

XVI. Hic rerum urbanarum status erat, cum
Pannonicas legiones seditio incessit, nullis novis
causis, nisi quod mutatus princeps licentiam turba-
rum et ex civili bello spem praemiorum ostendebat.

---

[1] ad *Ritter* : annum (annua *Lipsius, vulgo*) ad.

---

[1] For as consul designate, and present, he would have
been placed in the invidious position of voting first on the
question of his own preferment.

[2] Out of the twelve whom he nominated for the praetorship.

on behalf of Drusus was due to the circumstance that he was consul designate and in presence.[1]

For the praetorship Tiberius nominated twelve candidates, the number handed down by Augustus. The senate, pressing for an increase, was met by a declaration on oath that he would never exceed it.

XV. The elections were now for the first time transferred from the Campus to the senate: up to that day, while the most important were determined by the will of the sovereign, a few had still been left to the predilections of the Tribes. From the people the withdrawal of the right brought no protest beyond idle murmurs; and the senate, relieved from the necessity of buying or begging votes, was glad enough to embrace the change, Tiberius limiting himself to the recommendation of not more than four candidates,[2] to be appointed without rejection or competition. At the same time, the plebeian tribunes asked leave to exhibit games at their own expense—to be called after the late emperor and added to the calendar as the Augustalia. It was decided, however, that the cost should be borne by the treasury; also, that the tribunes should have the use of the triumphal robe in the Circus: the chariot was not to be permissible. The whole function, before long, was transferred to the praetor who happened to have the jurisdiction in suits between natives and aliens.

XVI. So much for the state of affairs in the capital: now came an outbreak of mutiny among the Pannonian legions. There were no fresh grievances; only the change of sovereigns had excited a vision of licensed anarchy and a hope of the emolu-

Castris aestivis tres simul legiones habebantur, praesidente Iunio Blaeso, qui, fine Augusti et initiis Tiberii auditis, ob iustitium aut gaudium intermiserat solita munia. Eo principio lascivire miles ; discordare, pessimi cuiusque sermonibus praebere auris, denique luxum et otium cupere, disciplinam et laborem aspernari. Erat in castris Percennius quidam, dux olim theatralium operarum, dein gregarius miles, procax lingua et miscere coetus histrionali studio doctus. Is imperitos animos et quaenam post Augustum militiae condicio ambigentis inpellere paulatim nocturnis conloquiis, aut, flexo in vesperam die et dilapsis[1] melioribus, deterrimum quemque congregare.

XVII. Postremo promptis iam et aliis seditionis ministris velut contionabundus[2] interrogabat cur paucis centurionibus, paucioribus tribunis in modum servorum oboedirent. Quando ausuros exposcere remedia, nisi novum et nutantem adhuc principem precibus vel armis adirent? Satis per tot annos ignavia peccatum, quod tricena aut quadragena stipendia senes et plerique truncato ex vulneribus corpore tolerent. Ne dimissis quidem finem esse militiae, sed apud vexillum tendentis[3] alio vocabulo

---

[1] dilapsis *Muretus* : delapsis.
[2] contionabundus *Beroaldus* : conditionabundus.
[3] tendentes *Jac. Gronovius* : t... | tentes.

ments of civil war. Three legions were stationed together in summer-quarters under the command of Junius Blaesus. News had come of the end of Augustus and the accession of Tiberius ; and Blaesus, to allow the proper interval for mourning or festivity, had suspended the normal round of duty. With this the mischief began. The ranks grew insubordinate and quarrelsome—gave a hearing to any glib agitator—became eager, in short, for luxury and ease, disdainful of discipline and work. In the camp there was a man by the name of Percennius, in his early days the leader of a claque at the theatres, then a private soldier with an abusive tongue, whose experience of stage rivalries had taught him the art of inflaming an audience. Step by step, by conversations at night or in the gathering twilight, he began to play on those simple minds, now troubled by a doubt how the passing of Augustus would affect the conditions of service, and to collect about him the off-scourings of the army when the better elements had dispersed.

XVII. At last, when they were ripe for action— some had now become his coadjutors in sedition— he put his question in something like a set speech :— " Why should they obey like slaves a few centurions and fewer tribunes? When would they dare to claim redress, if they shrank from carrying their petitions, or their swords, to the still unstable throne of a new prince? Mistakes enough had been made in all the years of inaction, when white-haired men, many of whom had lost a limb by wounds, were making their thirtieth or fortieth campaign. Even after discharge their warfare was not accomplished : still under canvas by the colours they endured the

eosdem labores perferre. Ac si quis tot casus vita
superaverit, trahi adhuc diversas in terras, ubi per
nomen agrorum uligines paludum vel inculta montium accipiant. Enimvero militiam ipsam gravem,
infructuosam: denis in diem assibus animam et
corpus aestimari; hinc vestem, arma, tentoria;
hinc saevitiam centurionum et vacationes munerum
redimi. At hercule verbera et vulnera, duram hiemem, exercitas aestates, bellum atrox aut sterilem
pacem sempiterna. Nec aliud levamentum quam
si certis sub legibus militia iniretur, ut singulos
denarios mererent, sextus decimus stipendii annus
finem adferret, ne ultra sub vexillis tenerentur, sed
isdem in castris praemium pecunia solveretur.
An praetorias cohortis, quae binos denarios acceperint,[1] quae post sedecim annos penatibus suis
reddantur, plus periculorum suscipere? Non obtrec-
tari a se urbanas excubias: sibi tamen apud horridas
gentis e contuberniis hostem aspici.

XVIII. Adstrepebat vulgus, diversis incitamentis,
hi verberum notas, illi canitiem, plurimi detrita

---

[1] acceperint *Beroaldus* : accepit.

---

[1] In 16 B.C., Augustus, the creator of the standing army,
fixed the period of service at sixteen consecutive years for the
legionaries and twelve for the guards. Two decades later, the
terms were prolonged to twenty and sixteen years respectively,
at the end of which the time-expired man was entitled to a
monetary bounty in lieu of the grant of land which had been
the rule for the past half-century. Veterans choosing, after
discharge, to remain in the service were kept, not with the
standard (*signum*), but under colours of their own (*vexillum*);
whence the *aliud vocabulum*, as Percennius puts it, of *vexillarii*.
Theoretically, at least, they were exempt from the routine
work of the legionaries, and formed a species of *corps d'élite*
of seasoned fighting men.

old drudgeries under an altered name.[1] And suppose
that a man survived this multitude of hazards: he
was dragged once more to the ends of earth to receive
under the name of a ' farm ' some swampy morass
or barren mountain-side.   In fact, the whole trade
of war was comfortless and profitless : ten asses a day
was the assessment of body and soul : with that they
had to buy clothes, weapons and tents, bribe the
bullying centurion and purchase a respite from duty![2]
But whip-cut and sword-cut, stern winter and
harassed summer, red war or barren peace,—these,
God knew, were always with them.   Alleviation
there would be none, till enlistment took place under
a definite contract—the payment to be a denarius a
day,[3] the sixteenth year to end the term of service,
no further period with the reserve to be required, but
the gratuity to be paid in money in their old
camp.   Or did the praetorian cohorts, who had
received two denarii a day—who were restored to
hearth and home on the expiry of sixteen years—
risk more danger ?   They did not disparage sentinel-
duty at Rome ; still, their own lot was cast among
savage clans, with the enemy visible from their
very tents."

XVIII. The crowd shouted approval, as one point
or the other told.   Some angrily displayed the marks
of the lash, some their grey hairs, most their thread-

[2] For a commentary on this sentence see the *Histories* I.
46.

[3] In the Second Punic War the value of the *as* sank from a
tenth to a sixteenth of the *denarius*.   As the troops still
received the same fraction (a third) of the *denarius*, their pay
was now 5½ *asses* a day , the amount was doubled by Julius
Caesar, and stood thenceforward at 10 *asses*, the fraction
being neglected.   Percennius now demands the full *denarius* (a
day-labourer's wage) of 16 *asses*.

tegmina et nudum corpus exprobrantes. Postremo eo furoris venere, ut tres legiones miscere in unam agitaverint. Depulsi aemulatione, quia suae quisque legioni eum honorem quaerebant, alio vertunt atque una tres aquilas et signa cohortium locant; simul congerunt caespites, exstruunt tribunal, quo magis conspicua sedes foret. Properantibus Blaesus advenit, increpabatque ac retinebat singulos, clamitans: " Mea potius caede imbuite manus: leviore flagitio legatum interficietis quam ab imperatore desciscitis. Aut incolumis fidem legionum retinebo, aut iugulatus paenitentiam adcelerabo."

XIX. Aggerabatur [1] nihilo minus caespes iamque pectori usque [2] adcreverat, cum tandem pervicacia victi inceptum omisere. Blaesus multa dicendi arte non per seditionem et turbas desideria militum ad Caesarem ferenda ait: neque veteres ab imperatoribus priscis, neque ipsos a divo Augusto tam nova petivisse; et parum in tempore incipientis principis curas onerari. Si tamen tenderent in pace temptare quae ne civilium quidem bellorum victores expostulaverint, cur contra morem obsequii, contra fas disciplinae vim meditentur? Decernerent legatos seque coram mandata darent. Adclamavere ut filius Blaesi tribunus legatione ea

[1] aggerabatur *Walther* : aggerebatur.
[2] usque *Beroaldus* : eiusque.

---

[1] *i.e.* the standards of the three maniples in each cohort—thirty in each legion.

bare garments and naked bodies. At last they
came to such a pitch of frenzy that they proposed
to amalgamate the three legions into one. Baffled
in the attempt by military jealousies, since each man
claimed the privilege of survival for his own legion,
they fell back on the expedient of planting the three
eagles and the standards of the cohorts[1] side by side.
At the same time, to make the site more conspicuous,
they began to collect turf and erect a platform.
They were working busily when Blaesus arrived.
He broke into reproaches, and in some cases dragged
the men back by force. " Dye your hands in my
blood," he exclaimed; " it will be a slighter crime
to kill your general than it is to revolt from your
emperor. Alive, I will keep my legions loyal, or,
murdered, hasten their repentance."

XIX. None the less, the turf kept mounting, and
had risen fully breast-high before his pertinacity
carried the day and they abandoned the attempt.
Blaesus then addressed them with great skill:—
" Mutiny and riot," he observed, " were not the best
ways of conveying a soldier's aspirations to his
sovereign. No such revolutionary proposals had been
submitted either by their predecessors to the captains
of an earlier day or by themselves to Augustus of
happy memory; and it was an ill-timed proceeding
to aggravate the embarrassments which confronted
a prince on his accession. But if they were resolved
to hazard during peace claims unasserted even by the
victors of the civil wars, why insult the principles
of discipline and the habit of obedience by an appeal
to violence? They should name deputies and give
them instructions in his presence." The answer came
in a shout, that Blaesus' son—a tribune—should

fungeretur peteretque militibus missionem ab sedecim annis; cetera mandaturos, ubi prima provenissent. Profecto iuvene, modicum otium: sed superbire miles, quod filius legati orator publicae causae
satis ostenderet necessitate expressa quae per modestiam non obtinuissent.

XX. Interea manipuli, ante coeptam seditionem
Nauportum missi ob itinera et pontes et alios usus,
postquam turbatum in castris accepere, vexilla
convellunt direptisque proximis vicis ipsoque Nau-
porto, quod municipii instar erat, retinentis centuriones inrisu et contumeliis, postremo verberibus
insectantur, praecipua in Aufidienum Rufum praefectum castrorum ira, quem dereptum vehiculo
sarcinis gravant aguntque primo in agmine, per
ludibrium rogitantes an tam immensa onera, tam
longa itinera libenter ferret. Quippe Rufus diu
manipularis, dein centurio, mox castris praefectus, antiquam duramque militiam revocabat,
vetus [1] operis ac laboris, et eo inmitior quia tole-
raverat.

XXI. Horum adventu redintegratur seditio et
vagi circumiecta populabantur. Blaesus paucos,
maxime praeda onustos, ad terrorem ceterorum adfici
verberibus, claudi carcere iubet; nam etiam tum

[1] vetus *Lipsius*: intus.

---

[1] Ober-Laybach, some ten miles to the south-west of
Laybach (the Jugoslav *Ljubljana*).

[2] A new class of officers, rendered necessary by the creation
of the standing army with its permanent camps for the legions.
Found only in the first two centuries after Christ, and recruited largely from centurions of long service, their disci-
plinary powers did not, in strictness, extend to capital punishment (see below, chap. 38).

undertake the mission and ask for the discharge of all soldiers of sixteen years' service and upwards: they would give him their other instructions when the first had borne fruit. The young man's departure brought comparative quiet. The troops, however, were elated, as the sight of their general's son pleading the common cause showed plainly enough that force had extracted what would never have been yielded to orderly methods.

XX. Meanwhile there were the companies dispatched to Nauportus[1] before the beginning of the mutiny. They had been detailed for the repair of roads and bridges, and on other service, but the moment news came of the disturbance in camp, they tore down their ensigns and looted both the neighbouring villages and Nauportus itself, which was large enough to claim the standing of a town. The centurions resisted, only to be assailed with jeers and insults, and finally blows; the chief object of anger being the camp-marshal, Aufidienus Rufus; who, dragged from his car, loaded with baggage, and driven at the head of the column, was plied with sarcastic inquiries whether he found it pleasant to support these huge burdens, these weary marches. For Rufus, long a private, then a centurion, and latterly a camp-marshal,[2] was seeking to reintroduce the iron discipline of the past, habituated as he was to work and toil, and all the more pitiless because he had endured.

XXI. The arrival of this horde gave the mutiny a fresh lease of life, and the outlying districts began to be overrun by wandering marauders. To cow the rest—for the general was still obeyed by the centurions and the respectable members of the rank

281

legato a centurionibus et optimo quoque manipu·
larium parebatur. Illi obniti trahentibus, prensare
circumstantium genua, ciere modo nomina singulorum, modo centuriam quisque cuius manipularis
erat, cohortem, legionem, eadem omnibus inminere
clamitantes. Simul probra in legatum cumulant,
caelum ac deos obtestantur, nihil reliqui faciunt quo
minus invidiam, misericordiam, metum et iras
permoverent. Adcurritur ab universis, et carcere
effracto solvunt vincula desertoresque ac rerum
capitalium damnatos sibi iam miscent.

XXII. Flagrantior inde vis, plures seditioni
duces. Et Vibulenus quidam, gregarius miles, ante
tribunal Blaesi adlevatus circumstantium umeris,
apud turbatos et quid pararet intentos : " Vos quidem "
inquit " his innocentibus et miserrimis lucem et spiritum reddidistis : sed quis fratri meo vitam, quis
fratrem mihi reddit? quem missum ad vos a Germanico exercitu de communibus commodis nocte proxima iugulavit per gladiatores suos, quos in exitium
militum habet atque armat. Responde, Blaese,
ubi cadaver abieceris [1] : ne hostes quidem sepultura
invident. Cum osculis, cum lacrimis dolorem meum
implevero, me quoque trucidari iube, dum interfectos
nullum ob scelus, sed quia utilitati legionum consu-
lebamus, hi [2] sepeliant."

XXIII. Incendebat [3] haec fletu et pectus atque os

---

[1] abieceris *Beroaldus* : ablegeris.
[2] hi *Lipsius* : ii.
[3] incendebat *Beroaldus* : incedebat.

---

[1] Actually, in order to give exhibitions in the province : a
custom afterwards prohibited by Nero (XIII. 31).

and file—Blaesus ordered a few who were especially heavy-laden with booty to be lashed and thrown into the cells. As the escort dragged them away, they began to struggle, to catch at the knees of the bystanders, to call on the names of individual friends, their particular century, their cohort, their legion, clamouring that a similar fate was imminent for all. At the same time they heaped reproaches on the general and invoked high heaven,—anything and everything that could arouse odium or sympathy, alarm or indignation. The crowd flew to the rescue, forced the guard-room, unchained the prisoners, and now took into fellowship deserters and criminals condemned for capital offences.

XXII. After this the flames burned higher; sedition found fresh leaders. A common soldier, Vibulenus by name, was hoisted on the shoulders of the bystanders in front of Blaesus' tribunal, and there addressed the turbulent and curious crowd:— " You, I grant," he said, " have restored light and breath to these innocent and much wronged men; but who restores the life to my brother—who my brother to me? He was sent to you by the army of Germany to debate our common interest—and yesterday night *he* did him to death by the hands of those gladiators whom he keeps and arms for the extermination of his soldiers.[1] Answer me, Blaesus: —Whither have you flung the body? The enemy himself does not grudge a grave! Then, when I have sated my sorrow with kisses, and drowned it with tears, bid them butcher me as well: only, let our comrades here lay us in earth—for we died, not for crime, but because we sought to serve the legions."

XXIII. He added to the inflammatory effect of

manibus verberans. Mox disiectis quorum per
umeros sustinebatur, praeceps et singulorum pedibus
advolutus, tantum consternationis invidiaeque conci-
vit, ut pars militum gladiatores, qui e servitio Blaesi
erant, pars ceteram eiusdem familiam vincirent,
alii ad quaerendum corpus effunderentur. Ac ni
propere neque corpus ullum reperiri, et servos adhibitis cruciatibus abnuere caedem, neque illi fuisse
umquam fratrem pernotuisset, haud multum ab
exitio legati aberant. Tribunos tamen ac praefectum castrorum extrusere, sarcinae fugientium direp-
tae, et centurio Lucilius interficitur, cui militaribus
facetiis vocabulum " cedo alteram " indiderant,
quia, fracta vite [1] in tergo militis, alteram clara voce
ac rursus aliam poscebat. Ceteros latebrae texere,
uno retento Clemente Iulio, qui perferendis militum mandatis habebatur idoneus ob promptum
ingenium. Quin ipsae inter se legiones octava et
quinta decuma ferrum parabant, dum centurionem cognomento Sirpicum illa morti deposcit,
quintadecumani tuentur, ni miles nonanus preces
et adversum aspernantis minas interiecisset.

XXIV. Haec audita quamquam abstrusum et
tristissima quaeque maxime occultantem Tiberium
perpulere, ut Drusum filium cum primoribus civitatis duabusque praetoriis cohortibus mitteret,

---

[1] fracta vite *Beroaldus* : facta vitae.

---

[1] The vine-rod, the familiar emblem of the centurionship.

his speech by weeping and striking his face and breast: then, dashing aside the friends on whose shoulders he was supported, he threw himself head-long and fawned at the feet of man after man, until he excited such consternation and hatred that one party flung into irons the gladiators in Blaesus' service; another, the rest of his household; while the others poured out in search of the corpse. In fact, if it had not come to light very shortly that no body was discoverable, that the slaves under torture denied the murder, and that Vibulenus had never owned a brother, they were within measurable distance of making away with the general. As it was, they ejected the tribunes and camp-marshal and plundered the fugitives' baggage. The centurion Lucilius also met his end. Camp humorists had surnamed him ''Fetch-Another,'' from his habit, as one cane[1] broke over a private's back, of calling at the top of his voice for a second, and ultimately a third. His colleagues found safety in hiding: Julius Clemens alone was kept, as the mutineers considered that his quick wits might be of service in presenting their claims. The eighth and fifteenth legions, it should be added, were on the point of turning their swords against each other upon the question of a centurion named Sirpicus,— demanded for execution by the eighth and protected by the fifteenth,—had not the men of the ninth intervened with entreaties and, in the event of their rejection, with threats.

XXIV. In spite of his secretiveness, always deepest when the news was blackest, Tiberius was driven by the reports from Pannonia to send out his son Drusus, with a staff of nobles and two praetorian

nullis satis certis mandatis, ex re consulturum. Et cohortes delecto milite supra solitum firmatae. Additur magna pars praetoriani equitis et robora Germanorum, qui tum custodes imperatori aderant; simul praetorii praefectus Aelius Seianus, collega Straboni patri suo datus, magna apud Tiberium auctoritate, rector iuveni et ceteris periculorum praemiorumque ostentator. Druso propinquanti quasi per officium obviae fuere legiones, non laetae, ut adsolet, neque insignibus fulgentes, sed inluvie deformi et vultu, quamquam maestitiam imitarentur, contumaciae propiores.

XXV. Postquam vallum introiit,[1] portas stationibus firmant, globos armatorum certis castrorum locis opperiri iubent; ceteri tribunal ingenti agmine circumveniunt. Stabat Drusus silentium manu poscens. Illi, quoties oculos ad multitudinem rettulerant,[2] vocibus truculentis strepere, rursum viso Caesare trepidare; murmur incertum, atrox clamor et repente quies; diversis animorum motibus pavebant terrebantque. Tandem interrupto tumultu litteras patris recitat, in quis perscriptum erat, praecipuam ipsi fortissimarum legionum curam, quibuscum plurima bella toleravisset; ubi primum a luctu requiesset animus, acturum apud patres de

---

[1] introiit *Lipsius* : introit.
[2] rettulerant *Beroaldus* : sed tulerant.

---

[1] That the *dona militaria*, worn on full-dress occasions, are meant seems to be shown by *Hist.* II. 89, *ceteri iuxta suam quisque centuriam, armis donisque fulgentes.*

[2] In order to exclude the main body of Drusus' escort.

[3] Once in 12–9 B.C., when he pushed forward the frontier to the Upper Danube; and again in 6–9 A.D., in the extremely grave crisis occasioned by the revolt of Pannonia and Dalmatia.

cohorts. He had no instructions that could be called definite: he was to suit his measures to the emergency. Drafts of picked men raised the cohorts to abnormal strength. In addition, a large part of the praetorian horse was included, as well as the flower of the German troops, who at that time formed the imperial bodyguard. The commandant of the household troops, Aelius Sejanus, who held the office jointly with his father Strabo and exercised a remarkable influence over Tiberius, went in attendance, to act as monitor to the young prince and to keep before the eyes of the rest the prospects of peril or reward. As Drusus approached, the legions met him, ostensibly to mark their loyalty; but the usual demonstrations of joy and glitter of decorations [1] had given place to repulsive squalor and to looks that aimed at sadness and came nearer to insolence.

XXV. The moment he passed the outworks, they held the gates with sentries,[2] and ordered bodies of armed men to be ready at fixed positions within the camp: the rest, in one great mass, flocked round the tribunal. Drusus stood, beckoning with his hand for silence. One moment, the mutineers would glance back at their thousands, and a roar of truculent voices followed; the next, they saw the Caesar and trembled: vague murmurings, savage yells and sudden stillnesses marked a conflict of passions which left them alternately terrified and terrible. At last, during a lull in the storm, Drusus read over his father's letter, in which it was written that " he had personally a special regard for the heroic legions in whose company he had borne so many campaigns;[3] that as soon as his thoughts found a rest from grief, he would state their case to the Conscript Fathers;

postulatis eorum; misisse interim filium, ut sine
cunctatione concederet quae statim tribui possent;
cetera senatui servanda, quem neque gratiae neque
severitatis expertem haberi par esset.

XXVI. Responsum est a contione mandata Clementi centurioni quae perferret. Is orditur de
missione a sedecim annis, de praemiis finitae militiae, ut denarius diurnum stipendium foret, ne
veterani sub vexillo haberentur. Ad ea Drusus
cum arbitrium senatus et patris obtenderet, clamore turbatur. Cur venisset, neque augendis militum stipendiis neque adlevandis laboribus, denique
nulla bene faciendi licentia? At hercule verbera
et necem cunctis permitti. Tiberium olim nomine
Augusti desideria legionum frustrari solitum: easdem artis Drusum rettulisse. Numquamne ad se
nisi[1] filios familiarum venturos? Novum id plane
quod imperator sola militis commoda ad senatum
reiciat. Eundem ergo senatum consulendum, quotiens supplicia aut proelia indicantur. An praemia
sub dominis, poenas sine arbitro esse?

XXVII. Postremo deserunt tribunal, ut quis
praetorianorum militum amicorumve Caesaris
occurreret, manus intentantes, causam discordiae
et initium armorum, maxime infensi Cn. Lentulo,
quod is ante alios aetate et gloria belli firmare Dru-

---

[1] ad se nisi *Lipsius*: nisi ad se.

---

[1] If he was thirty-five years of age at the time of his consulate (18 B.C.), he would be now in his sixty-seventh year;
his "military fame" rested on his campaign on the Danube
against the southern Daci (Getae). See the short and Roman
epitaph in IV. 44 *init.*

meantime he had sent his son to grant without delay
any reforms that could be conceded on the spot; the
others must be reserved for the senate, a body which
they would do well to reflect, could be both generous
and severe."

XXVI. The assembly replied that Clemens, the
centurion, was empowered to present their demands.
He began to speak of discharge at the end of sixteen
years, gratuities for service completed, payment on
the scale of a denarius a day, no retention of time-
expired men with the colours. Drusus attempted
to plead the jurisdiction of the senate and his father.
He was interrupted with a shout:—" Why had he
come, if he was neither to raise the pay of the troops
nor to ease their burdens—if, in short, he had no
leave to do a kindness? Yet death and the lash,
Heaven was their witness, were within the com-
petence of anyone! It had been a habit of Tiberius
before him to parry the requests of the legions by
references to Augustus, and now Drusus had repro-
duced the old trick. Were they never to be visited
by any but these young persons with a father? It
was remarkable indeed that the emperor should refer
the good of his troops, and nothing else, to the senate.
If so, he ought to consult the same senate when
executions or battles were the order of the day. Or
were rewards to depend on many masters, punishments to be without control?"

XXVII. At last they left the tribunal, shaking
their fists at any guardsman, or member of the
Caesar's staff, who crossed their road, in order to
supply a ground of quarrel and initiate a resort to
arms. They were bitterest against Gnaeus Lentulus,
whose superior age and military fame [1] led them to

sum credebatur et illa militiae flagitia primus aspernari. Nec multo post digredientem cum [1] Caesare
ac provisu periculi hiberna castra repetentem cir-
cumsistunt, rogitantes quo pergeret, ad imperatorem an ad patres, ut illic quoque commodis legionum adversaretur; simul ingruunt, saxa iaciunt.
Iamque lapidis ictu cruentus et exitii [2] certus, adcursu
multitudinis quae cum Druso advenerat protectus est.

XXVIII. Noctem minacem et in scelus erup-
turam fors lenivit: nam luna claro repente [3] caelo
visa languescere. Id miles rationis ignarus omen
praesentium accepit, suis [4] laboribus defectionem
sideris adsimulans, prospereque cessura qua [5] pergerent, si fulgor et claritudo deae redderetur. Igitur
aeris sono, tubarum cornuumque concentu strepere;
prout splendidior obscuriorve, laetari aut maerere;
et postquam ortae nubes offecere visui creditumque
conditam tenebris, ut sunt mobiles ad superstitionem perculsae semel mentes, sibi aeternum laborem portendi,[6] sua facinora aversari [7] deos lamen-
tantur. Vtendum inclinatione ea Caesar et quae

[1] cum *Beroaldus* : eum.   [2] exitii *Beroaldus* : exitu.
[3] claro repente *Lipsius* : clamore pena.
[4] suis *Freinsheim* : asuis.   [5] qua *Halm* : quae.
[6] portendi *Beroaldus* : potandi.
[7] aversari *Rhenanus* : adversari.

---

[1] September 26, at 3 A.M.
[2] *Procul auxiliantia gentes Aera crepant* (Stat. *Theb.* VI. 686).
References to this method of aiding the moon in her struggle
with witchcraft, sickness, or the jaws of malignant monsters,
are common enough : the custom, in fact, is (or has been)
world-wide. See, for example, the interesting account in the
first volume of Tylor's *Primitive Culture* (pp. 330–34), and,
for the views of a more sophisticated soldier, Amm. Marc.
XX. 3.

believe that he was hardening Drusus' heart and was the foremost opponent of this degradation of the service. Before long they caught him leaving with the prince: he had foreseen the danger and was making for the winter-camp. Surrounding him, they demanded whither he was going? To the emperor?—or to his Conscript Fathers, there also to work against the good of the legions? Simultaneously they closed in and began to stone him. He was bleeding already from a cut with a missile and had made up his mind that the end was come, when he was saved by the advent of Drusus' numerous escort.

XXVIII. It was a night of menace and foreboded a day of blood, when chance turned peace-maker: for suddenly the moon was seen to be losing light in a clear sky.[1] The soldiers, who had no inkling of the reason, took it as an omen of the present state of affairs: the labouring planet was an emblem of their own struggles, and their road would lead them to a happy goal, if her brilliance and purity could be restored to the goddess! Accordingly, the silence was broken by a boom of brazen gongs and the blended notes of trumpet and horn.[2] The watchers rejoiced or mourned[3] as their deity brightened or faded, until rising clouds curtained off the view and she set, as they believed, in darkness. Then—so pliable to superstition are minds once unbalanced— they began to bewail the eternal hardships thus foreshadowed and their crimes from which the face of heaven was averted. This turn of the scale, the Caesar reflected, must be put to use: wisdom should

[3] "In our own times, a writer on French folklore was surprised during a lunar eclipse to hear sighs and exclamations, ' Mon Dieu, qu'elle est souffrante.' "—Tylor, *l.c.*

casus obtulerat in sapientiam vertenda ratus, circumiri tentoria iubet; accitur centurio Clemens et si alii bonis artibus grati in vulgus. Hi [1] vigiliis, stationibus, custodiis portarum se inserunt, spem offerunt, metum intendunt: " Quo usque filium imperatoris obsidebimus? quis certaminum finis? Percennione et Vibuleno sacramentum dicturi sumus? Percennius et Vibulenus stipendia militibus, agros emeritis largientur? denique pro Neronibus et Drusis imperium populi Romani capessent? Quin potius, ut novissimi in culpam, ita primi ad paenitentiam sumus? Tarda sunt quae in commune expostulantur: privatam gratiam statim mereare, statim recipias." Commotis per haec mentibus et inter se suspectis, tironem a veterano, legionem a legione dissociant. Tum redire paulatim amor obsequii: omittunt portas, signa unum in locum principio seditionis congregata suas in sedes referunt.

XXIX. Drusus, orto die et vocata contione, quamquam rudis dicendi, nobilitate ingenita incusat priora, probat praesentia; negat se terrore et minis vinci: flexos ad modestiam si videat, si supplices audiat, scripturum patri ut placatus legionum preces exciperet. Orantibus rursum idem Blaesus

---

[1] hi *Weikert*: in.

reap where chance had sown. He ordered a round
of the tents to be made. Clemens, the centurion,
was sent for, along with any other officer whose
qualities had made him popular with the ranks.
These insinuated themselves everywhere, among
the watches, the patrols, the sentries at the gates,
suggesting hope and emphasizing fear. " How long
must we besiege the son of our emperor? What is
to be the end of our factions? Are we to swear
fealty to Percennius and Vibulenus? Will Percennius and Vibulenus give the soldier his pay—his
grant of land at his discharge? Are they, in fine,
to dispossess the stock of Nero and Drusus and take
over the sovereignty of the Roman People? Why,
rather, as we were the last to offend, are we not the
first to repent? Reforms demanded collectively are
slow in coming: private favour is quickly earned and
as quickly paid." The leaven worked; and under
the influence of their mutual suspicions they separated
once more recruit from veteran, legion from legion.
Then, gradually the instinct of obedience returned;
they abandoned the gates and restored to their
proper places the ensigns which they had grouped
together at the beginning of the mutiny.

XXIX. At break of day Drusus called a meeting.
He was no orator, but blamed their past and commended their present attitude with native dignity.
He was not to be cowed, he said, by intimidation and
threats; but if he saw them returning to their duty,
if he heard them speaking the language of suppliants,
he would write to his father and advise him to lend
an indulgent ear to the prayers of the legions. They
begged him to do so, and as their deputies to Tiberius
sent the younger Blaesus as before, together with

THE ANNALS OF TACITUS

et L. Aponius, eques Romanus e cohorte Drusi, Iustusque Catonius, primi ordinis centurio, ad Tiberium mittuntur. Certatum inde sententiis, cum alii opperiendos legatos atque interim comitate permulcendum militem censerent, alii fortioribus remediis agendum: nihil in vulgo modicum; terrere, ni paveant; ubi pertimuerint, inpune contemni; dum superstitio urgeat, adiciendos ex duce metus sublatis seditionis auctoribus. Promptum ad asperiora ingenium Druso erat: vocatos Vibulenum et Percennium interfici iubet. Tradunt plerique intra tabernaculum ducis obrutos, alii corpora extra vallum abiecta ostentui.

XXX. Tum, ut quisque praecipuus turbator, conquisiti, et pars, extra castra palantes, a centurionibus aut praetoriarum cohortium militibus caesi: quosdam ipsi manipuli documentum fidei tradidere. Auxerat militum curas praematura hiems imbribus continuis adeoque saevis, ut non egredi tentoria, congregari inter se, vix tutari signa possent, quae turbine atque unda raptabantur. Durabat et formido caelestis irae, nec frustra adversus impios hebescere sidera, ruere tempestates: non aliud malorum levamentum, quam si linquerent castra infausta temerataque et, soluti piaculo, suis quisque hibernis redderentur. Primum octava, dein quinta

BOOK I. XXIX.–XXX.

Lucius Aponius, a Roman knight on Drusus' staff, and Justus Catonius, a centurion of the first order. There was now a conflict of opinions, some proposing to wait for the return of the deputies and humour the troops in the meantime by a show of leniency, while others were for sterner remedies:—" A crowd was nothing if not extreme; it must either bluster or cringe: once terrified, it could be ignored with impunity; now that it was depressed by superstition was the moment for the general to inspire fresh terror by removing the authors of the mutiny." Drusus had a natural bias towards severity: Vibulenus and Percennius were summoned and their execution was ordered. Most authorities state that they were buried inside the general's pavilion: according to others, the bodies were thrown outside the lines and left on view.

XXX. There followed a hue and cry after every ringleader of note. Some made blindly from the camp and were cut down by the centurions or by members of the praetorian cohorts: others were handed over by the companies themselves as a certificate of their loyalty. The troubles of the soldiers had been increased by an early winter with incessant and pitiless rains. It was impossible to stir from the tents or to meet in common, barely possible to save the standards from being carried away by hurricane and flood. In addition their dread of the divine anger still persisted: not for nothing, it was whispered, was their impiety visited by fading planets and rushing storms; there was no relief from their miseries but to leave this luckless, infected camp, and, absolved from guilt, return every man to his winter-quarters. First the eighth legion, then

decuma legio rediere; nonanus opperiendas Tiberii epistulas clamitaverat, mox desolatus aliorum discessione imminentem necessitatem sponte praevenit. Et Drusus, non exspectato legatorum regressu, quia praesentia satis consederant,[1] in urbem rediit.

XXXI. Isdem ferme diebus isdem causis Germanicae legiones turbatae, quanto plures, tanto violentius, et magna spe fore ut Germanicus Caesar imperium alterius pati nequiret daretque se legionibus vi sua cuncta tracturis.[2] Duo apud ripam Rheni exercitus erant: cui nomen superiori sub C. Silio legato, inferiorem A. Caecina curabat. Regimen summae rei penes Germanicum, agendo Galliarum censui tum intentum. Sed quibus Silius moderabatur, mente ambigua fortunam seditionis alienae speculabantur: inferioris exercitus miles in rabiem prolapsus est, orto ab unetvicesimanis quintanisque initio, et tractis prima quoque ac vicesima legionibus: nam isdem aestivis in finibus Vbiorum habebantur per otium aut levia munia. Igitur, audito fine Augusti, vernacula multitudo, nuper acto in urbe dilectu, lasciviae sueta, labo-

---

[1] consederant *Rhenanus* : considerant.
[2] tracturis *Freinsheim* : tracturus.

---

[1] Four legions in the Upper Army and an equal number in the Lower, as against three in Pannonia. Of the two military districts (on the left bank of the Rhine), *Germania superior* extended from Lake Constance to Brohl, between Bonn and Coblenz; *Germania inferior* from Brohl to the sea.

[2] *i.e.* in receiving the returns of property, on the basis of which the tribute was periodically apportioned.

the fifteenth, departed. The men of the ninth had insisted loudly on waiting for Tiberius' letter: soon, isolated by the defection of the rest, they too made a virtue of what threatened to become a necessity. Drusus himself, since affairs were settled enough at present, went back to Rome without staying for the return of the deputies.

XXXI. During the same days almost, and from the same causes, the legions of Germany mutinied, in larger numbers[1] and with proportionate fury; while their hopes ran high that Germanicus Caesar, unable to brook the sovereignty of another, would throw himself into the arms of his legions, whose force could sweep the world. There were two armies on the Rhine bank: the Upper, under the command of Gaius Silius; the Lower, in charge of Aulus Caecina. The supreme command rested with Germanicus, then engaged in assessing the tribute of the Gaulish provinces.[2] But while the forces under Silius merely watched with doubtful sympathy the fortunes of a rising which was none of theirs, the lower army plunged into delirium. The beginning came from the twenty-first and fifth legions: then, as they were all stationed, idle or on the lightest of duty, in one summer camp on the Ubian frontier,[3] the first and twentieth as well were drawn into the current. Hence, on the report of Augustus' death, the swarm of city-bred recruits swept from the capital by the recent levy,[4] familiar with licence and

[3] In the Cologne district.
[4] After the loss of the seventeenth, eighteenth and nineteenth legions with Varus, Augustus by the most drastic methods enrolled two new legions, the twenty-first and twenty-second: the former (*Rapax*) was under Caecina; the latter (*Deiotariana*) stationed in Egypt.

rum intolerans, implere[1] ceterorum rudes animos:
venisse tempus quo veterani maturam missionem,
iuvenes largiora stipendia, cuncti modum miseriarum exposcerent saevitiamque centurionum ulciscerentur. Non unus haec, ut Pannonicas inter legiones Percennius, nec apud trepidas militum auris,
alios validiores exercitus respicientium, sed multa
seditionis ora vocesque: sua in manu sitam rem
Romanam, suis victoriis augeri rem publicam, in
suum cognomentum adscisci imperatores.

XXXII. Nec legatus obviam ibat: quippe plurium vaecordia constantiam exemerat. Repente
lymphati destrictis gladiis in centuriones invadunt:
ea vetustissima militaribus odiis materies et sae-
viendi principium. Prostratos verberibus mulcant,
sexagenis[2] singulos, ut numerum centurionum adaequarent: tum convulsos laniatosque et partim exa-
nimos ante vallum aut in amnem Rhenum proiciunt.
Septimius, cum perfugisset ad tribunal pedibusque
Caecinae advolveretur, eo usque flagitatus est,
donec ad exitium dederetur. Cassius Chaerea, mox
caede Gai Caesaris memoriam apud posteros adeptus,
tum adulescens et animi ferox, inter obstantis et
armatos ferro viam patefecit. Non tribunus ultra,

---

[1] implere] impellere *Acidalius.*
[2] sexagenis *Thiersch*: sexageni.

---

[1] They were *legiones Germanicae*, and a senatorial decree
had conferred the name *Germanicus* upon Tiberius' brother
Drusus and his posterity. It was borne, therefore, by their
present commander and his brother Claudius—occasionally
(ἔστιν ὅτε, D. Cass. LVII. 8) by Tiberius himself.

[2] According to Dio Cassius, he was ἐρρωμενέστατος ἀνδρῶν;
but *adulescens* hardly squares with Suetonius' assertion that he
was *iam senior* less than twenty-seven years later. Tacitus'
account of his dispatch of Caligula (Jan. 24, 41 A.D.) is un-

chafing at hardship, began to influence the simple minds of the rest :—" The time had come when the veteran should seek his overdue discharge, and the younger man a less niggardly pay ; when all should claim relief from their miseries and take vengeance on the cruelty of their centurions." These were not the utterances of a solitary Percennius declaiming to the Pannonian legions ; nor were they addressed to the uneasy ears of soldiers who had other and more powerful armies to bear in view : it was a sedition of many tongues and voices :—" Theirs were the hands that held the destinies of Rome ; theirs the victories by which the empire grew ; theirs the name which Caesars assumed ! "[1]

XXXII. The legate made no counter-move : indeed, the prevalent frenzy had destroyed his nerve. In a sudden paroxysm of rage the troops rushed with drawn swords on the centurions, the traditional objects of military hatred, and always the first victims of its fury. They threw them to the ground and applied the lash, sixty strokes to a man, one for every centurion in the legion ; then tossed them with dislocated limbs, mangled, in some cases unconscious, over the wall or into the waters of the Rhine. Septimius took refuge at the tribunal and threw himself at the feet of Caecina, but was demanded with such insistence that he had to be surrendered to his fate. Cassius Chaerea, soon to win a name in history as the slayer of Caligula, then a reckless stripling,[2] opened a way with his sword through an armed and challenging multitude. Neither tribune

luckily lost, but the details are striking enough even in the pages of Dio (LIX. 29), Josephus (*A.J.* XIX. 1-4), and Suetonius (*Calig.* 56–8).

non castrorum praefectus ius obtinuit: vigilias, stationes, et si qua alia praesens usus indixerat, ipsi partiebantur. Id militaris animos altius coniectantibus praecipuum indicium magni atque inplacabilis motus, quod disiecti nil neque [1] paucorum instinctu, set pariter ardescerent, pariter silerent, tanta aequalitate et constantia, ut regi crederes.

XXXIII. Interea Germanico per Gallias, ut diximus, census accipienti excessisse Augustum adfertur. Neptem eius Agrippinam in matrimonio pluresque ex ea liberos habebat, ipse Druso fratre Tiberii genitus, Augustae nepos, set anxius occultis in se patrui aviaeque odiis, quorum causae acriores quia iniquae. Quippe Drusi magna apud populum Romanum memoria, credebaturque, si rerum potitus foret, libertatem redditurus; unde in Germanicum favor et spes eadem. Nam iuveni civile ingenium, mira comitas et diversa ab [2] Tiberii sermone, vultu, adrogantibus et obscuris. Accedebant muliebres offensiones novercalibus Liviae in Agrippinam stimulis, atque ipsa Agrippina paulo commotior, nisi quod castitate et mariti amore quamvis indomitum animum in bonum vertebat.

XXXIV. Sed Germanicus quanto summae spei

---

[1] disiecti nil neque *Heraeus* : neque disiecti nil.
[2] ab *Weissenborn* (a *Beroaldus*) : ad.

nor camp-marshal kept authority longer: watches, patrols, every duty which circumstances indicated as vital, the mutineers distributed among themselves. Indeed, to a careful observer of the military temperament, the most alarming sign of acute and intractable disaffection was this: there were no spasmodic outbreaks instigated by a few firebrands, but everywhere one white heat of anger, one silence, and withal a steadiness and uniformity which might well have been accredited to discipline.

XXXIII. In the meantime, Germanicus, as we have stated, was traversing the Gallic provinces and assessing their tribute, when the message came that Augustus was no more. Married to the late emperor's granddaughter Agrippina, who had borne him several children, and himself a grandchild of the dowager (he was the son of Tiberius' brother Drusus), he was tormented none the less by the secret hatred of his uncle and grandmother—hatred springing from motives the more potent because iniquitous. For Drusus was still a living memory to the nation, and it was believed that, had he succeeded, he would have restored the age of liberty; whence the same affection and hopes centred on the young Germanicus with his unassuming disposition and his exceptional courtesy, so far removed from the inscrutable arrogance of word and look which characterized Tiberius. Feminine animosities increased the tension as Livia had a stepmother's irritable dislike of Agrippina, whose own temper was not without a hint of fire, though purity of mind and wifely devotion kept her rebellious spirit on the side of righteousness.

XXXIV. But the nearer Germanicus stood to the supreme ambition, the more energy he threw into

propior, tanto impensius pro Tiberio niti; seque et[1] proximos et Belgarum civitates in verba eius adigit. Dehinc, audito legionum tumultu, raptim profectus, obvias extra castra habuit, deiectis in terram oculis velut paenitentia. Postquam vallum iniit, dissoni questus audiri coepere. Et quidam prensa manu eius per speciem exosculandi inseruerunt digitos, ut vacua dentibus ora contingeret; alii curvata senio membra ostendebant. Adsistentem contionem, quia permixta videbatur, discedere in manipulos iubet: sic melius audituros responsum; vexilla praeferri, ut id saltem dicerneret cohortis; tarde obtemperavere. Tunc, a veneratione Augusti orsus, flexit ad victorias triumphosque Tiberii, praecipuis laudibus celebrans quae apud Germanias illis cum legionibus pulcherrima fecisset. Italiae inde consensum, Galliarum fidem extollit; nil usquam turbidum aut discors. Silentio haec vel murmure modico audita sunt.

XXXV. Vt seditionem attigit, ubi modestia militaris, ubi veteris disciplinae decus, quonam tribunos, quo centuriones exegissent, rogitans, nudant universi[2] corpora, cicatrices ex vulneribus, verberum notas exprobrant; mox indiscertis vocibus pretia vacationum, angustias stipendii, duri-

---

[1] seque et *Haase* : seque.
[2] universi *Lipsius* : universa.

---

[1] Tiberius—the foremost Roman general after the death of Agrippa—operated against the Germans, first in 9–8 B.C., then in 4–5 A.D., and finally, after the Varian disaster, in 9–11 A.D.

the cause of Tiberius. He administered the oath of fealty to himself, his subordinates, and the Belgic cities. Then came the news that the legions were out of hand. He set out in hot haste, and found them drawn up to meet him outside the camp, their eyes fixed on the ground in affected penitence. As soon as he entered the lines, a jangle of complaints began to assail his ears. Some of the men seized his hand, and with a pretence of kissing it pushed the fingers between their lips, so that he should touch their toothless gums; others showed him limbs bent and bowed with old age. When at last they stood ready to listen, as there appeared to be no sort of order, Germanicus commanded them to divide into companies: they told him they would hear better as they were. At least, he insisted, bring the ensigns forward; there must be something to distinguish the cohorts: they obeyed, but slowly. Then, beginning with a pious tribute to the memory of Augustus, he changed to the victories and the triumphs of Tiberius, keeping his liveliest praise for the laurels he had won in the Germanies at the head of those very legions.[1] Next he enlarged on the unanimity of Italy and the loyalty of the Gallic provinces, the absence everywhere of turbulence or disaffection.

XXXV. All this was listened to in silence or with suppressed murmurs. But when he touched on the mutiny and asked where was their soldierly obedience? where the discipline, once their glory? whither had they driven their tribunes—their centurions? with one impulse they tore off their tunics and reproachfully exhibited the scars of battle and the imprints of the lash. Then, in one undistinguished uproar, they taunted him with the fees

tiam operum ac propriis nominibus incusant vallum, fossas, pabuli, materiae, lignorum adgestus, et si qua alia ex necessitate aut adversus otium castrorum quaeruntur. Atrocissimus veteranorum clamor oriebatur, qui tricena aut supra stipendia numerantes, mederetur fessis, neu mortem in isdem laboribus obirent,[1] sed finem tam exercitae militiae neque inopem requiem orabant. Fuere etiam qui legatam a divo Augusto pecuniam reposcerent, faustis in Germanicum ominibus; et, si vellet imperium, promptos[2] ostentavere. Tum vero, quasi scelere contaminaretur, praeceps tribunali desiluit. Opposuerunt abeunti arma, minitantes, ni regrederetur; at ille moriturum potius quam fidem exueret clamitans, ferrum a latere deripuit[3] elatumque deferebat in pectus, ni proximi prensam dextram vi attinuissent. Extrema et conglobata inter se pars contionis ac, vix credibile dictu, quidam singuli, propius incedentes, feriret hortabantur; et miles nomine Calusidius strictum obtulit gladium, addito acutiorem esse. Saevum id malique moris etiam furentibus visum, ac spatium fuit quo Caesar ab amicis in tabernaculum raperetur.

---

[1] laboribus obirent *Ernesti* : laboribus.
[2] promptos *Rhenanus* : promtas.
[3] deripuit *Beroaldus* : diripuit.

---

[1] *i.e.* timber—a sense of *materia* which survives in the Spanish *madera*.

[2] For the legacy, see above (chap. 8). The implication of *reposcerent* is taken to be that they considered Germanicus the lawful heir : on the other hand, the phrase *faustis in Germanicum ominibus* can hardly be pressed into meaning much more than "with expressions of good-will to Germanicus." Cf. V. 4: *populus . . . circumsistit curiam faustisque in*

for exemption from duty, the miserly rate of pay, and the severity of the work,—parapet-making, entrenching, and the collection of forage, building material[1] and fuel were specifically mentioned, along with the other camp drudgeries imposed sometimes from necessity, sometimes as a precaution against leisure. The most appalling outcry arose from the veterans, who, enumerating their thirty or more campaigns, begged him to give relief to outworn men and not to leave them to end their days in the old wretchedness, but fix a term to this grinding service and allow them a little rest secured from beggary. There were some even who claimed the money bequeathed to them by the deified Augustus, with happy auguries for Germanicus;[2] and, should he desire the throne, they made it manifest that they were ready. On this he leapt straight from the platform as if he was being infected with their guilt. They barred his way with their weapons, threatening to use them unless he returned : but he, exclaiming that he would sooner die than turn traitor, snatched the sword from his side, raised it, and would have buried it in his breast, if the bystanders had not caught his arm and held it by force. The remoter and closely packed part of the assembly, and--though the statement passes belief—certain individual soldiers, advancing close to him, urged him to strike home. One private, by the name of Calusidius, drew his own blade and offered it with the commendation that " it was sharper." Even to that crowd of madmen the act seemed brutal and ill-conditioned, and there followed a pause long enough for the Caesar's friends to hurry him into his tent.

Caesarem ominibus falsas litteras et principe invito exitium domui eius intendi clamitat.

XXXVI. Consultatum ibi de remedio; etenim nuntiabatur parari legatos, qui superiorem exercitum ad causam eandem traherent; destinatum excidio Vbiorum oppidum, imbutasque praeda manus in direptionem Galliarum erupturas. Augebat metum gnarus Romanae seditionis et, si mitteretur ripa, invasurus hostis: at, si auxilia et socii adversum abscedentis legiones armarentur, civile bellum suscipi. Periculosa severitas, flagitiosa largitio; seu nihil militi, sive [1] omnia concederentur [2] in ancipiti res publica. Igitur, volutatis inter se rationibus, placitum ut epistulae nomine principis scriberentur: missionem dari vicena stipendia meritis, exauctorari qui sena dena fecissent ac retineri sub vexillo ceterorum inmunes nisi propulsandi hostis, legata quae petiverant exsolvi duplicarique.

XXXVII. Sensit miles in tempus conficta statimque flagitavit. Missio per tribunos maturatur, largitio differebatur in hiberna cuiusque. Non abscessere quintani unetvicesimanique, donec isdem in aestivis contracta ex viatico amicorum ipsiusque Caesaris pecunia persolveretur. Primam ac vicesimam legiones Caecina legatus in civitatem Vbiorum reduxit,

---

[1] sive *Jac. Gronovius* (seu *Beroaldus*): sibi.
[2] concederentur *Rhenanus*: concedentur.

---

[1] Cologne—later *Colonia Agrippinensis.* In the following chapter, *civitas Ubiorum* is merely synonymous.

[2] Yet in chap. 48 he reappears, not at Cologne but at Xanten (*Castra Vetera*); whence Mommsen's conjecture that the text of Tacitus, or of his authority, should run:—*primam ac vicesimam legiones Germanicus in civitatem Ubiorum reduxit, quintam et unetvicesimam Caecina legatus in Castra Vetera, turpi agmine e.q.s.*

XXXVI. There the question of remedies was debated. For reports were coming in that a mission was being organized to bring the upper army into line, that the Ubian capital[1] had been marked down for destruction, and that after this preliminary experiment in pillage the mutineers proposed to break out and loot the Gallic provinces. To add to the alarm, the enemy was cognizant of the disaffection in the Roman ranks, and invasion was certain if the Rhine bank was abandoned. Yet to arm the auxiliaries native and foreign against the seceding legions was nothing less than an act of civil war. Severity was dangerous, indulgence criminal: to concede the soldiery all or nothing was equally to hazard the existence of the empire. Therefore, after the arguments had been revolved and balanced, it was decided to have letters written in the name of the emperor, directing that all men who had served twenty years should be finally discharged; that any who had served sixteen should be released from duty and kept with the colours under no obligation beyond that of assisting to repel an enemy; and that the legacies claimed should be paid and doubled.

XXXVII. The troops saw that all this was invented for the occasion, and demanded immediate action. The discharges were expedited at once by the tribunes: the monetary grant was held back till the men should have reached their proper quarters for the winter. The fifth and twenty-first legions declined to move until the sum was made up and paid where they stood, in the summer camp, out of the travelling-chests of the Caesar's suite and of the prince himself. The legate Caecina led the first and twentieth legions back to the Ubian capital:[2] a dis-

turpi agmine, cum fisci de imperatore rapti inter signa interque aquilas veherentur. Germanicus, superiorem ad exercitum profectus, secundam et tertiam decumam et sextam decumam legiones nihil cunctatas sacramento adigit; quartadecumani paulum dubitaverant. Pecunia et missio quamvis non flagitantibus oblata est.

XXXVIII. At in Chaucis coeptavere seditionem praesidium agitantes vexillarii discordium legionum, et praesenti duorum militum supplicio paulum repressi sunt. Iusserat id M'. Ennius[1] castrorum praefectus, bono magis exemplo quam concesso iure. Deinde intumescente motu profugus repertusque, postquam intutae latebrae, praesidium ab audacia mutuatur: non praefectum ab iis, sed Germanicum ducem, sed Tiberium imperatorem violari. Simul exterritis qui obstiterant,[2] raptum vexillum ad ripam vertit, et, si quis agmine decessisset, pro desertore fore clamitans, reduxit in hiberna turbidos et nihil ausos.

XXXIX. Interea legati ab senatu regressum iam apud aram Vbiorum Germanicum adeunt. Duae ibi legiones, prima atque vicesima, veteranique nuper missi sub vexillo hiemabant. Pavidos et conscien-

---

[1] M'. Ennius *Ruperti* : mennius.
[2] obstiterant *Beroaldus* : obsisterant.

---

[1] Not a *vexillum veteranorum* (p. 276 n.)—for the veterans were in camp—but a detached body of legionaries on special service. The Chauci are the "Lesser Chauci" (*Chauci minores*, Καῦχοι οἱ μικροί) between the Ems and Weser.
[2] The deputation is that sent out to confer the *proconsulare imperium* (chap. 14): the Altar was at Cologne, dedicated

graceful march, with the general's plundered coffers borne flanked by ensigns and by eagles. Germanicus set out for the upper army, and induced the second, thirteenth, and sixteenth legions to take the oath of fidelity without demur; the fourteenth had shown some little hesitation. The money and discharges, though not demanded, were voluntarily conceded.

XXXVIII. Among the Chauci, however, a detachment,[1] drawn from the disaffected legions, which was serving on garrison duty, made a fresh attempt at mutiny, and was repressed for the moment by the summary execution of a couple of soldiers. The order had been given by Manius Ennius, the camp-marshal, and was more a wholesome example than a legal exercise of authority. Then as the wave of disorder began to swell, he fled, was discovered, and as his hiding offered no security, resolved to owe salvation to audacity :—" It was no camp-marshal," he cried, " whom they were affronting; it was Germanicus, their general—Tiberius, their emperor." At the same time, overawing resistance, he snatched up the standard, turned it towards the Rhine, and, proclaiming that anyone falling out of the ranks would be regarded as a deserter, led his men back to winter-quarters, mutinous enough but with nothing ventured.

XXXIX. Meanwhile the deputation from the senate found Germanicus, who had returned by then, at the Altar of the Ubians.[2] Two legions were wintering there, the first and twentieth; also the veterans recently discharged and now with their colours. Nervous as they were and distraught with

to Augustus, and serving apparently as a centre of the cult to the whole of Roman Germany.

tia vaecordes intrat metus venisse patrum iussu qui inrita facerent quae per seditionem expresserant. Vtque mos vulgo quamvis falsis reum subdere, Munatium Plancum consulatu functum, principem legationis, auctorem senatus consulti incusant: et nocte concubia vexillum in domo Germanici situm flagitare occipiunt, concursuque ad ianuam facto, moliuntur foris, extractum cubili Caesarem tradere vexillum intento mortis metu subigunt. Mox vagi per vias obvios habuere legatos, audita consternatione ad Germanicum tendentis. Ingerunt contumelias, caedem parant, Planco maxime, quem dignitas fuga impediverat; neque aliud periclitanti subsidium quam castra primae legionis. Illic signa et aquilam amplexus religione sese tutabatur, ac ni aquilifer Calpurnius vim extremam arcuisset, rarum etiam inter hostis, legatus populi Romani Romanis in castris sanguine suo altaria deum commaculavisset. Luce demum, postquam dux et miles et facta noscebantur, ingressus castra Germanicus perduci ad se Plancum imperat recepitque in tribunal. Tum fatalem increpans rabiem, neque militum sed deum ira resurgere, cur venerint legati aperit; ius legationis atque ipsius Planci gravem et

---

[1] The veterans, like Germanicus, are presumably quartered, not in camp, but in the town. They demand their *vexillum* as the symbol and guarantee of their status, in case the motives of the deputation should prove sinister.

[2] The standards and eagles (*propria legionum numina*, II. 17) were sacrosanct and adored as such.

[3] They stood with the standards in the *principia*.

the consciousness of guilt, the fear came over them that a senatorial commission had arrived to revoke all the concessions extorted by their rebellion. With the common propensity of crowds to find a victim, however false the charge, they accused Munatius Plancus, an ex-consul who was at the head of the deputation, of initiating the decree. Before the night was far advanced, they began to shout for the colours kept in Germanicus' quarters.[1] There was a rush to the gate; they forced the door, and, dragging the prince from bed, compelled him on pain of death to hand over the ensign. A little later, while roving the streets, they lit on the envoys themselves, who had heard the disturbance and were hurrying to Germanicus. They loaded them with insults, and contemplated murder; especially in the case of Plancus, whose dignity had debarred him from flight. Nor in his extremity had he any refuge but the quarters of the first legion. There, clasping the standards and the eagle, he lay in sanctuary;[2] and had not the eagle-bearer Calpurnius shielded him from the crowning violence, then—by a crime almost unknown even between enemies—an ambassador of the Roman people would in a Roman camp have defiled with his blood the altars of heaven.[3] At last, when the dawn came and officer and private and the doings of the night were recognized for what they were, Germanicus entered the camp, ordered Plancus to be brought to him, and took him on to the tribunal. Then, rebuking the "fatal madness, rekindled not so much by their own anger as by that of heaven," he gave the reasons for the deputies' arrival. He was plaintively eloquent upon the rights of ambassadors and the serious and undeserved

311

immeritum casum, simul quantum dedecoris adierit legio, facunde miseratur, attonitaque magis quam quieta contione, legatos praesidio auxiliarium equitum dimittit.

XL. Eo in metu arguere Germanicum omnes, quod non ad superiorem exercitum pergeret, ubi obsequia et contra rebellis auxilium: satis superque missione et pecunia et mollibus consultis peccatum. Vel si vilis ipsi salus, cur filium parvulum, cur gravidam coniugem inter furentis et omnis humani iuris violatores haberet? Illos saltem avo et rei publicae redderet. Diu cunctatus aspernantem uxorem, cum se divo Augusto ortam neque degenerem ad pericula testaretur, postremo uterum eius et communem filium multo cum fletu complexus, ut abiret perpulit. Incedebat muliebre et miserabile agmen, profuga ducis uxor, parvulum sinu filium gerens, lamentantes circum amicorum coniuges, quae simul trahebantur; nec minus tristes qui manebant.

XLI. Non florentis Caesaris neque suis in castris, sed velut in urbe victa facies; gemitusque ac planctus etiam militum auris oraque advertere: progrediuntur contuberniis. Quis ille flebilis sonus? quid [1] tam triste? Feminas inlustris, non centurionem ad tutelam, non militem, nihil imperatoriae uxoris aut comitatus soliti: pergere ad Treviros

---

[1] quid *Heinsius*: quod.

outrage to Plancus, as also upon the deep disgrace contracted by the legion. Then, after reducing his hearers to stupor, if not to peace, he dismissed the deputies under a guard of auxiliary cavalry.

XL. During these alarms, Germanicus was universally blamed for not proceeding to the upper army, where he could count on obedience and on help against the rebels:—"Discharges, donations, and softhearted measures had done more than enough mischief. Or, if he held his own life cheap, why keep an infant son and a pregnant wife among madmen who trampled on all laws, human or divine? These at any rate he ought to restore to their grandfather and the commonwealth." He was long undecided, and Agrippina met the proposal with disdain, protesting that she was a descendant of the deified Augustus, and danger would not find her degenerate. At last, bursting into tears, he embraced their common child, together with herself and the babe to be, and so induced her to depart. Feminine and pitiable the procession began to move—the commander's wife in flight with his infant son borne on her breast, and round her the tearful wives of his friends, dragged like herself from their husbands. Nor were those who remained less woe-begone.

XLI. The picture recalled less a Caesar at the zenith of fortune and in his own camp than a scene in a taken town. The sobbing and wailing drew the ears and eyes of the troops themselves. They began to emerge from quarters:—"Why," they demanded, "the sound of weeping? What calamity had happened? Here were these ladies of rank, and not a centurion to guard them, not a soldier, no sign of the usual escort or that this was the general's wife!

et externae tradi fidei.[1] Pudor inde et miseratio et
patris Agrippae, Augusti avi memoria, socer Drusus,
ipsa insigni fecunditate, praeclara pudicitia; iam
infans in castris genitus, in contubernio legionum
eductus, quem militari vocabulo Caligulam appella-
bant, quia plerumque ad concilianda vulgi studia eo
tegmine pedum induebatur. Sed nihil aeque flexit
quam invidia in Treviros; orant, obsistunt,[2] rediret,
maneret, pars Agrippinae occursantes, plurimi ad
Germanicum regressi. Isque, ut erat recens dolore
et ira, apud circumfusos ita coepit:

XLII. " Non mihi uxor aut filius patre et re publica
cariores sunt, sed illum quidem sua maiestas, imperium
Romanum ceteri exercitus defendent. Coniugem
et liberos meos, quos pro gloria vestra libens ad
exitium offerrem, nunc procul a furentibus sum-
moveo, ut quidquid istud sceleris imminet, meo
tantum sanguine pietur, neve occisus Augusti
pronepos, interfecta Tiberii nurus nocentiores vos
faciant.[3] Quid enim per hos dies inausum inteme-
ratumve vobis? Quod nomen huic coetui dabo?
militesne appellem, qui filium imperatoris vestri
vallo et armis circumsedistis? An civis, quibus

---

[1] tradi fidei *Wurm* : fidei.
[2] obsistunt *Beroaldus* : absistunt.
[3] faciant *Ritter* : faciat.

---

[1] A Gallic tribe, whose capital was the modern Trèves.
[2] " Little *caliga* "—the hob-nailed military (and rustic)
boot, not worn by officers above the rank of centurion, and
therefore regarded by the private soldier as typifying his
vocation. The tradition that Caligula was actually born in
camp is refuted by Suetonius (*Cal.* 8):—*ego in actis Anti
editum invenio.*

They were bound for the Treviri [1]—handed over to the protection of foreigners." There followed shame and pity and memories of her father Agrippa, of Augustus her grandfather. She was the daughter-in-law of Drusus, herself a wife of notable fruit-fulness and shining chastity. There was also her little son, born in the camp and bred the playmate of the legions; whom soldier-like they had dubbed "Bootikins" [2]—Caligula—because, as an appeal to the fancy of the rank and file, he generally wore the footgear of that name. Nothing, however, swayed them so much as their jealousy of the Treviri. They implored, they obstructed:—" She must come back, she must stay," they urged; some running to inter-cept Agrippina, the majority hurrying back to Ger-manicus. Still smarting with grief and indignation, he stood in the centre of the crowd, and thus began:—

XLII. "Neither my wife nor my son is dearer to me than my father and my country; but his own majesty will protect my father, and its other armies the empire. My wife and children I would cheerfully devote to death in the cause of your glory; as it is, I am remov-ing them from your madness. Whatever this impend-ing villainy of yours may prove to be, I prefer that it should be expiated by my own blood only, and that you should not treble your guilt by butchering the great-grandson of Augustus and murdering the daughter-in-law of Tiberius. For what in these latter days have you left unventured or unviolated? What name am I to give a gathering like this? Shall I call you soldiers—who have besieged the son of your emperor with your earthworks and your arms? Or citizens—who have treated the authority of the

tam proiecta senatus auctoritas? Hostium quoque ius et sacra legationis et fas gentium rupistis. Divus Iulius seditionem exercitus verbo uno compescuit, Quirites vocando qui sacramentum eius detrectabant; divus Augustus vultu et aspectu Actiacas legiones exterruit: nos, ut nondum eosdem, ita ex illis ortos, si Hispaniae Suriaeve miles aspernaretur, tamen mirum et indignum erat. Primane et vicesima legiones, illa signis a Tiberio acceptis, tu tot proeliorum socia, tot praemiis aucta, hanc tam [1] egregiam duci vestro gratiam refertis? Hunc ego nuntium patri, laeta omnia aliis e provinciis audienti, feram? ipsius tirones, ipsius veteranos non missione, non pecunia satiatos: hic tantum interfici centuriones, eici tribunos, includi legatos, infecta sanguine castra, flumina, meque precariam animam inter infensos trahere.

XLIII. "Cur enim primo contionis die ferrum illud, quod pectori meo infigere parabam, detraxistis, o inprovidi amici? Melius et amantius ille qui gladium offerebat. Cecidissem certe nondum tot flagitiorum exercitu meo conscius; legissetis ducem, qui meam quidem mortem inpunitam sineret, Vari tamen et trium legionum ulcisceretur. Neque enim di sinant

---

[1] aucta, hanc tam *Nipperdey, Andresen* : aucta.

---

[1] Citizens, as opposed to soldiers: the occasion was the mutiny of the tenth legion in 47 B.C. A dubious story runs that long afterwards Severus Alexander repeated the device at Antioch :—*Vos omnes hodie una voce, Quirites, dimittam, et incertum an Quirites* (Lampridius, chap. 53).

[2] At Brindisi, in the winter of 30 B.C. But Germanicus seems to embellish the facts.

[3] The scene is in the camp of the first legion (chap. 39), to which Germanicus addresses his direct appeal :—*tu tot proeliorum socia e.q.s.* The twentieth (*Valeria victrix*), one

senate as a thing so abject? You have outraged the
privileges due even to an enemy, the sanctity of
ambassadors, the law of nations. The deified Julius
crushed the insurrection of an army by one word:
they refused the soldiers' oath, and he addressed them
as *Quirites*.[1] A look, a glance, from the deified
Augustus, and the legions of Actium quailed.[2] I
myself am not yet as they, but I spring of their line,
and if the garrisons of Spain or Syria were to flout
me, it would still be a wonder and an infamy. And
is it the first and twentieth legions,—-the men who
took their standards from Tiberius, and you who
have shared his many fields and thriven on his
many bounties,[3]—that make this generous return
to their leader? Is this the news I must carry to
my father, while he hears from other provinces that
all is well—that his own recruits, his own veterans,
are not sated yet with money and dismissals; that
here only centurions are murdered, tribunes ejected,
generals imprisoned; that camp and river are red
with blood, while I myself linger out a precarious
life among men that seek to take it away?

XLIII. "For why, in the first day's meeting, my
short-sighted friends, did you wrench away the steel
I was preparing to plunge in my breast? Better and
more lovingly the man who offered me his sword!
At least I should have fallen with not all my army's
guilt upon my soul. You would have chosen a
general, who, while leaving my own death unpunished, would have avenged that of Varus and his three
legions. For, though the Belgians offer their ser-

of those raised, possibly by Tiberius himself, to cope with the
great Pannonian revolt of 6 A.D., is *illa* as the more remote in
thought, even if not in the order of words.

ut Belgarum quamquam offerentium decus istud et
claritudo sit, subvenisse Romano nomini, compres-
sisse Germaniae populos. Tua, dive Auguste, caelo
recepta mens, tua, pater Druse, imago, tui memoria,
isdem istis cum militibus, quos iam pudor et gloria
intrat, eluant hanc maculam irasque civilis in exitium
hostibus vertant. Vos quoque, quorum alia nunc ora,
alia pectora contueor, si legatos senatui, obsequium
imperatori, si mihi coniugem et filium redditis, disce-
dite a contactu ac dividite turbidos: id stabile ad
paenitentiam, id fidei vinculum erit."

XLIV. Supplices ad haec et vera exprobrari
fatentes, orabant puniret noxios, ignosceret lapsis
et duceret in hostem; revocaretur coniunx, rediret
legionum alumnus neve obses Gallis traderetur.
Reditum Agrippinae excusavit ob imminentem
partum et hiemem: venturum filium; cetera ipsi
exsequerentur. Discurrunt mutati et seditiosissi-
mum quemque vinctos trahunt ad legatum legionis
primae C. Caetronium, qui iudicium et poenas de
singulis in hunc modum exercuit. Stabant pro contione legiones destrictis gladiis: reus in suggestu
per tribunum ostendebatur; si nocentem adclama-

---

[1] It has been shown by Mommsen that the child, in all probability, was still-born.

vices, God forbid that theirs should be the honour and glory of vindicating the Roman name and quelling the nations of Germany! May thy spirit, Augustus, now received with thyself into heaven,—may thy image, my father Drusus, and the memory of thee, be with these same soldiers of yours, whose hearts are already opening to the sense of shame and of glory, to cancel this stain and convert our civil broils to the destruction of our enemies! And you yourselves—for now I am looking into changed faces and changed minds—if you are willing to restore to the senate its deputies, to the emperor your obedience, and to me my wife and children, then stand clear of the infection and set the malignants apart: that will be a security of repentance—that a guarantee of loyalty!"

XLIV. His words converted them into suppliants; they owned the justice of the charges and begged him to punish the guilty, forgive the erring, and lead them against the enemy. Let him recall his wife; let the nursling of the legions return: he must not be given in hostage to Gauls! His wife, he answered, must be excused: she could hardly return with winter and her confinement impending.[1] His son, however, should come back to them: what was still to be done they could do themselves.—They were changed men now; and, rushing in all directions, they threw the most prominent of the mutineers into chains and dragged them to Gaius Caetronius, legate of the first legion, who dealt out justice—and punishment—to them one by one by the following method. The legions were stationed in front with drawn swords; the accused was displayed on the platform by a tribune; if they cried "Guilty," he was thrown

319

verant, praeceps datus trucidabatur. Et gaudebat
caedibus miles, tamquam semet absolveret; nec
Caesar arcebat, quando nullo ipsius iussu penes
eosdem saevitia facti et invidia erat. Secuti exemplum veterani haud multo post in Raetiam mittuntur, specie defendendae provinciae ob imminentis Suebos, ceterum ut avellerentur castris, truci-
bus adhuc non minus asperitate remedii quam sceleris memoria. Centurionatum inde egit. Citatus
ab imperatore nomen, ordinem, patriam, numerum
stipendiorum, quae strenue in proeliis fecisset, et
cui erant dona [1] militaria, edebat. Si tribuni, si
legio industriam innocentiamque adprobaverant,
retinebat ordinem; [2] ubi avaritiam aut crudelitatem
consensu obiectavissent, solvebatur militia.

XLV. Sic compositis praesentibus, haud minor
moles supererat ob ferociam quintae et unetvice-
simae legionum, sexagesimum apud lapidem (loco
Vetera nomen est) hibernantium. Nam primi seditionem coeptaverant: atrocissimum quodque facinus horum manibus patratum; nec poena commilitonum exterriti nec paenitentia conversi iras reti-
nebant. Igitur Caesar arma, classem, socios demit-
tere Rheno parat, si imperium detrectetur, bello
certaturus.

XLVI. At Romae nondum cognito qui fuisset

----

[1] dona *Victorius*: donaria.
[2] ordinem *Kiessling*: ordines.

----

[1] The province, which included on the north the frontier-
district of Vindelicia, comprised the upper valleys of the
Danube and Inn, the Grisons, Tyrol, and part of Bavaria.
[2] By the group of tribes, east of the Elbe and north of the
Danube, which constituted the kingdom of Marbod (see II. 44).
[3] In the neighbourhood of Xanten.

down and hacked to death. The troops revelled in the butchery, which they took as an act of purification; nor was Germanicus inclined to restrain them—the orders had been none of his, and the perpetrators of the cruelty would have to bear its odium. The veterans followed the example, and shortly afterwards were ordered to Raetia[1]; nominally to defend the province against a threatened Suevian invasion,[2] actually to remove them from a camp grim even yet with remembered crimes and the equal horror of their purging. Then came a revision of the list of centurions. Each, on citation by the commander-in-chief, gave his name, company, and country; the number of his campaigns, his distinctions in battle and his military decorations, if any. If the tribunes and his legion bore testimony to his energy and integrity, he kept his post: if they agreed in charging him with rapacity or cruelty, he was dismissed from the service.

XLV. This brought the immediate troubles to a standstill; but there remained an obstacle of equal difficulty in the defiant attitude of the fifth and twenty-first legions, which were wintering some sixty miles away at the post known as the Old Camp.[3] They had been the first to break into mutiny; the worst atrocities had been their handiwork; and now they persisted in their fury, undaunted by the punishment and indifferent to the repentance of their comrades. The Caesar, therefore, arranged for the dispatch of arms, vessels, and auxiliaries down the Rhine, determined, if his authority were rejected, to try conclusions with the sword.

XLVI. Before the upshot of events in Illyricum[4]

[4] In the broad sense of Pannonia, Dalmatia, and Moesia.

exitus in Illyrico, et legionum Germanicarum motu
audito, trepida civitas incusare Tiberium quod,
dum patres et plebem, invalida et inermia, cunctatione ficta ludificetur, dissideat interim miles neque
duorum adulescentium nondum adulta auctoritate
comprimi queat. Ire ipsum et opponere maiestatem imperatoriam debuisse cessuris, ubi principem
longa experientia eundemque severitatis et muni-
ficentiae summum vidissent. An Augustum fessa
aetate totiens in Germanias commeare potuisse:
Tiberium vigentem annis sedere in senatu, verba
patrum cavillantem? Satis prospectum urbanae
servituti: militaribus animis adhibenda fomenta,
ut ferre pacem velint.

XLVII. Immotum adversus eos sermones fixum-
que Tiberio fuit non omittere caput rerum neque
se remque publicam in casum dare. Multa quippe
et diversa angebant: validior per Germaniam exercitus, propior apud Pannoniam; ille Galliarum
opibus subnixus, hic Italiae inminens: quos igitur
anteferret? ac ne postpositi contumelia incende-
rentur. At per filios pariter adiri maiestate salva,
cui maior e longinquo reverentia. Simul adulescentibus excusatum quaedam ad patrem reicere,
resistentisque Germanico aut Druso posse a se
mitigari vel infringi: quod aliud subsidium, si impe-

---

[1] The rhetoric is more effective than accurate, since the
latest expeditions of Augustus which can possibly be brought
under the description in the text are dated 16 B.C. and 8 B.C.
(D. Cass. LIV. 19; LV. 6). At the time of the latter, he was
fifty-four years of age, and Tiberius was now fifty-six.

was known at Rome, word came that the German legions had broken out. The panic-stricken capital turned on Tiberius :—" While with his hypocritical hesitation he was befooling the senate and commons, two powerless and unarmed bodies, meantime the troops were rising and could not be checked by the unripe authority of a pair of boys. He ought to have gone in person and confronted the rebels with the majesty of the empire : they would have yielded at sight of a prince, old in experience, and supreme at once to punish or reward. Could Augustus, in his declining years, make so many excursions into the Germanies? and was Tiberius, in the prime of life,[1] to sit idle in the senate, cavilling at the Conscript Fathers' words? Ample provision had been made for the servitude of Rome : it was time to administer some sedative to the passions of the soldiers, and so reconcile them to peace."

XLVII. To all this criticism Tiberius opposed an immutable and rooted determination not to endanger himself and the empire by leaving the centre of affairs. He had, indeed, difficulties enough of one sort or another to harass him. The German army was the stronger; that of Pannonia the nearer : the one was backed by the resources of the Gallic provinces; the other threatened Italy. Which, then, should come first? And what if those postponed should take fire at the slight? But in the persons of his sons he could approach both at once, without hazarding the imperial majesty, always most venerable from a distance. Further, it was excusable in the young princes to refer certain questions to their father, and it was in his power to pacify or crush resistance offered to Germanicus or Drusus; but

ratorem sprevissent? Ceterum ut iam iamque itu-
rus legit comites, conquisivit impedimenta, ador-
navit navis : mox hiemem aut negotia varie causatus,
primo prudentis, dein vulgum, diutissime provincias fefellit.

XLVIII. At Germanicus, quamquam contracto
exercitu et parata in defectores ultione, dandum
adhuc spatium ratus, si recenti exemplo sibi ipsi
consulerent, praemittit litteras ad Caecinam venire
se valida manu ac, ni supplicium in malos praesu-
mant, usurum promisca caede. Eas Caecina aquiliferis signiferisque et quod maxime castrorum sin-
cerum erat occulte recitat, utque cunctos infamiae,
se ipsos morti eximant hortatur : nam in pace causas
et merita spectari; ubi bellum ingruat, innocentis
ac noxios iuxta cadere. Illi, temptatis quos idoneos
rebantur, postquam maiorem legionum partem in
officio vident, de sententia legati statuunt tempus,
quo foedissimum quemque et seditioni promptum
ferro invadant. Tunc signo inter se dato inrumpunt
contubernia, trucidant ignaros, nullo nisi consciis
noscente quod caedis initium, quis finis.

XLIX. Diversa omnium, quae umquam acci-
dere, civilium armorum facies. Non proelio, non
adversis e castris, sed isdem e cubilibus, quos simul

let the emperor be scorned, and what resource was left?—However, as though any moment might see his departure, he chose his escort, provided his equipage, and fitted out vessels. Then with a variety of pleas, based on the wintry season or the pressure of affairs, he deceived at first the shrewdest; the populace, longer; the provinces, longest of all.

XLVIII. Meanwhile Germanicus had collected his force and stood prepared to exact a reckoning from the mutineers. Thinking it best, however, to allow them a further respite, in case they should consult their own safety by following the late precedent, he forwarded a letter to Caecina, saying that he was coming in strength, and, unless they forestalled him by executing the culprits, would put them impartially to the sword. Caecina read it privately to the eagle-bearers, the ensigns, and the most trustworthy men in the camp, urging them to save all from disgrace, and themselves from death. " For in peace," he said, " cases are judged on their merits; when war threatens, the innocent and the guilty fall side by side." Accordingly they tested the men whom they considered suitable, and, finding that in the main the legions were still dutiful, with the general's assent they fixed the date for an armed attack upon the most objectionable and active of the incendiaries. Then, passing the signal to one another, they broke into the tents and struck down their unsuspecting victims; while no one, apart from those in the secret, knew how the massacre had begun or where it was to end.

XLIX. No civil war of any period has presented the features of this. Not in battle, not from opposing camps, but comrades from the same bed—men who

325

vescentis dies, simul quietos nox habuerat, discedunt in partis, ingerunt tela. Clamor, vulnera, sanguis palam, causa in occulto; cuncta [1] fors regit. Et quidam bonorum caesi, postquam, intellecto in quos saeviretur, pessimi quoque arma rapuerant. Neque legatus aut tribunus moderator adfuit: permissa vulgo licentia atque ultio et satietas. Mox ingressus castra Germanicus, non medicinam illud plurimis cum lacrimis, sed cladem appellans cremari corpora iubet.

Truces etiam tum animos cupido involat eundi in hostem, piaculum furoris; nec aliter posse placari commilitonum manis, quam si pectoribus impiis honesta vulnera accepissent. Sequitur ardorem militum Caesar iunctoque ponte tramittit duodecim milia e legionibus, sex et viginti socias cohortis, octo equitum alas, quarum ea seditione intemerata modestia fuit.

L. Laeti neque procul Germani agitabant, dum iustitio ob amissum Augustum, post discordiis attinemur. At Romanus agmine propero silvam Caesiam limitemque a Tiberio coeptum scindit, castra in limite locat, frontem ac tergum vallo, latera concaedibus munitus. Inde saltus obscuros

---

[1] cuncta *Andresen* : cetera.

[1] With the Caesian Forest and the Tiberian *limes* alike unidentified, and the locality of the Marsi unknown (according to Strabo, 290, they had anticipated deportation into Gaul by retreating εἰς τὴν ἐν βάθει χώραν), the topography of Germanicus' raid must remain as obscure to the modern reader as it doubtless was to Tacitus. " It seems hardly possible to go beyond the likelihood that the Romans may have advanced, probably from Vetera, along the left bank of the Lippe, and then struck southward through a comparatively unknown country (*saltus obscuros*) towards the upper Ruhr,

had eaten together by day and rested together at dark—they took their sides and hurled their missiles. The yells, the wounds, and the blood were plain enough; the cause, invisible: chance ruled supreme. A number of the loyal troops perished as well: for, once it was clear who were the objects of attack, the malcontents also had caught up arms. No general or tribune was there to restrain: licence was granted to the mob, and it might glut its vengeance to the full. Before long, Germanicus marched into the camp. "This is not a cure, but a calamity," he said, with a burst of tears, and ordered the bodies to be cremated.

Even yet the temper of the soldiers remained savage and a sudden desire came over them to advance against the enemy : it would be the expiation of their madness; nor could the ghosts of their companions be appeased till their own impious breasts had been marked with honourable wounds. Falling in with the enthusiasm of his troops, the Caesar laid a bridge over the Rhine, and threw across twelve thousand legionaries, with twenty-six cohorts of auxiliaries and eight divisions of cavalry, whose discipline had not been affected by the late mutiny.

L. Throughout the pause, which the mourning for Augustus had begun and our discords prolonged, the Germans had been hovering gleefully in the neighbourhood. By a forced march, however, the Roman columns cut through the Caesian Forest and the line of delimitation commenced by Tiberius.[1] By this line they pitched the camp, with their front and rear protected by embankments and the flanks by a barricade of felled trees. Then came a threading of

and that the tribes living north of the Lippe endeavoured to intercept their retreat." Furneaux.

permeat consultatque ex duobus itineribus breve
et solitum sequatur, an inpeditius et intemptatum
eoque hostibus incautum. Delecta longiore via
cetera adcelerantur : etenim attulerant exploratores
festam eam Germanis noctem ac sollemnibus epulis
ludicram. Caecina cum expeditis cohortibus prae-
ire et obstantia silvarum amoliri iubetur; legiones
modico intervallo sequuntur. Iuvit nox sideribus
inlustris, ventumque ad vicos Marsorum et circum-
datae stationes stratis etiam tum per cubilia prop-
terque mensas, nullo metu, non antepositis vigiliis :
adeo cuncta incuria disiecta erant neque belli timor,
ac ne pax quidem nisi languida et soluta inter temu-
lentos.

LI. Caesar avidas legiones, quo latior populatio
foret, quattuor in cuneos dispertit; quinquaginta
milium spatium ferro flammisque pervastat. Non
sexus, non aetas miserationem attulit : profana simul
et sacra et celeberrimum illis gentibus templum
quod Tanfanae [1] vocabant solo aequantur. Sine vulnere milites, qui semisomnos, inermos aut palantis
ceciderant. Excivit ea caedes Bructeros, Tubantes,
Vsipetes, saltusque, per quos exercitui regressus,
insedere. Quod gnarum duci incessitque itineri et
proelio. Pars equitum et auxiliariae cohortes duce-

***

[1] Tanfanae *Beroaldus* : tāfanae.

***

[1] The " temple " was probably a consecrated grove and
altar; compare the well-known passage (*Germ.* 9) :—*nec
cohibere parietibus deos neque in ullam humani oris speciem
adsimulare ex magnitudine caelestium arbitrantur : lucos ac
nemora consecrant e.q.s.* For Tanfana the only other evidence
is a ninth- or tenth-century line :—*Zanfana sentit morgane
feiziu scâf cleiniu* (Zanfana sendet morgen kleine feiste Schafe).

gloomy forests and a consultation which of two roads
to follow; the one short and usual, the other more
difficult and unexplored, and therefore left unguarded
by the enemy. The longer route was chosen, but
otherwise all speed was made: for scouts had brought
in news that the night was a German festival and
would be celebrated with games and a solemn banquet.
Caecina was ordered to move ahead with the unencumbered cohorts and clear a passage through the
woods: the legions followed at a moderate interval.
The clear, starry night was in our favour; the
Marsian villages were reached, and a ring of pickets
was posted round the enemy, who were still lying,
some in bed, others beside their tables, without misgivings and with no sentries advanced. All was
disorder and improvidence: there was no apprehen-
sion of war, and even their peace was the nerveless
lethargy of drunkards.

LI. To extend the scope of the raid, the Caesar
divided his eager legions into four bodies, and, for
fifty miles around, wasted the country with sword
and flame. Neither age nor sex inspired pity;
places sacred and profane were razed indifferently to
the ground; among them, the most noted religious
centre of these tribes, known as the temple of
Tanfana.[1] The troops escaped without a wound:
they had been cutting down men half-asleep, unarmed
or dispersed.

The carnage brought the Bructeri, Tubantes, and
Usipetes into the field; and they occupied the forest
passes by which the army was bound to return.
This came to the prince's ear, and he took the road
prepared either to march or to fight. A detachment
of cavalry and ten auxiliary cohorts led the way, then

bant, mox prima legio, et mediis impedimentis sinistrum latus unetvicesimani, dextrum quintani clausere; vicesima legio terga firmavit, post ceteri sociorum. Sed hostes, donec agmen per saltus porrigeretur, immoti, dein latera et frontem modice adsultantes, tota vi novissimos incurrere. Turbabanturque densis Germanorum catervis leves cohortes, cum Caesar, advectus ad vicesimanos, voce magna hoc illud tempus obliterandae seditionis clamitabat: pergerent, properarent culpam in decus vertere. Exarsere animis unoque impetu perruptum hostem redigunt in aperta caeduntque: simul primi agminis copiae evasere silvas castraque communivere. Quietum inde iter, fidensque recentibus ac priorum oblitus miles in hibernis locatur.

LII. Nuntiata ea Tiberium laetitia curaque adfecere: gaudebat oppressam seditionem, sed quod largiendis pecuniis et missione festinata favorem militum quaesivisset, bellica quoque Germanici gloria angebatur. Rettulit tamen ad senatum de rebus gestis multaque de virtute eius memoravit, magis in speciem verbis adornata quam ut penitus sentire crederetur. Paucioribus Drusum et finem Illyrici motus laudavit, sed intentior et fida oratione. Cunctaque quae Germanicus indulserat servavit etiam apud Pannonicos exercitus.

came the first legion; the baggage-train was in the centre; the twenty-first legion guarded the left flank; the fifth, the right; the twentieth held the rear, and the rest of the allies followed. The enemy, however, made no move, till the whole line was defiling through the wood: then instituting a half-serious attack on the front and flanks, they threw their full force on the rear. The light-armed cohorts were falling into disorder before the serried German masses, when the Caesar rode up to the men of the twenty-first, and, raising his voice, kept crying that now was their time to efface the stain of mutiny :— " Forward, and make speed to turn disgrace into glory ! " In a flame of enthusiasm, they broke through their enemies at one charge, drove them into the open and cut them down. Simultaneously the forces in the van emerged from the forest and fortified a camp. From this point the march was unmolested, and the soldiers, emboldened by their late performances, and forgetful of the past, were stationed in winter quarters.

LII. The news both relieved and disquieted Tiberius. He was thankful that the rising had been crushed; but that Germanicus should have earned the good-will of the troops by his grants of money and acceleration of discharges—to say nothing of his laurels in the field—there was the rub ! However, in a motion before the senate, he acknowledged his services and enlarged on his courage ; but in terms too speciously florid to be taken as the expression of his inmost feelings. He expressed his satisfaction with Drusus and the conclusion of the trouble in Illyricum more briefly ; but he was in earnest, and his language honest. In addition, he confirmed to the Pannonian legions all concessions granted by Germanicus to his own.

LIII. Eodem anno Iulia supremum diem obiit, ob impudicitiam olim a patre Augusto Pandateria insula, mox oppido Reginorum, qui Siculum fretum accolunt, clausa. Fuerat in matrimonio Tiberii florentibus Gaio et Lucio Caesaribus spreveratque ut inparem; nec alia tam intima Tiberio causa cur Rhodum abscederet. Imperium adeptus extorrem, infamem et post interfectum Postumum Agrippam omnis spei egenam inopia ac tabe longa peremit, obscuram fore necem longinquitate exilii ratus. Par causa saevitiae in Sempronium Gracchum, qui, familia nobili, sollers ingenio et prave facundus, eandem Iuliam in matrimonio Marci Agrippae temeraverat. Nec is libidini finis: traditam Tiberio pervicax adulter contumacia et odiis in maritum accendebat; litteraeque, quas Iulia patri Augusto cum insectatione Tiberii scripsit, a Graccho compositae credebantur. Igitur amotus Cercinam, Africi maris insulam, quattuordecim annis exilium toleravit. Tunc milites ad caedem missi invenere in prominenti litoris, nihil laetum opperientem. Quorum adventu breve tempus petivit, ut suprema mandata uxori Alliariae per litteras daret, cervicemque

---

[1] Daughter of Augustus by Scribonia, and his only child (born 39 B.C., died 14 A.D.); married in 25 B.C. to her first cousin M. Marcellus, and upon his death without issue, two years later, to M. Vipsanius Agrippa, by whom she had three sons, C. and L. Caesar and Agrippa Postumus, with two daughters, Julia and Germanicus' wife Agrippina; transferred after Agrippa's death to Tiberius (11 B.C.), who was compelled to divorce his wife Vipsania for the occasion; disgraced and exiled in 2 B.C.

[2] Vandotena (Ventotene), a barren island north-west from the Bay of Naples.

[3] Reggio.

LIII. This year saw the decease of Julia;[1] whose
licentiousness had long ago driven her father,
Augustus, to confine her, first in the islet of Pandateria,[2] and latterly in the town of Rhegium[3] on the
Sicilian Strait.   Wedded to Tiberius while Gaius and
Lucius Caesar were still in their heyday, she had
despised him as her inferior; and this, in reality, was
the inner reason for his retirement to Rhodes.   Once
upon the throne, he left her, exiled, disgraced, and
(since the killing of Agrippa Postumus)[4] utterly
hopeless, to perish of destitution and slow decline:
the length of her banishment, he calculated, would
obscure the mode of her removal.   A similar motive
dictated his barbarous treatment of Sempronius
Gracchus, a man of high birth, shrewd wit and
perverted eloquence; who had seduced the same
Julia while she was still the wife of Marcus Agrippa.
Nor was this the close of the intrigue: for when
she was made over to Tiberius, her persevering
adulterer worked her into a fever of defiance and
hatred towards her husband; and her letter to her
father Augustus, with its tirade against Tiberius, was
believed to have been drafted by Gracchus.   He was
removed, in consequence, to Cercina,[5] an island in
African waters; where he endured his banishment
for fourteen years.   Now the soldiers sent to despatch
him found him on a projecting strip of shore, awaiting
the worst.   As they landed, he asked for a few
minutes' grace, so that he could write his final instructions to his wife Alliaria.   This done, he offered his

[4] See above, chaps. 5–6.   The implication is that she saw
no hope from her son-in-law, Germanicus.
[5] In reality, two small islands (Kerkena) in the Gulf of
Gabes.

percussoribus obtulit; constantia mortis haud indignus Sempronio nomine: vita degeneraverat. Quidam non Roma eos milites, sed ab L. Asprenate, pro consule Africae, missos tradidere, auctore Tiberio, qui famam caedis posse in Asprenatem verti frustra speraverat.

LIV. Idem annus novas caerimonias accepit addito sodalium Augustalium sacerdotio, ut quondam Titus Tatius retinendis Sabinorum sacris sodalis Titios[1] instituerat. Sorte ducti e primoribus civitatis unus et viginti: Tiberius Drususque et Claudius et Germanicus adiciuntur. Ludos Augustalis tunc primum coeptos turbavit discordia ex certamine histrionum. Indulserat ei ludicro Augustus, dum Maecenati obtemperat effuso in amorem Bathylli; neque ipse abhorrebat talibus studiis, et civile rebatur misceri voluptatibus vulgi. Alia Tiberio morum via: sed populum per tot annos molliter habitum nondum audebat ad duriora vertere.

LV. Druso Caesare C. Norbano consulibus, decernitur Germanico triumphus, manente bello; quod quamquam in aestatem summa ope parabat, initio veris et repentino in Chattos excursu praecepit.

---

[1] Titios *Vertranius*: tatios.

---

[1] An ancient priesthood, the origin and functions of which are equally obscure.

[2] Germanicus' brother, the future emperor. After his own deification, the full style of the association became *sodales Augustales Claudiales*.

[3] See above, chap. 15.

[4] He was a freedman and friend of Augustus, the rival of Pylades, and with him the creator of the pantomime.

[5] On the right bank of the Rhine in the Hesse-Nassau dis-

neck to the assassins, and met death with a firmness not unworthy of the Sempronian name from which his life had been a degeneration. Some state that the soldiers were not sent from Rome, but from Lucius Asprenas, proconsul of Africa: a version due to Tiberius, who had hoped, though vainly, to lay the scandal of the assassination at Asprenas' door.

LIV. The year also brought a novelty in religious ceremonial, which was enriched by a new college of Augustal priests, on the pattern of the old Titian brotherhood[1] founded by Titus Tatius to safeguard the Sabine rites. Twenty-one members were drawn by lot from the leading Roman houses: Tiberius, Drusus, Claudius,[2] and Germanicus were added. The Augustal Games,[3] now first instituted, were marred by a disturbance due to the rivalry of the actors. Augustus had countenanced these theatrical exhibitions in complaisance to Maecenas, who had fallen violently in love with Bathyllus.[4] Besides, he had no personal dislike for amusements of the type, and considered it a graceful act to mix in the pleasures of the crowd. The temper of Tiberius had other tendencies, but as yet he lacked the courage to force into the ways of austerity a nation which had been for so many years pampered.

LV. Drusus Caesar and Gaius Norbanus were now consuls, and a triumph was decreed to Germanicus with the war still in progress. He was preparing to prosecute it with his utmost power in the summer; but in early spring he anticipated matters by a sudden raid against the Chatti.[5] Hopes had arisen

A.V.C. 768 = A.D.15

trict. The tribe, hostile to Rome, was equally so to Arminius and the Cherusci.

Nam spes incesserat dissidere hostem in Arminium
ac Segestem, insignem utrumque perfidia in nos aut
fide. Arminius turbator Germaniae, Segestes parari
rebellionem saepe alias et supremo convivio, post
quod in arma itum, aperuit suasitque Varo ut se et
Arminium et ceteros proceres vinciret: nihil ausu-
ram plebem principibus amotis; atque ipsi tempus
fore, quo crimina et innoxios discerneret. Sed Varus
fato et vi Armini cecidit; Segestes quamquam consensu gentis in bellum tractus, discors manebat,
auctis privatim odiis, quod Arminius filiam eius
alii pactam, rapuerat, gener invisus inimici soceri;
quaeque apud concordes vincula caritatis, incita-
menta irarum apud infensos erant.

LVI. Igitur Germanicus ·quattuor legiones, quinque auxiliarium milia et tumultuarias catervas
Germanorum cis Rhenum colentium Caecinae tradit; totidem legiones, duplicem sociorum numerum
ipse ducit, positoque castello super vestigia paterni
praesidii in monte Tauno, expeditum exercitum in
Chattos rapit, L. Apronio ad munitiones viarum
et fluminum relicto. Nam (rarum illi caelo) siccitate et amnibus modicis inoffensum iter propera-
verat, imbresque et fluminum auctus regredienti

---

[1] A latinized form of *Hermann*. Most of the ascertainable
facts with regard to his career may be gleaned from the first
two books of the Annals: see the remarkable tribute in II. 88.

[2] See p. 248, n.

[3] The *Höhe*—though the ancient name has been restored—
between the Rhine and the Nidda.

that the enemy was becoming divided between Arminius[1] and Segestes: both famous names, one for perfidy towards us, the other for good faith. Arminius was the troubler of Germany: Segestes had repeatedly given warning of projected risings, especially at the last great banquet which preceded the appeal to arms; when he urged Varus to arrest Arminius, himself, and the other chieftains, on the ground that, with their leaders out of the way, the mass of the people would venture nothing, while he would have time enough later to discriminate between guilt and innocence. Varus, however, succumbed to his fate and the sword of Arminius[2]; Segestes, though forced into the war by the united will of the nation, continued to disapprove, and domestic episodes embittered the feud: for Arminius by carrying off his daughter, who was pledged to another, had made himself the hated son-in-law of a hostile father, and a relationship which cements the affection of friends now stimulated the fury of enemies.

LVI. Germanicus, then, after handing over to Caecina four legions, with five thousand auxiliaries and a few German bands drawn at summary notice from the west bank of the Rhine, took the field himself with as many legions and double the number of allies. Erecting a fort over the remains of his father's works on Mount Taunus,[3] he swept his army at full speed against the Chatti: Lucius Apronius was left behind to construct roads and bridges. For owing to the drought—a rare event under those skies—and the consequent shallowness of the streams, Germanicus had pushed on without a check; and rains and floods were to be apprehended on the

metuebantur.[1] Sed Chattis adeo inprovisus advenit,
ut quod imbecillum aetate ac sexu statim captum
aut trucidatum sit. Iuventus flumen Adranam
nando tramiserat,[2] Romanosque pontem coeptantis
arcebant. Dein tormentis sagittisque pulsi, temptatis frustra condicionibus pacis, cum quidam ad
Germanicum perfugissent, reliqui omissis pagis vicis-
que in silvas disperguntur. Caesar, incenso Mattio
(id genti caput), aperta populatus vertit ad Rhenum,
non auso hoste terga abeuntium lacessere, quod
illi moris, quotiens astu magis quam per formidinem cessit. Fuerat animus Cheruscis iuvare Chattos,
sed exterruit Caecina huc illuc ferens arma ; et Marsos
congredi ausos prospero proelio cohibuit.

LVII. Neque multo post legati a Segeste venerunt auxilium orantes adversus vim popularium
a quis circumsedebatur, validiore apud eos Arminio, quoniam bellum suadebat : nam barbaris, quanto
quis audacia promptus, tanto magis fidus rebusque
motis [3] potior habetur. Addiderat Segestes legatis
filium, nomine Segimundum ; sed iuvenis conscientia
cunctabatur. Quippe, anno quo Germaniae desci-
vere, sacerdos apud aram Vbiorum creatus, ruperat
vittas, profugus ad rebellis. Adductus tamen in

---

[1] metuebantur *Lipsius* : metuebatur.
[2] tramiserat *Acidalius* : tramiserit.
[3] rebusque motis *Lipsius* : rebus commotis.

---

[1] A stream falling into the Fulda (the tributary of the
Weser on which Cassel stands).
[2] North of the Eder, but unidentified.
[3] North-east of the Chatti, between the Weser and the
Elbe.
[4] See p. 306, n. 1.

return journey. Actually, his descent was so complete a surprise to the Chatti that all who suffered from the disabilities of age or sex were immediately taken or slaughtered. The able-bodied males had swum the Eder,[1] and, as the Romans began to bridge it, made an effort to force them back. Repelled by the engines and discharges of arrows, they tried, without effect, to negotiate terms of peace: a few then came over to Germanicus, while the rest abandoned their townships and villages, and scattered through the woods. First burning the tribal headquarters at Mattium,[2] the Caesar laid waste the open country, and turned back to the Rhine, the enemy not daring to harass the rear of the withdrawing force—their favourite manœuvre in cases where strategy rather than panic has dictated their retreat. The Cherusci[3] had been inclined to throw in their lot with the Chatti, but were deterred by a series of rapid movements on the part of Caecina: the Marsi, who hazarded an engagement, he checked in a successful action.

LVII. It was not long before envoys arrived from Segestes with a petition for aid against the violence of his countrymen, by whom he was besieged, Arminius being now the dominant figure, since he advocated war. For with barbarians the readier a man is to take a risk so much the more is he the man to trust, the leader to prefer when action is afoot. Segestes had included his son Segimundus in the embassy, though conscience gave the youth pause. For in the year when the Germanies revolted, priest though he was, consecrated at the Altar of the Ubians,[4] he had torn off his fillets and fled to join the rebels. Once persuaded, however, that he could still hope

spem clementiae Romanae, pertulit patris mandata, benigneque exceptus cum praesidio Gallicam in ripam missus est. Germanico pretium fuit convertere agmen, pugnatumque in obsidentis, et ereptus Segestes magna cum propinquorum et clientium manu. Inerant feminae nobiles, inter quas uxor Arminii eademque filia Segestis, mariti magis quam parentis animo neque victa in lacrimas neque voce supplex; compressis intra sinum manibus gravidum uterum intuens. Ferebantur et spolia Varianae cladis, plerisque eorum qui tum in deditionem veniebant praedae data: simul Segestes ipse, ingens visu et memoria bonae societatis inpavidus.

LVIII. Verba eius in hunc modum fuere: " Non hic mihi primus erga populum Romanum fidei et constantiae dies. Ex quo a divo Augusto civitate donatus sum, amicos inimicosque ex vestris utilitatibus delegi, neque odio patriae (quippe proditores etiam iis quos anteponunt invisi sunt[1]), verum quia Romanis Germanisque idem conducere et pacem quam bellum probabam. Ergo raptorem filiae meae, violatorem foederis vestri, Arminium, apud Varum, qui tum exercitui praesidebat, reum feci. Dilatus segnitia ducis, quia parum praesidii in legibus erat, ut me et Arminium et conscios vinciret flagitavi: testis illa nox, mihi utinam potius novissima!

---

[1] invisi sunt *Beroaldus* : invisunt.

in Roman clemency, he brought his father's message, and, after a kind reception, was sent over with a guard to the Gallic bank. Germanicus thought it worth his while to turn back, engaged the blockading forces, and rescued Segestes with a large company of his relatives and dependants. They included some women of high birth, among them the wife of Arminius, who was at the same time the daughter of Segestes, though there was more of the husband than the father in that temper which sustained her, unconquered to a tear, without a word of entreaty, her hands clasped tightly in the folds of her robe and her gaze fixed on her heavy womb. Trophies even of the Varian disaster were brought in—booty allotted in many cases to the very men now surrendering. Segestes himself was present, a huge figure, dauntless in the recollection of treaties honourably kept.

LVIII. His words were to the following effect:— "This is not my first day of loyalty and constancy to the people of Rome. From the moment when the deified Augustus made me a Roman citizen I have chosen my friends and my enemies with a view to your interests: not from hatred of my own country (for the traitor is loathsome even to the party of his choice), but because I took the advantage of Rome and Germany to be one, and peace a better thing than war. For that reason I accused Arminius—to me the abductor of a daughter, to you the violator of a treaty—in presence of Varus, then at the head of your army. Foiled by the general's delay, and knowing how frail were the protections of the law, I begged him to lay in irons Arminius, his accomplices, and myself. That night is my witness, which I would to God had been my last! What followed may

Quae secuta sunt, defleri magis quam defendi possunt: ceterum et inieci catenas Arminio, et a factione eius iniectas perpessus sum. Atque ubi primum tui copia, vetera novis et quieta turbidis antehabeo, neque ob praemium, sed ut me perfidia exsolvam, simul genti Germanorum idoneus conciliator, si paenitentiam quam perniciem maluerit. Pro iuventa et errore filii veniam precor: filiam necessitate huc adductam fateor. Tuum erit consultare utrum praevaleat quod ex Arminio concepit an quod ex me genita est." Caesar clementi responso liberis propinquisque eius incolumitatem, ipsi sedem vetere[1] in provincia pollicetur. Exercitum reduxit nomenque imperatoris, auctore Tiberio, accepit. Arminii uxor virilis sexus stirpem edidit: educatus Ravennae puer quo mox ludibrio conflictatus sit, in tempore memorabo.

LIX. Fama dediti benigneque excepti Segestis vulgata, ut quibusque bellum invitis aut cupientibus erat, spe vel dolore accipitur. Arminium, super insitam violentiam, rapta uxor, subiectus servitio uxoris uterus vaecordem agebant; volitabatque per Cheruscos, arma in Segestem, arma in Caesarem poscens. Neque probris temperabat: egregium patrem, magnum imperatorem, fortem exercitum, quorum tot manus unam mulierculam avexerint. Sibi tres legiones, totidem legatos procubuisse; non enim se proditione neque adversus

---

[1] uetere *Lipsius (et M[2])* : uetera.

---

[1] On the left—"Gallic"—bank. The German territory lost after the Varian disaster is regarded as being still in theory, though no longer in fact, a province.

[2] The account is lost, and in XI. 16 the plain implication is that the boy was already dead.

be deplored more easily than defended. Still, I have thrown my chains on Arminius: I have felt his partisans throw theirs on me. And now, at my first meeting with you, I prefer old things to new, calm to storm—not that I seek a reward, but I wish to free myself from the charge of broken trust, and to be at the same time a meet intercessor for the people of Germany, should it prefer repentance to destruction. For my son and the errors of his youth I ask a pardon. My daughter, I own, is here only by force. It is for you to settle which shall count the more—that she has conceived by Arminius, or that she was begotten by me."

The Caesar's reply was generous: to his relatives and children he promised indemnity: to himself, a residence in the old province.[1] Then he returned with his army, and at the instance of Tiberius took the title of *Imperator*. Arminius' wife gave birth to a male child, who was brought up at Ravenna: the humiliation which he had to suffer later I reserve for the proper place.[2]

LIX. The report of Segestes' surrender and his gracious reception, once it became generally known, was heard with hope or sorrow by the advocates or opponents of war. Arminius, violent enough by nature, was driven frantic by the seizure of his wife and the subjection to slavery of her unborn child. He flew through the Cherusci, demanding war against Segestes, war against the Caesar. There was no sparing of invectives:—" A peerless father! a great commander! a courageous army! whose united powers had carried off one wretched woman. Before his own sword three legions, three generals, had fallen. For he practised war, not by the help of

343

feminas gravidas, sed palam adversus armatos
bellum tractare; cerni adhuc Germanorum in lucis
signa Romana, quae dis patriis suspenderit. Coleret
Segestes victam ripam, redderet filio sacerdotium
hominum: Germanos numquam satis excusaturos,
quod inter Albim et Rhenum virgas et securis et
togam viderint. Aliis gentibus ignorantia imperii
Romani inexperta esse supplicia, nescia tributa:
quae quoniam exuerint, inritusque discesserit ille
inter numina dicatus Augustus, ille delectus Tiberius, ne inperitum adulescentulum, ne seditiosum
exercitum pavescerent. Si patriam, parentes, antiqua mallent quam dominos et colonias novas,
Arminium potius gloriae ac libertatis, quam Segestem flagitiosae servitutis ducem sequerentur."

LX. Conciti per haec non modo Cherusci, sed
conterminae gentes, tractusque in partis Inguiomerus, Arminii patruus, vetere[1] apud Romanos auctoritate; unde maior Caesari metus; et ne bellum
mole una ingrueret, Caecinam cum quadraginta
cohortibus Romanis distrahendo hosti per Bructeros ad flumen Amisiam mittit, equitem Pedo
praefectus finibus Frisiorum ducit. Ipse inpositas
navibus quattuor legiones per lacus vexit; simulque

---

[1] vetere *Wesenberg* : veteri.

---

[1] The sarcasm is evidently directed at the cult of Augustus.
[2] Actually Arminius was only a trifle the senior : compare
II. 73 with II. 88.
[3] A curious expression for his own four legions of the Lower
Army (chap. 31).

treason nor against pregnant women, but in open day
and against men who carried arms.   In the groves of
Germany were still to be seen the Roman standards
which he had hung aloft to the gods of their fathers.
Let Segestes inhabit the conquered bank, and make
his son once more a priest—to mortal deities:[1] one
fact the Germans could never sufficiently condone,
that their eyes had seen the Rods, the Axes, and
the Toga between the Elbe and the Rhine.   Other
nations, unacquainted with the dominion of Rome,
had neither felt her punishments nor known her
exactions: seeing that they had rid themselves of
both, and that the great Augustus, hallowed as deity,
and his chosen Tiberius had departed foiled, let them
never quail before a callow youth,[2] before a disaffected
army! If they loved their country, their parents, their
ancient ways, better than despots and new colonies,
then let them follow Arminius to glory and freedom
rather than Segestes to shame and slavery!"

LX. His appeal roused, not the Cherusci only, but
the bordering tribes as well; and it drew into the
confederacy his uncle Inguiomerus, whose prestige
had long stood high with the Romans.   This deepened
the alarm of Germanicus, and, to prevent the onslaught
from breaking in one great wave, he despatched
Caecina with forty Roman cohorts[3] through the
Bructeri to the Ems, so as to divide the enemy, while
the prefect Pedo[4] led the cavalry along the Frisian
frontier.

He himself, with four legions on board, sailed
through the lakes; and foot, horse, and fleet met

[4] Presumed to be Ovid's friend Pedo Albinovanus (*ex Ponto*,
IV. 10), author of a poem on the campaigns of Germanicus
(Sen. *suas*. I. 14). The Frisii occupied the coastal district
between the Zuydersee and the Ems (*Friesland*).

pedes, eques, classis [1] apud praedictum amnem
convenere. Chauci, cum auxilia pollicerentur, in
commilitium adsciti sunt. Bructeros sua urentis
expedita cum manu L. Stertinius missu Germanici
fudit; interque caedem et praedam repperit unde-
vicesimae legionis aquilam cum Varo amissam.
Ductum inde agmen ad ultimos Bructerorum, quantumque Amisiam et Lupiam amnis inter vastatum,
haud procul Teutoburgiensi saltu, in quo reliquiae
Vari legionumque insepultae dicebantur.

LXI. Igitur cupido Caesarem invadit solvendi
suprema militibus ducique, permoto ad miserationem
omni qui aderat exercitu ob propinquos, amicos,
denique ob casus bellorum et sortem hominum.
Praemisso Caecina, ut occulta saltuum scrutaretur
pontesque et aggeres umido paludum et fallacibus
campis inponeret, incedunt maestos locos visuque
ac memoria deformis.[2] Prima Vari castra lato ambitu
et dimensis principiis trium legionum manus ostentabant; dein semiruto vallo, humili fossa accisae
iam reliquiae consedisse intellegebantur: medio
campi albentia ossa, ut fugerant, ut restiterant,
disiecta vel aggerata. Adiacebant fragmina telorum equorumque artus, simul truncis arborum

---

[1] classis *Lipsius* : classes.
[2] deformis *Beroaldus* : deformides.

---

[1] The four legions are those of the Upper Army : the
" Lakes " are now one with the Zuydersee. The object of
Germanicus' vast détour, and, indeed, the course of the whole
campaign, are obscure in the extreme : for a discussion, see
Furneaux' *Excursus*.

[2] The whole army, not simply the advanced party under
Stertinius.

simultaneously on the river mentioned.[1] The Chauci promised a contingent, and were given a place in the ranks. The Bructeri began to fire their belongings, but were routed by Lucius Stertinius, who had been sent out by Germanicus with a detachment of light-armed troops; and while the killing and looting were in progress, he discovered the eagle of the nineteenth legion, which had been lost with Varus. Thence the column[2] moved on to the extremity of the Bructeran possessions, wasting the whole stretch of country between the Ems and the Lippe. They were now not far from the Teutoburgian Forest,[3] where, it was said, the remains of Varus and his legions lay unburied.

LXI. There came upon the Caesar, therefore, a passionate desire to pay the last tribute to the fallen and their leader, while the whole army present with him were stirred to pity at thought of their kindred, of their friends, ay! and of the chances of battle and of the lot of mankind. Sending Caecina forward to explore the secret forest passes and to throw bridges and causeways over the flooded marshes and treacherous levels, they pursued their march over the dismal tract, hideous to sight and memory. Varus' first camp, with its broad sweep and measured spaces for officers and eagles, advertised the labours of three legions: then a half-ruined wall and shallow ditch showed that there the now broken remnant had taken cover. In the plain between were bleaching bones, scattered or in little heaps, as the men had fallen, fleeing or standing fast. Hard by lay splintered spears and limbs of horses, while human skulls were

[3] The problem of its position has been endlessly debated, but appears not to be certainly soluble.

antefixa ora. Lucis propinquis barbarae arae, apud quas tribunos ac primorum ordinum centuriones mactaverant. Et cladis eius superstites, pugnam aut vincula elapsi, referebant hic cecidisse legatos, illic raptas aquilas; primum ubi vulnus Varo adactum, ubi infelici dextera et suo ictu mortem invenerit; quo tribunali contionatus Arminius, quot patibula captivis, quae scrobes, utque signis et aquilis per superbiam inluserit.

LXII. Igitur Romanus qui aderat exercitus, sextum post cladis annum, trium legionum ossa, nullo noscente alienas reliquias an suorum humo tegeret, omnis ut coniunctos, ut consanguineos, aucta in hostem ira, maesti simul et infensi condebant. Primum exstruendo tumulo caespitem Caesar posuit, gratissimo munere in defunctos et praesentibus doloris socius. Quod Tiberio haud probatum, seu cuncta Germanici in deterius trahenti, sive exercitum imagine caesorum insepultorumque tardatum ad proelia et formidolosiorem hostem credebat; neque imperatorem auguratu et vetustissimis caerimoniis praeditum adtrectare feralia debuisse.

LXIII. Sed Germanicus cedentem in avia Arminium secutus, ubi primum copia fuit, evehi

---

[1] For other Roman instances of the familiar prejudice against all contact, even ocular, between the consecrated and the dead, compare Sen. *Cons. ad Marc.* 15 (Tiberius delivering the funeral panegyric on his son *interiecto tantummodo velamento quod pontificis oculos a funere arceret*) and D. Cass. LX. 13 (the statue of Augustus removed by Claudius, τοῦ δὴ μήτε ἐφορᾶν αὐτὸν τοὺς φόνους νομίζεσθαι μήτε ἀεὶ κατακαλύπτεσθαι). For the Mosaic law, see *Levit.* xxi. 10–11; and for the primitive taboo on mourners, Sir J. G. Frazer in the *Golden Bough*.

nailed prominently on the tree-trunks. In the neighbouring groves stood the savage altars at which they had slaughtered the tribunes and chief centurions. Survivors of the disaster, who had escaped the battle or their chains, told how here the legates fell, there the eagles were taken, where the first wound was dealt upon Varus, and where he found death by the suicidal stroke of his own unhappy hand. They spoke of the tribunal from which Arminius made his harangue, all the gibbets and torture-pits for the prisoners, and the arrogance with which he insulted the standards and eagles.

LXII. And so, six years after the fatal field, a Roman army, present on the ground, buried the bones of the three legions; and no man knew whether he consigned to earth the remains of a stranger or a kinsman, but all thought of all as friends and members of one family, and, with anger rising against the enemy, mourned at once and hated.

At the erection of the funeral-mound the Caesar laid the first sod, paying a dear tribute to the departed, and associating himself with the grief of those around him. But Tiberius disapproved, possibly because he put an invidious construction on all acts of Germanicus, possibly because he held that the sight of the unburied dead must have given the army less alacrity for battle and more respect for the enemy, while a commander, invested with the augurate and administering the most venerable rites of religion, ought to have avoided all contact with a funeral ceremony.[1]

LXIII. Germanicus, however, followed Arminius as he fell back on the wilds, and at the earliest opportunity ordered the cavalry to ride out and clear the

349

equites campumque, quem hostis insederat, eripi
iubet. Arminius colligi suos et propinquare silvis
monitos vertit repente: mox signum prorumpendi
dedit iis quos per saltus occultaverat. Tunc nova
acie turbatus eques, missaeque subsidiariae cohortes
et fugientium agmine impulsae auxerant conster-
nationem; trudebanturque in paludem gnaram
vincentibus, iniquam nesciis, ni Caesar productas
legiones instruxisset: inde hostibus terror, fiducia
militi; et manibus aequis abscessum. Mox, reducto
ad Amisiam exercitu, legiones classe, ut advexerat,
reportat; pars equitum litore Oceani petere Rhenum
iussa; Caecina, qui suum militem ducebat, monitus, quamquam notis itineribus regrederetur, pontes
longos quam maturrime superare. Angustus is
trames vastas inter paludes et quondam a L. Domitio aggeratus, cetera limosa, tenacia gravi caeno
aut rivis incerta erant; circum silvae paulatim
adclives, quas tum Arminius inplevit, compendiis
viarum et cito agmine onustum sarcinis armisque
militem cum antevenisset. Caecinae dubitanti
quonam modo ruptos vetustate pontes reponeret

---

[1] The statement is suspiciously inaccurate. There is not
much weight in the argument that Caecina's four legions
would naturally be included in *exercitu*; but, of Germanicus'
own force, half travels by land, and the opening of chap. 70
seems to indicate that the subject has not been touched before.
Doederlein's *exercitu, ⟨II⟩ legiones* is only a palliative:
Nipperdey excised *legiones . . . reportat* as the note of a
reader.

[2] The inevitable conjectures as to the site are idle, since the
point where Caecina separated from Germanicus is unknown
and unknowable.

level ground in the occupation of the enemy. Arminius, who had directed his men to close up and retire on the woods, suddenly wheeled them round; then gave the signal for his ambush in the glades to break cover. The change of tactics threw our horse into confusion. Reserve cohorts were sent up; but, broken by the impact of the fugitive columns, they had only increased the panic, and the whole mass was being pushed towards swampy ground, familiar to the conquerors but fatal to strangers, when the Caesar came forward with the legions and drew them up in line of battle. This demonstration overawed the enemy and emboldened the troops, and they parted with the balance even.

Shortly afterwards, the prince led his army back to the Ems, and withdrew the legions as he had brought them, on shipboard :[1] a section of the cavalry was ordered to make for the Rhine along the coast of the Northern Ocean. Caecina, who led his own force, was returning by a well-known route, but was none the less warned to cross the Long Bridges as rapidly as possible.[2] These were simply a narrow causeway, running through a wilderness of marshes and thrown up, years before, by Lucius Domitius ;[3] the rest was a slough—foul, clinging mud intersected by a maze of rivulets. Round about, the woods sloped gently from the plain; but now they were occupied by Arminius, whose forced march along the shorter roads had been too quick for the Roman soldier, weighted with his baggage and accoutrements. Caecina, none too certain how to relay the old, broken-down bridges and at the same time hold off the enemy, decided to

[3] L. Domitius Ahenobarbus, grandfather of the emperor Nero (ob. 25 A.D.) : see the notice of him in IV. 44.

simulque propulsaret hostem, castra metari in loco placuit, ut opus et alii proelium inciperent.

LXIV. Barbari perfringere stationes seque [1] inferre munitoribus nisi lacessunt, circumgrediuntur, occursant: miscetur operantium bellantiumque clamor. Et cuncta pariter Romanis adversa: locus uligine profunda; idem ad gradum instabilis, procedentibus lubricus; corpora gravia loricis; neque librare [2] pila inter undas poterant. Contra Cheruscis sueta apud paludes proelia, procera membra, hastae ingentes ad vulnera facienda, quamvis procul. Nox [3] demum inclinantis iam [4] legiones adversae pugnae exemit. Germani, ob prospera indefessi, ne tum quidem sumpta quiete, quantum aquarum circum surgentibus iugis oritur vertere in subiecta, mersaque humo et obruto quod effectum operis, duplicatus militi labor. Quadragesimum id stipendium Caecina parendi aut imperitandi habebat, secundarum ambiguarumque rerum sciens eoque interritus. Igitur, futura volvens, non aliud repperit quam ut hostem silvis coerceret, donec saucii quantumque gravioris agminis anteirent; nam medio montium et paludum porrigebatur planities, quae tenuem aciem pateretur. Deliguntur legiones quinta dextro lateri, unetvicesima in laevum, primani ducendum ad agmen, vicesimanus adversum secuturos.

---

[1] seque *Beroaldus* : sequi.
[2] librare *Beroaldus* : liberare.
[3] nox *Frobeniana* (1519) : mox.
[4] iam *Freinsheim* : tam.

mark out a camp where he stood, so that part of the men could begin work while the others accepted battle.

LXIV. Skirmishing, enveloping, charging, the barbarians struggled to break the line of outposts and force their way to the working parties. Labourers and combatants mingled their cries. Everything alike was to the disadvantage of the Romans—the ground, deep in slime and ooze, too unstable for standing fast and too slippery for advancing—the weight of armour on their backs—their inability amid the water to balance the pilum for a throw. The Cherusci, on the other hand, were habituated to marsh-fighting, long of limb, and armed with huge lances to wound from a distance. In fact, the legions were already wavering when night at last released them from the unequal struggle.

Success had made the Germans indefatigable. Even now they took no rest, but proceeded to divert all streams, springing from the surrounding hills, into the plain below, flooding the ground, submerging the little work accomplished, and doubling the task of the soldiery. Still, it was Caecina's fortieth year of active service as commander or commanded, and he knew success and danger too well to be easily perturbed. On balancing the possibilities, he could see no other course than to hold the enemy to the woods until his wounded and the more heavily laden part of the column passed on: for extended between mountain and morass was a level patch which would just allow an attenuated line of battle. The fifth legion was selected for the right flank, the twenty-first for the left; the first was to lead the van, the twentieth to stem the inevitable pursuit.

LXV. Nox per diversa inquies, cum barbari festis epulis, laeto cantu aut truci sonore subiecta vallium ac resultantis saltus complerent, apud Romanos invalidi ignes, interruptae voces atque ipsi passim adiacerent vallo, oberrarent tentoriis, insomnes magis quam pervigiles. Ducemque terruit dira quies: nam Quintilium Varum sanguine oblitum et paludibus emersum cernere et audire visus est velut vocantem, non tamen obsecutus et manum intendentis reppulisse. Coepta luce missae in latera legiones, metu an contumacia, locum deseruere, capto propere campo umentia ultra. Neque tamen Arminius, quamquam libero incursu, statim prorupit; sed ut haesere caeno fossisque impedimenta, turbati circum milites, incertus signorum ordo, utque tali in tempore sibi quisque properus et lentae adversum imperia aures, inrumpere Germanos iubet, clamitans: "En Varus eodemque[1] iterum fato vinctae legiones!" Simul haec et cum delectis scindit agmen equisque maxime vulnera ingerit. Illi, sanguine suo et lubrico paludum lapsantes, excussis rectoribus, disicere obvios, proterere iacentis. Plurimus circa aquilas labor, quae neque ferri adversum ingruentia tela neque figi limosa humo poterant. Caecina, dum sustentat aciem, suffosso equo delapsus,

---

[1] eodemque *Ritter* : et eodemque.

LXV. It was a night of unrest, though in con-
trasted fashions. The barbarians, in high carousal,
filled the low-lying valleys and echoing woods with
chants of triumph or fierce vociferations: among the
Romans were languid fires, broken challenges, and
groups of men stretched beside the parapet or stray-
ing amid the tents, unasleep but something less than
awake. The general's night was disturbed by a
sinister and alarming dream: for he imagined that he
saw Quintilius Varus risen, blood-bedraggled, from
the marsh, and heard him calling, though he refused
to obey and pushed him back when he extended his
hand. Day broke, and the legions sent to the wings,
either through fear or wilfulness, abandoned their
post, hurriedly occupying a level piece of ground
beyond the morass. Arminius, however, though the
way was clear for the attack, did not immediately
deliver his onslaught. But when he saw the baggage-
train caught in the mire and trenches; the troops
around it in confusion; the order of the standards
broken, and (as may be expected in a crisis) every
man quick to obey his impulse and slow to hear the
word of command, he ordered the Germans to break
in. "Varus and the legions," he cried, "enchained
once more in the old doom!" And, with the word,
he cut through the column at the head of a picked
band, their blows being directed primarily at the
horses. Slipping in their own blood and the marsh-
slime, the beasts threw their riders, scattered all they
met, and trampled the fallen underfoot. The eagles
caused the greatest difficulty of all, as it was impossible either to advance them against the storm of spears
or to plant them in the water-logged soil. Caecina,
while attempting to keep the front intact, fell with

circumveniebatur, ni prima legio sese opposuisset.
Iuvit hostium aviditas, omissa caede praedam
sectantium, enisaeque legiones vesperascente die
in aperta et solida. Neque is miseriarum finis.
Struendum vallum, petendus agger; amissa magna
ex parte per quae egeritur [1] humus aut exciditur caespes; non tentoria manipulis, non fomenta sauciis;
infectos caeno aut cruore cibos dividentes, funestas
tenebras et tot hominum milibus unum iam reliquum diem lamentabantur.

LXVI. Forte equus, abruptis vinculis, vagus et
clamore territus, quosdam occurrentium obturbavit.
Tanta inde consternatio inrupisse Germanos cre-
dentium, ut cuncti ruerent ad portas, quarum decu-
mana maxime petebatur, aversa hosti et fugientibus
tutior. Caecina, comperto vanam esse formidinem,
cum tamen neque auctoritate neque precibus, ne
manu quidem obsistere aut retinere militem quiret,
proiectus in limine portae, miseratione demum, quia
per corpus legati eundum erat, clausit viam; simul
tribuni et centuriones falsum pavorem esse docue-
runt.

LXVII. Tunc contractos in principia iussosque
dicta cum silentio accipere temporis ac necessitatis
monet. Vnam in armis salutem, sed ea consilio

[1] egeritur *Rhenanus* : geritur.

his horse stabbed under him, and was being rapidly surrounded when the first legion interposed. A point in our favour was the rapacity of the enemy, who left the carnage to pursue the spoils; and towards evening the legions struggled out on to open and solid ground. Nor was this the end of their miseries. A rampart had to be raised and material sought for the earthwork; and most of the tools for excavating soil or cutting turf had been lost. There were no tents for the companies, no dressings for the wounded, and as they divided their rations, foul with dirt or blood, they bewailed the deathlike gloom and that for so many thousands of men but a single day now remained.

LXVI. As chance would have it, a stray horse which had broken its tethering and taken fright at the shouting, threw into confusion a number of men who ran to stop it. So great was the consequent panic (men believed the Germans had broken in) that there was a general rush to the gates, the principal objective being the decuman, which faced away from the enemy and opened the better prospects of escape. Caecina, who had satisfied himself that the fear was groundless, but found command, entreaty, and even physical force, alike powerless to arrest or detain the men, threw himself flat in the gateway; and pity in the last resort barred a road which led over the general's body. At the same time, the tribunes and centurions explained that it was a false alarm.

LXVII. He now collected the troops in front of his quarters, and, first ordering them to listen in silence, warned them of the crisis and its urgency :— " Their one safety lay in the sword; but their resort

temperanda manendumque intra vallum, donec expugnandi hostes spe propius succederent; mox undique erumpendum: illa eruptione ad Rhenum perveniri. Quod si fugerent, pluris silvas, profundas magis paludes, saevitiam hostium superesse; at victoribus decus, gloriam. Quae domi cara, quae in castris honesta, memorat; reticuit de adversis. Equos dehinc, orsus a suis, legatorum tribunorumque nulla ambitione fortissimo cuique bellatori tradit, ut hi, mox pedes in hostem invaderent.

LXVIII. Haud minus inquies Germanus spe, cupidine et diversis ducum sententiis agebat, Arminio sinerent egredi egressosque rursum per umida et inpedita circumvenirent suadente, atrociora Inguiomero et laeta barbaris, ut vallum armis ambirent: promptam expugnationem, plures captivos, incorruptam praedam fore. Igitur orta die proruunt fossas, iniciunt cratis, summa valli prensant, raro super milite et quasi ob metum defixo. Postquam haesere munimentis, datur cohortibus signum cornuaque ac tubae concinuere. Exim clamore et impetu tergis Germanorum circumfunduntur, exprobrantes non hic silvas nec paludes, sed aequis locis aequos deos. Hosti, facile excidium et paucos ac semermos cogitanti, sonus tubarum, fulgor ar-

to it should be tempered with discretion, and they must remain within the rampart till the enemy approached in the hope of carrying it by assault. Then, a sally from all sides—and so to the Rhine! If they fled, they might expect more forests, deeper swamps, and a savage enemy: win the day, and glory and honour were assured." He reminded them of all they loved at home, all the honour they had gained in camp: of disaster, not a word. Then, with complete impartiality, he distributed the horses of the commanding officers and tribunes—he had begun with his own—to men of conspicuous gallantry; the recipients to charge first, while the infantry followed.

LXVIII. Hope, cupidity, and the divided counsels of the chieftains kept the Germans in equal agitation. Arminius proposed to allow the Romans to march out, and, when they had done so, to entrap them once more in wet and broken country; Inguiomerus advocated the more drastic measures dear to the barbarian:—" Let them encircle the rampart in arms. Storming would be easy, captives more plentiful, the booty intact!" So, at break of day, they began demolishing the fosses, threw in hurdles, and struggled to grasp the top of the rampart; on which were ranged a handful of soldiers apparently petrified with terror. But as they swarmed up the fortifications, the signal sounded to the cohorts, and cornets and trumpets sang to arms. Then, with a shout and a rush, the Romans poured down on the German rear. " Here were no trees," they jeered, " no swamps, but a fair field and an impartial Heaven." Upon the enemy, whose thoughts were of a quick despatch and a few half-armed

morum, quanto inopina, tanto maiora offunduntur,[1] cadebantque, ut rebus secundis avidi, ita adversis incauti. Arminius integer, Inguiomerus [2] post grave vulnus pugnam deseruere; vulgus trucidatum est, donec ira et dies permansit. Nocte demum reversae legiones, quamvis plus vulnerum, eadem ciborum egestas fatigaret, vim, sanitatem, copias, cuncta in victoria habuere.

LXIX. Pervaserat interim circumventi exercitus fama et infesto Germanorum agmine Gallias peti, ac ni Agrippina inpositum Rheno pontem solvi prohibuisset, erant qui id flagitium formidine auderent. Sed femina ingens animi munia ducis per eos dies induit, militibusque, ut quis inops aut saucius, vestem et fomenta dilargita est. Tradit C. Plinius, Germanicorum bellorum scriptor, stetisse apud principium pontis [3] laudes et grates reversis legionibus habentem. Id Tiberii animum altius penetravit: non enim simplicis eas curas, nec adversus externos studia militum [4] quaeri. Nihil relictum imperatoribus, ubi femina manipulos intervisat, signa adeat, largitionem temptet, tamquam parum ambitiose filium ducis gregali habitu circumferat Caesaremque Caligulam appellari velit. Potiorem iam

[1] offunduntur *Rhenanus* : offenduntur.
[2] Inguiomerus *Beroaldus* : Ingoiomerus.
[3] pontis *vulgo* (ponti *Beroaldus*) : poti.
[4] studia militum *Doederlein* : militum.

---

[1] At Vetera (Xanten).
[2] The elder Pliny—Gaius Plinius Secundus (23–79 A.D.). His account of the German wars (*inchoavit cum in Germania militaret*, says his nephew, *Epp.* III. 5), now lost, though once believed to have been seen by Conrad Gesner at Augsburg, comprised twenty books and was in all probability a main source for the *Germania* of Tacitus.

defenders, the blare of trumpets and the flash of weapons burst with an effect proportioned to the surprise, and they fell—as improvident in failure as they had been headstrong in success. Arminius and Inguiomerus abandoned the fray, the former unhurt, the latter after a serious wound; the rabble was slaughtered till passion and the daylight waned. It was dusk when the legions returned, weary enough—for wounds were in greater plenty than ever, and provisions in equal scarcity—but finding in victory strength, health, supplies, everything.

LXIX. In the meantime a rumour had spread that the army had been trapped and the German columns were on the march for Gaul; and had not Agrippina prevented the demolition of the Rhine bridge,[1] there were those who in their panic would have braved that infamy. But it was a great-hearted woman who assumed the duties of a general throughout those days; who, if a soldier was in need, clothed him, and, if he was wounded, gave him dressings. Pliny, the historian of the German Wars,[2] asserts that she stood at the head of the bridge, offering her praises and her thanks to the returning legions. The action sank deep into the soul of Tiberius. "There was something behind this officiousness; nor was it the foreigner against whom her courtship of the army was directed. Commanding officers had a sinecure nowadays, when a woman visited the maniples, approached the standards and took in hand to bestow largesses—as though it were not enough to curry favour by parading the general's son in the habit of a common soldier, with the request that he should be called Caesar Caligula![3] Already

[3] See p. 314, n. 2.

apud exercitus Agrippinam quam legatos, quam
duces; conpressam a muliere seditionem, cui nomen
principis obsistere non quiverit. Accendebat haec
onerabatque Seianus, peritia morum Tiberii odia
in longum iaciens, quae reconderet auctaque promeret.

LXX. At Germanicus legionum, quas navibus
vexerat, secundam et quartam decimam itinere
terrestri P. Vitellio ducendas tradit, quo levior
classis vadoso mari innaret vel reciproco sideret.
Vitellius primum iter sicca humo aut modice adla-
bente aestu quietum habuit; mox inpulsu aquilonis,
simul sidere aequinoctii, quo maxime tumescit
Oceanus, rapi agique agmen. Et opplebantur terrae: eadem freto, litori, campis facies, neque discerni poterant incerta ab solidis, brevia a profundis.
Sternuntur fluctibus, hauriuntur gurgitibus; iumenta, sarcinae, corpora exanima interfluunt, occursant. Permiscentur inter se manipuli, modo
pectore, modo ore tenus extantes, aliquando sub-
tracto solo disiecti aut obruti. Non vox et mutui
hortatus iuvabant adversante unda; nihil strenuus
ab ignavo, sapiens ab inprudenti,[1] consilia a casu
differre: cuncta pari violentia involvebantur. Tan-

1 ab imprudenti *Lipsius*: aprudenti.

---

1 See above, chap. 63, with the note.
2 Legate of Germanicus and uncle of the future emperor.
For other references to him see II. 6, 74; for his part in the
trial of Piso, III. 10 sqq.; for his death, V. 8.

Agrippina counted for more with the armies than any general or generalissimo, and a woman had suppressed a mutiny which the imperial name had failed to check." Sejanus inflamed and exacerbated his jealousies; and, with his expert knowledge of the character of Tiberius, kept sowing the seed of future hatreds—grievances for the emperor to store away and produce some day with increase.

LXX. Meanwhile Germanicus,[1] in order to lighten the fleet in case it should have to navigate shallow water or should find itself grounded at ebb-tide, transferred two of the legions he had brought on shipboard—the second and fourteenth—to Publius Vitellius,[2] who was to march them back by the land route. At first Vitellius had an uneventful journey over dry ground or through gently running tides. Before long, however, a northerly gale, aggravated by the equinox, during which the Ocean is always at its wildest, began to play havoc with the column. Then the whole land became a flood: sea, shore, and plain wore a single aspect; and it was impossible to distinguish solid from fluid, deep from shallow. Men were dashed over by the billows or drawn under by the eddies: packhorses—their loads—lifeless bodies—came floating through, or colliding with, the ranks. The companies became intermingled, the men standing one moment up to the breast, another up to the chin, in water; then the ground would fail beneath them, and they were scattered or submerged. Words and mutual encouragement availed nothing against the deluge: there was no difference between bravery and cowardice, between wisdom and folly, circumspection or chance; everything was involved in the same fury of the elements. At last

dem Vitellius, in editiora enisus, eodem agmen sub-
duxit. Pernoctavere sine utensilibus, sine igni,
magna pars nudo aut mulcato corpore, haud minus
miserabiles quam quos hostis circumsidebat:[1] quippe
illic etiam honestae mortis usus, his inglorium
exitium. Lux reddidit terram, penetratumque ad
amnem,[2] quo Caesar classe contenderat. Inpositae
dein legiones, vagante fama submersas; nec fides
salutis, antequam Caesarem exercitumque reducem
videre.

LXXI. Iam Stertinius, ad accipiendum in deditionem Segimerum, fratrem Segestis, praemissus
ipsum et filium eius in civitatem Vbiorum perdu-
xerat. Data utrique venia, facile Segimero, cunc-
tantius filio, quia Quintilii Vari corpus inlusisse
dicebatur. Ceterum ad supplenda exercitus damna
certavere Galliae, Hispaniae, Italia, quod cuique
promptum, arma, equos, aurum offerentes. Quorum
laudato studio Germanicus, armis modo et equis
ad bellum sumptis, propria pecunia militem iuvit.
Vtque cladis memoriam etiam comitate leniret,
circumire saucios, facta singulorum extollere, vulnera intuens, alium spe, alium gloria, cunctos adlo-
quio et cura sibique et proelio firmabat.

---

[1] circumsidebat *Urlichs* : circumsidet.
[2] amnem *Mercer* : amnem Visurgin.

---

[1] The force under Caecina.
[2] As they were returning from the Ems to the Rhine, the
Visurgin (Weser) of the Mediceus is an absurdity. If Vitellius

Vitellius struggled out on to rising ground and led his columns after him. They spent the night without necessaries, without fire, many of them naked or badly maimed,—every whit as wretched as their comrades in the invested camp.[1] For those at least had the resource of an honourable death; here was destruction without the glory. Day brought back the land, and they pushed on to the river [2] to which Germanicus had preceded them with the fleet. The legions then embarked. Current report proclaimed them drowned, and the doubts of their safety were only dispelled by the sight of the Caesar returning with his army.

LXXI. By this time, Stertinius, who had been sent forward to receive the submission of Segestes' brother Segimerus, had brought him and his son through to the Ubian capital. Both were pardoned; Segimerus without any demur, his son with more hesitation, as he was said to have insulted the corpse of Quintilius Varus. For the rest, the two Gauls, the Spains, and Italy vied in making good the losses of the army with offers of weapons, horses, or gold, according to the special capacity of each province. Germanicus applauded their zeal, but took only arms and horses for the campaign: the soldiers he assisted from his private means. To soften by kindness also their recollections of the late havoc, he made a round of the wounded, praised their individual exploits; and, while inspecting their injuries, confirmed their enthusiasm for himself and battle, here by the stimulus of hope, there by that of glory, and everywhere by his consolations and solicitude.

took only two days and a night for his march, the river in question was presumably the Hunse.

THE ANNALS OF TACITUS

LXXII. Decreta eo anno triumphalia insignia
A. Caecinae, L. Apronio, C. Silio ob res cum Germanico gestas. Nomen patris patriae Tiberius, a populo
saepius ingestum repudiavit; neque in acta sua
iurari, quamquam censente senatu, permisit, cuncta
mortalium incerta, quantoque plus adeptus foret,
tanto se magis in lubrico dictitans.[1] Non tamen
ideo faciebat fidem civilis animi; nam legem maiestatis reduxerat, cui nomen apud veteres idem, sed
alia in iudicium veniebant, si quis proditione exercitum aut [2] plebem seditionibus, denique male gesta
re publica maiestatem populi Romani minuisset:
facta arguebantur, dicta inpune erant. Primus
Augustus cognitionem de famosis libellis specie
legis eius tractavit, commotus Cassii Severi libidine,
qua viros feminasque inlustris procacibus scriptis
diffamaverat; mox Tiberius, consultante Pompeio
Macro praetore an iudicia maiestatis redderentur,

---

[1] dictitans *Muretus* : dictan.
[2] aut *Beroaldus* : ut.

---

[1] The triumph proper (*iustus triumphus*) has now, as a logical
consequence of the imperial system, become the exclusive
privilege of the sovereign and his co-regents, the only holders
of true *imperium*. The *triumphalia insignia* (*ornamenta*)
carried with them the prestige and external distinctions of the
triumph, which was itself unheld.

[2] Conferred upon Augustus by the senate in 2 B.C. Tiberius'
refusal was never withdrawn (II. 89, D. Cass. LVIII. 12), nor
does the title figure upon his coins.

[3] The annual oath, taken on the first of January by the
magistrates and senate to treat as valid all *acta* of the emperor
and, save in the case of *damnatio memoriae*, his predecessors,
including the dictator Julius.

[4] *Civilis* is apt to necessitate a loose paraphrase. Tiberius
wishes to convey the impression that he is a kind of " empereur
citoyen," a *civis inter cives*: the pose is discredited by the

LXXII. In this year triumphal distinctions[1] were voted to Aulus Caecina, Lucius Apronius, and Caius Silius, in return for their services with Germanicus. Tiberius rejected the title *Father of his Country*,[2] though it had been repeatedly pressed upon him by the people: and, disregarding a vote of the senate, refused to allow the taking of an oath to obey his enactments.[3] "All human affairs," so ran his comment, "were uncertain, and the higher he climbed the more slippery his position." Yet even so he failed to inspire the belief that his sentiments were not monarchical.[4] For he had resuscitated the *Lex Majestatis*, a statute which in the old jurisprudence had carried the same name but covered a different type of offence—betrayal of an army; seditious incitement of the populace; any act, in short, of official maladministration diminishing the "majesty of the Roman nation." Deeds were challenged, words went immune. The first to take cognizance of written libel under the statute was Augustus; who was provoked to the step by the effrontery with which Cassius Severus[5] had blackened the characters of men and women of repute in his scandalous effusions: then Tiberius, to an inquiry put by the praetor, Pompeius Macer, whether process should still be granted on this statute, replied that "the

fact that, if the *lex maiestatis* is to apply to the *princeps*, it can only be because he has ceased to be a citizen and has become the State.

[5] The famous orator, *quem primum adfirmant flexisse ab illa vetere atque derecta dicendi via* (*Dial.* 19); banished by Augustus to Crete in 8 A.D. (Jerome) or 12 A.D. (*cf.* D. Cass. LVI. 27); removed by Tiberius to Seriphus and his property confiscated in 24 A.D. (below, IV. 21); died in the twenty-fifth year of his exile.

exercendas leges esse respondit. Hunc quoque aspe-
ravere carmina incertis auctoribus vulgata in saevitiam superbiamque eius et discordem cum matre
animum.

LXXIII. Haud pigebit referre in Falanio et
Rubrio, modicis equitibus Romanis, praetemptata
crimina, ut quibus initiis, quanta Tiberii arte gra-
vissimum exitium inrepserit, dein repressum sit,
postremo arserit cunctaque corripuerit, noscatur.
Falanio obiciebat accusator, quod inter cultores
Augusti, qui per omnis domos in modum collegio-
rum habebantur, Cassium quendam, mimum corpore
infamem, adscivisset, quodque venditis hortis statuam Augusti simul mancipasset. Rubrio crimini
dabatur violatum periurio numen [1] Augusti. Quae
ubi Tiberio notuere, scripsit consulibus non ideo
decretum patri suo caelum, ut in perniciem civium
is honor verteretur. Cassium histrionem solitum
inter alios eiusdem artis interesse ludis, quos mater
sua in memoriam Augusti sacrasset; nec contra
religiones fieri, quod effigies eius, ut alia numinum
simulacra, venditionibus hortorum et domuum acce-
dant. Ius iurandum perinde aestimandum quam si
Iovem fefellisset: deorum iniurias dis curae.

LXXIV. Nec multo post Granium Marcellum,
praetorem Bithyniae, quaestor ipsius Caepio Cris-

---

[1] numen *Freinsheim* : nomen.

---

[1] It is not clear whether the close of the sentence refers only
to the principate of Tiberius or whether the " conflagration "
is the reign of terror occasioned by the merciless abuse of the
lex maiestatis in the closing years of Domitian.

[2] The scenic *ludi Palatini* (see D. Cass. LVI. 46), which
witnessed the assassination of Caligula.

[3] Tiberius repeats a maxim of Roman law :—*iurisiurandi
contempta religio satis deum ultorem habet* (*Cod.* IV. 1, 2).

law ought to take its course." He, too, had been ruffled by verses of unknown authorship satirizing his cruelty, his arrogance, and his estrangement from his mother.

LXXIII. It will not be unremunerative to recall the first, tentative charges brought in the case of Falanius and Rubrius, two Roman knights of modest position; if only to show from what beginnings, thanks to the art of Tiberius, the accursed thing crept in, and, after a temporary check, at last broke out, an all-devouring conflagration.[1] Against Falanius the accuser alleged that he had admitted a certain Cassius, mime and catamite, among the "votaries of Augustus," who were maintained, after the fashion of fraternities, in all the great houses: also, that when selling his gardens, he had parted with a statue of Augustus as well. To Rubrius the crime imputed was violation of the deity of Augustus by perjury. When the facts came to the knowledge of Tiberius, he wrote to the consuls that a place in heaven had not been decreed to his father in order that the honour might be turned to the destruction of his countrymen. Cassius, the actor, with others of his trade, had regularly taken part in the games which his own mother had consecrated to the memory of Augustus[2]; nor was it an act of sacrilege, if the effigies of that sovereign, like other images of other gods, went with the property, whenever a house or garden was sold. As to the perjury, it was on the same footing as if the defendant had taken the name of Jupiter in vain: the gods must look to their own wrongs.[3]

LXXIV. Before long, Granius Marcellus, praetor of Bithynia, found himself accused of treason by his

pinus maiestatis postulavit, subscribente Romano Hispone: qui formam vitae iniit, quam postea celebrem miseriae temporum et audacia hominum fecerunt. Nam egens, ignotus, inquies, dum occultis libellis saevitiae principis adrepit, mox clarissimo cuique periculum facessit, potentiam apud unum, odium apud omnis adeptus, dedit exemplum, quod secuti ex pauperibus divites, ex contemptis metuendi perniciem aliis, ac postremum sibi invenere. Sed Marcellum insimulabat sinistros de Tiberio sermones habuisse, inevitabile crimen, cum ex moribus principis foedissima quaeque deligeret accusator obiectaretque reo. Nam quia vera erant, etiam dicta credebantur. Addidit Hispo statuam Marcelli altius quam Caesarum sitam et alia in statua amputato capite Augusti effigiem Tiberii inditam. Ad quod exarsit adeo, ut rupta taciturnitate proclamaret se quoque in ea causa laturum sententiam palam et iuratum, quo ceteris eadem necessitas fieret. Manebant etiam tum vestigia morientis libertatis. Igitur Cn. Piso " Quo " inquit " loco censebis, Caesar ? si primus, habebo quod sequar; si post omnis, vereor ne inprudens dissentiam." Permotus his, quantoque incautius efferverat, paenitentia patiens, tulit absolvi reum criminibus maiestatis; de pecuniis repetundis ad reciperatores itum est.

---

[1] As Rome lacked a public prosecutor, the law had to be set in motion by individuals. Hence the rise of the hated class of professional informers, " delatores," *genus hominum publico exitio repertum* (IV. 30); who speculated on the rewards offered by the statutes in the event of a successful prosecution.

own quaestor, Caepio Crispinus, with Hispo Romanus
to back the charge. Caepio was the pioneer in a
walk of life which the miseries of the age and the
effronteries of men soon rendered popular.[1] Indigent,
unknown, unresting, first creeping, with his private
reports, into the confidence of his pitiless sovereign,
then a terror to the noblest, he acquired the favour
of one man, the hatred of all, and set an example,
the followers of which passed from beggary to wealth,
from being despised to being feared, and crowned
at last the ruin of others by their own. He alleged
that Marcellus had retailed sinister anecdotes about
Tiberius: a damning indictment, when the accuser
selected the foulest qualities of the imperial character, and attributed their mention to the accused.
For, as the facts were true, they were also believed
to have been related! Hispo added that Marcellus'
own statue was placed on higher ground than those
of the Caesars, while in another the head of Augustus
had been struck off to make room for the portrait
of Tiberius. This incensed the emperor to such a
degree that, breaking through his taciturnity, he
exclaimed that, in this case, he too would vote,
openly and under oath,—the object being to impose
a similar obligation on the rest. There remained
even yet some traces of dying liberty. Accordingly
Gnaeus Piso inquired: "In what order will you
register your opinion, Caesar? If first, I shall have
something to follow: if last of all, I fear I may
inadvertently find myself on the other side." The
words went home; and with a meekness that showed
how profoundly he rued his unwary outburst, he
voted for the acquittal of the defendant on the
counts of treason. The charge of peculation went
before the appropriate commission.

LXXV. Nec patrum cognitionibus satiatus iudiciis adsidebat in cornu tribunalis, ne praetorem curuli depelleret; multaque eo coram adversus ambitum et potentium preces constituta. Sed dum veritati consulitur, libertas corrumpebatur. Inter quae Pius Aurelius senator, questus mole publicae viae ductuque aquarum labefactas aedis suas, auxilium patrum invocabat. Resistentibus aerarii praetoribus subvenit Caesar pretiumque aedium Aurelio tribuit, erogandae per honesta pecuniae cupiens: quam virtutem diu retinuit, cum ceteras exueret. Propertio Celeri praetorio, veniam ordinis ob paupertatem petenti, decies sestertium largitus est, satis conperto paternas ei angustias esse. Temptantis eadem alios probare causam [1] senatui iussit, cupidine severitatis in iis etiam quae rite faceret acerbus. Vnde ceteri silentium et paupertatem confessioni et beneficio praeposuere.

LXXVI. Eodem anno continuis imbribus auctus Tiberis plana urbis stagnaverat; relabentem secuta est aedificiorum et hominum strages. Igitur censuit Asinius Gallus ut libri Sibyllini adirentur. Renuit Tiberius, perinde divina humanaque obtegens; sed remedium coercendi fluminis Ateio Capitoni et L. Arruntio mandatum. Achaiam ac Macedoniam

---

[1] causam *Beroaldus* (causas *Sirker*): causa.

---

[1] Roughly £10,000—the property qualification fixed by Augustus as the minimum necessary for membership of the senate. Similar grants are mentioned with fair frequency (*e.g.* II. 37).

[2] He was sceptical, in any case, about the Sibylline canon (see VI. 12 and D. Cass. LVII. 18). The collection, transferred by Augustus in 12 B.C. from the Capitol to the temple of the Palatine Apollo, could only be consulted by the *quindecimviri* with the authorization of the senate.

LXXV. Not satiated with senatorial cases, he took to sitting in the common courts,—at a corner of the tribunal, so as not to dispossess the praetor of his chair. As a result of his presence, many verdicts were recorded in defiance of intrigue and of the solicitations of the great. Still, while equity gained, liberty suffered.—Among these cases, Aurelius Pius, a member of the senate, complained that by the construction of a public road and aqueduct his house had been left insecure; and he asked compensation from the Fathers. As the treasury officials were obdurate, Tiberius came to the rescue, and paid him the value of his mansion: for, given a good cause, he was ready and eager to spend—a virtue which he long retained, even when he was denuding himself of every other. When Propertius Celer, the ex-praetor, applied to be excused from his senatorial rank on the score of poverty, he satisfied himself that his patrimony was in fact embarrassed, and made him a gift of one million sesterces.[1] Others who tried a similar experiment were ordered to make out a case before the senate: for in his passion for austerity, even where he acted justly, he contrived to be harsh. The rest, therefore, preferred silence and poverty to confession and charity.

LXXVI. In the same year, the Tiber, rising under the incessant rains, had flooded the lower levels of the city, and its subsidence was attended by much destruction of buildings and life. Accordingly, Asinius Gallus moved for a reference to the Sibylline Books. Tiberius objected, preferring secrecy as in earth so in heaven:[2] still, the task of coercing the stream was entrusted to Ateius Capito and Lucius Arruntius. Since Achaia and Macedonia protested

onera deprecantis levari in praesens proconsulari imperio tradique Caesari placuit. Edendis gladiatoribus, quos Germanici fratris ac suo nomine obtulerat, Drusus praesedit, quamquam vili sanguine nimis gaudens; quod in vulgus formidolosum et pater arguisse dicebatur. Cur abstinuerit spectaculo ipse, varie trahebant: alii taedio coetus, quidam tristitia ingenii et metu conparationis, quia Augustus comiter interfuisset. Non crediderim ad ostentandam saevitiam movendasque populi offensiones concessam filio materiem, quamquam id quoque[1] dictum est.

LXXVII. At theatri licentia, proximo priore anno coepta, gravius tum erupit, occisis non modo e plebe, sed[2] militibus et centurione, vulnerato tribuno praetoriae cohortis, dum probra in magistratus et dissensionem vulgi prohibent. Actum de ea seditione apud patres, dicebanturque sententiae, ut praetoribus ius virgarum in histriones esset. Intercessit Haterius Agrippa, tribunus plebei, increpitusque est Asinii Galli oratione, silente Tiberio, qui ea simulacra libertatis senatui praebebat. Valuit

---

[1] quoque *Lipsius* : quod.   [2] sed *marg.* : et.

---

[1] In 27 B.C. Augustus introduced the classification of the provinces as public and imperial : the former still administered by ex-consuls and ex-praetors chosen by lot under supervision of the senate, the latter, by *legati* appointed by and responsible to the sovereign. Achaia (Greece proper with Thessaly and Epirus) was then separated from Macedonia and converted into a senatorial province : it now, in 15 A.D., became imperial, and so remained for twenty-nine years. The financial relief consequent on the change would be due in part to the fact that the expense of a separate staff was saved by placing the province

against the heavy taxation, it was decided to relieve them of their proconsular government for the time being and transfer them to the emperor.[1] A show of gladiators, given in the name of his brother Germanicus, was presided over by Drusus, who took an extravagant pleasure in the shedding of blood however vile—a trait so alarming to the populace that it was said to have been censured by his father. Tiberius' own absence from the exhibition was variously explained. Some ascribed it to his impatience of a crowd; others, to his native morosity and his dread of comparisons: for Augustus had been a good-humoured spectator. I should be slow to believe that he deliberately furnished his son with an occasion for exposing his brutality and arousing the disgust of the nation; yet even this was suggested.

LXXVII. The disorderliness of the stage, which had become apparent the year before,[2] now broke out on a more serious scale. Apart from casualties among the populace, several soldiers and a centurion were killed, and an officer of the Praetorian Guards wounded, in the attempt to repress the insults levelled at the magistracy and the dissension of the crowd. The riot was discussed in the senate, and proposals were mooted that the praetors should be empowered to use the lash on actors. Haterius Agrippa, a tribune of the people, interposed his veto, and was attacked in a speech by Asinius Gallus. Tiberius said nothing: these were the phantoms of liberty which he permitted to the senate. Still the

under the governor of Moesia, but in the main, no doubt, to a more efficient administration.

[2] See above, chap. 54.

tamen intercessio, quia divus Augustus immunis verberum histriones quondam responderat, neque fas Tiberio infringere dicta eius. De modo lucaris et adversus lasciviam fautorum multa decernuntur; ex quis maxime insignia, ne domos pantomimorum senator introiret, ne egredientis in publicum equites Romani cingerent aut alibi quam in theatro sectarentur,[1] et spectantium immodestiam exilio [2] multandi potestas praetoribus fieret.

LXXVIII. Templum ut in colonia Tarraconensi [3] strueretur Augusto petentibus Hispanis permissum, datumque in omnis provincias exemplum. Centesimam rerum venalium, post bella civilia institutam, deprecante populo, edixit Tiberius militare aerarium eo subsidio niti; simul imparem oneri rem publicam, nisi vicesimo militiae anno veterani dimitterentur. Ita proximae seditionis male consulta, quibus sedecim stipendiorum finem expresserant, abolita in posterum.

LXXIX. Actum deinde in senatu ab Arruntio et Ateio, an ob moderandas Tiberis exundationes verterentur flumina et lacus, per quos augescit; auditaeque municipiorum et coloniarum legationes,

[1] sectarentur *Wölfflin :* spectarentur.
[2] exilio *Beroaldus :* exitio.
[3] Tarraconensi *Beroaldus :* terra conensi.

---

[1] The chief town of north-eastern Spain (*Hispania Tarraconensis*)—now Tarragona.
[2] Instituted and endowed by Augustus in 6 A.D., with the primary object of providing pensions and gratuities to time-expired men.
[3] But not wholly so; for, apart from occasional sources of revenue, the proceeds of a five per cent. succession duty

veto held good: for the deified Augustus had once remarked, in answer to a question, that players were immune from the scourge; and it would be blasphemy in Tiberius to contravene his words. Measures in plenty were framed to limit the expenditure on entertainments and to curb the extravagance of the partisans. The most striking were: that no senator was to enter the houses of the pantomimes; that. if they came out into public, Roman knights were not to gather round, nor were their performances to be followed except in the theatre; while the praetors were to be authorized to punish by exile any disorder among the spectators.

LXXVIII. Permission to build a temple to Augustus in the colony of Tarraco[1] was granted to the Spaniards, and a precedent set for all the provinces. A popular protest against the one per cent. duty on auctioned goods (which had been imposed after the Civil Wars) brought from Tiberius a declaration that " the military exchequer[2] was dependent on that resource;[3] moreover, the commonwealth was not equal to the burden, unless the veterans were discharged only at the end of twenty years' service." Thus the misconceived reforms of the late mutiny, in virtue of which the legionaries had extorted a maximum term of sixteen years, were cancelled for the future.

LXXIX. Next, a discussion was opened in the senate by Arruntius and Ateius, whether the invasions of the Tiber should be checked by altering the course of the rivers and lakes swelling its volume. Deputations from the municipalities and colonies

(*vicesima hereditatum*) had also been ear-marked by Augustus for the new treasury.

377

orantibus Florentinis ne Clanis solito alveo demotus in amnem Arnum transferretur idque ipsis perniciem adferret. Congruentia his Interamnates [1] disseruere : pessum ituros fecundissimos Italiae campos, si amnis Nar (id enim parabatur) in rivos diductus [2] superstagnavisset. Nec Reatini silebant, Velinum lacum, qua in Narem effunditur, obstrui recusantes, quippe in adiacentia erupturum; optume rebus mortalium consuluisse naturam, quae sua ora fluminibus, suos cursus, utque originem, ita finis dederit ; spectandas etiam religiones maiorum,[3] qui sacra et lucos et aras patriis amnibus dicaverint; quin ipsum Tiberim nolle prorsus accolis fluviis orbatum minore gloria fluere. Seu preces coloniarum, seu difficultas operum, sive superstitio valuit, ut in sententiam Pisonis [4] concederetur,[5] qui nil mutandum censuerat.

LXXX. Prorogatur Poppaeo Sabino provincia Moesia, additis Achaia ac Macedonia. Id quoque morum Tiberii fuit, continuare imperia ac plerosque ad finem vitae in isdem exercitibus aut iurisdictionibus habere. Causae variae traduntur: alii taedio novae curae semel placita pro aeternis serva-

[1] Interamnates *Beroaldus* : ante manates.
[2] diductus *Beroaldus* : deductus.
[3] maiorum *Nipperdey* : sociorum.
[4] Pisonis] Cn. Pisonis *Nipperdey*.
[5] concederetur *Lipsius* : concederet.

---

[1] Chiana.

[2] Of Interamna Nahartium (now Terni) in Umbria. As the town was the birthplace of the emperor Tacitus, it erected a tomb to the historian also—only, it is said, to destroy it at the order of Pius V as that of an enemy of Christianity.

[3] Nera.

[4] Of Reate (the modern Rieti).

were heard. The Florentines pleaded that the Clanis[1] should not be deflected from its old bed into the Arno, to bring ruin upon themselves. The Interamnates'[2] case was similar:—" The most generous fields of Italy were doomed, if the Nar[3] should overflow after this scheme had split it into rivulets." Nor were the Reatines[4] silent:—" They must protest against the Veline Lake[5] being dammed at its outlet into the Nar, as it would simply break a road into the surrounding country. Nature had made the best provision for the interests of humanity, when she assigned to rivers their proper mouths—their proper courses—their limits as well as their origins. Consideration, too, should be paid to the faith of their fathers, who had hallowed rituals and groves and altars to their country streams. Besides, they were reluctant that Tiber himself, bereft of his tributary streams, should flow with diminished majesty." Whatever the deciding factor—the prayers of the colonies, the difficulty of the work, or superstition— the motion of Piso, " that nothing be changed," was agreed to.

LXXX. Poppaeus Sabinus was continued in his province of Moesia[6], to which Achaia and Macedonia were added. It was one of the peculiarities of Tiberius to prolong commands, and, as often as not, to retain the same man at the head of the same army or administrative district till his dying day. Various reasons are given. Some hold it was the weary dislike of recurring trouble which caused

---

[5] Lago di Piè-di-Lugo. The lake lay between Reate and Interamna : the outlet was in reality artificial (Cic. *ad Att.* IV. 15).

[6] An imperial province corresponding pretty closely to the Servia and Bulgaria of twenty years ago.

visse; quidam invidia, ne plures fruerentur; sunt
qui existiment, ut callidum eius ingenium, ita anxium iudicium; neque enim eminentis virtutes
sectabatur, et rursum vitia oderat: ex optimis periculum sibi,[1] a pessimis dedecus publicum metuebat.
Qua haesitatione postremo eo provectus est, ut
mandaverit quibusdam provincias, quos egredi urbe
non erat passurus.

LXXXI. De comitiis consularibus, quae tum
primum illo principe ac deinceps fuere, vix quicquam firmare ausim: adeo diversa non modo apud
auctores, sed in ipsius orationibus reperiuntur.
Modo, subtractis candidatorum nominibus, originem
cuiusque et vitam et stipendia descripsit, ut qui forent
intellegeretur; aliquando, ea quoque significatione
subtracta, candidatos hortatus ne ambitu comitia
turbarent, suam ad id curam pollicitus est. Plerumque eos tantum apud se professos disseruit,
quorum nomina consulibus edidisset; posse et alios
profiteri, si gratiae aut meritis confiderent: speciosa
verbis, re inania aut subdola, quantoque maiore
libertatis imagine tegebantur, tanto eruptura ad
infensius servitium.

[1] sibi *Victorius* : sibi sibi.

him to treat a decision once framed as eternally
valid; others that he grudged to see too many
men enjoying preferment; while there are those
who believe that as his intellect was shrewd so his
judgment was hesitant; for, on the one hand, he did
not seek out pre-eminent virtue, and, on the other,
he detested vice: the best he feared as a private
danger, the worst as a public scandal. In the end,
this vacillation carried him so far that he gave provinces to men whom he was never to allow to
leave Rome.

LXXXI. As to the consular elections, from this
year's—the first—down to the last of the reign, I
can hardly venture a single definite assertion: so
conflicting is the evidence, not of the historians alone,
but of the emperor's own speeches. Sometimes, he
withheld the candidate's names, but described the
birth, career, and campaigns of each in terms that
left his identity in no doubt. Sometimes even these
clues were suppressed, and he urged " the candidates " not to vitiate the election by intrigue, and
promised his own efforts to that end. Generally, he
declared that no one had applied to him for nomination, except those whose names he had divulged to
the consuls: others might still apply, if they had
confidence in their influence or their merits. In
words the policy was specious; in reality, it was
nugatory or perfidious and destined to issue in a
servitude all the more detestable the more it was
disguised under a semblance of liberty!

BOOK II

LIBER II

I. Sisenna Statilio,[1] L. Libone consulibus, mota Orientis regna provinciaeque Romanae, initio apud Parthos orto, qui petitum Roma, acceptumque regem, quamvis gentis Arsacidarum, ut externum aspernabantur. Is fuit Vonones, obses Augusto datus a Phraate. Nam Phraates, quamquam depulisset exercitus ducesque Romanos, cuncta venerantium officia ad Augustum verterat partemque prolis firmandae amicitiae miserat, haud perinde nostri metu quam fidei popularium diffisus.

II. Post finem Phraatis et sequentium regum ob internas caedis venere in urbem legati a primoribus Parthis, qui Vononem vetustissimum liberorum eius accirent. Magnificum id sibi credidit Caesar auxitque opibus. Et accepere barbari laetantes, ut ferme ad nova imperia. Mox subiit pudor degeneravisse Parthos : petitum alio ex orbe regem, hostium artibus infectum ; iam inter provincias Romanas solium Arsacidarum haberi darique. Vbi

---

[1] Statilio *Ritter* : Statilio Tauro.

---

[1] *Statilio Tauro* is correct in point of fact, but the two cognomina are against the usage of Tacitus.

[2] The royal house of Parthia, lasting approximately from 250 B.C. to 230 A.D., when it fell before the new Persian Empire of the Sassanids.

[3] Phraates IV (37 B.C.–2 A.D.). The reference in the beginning of the next sentence is to Antony's great and ill-starred expedition against Parthia in 36 B.C. See Plut. *Ant.* 37 *sqq.*; D. Cass. XLIX. 24 *sqq.*

BOOK II

I. With the consulate of Statilius Sisenna[1] and Lucius Libo came an upheaval among the independent kingdoms and Roman provinces of the East. The movement started with the Parthians, who despised as an alien the sovereign whom they had sought and received from Rome, member though he was of the Arsacian house.[2] This was Vonones, once given by Phraates[3] as a hostage to Augustus. For, though he had thrown back Roman armies and commanders, to the emperor Phraates had observed every point of respect, and, to knit the friendship closer, had sent him part of his family, more from distrust of his countrymen's loyalty than from any awe of ourselves.

II. After domestic murders had made an end of Phraates and his successors, a deputation from the Parthian nobility arrived in Rome, to summon Vonones,[4] as the eldest of his children, to the throne. The Caesar took this as an honour to himself and presented the youth with a considerable sum. The barbarians, too, accepted him with the pleasure they usually evince at a change of sovereigns. It quickly gave place to shame:—" The Parthians had degenerated: they had gone to another continent for a king tainted with the enemy's arts, and now the throne of the Arsacidae was held, or given away, as one of the provinces of Rome. Where was the glory

[4] Vonones I (7 or 8–11 A.D.).

illam gloriam trucidantium Crassum, exturbantium
Antonium, si mancipium Caesaris, tot per annos
servitutem perpessum, Parthis imperitet? Accendebat dedignantis et ipse diversus a maiorum institutis, raro venatu, segni equorum cura; quotiens
per urbes incederet, lecticae gestamine fastuque erga
patrias epulas. Inridebantur et Graeci comites ac
vilissima utensilium anulo clausa. Sed prompti
aditus, obvia comitas, ignotae Parthis virtutes,
nova vitia; et quia ipsorum moribus [1] aliena perinde
odium pravis et honestis.

III. Igitur Artabanus Arsacidarum e sanguine
apud Dahas adultus excitur, primoque congressu
fusus reparat viris regnoque potitur. Victo Vononi
perfugium Armenia fuit, vacua tunc interque Parthorum et Romanas opes infida ob scelus Antonii,
qui Artavasden regem Armeniorum, specie amicitiae inlectum, dein catenis oneratum, postremo
interfecerat. Eius filius Artaxias, memoria patris

---

[1] moribus *Muretus* : maioribus.

---

[1] At Carrhae (53 B.C.).

[2] The *locus classicus* is Justin XLI. 3 : *Carne non nisi
venatibus quaesita vescuntur. Equis omni tempore vectantur :
illis bella, illis convivia, illis publica ac privata officia obeunt
e.q.s.*

[3] Of the king with his grandees (*megistanes*). So, on the
death of Germanicus, it was said *regum etiam regem et exerci-
tatione venandi et convictu megistanum abstinuisse, quod apud
Parthos iustiti instar est* (Suet. *Cal.* 7).

[4] Artabanus III (11–40 A.D.).

[5] A Scythian race to the south-east of the Caspian Sea.

[6] The following list of Armenian sovereigns may make this
and the following chapter a little clearer : 56 or 55 B.C.–
34 B.C. *Artavasdes I* (played Antony false in his Parthian
campaign of 36 B.C.; entrapped by him two years later and
handed to Cleopatra; executed by her in 30 B.C.) : 33 B.C.–

of the men who slew Crassus[1] and ejected Antony,
if a chattel of the Caesar, who had brooked his
bondage through all these years, was to govern
Parthians?" Their contempt was heightened by
the man himself, with his remoteness from ancestral
traditions, his rare appearances in the hunting-field,
his languid interest in horseflesh,[2] his use of a litter
when passing through the towns, and his disdain of
the national banquets.[3] Other subjects for mirth
were his Greek retinue and his habit of keeping
even the humblest household necessaries under seal.
His easy accessibility, on the other hand, and his
unreserved courtesy—virtues unknown to Parthia—
were construed as exotic vices; and the good and
ill in him, as they were equally strange to the
national character, were impartially abhorred.

III. Consequently Artabanus,[4] an Arsacian of the
blood, who had grown to manhood among the Dahae,[5]
was brought into the lists, and, though routed in the
first engagement, rallied his forces and seized the
kingdom.

The defeated Vonones found shelter in Armenia,
then a masterless land between the Parthian and
Roman empires—a dubious neighbour to the latter
owing to the criminal action of Antony, who, after
entrapping the late king, Artavasdes, by a parade
of friendship, had then thrown him into irons and
finally executed him.[6] His son Artaxias, hostile to

20 B.C. *Artaxias II* (" nobis infensus "; massacred all Romans
in his dominions): 20 B.C.-6 B.C., approximately, *a. Tigranes
II* ("datus a Caesare Armeniis"; established on the throne
by Tiberius—see Hor. *Epp.* I. 12, 16); *b. Tigranes III* and
Erato (husband and wife as well as brother and sister; joint
sovereigns); 6 B.C.-1 B.C., approximately, *a. Artavasdes II*
("iussu Augusti impositus"); *b. Tigranes III* and *Erato*

nobis infensus, Arsacidarum vi seque regnumque
tutatus est. Occiso Artaxia per dolum propinquorum, datus a Caesare Armeniis Tigranes deduc-
tusque in regnum a Tiberio Nerone. Nec Tigrani
diuturnum imperium fuit neque liberis eius, quamquam sociatis more externo in matrimonium regnumque.

IV. Dein iussu Augusti inpositus Artavasdes et
non sine clade nostra deiectus. Tum Gaius Caesar
componendae Armeniae deligitur. Is Ariobarzanen,
origine Medum, ob insignem corporis formam et
praeclarum animum volentibus Armeniis praefecit.
Ariobarzane morte fortuita absumpto stirpem eius
haud toleravere; temptatoque feminae imperio,
cui nomen Erato, eaque brevi pulsa, incerti solutique
et magis sine domino quam in libertate profugum
Vononen in regnum accipiunt. Sed ubi minitari
Artabanus et parum subsidii in Armeniis, vel, si
nostra vi defenderetur, bellum adversus Parthos
sumendum erat, rector Syriae Creticus Silanus exci-
tum custodia circumdat, manente luxu et regio
nomine. Quod ludibrium ut effugere agitaverit
Vonones in loco reddemus.

(restored): 1 B.C.–11 A.D., approximately, *a. Ariobarzanes*
("origine Medus"); *b. Artavasdes III* (his son); *c. Tigranes IV*
(cf. VI. 40): *d. Erato* (again restored?): 11 or 12 A.D. *Vonones*.

[1] The allusion, of course, is to the custom of sister-marriage
—the survival probably of a period when the blood royal could
be transmitted only in the female line. Familiar instances
are the Carian dynasts (Mausolus–Artemisia, Idrieus–Ada)
and the native and even Ptolemaic sovereigns of Egypt
(Ptolemy Philadelphus–Arsinoë, Ptolemy Philopator–Arsinoë).

[2] See I. 3. Invested with proconsular power and sent out
as vice-regent to the eastern provinces in 1 B.C., he was
treacherously wounded in Armenia (3 A.D.), and died before
reaching Italy (Feb. 21, 4 A.D.).

ourselves on account of his father's memory, was able to protect himself and his crown by the arms of the Arsacidae. After his assassination by the treachery of his own relatives, the Caesar assigned Tigranes to Armenia, and he was settled in his dominions by Tiberius Nero. Tigranes' term of royalty was brief; and so was that of his children, though associated by the regular oriental ties of marriage and joint government.[1]

IV. In the next place, by the mandate of Augustus, Artavasdes was imposed upon his countrymen—only to be shaken off, not without a measure of discredit to our arms. Then came the appointment of Gaius Caesar[2] to compose the affairs of Armenia. He gave the crown to Ariobarzanes, a Mede[3] by extraction; to whose good looks and brilliant qualities the Armenians raised no objection. But when an accident carried off Ariobarzanes, their tolerance did not reach to his family; and after an experiment in female government with a queen called Erato, who was quickly expelled, the drifting, disintegrated people, ownerless rather than emancipated, welcomed the fugitive Vonones to the throne. But as Artabanus became threatening and little support could be expected from the Armenians, while the armed protection of Rome would entail a Parthian war, Creticus Silanus, governor of Syria, obtained his eviction, and placed him under a surveillance which still left him his luxuries and his title. His attempt to escape from this toy court we shall notice in its proper place.[4]

---

[3] From Media Atropatene (*Azerbeidján*), between Armenia and Media proper : an appanage of the Arsacidae.

[4] See below, chap. 68.

V. Ceterum Tiberio haud ingratum accidit turbari res Orientis, ut ea specie Germanicum suetis legionibus abstraheret novisque provinciis impositum dolo simul et casibus obiectaret. At ille, quanto acriora in eum studia militum et aversa patrui voluntas, celerandae victoriae intentior, tractare proeliorum vias et quae sibi tertium iam annum belligeranti saeva vel prospera evenissent. Fundi Germanos acie et iustis locis, iuvari silvis, paludibus, brevi aestate et praematura hieme; suum militem haud perinde vulneribus quam spatiis itinerum, damno armorum adfici; fessas Gallias ministrandis equis; longum impedimentorum agmen opportunum ad insidias, defensantibus iniquum. At si mare intretur, promptam ipsis possessionem et hostibus ignotam, simul bellum maturius incipi legionesque et commeatus pariter vehi; integrum equitem equosque per ora et alveos fluminum media in Germania fore.

VI. Igitur huc intendit, missis ad census Galliarum P. Vitellio et C. Antio.[1] Silius et Caecina[2] fabricandae classi praeponuntur. Mille naves sufficere visae properataeque, aliae breves, angusta puppi

---

[1] C. Antio *Ursinius* : cantio.
[2] Silius et Caecina *Urlichs* : Silius et Anteius et Caecina.

V. For Tiberius the disturbances in the East were
a not unwelcome accident, as they supplied him with
a pretext for removing Germanicus from his familiar
legions and appointing him to unknown provinces,
where he would be vulnerable at once to treachery
and chance. But the keener the devotion of his
soldiers and the deeper the aversion of his uncle,
the more anxious grew the prince to accelerate his
victory; and he began to consider the ways and
means of battle in the light of the failures and
successes which had fallen to his share during the
past two years of campaigning. In a set engagement and on a fair field, the Germans, he reflected,
were beaten—their advantage lay in the forests and
swamps, the short summer and the premature
winter. His own men were not so much affected by
their wounds as by the dreary marches and the loss
of their weapons. The Gallic provinces were weary
of furnishing horses; and a lengthy baggage-train
was easy to waylay and awkward to defend. But if
they ventured on the sea, occupation would be easy
for themselves and undetected by the enemy; while
the campaign might begin at an earlier date, and
the legions and supplies be conveyed together: the
cavalry and horses would be taken up-stream
through the river-mouths and landed fresh in the
centre of Germany.

VI. To this course, then, he bent his attention.
Publius Vitellius and Gaius Antius were sent to
assess the Gallic tribute: Silius and Caecina were
made responsible for the construction of a fleet. A
thousand vessels were considered enough, and these
were built at speed. Some were short craft with
very little poop or prow, and broad-bellied, the more

proraque et lato utero, quo facilius fluctus tolerarent;
quaedam planae carinis, ut sine noxa siderent;
plures adpositis utrimque gubernaculis, converso ut
repente remigio hinc vel illinc adpellerent; multae
pontibus stratae, super quas tormenta veherentur,
simul aptae ferendis equis aut commeatui; velis
habiles, citae remis augebantur alacritate militum
in speciem ac terrorem. Insula Batavorum in
quam convenirent praedicta, ob facilis adpulsus
accipiendisque copiis et transmittendum ad bellum
opportuna. Nam Rhenus uno alveo continuus aut
modicas insulas circumveniens apud principium agri
Batavi velut in duos amnis dividitur, servatque
nomen et violentiam cursus, qua Germaniam prae-
vehitur, donec Oceano misceatur; ad Gallicam ripam
latior et placidior adfluens (verso cognomento Vaha-
lem accolae dicunt), mox id quoque vocabulum
mutat Mosa flumine eiusque inmenso ore eundem
in Oceanum effunditur.

VII. Sed Caesar, dum adiguntur naves, Silium
legatum cum expedita manu inruptionem in Chattos
facere iubet: ipse audito castellum Lupiae flumini
adpositum obsideri, sex legiones eo duxit. Neque
Silio ob subitos imbris aliud actum quam ut modicam
praedam et Arpi principis Chattorum coniugem
filiamque raperet, neque Caesari copiam pugnae

---

[1] The Rhine delta, as explained below.

[2] Now the Old (" Crooked ") Rhine—little better than a
ditch—on which Utrecht and Leyden stand.

[3] If this is not the Fort Aliso mentioned below, its position
cannot be even conjectured.

easily to withstand a heavy sea: others had flat
bottoms, enabling them to run aground without
damage; while still more were fitted with rudders at
each end, so as to head either way the moment the
oarsmen reversed their stroke. Many had a deck-
flooring to carry the military engines, though they
were equally useful for transporting horses or supplies. The whole armada, equipped at once for
sailing or propulsion by the oar, was a striking and
formidable spectacle, rendered still more so by the
enthusiasm of the soldiers. The Isle of Batavia[1] was
fixed for the meeting-place, since it afforded an easy
landing and was convenient both as a rendezvous
for the troops and as the base for a campaign across
the water. For the Rhine, which so far has flowed
in a single channel, save only where it circles some
unimportant islet, branches at the Batavian frontier
into what may be regarded as two rivers. On the
German side, it runs unchanged in name and vehemence till its juncture with the North Sea:[2] the
Gallic bank it washes with a wider, gentler stream,
known locally as the Waal, though before long it
changes its style once more and becomes the river
Meuse, through whose immense estuary it discharges, also into the North Sea.

VII. However, while the ships were coming in, the
Caesar ordered his lieutenant Silius to take a mobile
force and raid the Chattan territory: he himself,
hearing that the fort on the Lippe[3] was invested,
led six legions to its relief. But neither could Silius,
in consequence of the sudden rains, effect anything
beyond carrying off a modest quantity of booty,
together with the wife and daughter of the Chattan
chief, Arpus, nor did the besiegers allow the prince

obsessores fecere, ad famam adventus eius dilapsi: tumulum tamen nuper Varianis legionibus structum et veterem aram Druso sitam disiecerant. Restituit aram honorique patris princeps ipse cum legionibus decucurrit; tumulum iterare haud visum. Et cuncta inter castellum Alisonem ac Rhenum novis limitibus aggeribusque permunita.

VIII. Iamque classis advenerat, cum praemisso commeatu et distributis in legiones ac socios navibus fossam, cui Drusianae nomen, ingressus precatusque Drusum patrem ut se eadem ausum libens placatusque exemplo ac memoria consiliorum atque operum iuvaret, lacus inde et Oceanum usque ad Amisiam flumen secunda navigatione pervehitur. Classis Amisiae ore[1] relicta laevo amne, erratumque in eo quod non subvexit aut[2] transposuit militem dextras in terras iturum; ita plures dies efficiendis pontibus absumpti. Et eques quidem ac legiones prima aestuaria, nondum adcrescente unda, intrepidi transiere: postremum auxiliorum agmen Batavique in parte ea, dum insultant aquis artemque nandi ostentant, turbati et quidam hausti sunt.

[1] Amisiae ore *Seyffert*: Amisiae.
[2] subvexit aut *Wurm*: subvexit.

---

[1] See I. 62.

[2] Almost certainly the fort constructed by Drusus at the confluence of the Lippe and "Eliso" (ἥ ὅ τε Λουπίας καὶ ὁ Ἐλίσων συμμίγνυνται, D. Cass. LIV. 33). If the Eliso is the Alme (the oldest and perhaps most probable view), the fort must be placed near Paderborn; if the Ahse, then near Hamm; and if the Stever, about Haltern.

[3] The name here includes not only the canal, some two miles long, by which Drusus connected the northern branch of the Rhine near Arnheim with the Yssel, but the widened course of the stream itself.

an opportunity of battle, but melted away at the
rumour of his approach. Still, they had demolished
the funeral mound just raised in memory of the
Varian legions,[1] as well as an old altar set up to
Drusus. He restored the altar and himself headed
the legions in the celebrations in honour of his
father; the tumulus it was decided not to recon-
struct. In addition, the whole stretch of country
between Fort Aliso[2] and the Rhine was thoroughly
fortified with a fresh line of barriers and earthworks.

VIII. The fleet had now arrived. Supplies were
sent forward, ships assigned to the legionaries and
allies, and he entered the so-called Drusian Fosse.[3]
After a prayer to his father, beseeching him of his
grace and indulgence to succour by the example and
memory of his wisdom and prowess a son who had
ventured in his footsteps,[4] he pursued his voyage
through the lakes[5] and the high sea, and reached the
Ems without misadventure. The fleet stayed in the
mouth of the river on the left side, and an error
was committed in not carrying the troops further
up-stream or disembarking them on the right bank
for which they were bound; the consequence being
that several days were wasted in bridge-building.
The estuaries immediately adjoining were crossed
intrepidly enough by the cavalry and legions, before
the tide had begun to flow: the auxiliaries in the
extreme rear and the Batavians in the same part of
the line, while dashing into the water and exhibiting
their powers of swimming, were thrown into disorder,
and a number of them drowned. As the Caesar

[4] Suet. *Claud.* 1 : *Drusus . . . Oceanum septemtrionalem
primus Romanorum ducum navigavit.*

[5] The Zuyderzee.

Metanti castra Caesari Angrivariorum[1] defectio a
tergo nuntiatur: missus ilico Stertinius cum equite
et armatura levi igne et caedibus perfidiam ultus est.

IX. Flumen Visurgis Romanos Cheruscosque
interfluebat; eius in ripa cum ceteris primoribus
Arminius adstitit, quaesitoque an Caesar venisset,
postquam adesse responsum est, ut liceret cum fratre
conloqui oravit. Erat is in exercitu cognomento
Flavus, insignis fide et amisso per vulnus oculo
paucis ante annis duce Tiberio. Tum permissu * *[2]
progressusque salutatur ab Arminio; qui amotis
stipatoribus, ut sagittarii nostra pro ripa dispositi
abscederent postulat, et postquam digressi, unde
ea deformitas oris interrogat fratrem. Illo locum et
proelium referente, quodnam praemium recepisset
exquirit. Flavus aucta stipendia, torquem et coronam aliaque militaria dona memorat, inridente Arminio vilia servitii pretia.

X. Exim diversi ordiuntur, hic magnitudinem
Romanam, opes Caesaris et victis gravis poenas,
in deditionem venienti paratam clementiam; neque
coniugem et filium eius hostiliter haberi: ille fas

[1] Angrivariorum] Ampsivariorum *Giefers.*
[2] **Nipperdey.*

---

[1] In chap. 19 the tribe is found east of the Weser;
whence Giefers' conjecture *Ampsivariorum.* No certainty
can be felt on the point; and it is possible, even, that something is lost before *metanti castra,* as it is difficult to suppose
that the march from the Ems to the west bank of the Weser
could have been passed over without a word.

[2] Merivale pointed out that the breadth of the Weser
makes the following narrative questionable. Other over-
picturesque touches in Tacitus' sources are Germanicus'
dream (chap. 14) and the apparition of the eight eagles
(chap. 17).

was arranging his encampment, news came of an Angrivarian [1] rising in his rear: Stertinius, who was instantly despatched with a body of horse and light-armed infantry, repaid the treachery with fire and bloodshed.

IX. The river Weser ran between the Roman and Cheruscan forces. Arminius came to the bank and halted with his fellow-chieftains:—" Had the Caesar come? " he inquired.[2] On receiving the reply that he was in presence, he asked to be allowed to speak with his brother. That brother, Flavus by name, was serving in the army, a conspicuous figure both from his loyalty and from the loss of an eye through a wound received some few years before during Tiberius' term of command. Leave was granted, ⟨and Stertinius took him down to the river⟩.[3] Walking forward, he was greeted by Arminius; who, dismissing his own escort, demanded that the archers posted along our side of the stream should be also withdrawn. When these had retired, he asked his brother, whence the disfigurement of his face? On being told the place and battle, he inquired what reward he had received. Flavus mentioned his increased pay, the chain, the crown, and other military decorations; Arminius scoffed at the cheap rewards of servitude.

X. They now began to argue from their opposite points of view. Flavus insisted on " Roman greatness, the power of the Caesar; the heavy penalties for the vanquished; the mercy always waiting for him who submitted himself. Even Arminius' wife and child were not treated as enemies." His brother

---

[3] The text translates roughly Nipperdey's proposal : *Tum permissu ⟨imperatoris deducitur a Stertinio⟩, progressusque e.q.s.*

patriae, libertatem avitam, penetralis Germaniae
deos, matrem precum sociam, ne propinquorum et
adfinium, denique gentis suae desertor et proditor
quam liberator[1] esse mallet. Paulatim inde ad iurgia
prolapsi quo minus pugnam consererent ne flumine
quidem interiecto cohibebantur, ni Stertinius adcur-
rens plenum irae armaque et equum poscentem
Flavum attinuisset. Cernebatur contra minitabun-
dus Arminius proeliumque denuntians; nam pleraque Latino sermone interiaciebat, ut qui Romanis
in castris ductor popularium meruisset.

XI. Postero die Germanorum acies trans Visurgim stetit. Caesar nisi pontibus praesidiisque inpo-
sitis dare in discrimen legiones haud imperatorium
ratus, equitem vado tramittit. Praefuere Stertinius
et e numero primipilarium Aemilius, distantibus locis
invecti, ut hostem diducerent:[2] qua celerrimus
amnis, Chariovalda, dux Batavorum, erupit. Eum
Cherusci, fugam simulantes, in planitiem saltibus
circumiectam traxere: dein coorti et undique effusi
trudunt adversos, instant cedentibus collectosque in
orbem pars congressi, quidam eminus proturbant.
Chariovalda, diu sustentata hostium saevitia, horta-

---

[1] liberator *Jacob*: imperator.
[2] diducerent *Rhenanus*: deducerent.

---

[1] The leading centurion of the sixty in a legion was the
primipilus—the first centurion of the first maniple of the first
cohort. On the completion of his service he frequently
received equestrian rank, and was employed in positions of
very considerable responsibility. Here Aemilius (probably
the *vir militaris* of IV. 42) acts as *praefectus equitum*. An
inscription. which should apparently be referred to him,
runs: Paulo Aemilio, D. f., primo pilo, bis praefecto equitum,
tribuno cohortis IIII praetoriae (C.I.L. X. 3881).

urged " the sacred call of their country; their
ancestral liberty; the gods of their German hearths;
and their mother, who prayed, with himself, that he
would not choose the title of renegade and traitor to
his kindred, to the kindred of his wife, to the whole
of his race in fact, before that of their liberator."
From this point they drifted, little by little, into
recriminations; and not even the intervening river
would have prevented a duel, had not Stertinius
run up and laid a restraining hand on Flavus, who
in the fullness of his anger was calling for his weapons
and his horse. On the other side Arminius was
visible, shouting threats and challenging to battle:
for he kept interjecting much in Latin, as he had seen
service in the Roman camp as a captain of native
auxiliaries.

XI. On the morrow, the German line drew up
beyond the Weser. The Caesar, as he held it doubtful generalship to risk the legions without providing
adequately guarded bridges, sent his cavalry across
by a ford. Stertinius and Aemilius—a retired centurion of the first rank[1]—were in command, and, in
order to distract the enemy, delivered the assault
at widely separate points: where the current ran
fiercest, Chariovalda, the Batavian leader, dashed
out. By a feigned retreat the Cherusci drew him on
to a level piece of ground fringed with woods: then,
breaking cover, they streamed out from all quarters,
overwhelmed the Batavians where they stood their
ground, harassed them where they retired, and, when
they rallied in circular formation, flung them back,
partly by hand-to-hand fighting, partly by discharges
of missiles. After long sustaining the fury of the
enemy, Chariovalda exhorted his men to hack a way,

tus suos ut ingruentis catervas globo perfringerent,[1]
atque ipse [2] densissimos inrumpens, congestis telis
et suffosso equo labitur, ac multi nobilium circa:
ceteros vis sua aut equites cum Stertinio Aemilioque
subvenientes periculo exemere.

XII. Caesar transgressus Visurgim indicio perfugae cognoscit delectum ab Arminio locum pugnae;
convenisse et alias nationes in silvam Herculi sacram
ausurosque nocturnam castrorum oppugnationem.
Habita indici fides et cernebantur ignes, suggres-
sique propius speculatores audiri fremitum equorum
inmensique et inconditi agminis murmur attulere.
Igitur propinquo summae rei discrimine explorandos
militum animos ratus, quonam id modo incorruptum
foret secum agitabat. Tribunos et centuriones
laeta saepius quam comperta nuntiare, libertorum
servilia ingenia, amicis inesse adulationem; si
contio vocetur, illic quoque quae pauci incipiant
reliquos adstrepere. Penitus noscendas mentes,
cum secreti et incustoditi inter militaris cibos spem
aut metum proferrent.

XIII. Nocte coepta egressus augurali per occulta
et vigilibus ignara, comite uno, contectus umeros
ferina pelle, adit castrorum vias, adsistit tabernacu-

---

[1] perfringerent *Bezzenberger* : fringerent.
[2] ipse *Weissenborn* : ipsis.

---

[1] *Germ.* 3 : *Fuisse apud eos et Herculem memorant,*
primumque omnium virorum fortium ituri in proelia canunt.
[2] His object may have been to pass for a native auxiliary.

in mass, through the assailing bands; then threw himself into the thickest of the struggle, and fell under a shower of spears, with his horse stabbed under him and many of his nobles around. The rest were extricated from danger by their own efforts or by the mounted men who advanced to the rescue under Stertinius and Aemilius.

XII. After crossing the Weser, Germanicus gathered from the indications of a deserter that Arminius had chosen his ground for battle: that other nations also had mustered at the holy forest of Hercules,[1] and that the intention was to hazard a night attack on the camp. The informer's account carried conviction: indeed, the German fires could be discerned; and scouts, who ventured closer up, came in with the news that they could hear the neigh of horses and the murmur of a vast and tumultuous array. The Caesar, who thought it desirable, with the supreme decision hard at hand, to probe the feeling of his troops, debated with himself how to ensure that the experiment should be genuine. The reports of tribunes and centurions were more often cheering than accurate; the freedman was a slave at heart; in friends there was a strain of flattery; should he convoke an assembly, even there a few men gave the lead and the rest applauded. He must penetrate into the soldiers' thoughts while, private and unguarded, they expressed their hope or fear over their rations.

XIII. At fall of night, leaving his pavilion by a secret outlet unknown to the sentries, with a single attendant, a wild-beast's skin over his shoulders,[2] he turned into the streets of the camp, stood by the tents and tasted his own popularity, while the men—

lis fruiturque fama sui, cum hic nobilitatem ducis, decorem alius, plurimi patientiam, comitatem, per seria, per iocos eundem in animum [1] laudibus ferrent reddendamque gratiam in acie faterentur; simul perfidos et ruptores pacis ultioni et gloriae mactandos. Inter quae unus hostium, Latinae linguae sciens, acto ad vallum equo, voce magna, coniuges et agros et stipendii in dies, donec bellaretur, sestertios centenos, si quis transfugisset, Arminii nomine pollicetur. Intendit ea contumelia legionum iras : veniret dies, daretur pugna; sumpturum militem Germanorum agros, tracturum coniuges; accipere omen et matrimonia ac pecunias hostium praedae destinare. Tertia ferme vigilia adsultatum est castris sine coniectu teli, postquam crebras pro munimentis cohortes et nihil remissum sensere.

XIV. Nox eadem laetam Germanico quietem tulit, viditque se operatum et sanguine sacro [2] respersa praetexta pulchriorem aliam manibus aviae Augustae accepisse. Auctus omine, addicentibus auspiciis, vocat contionem et quae sapientia provisa [3] aptaque inminenti pugnae disserit. Non campos modo militi Romano ad proelium bonos, sed si ratio adsit, silvas et saltus; nec enim inmensa

[1] in animum *Nipperdey* : animum.
[2] sacro *Beroaldus* : sacri.
[3] provisa *J. F. Gronovius* : praevisa.

---

[1] Twenty-five denarii—an offer which, if made, could never have been taken seriously by the legionaries (see I. 17).

serious or jesting but unanimous—praised some the commander's lineage, others his looks, the most his patience and his courtesy; admitting that they must settle their debt of gratitude in the field and at the same time sacrifice to glory and revenge their perfidious and treaty-breaking foe. In the midst of all this, one of the enemy, with a knowledge of Latin, galloped up to the wall, and in loud tones proffered to each deserter in the name of Arminius, wives and lands and a daily wage of one hundred sesterces[1] for the duration of the war. This insult fired the anger of the legions:—" Wait till the day broke and they had the chance of battle! The Roman soldier would help himself to German lands and come back dragging German wives. The omen was welcome: the enemy's women and his money were marked down for prey! "—Some time about the third watch, a demonstration was made against the camp, though not a spear was thrown, when the assailants realized that the ramparts were lined with cohorts and that no precaution had been omitted.

XIV. The same night brought Germanicus a reassuring vision: for he dreamed that he was offering sacrifice, and that—as his vestment was bespattered with the blood of the victim—he had received another, more beautiful, from the hand of his grandmother, Augusta. Elated by the omen, and finding the auspices favourable, he summoned a meeting of the troops and laid before them the measures his knowledge had suggested and the points likely to be of service in the coming struggle :—
" A plain was not the only battle-field favourable to a Roman soldier: if he used judgment, woods and glades were equally suitable. The barbarians'

barbarorum scuta, enormis hastas inter truncos
arborum et enata humo virgulta perinde haberi
quam pila et gladios et haerentia corpori tegmina.
Denserent ictus, ora mucronibus quaererent: non
loricam Germano, non galeam, ne scuta quidem ferro
nervove firmata, sed viminum textus vel tenuis et
fucatas colore tabulas; primam utcumque aciem
hastatam, ceteris praeusta aut brevia tela. Iam corpus ut visu torvum et ad brevem impetum validum,
sic nulla vulnerum patientia. Sine pudore flagitii,
sine cura ducum abire, fugere, pavidos adversis,
inter secunda non divini, non humani iuris memores.
Si taedio viarum ac maris finem cupiant, hac acie
parari: propiorem iam Albim quam Rhenum neque
bellum ultra, modo se patris patruique vestigia
prementem isdem in terris victorem sisterent.

XV. Orationem ducis secutus militum ardor,
signumque pugnae datum. Nec Arminius aut ceteri
Germanorum proceres omittebant suos quisque
testari, hos esse Romanos Variani exercitus fugacis-
simos qui, ne bellum tolerarent, seditionem induérint;
quorum pars onusta vulneribus terga,[1] pars fluctibus et procellis fractos artus infensis rursum hostibus, adversis dis obiciant, nulla boni spe. Classem

---

[1] terga *Muretus* : tergum.

---

[1] One of the three reminiscences of Horace which have been
detected in Tacitus : see *Carm.* Ⅲ. 6, 7, *lasso maris et viarum*
and *Epp.* I. 11, 6, *odio maris atque viarum.* The other two
may be found at XI. 15, *laeta . . . in praesens = Carm.* II.
16, 25, *laetus in praesens,* and XV. 37 *contaminatorum grege =
Carm.* I. 37, 9 *contaminato cum grege.*

[2] On the east of the Elba, the Suebi and Marbod (see
I. 44 and the note, and, for an interesting account of Marbod's
position, Seeck's *Untergang der antiken Welt* I. 228, *sqq.*) were
friendly, or at least neutral.

huge shields, their enormous spears, could not be
so manageable among tree-trunks and springing
brushwood as the pilum, the short sword, and close-
fitting body-armour. Their policy was to strike thick
and fast, and to direct the point to the face. The
Germans carried neither corselet nor headpiece—
not even shields with a toughening of metal or hide,
but targes of wickerwork or thin, painted board.
Their first line alone carried spears of a fashion:
the remainder had only darts, fire-pointed or too
short. Their bodies, again, while grim enough to
the eye and powerful enough for a short-lived onset,
lacked the stamina to support a wound. They were
men who could turn and run without a blush for
their disgrace and without a thought for their
leaders, faint-hearted in adversity, in success regardless of divine and human law.—If they were weary
of road and sea,[1] and desired the end, this battle
could procure it. Already the Elbe was nearer
than the Rhine, and there would be no fighting
further,[2] if once, treading as he was in the footsteps
of his father and his uncle, they established him
victorious in the same region! "

XV. The commander's speech was followed by an
outburst of military ardour, and the signal was given
to engage.

Nor did Arminius or the other German chieftains
fail to call their several clans to witness that " these
were the Romans of Varus' army who had been the
quickest to run, men who rather than face war had
resorted to mutiny; half of whom were again exposing their spear-scored backs, half their wave and
tempest-broken limbs, to a revengeful foe, under the
frowns of Heaven and hopeless of success! For it

quippe et avia Oceani quaesita ne quis venientibus
occurreret, ne pulsos premeret: sed ubi miscuerint
manus, inane victis ventorum remorumve subsidium. Meminissent modo avaritiae, crudelitatis,
superbiae : aliud sibi reliquum quam tenere libertatem aut mori ante servitium?

XVI. Sic accensos et proelium poscentis in campum, cui Idisiaviso[1] nomen, deducunt. Is medius
inter Visurgim et collis, ut ripae fluminis cedunt
aut prominentia montium resistunt, inaequaliter
sinuatur. Pone tergum insurgebat silva, editis in
altum ramis et pura humo inter arborum truncos.
Campum et prima silvarum barbara acies tenuit:
soli Cherusci iuga insedere ut proeliantibus Romanis
desuper incurrerent. Noster exercitus sic incessit:
auxiliares Galli Germanique in fronte, post quos
pedites sagittarii; dein quattuor legiones et cum
duabus praetoriis cohortibus ac delecto equite Caesar; exim totidem aliae legiones et levis armatura
cum equite sagittario ceteraeque sociorum cohortes.
Intentus paratusque miles ut ordo agminis in aciem
adsisteret.

XVII. Visis Cheruscorum catervis, quae per
ferociam proruperant, validissimos equitum incurrere latus, Stertinium cum ceteris turmis circumgredi
tergaque[2] invadere iubet, ipse in tempore adfuturus.

---

[1] Idisiaviso *Grimm* : idista viso.
[2] tergaque *Lipsius* : tergave.

---

[1] Grimm interpreted his emendation by *Elfenwiese*:
attempted identifications are highly speculative.

was to ships and pathless seas they had had recourse, so that none might oppose them as they came or chase them when they fled. But if once the fray was joined, winds and oars were a vain support for beaten men!—They had only to remember Roman greed, cruelty, and pride: was there another course left for them but to hold their freedom or to die before enslavement?"

XVI. Thus inflamed and clamouring for battle, they followed their leaders down into a plain known as Idisiaviso.[1] Lying between the Weser and the hills, it winds irregularly along, with here a concession from the river and there an encroachment by some mountain-spur. Behind rose the forest, lifting its branches high in air, and leaving the ground clear between the trunks. The barbarian line was posted on the level and along the skirts of the wood: the Cherusci alone were planted on the hill-tops, ready to charge from the height when the Romans engaged. Our army advanced in the following order: in the van, the auxiliary Gauls and Germans with the unmounted archers behind; next, four legions, and the Caesar with two praetorian cohorts and the flower of the cavalry; then, four other legions, the light-armed troops with the mounted archers and the rest of the allied cohorts. The men were alert and ready, so arranged that the order of march could come to a halt in line of battle.

XVII. On sighting the Cheruscan bands, whose wild hardihood had led them to dash forward, the prince ordered his best cavalry to charge the flank; Stertinius with the remaining squadrons was to ride round and attack the rear, while he himself would not be wanting when the time came. Meanwhile

407

Interea pulcherrimum augurium, octo aquilae petere
silvas et intrare visae imperatorem advertere.
Exclamat irent, sequerentur Romanas avis, propria
legionum numina. Simul pedestris acies infertur
et praemissus eques postremos ac latera impulit. Mi-
rumque dictu, duo hostium agmina diversa fuga,
qui silvam tenuerant, in aperta, qui campis adsti-
terant, in silvam ruebant. Medii inter hos Cherusci collibus detrudebantur, inter quos insignis
Arminius manu, voce, vulnere sustentabat pugnam.
Incubueratque sagittariis, illa rupturus, ni Rae-
torum Vindelicorumque et Gallicae cohortes signa
obiecissent. Nisu tamen corporis et impetu equi
pervasit, oblitus faciem suo cruore ne nosceretur.
Quidam adgnitum a Chaucis inter auxilia Romana
agentibus emissumque tradiderunt. Virtus seu fraus
eadem Inguiomero effugium dedit: ceteri passim
trucidati. Et plerosque tranare Visurgim conantis
iniecta tela aut vis fluminis, postremo moles ruen-
tium et incidentes ripae operuere. Quidam turpi
fuga in summa arborum nisi ramisque se occultantes
admotis sagittariis per ludibrium figebantur, alios
prorutae arbores adflixere.

---

[1] One for each legion. " Critics have superfluously noted
that eagles are now rarely if ever seen in those parts, and that
their nearest representative, the ' vultur albucillus,' is not
gregarious ": Furneaux.

his attention was arrested by a curiously happy
omen—eight [1] eagles seen aiming for, and entering,
the glades. " Forward," he exclaimed, " and follow
the birds of Rome, the guardian spirits of the legions!"
At the same moment the line of infantry charged
and the advanced cavalry broke into the rear and
flanks. Thus, remarkably enough, two columns of
the enemy were following directly opposed lines of
flight—the troops who had held the forest, rushing
into the open; those who had been stationed in the
plain, diving into the forest. Midway between both,
the Cherusci were being pushed from the hills—
among them the unmistakable figure of Arminius,
striking, shouting, bleeding, in his effort to maintain
the struggle. He had flung himself on the archers,
and would have broken through at that point, had
not the Raetian, Vindelician, and Gallic cohorts
opposed their standards. Even so, a great physical
effort, together with the impetus of his horse, carried
him clear. To avoid recognition, he had stained his
face with his own blood; though, according to some
authorities, the Chauci serving among the Roman
auxiliaries knew him and gave him passage. The
like courage or the like treachery won escape for
Inguiomerus: the rest were butchered in crowds.
Numbers were overwhelmed in an attempt to swim
the Weser, at first by the discharge of spears or the
sweep of the current, later by the weight of the
plunging masses and the collapse of the river-banks.
Some clambered to an ignominious refuge in the tree-
tops, and, while seeking cover among the branches,
were shot down in derision by a body of archers,
who had been moved up; others were brought down
by felling the trees.

XVIII. Magna ea victoria neque cruenta nobis fuit. Quinta ab hora diei ad noctem caesi hostes decem milia passuum cadaveribus atque armis opplevere, repertis inter spolia eorum catenis quas in Romanos ut non dubio eventu portaverant.

Miles in loco proelii Tiberium imperatorem salutavit struxitque aggerem et in modum tropaeorum arma subscriptis victarum gentium nominibus imposuit.

XIX. Haut perinde Germanos vulnera, luctus, excidia quam ea species dolore et ira adfecit. Qui modo abire sedibus, trans Albim concedere parabant, pugnam volunt, arma rapiunt; plebes, primores, iuventus, senes agmen Romanum repente incursant, turbant. Postremo deligunt locum flumine et silvis clausum, arta intus planitie et umida; silvas quoque profunda palus ambibat nisi quod latus unum Angrivarii lato aggere extulerant quo a Cheruscis dirimerentur. Hic pedes adstitit: equitem propinquis lucis texere ut ingressis silvam legionibus a tergo foret.

XX. Nihil ex his[1] Caesari incognitum: consilia, locos, prompta, occulta noverat astusque hostium in perniciem ipsis vertebat. Seio Tuberoni legato tradit equitem campumque; peditum aciem ita

[1] his *Oberlin* : iis.

---

[1] This not improbable detail is found rather too frequently in the ancient historians. Furneaux cites Polyb. III. 82 and Florus III. 7, 2: one might add Hdt. I. 66; D. Sic. XX. 13; 1 Macc. iii. 41.

[2] The *salutatio imperatoria*, by which, under the republic, the victorious general was acclaimed as *imperator* by his troops, and crowned with bays, was now, with the triumph, a prerogative of the *princeps* : a fact symbolized by the laurel planted before the palace. See below, III. 74.

XVIII. It was a brilliant, and to us not a bloody, victory. The enemy were slaughtered from the fifth hour of daylight to nightfall, and for ten miles the ground was littered with corpses and weapons. Among the spoils were found the chains which, without a doubt of the result, they had brought in readiness for the Romans.[1]

After proclaiming Tiberius *Imperator* on the field of battle,[2] the troops raised a mound, and decked it with arms in the fashion of a trophy, inscribing at the foot the names of the defeated clans.

XIX. The sight affected the Germans with an anguish and a fury which wounds, distress, and ruin had been powerless to evoke. Men, who a moment ago had been preparing to leave their homesteads and migrate across the Elbe, were now eager for battle and flew to arms. Commons and nobles, youth and age, suddenly assailed the Roman line of march and threw it into disorder. At last they fixed on a position pent in between a stream and the forests, with a narrow, waterlogged plain in the centre; the forests too were encircled by a deep swamp, except on one side, where the Angrivarii had raised a broad earthen barrier to mark the boundary between themselves and the Cherusci. Here the infantry took up their station; the mounted men they concealed in the neighbouring groves, so as to be in the rear of the legions when they entered the forest.

XX. None of these points escaped the Caesar. He was aware of their plans, their position, their open and secret arrangements, and he proposed to turn the devices of the enemy to their own ruin. To his legate, Seius Tubero, he assigned the cavalry and the plain; the line of infantry he drew up so

instruxit ut pars aequo in silvam aditu incederet,
pars obiectum aggerem eniteretur; quod arduum
sibi, cetera legatis permisit. Quibus plana evenerant, facile inrupere: quis inpugnandus agger, ut
si murum succederent, gravibus superne ictibus
conflictabantur. Sensit dux inparem comminus
pugnam remotisque paulum legionibus funditores
libritoresque excutere tela et proturbare hostem
iubet. Missae e tormentis hastae, quantoque conspicui magis propugnatores, tanto pluribus vulneribus deiecti. Primus Caesar cum praetoriis cohortibus, capto vallo, dedit impetum in silvas. Con-
lato illic gradu certatum: hostem a tergo palus,
Romanos flumen aut montes claudebant; utrisque
necessitas in loco, spes in virtute, salus ex
victoria.

XXI. Nec minor Germanis animus, sed genere
pugnae et armorum superabantur, cum ingens multitudo artis locis praelongas hastas non protenderet,
non colligeret, neque adsultibus et velocitate corporum uteretur, coacta stabile ad proelium; contra
miles, cui scutum pectori adpressum et insidens
capulo manus, latos barbarorum artus, nuda ora
foderet viamque strage hostium aperiret, inprompto
iam Arminio [1] ob continua pericula, sive illum recens

---

[1] iam Arminio *Beroaldus*: iam.

that one part should march by the level track to the forest, while the other scaled the obstacle presented by the barrier. The difficult part of the enterprise he reserved for himself, the rest he left to his deputies. The party to which the even ground had been allotted broke in without trouble; their comrades with the barrier to force, much as if they had been scaling a wall, suffered considerably from the heavy blows delivered from higher ground. Feeling that the odds were against him at close quarters, Germanicus withdrew the legionaries a short distance, and ordered his slingers and marksmen to make play with their missiles and disperse the enemy. Spears were flung from the engines; and the more conspicuous the defenders, the more numerous the wounds under which they fell. On the capture of the rampart, the Caesar charged foremost into the forest with the praetorian cohorts. There the conflict raged foot to foot. The enemy was hemmed in by the morass in his rear, the Romans by the river or the hills: the position left no choice to either, there was no hope but in courage, no salvation but from victory.

XXI. In hardihood the Germans held their own; but they were handicapped by the nature of the struggle and the weapons. Their extraordinary numbers—unable in the restricted space to extend or recover their tremendous lances, or to make use of their rushing tactics and nimbleness of body— were compelled to a standing fight; while our own men, shields tight to the breast and hand on hilt, kept thrusting at the barbarians' great limbs and bare heads and opening a bloody passage through their antagonists—Arminius being now less active, whether owing to the succession of dangers or to

acceptum vulnus tardaverat. Quin et Inguiomerum,
tota volitantem acie, fortuna magis quam virtus
deserebat. Et Germanicus, quo magis adgnosceretur, detraxerat tegimen capiti orabatque insisterent
caedibus : nil opus captivis, solam internicionem
gentis finem bello fore. Iamque sero diei subducit
ex acie legionem faciendis castris : ceterae ad noctem cruore hostium satiatae sunt. Equites ambigue
certavere.

XXII. Laudatis pro contione victoribus Caesar
congeriem armorum struxit, superbo cum titulo :
debellatis inter Rhenum Albimque nationibus exercitum Tiberii Caesaris ea monimenta[1] Marti et
Iovi et Augusto sacravisse. De se nihil addidit,
metu invidiae an ratus conscientiam facti[2] satis esse.
Mox bellum in Angrivarios[3] Stertinio mandat, ni
deditionem properavissent. Atque illi supplices nihil
abnuendo veniam omnium accepere.

XXIII. Sed aestate iam adulta legionum aliae
itinere terrestri in hibernacula remissae; pluris
Caesar classi inpositas per flumen Amisiam Oceano
invexit. Ac primo placidum aequor mille navium
velis strepere aut remis[4] inpelli : mox atro nubium

---

[1] monimenta *Lipsius* : munimenta.
[2] facti *Aldus* : factis.
[3] Angrivarios] Ampsivarios *Giefers*.
[4] velis . . . remis *Jackson* : remis . . . velis.

---

[1] In order to complete the suppression of the revolt
mentioned at the close of chap. 8 : the same doubt as to the
reading exists, of course, here.

[2] The period would be July. The summer, like the other
seasons, was divided into three months : in the first, it was

the hampering effects of his recent wound. Inguio-merus, moreover, as he flew over the battle-field, found himself deserted less by his courage than by fortune. Germanicus, also, to make recognition the easier had torn off his headpiece and was adjuring his men to press on with the carnage:—" Prisoners were needless: nothing but the extermination of the race would end the war."—At last, in the decline of day, he withdrew one legion from the front to begin work on the camp; while the others satiated them-selves with the enemies' blood till night. The cavalry engagement was indecisive.

XXII. First eulogizing the victors in an address, the Caesar raised a pile of weapons, with a legend boasting that " the army of Tiberius Caesar, after subduing the nations between the Rhine and the Elbe, had consecrated that memorial to Mars, to Jupiter, and to Augustus." Concerning himself he added nothing, either apprehending jealousy or holding the consciousness of his exploit to be enough. Shortly afterwards he commissioned Stertinius to open hostilities against the Angrivarii,[1] unless they forestalled him by surrender. And they did, in fact, come to their knees, refusing nothing, and were forgiven all.

XXIII. However, as summer was already at the full,[2] a part of the legions were sent back to winter quarters by the land route: the majority were put on shipboard by the prince, who took them down the Ems into the North Sea. At first it was a tranquil expanse, troubled only by the sound and impulse of the sails and oars of a thousand ships. But soon

nova; in the second, adulta; in the third, praeceps (Servius on Georg. I. 43).

globo effusa grando, simul variis undique procellis
incerti fluctus prospectum adimere, regimen inpe-
dire; milesque pavidus et casuum maris ignarus,
dum turbat nautas vel intempestive iuvat, officia
prudentium corrumpebat. Omne dehinc caelum et
mare omne in austrum cessit, qui tumidis [1] Germaniae
terris, profundis amnibus, immenso nubium tractu
validus et rigore vicini septentrionis horridior rapuit
disiecitque navis in aperta Oceani aut insulas saxis
abruptis vel per occulta vada infestas. Quibus
paulum aegreque vitatis, postquam mutabat aestus
eodemque quo ventus ferebat, non adhaerere ancoris,
non exhaurire inrumpentis undas poterant : equi,
iumenta, sarcinae, etiam arma praecipitantur quo
levarentur alvei manantes per latera et fluctu super-
urgente.

XXIV. Quanto violentior cetero mari Oceanus
et truculentia caeli praestat Germania, tantum illa
clades novitate et magnitudine excessit, hostilibus
circum litoribus aut ita vasto et profundo ut credatur
novissimum ac sine terris mare. Pars navium haus-
tae sunt, plures apud insulas longius sitas eiectae;
milesque nullo illic hominum cultu fame absumptus,
nisi quos corpora equorum eodem elisa tolerave-
rant. Sola Germanici triremis Chaucorum terram
adpulit; quem per omnis illos dies noctesque apud

----

[1] tumidis] humidis *Rhenanus*.

----

[1] The underlying theory is that the sodden lands and the
rivers form the clouds by evaporation; the clouds, in their
turn, give rise to the wind (Sen. *Q.N.* V. 5; *ib.* 13).

[2] Between the Weser and Holland : the *saxa abrupta*,
like the *Scopuli* of the next chapter, can be only a mistaken
literary embellishment.

[3] The open ocean as opposed to land-locked seas.

[4] Presumably off the coast of Schleswig.

the hail poured from a black mass of clouds, and simultaneously the waves, buffeted by conflicting gales from every quarter, began to blot out the view and impede the steering. The soldiers—struck by alarm, and unfamiliar with the sea and its hazards— nullified by their obstruction or mistimed help the services of the professional sailors. Then all heaven, all ocean, passed into the power of the south wind; which, drawing its strength from the sodden lands of Germany, the deep rivers, the endless train of clouds,[1] with its grimness enhanced by the rigour of the neighbouring north, caught and scattered the vessels to the open ocean or to islands[2] either beetling with crags or perilous from sunken shoals. These were avoided with time and difficulty; but, when the tide began to change and set in the same direction as the wind, it was impossible either to hold anchor or to bale out the inrushing flood. Chargers, pack-horses, baggage, even arms, were jettisoned, in order to lighten the hulls, which were leaking through the sides and overtopped by the waves.

XXIV. Precisely as Ocean[3] is more tempestuous than the remaining sea, and Germany unequalled in the asperity of its climate, so did that calamity transcend others in extent and novelty—around them lying hostile shores or a tract so vast and profound that it is believed the last and landless deep. Some of the ships went down; more were stranded on remote islands;[4] where, in the absence of human life, the troops died of starvation, except for a few who supported themselves on the dead horses washed up on the same beach. Germanicus' galley put in to the Chaucian coast alone. Throughout all those days and nights, posted on some cliff or projection

417

scopulos et prominentis oras, cum se tanti exitii reum clamitaret, vix cohibuere amici quo minus eodem mari oppeteret. Tandem relabente aestu et secundante vento claudae naves raro remigio aut intentis vestibus, et quaedam a validioribus tractae, revertere; quas raptim refectas misit ut scrutarentur insulas. Collecti ea cura plerique: multos Angrivarii nuper in fidem accepti redemptos ab interioribus reddidere; quidam in Britanniam rapti et remissi a regulis. Vt quis ex longinquo revenerat, miracula narrabant, vim turbinum et inauditas volucris, monstra maris, ambiguas hominum et beluarum formas, visa sive ex metu credita.

XXV. Sed fama classis amissae ut Germanos ad spem belli, ita Caesarem ad coercendum erexit. C. Silio cum triginta peditum, tribus equitum milibus ire in Chattos imperat; ipse maioribus copiis Marsos inrumpit, quorum dux Mallovendus nuper in deditionem acceptus propinquo luco [1] defossam Varianae legionis aquilam modico praesidio servari indicat. Missa extemplo manus quae hostem a fronte eliceret, alii qui terga circumgressi recluderent humum; et utrisque adfuit fortuna. Eo promptior Caesar pergit introrsus, populatur, excindit non ausum congredi hostem aut, sicubi restiterat,

---

[1] luco *Lipsius* : loco.

---

[1] The influence of Pedo Albinovanus' poem (see p. 345, n.) has been plausibly suspected in more places than one of this narrative.

of the shore, he continued to exclaim that he was guilty of the great disaster; and his friends with difficulty prevented him from finding a grave in the same waters. At length, with the turning tide and a following wind, the crippled vessels began to come in, some with a few oars left, others with clothing hoisted for canvas, and a few of the weaker in tow. They were instantly refitted and sent out to examine the islands. By that act of forethought a large number of men were gathered in, while many were restored by our new subjects, the Angrivarians, who had ransomed them from the interior. A few had been swept over to Britain, and were sent back by the petty kings. Not a man returned from the distance without his tale of marvels—furious whirl-winds, unheard-of birds, enigmatic shapes half-human and half-bestial:[1] things seen, or things believed in a moment of terror.

XXV. But though the rumoured loss of the fleet inspired the Germans to hope for war, it also inspired the Caesar to hold them in check. Gaius Silius he ordered to take the field against the Chatti with thirty thousand foot and three thousand horse: he himself with a larger force invaded the Marsi; whose chieftain, Mallovendus, had lately given in his sub-mission, and now intimated that the eagle of one of Varus' legions was buried in an adjacent grove, with only a slender detachment on guard. One com-pany was despatched immediately to draw the enemy by manœuvring on his front; another, to work round the rear and excavate. Both were attended by good fortune; and the Caesar pushed on to the interior with all the more energy, ravaging and destroying an enemy who either dared not engage

statim pulsum nec umquam magis, ut ex captivis cognitum est, paventem. Quippe invictos et nullis casibus superabilis Romanos praedicabant, qui perdita classe, amissis armis, post constrata equorum virorumque corporibus litora eadem virtute, pari ferocia et velut aucto numero inrupissent.

XXVI. Reductus inde in hiberna[1] miles, laetus animi quod adversa maris expeditione prospera pensavisset. Addidit munificentiam Caesar, quantum quis damni professus erat exsolvendo. Nec dubium habebatur labare hostis petendaeque pacis consilia sumere et, si proxima aestas adiceretur, posse bellum patrari. Sed crebris epistulis Tiberius monebat rediret ad decretum triumphum: satis iam eventuum, satis casuum. Prospera illi et magna proelia: eorum quoque meminisset, quae venti et fluctus, nulla ducis culpa, gravia tamen et saeva damna intulissent. Se novies a divo Augusto in Germaniam missum plura consilio quam vi perfecisse: sic Sugambros in deditionem acceptos, sic Suebos regemque Maroboduum pace obstrictum. Posse et Cheruscos ceterasque rebellium gentis, quoniam Romanae ultioni consultum esset,[2] internis discordiis relinqui. Precante Germanico annum efficiendis

---

[1] hiberna *Beroaldus* : hiona.   [2] esset *Muretus* : est.

---

[1] The verdict of history upon these campaigns must, however, coincide with that of Tiberius.

or was immediately routed wherever he turned to
bay. It was gathered from the prisoners that the
Germans had never been more completely demoralized. Their cry was that "the Romans were
invincible—proof against every disaster! They had
wrecked their fleet, lost their arms; the shores had
been littered with the bodies of horses and men;
yet they had broken in again, with the same courage,
with equal fierceness, and apparently with increased
numbers!"

XXVI. The army was then marched back to
winter quarters, elated at having balanced the
maritime disaster by this fortunate expedition.
Moreover, there was the liberality of the Caesar,
who compensated every claimant in full for the loss
he professed to have sustained. Nor was any doubt
felt that the enemy was wavering and discussing an
application for peace; and that with another effort
in the coming summer, the war might see its close.[1]
But frequent letters from Tiberius counselled the
prince "to return for the triumph decreed him:
there had been already enough successes, and
enough mischances. He had fought auspicious and
great fields: he should also remember the losses
inflicted by wind and wave—losses not in any way
due to his leadership, yet grave and deplorable. He
himself had been sent nine times into Germany by
the deified Augustus; and he had effected more by
policy than by force. Policy had procured the
Sugambrian surrender; policy had bound the Suebi
and King Maroboduus to keep the peace. The
Cherusci and the other rebel tribes, now that enough
had been done for Roman vengeance, might similarly
be left to their intestine strife." When Germanicus

coeptis, acrius modestiam eius adgreditur alterum
consulatum offerendo cuius munia praesens obiret.
Simul adnectebat, si foret adhuc bellandum, relinqueret materiem Drusi fratris gloriae, qui nullo
tum alio hoste non nisi apud Germanias adsequi
nomen imperatorium et deportare lauream posset.
Haud cunctatus est ultra Germanicus, quamquam
fingi ea seque per invidiam parto iam decori abstrahi
intellegeret.

XXVII. Sub idem tempus e familia Scriboniorum
Libo Drusus defertur moliri res novas. Eius
negotii initium, ordinem, finem curatius disseram,
quia tum primum reperta sunt quae per tot annos
rem publicam exedere. Firmius Catus senator,
ex intima Libonis amicitia, iuvenem inprovidum
et facilem inanibus ad Chaldaeorum promissa,
magorum sacra, somniorum etiam interpretes impulit, dum proavum Pompeium, amitam Scriboniam,
quae quondam Augusti coniunx fuerat, consobrinos
Caesares,[1] plenam imaginibus domum ostentat,
hortaturque ad luxum et aes alienum, socius libidi-
num et necessitatum, quo pluribus indiciis inligaret.

XXVIII. Vt satis testium et qui servi eadem
noscerent repperit, aditum ad principem postulat,

---

[1] consobrinos Caesares *Beroaldus* : consobrinus caesaris.

---

[1] Seneca's epigram (*Epp.* 70, 10) deserves quotation :—
*Adulescens tam stolidus quam nobilis, maiora sperans quam illo
saeculo quisquam sperare poterat aut ipse ullo.*

asked for one year more in which to finish his work, he delivered a still shrewder attack on his modesty, and offered him a second consulate, the duties of which he would assume in person. A hint was appended that " if the war must be continued, he might leave his brother, Drusus, the material for a reputation; since at present there was no other national enemy, and nowhere but in the Germanies could he acquire the style of *Imperator* and a title to the triumphal bays."—Germanicus hesitated no longer, though he was aware that these civilities were a fiction, and that jealousy was the motive which withdrew him from a glory already within his grasp.

XXVII. Nearly at the same time, a charge of revolutionary activities was laid against Libo Drusus,[1] a member of the Scribonian family. I shall describe in some detail the origin, the progress, and the end of this affair, as it marked the discovery of the system destined for so many years to prey upon the vitals of the commonwealth. Firmius Catus, a senator, and one of Libo's closest friends, had urged that short-sighted youth, who had a foible for absurdities, to resort to the forecasts of astrologers, the ritual of magicians, and the society of interpreters of dreams; pointing to his great-grandfather Pompey, to his great-aunt Scribonia (at one time the consort of Augustus), to his cousinship with the Caesars, and to his mansion crowded with ancestral portraits; encouraging him in his luxuries and loans; and, to bind him in a yet stronger chain of evidence, sharing his debaucheries and his embarrassments.

XXVIII. When he had found witnesses enough, and slaves to testify in the same tenor, he asked for

demonstrato crimine et reo per Flaccum Vescularium equitem Romanum, cui propior cum Tiberio usus erat. Caesar indicium haud aspernatus congressus abnuit: posse enim eodem Flacco internuntio sermones commeare. Atque interim Libonem ornat praetura, convictibus adhibet, non vultu alienatus, non verbis commotior (adeo iram condiderat); cunctaque eius dicta factaque, cum prohibere posset, scire malebat, donec Iunius quidam, temptatus ut infernas umbras carminibus eliceret, ad Fulcinium Trionem indicium detulit. Celebre inter accusatores Trionis ingenium erat avidumque famae malae. Statim corripit reum, adit consules, cognitionem senatus poscit. Et vocantur patres, addito consultandum super re magna et atroci.

XXIX. Libo interim veste mutata cum primoribus feminis circumire domos, orare adfinis, vocem adversum pericula poscere, abnuentibus cunctis, cum diversa praetenderent, eadem formidine. Die senatus metu et aegritudine fessus, sive, ut tradidere quidam, simulato morbo, lectica delatus ad foris curiae innisusque fratri et manus ac supplices voces

---

[1] See VI. 10.
[2] In order to question them as to the future. An interesting account of the procedure may be found in Heliodorus, *Aeth.* VI. sub fin.

an interview with the sovereign, to whom the charge
and the person implicated had been notified by
Vescularius Flaccus,[1] a Roman knight on familiar
terms with Tiberius. The Caesar, without rejecting
the information, declined a meeting, as " their conversations might be carried on through the same
intermediary, Flaccus." In the interval, he distinguished Libo with a praetorship and several
invitations to dinner. There was no estrangement
on his brow, no hint of asperity in his speech : he
had buried his anger far too deep. He could have
checked every word and action of Libo : he preferred,
however, to know them. At length, a certain Junius,
solicited by Libo to raise departed spirits by incanta-
tion,[2] carried his tale to Fulcinius Trio.[3] Trio's genius,
which was famous among the professional informers,
hungered after notoriety. He swooped immediately
on the accused, approached the consuls, and demanded a senatorial inquiry. The Fathers were
summoned, to deliberate (it was added) on a case of
equal importance and atrocity.

XXIX. Meanwhile, Libo changed into mourning,
and with an escort of ladies of quality made a circuit
from house to house, pleading with his wife's relatives,
and conjuring them to speak in mitigation of his
danger,—only to be everywhere refused on different
pretexts and identical grounds of alarm. On the
day the senate met, he was so exhausted by fear and
distress—unless, as some accounts have it, he
counterfeited illness—that he was borne to the doors
of the Curia in a litter, and, leaning on his brother,
extended his hands and his appeals to Tiberius, by

[3] His subsequent career may be traced from III. 9 and 19;
V. 11; VI. 4 and 38.

ad Tiberium tendens immoto eius vultu excipitur.
Mox libellos et auctores recitat Caesar ita moderans
ne lenire neve asperare [1] crimina videretur.

XXX. Accesserant praeter Trionem et Catum
accusatores Fonteius Agrippa et C. Vibius,[2] certabantque cui ius perorandi in reum daretur, donec
Vibius, quia nec ipsi inter se concederent et Libo
sine patrono introisset, singillatim se crimina obiec-
turum professus, protulit libellos vaecordes adeo
ut consultaverit Libo an habiturus foret opes quis
viam Appiam Brundisium usque pecunia operiret.
Inerant et alia huiusce modi stolida, vana, si mollius
acciperes, miseranda. Vno tamen libello manu
Libonis nominibus Caesarum aut senatorum additas
atrocis vel occultas notas accusator arguebat. Ne-
gante reo adgnoscentis servos per tormenta interrogari [3] placuit. Et quia vetere senatus consulto
quaestio in caput domini prohibebatur, callidus et
novi iuris repertor Tiberius mancipari singulos actori
publico iubet, scilicet ut in Libonem ex servis salvo
senatus consulto quaereretur. Ob quae posterum
diem reus petivit domumque digressus extremas
preces P. Quirinio propinquo suo ad principem man-
davit.

[1] asperare *Beroaldus* : asperari.
[2] Vibius *Gruter ut infra* : livius.
[3] interrogari *Lipsius* : interrogare.

---

[1] So that Libo could answer each immediately, and no
continuous speech would be needed on either side.
[2] Otherwise their testimony was not admissible.

whom he was received without the least change of countenance. The emperor then read over the indictment and the names of the sponsors, with a self-restraint that avoided the appearance of either palliating or aggravating the charges.

XXX. Besides Trio and Catus, Fonteius Agrippa and Gaius Vibius had associated themselves with the prosecution, and it was disputed which of the four should have the right of stating the case against the defendant. Finally, Vibius announced that, as no one would give way and Libo was appearing without legal representation, he would take the counts one by one.[1] He produced Libo's papers, so fatuous that, according to one, he had inquired of his prophets if he would be rich enough to cover the Appian Road as far as Brundisium with money. There was more in the same vein, stolid, vacuous, or, if indulgently read, pitiable. In one paper, however, the accuser argued, a set of marks, sinister or at least mysterious, had been appended by Libo's hand to the names of the imperial family and a number of senators. As the defendant denied the allegation, it was resolved to question the slaves, who recognized the handwriting, under torture;[2] and, since an old decree prohibited their examination in a charge affecting the life of their master, Tiberius, applying his talents to the discovery of a new jurisprudence, ordered them to be sold individually to the treasury agent: all to procure servile evidence against a Libo, without overriding a senatorial decree! In view of this, the accused asked for an adjournment till next day, and left for home, after commissioning his relative, Publius Quirinius, to make a final appeal to the emperor.

XXXI. Responsum est ut senatum rogaret. Cinge-
batur interim milite domus, strepebant etiam in
vestibulo ut audiri, ut aspici possent, cum Libo,
ipsis quas in novissimam voluptatem adhibuerat
epulis excruciatus, vocare percussorem, prensare
servorum dextras, inserere gladium. Atque illis,
dum trepidant, dum refugiunt, evertentibus adpositum cum mensa lumen, feralibus iam sibi tenebris
duos ictus in viscera derexit. Ad gemitum conla-
bentis adcurrere liberti, et caede visa miles abstitit.
Accusatio tamen apud patres adseveratione eadem
peracta, iuravitque Tiberius petiturum se vitam
quamvis nocenti, nisi voluntariam mortem prope-
ravisset.

XXXII. Bona inter accusatores dividuntur, et
praeturae extra ordinem datae iis qui senatorii
ordinis erant. Tunc Cotta Messalinus, ne imago
Libonis exequias posterorum comitaretur, censuit,
Cn. Lentulus, ne quis Scribonius cognomentum
Drusi adsumeret. Supplicationum dies Pomponii
Flacci sententia constituti, dona Iovi, Marti, Concordiae, utque iduum Septembrium dies, quo se
Libo interfecerat, dies festus haberetur, L. Piso
et Gallus Asinius et Papius Mutilus et L. Apronius
decrevere; quorum auctoritates adulationesque rettuli ut sciretur vetus id in re publica malum. Facta

---

[1] A professional whose hand would be steadier than his own.
So Nero *Spiculum murmillonem vel quemlibet percussorem,
cuius manu periret, requisivit* (Suet. *Ner.* 47).

XXXI. The reply ran, that he must address his petitions to the senate. Meanwhile, his house was picketed by soldiers; they were tramping in the portico itself, within eyeshot and earshot, when Libo, thus tortured at the very feast which he had arranged to be his last delight on earth, called out for a slayer,[1] clutched at the hands of his slaves, strove to force his sword upon them. They, as they shrank back in confusion, overturned lamp and table together; and he, in what was now for him the darkness of death, struck two blows into his vitals. He collapsed with a moan, and his freedmen ran up: the soldiers had witnessed the bloody scene, and retired.

In the senate, however, the prosecution was carried through with unaltered gravity, and Tiberius declared on oath that, guilty as the defendant might have been, he would have interceded for his life, had he not laid an over-hasty hand upon himself.

XXXII. His estate was parcelled out among the accusers, and extraordinary praetorships were conferred on those of senatorial status. Cotta Messalinus then moved that the effigy of Libo should not accompany the funeral processions of his descendants; Gnaeus Lentulus, that no member of the Scribonian house should adopt the surname of Drusus. Days of public thanksgiving were fixed at the instance of Pomponius Flaccus. Lucius Piso, Asinius Gallus, Papius Mutilus, and Lucius Apronius procured a decree that votive offerings should be made to Jupiter, Mars, and Concord; and that the thirteenth of September, the anniversary of Libo's suicide, should rank as a festival. This union of sounding names and sycophancy I have recorded as showing how long that evil has been rooted in the State.—

et de mathematicis magisque Italia pellendis senatus consulta ; quorum e numero L. Pituanius saxo deiectus est, in P. Marcium consules extra portam Esquilinam, cum classicum canere iussissent, more prisco advertere.

XXXIII. Proximo senatus die multa in luxum civitatis dicta a Q. Haterio consulari, Octavio Frontone praetura functo ; decretumque ne vasa auro solida ministrandis cibis fierent, ne vestis serica viros foedaret. Excessit Fronto ac postulavit modum argento, supellectili, familiae : erat quippe adhuc frequens senatoribus, si quid e re publica crederent, loco sententiae promere. Contra Gallus Asinius disseruit : auctu imperii adolevisse etiam privatas opes, idque non novum, sed e vetustissimis moribus : aliam apud Fabricios, aliam apud Scipiones pecuniam ; et cuncta ad rem publicam referri, qua tenui angustas civium domos, postquam eo magnificentiae venerit, gliscere singulos. Neque in familia et argento quaeque ad usum parentur nimium aliquid aut modicum nisi ex fortuna possidentis. Distinctos senatus et equitum census, non

---

[1] *Genus hominum potentibus infidum, sperantibus fallax, quod in civitate nostra et vetabitur semper et retinebitur* (*Hist.* I. 22). For another decree—*atrox et inritum*—see XII. 52 ; for Tiberius' interest in the art, and Tacitus' verdict upon it, VI. 20 *sqq.* ; and for a large collection of literary and historical references, Mayor on Juv. XIV. 248.

Other resolutions of the senate ordered the expulsion of the astrologers [1] and magic-mongers from Italy. One of their number, Lucius Pituanius, was flung from the Rock; another—Publius Marcius—was executed by the consuls outside the Esquiline Gate according to ancient usage [2] and at sound of trumpet.

XXXIII. At the next session, the ex-consul, Quintus Haterius,[3] and Octavius Fronto, a former praetor, spoke at length against the national extravagance; and it was resolved that table-plate [4] should not be manufactured in solid gold, and that Oriental silks should no longer degrade the male sex. Fronto went further, and pressed for a statutory limit to silver, furniture, and domestics: for it was still usual for a member to precede his vote by mooting any point which he considered to be in the public interest. Asinius Gallus opposed:—" With the expansion of the empire, private fortunes had also grown; nor was this new, but consonant with extremely ancient custom. Wealth was one thing with the Fabricii, another with the Scipios; and all was relative to the state. When the state was poor, you had frugality and cottages: when it attained a pitch of splendour such as the present, the individual also throve. In slaves or plate or anything procured for use there was neither excess nor moderation except with reference to the means of the owner. Senators and knights had a special property

---

[2] The procedure, unknown to Nero (Suet. *Ner.* 49) and rare enough to be an interesting spectacle to the antiquarian Claudius (*Claud.* 34). was decapitation.

[3] The famous and now aged orator: see I. 13, III. 57, and the short notice in IV. 61.

[4] As distinct from vessels consecrated to religious uses.

quia diversi natura, sed ut sicut[1] locis, ordinibus, dignationibus antistent, ita iis[2] quae ad requiem animi aut salubritatem corporum parentur, nisi forte clarissimo cuique pluris curas, maiora pericula sube- unda, delenimentis curarum et periculorum carendum esse. Facilem adsensum Gallo sub nominibus honestis confessio vitiorum et similitudo audientium dedit. Adiecerat et Tiberius non id tempus censurae nec, si quid in moribus labaret, defuturum corrigendi auctorem.

XXXIV. Inter quae L. Piso ambitum fori, cor- rupta iudicia, saevitiam oratorum accusationes minitantium increpans, abire se et cedere urbe, victurum in aliquo abdito et longinquo rure testaba- tur; simul curiam relinquebat. Commotus est Tiberius, et quamquam mitibus verbis Pisonem permulsisset, propinquos quoque eius impulit ut abeuntem auctoritate vel precibus tenerent. Haud minus liberi doloris documentum idem Piso mox dedit vocata in ius Vrgulania, quam supra leges amicitia Augustae extulerat. Nec aut Vrgulania obtempera- vit, in domum Caesaris spreto Pisone vecta, aut ille abscessit, quamquam Augusta se violari et immi- nui quereretur. Tiberius hactenus indulgere matri

---

[1] ut sicut *Urlichs* : ut.   [2] ita iis *Ruperti* : talis.

---

[1] The former, one million sesterces; the latter, four hundred thousand.

qualification,[1] not because they differed in kind from their fellow-men, but in order that those who enjoyed precedence in place, rank, and dignity should enjoy it also in the easements that make for mental peace and physical well-being. And justly so—unless your distinguished men, while saddled with more responsibilities and greater dangers, were to be deprived of the relaxations compensating those responsibilities and those dangers."—With his virtuously phrased confession of vice, Gallus easily carried with him that audience of congenial spirits. Tiberius, too, had added that it was not the time for a censorship, and that, if there was any loosening of the national morality, a reformer would be forthcoming.

XXXIV. During the debate, Lucius Piso, in a diatribe against the intrigues of the Forum, the corruption of the judges, and the tyranny of the advocates with their perpetual threats of prosecution, announced his retirement—he was migrating from the capital, and would live his life in some sequestered, far-away country nook. At the same time, he started to leave the Curia. Tiberius was perturbed; and, not content with having mollified him by a gentle remonstrance, induced his relatives also to withhold him from departure by their influence or their prayers.—It was not long before the same Piso gave an equally striking proof of the independence of his temper by obtaining a summons against Urgulania, whose friendship with the ex-empress had raised her above the law. Urgulania declined to obey, and, ignoring Piso, drove to the imperial residence : her antagonist, likewise. stood his ground, in spite of Livia's complaint that his act was an outrage and humiliation to herself. Tiberius, who

433

civile ratus, ut se iturum ad praetoris tribunal,
adfuturum Vrgulaniae diceret, processit Palatio,
procul sequi iussis militibus. Spectabatur occur-
sante populo compositus ore et sermonibus variis
tempus atque iter ducens, donec, propinquis Pisonem frustra coercentibus, deferri Augusta pecuniam
quae petebatur iuberet. Isque finis rei, ex qua neque
Piso inglorius et Caesar maiore fama fuit. Ceterum
Vrgulaniae potentia adeo nimia civitati erat ut testis
in causa quadam, quae apud senatum tractabatur,
venire dedignaretur: missus est praetor qui domi in-
terrogaret, cum virgines Vestales in foro et iudicio
audiri, quotiens testimonium dicerent, vetus mos
fuerit.

XXXV. Res eo anno prolatas haud referrem, ni
pretium foret Cn. Pisonis et Asinii Galli super eo
negotio diversas sententias noscere. Piso, quamquam afuturum se dixerat Caesar, ob id magis agendas censebat, ut absente principe senatum et equites
posse sua munia sustinere decorum rei publicae
foret. Gallus, quia speciem libertatis Piso prae-
ceperat, nihil satis inlustre aut ex dignitate populi
Romani nisi coram et sub oculis Caesaris, eoque

---

[1] The vacation of the senate and law-courts. In this case,
the embarrassing point was that, if the vacation was arranged
to coincide with the absence of the emperor, it would coincide
also with the presence in the capital of a multitude of Italians
and provincials with important legal business, public or private,
to transact.

reflected that it would be no abuse of his position
to indulge his mother up to the point of promising
to appear at the praetorian court and lend his support
to Urgulania, set out from the palace, ordering his
guards to follow at a distance. The people, flocking
to the sight, watched him while with great composure
of countenance he protracted the time and the
journey by talking on a variety of topics, until,
as his relatives failed to control Piso, Livia gave
orders for the sum in demand to be paid. This
closed an incident of which Piso had some reason to
be proud, while at the same time it added to the
emperor's reputation. For the rest, the influence
of Urgulania lay so heavy on the state that, in one
case on trial before the senate, she disdained to
appear as a witness, and a praetor was sent to
examine her at home, although the established
custom has always been for the Vestal Virgins, when
giving evidence, to be heard in the Forum and courts
of justice.

XXXV. Of this year's adjournment[1] I should say
nothing, were it not worth while to note the
divergent opinions of Gnaeus Piso and Asinius Gallus
on the subject. Piso, although the emperor had
intimated that he would not be present, regarded it
as a further reason why public business should go
forward, so that the ability of the senators and
knights to carry out their proper duties in the
absence of the sovereign might redound to the credit
of the state. Forestalled by Piso in this show of
independence, Gallus objected that business, not
transacted under the immediate eye of their prince,
lacked distinction and fell short of the dignity of
the Roman people; and for that reason the concourse

conventum Italiae et adfluentis provincias prae-
sentiae eius servanda dicebat.   Audiente haec Tiberio
ac silente magnis utrimque contentionibus acta, sed
res dilatae.

XXXVI. Et certamen Gallo adversus Caesarem
exortum est.   Nam censuit in quinquennium magistratuum comitia habenda, utque legionum legati,
qui ante praeturam ea militia fungebantur, iam
tum praetores destinarentur, princeps duodecim
candidatos in annos singulos nominaret.   Haud
dubium erat eam sententiam altius penetrare et
arcana imperii temptari.   Tiberius tamen, quasi
augeretur potestas eius, disseruit: grave modera-
tioni suae tot eligere, tot differre.   Vix per singulos
annos offensiones vitari, quamvis repulsam propinqua spes soletur: quantum odii fore ab iis qui
ultra quinquennium proiciantur?   Vnde prospici
posse quae cuique tam longo temporis spatio mens,
domus, fortuna?   Superbire homines etiam annua
designatione: quid si honorem per quinquennium
agitent?   Quinquiplicari prorsus magistratus, subverti leges, quae sua spatia exercendae candidatorum
industriae quaerendisque aut potiundis honoribus
statuerint.   Favorabili in speciem oratione vim
imperii tenuit.

---

[1] If the motion were carried, the elections would continue
to be held annually.   At the first, however, all magistracies
for the next five years would be allotted; at the second (held
in the following year) those for the fifth year from that date;
and so indefinitely.   But, if the holders of all magistracies
were unalterably predetermined for five years, the result must
obviously be not only to fetter the inclinations of the sovereign
to an appreciable extent, but to render the prospective officials,
whose position was secured in advance, considerably less pliant
than would otherwise have been the case.

of Italy and the influx from the provinces ought to be reserved for his presence. The debate was conducted with much vigour on both sides, while Tiberius listened and was mute: the adjournment, however, was carried.

XXXVI. Another passage of arms arose between Gallus and the Caesar. The former moved that the elections should determine the magistrates for the next five years,[1] and that legionary commanders, serving in that capacity before holding the praetor-ship, should become praetors designate at once, the emperor nominating twelve candidates for each year. There was no doubt that the proposal went deeper than this, and trespassed on the arcana of sovereignty. Tiberius, however, replied by treat-ing it as an extension of his own prerogative :—" To his moderate temper it was an ungrateful task to mete out so many appointments and disappointments. Even on the annual system, it was difficult to avoid offences, though hope of office in the near future softened the rebuff: how much odium must he incur from those whom he threw aside for above five years ! And how could it be foreseen what would be the frame of mind, the family, the fortune of each over so long an interval of time? Men grew arrogant enough even in the twelve months after nomination : what if they had a whole quinquennium in which to play the official ? The proposal actually multiplied the number of magistrates by five, and subverted the laws which had fixed the proper periods for exercising the industry of candidates and for soliciting or enjoying preferment." With this speech, which outwardly had a popular appearance, he kept his hold upon the essentials of sovereignty.

XXXVII. Censusque quorundam senatorum iuvit. Quo magis mirum fuit quod preces Marci Hortali, nobilis iuvenis, in paupertate manifesta superbius accepisset. Nepos erat oratoris Hortensii, inlectus a divo Augusto liberalitate decies sestertii ducere uxorem, suscipere liberos, ne clarissima familia extingueretur. Igitur quattuor filiis ante limen curiae adstantibus, loco sententiae, cum in Palatio senatus haberetur, modo Hortensii inter oratores sitam imaginem, modo Augusti intuens, ad hunc modum coepit: " Patres conscripti, hos, quorum numerum et pueritiam videtis, non sponte sustuli sed quia princeps monebat; simul maiores mei meruerant ut posteros haberent. Nam ego, qui non pecuniam, non studia populi neque eloquentiam, gentile domus nostrae bonum, varietate temporum accipere vel parare potuissem, satis habebam, si tenues res meae nec mihi pudori nec cuiquam oneri forent. Iussus ab imperatore uxorem duxi. En stirps et progenies tot consulum, tot dictatorum. Nec ad invidiam ista, sed conciliandae misericordiae refero. Adsequentur florente te, Caesar, quos dederis honores: interim Q. Hortensii [1] pronepotes, divi Augusti alumnos ab inopia defende."

---

[1] interim Q. Hortensii *Beroaldus* : interimq; hortensq.

---

[1] The senatorial census (see I. 75).

[2] In the Latin library of the Palatium (Suet. *Aug.* 29; D. Cass. LIII. 1), where the senate was frequently convened in the declining years of Augustus. For the portrait-medallions of the orators see chap. 83. below.

[3] The list, in reality, only includes one dictator, one consul, and a consul designate.

XXXVII. In addition, he gave monetary help to several senators; so that it was the more surprising when he treated the application of the young noble, Marcus Hortalus, with a superciliousness uncalled for in view of his clearly straitened circumstances. He was a grandson of the orator Hortensius; and the late Augustus, by the grant of a million sesterces,[1] had induced him to marry and raise a family, in order to save his famous house from extinction. With his four sons, then, standing before the threshold of the Curia, he awaited his turn to speak; then, directing his gaze now to the portrait of Hortensius among the orators (the senate was meeting in the Palace),[2] now to that of Augustus, he opened in the following manner:—"Conscript Fathers, these children whose number and tender age you see for yourselves, became mine not from any wish of my own, but because the emperor so advised, and because, at the same time, my ancestors had earned the right to a posterity. For to me, who in this changed world had been able to inherit nothing and acquire nothing, —not money, nor popularity, nor eloquence, that general birthright of our house,—to me it seemed enough if my slender means were neither a disgrace to myself nor a burden to my neighbour. At the command of the sovereign, I took a wife; and here you behold the stock of so many consuls, the offspring of so many dictators![3] I say it, not to awaken odium, but to woo compassion. Some day, Caesar, under your happy sway, they will wear whatever honours you have chosen to bestow: in the meantime, rescue from beggary the great-grandsons of Quintus Hortensius, the fosterlings of the deified Augustus!"

439

XXXVIII. Inclinatio senatus incitamentum Tiberio fuit quo promptius adversaretur, his ferme verbis usus: "Si quantum pauperum est venire huc et liberis suis petere pecunias coeperint, singuli numquam exsatiabuntur, res publica deficiet. Nec sane ideo a maioribus concessum est egredi aliquando relationem et quod in commune conducat loco sententiae proferre, ut privata negotia et res familiaris nostras hic augeamus, cum invidia senatus et principum, sive indulserint largitionem sive abnuerint. Non enim preces sunt istud, sed efflagitatio, intempestiva quidem et inprovisa, cum aliis de rebus convenerint patres, consurgere et numero atque aetate liberum suorum urgere modestiam senatus, eandem vim in me transmittere ac velut perfringere aerarium, quod si ambitione exhauserimus, per scelera supplendum erit. Dedit tibi, Hortale, divus Augustus pecuniam, sed non conpellatus nec ea lege ut semper daretur. Languescet alioqui industria, intendetur socordia, si nullus ex se metus aut spes, et securi omnes aliena subsidia expectabunt, sibi ignavi, nobis graves." Haec atque talia, quamquam cum adsensu audita ab iis quibus omnia principum, honesta atque inhonesta, laudare mos est, plures per silentium aut occultum murmur excepere. Sensitque Tiberius; et cum paulum reticuisset,

XXXVIII. The senate's inclination to agree incited Tiberius to a more instant opposition. His speech in effect ran thus:—" If all the poor of the earth begin coming here and soliciting money for their children, we shall never satisfy individuals, but we shall exhaust the state. And certainly, if our predecessors ruled that a member, in his turn to speak, might occasionally go beyond the terms of the motion and bring forward a point in the public interest, it was not in order that we should sit here to promote our private concerns and personal fortunes, while rendering the position of the senate and its head equally invidious whether they bestow or withhold their bounty. For this is no petition, but a demand—an unseasonable and unexpected demand, when a member rises in a session convened for other purposes, puts pressure on the kindly feeling of the senate by a catalogue of the ages and number of his children, brings the same compulsion to bear indirectly upon myself, and, so to say, carries the Treasury by storm; though, if we drain it by favouritism, we shall have to refill it by crime. The deified Augustus gave you money, Hortalus; but not under pressure, nor with a proviso that it should be given always. Otherwise, if a man is to have nothing to hope or fear from himself, industry will languish, indolence thrive, and we shall have the whole population waiting, without a care in the world, for outside relief, incompetent to help itself, and an incubus to us." These sentences and the like, though heard with approval by the habitual eulogists of all imperial actions honourable or dishonourable, were by most received with silence or a suppressed murmur. Tiberius felt the chill, and, after a short

Hortalo se respondisse ait: ceterum si patribus videretur, daturum liberis eius ducena sestertia singulis, qui sexus virilis essent. Egere alii grates: siluit Hortalus, pavore an avitae nobilitatis etiam inter angustias fortunae retinens. Neque miseratus est posthac Tiberius, quamvis domus Hortensii pudendam ad inopiam delaberetur.[1]

XXXIX. Eodem anno mancipii unius audacia, ni mature subventum foret, discordiis armisque civilibus rem publicam perculisset. Postumi Agrippae servus, nomine Clemens, comperto fine Augusti, pergere in insulam Planasiam et fraude aut vi raptum Agrippam ferre ad exercitus Germanicos non servili animo concepit. Ausa eius inpedivit tarditas onerariae navis: atque interim patrata[2] caede ad maiora et magis praecipitia conversus furatur cineres vectusque Cosam,[3] Etruriae promunturium, ignotis locis sese abdit, donec crinem barbamque promitteret: nam aetate et forma haud dissimili in dominum erat. Tum per idoneos et secreti eius socios crebrescit vivere Agrippam, occultis primum sermonibus, ut vetita solent, mox vago rumore apud inperitissimi cuiusque promptas auris aut rursum apud turbidos eoque nova cupientis. Atque ipse adire municipia obscuro diei, neque propalam

---

[1] delaberetur *Ernesti*: dilabaretur.
[2] patrata *Rhenanus*: parata.
[3] Cosam *Lipsius*: coram.

---

[1] See above, I. 3, 5, 6.
[2] In reality, the town at the neck of the promontory Mons Argentarius (*M. Argentaro*), which lay a little to the southeast of Planasia (*Pianosa*), and a few miles from Igilium (*Giglio*).

pause, observed that Hortalus had had his answer;
but, if the senate thought it proper, he would present
each of his male children with two hundred thousand
sesterces. Others expressed their thanks; Hortalus
held his peace: either his nerve failed him, or even
in these straits of fortune he clung to the traditions
of his race. Nor in the future did Tiberius repeat
his charity, though the Hortensian house kept
sinking deeper into ignominious poverty.

XXXIX. In the same year, the country, but for
prompt measures, would have been plunged into
faction and civil war by the hardihood of a solitary
serf. Clemens by name, he was the slave of Agrippa
Postumus;[1] but there was nothing servile in the
imagination which, on the news of Augustus' death,
conceived the idea of making for the isle of Planasia,
rescuing Agrippa by fraud or force, and conveying
him to the armies of Germany. The tardy movements of a cargo-boat interfered with his venture;
and since in the meantime the execution had been
carried out, he fell back on a more ambitious and
precarious scheme; purloined the funeral ashes,
and sailing to Cosa,[2] a promontory on the Etrurian
coast, vanished into hiding until his hair and beard
should have grown: for in age and general appearance he was not unlike his master. Then, through
fitting agents, partners in his secret, a report that
Agrippa lived began to circulate; at first, in whispered dialogues, as is the way with forbidden news;
soon, in a rumour which ran wherever there were
fools with open ears, or malcontents with the usual
taste for revolution. He himself took to visiting
the provincial towns in the dusk of the day. He
was never to be seen in the open, and never over-

443

aspici neque diutius isdem locis, sed quia veritas visu et mora, falsa festinatione et incertis valescunt, relinquebat famam aut praeveniebat.

XL. Vulgabatur interim per Italiam servatum munere deum Agrippam, credebatur Romae; iamque Ostiam invectum multitudo ingens, iam in urbe clandestini coetus celebrabant, cum Tiberium anceps cura distrahere, vine militum servum suum coerceret an inanem credulitatem tempore ipso vanescere sineret: modo nihil spernendum, modo non omnia metuenda ambiguus pudoris ac metus reputabat. Postremo dat negotium Sallustio Crispo. Ille e clientibus duos (quidam milites fuisse tradunt) deligit atque hortatur, simulata conscientia adeant, offerant pecuniam, fidem atque pericula polliceantur. Exequuntur ut iussum erat. Dein speculati noctem incustoditam, accepta idonea manu, vinctum clauso ore in Palatium traxere. Percontanti Tiberio quo modo Agrippa factus esset respondisse fertur " quo modo tu Caesar." Vt ederet socios subigi non potuit. Nec Tiberius poenam eius palam ausus, in secreta Palatii parte interfici iussit corpusque clam auferri. Et quamquam multi e domo principis equitesque ac senatores sustentasse opibus, iuvisse consiliis dicerentur, haud quaesitum.

---

[1] See I. 6 and III. 30.
[2] If not *per uxorium ambitum et senili adoptione* (I. 7), at least by methods not more discreditable.

long in one neighbourhood: rather, as truth acquires strength by publicity and delay, falsehood by haste and incertitudes, he either left his story behind him or arrived in advance of it.

XL. Meanwhile, it was rumoured through Italy that Agrippa had been saved by the special grace of Heaven: at Rome the rumour was believed. Already huge crowds were greeting his arrival in Ostia, already there were clandestine receptions in the capital itself, when the dilemma began to distract Tiberius:—Should he call in the military to suppress one of his own slaves, or leave this bubble of credulity to vanish with the mere lapse of time? Tossed between shame and alarm, he reflected one moment that nothing was despicable; the next, that not everything was formidable. At last he handed over the affair to Sallustius Crispus,[1] who chose two of his clients (soldiers according to some accounts) and instructed them to approach the pretender in the character of accomplices, offer him money, and promise fidelity whatever the perils. These orders they carried out: then, waiting for a night when the impostor was off his guard, they took an adequate force and haled him, chained and gagged, to the palace. To the inquiry of Tiberius, how he had turned himself into Agrippa, he is said to have answered: "As you turned yourself into a Caesar." [2] He could not be forced to divulge his confederates. Nor did Tiberius hazard a public execution, but gave orders for him to be killed in a secret quarter of the palace, and the body privately removed: and notwithstanding that many of the imperial household, as well as knights and senators, were said to have given him the support of their wealth and the benefit of their advice, no investigation followed.

445

XLI. Fine anni arcus propter aedem Saturni ob recepta signa cum Varo amissa ductu Germanici, auspiciis Tiberii, et aedes Fortis Fortunae Tiberim iuxta in hortis, quos Caesar dictator populo Romano legaverat, sacrarium genti Iuliae effigiesque divo Augusto apud Bovillas dicantur.

C. Caelio L. Pomponio consulibus Germanicus Caesar a.d. VII. Kal. Iunias triumphavit de Cheruscis Chattisque et Angrivariis quaeque aliae nationes usque ad Albim colunt. Vecta spolia, captivi, simulacra montium, fluminum, proeliorum; bellumque, quia conficere prohibitus erat, pro confecto accipiebatur. Augebat intuentium visus eximia ipsius species currusque quinque liberis onustus. Sed suberat occulta formido, reputantibus haud prosperum in Druso patre eius favorem vulgi, avunculum eiusdem Marcellum flagrantibus plebis studiis intra iuventam ereptum, brevis et infaustos populi Romani amores.

XLII. Ceterum Tiberius nomine Germanici trecenos plebi sestertios viritim dedit seque collegam consulatui eius destinavit. Nec ideo sincerae caritatis fidem adsecutus amoliri iuvenem specie honoris statuit struxitque causas aut forte oblatas arripuit.

---

¹ In the Forum, near the Golden Milestone.

² See I. 60 and II. 25: the third was only recovered under Claudius (D. Cass. LX. 8).

³ On the right bank of the Tiber.

⁴ In Latium, some little distance west of the head of the Alban Lake. The long-standing connection of the Julii with the town was due to the fact that traditionally it was planted from Alba Longa, itself founded by Iulus.

⁵ This name and C. Caecilius are equally well attested: for a possible explanation, see Nipperdey *ad loc.*

⁶ Marcellus (half-brother of Germanicus' mother) died at the age of twenty (21 B.C.); Drusus at that of thirty (9 B.C.).

446

XLI. The close of the year saw dedicated an arch near the temple of Saturn[1] commemorating the recovery, "under the leadership of Germanicus and the auspices of Tiberius," of the eagles lost with Varus;[2] a temple to Fors Fortuna on the Tiber bank, in the gardens which the dictator Caesar had bequeathed to the nation;[3] a sanctuary to the Julian race, and an effigy to the deity of Augustus, at Bovillae.[4]

In the consulate of Gaius Caelius[5] and Lucius Pomponius, Germanicus Caesar, on the twenty-sixth day of May, celebrated his triumph over the Cherusci, the Chatti, the Angrivarii, and the other tribes lying west of the Elbe. There was a procession of spoils and captives, of mimic mountains, rivers, and battles; and the war, since he had been forbidden to complete it, was assumed to be complete. To the spectators the effect was heightened by the noble figure of the commander himself, and by the five children who loaded his chariot. Yet beneath lay an unspoken fear, as men reflected that to his father Drusus the favour of the multitude had not brought happiness—that Marcellus, his uncle,[6] had been snatched in youth from the ardent affections of the populace—that the loves of the Roman nation were fleeting and unblest!

XLII. For the rest, Tiberius, in the name of Germanicus, made a distribution to the populace of three hundred sesterces a man: as his colleague in the consulship he nominated himself. All this, however, won him no credit for genuine affection, and he decided to remove the youth under a show of honour; some of the pretexts he fabricated, others he accepted as chance offered. For fifty

A.V.C. 796 = A.D. 17

447

Rex Archelaus quinquagesimum annum Cappadocia
potiebatur, invisus Tiberio quod eum Rhodi agentem nullo officio coluisset. Nec id Archelaus per
superbiam omiserat, sed ab intimis Augusti monitus,
quia florente Gaio Caesare missoque ad res Orientis
intuta Tiberii amicitia credebatur. Vt versa Caesarum subole imperium adeptus est, elicit Archelaum
matris litteris, quae non dissimulatis filii offensionibus
clementiam offerebat, si ad precandum¹ veniret. Ille
ignarus doli vel, si intellegere crederetur, vim
metuens in urbem properat; exceptusque immiti a
principe et mox accusatus in senatu, non ob crimina
quae fingebantur, sed angore, simul fessus senio et
quia regibus aequa, nedum infima insolita sunt, finem
vitae sponte an fato implevit. Regnum in provinciam redactum est, fructibusque eius levari posse
centesimae vectigal professus Caesar ducentesimam
in posterum statuit. Per idem tempus Antiocho
Commagenorum, Philopatore Cilicum regibus defunctis turbabantur nationes, plerisque Romanum, aliis
regium imperium cupientibus; et provinciae Suria

---

¹ precandum] deprecandum *Haase.*

---

¹ The sentence, to be exact, must be taken as reverting to
the accession of Tiberius (14 A.D.): for it was in 36 B.C. that
Archelaus (grandson and namesake of Sulla's antagonist in
the Mithridatic War) was presented by Antony with the
kingdom of Cappadocia; to which Augustus had subsequently
added Lesser Armenia and part of Cilicia.
² See I. 4.   ³ See I. 78.
⁴ This little kingdom, a remnant of the Seleucian empire,
lay pent in between Cappadocia on the north, Syria on the
south, Cilicia on the west, and the Euphrates on the east;
the capital being Lucian's birthplace, Samosata. The
country was important only as commanding the passage of the
Upper Euphrates.

years King Archelaus had been in possession of Cappadocia;[1] to Tiberius a hated man, since he had offered him none of the usual attentions during his stay in Rhodes.[2] The omission was due not to insolence, but to advice from the intimates of Augustus; for, as Gaius Caesar was then in his heyday and had been despatched to settle affairs in the East, the friendship of Tiberius was believed unsafe. When, through the extinction of the Caesarian line, Tiberius attained the empire, he lured Archelaus from Cappadocia by a letter of his mother; who, without dissembling the resentment of her son, offered clemency, if he came to make his petition. Unsuspicious of treachery, or apprehending force, should he be supposed alive to it, he hurried to the capital, was received by an unrelenting sovereign, and shortly afterwards was impeached in the senate. Broken, not by the charges, which were fictitious, but by torturing anxiety, combined with the weariness of age and the fact that to princes even equality—to say nothing of humiliation—is an unfamiliar thing, he ended his days whether deliberately or in the course of nature. His kingdom was converted into a province; and the emperor, announcing that its revenues made feasible a reduction of the one per cent. sale-tax,[3] fixed it for the future at one half of this amount.—About the same time, the death of the two kings, Antiochus of Commagene[4] and Philopator of Cilicia,[5] disturbed the peace of their countries, where the majority of men desired a Roman governor, and the minority a monarch. The provinces, too, of Syria and Judaea,

[5] Philopator's sovereignty, however, extended only to a petty principality in the east of the country.

atque Iudaea, fessae oneribus, deminutionem tributi
orabant.

XLIII. Igitur haec et de Armenia quae supra
memoravi apud patres disseruit, nec posse motum
Orientem nisi Germanici sapientia conponi: nam
suam aetatem vergere, Drusi nondum satis adolevisse. Tunc decreto patrum permissae Germanico
provinciae quae mari dividuntur, maiusque imperium, quoquo adisset, quam iis qui sorte aut missu
principis obtinerent. Sed Tiberius demoverat Suria
Creticum Silanum, per adfinitatem conexum Germanico, quia Silani filia Neroni vetustissimo liberorum eius pacta erat, praefeceratque Cn. Pisonem,
ingenio violentum et obsequii ignarum, insita ferocia a patre Pisone qui civili bello resurgentis in Africa
partis acerrimo ministerio adversus Caesarem iuvit,
mox Brutum et Cassium secutus concesso reditu
petitione honorum abstinuit, donec ultro ambiretur
delatum ab Augusto consulatum accipere. Sed
praeter paternos spiritus uxoris quoque Plancinae
nobilitate et opibus accendebatur; vix Tiberio
concedere, liberos eius ut multum infra despec-

---

[1] The statement is rather highly coloured: for Tiberius
was only fifty-nine years of age, Germanicus thirty-one, and
Drusus twenty-nine.

[2] See above, chap. 4.

[3] Munatia Plancina (D. Cass. LVIII. 22); presumably a
daughter of the celebrated L. Munatius Plancus—*morbo*

exhausted by their burdens, were pressing for a diminution of the tribute.

XLIII. These circumstances, then, and the events in Armenia, which I mentioned above, were discussed by Tiberius before the senate. "The commotion in the East," he added, " could only be settled by the wisdom of Germanicus: for his own years were trending to their autumn, and those of Drusus were as yet scarcely mature." [1] There followed a decree of the Fathers, delegating to Germanicus the provinces beyond the sea, with powers overriding, in all regions he might visit, those of the local governors holding office by allotment or imperial nomination. Tiberius, however, had removed Creticus Silanus [2] from Syria—he was a marriage connection of Germanicus, whose eldest son, Nero, was plighted to his daughter—and had given the appointment to Gnaeus Piso, a man of ungoverned passions and constitutional insubordinacy. For there was a strain of wild arrogance in the blood—a strain derived from his father Piso; who in the Civil War lent strenuous aid against Caesar to the republican party during its resurrection in Africa, then followed the fortunes of Brutus and Cassius, and, on the annulment of his exile, refused to become a suitor for office, until approached with a special request to accept a consulate proffered by Augustus. But, apart from the paternal temper, Piso's brain was fired by the lineage and wealth of his wife Plancina : [3] to Tiberius he accorded a grudging precedence : upon his children he looked down as far beneath him.

proditor—to whom Horace addresses the ode *Laudabunt alii e.q.s.* (I. 7).

tare. Nec dubium habebat se delectum qui Suriae imponeretur ad spes Germanici coercendas. Credidere quidam data et a Tiberio occulta mandata; et Plancinam haud dubie Augusta monuit aemulatione muliebri Agrippinam insectandi.[1] Divisa namque et discors aula erat tacitis in Drusum aut Germanicum studiis. Tiberius ut proprium et sui sanguinis Drusum fovebat: Germanico alienatio patrui amorem apud ceteros auxerat, et quia claritudine materni[2] generis anteibat, avum M. Antonium, avunculum Augustum ferens. Contra Druso proavus eques Romanus Pomponius Atticus dedecere Claudiorum imagines videbatur: et coniunx Germanici Agrippina fecunditate ac fama Liviam uxorem Drusi praecellebat. Sed fratres egregie concordes et proximorum certaminibus inconcussi.

XLIV. Nec multo post Drusus in Illyricum missus est ut suesceret militiae studiaque exercitus pararet; simul iuvenem urbano luxu lascivientem melius in castris haberi Tiberius seque tutiorem

---

[1] insectandi] insectans *Madvig.*
[2] materni *Rhenanus* : mater.

---

[1] " The proudest member of one of the noblest houses yet left, he had spoken out in the senate (I. 74) and had perhaps been noted by Augustus as dangerous (I. 13). Yet his wife stood high in the favour of Augustus, and he could hardly be passed over in the award of provinces. It is reasonable to suppose that the one mistrust was set against the other, that he was to be some check on his young ' imperator,' who, in turn, was to check him by an ' imperium maius ' on the spot."—Furneaux.

Nor did he entertain a doubt that he had been selected
for the governorship of Syria in order to repress the
ambitions of Germanicus.[1] The belief has been held
that he did in fact receive private instructions from
Tiberius; and Plancina, beyond question, had advice
from the ex-empress, bent with feminine jealousy
upon persecuting Agrippina. For the court was
split and torn by unspoken preferences for Germanicus or for Drusus. Tiberius leaned to the latter as
his own issue and blood of his blood. Germanicus,
owing to the estrangement of his uncle, had risen
in the esteem of the world; and he had a further
advantage in the distinction of his mother's family,
among whom he could point to Mark Antony for a
grandfather and to Augustus for a great-uncle. On
the other hand, the plain Roman knight, Pomponius
Atticus, who was great-grandfather to Drusus,[2]
seemed to reflect no credit upon the ancestral effigies
of the Claudian house; while both in fecundity and
in fair fame Agrippina, the consort of Germanicus,
ranked higher than Drusus' helpmeet, Livia.[3] The
brothers, however, maintained a singular unanimity,
unshaken by the contentions of their kith and kin.

XLIV. Shortly afterwards, Drusus was despatched
to Illyricum, in order to serve his apprenticeship to
war and acquire the favour of the army. At the
same time, Tiberius believed that the young prince,
who was running riot among the extravagances of
the capital, was better in camp,[4] and that he himself

[2] Agrippa's first wife was Pomponia, daughter of Cicero's
friend. The child of the union was Vipsania Agrippina, first
wife of Tiberius and mother of Drusus.
[3] Sister of Germanicus and Claudius; first cousin, wife, and
poisoner of Drusus.
[4] See III. 32 (and perhaps I. 76).

rebatur utroque filio legiones obtinente. Sed Suebi praetendebantur auxilium adversus Cheruscos orantes; nam discessu Romanorum ac vacui externo metu gentis adsuetudine et tum aemulatione gloriae arma in se verterant. Vis nationum, virtus ducum in aequo; set Maroboduum regis nomen invisum apud popularis, Arminium pro libertate bellantem favor habebat.

XLV. Igitur non modo Cherusci sociique eorum, vetus Arminii miles, sumpsere bellum, sed e regno etiam Marobodui Suebae gentes, Semnones ac Langobardi, defecere ad eum. Quibus additis praepollebat, ni Inguiomerus cum manu clientium ad Maroboduum perfugisset, non aliam ob causam quam quia fratris filio iuveni patruus senex parere dedignabatur. Deriguntur acies, pari utrimque spe, nec, ut olim apud Germanos, vagis incursibus aut disiectas per catervas: quippe longa adversum nos militia insueverant sequi signa, subsidiis firmari, dicta imperatorum accipere. Ac tunc Arminius equo conlustrans cuncta, ut quosque advectus erat, reciperatam libertatem, trucidatas legiones, spolia adhuc et tela Romanis derepta in manibus multorum ostentabat; contra fugacem Maroboduum appel-

---

[1] See I. 44.   [2] East of the Elbe, north of Bohemia.
[3] See I. 60.

would be all the safer with both his sons at the head
of legions. The pretext, however, was a Suebian[1]
request for help against the Cherusci: for, now that
the Romans had withdrawn and the foreign menace
was removed, the tribes—obedient to the national
custom, and embittered in this case by their rivalry
in prestige—had turned their weapons against each
other. The power of the clans and the prowess of
their leaders were upon a level; but while his kingly
title rendered Maroboduus unpopular with his
countrymen, Arminius aroused enthusiasm as the
champion of liberty.

XLV. The result was that not only the veteran
soldiery of Arminius—the Cherusci and their confederates—took up the campaign, but even from
the dominions of Maroboduus two Suebian tribes,
the Semnones and Langobardi,[2] revolted to his
cause. This accession assured him the preponderance,
had not Inguiomerus[3] with a band of his retainers
deserted to the enemy, for the sole reason that as an
old man and an uncle he scorned to obey the youthful
son of his brother. Hope ran high on both sides as
the lines of battle drew up, no longer to the old
German accompaniment of charges either desultory
or executed by scattered parties: for their long
campaigns against ourselves had accustomed them
to follow their standards, to secure their main body
by reserves, and to give attention to their generals'
orders. So, in this instance, Arminius on horseback
passed in review the whole of his forces, and, as
he came to the several divisions, pointed to the
liberties they had recovered, the legions they had
butchered, and the spoils and spears, torn from
Roman dead, which many of them carried in their

lans, proeliorum expertem, Hercyniae latebris defensum; ac mox per dona et legationes petivisse foedus, proditorem patriae, satellitem Caesaris, haud minus infensis animis exturbandum quam Varum Quintilium interfecerint. Meminissent modo tot proeliorum, quorum eventu et ad postremum eiectis Romanis satis probatum, penes utros summa belli fuerit.

XLVI. Neque Maroboduus iactantia sui aut probris in hostem abstinebat, sed Inguiomerum tenens illo in corpore decus omne Cheruscorum, illius consiliis gesta quae prospere ceciderint testabatur: vaecordem Arminium et rerum nescium alienam gloriam in se trahere, quoniam tres vagas [1] legiones et ducem fraudis ignarum perfidia deceperit, magna cum clade Germaniae et ignominia sua, cum coniunx, cum filius eius servitium adhuc tolerent. At se duodecim legionibus petitum duce Tiberio inlibatam Germanorum gloriam servavisse, mox condicionibus aequis discessum; neque paenitere quod ipsorum in manu sit, integrum adversum Romanos bellum an pacem incruentam malint. His vocibus instinctos exercitus propriae quoque causae stimulabant, cum a Cheruscis Langobardisque pro anti-

---

[1] vagas *Dräger* : vacuas.

---

[1] *i.e.* in Bohemia.
[2] The reference is to the events of 6 A.D., when the decision was taken to crush the new and formidable power created by Marbod. A double invasion of Bohemia in overwhelming force was about to be launched when the operations were effectively arrested by the great revolt of Pannonia and Dalmatia, which appeared to threaten Italy itself. To the accidental nature of his deliverance Marbod naturally does not

hands. Maroboduus, in contrast, was described as " the fugitive who, without one stricken field, had lain safe in the coverts of the Hercynian Forest [1] and then sued for a treaty with gifts and embassies, a betrayer of his country, a satellite of the Caesar; whom it was their duty to expel with as little compunction as they felt when they slew Quintilius Varus. Let them only recall the series of their stricken fields! The issue of those, and the final ejection of the Romans showed plainly enough with whom had rested the mastery in the war!"

XLVI. Nor could Maroboduus refrain from a panegyric upon himself and an invective against the enemy, but holding Inguiomerus by the hand, " There was the one person," he declared, " in whom resided the whole glory of the Cherusci—by whose counsels had been won whatsoever success they had achieved! Arminius was a fool, a novice in affairs, who usurped another man's fame, because by an act of perfidy he had entrapped three straggling legions and a commander who feared no fraud: a feat disastrous to Germany and disgraceful to its author, whose wife and child were even yet supporting their bondage. For himself, when he was attacked by twelve legions, with Tiberius at their head, he had kept the German honour unstained, and soon afterwards the combatants had parted on equal terms: [2] nor could he regret that it was now in their power to choose with Rome either a war uncompromised or a bloodless peace!" Fired by the oratory, the armies were stimulated also by motives of their own, as the Cherusci and Langobardi were striking for ancient

here allude : Arminius has done so above in the words *proeliorum expertem.*

457

quo decore aut recenti libertate et contra augendae dominationi certaretur. Non alias maiore mole concursum neque ambiguo magis eventu, fusis utrimque dextris cornibus; sperabaturque rursum pugna, ni Maroboduus castra in collis subduxisset. Id signum perculsi fuit et, transfugiis paulatim nudatus, in Marcomanos concessit misitque legatos ad Tiberium oraturos auxilia. Responsum est non iure eum adversus Cheruscos arma Romana invocare, qui pugnantis in eundem hostem Romanos nulla ope iuvisset. Missus tamen Drusus, ut rettulimus, paci firmator.

XLVII. Eodem anno duodecim celebres Asiae urbes conlapsae nocturno motu terrae, quo inprovisior graviorque pestis fuit. Neque solitum in tali casu effugium subveniebat in aperta prorumpendi, quia diductis terris hauriebantur. Sedisse inmensos montes, visa in arduo quae plana fuerint, effulsisse inter ruinam ignis memorant. Asperrima in Sardianos lues plurimum in eosdem misericordiae traxit: nam centies sestertium pollicitus Caesar, et quantum aerario aut fisco pendebant in quinquennium remisit. Magnetes a Sipylo proximi damno ac remedio habiti. Temnios, Philadelphenos, Aegeatas, Apollonidenses,[1] quique Mosteni aut Macedones Hyrcani vocantur, et Hierocaesariam, Myrinam, Cymen, Tmolum levari idem in tempus tributis

---

[1] Apollonidenses *Ernesti* : apolloniensis.

---

[1] Presumably " the men of the marches "; a powerful tribe, driven by the campaigns of Germanicus' father from the banks of the Main into Bohemia, from which they expelled the Celtic inhabitants.

[2] Of the twelve, Temnos, Aegeae, Myrina and Cyme were in Aeolis; the remainder, further inland in Lydia.

fame or recent liberty; their adversaries for the extension of a realm. No field ever witnessed a fiercer onset or a more ambiguous event; for on both sides the right wing was routed. A renewal of the conflict was expected, when Maroboduus shifted his camp to the hills. It was the sign of a beaten man; and stripped gradually of his forces by desertions, he fell back upon the Marcomani[1] and sent a deputation to Tiberius asking assistance. The reply ran that " to invoke the Roman arms against the Cherusci was not the part of a man who had brought no help to Rome when she was herself engaged against the same enemy." Drusus, however, as we have mentioned, was sent out to consolidate a peace.

XLVII. In the same year, twelve important cities of Asia collapsed in an earthquake, the time being night, so that the havoc was the less foreseen and the more devastating. Even the usual resource in these catastrophes, a rush to open ground, was unavailing, as the fugitives were swallowed up in yawning chasms. Accounts are given of huge mountains sinking, of former plains seen heaved aloft, of fires flashing out amid the ruin. As the disaster fell heaviest on the Sardians, it brought them the largest measure of sympathy, the Caesar promising ten million sesterces, and remitting for five years their payments to the national and imperial exchequers. The Magnesians of Sipylus were ranked second in the extent of their losses and their indemnity. In the case of the Temnians, Philadelphenes, Aegeates, Apollonideans, the so-called Mostenians and Hyrcanian Macedonians, and the cities of Hierocaesarea, Myrina, Cyme, and Tmolus,[2] it was decided to exempt them

mittique ex senatu placuit, qui praesentia spectaret
refoveretque. Delectus est M. Ateius [1] e praetoriis,
ne consulari obtinente Asiam aemulatio inter pares
et ex eo impedimentum oreretur.

XLVIII. Magnificam in publicum largitionem
auxit Caesar haud minus grata liberalitate, quod
bona Aemiliae Musae, locupletis intestatae, petita
in fiscum, Aemilio Lepido, cuius e domo videbatur,
et Pantulei divitis equitis Romani hereditatem,
quamquam ipse heres in parte legeretur, tradidit
M. Servilio, quem prioribus neque suspectis tabulis
scriptum compererat, nobilitatem utriusque pecunia
iuvandam praefatus. Neque hereditatem cuiusquam
adiit nisi cum amicitia meruisset: ignotos et aliis
infensos eoque principem nuncupantis procul arcebat. Ceterum ut honestam innocentium paupertatem levavit, ita prodigos et ob flagitia egentis,
Vibidium Virronem,[2] Marium Nepotem, Appium
Appianum, Cornelium Sullam, Q. Vitellium movit
senatu aut sponte cedere passus est.

XLIX. Isdem temporibus deum aedis vetustate
aut igni abolitas coeptasque ab Augusto dedicavit,
Libero Liberaeque et Cereri iuxta Circum Maximum,

[1] Ateius *Mommsen* : aletus.
[2] Virronem *Nipperdey* : Varronem.

---

[1] The fire in question was probably that of 31 B.C., ascribed
(D. Cass. L. 10) to an *émeute* of freedmen occasioned by a
property-levy.

[2] Dionysus, Persephone, and Demeter. This is stated to
have been vowed by Postumius before the battle of Lake
Regillus (496 B.C.) and to have been completed three years
later.

from tribute for the same term and to send a senatorial commissioner to view the state of affairs and administer relief. Since Asia was held by a consular governor, an ex-praetor—Marcus Ateius—was selected, so as to avoid the difficulties which might arise from the jealousy of two officials of similar standing.

XLVIII. The emperor supplemented his imposing benefaction on behalf of the state by an equally popular display of private liberality. The property of Aemilia Musa, a woman of means and intestate, which had been claimed as escheating to the imperial exchequer, he transferred to Aemilius Lepidus, to whose family she apparently belonged; and the inheritance of the wealthy Roman knight Pantuleius, though he was himself mentioned as part heir, he handed over to Marcus Servilius, on discovering that he had figured in an earlier and unsuspected testament. In both cases, he remarked before doing so, that high birth required the help of money. He entered upon no bequest unless he had earned it by his friendship: strangers, and persons who were at variance with others and consequently named the sovereign as their heir, he kept at a distance. But as he relieved the honourable poverty of the innocent, so he procured the removal, or accepted the resignation, of the following senators :—Vibidius Virro, Marius Nepos, Appius Appianus, Cornelius Sulla, and Quintus Vitellius; prodigals, beggared by their vices.

XLIX. Nearly at the same time, he consecrated the temples, ruined by age or fire,[1] the restoration of which had been undertaken by Augustus. They included a temple to Liber, Libera, and Ceres,[2] close

quam ¹ A. Postumius dictator voverat, eodemque in loco aedem Florae ab Lucio et Marco Publiciis aedilibus constitutam, et Iano templum, quod apud forum holitorium C. Duilius struxerat, qui primus rem Romanam prospere mari gessit triumphumque navalem de Poenis meruit. Spei aedes a ² Germanico sacratur : hanc A. Atilius ³ voverat eodem bello.

L. Adolescebat interea lex maiestatis. Et Appuleiam Varillam,⁴ sororis Augusti neptem, quia probrosis sermonibus divum Augustum ac Tiberium et matrem eius inlusisset Caesarique conexa adulterio teneretur, maiestatis delator arcessebat. De adulterio satis caveri lege Iulia visum : maiestatis crimen distingui Caesar postulavit damnarique, si qua de Augusto inreligiose dixisset : in se iacta nolle ad cognitionem vocari. Interrogatus a consule quid de iis censeret quae de matre eius locuta secus argueretur reticuit : dein proximo senatus die illius quoque nomine oravit ne cui verba in eam quoquo modo habita crimini forent. Liberavitque Appuleiam lege maiestatis : adulterii graviorem poenam

---

¹ quam *Lipsius* : quas.
² a *Beroaldus* : in.
³ A. Atilius *Nipperdey* : iatillius.
⁴ Varillam *Furlanetto* : variliam.

---

¹ About 240 B.C.
² Between the Capitoline Hill and the Tiber. Dui'ius' victory with the first Roman fleet was gained off Mylae in Sicily in 260 B.C. (Polyb. I. 20–23), his triumph being commemorated by the *columna rostrata*.
³ Aulus Atilius Calatinus, consul 258 B.C. and 254 B.C., dictator 249 B.C.
⁴ *Lex Iulia de adulteriis et stupris* (17 B.C.).
⁵ Forfeiture of half her dowry and a third of her property, together with relegation to an island.—*Exemplo maiorum*

to the Circus Maximus, and vowed by Aulus Postumius, the dictator; another, on the same site, to Flora, founded by Lucius and Marcus Publicius in their aedileship,[1] and a shrine of Janus, built in the Herb Market[2] by Gaius Duilius, who first carried the Roman cause to success on sea and earned a naval triumph over the Carthaginians. The temple of Hope, vowed by Aulus Atilius[3] in the same war, was dedicated by Germanicus.

L. Meanwhile, the law of treason was coming to its strength; and Appuleia Varilla, the niece of Augustus' sister, was summoned by an informer to answer a charge under the statute, on the ground that she had insulted the deified Augustus, as well as Tiberius and his mother, by her scandalous conversations, and had sullied her connection with the Caesar by the crime of adultery. The adultery, it was decided, was sufficiently covered by the Julian Law;[4] and as to the charge of treason, the emperor requested that a distinction should be drawn, conviction to follow, should she have said anything tantamount to sacrilege against Augustus: remarks levelled at himself he did not wish to be made the subject of inquiry. To the consul's question: "What was his opinion of the reprehensible statements she was alleged to have made about his mother?" he gave no answer; but at the next meeting of the senate he asked, in her name also, that no one should be held legally accountable for words uttered against her in any circumstances whatever. After freeing Appuleia from the operation of the statute, he deprecated the heavier penalty[5] for adultery, and

applies, not to the penalty, but to the fact that its execution was entrusted to her relatives.

deprecatus, ut exemplo maiorum propinquis suis ultra ducentesimum lapidem removeretur suasit. Adultero Manlio Italia atque Africa interdictum est.

LI. De praetore in locum Vipstani Galli, quem mors abstulerat, subrogando certamen incessit. Germanicus atque Drusus (nam etiam tum Romae erant) Haterium Agrippam propinquum Germanici fovebant. Contra plerique nitebantur ut numerus liberorum in candidatis praepolleret, quod lex iubebat. Laetabatur Tiberius, cum inter filios eius et leges senatus disceptaret. Victa est sine dubio lex, sed neque statim et paucis suffragiis, quo modo etiam cum valerent leges vincebantur.

LII. Eodem anno coeptum in Africa bellum, duce hostium Tacfarinate. Is natione Numida, in castris Romanis auxiliaria [1] stipendia meritus, mox desertor vagos primum et latrociniis suetos ad praedam et raptus congregare, dein more militiae per vexilla et turmas componere, postremo non inconditae turbae sed Musulamiorum dux haberi. Valida ea gens et solitudinibus Africae propinqua, nullo etiam tum urbium cultu, cepit arma Maurosque accolas in bellum traxit: dux et his, Mazippa. Divisusque exercitus, ut Tacfarinas lectos viros et Romanum in modum armatos castris attineret, disciplina et impe-

---

[1] auxiliaria] auxiliaris *Lipsius.*

---

[1] In strictness, he should have lost half his estate and been relegated to a different island from Appuleia.

[2] According to the *Lex Papia Poppaea* (see III. 25–28).

[3] For his later activities, see III. 20, 22, 73; IV. 23.

[4] South of the Saltus Aurasius (*Mt. Aurez*), where the desert frontier of the Roman province began.

[5] Numidian tribes inhabiting eastern Mauretania.

suggested that in accordance with the old-world precedents she might be handed to her relatives and removed to a point beyond the two-hundredth milestone. Her lover, Manlius, was banned from residence in Italy or Africa.[1]

LI. The appointment of a praetor to replace Vipstanus Gallus, cut off by death, gave rise to dispute. Germanicus and Drusus—for they were still at Rome—supported Haterius Agrippa, a kinsman of Germanicus. On the other hand, many insisted that the deciding factor should be the number of a candidate's children—legally the correct position.[2] Tiberius was overjoyed to see the senate divided between his sons and the laws. The law was certainly defeated, but not immediately and by a few votes only,—the mode in which laws were defeated even in days when laws had force!

LII. In the course of the same year, war broke out in Africa; where the enemy was commanded by Tacfarinas.[3] By nationality a Numidian, who had served as an auxiliary in the Roman camp and then deserted, he began by recruiting gangs of vagrants, accustomed to robbery, for the purposes of plunder and of rapine: then he marshalled them into a body in the military style by companies and troops; finally, he was recognized as the head, not of a chaotic horde, but of the Musulamian people.[4] That powerful tribe, bordering on the solitudes of Africa, and even then innocent of city life, took up arms and drew the adjacent Moors[5] into the conflict. They, too, had their leader, Mazippa; and the confederate army was so divided that Tacfarinas could retain in camp a picked corps, equipped on the Roman model, and there inure it to discipline and

riis compesceret, Mazippa levi cum copia incendia et caedis et terrorem circumferret. Conpulerantque Cinithios, haud spernendam nationem, in eadem, cum Furius Camillus pro consule Africae legionem et quod sub signis sociorum in unum conductos ad hostem duxit, modicam manum, si multitudinem Numidarum atque Maurorum spectares; sed nihil aeque cavebatur quam ne bellum metu eluderent; spe victoriae inducti sunt ut vincerentur. Igitur legio medio, leves cohortes duaeque alae in cornibus locantur. Nec Tacfarinas pugnam detrectavit. Fusi Numidae, multosque post annos Furio nomini partum decus militiae. Nam post illum reciperatorem urbis filiumque eius Camillum penes alias familias imperatoria laus fuerat; atque hic, quem memoramus, bellorum expers habebatur. Eo pronior Tiberius res gestas apud senatum celebravit: et decrevere patres triumphalia insignia, quod Camillo ob modestiam vitae impune fuit.

LIII. Sequens annus Tiberium tertio, Germanicum iterum consules habuit. Sed eum honorem Germanicus iniit apud urbem Achaiae Nicopolim, quo venerat per Illyricam oram viso fratre Druso in Delmatia agente, Hadriatici ac mox Ionii maris

---

[1] Further eastward on the Lesser Syrtis (Gulf of Gabes).

[2] The allusion is to the defeat of the Gauls after Allia (390 B.C.) by M. Furius Camillus.—In what follows, Tacitus is charged with confusing the grandson of the dictator with his son, while overlooking two minor triumphs won by the family.

[3] The implication is that he was not the type of commander who could inspire jealousy.

obedience, while Mazippa, with a light-armed band, disseminated fire, slaughter, and terror. They had forced the Cinithians,[1] by no means a negligible tribe, to join them, when Furius Camillus, proconsul of Africa, combined his legion with the whole of the auxiliaries under the standards, and led them towards the enemy—a modest array in view of the multitude of Numidians and Moors; yet the one thing he was anxious above all to avoid was that they should take fright and evade a trial of arms. The hope of victory, however, lured them into defeat. The legion, then, was posted in the centre; the light cohorts and two squadrons of horse on the wings. Nor did Tacfarinas decline the challenge: the Numidians were routed; and after many years the Furian name won martial honours. For, since the days of Rome's great recoverer [2] and his son, the laurels of high command had passed to other houses; and the Camillus with whom we are here concerned was not regarded as a soldier. Tiberius, therefore, was the readier to laud his exploits before the senate; while the Fathers voted him the insignia of triumph— to the unassuming Camillus an innocuous compliment.[3]

LIII. The following year found Tiberius consul for a third time; Germanicus, for a second. The latter, however, entered upon that office in the Achaian town of Nicopolis,[4] which he had reached by skirting the Illyrian coast after a visit to his brother Drusus, then resident in Dalmatia: the passage had been stormy both in the Adriatic and,

---

[4] On the northern side of the entrance to the Sinus Ambracicus (Gulf of Arta); founded by Augustus on the site of his camp before the battle of Actium.

adversam navigationem perpessus. Igitur paucos
dies insumpsit reficiendae classi; simul sinus Actiaca
victoria inclutos et sacratas ab Augusto manubias
castraque Antonii cum recordatione maiorum suorum adiit. Namque ei, ut memoravi, avunculus
Augustus, avus Antonius erant, magnaque illic
imago tristium laetorumque. Hinc ventum Athenas
foederique sociae et vetustae urbis datum ut uno
lictore uteretur. Excepere [1] Graeci quaesitissimis
honoribus, vetera suorum facta dictaque praeferentes
quo plus dignationis adulatio haberet.

LIV. Petita inde Euboea tramisit Lesbum, ubi
Agrippina novissimo partu Iuliam edidit. Tum
extrema Asiae Perinthumque ac Byzantium, Thra-
cias urbes, mox Propontidis angustias et os Pon-
ticum intrat, cupidine veteres locos et fama cele-
bratos noscendi; pariterque provincias internis
certaminibus aut magistratuum iniuriis fessas refo-
vebat. Atque illum in regressu sacra Samothracum
visere nitentem obvii aquilones depulere. Igitur
adito Ilio [2] quaeque ibi varietate fortunae et nostri
origine veneranda, relegit Asiam adpellitque Colo-

---

[1] Excepere *Beroaldus* : excipere.
[2] adito Ilio *Sev. Vater* : alio.

---

[1] At Actium, on the southern side of the gulf.
[2] See above, chap. 43.
[3] The custom was for a Roman magistrate, on entering the
territory of a *civitas libera* such as Athens, to leave behind him
the fasces and lictors. In the present case, Germanicus'
single lictor has no official significance whatever.
[4] Julia Livilla, married to M. Vinicius in 33 A.D. (VI. 15);
banished by her brother Caligula four years later (D. Cass.
LIX. 3, Suet. *Cal.* 24, 29); recalled by her uncle Claudius, but
afterwards put to death at the instigation of Messalina, on the
ground of her alleged adultery with Seneca (D. Cass. LX. 4;
ib. 8; Suet. *Cal.* 59; *Claud.* 29).

later, in the Ionian Sea. He spent a few days,
therefore, in refitting the fleet; while at the same
time, evoking the memory of his ancestors, he viewed
the gulf immortalized by the victory of Actium,
together with the spoils which Augustus had consecrated, and the camp of Antony.[1] For Augustus, as
I have said,[2] was his great-uncle, Antony his grandfather; and before his eyes lay the whole great
picture of disaster and of triumph.—He next arrived
at Athens; where, in deference to our treaty with
an allied and time-honoured city, he made use of
one lictor alone.[3] The Greeks received him with
most elaborate compliments, and, in order to temper
adulation with dignity, paraded the ancient doings
and sayings of their countrymen.

LIV. From Athens he visited Euboea, and crossed
over to Lesbos; where Agrippina, in her last confinement, gave birth to Julia.[4] Entering the out-
skirts of Asia, and the Thracian towns of Perinthus
and Byzantium, he then struck through the straits
of the Bosphorus and the mouth of the Euxine, eager
to make the acquaintance of those ancient and
storied regions, though simultaneously he brought
relief to provinces outworn by internecine feud or
official tyranny. On the return journey, he made
an effort to visit the Samothracian Mysteries,[5] but
was met by northerly winds, and failed to make the
shore. So, after an excursion to Troy and those
venerable remains which attest the mutability of
fortune and the origin of Rome, he skirted the Asian
coast once more, and anchored off Colophon, in order

[5] The reference is to the cult of the Cabiri; the late identi-
fication of whom with the Penates may have suggested
Germanicus' visit.

phona ut Clarii Apollinis oraculo uteretur. Non femina illic, ut apud Delphos, sed certis e familiis et ferme Mileto accitus sacerdos numerum modo consultantium et nomina audit; tum in specum degressus, hausta fontis arcani aqua, ignarus plerumque litterarum et carminum, edit responsa versibus compositis super rebus quas quis mente concepit. Et ferebatur Germanico per ambages, ut mos oraculis, maturum exitum [1] cecinisse.

LV. At Cn. Piso quo properantius destinata inciperet civitatem Atheniensium turbido incessu exterritam oratione saeva increpat, oblique Germanicum perstringens quod contra decus Romani nominis non Atheniensis, tot cladibus extinctos, sed conluviem illam nationum comitate nimia coluisset: hos enim esse Mithridatis adversus Sullam, Antonii adversus divum Augustum socios. Etiam vetera obiectabat, quae in Macedones inprospere, violenter in suos fecissent, offensus urbi propria quoque ira quia Theophilum quendam Areo iudicio falsi damnatum precibus suis non concederent. Exim navigatione celeri per Cycladas et compendia maris adsequitur Germanicum apud insulam Rhodum, haud nescium quibus insectationibus petitus foret; sed

<hr>

[1] exitum *Heraeus*: exitium.

<hr>

[1] Augustus had found it necessary to prohibit the practice of selling Athenian citizenship (D. Cass. LIV. 7).
[2] In the first Mithridatic War (87–86 B.C.).
[3] At Actium.

to consult the oracle of the Clarian Apollo. Here it is not a prophetess, as at Delphi, but a male priest, chosen out of a restricted number of families, and in most cases imported from Miletus, who hears the number and the names of the consultants, but no more, then descends into a cavern, swallows a draught of water from a mysterious spring, and—though ignorant generally of writing and of metre—delivers his response in set verses dealing with the subject each inquirer has in mind. Rumour said that he had predicted to Germanicus his hastening fate, though in the equivocal terms which oracles affect.

LV. Meanwhile Gnaeus Piso, in haste to embark upon his schemes, first alarmed the community of Athens by a tempestuous entry, then assailed them in a virulent speech, which included an indirect attack on Germanicus for " compromising the dignity of the Roman name by his exaggerated civilities, not to the Athenians (whose repeated disasters had extinguished the breed) but to the present cosmopolitan rabble.[1] For these were the men who had leagued themselves with Mithridates against Sulla,[2] with Antony against the deified Augustus! "[3] He upbraided them even with their ancient history; their ill-starred outbreaks against Macedon and their violence towards their own countrymen. Private resentment, also, embittered him against the town, as the authorities refused to give up at his request a certain Theophilus, whom the verdict of the Areopagus had declared guilty of forgery. After this, quick sailing by a short route through the Cyclades brought him up with Germanicus at Rhodes. The prince was aware of the invectives with which he

tanta mansuetudine agebat ut, cum orta tempestas
raperet in abrupta possetque interitus inimici ad
casum referri, miserit triremis quarum subsidio dis-
crimini eximeretur. Neque tamen mitigatus Piso,
et vix diei moram perpessus linquit Germanicum
praevenitque. Et postquam Suriam ac legiones
attigit, largitione, ambitu, infimos manipularium
iuvando, cum veteres centuriones, severos tribunos
demoveret locaque eorum clientibus suis vel deterrimo cuique attribueret, desidiam in castris, licentiam in urbibus, vagum ac lascivientem per agros
militem sineret, eo usque corruptionis provectus
est, ut sermone vulgi parens legionum haberetur.
Nec Plancina se intra decora feminis tenebat, sed
exercitio equitum, decursibus cohortium interesse,
in Agrippinam, in Germanicum contumelias iacere,
quibusdam etiam bonorum militum ad mala obsequia promptis, quod haud invito imperatore ea fieri
occultus rumor incedebat. Nota haec Germanico,
sed praeverti ad Armenios instantior cura fuit.

LVI. Ambigua gens ea antiquitus hominum
ingeniis et situ terrarum, quoniam nostris provinciis
late praetenta penitus ad Medos porrigitur; maxi-
misque imperiis interiecti et saepius discordes sunt,

had been assailed; yet he behaved with such mildness that, when a rising storm swept Piso towards the rock-bound coast, and the destruction of his foe could have been referred to misadventure, he sent warships to help in extricating him from his predicament. Even so, Piso was not mollified; and, after reluctantly submitting to the loss of a single day, he left Germanicus and completed the journey first. Then, the moment he reached Syria and the legions, by bounties and by bribery, by attentions to the humblest private, by dismissals of the veteran centurions and the stricter commanding officers, whom he replaced by dependants of his own or by men of the worst character, by permitting indolence in the camp, licence in the towns, and in the country a vagrant and riotous soldiery, he carried corruption to such a pitch that in the language of the rabble he was known as the Father of the Legions. Nor could Plancina contain herself within the limits of female decorum: she attended cavalry exercises and infantry manœuvres; she flung her gibes at Agrippina or Germanicus; some even of the loyal troops being ready to yield her a disloyal obedience; for a whispered rumour was gaining ground that these doings were not unacceptable to the emperor. The state of affairs was known to Germanicus, but his more immediate anxiety was to reach Armenia first.

LVI. That country, from the earliest period, has owned a national character and a geographical situation of equal ambiguity, since with a wide extent of frontier conterminous with our own provinces, it stretches inland right up to Media; so that the Armenians lie interposed between two vast empires, with which, as they detest Rome and envy the

adversus Romanos odio et in Parthum invidia. Regem illa tempestate non habebant, amoto Vonone : sed favor nationis inclinabat in Zenonem, Polemonis regis Pontici filium, quod is prima ab infantia instituta et cultum Armeniorum aemulatus, venatu, epulis et quae alia barbari celebrant, proceres plebemque iuxta devinxerat. Igitur Germanicus in urbe Artaxata adprobantibus nobilibus, circumfusa multitudine, insigne regium capiti eius imposuit. Ceteri venerantes regem Artaxiam consalutavere, quod illi vocabulum indiderant ex nomine urbis. At Cappadoces in formam provinciae redacti Q. Veranium legatum accepere ; et quaedam ex regiis tributis deminuta quo mitius Romanum imperium speraretur. Commagenis Q. Servaeus praeponitur, tum primum ad ius praetoris translatis.

LVII. Cunctaque socialia prospere composita non ideo laetum Germanicum habebant ob superbiam Pisonis qui iussus partem legionum ipse aut per filium in Armeniam ducere utrumque neglexerat. Cyrri demum apud hiberna decumae legionis convenere,[1] firmato vultu, Piso adversus metum, Germanicus, ne minari crederetur ; et erat, ut rettuli, clementior. Sed amici accendendis offensionibus

---

[1] convenere *Rhenanus* : convenire.

---

[1] See above, chaps. 1–4.

[2] Long dead, Pontus being now governed by his widow.

[3] On the Araxes (*Arás*), near the foot of Ararat, the ruins still carrying the name Ardaschar; according to Plutarch (*Luc.* 31), a μέγα καὶ πάγκαλον χρῆμα πόλεως, designed by Hannibal for Artaxias I; fired and razed by Corbulo in 58 A.D. (XIII. 41).

[4] Rather by his two predecessors of the name.

[5] Only a temporary expedient, as he and Servaeus soon reappear in Germanicus' suite (III. 10, 13, 19).

Parthian, they are too frequently at variance. At
the moment they lacked a king, owing to the removal
of Vonones,[1] but the national sentiment leaned to
Zeno, a son of the Pontic sovereign Polemo:[2] for
the prince, an imitator from earliest infancy of
Armenian institutions and dress, had endeared himself equally to the higher and the lower orders by
his affection for the chase, the banquet, and the
other favourite pastimes of barbarians. Accordingly,
in the town of Artaxata,[3] before the consenting nobles
and a great concourse of the people, Germanicus
placed on his head the emblem of royalty. All save
the Romans did homage and acclaimed King Artaxias
—an appellation suggested by the name of the city.[4]
On the other hand, Cappadocia, reduced to the rank
of a province, received Quintus Veranius as governor;[5]
and, to encourage hope in the mildness of Roman
sway, a certain number of the royal tributes were
diminished. Quintus Servaeus was appointed to
Commagene, now for the first time transferred to
praetorian jurisdiction.

LVII. Complete and happy as was his adjustment
of the allies' affairs, it gave Germanicus no satisfaction,
in view of the insolence of Piso; who, when ordered
to conduct part of the legions into Armenia either
in his own person or in that of his son, had ignored
both alternatives. In Cyrrus,[6] the winter-quarters
of the tenth legion, they met at last, their features
schooled to exclude, in Piso's case, all evidence of
alarm; in the Caesar's, all suggestion of a threat.
He was, in fact, as I have stated, indulgent to a fault.
But his friends had the craft to inflame his resent-

* In N. Syria (now *Khoros*).

callidi intendere vera, adgerere falsa ipsumque et
Plancinam et filios variis modis criminari.   Postremo
paucis familiarium adhibitis sermo coeptus a Caesare, qualem ira et dissimulatio gignit, responsum
a Pisone precibus contumacibus; discesseruntque [1]
apertis [2] odiis.   Post quae [3] rarus in tribunali Caesaris
Piso et, si quando adsideret, atrox ac dissentire
manifestus.   Vox quoque eius audita est in convivio,
cum apud regem Nabataeorum coronae aureae
magno pondere Caesari et Agrippinae, leves Pisoni
et ceteris offerrentur, principis Romani, non Parthi
regis filio eas epulas dari; abiecitque simul coronam
et multa in luxum addidit quae Germanico quamquam acerba tolerabantur tamen.

LVIII. Inter quae ab rege Parthorum Artabano
legati venere.   Miserat amicitiam ac foedus memo-
raturos, et cupere novari [4] dextras, daturumque honori
Germanici ut ripam Euphratis accederet: petere
interim ne Vonones in Suria haberetur neu proceres
gentium propinquis nuntiis ad discordias traheret.
Ad ea Germanicus de societate Romanorum Par-
thorumque magnifice, de adventu regis et cultu sui
cum decore ac modestia respondit.   Vonones Pom-
peiopolim, Ciliciae maritimam urbem, amotus est.

---

[1] discesseruntque *Pichena* : discesserantque.
[2] apertis *Lipsius* : opertis.
[3] post quae *Muretus* : postque.
[4] cupere novari *Nipperdey* : cuperere novari (cupere
renovari *vetus vulgata*).

---

[1] The Nabataeans at this time formed a dependent kingdom
n N.W. Arabia; later (105 A.D.), the province of Arabia
Petraea.
[2] The contrast between *regis* and *principis*—the " king of
kings " and the " first of citizens "—is necessarily obliterated
in the translation.

ments: they aggravated truths, accumulated falsehoods, levelled a miscellany of charges at Piso,
Plancina, and their sons. Finally, in the presence
of a few intimates, the prince opened the conversation
in the key always struck by dissembled anger; Piso
returned a defiant apology, and they parted in open
hatred. From now onward, Piso's appearances at
the tribunal of Germanicus were rare; and, on the
occasions when he took his seat, it was with the
sullen air of undisguised opposition. Again. he
was heard to remark in a banquet at the Nabataean
court,[1] when massive golden crowns were offered to
Germanicus and Agrippina, and lighter specimens
to Piso and the rest, that this was a dinner given to
the son, not of a Parthian king, but of a Roman
prince.[2] At the same time, he tossed his crown
aside, and added a diatribe on luxury, which Germanicus, in spite of its bitterness, contrived to
tolerate.

LVIII. Meanwhile deputies arrived from the
Parthian king, Artabanus. They had been sent to
mention the friendship and the treaty between the
nations, and to add that " the king desired a fresh
exchange of pledges; and, in compliment to Germanicus, would meet him on the bank of the
Euphrates. In the interval, he asked that Vonones
should not be kept in Syria[3] to lure the tribal chieftains
into discord by agents from over the border." As
to the alliance between Rome and Parthia, Germanicus replied in florid terms; of the king's coming
and his courtesy to himself he spoke with dignity
and modesty: Vonones was removed to Pompeiopolis,[4]
a maritime town of Cilicia. The concession was not

[3] See above, chap. 4.   [4] Formerly Soli, now Mezetlü.

Datum id non modo precibus Artabani, sed contumeliae Pisonis cui gratissimus erat ob plurima officia et dona quibus Plancinam devinxerat.[1]

LXII. Dum ea aestas Germanico pluris per provincias transigitur, haud leve decus Drusus quaesivit inliciens Germanos ad discordias utque fracto iam Maroboduo usque in exitium insisteretur. Erat inter Gotones nobilis iuvenis nomine Catualda, profugus olim vi Marobodui et tunc dubiis rebus eius ultionem ausus. Is valida manu finis Marcomanorum ingreditur corruptisque primoribus ad societatem inrumpit regiam castellumque iuxta situm. Veteres illic Sueborum praedae et nostris e provinciis lixae ac negotiatores reperti quos ius commercii, dein cupido augendi pecuniam, postremo oblivio patriae suis quemque ab sedibus hostilem in agrum transtulerat.

LXIII. Maroboduo undique deserto non aliud subsidium quam misericordia Caesaris fuit. Transgressus Danuvium, qua Noricam provinciam praefluit, scripsit Tiberio non ut profugus aut supplex,

[1] *Sequuntur in codd. cc.* 59–61 : *post c.* 67 *traiecit* Steup.

---

[1] Steup (*Rh. Mus.* XXIV. 72) first drew attention to the grave difficulties involved by the traditional order of the chapters. According to that order, the events of chaps. 62–67 fall, together with Germanicus' Egyptian tour, in the year 19 A.D. Yet the opening words of chap. 62 refer unmistakably to the prince's actions in 18 A.D. Again, the announcements of Marbod's fall and Artaxias' coronation arrive simultaneously at Rome (chap. 64 *init.*); but a year divides the two happenings. In addition, it is at least surprising that Drusus should have left for Illyricum in 17 A.D. (see chaps. 44, 51, 53), and that nothing should be heard of him until 19 A.D.

simply a compliance with Artabanus' request but also an affront to Piso; to whom the pretender was highly acceptable in consequence of the numerous civilities and presents for which Plancina was indebted to him.

LXII.[1] While Germanicus was passing the summer in various provinces, Drusus earned considerable credit by tempting the Germans to revive their feuds and, as the power of Maroboduus was already shattered, to press on his complete destruction. Among the Gotones[2] was a youth of good family, named Catualda, exiled some time ago by the arms of Maroboduus, and now, as his fortunes waned, emboldened to revenge. With a strong following, he entered Marcomanian territory, seduced the chieftains into complicity, and burst into the palace and adjoining fortress. There they discovered the ancient Suebian spoils, together with a number of sutlers and traders out of the Roman provinces, drawn from their respective homes and implanted on hostile soil first by the commercial privileges,[3] then by the lure of increased profits, and finally by oblivion of their country.

LXIII. Forsaken on every side, Maroboduus had no other refuge than the imperial clemency. Crossing the Danube where it flows by the province of Noricum[4] he wrote to Tiberius, not in the tone of a landless man

[2] On the eastern bank of the lower Vistula. After their migration in the latter part of the second century they are found on the Euxine under the more famous title of Goths.

[3] Conferred by the treaty which excites the indignation of Arminius in chap. 45.

[4] Between Raetia and Pannonia, the northern frontier being the Danube from Passau nearly to Vienna.

479

sed ex memoria prioris fortunae: nam multis nationibus clarissimum quondam regem ad se vocantibus
Romanam amicitiam praetulisse. Responsum a
Caesare tutam ei honoratamque sedem in Italia
fore, si maneret: sin rebus eius aliud conduceret,
abiturum fide qua venisset. Ceterum apud senatum
disseruit non Philippum Atheniensibus, non Pyrrhum
aut Antiochum populo Romano perinde metuendos
fuisse. Extat oratio qua magnitudinem viri, violentiam subiectarum ei gentium et quam propinquus Italiae hostis, suaque in destruendo eo consilia
extulit. Et Maroboduus quidem Ravennae habitus,
si¹ quando insolescerent Suebi, quasi rediturus in
regnum ostentabatur: sed non excessit Italia per
duodeviginti annos consenuitque multum imminuta
claritate ob nimiam vivendi cupidinem. Idem Catual-
dae casus neque aliud perfugium. Pulsus haud multo
post Hermundurorum opibus et Vibilio duce recep-
tusque, Forum Iulium, Narbonensis Galliae coloniam, mittitur. Barbari utrumque comitati, ne
quietas provincias immixti turbarent, Danuvium
ultra inter flumina Marum et Cusum locantur, dato
rege Vannio gentis Quadorum.

LXIV. Simul nuntiato regem Artaxian Armeniis a

¹ si . . . rediturus *Beroaldus* : nesi . . . reditus.

---

¹ A friendly branch of the Suebi, north of Raetia, to which
they were allowed free access : see *Germ.* 41. Vibilius appears
again in XII. 29.
² On the Via Aurelia, which ran to Arles. Now Fréjus, in
the *département* of Vat.
³ In Moravia and Upper Hungary; neighbours of the
Marcomani, with whom they played a leading part in the
great barbarian coalition against Rome under Marcus Aurelius.
—For the fate of Vannius' kingdom see XII. 29–30.

or a suppliant, but in one reminiscent of his earlier
fortune: for " though many nations offered to
welcome a king once so glorious, he had preferred
the friendship of Rome." The Caesar replied that
" he would have a safe and honoured seat in Italy,
if he remained ; but, should his interests make a
change advisable, he might depart as securely as
he had come." He asserted, however, in the senate
that " not Philip himself had been so grave a menace
to Athens—not Pyrrhus nor Antiochus to the Roman
people." The speech is still extant, in which he
emphasized " the greatness of the man, the violence
of the peoples beneath his rule, the nearness of the
enemy to Italy, and the measures he had himself
taken to destroy him." Maroboduus, in fact, was
detained at Ravenna; where the possibility of his
restoration was held out to the Suebians, whenever
they became unruly : but for eighteen years he
never set foot out of Italy and grew into an old man,
his fame much tarnished by too great love of life.
An identical disaster and a similar haven awaited
Catualda. A short while afterwards, broken by the
power of the Hermunduri[1] and the generalship of
Vibilius, he received asylum, and was sent to Forum
Julium,[2] a colony of Narbonensian Gaul. Since the
barbarian retainers of the two princes might, if
intermingled with the native population, have disturbed the peace of the provinces, they were assigned
a king in the person of Vannius, from the Quadian
tribe,[3] and settled on the further bank of the Danube,
between the rivers Marus and Cusus.[4]

LXIV. As news had come at the same time that

[4] Marus is the March (Morava); Cusus, the Waag or Gran
or Gusen.

Germanico datum, decrevere patres ut Germanicus atque Drusus ovantes urbem introirent. Structi et arcus circum latera templi Martis Vltoris cum effigie Caesarum, laetiore Tiberio quia pacem sapientia firmaverat quam si bellum per acies confecisset. Igitur Rhescuporim quoque, Thraeciae regem, astu adgreditur. Omnem eam nationem Rhoemetalces tenuerat; quo defuncto Augustus partem Thraecum Rhescuporidi fratri eius, partem filio Cotyi permisit. In ea divisione arva et urbes et vicina Graecis Cotyi, quod incultum, ferox, adnexum hostibus, Rhescuporidi cessit: ipsorumque regum ingenia, illi mite et amoenum, huic atrox, avidum et societatis impatiens erat. Sed primo subdola concordia egere: mox Rhescuporis egredi finis, vertere in se Cotyi data et resistenti vim facere, cunctanter sub Augusto, quem auctorem utriusque regni, si sperneretur, vindicem metuebat. Enimvero audita mutatione principis immittere latronum globos, excindere castella, causas bello.

LXV. Nihil aeque Tiberium anxium habebat quam ne composita turbarentur. Deligit centurionem qui nuntiaret regibus ne armis disceptarent;

---

[1] Built in the Forum of Augustus to commemorate his vengeance on the slayers of the dictator Julius. For its military associations, cf. Suet. *Aug.* 29; Ov. *Fast.* V. 567 *sqq.*; and below III. 18 and XIII. 8. A few columns still remain.

[2] The country only became a province under Claudius (46 A.D.). Under Tiberius, with the exception of the southern coast on the Aegean (which belonged to the province of Macedonia) and the Thracian Chersonese (which was private imperial property), it was governed by semi-independent native princes.

[3] For his poetical attainments, see Ovid's appeal to him (*ex P.* II. 9): Antipater is still more florid (*Anth. Pal.* IV. 75, Ζηνὶ καὶ ᾿Απόλλωνι καὶ ῎Αρεϊ τέκνον ἀνάκτων Εἴκελον κτέ).

Germanicus had presented the throne of Armenia
to Artaxias, the senate resolved that he and Drusus
should receive an ovation upon entering the capital.
In addition, arches bearing the effigy of the two
Caesars were erected on each side of the temple of
Mars the Avenger;[1] while Tiberius showed more
pleasure at having kept the peace by diplomacy
than if he had concluded a war by a series of stricken
fields. Accordingly, he now brought his cunning to
bear against Rhescuporis, the king of Thrace.[2] The
whole of that country had been subject to Rhoemetalces; after whose death Augustus conferred one
half on his brother Rhescuporis, the other on his son
Cotys. By this partition the agricultural lands, the
towns, and the districts adjoining the Greek cities
fell to Cotys; the remainder,—a sterile soil, a wild
population, with enemies at the very door,—to
Rhescuporis. So, too, with the character of the
kings: one was gentle and genial;[3] the other, sullen,
grasping, and intolerant of partnership. At the first,
however, they acted with a deceptive show of concord: then Rhescuporis began to overstep his frontiers, to appropriate districts allotted to Cotys, and
to meet opposition with force: hesitantly during
the lifetime of Augustus, whom he feared as the
creator of both kingdoms and, if slighted, their
avenger. The moment, however, that he heard of
the change of sovereigns, he began to throw preda-
tory bands across the border, to demolish fortresses,
and to sow the seeds of war.

LXV. Nothing gave Tiberius so much anxiety as
that settlements once made should not be disturbed.
He chose a centurion to notify the kings that there
must be no appeal to arms; and Cotys at once dis-

statimque a Cotye dimissa sunt quae paraverat auxilia. Rhescuporis ficta modestia postulat eundem in locum coiretur: posse de controversiis conloquio transigi. Nec diu dubitatum de tempore, loco, dein condicionibus, cum alter facilitate, alter fraude cuncta inter se concederent acciperentque. Rhescuporis sanciendo, ut dictitabat, foederi convivium adicit, tractaque in multam noctem laetitia per epulas ac vinolentiam incautum Cotyn et, postquam dolum intellexerat, sacra regni, eiusdem familiae deos et hospitalis mensas obtestantem catenis onerat. Thraeciaque omni potitus scripsit ad Tiberium structas sibi insidias, praeventum insidiatorem; simul bellum adversus Bastarnas Scythasque praetendens novis peditum et equitum copiis sese firmabat. Molliter rescriptum, si fraus abesset, posse eum innocentiae fidere, ceterum neque se neque senatum nisi cognita causa ius et iniuriam discreturos: proinde tradito Cotye veniret transferretque invidiam criminis.

LXVI. Eas litteras Latinius Pandusa[1] pro praetore Moesiae cum militibus quis Cotys traderetur in Thraeciam misit. Rhescuporis inter metum et iram cunctatus maluit patrati quam incepti facinoris reus esse: occidi Cotyn iubet mortemque

---

[1] Pandusa *Nipperdey*: pandus.

---

[1] To those of Cotys.

banded the auxiliaries he had collected. Rhescuporis, with assumed moderation, asked for a personal
meeting: their differences, he said, could be adjusted
verbally. Small difficulty was made about the time,
the place, and, finally, the conditions, when one
party through good nature, and the other through
duplicity, conceded and accepted everything. To
ratify the treaty, as he said, Rhescuporis added a
banquet. When the merriment had been prolonged
far into the night with the help of good cheer and
wine, he laid in irons the unsuspecting Cotys, who,
on discovering the treachery, appealed in vain to the
sanctities of kingship, the deities of their common
house, and the immunities of the hospitable board.
Master of the whole of Thrace, he wrote to Tiberius
that a plot had been laid for him, but he had forestalled the plotter: at the same time, under the
pretext of a campaign against the Bastarnae and
Scythians, he strengthened himself by fresh levies
of infantry and cavalry. A smooth letter came
back:—" If his conscience was clear, he might trust
to his innocence; but neither the emperor nor
the senate could discriminate between the rights
and wrongs of the case unless they heard it. He
had better, then, surrender Cotys, come to Rome,
and shift the odium of the charge from his own
shoulders."[1]

LXVI. The letter was despatched into Thrace by
Latinius Pandusa, the propraetor of Moesia, together
with a company of soldiers, who were to take over
Cotys. After some fluctuation between fear and
anger, Rhescuporis, deciding to stand his trial for the
commission, not the inception, of a crime, ordered
the execution of Cotys; and promulgated a lie that

sponte sumptam ementitur. Nec tamen Caesar placitas semel artes mutavit, sed defuncto Pandusa,[1] quem sibi infensum Rhescuporis arguebat, Pomponium Flaccum, veterem stipendiis et arta cum rege amicitia eoque accommodatiorem ad fallendum, ob id maxime Moesiae praefecit.

LXVII. Flaccus in Thraeciam transgressus per ingentia promissa quamvis ambiguum et scelera sua reputantem perpulit ut praesidia Romana intraret. Circumdata hinc regi specie honoris valida manus, tribunique et centuriones monendo, suadendo, et quanto longius abscedebatur, apertiore custodia, postremo gnarum necessitatis in urbem traxere. Accusatus in senatu ab uxore Cotyis damnatur, ut procul regno teneretur. Thraecia in Rhoemetalcen filium, quem paternis consiliis adversatum constabat, inque liberos Cotyis dividitur; iisque nondum adultis Trebellenus Rufus praetura functus datur qui regnum interim tractaret, exemplo quo maiores M. Lepidum Ptolemaei liberis tutorem in Aegyptum miserant. Rhescuporis Alexandriam devectus atque illic fugam temptans an ficto crimine interficitur.

LIX. M. Silano L. Norbano consulibus Germanicus Aegyptum proficiscitur cognoscendae antiquitatis. Sed cura provinciae praetendebatur, leva-

---

[1] Pandusa *Nipperdey* : padusa.

---

[1] Scandal also accused him of being a boon-companion of Tiberius—*omnium horarum amicus* (Suet. *Tib.* 42).

[2] They did not, however, return with Rufus to Thrace, but were detained by Tiberius in Rome and educated in company with Caligula.

[3] Philometer and Physcon, sons of Ptolemy Epiphanes (*ob.* 181 B.C.).

[4] *Quod vero Alexandriam propter immensam et repentinam famem inconsulto se adisset, questus est* (Tiberius) *in senatu*

his death had been self-inflicted. Still, the Caesar made no change in the methods he had once resolved upon, but, on the death of Pandusa—whom Rhescuporis accused of animus against himself—appointed Pomponius Flaccus to the government of Moesia; chiefly because that veteran campaigner was a close friend of the king, and, as such, the better adapted to deceive him.[1]

LXVII. Flaccus crossed into Thrace, and by un-stinted promises induced Rhescuporis to enter the Roman lines, though he felt some hesitation, as he reflected on his guilt. He was then surrounded by a strong body-guard, ostensibly out of respect for his royalty; and by advice, suasion, and a surveillance which grew more obvious at each remove, till at last he realized the inevitable, the tribunes and cen-turions haled him to Rome. He was accused in the senate by Cotys' wife, and condemned to detention at a distance from his kingdom. Thrace was divided between his son Rhoemetalces, who was known to have opposed his father's designs, and the children of Cotys. As these were not of mature age, they were put under the charge of Trebellenus Rufus,[2] an ex-praetor, who was to manage the kingdom in the interregnum; a parallel from an earlier generation being the despatch of Marcus Lepidus to Egypt as the guardian of Ptolemy's children.[3] Rhescuporis was deported to Alexandria, and perished in a genuine, or imputed, attempt at escape.

LIX. In the consulate of Marcus Silanus and Lucius Norbanus, Germanicus set out for Egypt to view its antiquities, though the reason given was solicitude for the province.[4] He did, in fact, lower

A.V.C. 772 = A.D. 19

(Suet. *Tib.* 52). To the opening of the granaries there is an incidental allusion in Jos. *c. Ap.* II. 5.

vitque apertis horreis pretia frugum multaque in vulgus grata usurpavit: sine milite incedere, pedibus intectis et pari cum Graecis amictu, P. Scipionis aemulatione, quem eadem factitavisse apud Siciliam, quamvis flagrante adhuc Poenorum bello, accepimus. Tiberius cultu habituque eius lenibus verbis perstricto, acerrime increpuit quod contra instituta Augusti non sponte principis Alexandriam introisset. Nam Augustus, inter alia dominationis arcana, vetitis nisi permissu ingredi senatoribus aut equitibus Romanis inlustribus, seposuit Aegyptum, ne fame urgeret Italiam quisquis eam provinciam claustraque terrae ac maris quamvis levi praesidio adversum ingentis exercitus insedisset.

LX. Sed Germanicus nondum comperto profectionem eam incusari Nilo subvehebatur, orsus oppido a Canopo. Condidere id Spartani ob sepultum illic rectorem navis Canopum, qua tempestate Menelaus Graeciam repetens diversum ad mare terramque Libyam deiectus est.[1] Inde proximum amnis os dicatum Herculi, quem indigenae ortum apud se et antiquissimum perhibent eosque, qui postea pari vir-

---

¹ deiectus est *J. Gronovius, Pichena*: delectus.

---

¹ Liv. XXIX. 19 *ad fin.*

² Men of the type of Maecenas and Sallustius Crispus, possessed of senatorial census, but remaining within the equestrian order by choice and constituting a sort of *noblesse de l'empire*.

³ Egypt was never a province in the true sense of the term, but a private imperial domain, administered on behalf of the princeps, as representing its kings, by a *praefectus* drawn from the equestrian order. See *Hist.* I. 11 :—*Aegyptum . . . iam inde a divo Augusto equites Romani obtinent loco regum : ita visum expedire provinciam aditu difficilem, annonae fecundam . . . domi retinere.*

the price of corn by opening the state granaries, and adopted many practices popular with the multitude, walking without his guards, his feet sandalled and his dress identical with that of the Greeks: an imitation of Publius Scipio, who is recorded to have done the like in Sicily, although the Carthaginian war was still raging.[1] Tiberius passed a leniently worded criticism on his dress and bearing, but rebuked him with extreme sharpness for overstepping the prescription of Augustus by entering Alexandria without the imperial consent. For Augustus, among the other secrets of absolutism, by prohibiting all senators or Roman knights of the higher rank [2] from entering the country without permission, kept Egypt isolated;[3] in order that Italy might not be subjected to starvation by anyone who contrived, with however slight a garrison against armies however formidable, to occupy the province and the key-positions by land and sea.[4]

LX. Not yet aware, however, that his itinerary was disapproved, Germanicus sailed up the Nile, starting from the town of Canopus—founded by the Spartans in memory of the helmsman so named, who was buried there in the days when Menelaus, homeward bound for Greece, was blown to a distant sea and the Libyan coast. From Canopus he visited the next of the river-mouths, which is sacred to Hercules [5] (an Egyptian born, according to the local account, and the eldest of the name, the others of

[4] Pharus by sea, Pelusium by land (Hirt. *bell. Alex.* 26). For the dependence of Italy on foreign grain, see, for instance, III. 54 and XII. 43.

[5] The " Egyptian Hercules " is discussed at length by Herodotus (II. 43 *sqq.*): Brugsch identified him with the Theban Khonsu-neferhetep, a sun-deity.

THE ANNALS OF TACITUS

tute fuerint, in cognomentum eius adscitos; mox visit veterum Thebarum magna vestigia. Et manebant structis molibus litterae Aegyptiae, priorem opulentiam complexae: iussusque e senioribus sacerdotum patrium sermonem interpretari, referebat habitasse quondam septingenta milia aetate militari atque eo cum exercitu regem Rhamsen Libya, Aethiopia Medisque et Persis et Bactriano ac Scytha potitum quasque terras Suri Armeniique et contigui Cappadoces colunt, inde Bithynum, hinc Lycium ad mare imperio tenuisse. Legebantur et indicta gentibus tributa, pondus argenti et auri, numerus armorum equorumque et dona templis, ebur atque odores, quasque copias frumenti et omnium utensilium quaeque natio penderet, haud minus magnifica quam nunc vi Parthorum aut potentia Romana iubentur.

LXI. Ceterum Germanicus aliis quoque miraculis intendit animum, quorum praecipua Memnonis saxea effigies, ubi radiis solis icta est, vocalem sonum reddens, disiectasque inter et vix pervias arenas instar montium eductae pyramides certamine et opibus regum, lacusque effossa humo, superfluentis Nili receptacula; atque alibi angustiae et profunda altitudo, nullis inquirentium spatiis pentrabilis. Exim ventum Elephantinen ac Syenen, claustra

---

[1] *Uast, (Ta-) Àpet;* now the ruins of Karnak, Luxor, and Medinet-Habu.

[2] Ramessu II (1333 B.C.); the semi-mythical Sesostris (Sesosis) of Herodotus and Diodorus: the list of his conquests is, of course, mainly fabulous.

[3] The northern colossus of the two at Medinet-Habu, which represent Amen-hetep III (*ca.* 1450 B.C.). Another imperial antiquary, in the person of Hadrian, has left his name on the statue: the "vocal sound" of the familiar story ceased when the colossus was restored by Severus.

later date and equal virtue being adopted into the title); then, the vast remains of ancient Thebes.[1] On piles of masonry Egyptian letters still remained, embracing the tale of old magnificence, and one of the senior priests, ordered to interpret his native tongue, related that " once the city contained seven hundred thousand men of military age, and with that army King Rhamses,[2] after conquering Libya and Ethiopia, the Medes and the Persians, the Bactrian and the Scyth, and the lands where the Syrians and Armenians and neighbouring Cappadocians dwell, had ruled over all that lies between the Bithynian Sea on the one hand and the Lycian on the other." The tribute-lists of the subject nations were still legible: the weight of silver and gold, the number of weapons and horses, the temple-gifts of ivory and spices, together with the quantities of grain and other necessaries of life to be paid by the separate countries; revenues no less imposing than those which are now exacted by the might of Parthia or by Roman power.

LXI. But other marvels, too, arrested the attention of Germanicus: in especial, the stone colossus of Memnon,[3] which emits a vocal sound when touched by the rays of the sun; the pyramids reared mountain high by the wealth of emulous kings among wind-swept and all but impassable sands; the excavated lake which receives the overflow of Nile;[4] and, elsewhere, narrow gorges and deeps impervious to the plummet of the explorer. Then he proceeded to Elephantine and Syene,[5] once the limits of the

[4] The Lake Moeris of Herodotus, south of Memphis; now the Birket al-Ḳarûn in the Fayyûm.
[5] Assouan; Elephantine (termed Ābu, *i.e.* " elephant," in the inscriptions) being an island opposite.

olim Romani imperii, quod nunc rubrum ad mare patescit.

LXVIII. Per idem tempus Vonones, quem amotum in Ciliciam memoravi, corruptis custodibus effugere ad Armenios, inde[1] Albanos Heniochosque et consanguineum sibi regem Scytharum conatus est. Specie venandi omissis maritimis locis avia saltuum petiit, mox pernicitate equi ad amnem Pyramum contendit, cuius pontes accolae ruperant audita regis fuga, neque vado penetrari poterat. Igitur in ripa fluminis a Vibio Frontone praefecto equitum vincitur; mox Remmius evocatus, priori custodiae regis adpositus, quasi per iram gladio eum transigit. Vnde maior fides conscientia sceleris et metu indicii mortem Vononi inlatam.

LXIX. At Germanicus Aegypto remeans cuncta quae apud legiones aut urbes iusserat abolita vel in contrarium versa cognoscit. Hinc graves in Pisonem contumeliae, nec minus acerba quae ab illo in Caesarem intentabantur.[2] Dein Piso abire Suria statuit. Mox adversa Germanici valetudine detentus, ubi recreatum accepit votaque pro incolumitate solvebantur, admotas hostias, sacrificalem apparatum, festam Antiochensium plebem per lictores proturbat. Tum Seleuciam degreditur, opperiens aegritudinem, quae rursum Germanico acciderat.

---

[1] inde *Wopkens* (dein *Haase*) : inde in.
[2] intentabantur *Wurm* : temptabantur.

---

[1] About 115 A.D., after the conquests of Trajan.
[2] Chap. 58.   [3] Caucasian tribes.
[4] The upper reaches of the Djihân in Cilicia.
[5] Seleucia Pieria (Σ. ἡ ἐν Πιερίᾳ), the port of Antioch : see *Acts* xiii. 1–4.

Roman Empire, which now [1] stretches to the Persian Gulf.

LXVIII. About this time, Vonones—whose sequestration in Cilicia I have mentioned [2]—attempted by bribing his warders to escape into Armenia, then to the Albani, [3] the Heniochi, [3] and his relative, the king of Scythia. Leaving the coast under the pretext of a hunting excursion, he made for the trackless forest country, and, availing himself of the speed of his horse, hurried to the river Pyramus; [4] where, on the news of his escape, the bridges had been demolished by the people of the district: the stream itself was not fordable. He was arrested, therefore, on the river-bank by the cavalry prefect, Vibius Fronto; and a little later, Remmius, a time-expired veteran who had been in command of his former guards, ran him through with his sword, as though in an outburst of anger: a fact which makes it the more credible that conscious guilt and a fear of disclosures dictated the murder.

LXIX. On the way from Egypt, Germanicus learned that all orders issued by him to the legions or the cities had been rescinded or reversed. Hence galling references to Piso: nor were the retorts directed by him against the prince less bitter. Then Piso determined to leave Syria. Checked almost immediately by the ill-health of Germanicus, then hearing that he had rallied and that the vows made for his recovery were already being paid, he took his lictors and swept the streets clear of the victims at the altars, the apparatus of sacrifice, and the festive populace of Antioch. After this, he left for Seleucia, [5] awaiting the outcome of the malady which had again attacked Germanicus. The cruel virulence of the

493

Saevam vim morbi augebat persuasio veneni a Pisone accepti; et reperiebantur solo ac parietibus erutae humanorum corporum reliquiae, carmina et devotiones et nomen Germanici plumbeis tabulis insculptum, semusti cineres ac tabo [1] obliti aliaque malefica quis creditur animas numinibus infernis sacrari. Simul missi a Pisone incusabantur ut valetudinis adversa rimantes.

LXX. Ea Germanico haud minus ira quam per metum accepta. Si limen obsideretur, si effundendus spiritus sub oculis inimicorum foret, quid deinde miserrimae coniugi, quid infantibus liberis eventurum? Lenta videri veneficia: festinare et urgere, ut provinciam, ut legiones solus habeat. Sed non usque eo defectum Germanicum, neque praemia caedis apud interfectorem mansura. Componit epistulas quis amicitiam ei renuntiabat: addunt plerique iussum provincia decedere. Nec Piso moratus ultra navis solvit moderabaturque cursui quo propius regrederetur, si mors Germanici Suriam aperuisset.

LXXI. Caesar paulisper ad spem erectus, dein fesso corpore, ubi finis aderat, adsistentis amicos in hunc modum adloquitur: " Si fato concederem, iustus mihi dolor etiam adversus deos esset, quod

---

[1] tabo *Lipsius* : tabe.

---

[1] The tablets were employed in the ancient and almost ubiquitous rite of defixion (*defixio*, κατάδεσις), which consisted essentially in running a nail or needle through the effigy or the name of the person marked down for destruction. For an account of the procedure and the theory underlying it, the reader may be referred to F. B. Jevons in *Anthropology and the Classics* (p. 106 *sqq.*).

[2] Half-burnt human remains from the funeral-pyre.

[3] Besides the infant Julia (chap. 54), Caligula was with him

disease was intensified by the patient's belief that
Piso had given him poison; and it is a fact that
explorations in the floor and walls brought to light
the remains of human bodies, spells, curses, leaden
tablets engraved with the name *Germanicus*,[1] charred
and blood-smeared ashes,[2] and others of the implements of witchcraft by which it is believed the living
soul can be devoted to the powers of the grave.
At the same time, emissaries from Piso were accused
of keeping a too inquisitive watch upon the ravages
of the disease.

LXX. Of all this Germanicus heard with at least
as much anger as alarm:—" If his threshold was
besieged, if he must surrender his breath under the
eye of his enemies, what must the future hold in
store for his unhappy wife—for his infant children?[3]
Poison was considered too dilatory; Piso was growing urgent—imperative—to be left alone with his
province and his legions! But Germanicus had not
fallen from himself so far, nor should the price of
blood remain with the slayer!" He composed a
letter renouncing his friendship: the general account
adds that he ordered him to leave the province.
Delaying no longer, Piso weighed anchor, and regu-
lated his speed so that the return journey should be
the shorter, if Germanicus' death opened the door
in Syria.

LXXI. For a moment the Caesar revived to hope:
then his powers flagged, and, with the end near,
he addressed his friends at the bedside to the following effect:—" If I were dying by the course of
nature, I should have a justified grievance against
Heaven itself for snatching me from parents, children,

(III. 1, *duobus cum liberis*; Suet. *Cal.* 10, *comitatus est patrem
et Syriaca expeditione*).

me parentibus, liberis, patriae intra iuventam prae-
maturo exitu raperent: nunc scelere Pisonis et Plancinae interceptus ultimas preces pectoribus vestris
relinquo: referatis patri ac fratri, quibus acerbita-
tibus dilaceratus, quibus insidiis circumventus miser-
rimam vitam pessima morte finierim. Si quos spes
meae, si quos propinquus sanguis, etiam quos invidia erga viventem movebat, inlacrimabunt quondam florentem et tot bellorum superstitem muliebri
fraude cecidisse. Erit vobis locus querendi apud
senatum, invocandi leges. Non hoc praecipuum amicorum munus est, prosequi defunctum ignavo questu,
sed quae voluerit meminisse, quae mandaverit
exequi. Flebunt Germanicum etiam ignoti: vindi-
cabitis vos, si me potius quam fortunam meam fove-
batis. Ostendite populo Romano divi Augusti
neptem eandemque coniugem meam, numerate sex
liberos. Misericordia cum accusantibus erit fingenti-
busque scelesta mandata aut non credent homines
aut non ignoscent." Iuravere amici dextram morientis contingentes spiritum ante quam ultionem
amissuros.

LXXII. Tum ad uxorem versus per memoriam
sui, per communis liberos oravit exueret ferociam,
saevienti fortunae summitteret animum, neu regressa
in urbem aemulatione potentiae validiores inritaret.
Haec palam et alia secreto, per quae ostendisse
credebatur metum ex Tiberio. Neque multo post

and country, by a premature end in the prime of life. Now, cut off as I am by the villainy of Piso and Plancina, I leave my last prayers in the keeping of your breasts: report to my father and brother the agonies that rent me, the treasons that encompassed me, before I finished the most pitiable of lives by the vilest of deaths. If any were ever stirred by the hopes I inspired, by kindred blood,— even by envy of me while I lived,—they must shed a tear to think that the once happy survivor of so many wars has fallen by female treachery. You will have your opportunity to complain before the senate and to invoke the law. The prime duty of friends is not to follow their dead with passive laments, but to remember his wishes and carry out his commands. Strangers themselves will bewail Germanicus: *you* will avenge him—if you loved me, and not my fortune. Show to the Roman people the granddaughter of their deified Augustus, who was also my wife; number her six children: pity will side with the accusers, and, if the murderers allege some infamous warrant, they will find no credence in men—or no forgiveness!" His friends touched the dying hand and swore to forgo life sooner than revenge.

LXXII. Then he turned to his wife, and implored her " by the memory of himself, and for the sake of their common children, to strip herself of pride, to stoop her spirit before the rage of fortune, and never—if she returned to the capital—to irritate those stronger than herself by a competition for power." These words in public: in private there were others, in which he was believed to hint at danger from the side of Tiberius. Soon afterwards

extinguitur, ingenti luctu provinciae et circumiacentium populorum. Indoluere exterae nationes regesque: tanta illi comitas in socios, mansuetudo in hostis: visuque et auditu iuxta venerabilis, cum magnitudinem et gravitatem summae fortunae retineret, invidiam et adrogantiam effugerat.

LXXIII. Funus sine imaginibus et pompa per laudes ac memoriam virtutum eius celebre fuit. Et erant qui formam, aetatem,[1] genus mortis, ob propinquitatem etiam locorum in quibus interiit, magni Alexandri fatis adaequarent. Nam utrumque corpore decoro, genere insigni, haud multum triginta annos egressum, suorum insidiis externas inter gentis occidisse: sed hunc mitem erga amicos, modicum voluptatum, uno matrimonio, certis liberis egisse, neque minus proeliatorem, etiam si temeritas afuerit praepeditusque sit perculsas tot victoriis Germanias servitio premere. Quod si solus arbiter rerum, si iure et nomine regio fuisset, tanto promptius adsecuturum gloriam militiae quantum clementia, temperantia, ceteris bonis artibus praestitisset. Corpus antequam cremaretur nudatum in foro Antiochensium, qui locus sepulturae destinabatur, praetuleritne veneficii signa parum constitit; nam ut quis misericordia in Germanicum et praesumpta suspicione

---

[1] formam, fortunam, aetatem, *Johann Mueller.*

---

[1] A circumstantial account is given in Suet. *Cal.* 5.

[2] *Annum agens aetatis quartum et tricensimum diuturno morbo Antiochiae obiit* (Germanicus), Suet. *Cal.* 1. Alexander was a year younger.

[3] The tales of the poisoning of Alexander may be read in Plut. *Alex.* 77; Arr. *Anab.* VII. 27; Q. Curt. X. 10; Just. XII. 13; or—perhaps with equal profit—in the Pseudo-Callisthenes, III. *fin.*

he passed away, to the boundless grief of the province and the adjacent peoples.[1] Foreign nations and princes felt the pang—so great had been his courtesy to allies, his humanity to enemies : in aspect and address alike venerable, while he maintained the magnificence and dignity of exalted fortune, he had escaped envy and avoided arrogance.

LXXIII. His funeral, devoid of ancestral effigies or procession, was distinguished by eulogies and recollections of his virtues. There were those who, considering his personal appearance, his early age, and the circumstances of his death,—to which they added the proximity of the region where he perished,— compared his decease with that of Alexander the Great :—" Each eminently handsome, of famous lineage, and in years not much exceeding thirty,[2] had fallen among alien races by the treason of their countrymen.[3] But the Roman had borne himself as one gentle to his friends, moderate in his pleasures, content with a single wife and the children of lawful wedlock. Nor was he less a man of the sword; though he lacked the other's temerity, and, when his numerous victories had beaten down the Germanies, was prohibited from making fast their bondage. But had he been the sole arbiter of affairs, of kingly authority and title, he would have overtaken the Greek in military fame with an ease proportioned to his superiority in clemency, self-command, and all other good qualities." The body, before cremation, was exposed in the forum of Antioch, the place destined for the final rites. Whether it bore marks of poisoning was disputable : for the indications were variously read, as pity and preconceived suspicion swayed the spectator to the

aut favore in Pisonem pronior, diversi interpretabantur.

LXXIV. Consultatum inde inter legatos quique alii senatorum aderant quisnam Suriae praeficeretur. Et ceteris modice nisis, inter Vibium Marsum et Cn. Sentium diu quaesitum: dein Marsus seniori et acrius tendenti Sentio concessit. Isque infamem veneficiis ea in provincia et Plancinae percaram nomine Martinam in urbem misit, postulantibus Vitellio ac Veranio ceterisque qui crimina et accusationem tamquam adversus receptos iam reos instruebant.

LXXV. At Agrippina, quamquam defessa luctu et corpore aegro, omnium tamen quae ultionem morarentur intolerans ascendit classem cum cineribus Germanici et liberis, miserantibus cunctis quod femina nobilitate princeps, pulcherrimo modo matrimonio, inter venerantis gratantisque aspici solita, tunc feralis reliquias sinu ferret, incerta ultionis, anxia sui et infelici fecunditate fortunae totiens obnoxia. Pisonem interim apud Coum insulam nuntius adsequitur excessisse Germanicum. Quo intemperanter accepto caedit victimas, adit templa, neque ipse gaudium moderans et magis insolescente Plancina, quae

---

[1] All legati must have held at least the quaestorship, and were therefore senators.

[2] Consul suffectus in 17 A.D.; proconsul of Africa for three years (27–30 A.D.?); governor of Syria under Claudius. He appears again in the *Annals* at II. 79; IV. 56; VI. 47–8; XI. 10; and, since he had literary tastes (*vetustis honoribus et inlustris studiis*, VI. 47), it has been conjectured that some of the details of Germanicus' last days may rest ultimately on his authority.

[3] Cn. Sentius Saturninus, consul suffectus in 4 A.D. A

side of Germanicus, or his predilections to that of Piso.

LXXIV. A consultation followed between the legates and other senators[1] present, to determine the new governor of Syria. When the rest had made a half-hearted effort, the claims of Vibius Marsus[2] and Gnaeus Sentius[3] were canvassed at length; then Marsus gave way to the superior age and greater keenness of his competitor. And he, on the demand of Vitellius, Veranius, and the others (who were drawing up the articles of indictment as though the case had already been entered), despatched to Rome a woman by the name of Martina, infamous in the province for her poisonings and beloved of Plancina.

LXXV. Agrippina herself, worn out with grief and physically ill, yet intolerant of every obstacle to revenge, went on board the fleet with her children and the ashes of Germanicus; amid universal pity for this woman of sovereign lineage, her wedded glory wont but yesterday to attract the gaze of awed and gratulatory crowds, now carrying in her bosom the relics of the dead, uncertain of her vengeance, apprehensive for herself, cursed in that fruitfulness which had borne but hostages to fortune.

Piso, in the meantime, was overtaken at the isle of Cos[4] by a message that Germanicus was dead. He received it with transport. Victims were immolated, temples visited; and, while his own joy knew no bounds, it was overshadowed by the insolence of Plancina, who had been in mourning for the

fragmentary inscription proves that his appointment was recognized as valid by Tiberius.

[4] Off the Carian coast, in the province of Asia.

luctum amissae sororis tum primum laeto cultu mutavit.

LXXVI. Adfluebant centuriones monebantque prompta illi legionum studia: repeteret provinciam non iure ablatam et vacuam. Igitur quid agendum consultanti M. Piso filius properandum in urbem censebat: nihil adhuc inexpiabile admissum neque suspiciones imbecillas aut inania famae pertimescenda. Discordiam erga Germanicum odio fortasse dignam, non poena; et adeptione provinciae satis factum inimicis. Quod si regrederetur obsistente Sentio civile bellum incipi; nec duraturos in partibus centuriones militesque apud quos recens imperatoris sui memoria et penitus infixus in Caesares amor praevaleret.

LXXVII. Contra Domitius Celer, ex intima eius amicitia, disseruit utendum eventu: Pisonem, non Sentium Suriae praepositum; huic fascis et ius praetoris, huic legiones datas. Si quid hostile ingruat, quem iustius arma oppositurum quam qui[1] legati auctoritatem et propria mandata acceperit? Relinquendum etiam rumoribus tempus quo senescant: plerumque innocentis recenti invidiae imparis. At si teneat exercitum, augeat viris, multa quae provi-

---

[1] quam qui *Lipsius* : qui.

---

[1] From the Syrian legions: men, presumably, who owed their promotion to Piso (see above, chap. 55).

loss of a sister, and now changed for the first time into the garb of joy.

LXXVI. Centurions [1] came streaming in with their advice:—" The legions were eager to declare for him—he must return to the province illegally wrested from him and now masterless." At a council, then, to decide what action should be taken, his son, Marcus Piso, held that he must hurry to the capital:—" So far, he had been guilty of nothing that was past expiation; nor were feeble suspicions or unsubstantial rumours a matter for alarm. His difference with Germanicus might perhaps earn him a measure of unpopularity, but not punishment; while the forfeiture of his province had satisfied his private enemies. To go back was to embark on a civil war, if Sentius resisted; nor would the centurions and private soldiers stand fast in his cause, since with them the yet recent memory of their commander, and their deep-seated affection for the Caesars, outweighed all else."

LXXVII. Domitius Celer, one of his most intimate associates, argued upon the other side:—" He had better profit by the occasion: not Sentius, but Piso, had been created governor of Syria: to him had been entrusted the symbols of magistracy, the praetorian jurisdiction,—ay, and the legions. If hostilities threatened, who could more justly take the field than a man who had received the powers of a legate, in addition to private instructions? Besides, rumours ought to be allowed an interval in which to grow stale: innocence too often was unable to face the first blast of unpopularity. But if he kept the army and augmented his powers, chance would give a favourable turn to much that could not at

deri non possint fortuito in melius casura. " An fes-
tinamus cum Germanici cineribus adpellere, ut te
inauditum et indefensum planctus Agrippinae ac
vulgus imperitum primo rumore rapiant? Est tibi
Augustae conscientia, est Caesaris favor, sed in
occulto; et perisse Germanicum nulli iactantius
maerent quam qui maxime laetantur."

LXXVIII. Haud magna mole Piso promptus fero-
cibus in sententiam trahitur missisque ad Tiberium
epistulis incusat Germanicum luxus et superbiae;
seque pulsum, ut locus rebus novis patefieret, curam
exercitus eadem fide qua tenuerit repetivisse. Simul
Domitium impositum triremi vitare litorum oram
praeterque insulas alto [1] mari pergere in Suriam
iubet. Concurrentis desertores per manipulos componit, armat lixas traiectisque in continentem navibus vexillum tironum in Suriam euntium intercipit,
regulis Cilicum ut se auxiliis iuvarent scribit, haud
ignavo ad ministeria belli iuvene Pisone, quamquam
suscipiendum bellum abnuisset.

LXXIX. Igitur oram Lyciae ac Pamphyliae prae-
legentes, obviis navibus quae Agrippinam vehebant,
utrimque infensi arma primo expediere: dein mutua
formidine non ultra iurgium processum est, Mar-
susque Vibius nuntiavit Pisoni Romam ad dicendam

---

[1] alto *Lipsius* : lato.

---

[1] Since the death of Philopator (chap. 42) there were two
of these principalities remaining : Olba, north of Pompeiopolis;
and Trachea, the western part of Cilicia, then held by Archelaus
of Cappadocia.

present be foreseen. Or," he continued, "are we racing to make the harbour at the same moment as the ashes of Germanicus, so that with the first breath of scandal you may be swept to your doom, unheard and undefended, by a sobbing wife and a fatuous crowd? You have the complicity of Augusta, the favour of the Caesar,—but only in private; and none more ostentatiously bewail the fate of Germanicus than they who most rejoice at it."

LXXVIII. There was no great difficulty in converting Piso, with his taste for audacity, to this opinion; and, in a letter forwarded to Tiberius, he accused Germanicus of luxury and arrogance: as for himself, " he had been expelled so as to leave scope for a revolution, but had now gone to resume charge of the army, with the same loyalty as he had shown when he was at its head." At the same time, he placed Domitius on a warship, with orders to avoid the coasting-route and to make straight for Syria, past the islands and through the high seas. As deserters flocked in, he organized them by maniples; armed the camp-followers; then, crossing with his fleet to the mainland, intercepted a body of recruits bound for Syria, and wrote to the Cilician kinglets [1] to support him with auxiliaries—the young Piso assisting actively in the preparations for war, though he had protested against engaging in it.

LXXIX. As they were skirting, then, the coast of Lycia and Pamphylia, they were met by the squadron convoying Agrippina. On each side the hostility was such that at first they prepared for action: then, owing to their mutual fears, the affair went no further than high words; in the course of which Vibius Marsus summoned Piso to return to

causam veniret. Ille eludens respondit adfuturum ubi praetor qui de veneficiis quaereret reo atque accusatoribus diem prodixisset. Interim Domitius Laodiciam urbem Syriae adpulsus, cum hiberna sextae legionis peteret, quod eam maxime novis consiliis idoneam rebatur, a Pacuvio legato praevenitur. Id Sentius Pisoni per litteras aperit monetque ne castra corruptoribus, ne provinciam bello temptet. Quosque Germanici memores aut inimicis eius adversos cognoverat, contrahit, magnitudinem imperatoris identidem ingerens et rem publicam armis peti; ducitque validam manum et proelio paratam.

LXXX. Nec Piso, quamquam coepta secus cadebant, omisit tutissima e praesentibus, sed castellum Ciliciae munitum admodum, cui nomen Celenderis, occupat; nam admixtis desertoribus et tirone nuper intercepto suisque et Plancinae servitiis auxilia Cilicum quae reguli miserant in numerum legionis composuerat. Caesarisque se legatum testabatur provincia quam is dedisset arceri, non a legionibus (earum quippe accitu **venire**), sed a Sentio privatum odium falsis criminibus **tegente**. Consisterent in acie, non pugnaturis militibus ubi Pisonem ab ipsis

---

[1] Marsus' citation had no legal force, as it was only when the president of the court had formally received the charge that a day (normally the tenth from the date) was fixed for the appearance of the parties. The true insolence of the answer lies, however, in the tacit assumption that the case had no features so exceptional as to necessitate a change from the usual procedure.

[2] The modern Ladikîeh (Latakia), nearly opposite the north-eastern extremity of Cyprus : the other Syrian town of the name lay near Lebanon.

Rome and enter his defence. He gave a sarcastic answer that he would be there when the praetor with cognizance of poisoning cases had notified a date to the accusers and accused.[1]

Meanwhile, Domitius had landed at the Syrian town of Laodicea.[2] He was making for the winter quarters of the sixth legion, which he thought the best adapted for his revolutionary designs, when he was forestalled by the commanding officer, Pacuvius. Sentius notified Piso of the incident by letter, and warned him to make no attempt upon the camp by his agents or upon the province by his arms. He then collected the men whom he knew to be attached to the memory of Germanicus,—or, at least, opposed to his enemies,—impressed upon them the greatness of the emperor and the fact that this was an armed attack on the state, then took the field at the head of a powerful force ready for battle.

LXXX. Piso, too, though his enterprise was developing awkwardly, adopted the safest course in the circumstances by seizing an extremely strong post in Cilicia, named Celenderis.[3] For by an admixture of the deserters, the recently intercepted recruits, and his own and Plancina's slaves, he had arranged the Cilician auxiliaries, sent by the petty kings, in what was numerically a legion. He called them to witness that " he, the representative of the Caesar, was being excluded from the province which the Caesar had given, not by the legions—it was at their invitation he came!—but by Sentius, who was veiling his private hatred under a tissue of calumnies. They must take their stand in line of battle: the soldiers would never strike, when they had seen

[3] Now Kilindria (the Turkish *Tchilindere*).

parentem quondam appellatum, si iure ageretur,
potiorem, si armis, non invalidum vidissent. Tum
pro munimentis castelli manipulos explicat colle
arduo et derupto; nam cetera mari cinguntur. Contra veterani ordinibus ac subsidiis instructi: hinc
militum, inde locorum asperitas, sed non animus,
non spes, ne tela quidem nisi agrestia aut subitum
in [1] usum properata. Vt venere in manus, non ultra
dubitatum quam dum Romanae cohortes in aequum
eniterentur: vertunt terga Cilices seque castello
claudunt.

LXXXI. Interim Piso classem haud procul opperientem adpugnare frustra temptavit; regressusque
et pro muris, modo semet adflictando, modo singulos
nomine ciens, praemiis vocans, seditionem coeptabat: [2] adeoque commoverat ut signifer legionis [3]
sextae signum ad eum transtulerit, cum Sentius occa-
nere cornua tubasque et peti aggerem, erigi scalas
iussit ac promptissimum quemque succedere, alios
tormentis hastas, saxa et faces ingerere. Tandem
victa pertinacia Piso oravit ut traditis armis maneret
in castello, dum Caesar cui Suriam permitteret consulitur. Non receptae condiciones nec aliud quam
naves et tutum in urbem iter concessum est.

---

[1] subitum in *Doederlein*: subitum.
[2] coeptabat: adeoque . . . transtulerit, cum *Jackson*:
coeptabat, adeoque . . . transtulerit. Tum.
[3] legionis *edd.*: legionis vocans.

---

[1] The legion in which Piso's influence was strongest (see
above, chap. 79).

Piso; whom once they called Father; who, if the verdict went by justice, was the superior; and, if by arms, not wholly powerless." He then deployed his maniples in front of the fortress lines on a high and precipitous hill (the rest of the position is secured by the sea): confronting them stood the veterans, drawn up in centuries and with reserves. On the one side was a grim soldiery; on the other, a position not less grim,—but no courage, no hope, not even weapons, apart from rustic spears or makeshifts improvised to meet the sudden demand. When the collision came, doubt only lasted until the Roman cohorts scrambled up to level ground: the Cilicians took to their heels and barricaded themselves in the fortress.

LXXXI. In the meantime, Piso attempted, without effect, to attack the fleet, which was waiting at some little distance. On his return, he took his station on the walls; and, now beating his breast, now summoning particular soldiers by name and weighting the call with a bribe, endeavoured to create a mutiny. He had, indeed, produced enough impression for one ensign of the sixth[1] legion to come over with his standard, when Sentius ordered the cornets and trumpets to sound, the materials for a mound to be collected, ladders raised; the readiest to go forward to the escalade, others to discharge spears, stones, and firebrands, from the military engines. At last Piso's obstinacy was broken, and he applied for permission to hand over his arms and remain in the fort while the Caesar's award of the Syrian governorship was being ascertained. The terms were not accepted, and the only concessions made were a grant of ships and a safe-conduct to the capital.

LXXXII. At Romae, postquam Germanici valetudo percrebuit cunctaque ut ex longinquo aucta
in deterius adferebantur, dolor, ira, et erumpebant
questus. Ideo nimirum in extremas terras rele-
gatum, ideo Pisoni permissam provinciam; hoc
egisse secretos Augustae cum Plancina sermones.
Vera prorsus de Druso seniores locutos: displicere
regnantibus civilia filiorum ingenia, neque ob aliud
interceptos quam quia populum Romanum aequo
iure complecti reddita libertate agitaverint. Hos
vulgi sermones audita mors adeo incendit ut ante
edictum magistratuum, ante senatus consultum
sumpto iustitio desererentur fora, clauderentur domus. Passim silentia et gemitus, nihil compositum
in ostentationem; et, quamquam neque insignibus
lugentium abstinerent, altius animis maerebant.
Forte negotiatores vivente adhuc Germanico Suria
egressi laetiora de valetudine eius attulere. Statim
credita, statim vulgata sunt: ut quisque obvius,
quamvis leviter audita in alios atque illi in plures
cumulata gaudio transferunt. Cursant per urbem,
moliuntur templorum foris; iuvat credulitatem nox

---

[1] Drusus was the step-son of Augustus, Germanicus the
adopted son of Tiberius.

[2] For the belief that Drusus designed to restore the republic,
see I. 33 and Suet. *Claud.* 1. He died in Germany from the
consequences of a riding accident (Liv. *epit.* 140; νόσῳ τινί,
D. Cass. LV. 1): the absurd and inevitable story of his
poisoning by order of Augustus is mentioned and rejected by
Suetonius, *l.c.*

[3] Suetonius is more explicit (*Cal.* 6) :—*Passim cum luminibus
et victimis in Capitolium concursum est ac paene revolsae templi*

LXXXII. But at Rome, when the failure of Germanicus' health became current knowledge, and every circumstance was reported with the aggravations usual in news that has travelled far, all was grief and indignation. A storm of complaints burst out:—" So for this he had been relegated to the ends of earth; for this Piso had received a province; and this had been the drift of Augusta's colloquies with Plancina! It was the mere truth, as the elder men said of Drusus, that sons with democratic tempers were not pleasing to fathers on a throne[1]; and both had been cut off for no other reason than because they designed to restore the age of freedom and take the Roman people into a partnership of equal rights."[2] The announcement of his death inflamed this popular gossip to such a degree that before any edict of the magistrates, before any resolution of the senate, civic life was suspended, the courts deserted, houses closed. It was a town of sighs and silences, with none of the studied advertisements of sorrow; and, while there was no abstention from the ordinary tokens of bereavement, the deeper mourning was carried at the heart. Accidentally, a party of merchants, who had left Syria while Germanicus was yet alive, brought a more cheerful account of his condition. It was instantly believed and instantly disseminated. No man met another without proclaiming his unauthenticated news; and by him it was passed to more, with supplements dictated by his joy. Crowds were running in the streets and forcing temple-doors.[3] Credulity throve

fores, ne quid gestientis vota reddere moraretur. He quotes the verse with which they woke Tiberius :—*Salva Roma, salva patria, salvus est Germanicus.*

THE ANNALS OF TACITUS

et promptior inter tenebras adfirmatio. Nec obstitit falsis Tiberius donec tempore ac spatio vanescerent: et populus quasi rursum ereptum acrius doluit.

LXXXIII. Honores ut quis amore in Germanicum aut ingenio validus reperti decretique: ut nomen eius Saliari carmine caneretur; sedes curules sacerdotum Augustalium locis superque eas querceae coronae statuerentur; ludos circensis eburna effigies praeiret neve quis flamen aut augur in locum Germanici nisi gentis Iuliae crearetur. Arcus additi Romae et apud ripam Rheni et in monte Syriae Amano cum inscriptione rerum gestarum ac mortem ob rem publicam obisse. Sepulchrum Antiochiae ubi crematus, tribunal Epidaphnae quo in loco vitam finierat. Statuarum locorumve in quis coleretur [1] haud facile quis numerum inierit. Cum censeretur clipeus auro et magnitudine insignis inter auctores eloquentiae, adseveravit Tiberius solitum paremque ceteris dicaturum: neque enim eloquentiam fortuna discerni et satis inlustre si veteres inter scriptores haberetur. Equester ordo cuneum Germanici appel-

---

[1] coleretur *Beroaldus* : colerentur.

---

[1] In addition to lays in honour of the gods severally, this primitive and unintelligible hymn (*Saliorum carmina vix sacerdotibus suis satis intellecta*, Quint. I. 6, 40) contained *carmina in universos sermones composita*, in which the name of Augustus had already been inserted.

[2] See I. 54.

[3] In company with the images of the gods.

[4] Augustalis.

[5] Ὁ μὲν γὰρ Ἀμανὸς . . . περικλείει τὸν Ἰσσικὸν κόλπον ἅπαντα Strab 535: Nipperdey gives the modern name as Akma Dagh.

[6] Actually the suburb was Daphne, the city Ἀντιόχεια ἡ ἐπὶ Δάφνῃ : a rather curious inaccuracy in view of the great celebrity of Daphne (see, for instance, Munro, *Aetna*, pp. 40–43).

—it was night, and affirmation is boldest in the dark. Nor did Tiberius check the fictions, but left them to die out with the passage of time; and the people mourned with added bitterness for what seemed a second bereavement.

LXXXIII. Affection and ingenuity vied in dis-covering and decreeing honours to Germanicus: his name was to be chanted in the Saliar Hymn;[1] curule chairs surmounted by oaken crowns were to be set for him wherever the Augustal priests[2] had right of place; his effigy in ivory was to lead the procession at the Circus Games,[3] and no flamen[4] or augur, unless of the Julian house, was to be created in his room. Arches were added, at Rome, on the Rhine bank, and on the Syrian mountain of Amanus,[5] with an inscription recording his achievements and the fact that he had died for his country. There was to be a sepulchre in Antioch, where he had been cremated; a funeral monument in Epidaphne,[6] the suburb in which he had breathed his last. His statues, and the localities in which his cult was to be practised, it would be difficult to enumerate. When it was proposed to give him a gold medallion, as remarkable for the size as for the material, among the portraits of the classic orators,[7] Tiberius declared that he would dedicate one himself " of the customary type, and in keeping with the rest: for eloquence was not measured by fortune, and it was distinction enough if he ranked with the old masters." The equestrian order renamed the so-called " junior section " in

[7] In the Palatine Library (see above, chap. 37). The *clipeus* was a disk, usually of bronze, with the portrait en-graved on it: Pliny actually derives the word from γλύφω (*H.N.* XXXV. 3).

lavit qui iuniorum dicebatur, instituitque uti turmae idibus Iuliis imaginem eius sequerentur. Pleraque manent: quaedam statim omissa sunt aut vetustas oblitteravit.

LXXXIV. Ceterum recenti adhuc maestitia soror Germanici Livia, nupta Druso, duos virilis sexus simul enixa est. Quod rarum laetumque etiam modicis penatibus tanto gaudio principem adfecit, ut non temperaverit quin iactaret apud patres nulli ante Romanorum eiusdem fastigii viro geminam stirpem editam: nam cuncta, etiam fortuita. ad gloriam vertebat. Sed populo tali in tempore id quoque dolorem tulit, tamquam auctus liberis Drusus domum Germanici magis urgeret.

LXXXV. Eodem anno, gravibus senatus decretis libido feminarum coercita cautumque ne quaestum corpore faceret cui avus aut pater aut maritus eques Romanus fuisset. Nam Vistilia, praetoria familia genita, licentiam stupri apud aedilis vulgaverat, more inter veteres recepto, qui satis poenarum adversum impudicas in ipsa professione flagitii credebant. Exactum et a Titidio Labeone Vistiliae marito cur in uxore delicti manifesta ultionem legis omisisset. Atque illo praetendente sexaginta dies ad consultandum datos necdum praeterisse, satis visum de

---

[1] The date of the annual *travectio*, or review of the *equites Romani equo publico*; long obsolete, but revived by Augustus (Suet. *Aug.* 38).

[2] Pliny (*H.N.* XXXV. 4) describes him as recently dead at an advanced age; as having held the proconsulate of Gallia

their part of the theatre after Germanicus, and ruled that on the fifteenth of July [1] the cavalcade should ride behind his portrait. Many of these compliments remain: others were discontinued immediately, or have lapsed with the years.

LXXXIV. While the public mourning was still fresh, Germanicus' sister, Livia, who had married Drusus, was delivered of twin sons. The event, a rare felicity even in modest households, affected the emperor with so much pleasure that he could not refrain from boasting to the Fathers that never before had twins been born to a Roman of the same eminence: for he converted everything, accidents included, into material for self-praise. To the people, however, coming when it did, even this incident was a regret; as though the increase in Drusus' family was a further misfortune for the house of Germanicus.

LXXXV. In the same year, bounds were set to female profligacy by stringent resolutions of the senate; and it was laid down that no woman should trade in her body, if her father, grandfather, or husband had been a Roman knight. For Vistilla, the daughter of a praetorian family, had advertised her venality on the aediles' list— the normal procedure among our ancestors, who imagined the unchaste to be sufficiently punished by the avowal of their infamy. Her husband, Titidius Labeo,[2] was also required to explain why, in view of his wife's manifest guilt, he had not invoked the penalty of the law. As he pleaded that sixty days, not yet elapsed, were allowed for deliberation, it was thought

Narbonensis; and as being an enthusiastic amateur of painting —*sed ea res inrisu et contumeliae erat.*

Vistilia statuere; eaque in insulam Seriphon abdita
est. Actum et de sacris Aegyptiis Iudaicisque pellendis factumque patrum consultum ut quattuor
milia libertini generis ea superstitione infecta quis
idonea aetas in insulam Sardiniam veherentur, coercendis illic latrociniis et, si ob gravitatem caeli
interissent, vile damnum; ceteri cederent Italia nisi
certam ante diem profanos ritus exuissent.

LXXXVI. Post quae rettulit Caesar capiendam
virginem in locum Occiae, quae septem et quinquaginta per annos summa sanctimonia Vestalibus sacris
praesederat; egitque grates Fonteio Agrippae et
Domitio Pollioni quod offerendo filias de officio in
rem publicam certarent. Praelata est Pollionis filia,
non ob aliud quam quod mater eius in eodem coniugio
manebat; nam Agrippa discidio domum imminuerat.
Et Caesar quamvis posthabitam decies sestertii dote
solatus est.

LXXXVII. Saevitiam annonae incusante plebe
statuit frumento pretium quod emptor penderet,
binosque nummos se additurum negotiatoribus in
singulos modios. Neque tamen ob ea parentis patriae
delatum et antea vocabulum adsumpsit, acerbeque
increpuit eos qui divinas occupationes ipsumque

---

[1] A proverbially insignificant and barren island (now
Serpho[s]) in the Cyclades between Cythnus and Siphnus.

[2] The scandals which roused Tiberius to action may be read
in Jos. A.J. XVIII. 3, 4–5.

[3] The eligible age was from six to ten years, the vows being
obligatory for thirty.

enough to pass sentence on Vistilia, who was removed to the island of Seriphos.[1]—Another debate dealt with the proscription of the Egyptian and Jewish rites,[2] and a senatorial edict directed that four thousand descendants of enfranchised slaves, tainted with that superstition and suitable in point of age, were to be shipped to Sardinia and there employed in suppressing brigandage: "if they succumbed to the pestilential climate, it was a cheap loss." The rest had orders to leave Italy, unless they had renounced their impious ceremonial by a given date.

LXXXVI. The emperor then moved for the appointment of a Virgin to replace Occia, who for fifty-seven years had presided over the rites of Vesta with unblemished purity: Fonteius Agrippa and Domitius Pollio he thanked for the public-spirited rivalry which had led them to proffer their own daughters. Pollio's child[3] was preferred, for no reason save that her mother was still living with the same husband, while Agrippa's divorce had impaired the credit of his household. As a solatium to the rejected candidate, the Caesar presented her with a dowry of a million sesterces.[4]

LXXXVII. As the commons protested against the appalling dearness of corn, he fixed a definite price to be paid by the buyer, and himself guaranteed the seller a subsidy of two sesterces the peck. Yet he would not on that score accept the title " Father of his Country," which had indeed been offered previously ;[5] and he administered a severe reprimand to those who had termed his occupations " divine,"

---

[4] " Though a large, not an unusual dowry," Mayor on Juv. X. 335. He quotes, *inter alia*, Sen. *Cons. ad Helv.* 12, 6, *pantomimae deciens sestertio nubunt.*   [5] I. 72.

dominum dixerant. Vnde angusta et lubrica oratio
sub principe qui libertatem metuebat, adulationem
oderat.

LXXXVIII. Reperio apud scriptores senatoresque
eorundem temporum Adgandestrii principis Chattorum lectas in senatu litteras, quibus mortem Arminii
promittebat si patrandae neci venenum mitteretur,
responsumque esse non fraude neque occultis, sed
palam et armatum populum Romanum hostis suos
ulcisci. Qua gloria aequabat se Tiberius priscis
imperatoribus qui venenum in Pyrrhum regem
vetuerant prodiderantque. Ceterum Arminius abs-
cedentibus Romanis et pulso Maroboduo regnum
adfectans libertatem popularium adversam habuit,
petitusque armis cum varia fortuna certaret, dolo
propinquorum cecidit. Liberator haud dubie Germaniae et qui non primordia populi Romani, sicut alii
reges ducesque, sed florentissimum imperium laces-
sierit, proeliis ambiguus, bello non victus, septem
et triginta annos vitae, duodecim potentiae explevit,
caniturque adhuc barbaras apud gentis, Graecorum
annalibus ignotus, qui sua tantum mirantur, Romanis
haud perinde celebris, dum vetera extollimus recentium incuriosi.

---

[1] By his own definition (D. Cass. LVII. 8), to his slaves he
was " dominus "; to his soldiers, " imperator "; to the rest of
the world, " princeps."—For his occupations he preferred
‚' laborious " rather than " sacred " as an adjective (Suet.
Tib. 27). Diocletian introduced the " dominate."

[2] Since his power must be reckoned from the defeat of Varus,
his death would fall in 21 A.D.

and himself "Lord."[1] The speaker, consequently, had to walk a strait and slippery road under a prince who feared liberty and detested flattery.

LXXXVIII. I find from contemporary authors, who were members of the senate, that a letter was read in the curia from the Chattan chief Adgandestrius, promising the death of Arminius, if poison were sent to do the work; to which the reply went back that "it was not by treason nor in the dark but openly and in arms that the Roman people took vengeance on their foes": a high saying intended to place Tiberius on a level with the old commanders who prohibited, and disclosed, the offer to poison King Pyrrhus. Arminius himself, encouraged by the gradual retirement of the Romans and the expulsion of Maroboduus, began to aim at kingship, and found himself in conflict with the independent temper of his countrymen. He was attacked by arms, and, while defending himself with chequered results, fell by the treachery of his relatives. Undoubtedly the liberator of Germany; a man who, not in its infancy as captains and kings before him, but in the high noon of its sovereignty, threw down the challenge to the Roman nation, in battle with ambiguous results, in war without defeat; he completed thirty-seven years of life, twelve of power,[2] and to this day is sung in tribal lays, though he is an unknown being to the Greek historians, who admire only the history of Greece, and receives less than his due from us of Rome, who glorify the ancient days and show little concern for our own.

BOOK III

LIBER III

I. Nihil intermissa navigatione hiberni maris Agrippina Corcyram insulam advehitur, litora Calabriae contra sitam. Illic paucos dies componendo animo insumit, violenta luctu et nescia tolerandi. Interim, adventu eius audito, intimus quisque amicorum et plerique militares, ut quique sub Germanico stipendia fecerant, multique etiam ignoti vicinis e municipiis, pars officium in principem rati, plures illos secuti, ruere ad oppidum Brundisium, quod naviganti celerrimum fidissimumque adpulsu erat. Atque ubi primum ex alto visa classis, complentur non modo portus et proxima mari,[1] sed moenia ac tecta, quaque longissime prospectari poterat, maerentium turba et rogitantium inter se silentione an voce aliqua egredientem exciperent. Neque satis constabat quid pro tempore foret, cum classis paulatim successit, non alacri, ut adsolet, remigio, sed cunctis ad tristitiam compositis. Postquam duobus cum liberis, feralem urnam tenens, egressa navi defixit oculos, idem omnium gemitus; neque discerneres proximos alienos, virorum feminarumve

---

[1] mari *Muretus*: maris.

---

[1] Since Agrippina's voyage had begun in the previous year (II. 75; 79), the narrative passes to 20 A.D. without the normal preliminary mention of the new consuls.

[2] Corfu.

BOOK III

I. Without [1] once pausing in her navigation of the
wintry sea, Agrippina reached the island of Corcyra [2]
opposite the Calabrian coast. There, frantic with
grief and unschooled to suffering, she spent a few
days in regaining her composure. Meanwhile, at
news of her advent, there was a rush of people to
Brundisium, as the nearest and safest landing-place
for the voyager. Every intimate friend was present;
numbers of military men, each with his record of
service under Germanicus; even many strangers
from the local towns, some thinking it respectful to
the emperor, the majority following their example.
The moment her squadron was sighted in the offing,
not only the harbour and the points nearest the sea
but the city-walls and house-roofs, all posts, indeed,
commanding a wide enough prospect, were thronged
by a crowd of mourners, who asked each other if
they ought to receive her landing in silence, or with
some audible expression of feeling. It was not yet
clear to them what the occasion required, when little
by little the flotilla drew to shore, not with the
accustomed eager oarsmanship, but all with an
ordered melancholy. When, clasping the fatal urn,
she left the ship with her two children, and fixed her
eyes on the ground, a single groan arose from the
whole multitude; nor could a distinction be traced
between the relative and the stranger, the wailings of
women or of men: only, the attendants of Agrippina,

A.U.C. 773 =
A.D. 20

planctus, nisi quod comitatum Agrippinae longo maerore fessum obvii et recentes in dolore anteibant.

II. Miserat duas praetorias cohortis Caesar, addito ut magistratus Calabriae Apulique et Campani suprema erga memoriam filii sui munia[1] fungerentur. Igitur tribunorum centurionumque umeris cineres portabantur; praecedebant incompta signa, versi fasces; atque ubi colonias transgrederentur, atrata plebes, trabeati equites pro opibus loci vestem, odores aliaque funerum sollemnia cremabant. Etiam quorum diversa oppida, tamen obvii et victimas atque aras dis manibus statuentes lacrimis et conclamationibus dolorem testabantur. Drusus Tarracinam progressus est cum Claudio fratre liberisque Germanici, qui in urbe fuerant. Consules M. Valerius et M.[2] Aurelius (iam enim magistratum occeperant) et senatus ac magna pars populi viam complevere, disiecti et ut cuique libitum flentes; aberat quippe adulatio, gnaris omnibus laetam Tiberio Germanici mortem male dissimulari.

III. Tiberius atque Augusta publico abstinuere, inferius maiestate sua rati si palam lamentarentur, an ne omnium oculis vultum eorum scrutantibus falsi intellegerentur. Matrem Antoniam non apud

---

[1] munia *Ritter* : munera.   [2] M. *Panvinius* : c.

---

[1] The purple-striped mantle (*trabea*), worn on such occasions as the annual *travectio* (II. 83, note).

[2] Formerly Anxur, now Terracina; an old coastal town of Latium on the Appian Way, some 60 miles from Rome.

[3] Son of the Valerius Messala (Messalinus) of I. 8.

exhausted by long-drawn sorrow, were less demon-
strative than the more recent mourners by whom
they were met.

II. The Caesar had sent two cohorts of the Guard;
with further orders that the magistrates of Calabria,
Apulia, and Campania should render the last offices
to the memory of his son. And so his ashes were
borne on the shoulders of tribunes and centurions:
before him the standards went unadorned, the Axes
reversed; while, at every colony they passed, the
commons in black and the knights in official purple [1]
burned raiment, perfumes, and other of the customary funeral tributes, in proportion to the resources
of the district. Even the inhabitants of outlying
towns met the procession, devoted their victims and
altars to the departed spirit, and attested their grief
with tears and cries. Drusus came up to Tarracina,[2]
with Germanicus' brother Claudius and the children
who had been left in the capital. The consuls,
Marcus Valerius [3] and Marcus Aurelius [4] (who had
already begun their magistracy), the senate, and a
considerable part of the people, filled the road,
standing in scattered parties and weeping as they
pleased: for of adulation there was none, since all
men knew that Tiberius was with difficulty dissembling his joy at the death of Germanicus.

III. He and Augusta abstained from any appearance in public, either holding it below their majesty
to sorrow in the sight of men, or apprehending that,
if all eyes perused their looks, they might find
hypocrisy legible. I fail to discover, either in the

---

[4] Identified with the Cotta Messalinus of II. 32; a friend
of Ovid; brother of Valerius Messala, and therefore uncle of
his colleague.

auctores rerum, non diurna actorum scriptura, reperio ullo insigni officio functam, cum super Agrippinam et Drusum et Claudium ceteri quoque consanguinei nominatim perscripti sint, seu valetudine praepediebatur seu victus luctu animus magnitudinem mali perferre visu non toleravit. Facilius crediderim Tiberio et Augustae [1] qui domo non excedebant, cohibitam, ut par maeror et matris exemplo avia quoque et patruus attineri viderentur.

IV. Dies quo reliquiae tumulo Augusti inferebantur modo per silentium vastus, modo ploratibus inquies; plena urbis itinera, conlucentes per campum Martis faces. Illic miles cum armis, sine insignibus magistratus, populus per tribus concidisse rem publicam, nihil spei reliquum clamitabant, promptius apertiusque quam ut meminisse imperitantium crederes. Nihil tamen Tiberium magis penetravit quam studia hominum accensa in Agrippinam, cum decus patriae, solum Augusti sanguinem, unicum antiquitatis specimen appellarent versique ad caelum ac deos integram illi subolem ac superstitem iniquorum precarentur.

V. Fuere qui publici funeris pompam requirerent

[1] Augustae *Kritz, Doederlein* : Augusta.

---

[1] An official newspaper dating, like the *acta senatus*, from Caesar's consulship of 59 B.C. (Suet. *Jul.* 20). The style and matter may be fairly well conjectured from the amusing parody in Petr. *Sat.* 53, coupled with the disdainful verdict of Tacitus (XIII. 31 *init.*).

[2] The younger of the two daughters of Antony by Augustus' sister, Octavia; born about 36 B.C.; wife of Drusus, the brother of Tiberius; survived till the reign of Caligula.

historians or in the government journals,[1] that the
prince's mother, Antonia,[2] bore any striking part in
the ceremonies, although, in addition to Agrippina
and Drusus and Claudius, his other blood-relations
are recorded by name. Ill-health may have been
the obstacle; or a spirit broken with grief may have
shrunk from facing the visible evidence of its great
affliction; but I find it more credible that Tiberius
and Augusta, who did not quit the palace, kept her
there, in order to give the impression of a parity of
sorrow—of a grandmother and uncle detained at
home in loyalty to the example of a mother.

IV. The day on which the remains were consigned
to the mausoleum of Augustus[3] was alternately a
desolation of silence and a turmoil of laments. The
city-streets were full, the Campus Martius alight
with torches. There the soldier in harness,[4] the
magistrate lacking his insignia, the burgher in his
tribe, iterated the cry that " the commonwealth had
fallen and hope was dead " too freely and too openly
for it to be credible that they remembered their
governors. Nothing, however, sank deeper into
Tiberius' breast than the kindling of men's enthusiasm
for Agrippina—" the glory of her country, the last
scion of Augustus, the peerless pattern of ancient
virtue." So they styled her; and, turning to heaven
and the gods, prayed for the continuance of her
issue—" and might they survive their persecutors ! "

V. There were those who missed the pageantry

---

[3] See I. 8, with the note.
[4] On ordinary occasions the Guards in the capital wore the
toga, not the military *sagum*, and carried sword and spear, but
neither shield, helmet, nor breastplate. Other allusions to
the custom may be seen at XII. 36, XVI. 27, *Hist.* I. 38 and 80.

compararentque quae in Drusum patrem Germanici
honora et magnifica Augustus fecisset. Ipsum quippe
asperrimo hiemis Ticinum usque progressum neque
abscedentem a corpore simul urbem intravisse; cir-
cumfusas lecto Claudiorum Liviorumque [1] imagines;
defletum in foro, laudatum pro rostris, cuncta a
maioribus reperta aut quae posteri invenerint cumulata: at Germanico ne solitos quidem et cuicumque
nobili debitos honores contigisse. Sane corpus ob
longinquitatem itinerum externis terris quoquo modo
crematum; sed tanto plura decora mox tribui par
fuisse quanto prima fors negavisset. Non fratrem
nisi unius diei via, non patruum saltem porta tenus
obvium. Vbi illa veterum instituta, propositam [2]
toro effigiem, meditata ad memoriam virtutis carmina
et laudationes et lacrimas vel doloris imitamenta?

VI. Gnarum id Tiberio fuit; utque premeret vulgi
sermones, monuit edicto multos inlustrium Romanorum ob rem publicam obisse, neminem tam flagranti
desiderio celebratum. Idque et sibi et cunctis egregium, si modus adiceretur. Non enim eadem decora
principibus viris et imperatori populo quae modicis

---

[1] The modern Pavia.—Drusus died in Germany (9 B.C.),
and Tiberius posted on a celebrated journey of 200 miles,
tribus vehiculis, to his death-bed (D. Cass. LV. 2; Plin. *H.N.*
VII. 20; Sen. *Cons. ad Pol.* 34). The corpse was met by
Augustus at Ticinum and borne to Rome *per municipiorum
coloniarumque primores* (Suet. *Claud.* 1).

[2] *Insertus est* (Tiberius) *et Liviorum familiae, adoptato in
eam materno avo,* Suet. *Tib.* 3.

[3] The oration in the Forum was delivered by Tiberius
himself; Augustus spoke in the Flaminian Circus (D. Cass.
LV. 2).

of a state-funeral and compared the elaborate
tributes rendered by Augustus to Germanicus' father,
Drusus:—" In the bitterest of the winter, the
sovereign had gone in person as far as Ticinum,[1] and,
never stirring from the corpse, had entered the capital
along with it. The bier had been surrounded with
the family effigies of the Claudian and Livian[2] houses;
the dead had been mourned in the Forum,[3] eulogized
upon the Rostra; every distinction which our ancestors had discovered, or their posterity invented, was
showered upon him. But to Germanicus had fallen
not even the honours due to every and any noble!
Granted that the length of the journey was a reason
for cremating his body, no matter how, on foreign
soil, it would only have been justice that he should
have been accorded all the more distinctions later,
because chance had denied them at the outset. His
brother[4] had gone no more than one day's journey
to meet him; his uncle not even to the gate. Where
were those usages of the ancients—the image placed
at the head of the couch, the set poems to the
memory of departed virtue, the panegyrics, the tears,
the imitations (if no more) of sorrow? "

VI. All this Tiberius knew; and, to repress the
comments of the crowd, he reminded them in a
manifesto that " many illustrious Romans had died
for their country, but none had been honoured with
such a fervour of regret: a compliment highly valued
by himself and by all, if only moderation were
observed. For the same conduct was not becoming
to ordinary families or communities and to leaders

---

[4] Since the movements of Claudius were negligible, this must
refer to Germanicus' brother by adoption, Drusus. With
patruum (instead of *patrem*) Tacitus reverts from the adoptive
to the natural relationship.

domibus aut civitatibus. Convenisse recenti dolori
'uctum et ex maerore solacia; sed referendum iam
animum ad firmitudinem, ut quondam divus Iulius
amissa unica filia, ut divus Augustus ereptis nepoti-
bus abstruserint tristitiam. Nil opus vetustioribus
exemplis, quotiens populus Romanus cladis exercituum, interitum ducum, funditus amissas nobilis
familias constanter tulerit. Principes mortales, rem
publicam aeternam esse. Proin repeterent sollemnia,
et quia ludorum Megalesium spectaculum suberat,
etiam voluptates resumerent.

VII. Tum exuto iustitio reditum ad munia et
Drusus Illyricos ad exercitus profectus est, erectis
omnium animis spe petendae [1] e Pisone ultionis et
crebro questu, quod vagus interim per amoena Asiae
atque Achaiae adroganti et subdola mora scelerum
probationes subverteret. Nam vulgatum erat missam, ut dixi, a Cn. Sentio famosam veneficiis Martinam subita morte Brundisii extinctam, venenumque
nodo crinium ejus occultatum nec ulla in corpore
signa sumpti exitii reperta.

VIII. At Piso, praemisso in urbem filio datisque

---

[1] animis spe petendae *Freinsheim* : animis petendae.

---

[1] Daughter of Caesar and Cornelia: born 83–82 B.C.;
married to Pompey in 59 B.C.; died five years later. For the
circumstances of her death, see Plut. *Pomp.* 53; and for her
father's stoicism, Cic. *ad Q. fr.* III. 8, 3.

[2] Gaius and Lucius Caesar (see above I. 3).

[3] April 4–10. The Games, mainly theatrical, were in
honour of the Great Mother, Cybele: the well-known story
of their institution towards the end of the Hannibalian War
will be found in Liv. XXIX. 10–14.

[4] II. 74.

of the state and to an imperial people. Mourning and the solace of tears had suited the first throes of their affliction; but now they must recall their minds to fortitude, as once the deified Julius at the loss of his only daughter,[1] and the deified Augustus at the taking of his grandchildren,[2] had thrust aside their anguish. There was no need to show by earlier instances how often the Roman people had borne unshaken the slaughter of armies, the death of generals, the complete annihilation of historic houses. Statesmen were mortal, the state eternal. Let them return, therefore, to their usual occupations and— as the Megalesian Games[3] would soon be exhibited— resume even their pleasures!"

VII. The period of mourning now closed; men went back to their avocations, and Drusus left for the armies of Illyricum. All minds were elated at the prospect of calling Piso to account, and complaints were frequent that, during the interval, he should be roaming amid the landscapes of Asia and Achaia, destroying the evidences of his guilt by presumptuous and fraudulent delays. For news had spread that Martina—the notorious poisoner, despatched to Rome, as I have said,[4] by Gnaeus Sentius —had suddenly yielded up the ghost at Brundisium; that poison had been concealed in a knot of her hair; and that no indications of self-murder had been found on the body.[5]

VIII. Meanwhile, Piso, sending his son in advance

[5] The gossips reasoned that Piso had, beyond doubt, forced Martina to poison herself: but, if her drugs could kill without leaving a trace on the body, then obviously it was idle to debate, in the case of Germanicus, whether the corpse *praetulerit veneficii signa* (II. 73 *fin.*).

mandatis per quae principem molliret, ad Drusum
pergit, quem haud fratris interitu trucem quam re-
moto aemulo aequiorem sibi sperabat. Tiberius, quo
integrum iudicium ostentaret, exceptum comiter
iuvenem sueta erga filios familiarum nobilis liberalitate auget. Drusus Pisoni, si vera forent quae
iacerentur, praecipuum in dolore suum locum respondit; sed malle falsa et inania nec cuiquam mortem
Germanici exitiosam esse. Haec palam et vitato
omni secreto; neque dubitabantur praescripta ei
a Tiberio, cum incallidus alioqui et facilis iuventa
senilibus tum artibus uteretur.

IX. Piso, Delmatico mari tramisso relictisque apud
Anconam navibus, per Picenum ac mox Flaminiam
viam adsequitur legionem, quae e Pannonia in urbem, dein praesidio Africae ducebatur; eaque res
agitata rumoribus ut in agmine atque itinere crebro
se militibus ostentavisset. Ab Narnia, vitandae sus-
picionis an quia pavidis consilia in incerto sunt,
Nare ac mox Tiberi devectus auxit vulgi iras, quia
navem tumulo Caesarum adpulerat dieque et ripa
frequenti, magno clientium agmine ipse, feminarum

---

[1] The Adriatic.

[2] The great highway running from Rome to Ariminum
(Rimini). Piso strikes westward through northern Picenum,
joins the *via Flaminia* in Umbria, and follows it in company
with the legion as far as Narnia (the ancient Nequinum, now
Narni). Then, to avoid the appearance of tampering with the
soldiers, he descends the Nar (Nera) by boat until its confluence with the Tiber, and so proceeds by water to Rome.

[3] As an additional precaution against Tacfarinas. The
legion (*IX. Hispana*) was rather prematurely withdrawn by
Tiberius (IV. 23).

to the capital with a message designed to pacify the
emperor, bent his way to Drusus; whom he hoped
to find not so much angered at a brother's death as
reconciled to himself by the suppression of a rival.
To make a display of impartiality, Tiberius gave the
young envoy a civil reception, and treated him with
the liberality he was in the habit of showing to the
cadets of noble families. To the father, Drusus'
answer was that, " if the current imputations were
true, his own resentment must rank foremost of all;
but he preferred to believe they were false and
unfounded, and that Germanicus' death involved
the doom of no one." The reply was given in public,
all secrecy having been avoided; and no doubts
were felt that the phrasing was dictated by Tiberius,
when a youth, who had otherwise the simple and
pliant character of his years, resorted for the nonce
to the disingenuities of age.

IX. After crossing the sea of Dalmatia,[1] Piso left
his vessels at Ancona, and, travelling through
Picenum, then by the Flaminian Road,[2] came up
with a legion marching from Pannonia to Rome, to
join later on the garrison in Africa:[3] an incident
which led to much gossip and discussion as to the
manner in which he had kept showing himself to the
soldiers on the march and by the wayside. From
Narnia, either to avoid suspicion or because the
plans of a frightened man are apt to be inconsistent,
he sailed down the Nar, then down the Tiber, and
added to the exasperation of the populace by bringing his vessel to shore at the mausoleum of the
Caesars. It was a busy part of the day and of the
river-side; yet he with a marching column of
retainers, and Plancina with her escort of women,

comitatu Plancina et vultu alacres incessere. Fuit
inter inritamenta invidiae domus foro imminens festa
ornatu conviviumque et epulae et celebritate loci
nihil occultum.

X. Postera die Fulcinius Trio Pisonem apud consules postulavit. Contra Vitellius ac Veranius ceterique Germanicum comitati tendebant, nullas esse
partis Trioni; neque se accusatores, sed rerum indices
et testis mandata Germanici perlaturos. Ille dimissa
eius causae delatione, ut priorem vitam accusaret
obtinuit petitumque est a principe cognitionem
exciperet. Quod ne reus quidem abnuebat, studia
populi et patrum metuens; contra Tiberium sper-
nendis rumoribus validum et conscientiae matris
innexum esse; veraque aut in deterius credita iudice
ab uno facilius discerni, odium et invidiam apud
multos valere. Haud fallebat Tiberium moles cognitionis quaque ipse fama distraheretur. Igitur paucis
familiarium adhibitis minas accusantium et hinc
preces audit integramque causam ad senatum
remittit.

XI. Atque interim Drusus rediens Illyrico, quamquam patres censuissent ob receptum Maroboduum

---

[1] See II. 28 with the note.

[2] Before the senate.—The case might have gone: (a) before
a praetor and jury; (b) before the consuls and senate;
(c) before a private court of the emperor, assisted by an informal board of advisers. Actually, it comes before Tiberius,
who naturally decides to transfer the responsibility to the
senate.

[3] Since the " achievements " must have fallen in 18 A.D.,
either Tacitus has slipped or the words *priore aestate* are

proceeded beaming on their way. There were other irritants also; among them, festal decorations upon his mansion looming above the forum; guests and a dinner; and, in that crowded quarter, full publicity for everything.

X. Next day, Fulcinius Trio[1] applied to the consuls for authority to prosecute Piso.[2] He was opposed by Vitellius, Veranius, and the other members of Germanicus' suite: Trio, they argued, had no standing in the case; nor were they themselves acting as accusers, but as deponents and witnesses to the facts, carrying out the instructions of the prince. Waiving the indictment on this head, Trio secured the right of arraigning Piso's previous career, and the emperor was asked to take over the trial. To this even the defendant made no demur, as he distrusted the prepossessions of the people and senate; while Tiberius, he knew, had the strength of mind to despise scandal, and was involved in his mother's accession to the plot. Besides, truth was more easily distinguished from accepted calumny by one judge; where there were more, odium and malevolence carried weight. The difficulties of the inquiry, and the rumours busy with his own character, were not lost upon Tiberius. Therefore with a few intimate friends for assessors, he heard the threats of the accusers, the prayers of the accused; and remitted the case in its integrity to the senate.

XI. In the interval, Drusus returned from Illyricum. The Fathers had decreed him an ovation at his entry, in return for the submission of Maroboduus and his achievements of the preceding summer;[3] but

spurious, as they almost certainly are at the opening of chap. 20.

et res priore aestate [1] gestas ut ovans iniret, prolato
honore urbem intravit. Post quae reo L.[2] Arruntium, P. Vinicium,[3] Asinium Gallum, Aeserninum
Marcellum, Sex. Pompeium patronos petenti iisque
diversa excusantibus M'.[4] Lepidus et L. Piso et
Livineius Regulus adfuere, arrecta omni civitate,
quanta fides amicis Germanici, quae fiducia reo;
satin cohiberet ac premeret sensus suos Tiberius.
Haud [5] alias intentior populus plus sibi in principem
occultae vocis aut suspicacis silentii permisit.

XII. Die senatus Caesar orationem habuit medi-
tato temperamento. Patris sui legatum atque ami-
cum Pisonem fuisse adiutoremque Germanico datum
a se, auctore senatu, rebus apud Orientem adminis-
trandis. Illic contumacia et certaminibus asperasset
iuvenem exituque eius laetatus esset an scelere
extinxisset, integris animis diiudicandum. "Nam
si legatus officii terminos, obsequium erga imperatorem exuit eiusdemque morte et luctu meo laetatus
est, odero seponamque a domo mea et privatas ini-
micitias non vi [6] principis ulciscar; sin facinus in
cuiuscumque mortalium nece vindicandum dete-

[1] [priore aestate] *Nipperdey.*
[2] L. *N. Faber* : T.
[3] P. Vinicium *Borghesi* : fulnicium.
[4] M'. *Lipsius* : M.
[5] haud *Acidalius* : is haud.
[6] non vi *Muretus* (non *Becher*) : novi.

---

[1] As the governor (*legatus pro praetore Augusti*) of Hither
Spain : see chap. 13.

he postponed the honour and made his way into the
capital privately.

As his advocates the defendant now specified
Lucius Arruntius, Publius Vinicius, Asinius Gallus,
Marcellus Aeserninus and Sextus Pompeius. They
declined on various pretexts, and Manius Lepidus,
Lucius Piso, and Livineius Regulus came to his
support. The whole nation was eagerly specu-
lating upon the loyalty of Germanicus' friends, the
criminal's grounds for confidence, the chances that
Tiberius would be able to keep his sentiments
effectively under lock and key. Never had the
populace been more keenly on the alert: never had
it shown more freedom of whispered criticism and
suspicious silence towards the emperor.

XII. On the day the senate met, the Caesar spoke
with calculated moderation. " Piso," he said, " had
been his father's lieutenant[1] and friend; and he himself, at the instance of the senate, had assigned him
to Germanicus as his coadjutor in the administration of the East. Whether, in that position, he had
merely exasperated the youthful prince by perversity
and contentiousness, and then betrayed pleasure at
his death, or whether he had actually cut short his
days by crime, was a question they must determine
with open minds. For " (he proceeded) " if the
case is one of a subordinate who, after ignoring the
limits of his commission and the deference owed to
his superior, has exulted over that superior's death
and my own sorrow, I shall renounce his friendship,
banish him from my house, and redress my grievances
as a man without invoking my powers as a sovereign.
But if murder comes to light—and it would call for
vengeance, were the victim the meanest of mankind

537

gitur, vos vero et liberos Germanici et nos parentes
iustis solaciis adficite. Simulque illud reputate, tur-
bide et seditiose tractaverit exercitus Piso, quaesita
sint per ambitionem studia militum, armis repetita
provincia, an falsa haec in maius vulgaverint accusatores, quorum ego nimiis studiis iure suscenseo.
Nam quo pertinuit nudare corpus et contrectandum
vulgi oculis permittere differrique etiam per externos
tamquam veneno interceptus esset, si incerta adhuc
ista et scrutanda sunt? Defleo equidem filium
meum semperque deflebo; sed neque reum prohibeo
quo minus cuncta proferat, quibus innocentia eius
sublevari aut, si qua fuit iniquitas Germanici, coargui
possit, vosque oro ne, quia dolori meo causa conexa
est, obiecta crimina pro adprobatis accipiatis. Si
quos propinquus sanguis aut fides sua patronos dedit,
quantum quisque eloquentia et cura valet, iuvate
periclitantem; ad eundem laborem, eandem constantiam accusatores hortor. Id solum Germanico
super leges praestiterimus, quod in curia potius quam
in foro, apud senatum quam apud iudices de morte
eius anquiritur; cetera pari modestia tractentur.
Nemo Drusi lacrimas, nemo maestitiam meam spec-
tet, nec si qua in nos adversa finguntur."

---

[1] Tiberius, therefore, endorses the view of Piso (II. 79,
note).

—then do *you* see to it that proper requital is made to the children of Germanicus and to us, his parents. At the same time, consider the following points:—Did Piso's treatment of the armies make for disorder and sedition? Did he employ corrupt means to win the favour of the private soldiers? Did he levy war in order to reposssess himself of the province? Or are these charges falsehoods, published with enlargements by the accusers; at whose zealous indiscretions I myself feel some justifiable anger? For what was the object in stripping the corpse naked and exposing it to the degrading contact of the vulgar gaze? Or in diffusing the report— and among foreigners—that he fell a victim to poison, if that is an issue still uncertain and in need of scrutiny? True, I lament my son, and shall lament him always. But far from hampering the defendant in adducing every circumstance which may tend to relieve his innocence or to convict Germanicus of injustice (if injustice there was), I beseech you that, even though the case is bound up with a personal sorrow of my own, you will not therefore receive the assertion of guilt as a proof of guilt. If kinship or a sense of loyalty has made some of you his advocates, then let each, with all the eloquence and devotion he can command, aid him in his hour of danger. To the accusers I commend a similar industry, a similar constancy. The only extra-legal concession we shall be found to have made to Germanicus is this, that the inquiry into his death is being held not in the Forum but in the Curia, not before a bench of judges but the senate.[1] Let the rest of the proceedings show the like restraint: let none regard the tears of Drusus, none my own sadness, nor yet any fictions invented to our discredit."

XIII. Exim biduum criminibus obiciendis statuitur utque sex dierum spatio interiecto reus per triduum defenderetur. Tum Fulcinius vetera et inania orditur, ambitiose avareque habitam Hispaniam; quod neque convictum noxae reo si recentia purgaret, neque defensum absolutioni erat si teneretur maioribus flagitiis. Post quem[1] Servaeus et Veranius et Vitellius consimili studio et multa eloquentia Vitellius obiecere odio Germanici et rerum novarum studio Pisonem vulgus militum per licentiam et sociorum iniurias eo usque conrupisse ut parens legionum a deterrimis appellaretur; contra in optimum quemque, maxime in comites et amicos Germanici saevisse; postremo ipsum devotionibus et veneno peremisse; sacra hinc et immolationes nefandas ipsius atque Plancinae, petitam armis rem publicam, utque reus agi posset, acie victum.

XIV. Defensio in ceteris trepidavit; nam neque ambitionem militarem neque provinciam pessimo cuique obnoxiam, ne contumelias quidem adversum imperatorem infitiari poterat: solum veneni crimen visus est diluisse, quod ne accusatores quidem satis firmabant, in convivio Germanici, cum super eum

---

[1] post quem *Rhenanus* (post quae *Baiter*) : postq.

---

[1] The speech had been read by the elder Pliny (*H.N.* XI. 187).
[2] At Cos (II. 75 *fin.*).
[3] At Celenderis (II. 80).

XIII. It was then resolved to allow two days for the formulation of the charges: after an interval of six days, the case for the defence would occupy another three. Fulcinius opened with an old and futile tale of intrigue and cupidity during Piso's administration of Spain. The allegations, if established, could do the defendant no harm, should he dispel the more recent charge: if they were rebutted, there was still no acquittal, if he was found guilty of the graver delinquencies. Serraeus, Veranius, and Vitellius followed—with equal fervour; and Vitellius with considerable eloquence.[1] "Through his hatred of Germanicus and his zeal for anarchy," so ran the indictment, "Piso had, by relaxing discipline and permitting the maltreatment of the provincials, so far corrupted the common soldiers that among the vilest of them he was known as the Father of the Legions. On the other hand, he had been ruthless to the best men, especially the companions and friends of Germanicus, and at last, with the help of poison and the black arts, had destroyed the prince himself. Then had come the blasphemous rites and sacrifices[2] of Plancina and himself, an armed assault on the commonwealth, and—in order that he might be put on his trial—defeat upon a stricken field."[3]

XIV. On all counts but one the defence wavered. There was no denying that he had tampered with the soldiery, that he had abandoned the province to the mercies of every villain, that he had even insulted the commander-in-chief. The single charge which he seemed to have dissipated was that of poisoning. It was, indeed, none too plausibly sustained by the accusers, who argued that, at a dinner given by Germanicus, Piso (who was seated above

Piso discumberet, infectos manibus eius cibos arguentes. Quippe absurdum videbatur inter aliena servitia et tot adstantium visu, ipso Germanico coram, id ausum; offerebatque familiam reus et ministros in tormenta flagitabat. Sed iudices per diversa implacabiles erant, Caesar ob bellum provinciae inlatum, senatus numquam satis credito sine fraude Germanicum interisse. . . .[1] scripsissent expostulantes, quod haud minus Tiberius quam Piso abnuere. Simul populi ante curiam voces audiebantur: non temperaturos manibus si patrum sententias evasisset. Effigiesque Pisonis traxerant in Gemonias ac divellebant, ni iussu principis protectae repositaeque forent. Igitur inditus lecticae et a tribuno praetoriae cohortis deductus est, vario rumore custos saluti an mortis exactor sequeretur.

XV. Eadem Plancinae invidia, maior gratia; eoque ambiguum habebatur quantum Caesari in eam liceret. Atque ipsa, donec mediae Pisoni spes, sociam se

[1] . . . *Ferretti.*

---

[1] As a member of the senate he was necessarily one of the judges.

[2] The gap in the text—evidently considerable—must have contained a mention of the adjournment (*comperendinatio*) of the trial, followed by a second hearing (*redintegrata accusatio*, chap. 15). The correspondence, demanded by the accusers and refused by the defendant and the emperor alike, can hardly have been other than letters from Piso and Plancina to Tiberius and Augusta.

him) introduced the dose into his food. Certainly, it seemed folly to assume that he could have ventured the act among strange servants, under the eyes of so many bystanders, and in the presence of the victim himself: also, he offered his own slaves for torture, and insisted on its application to the attendants at the meal. For one reason or other, however, the judges were inexorable: the Caesar,[1] because war had been levied on a province; the senate, because it could never quite believe that Germanicus had perished without foul play. . . .[2] A demand for the correspondence was rejected as firmly by Tiberius as by Piso. At the same time, shouts were heard: it was the people at the senate-doors, crying that, if he escaped the suffrages of the Fathers, they would take the law into their own hands. They had, in fact, dragged his effigies to the Gemonian Stairs,[3] and were engaged in dismembering them, when they were rescued and replaced at the imperial command. He was therefore put in a litter and accompanied home by an officer of one of the praetorian cohorts; while rumour debated whether the escort was there for the preservation of his life or the enforcement of his death.

XV. Plancina, equally hated, had more than equal influence; so that it was considered doubtful how far the sovereign would be allowed to proceed against her. She herself, so long as hope remained for Piso,

---

[3] A flight of stairs leading from the Capitol to the Forum Romanum, on which the bodies of criminals garotted in the *carcer* were exposed before being consigned to the Tiber: cf. V. 9, VI. 25, *Hist.* III. 74 and 85. For the fury of the mob venting itself on statues, see Mayor's collection of instances at Juv. X. 58.

cuiuscumque fortunae et si ita ferret comitem exitii
promittebat; ut secretis Augustae precibus veniam
obtinuit, paulatim segregari a marito, dividere defensionem coepit. Quod reus postquam sibi exitiabile
intelligit, an adhuc experiretur dubitans, hortantibus
filiis durat mentem senatumque rursum ingreditur;
redintegratamque accusationem, infensas patrum
voces, adversa et saeva cuncta perpessus, nullo magis
exterritus est quam quod Tiberium sine miseratione,
sine ira, obstinatum clausumque vidit, ne quo adfectu
perrumperetur. Relatus domum, tamquam defensionem in posterum meditaretur, pauca conscribit
obsignatque et liberto tradit; tum solita curando
corpori exequitur. Dein multam post noctem,
egressa cubiculo uxore, operiri foris iussit; et coepta
luce perfosso iugulo, iacente humi gladio, repertus
est.

XVI. Audire me memini ex senioribus visum saepius inter manus Pisonis libellum quem ipse non
vulgaverit; sed amicos eius dictitavisse litteras
Tiberii et mandata in Germanicum contineri, ac
destinatum promere apud patres principemque arguere, ni elusus a Seiano per vana promissa foret;
nec illum sponte exstinctum, verum immisso per-
cussore. Quorum neutrum adseveraverim; neque

protested that she would share his fortune for good
or ill, or, if the need arose, would meet destruction
in his company. But once her pardon had been
procured by the private intercessions of Livia, she
began step by step to dissociate herself from her
husband and to treat her own defence as a distinct
issue. It was a fatal symptom, and the defendant
knew it. He was doubtful whether to make another
effort or not; but, as his sons pressed him, he
hardened his heart and entered the senate once
more. He faced the repetition of the charges, the
hostile cries of the Fathers, the fierce opposition
evident in every quarter; but nothing daunted him
more than the sight of Tiberius, pitiless and anger-
less, barred and bolted against the ingress of any
human emotion. After being carried home, he wrote
a little, apparently notes for his defence the next
day; sealed the paper, and handed it to a freedman.
Then he gave the usual attention to his person;
and finally, late at night, when his wife had left the
bedroom, he ordered the door to be closed, and was
found at daybreak with his throat cut and a sword
lying on the floor.

XVI. I remember hearing my elders speak of a
document seen more than once in Piso's hands. The
purport he himself never disclosed, but his friends
always asserted that it contained a letter from
Tiberius with his instructions in reference to Germanicus; and that, if he had not been tricked by
the empty promises of Sejanus, he was resolved to
produce it before the senate and to put the emperor
upon his defence. His death, they believed, was
not self-inflicted: an assassin had been let loose to
do the work. I should hesitate to endorse either

tamen occulere debui narratum ab iis qui nostram ad iuventam duraverunt. Caesar flexo in maestitiam ore suam invidiam tali morte quaesitam apud senatum . . .[1] crebrisque interrogationibus exquirit qualem Piso diem supremum noctemque exegisset. Atque illo pleraque sapienter, quaedam inconsultius respondente, recitat codicillos a Pisone in hunc ferme modum compositos: " Conspiratione inimicorum et invidia falsi criminis oppressus, quatenus veritati et innocentiae meae nusquam locus est, deos inmortalis testor vixisse me, Caesar, cum fide adversum te neque alia in matrem tuam pietate; vosque oro liberis meis consulatis, ex quibus Cn. Piso qualicumque fortunae meae non est adiunctus, cum omne hoc tempus in urbe egerit, M. Piso repetere Suriam dehortatus est. Atque utinam ego potius filio iuveni quam ille patri seni cessisset. Eo impensius precor ne meae pravitatis poenas innoxius luat. Per quinque et quadraginta annorum obsequium, per collegium consulatus, quondam divo Augusto parenti tuo probatus et tibi amicus nec quicquam post haec rogaturus salutem infelicis filii rogo." De Plancina nihil addidit.

XVII. Post quae Tiberius adulescentem crimine civilis belli purgavit, patris quippe iussa nec potuisse

[1] . . . *Boxhorn.*

---

[1] The smallest possible supplement is Weissenborn's: *apud senatum* ⟨conquestus M. Pisonem vocari iubet⟩ *crebrisque e.q.s.* As it is natural to suppose, however, that both this lacuna and the not inconsiderable one above (chap. 14) are due to the mutilation of the same leaf in the archetype, the loss is probably greater.

[2] His public life was therefore virtually co-extensive with the principate.

[3] He was consul with Tiberius in 7 B.C.

theory: at the same time. it was my duty not to suppress a version given by contemporaries who were still living in my early years.

With his lineaments composed to melancholy, the Caesar expressed his regret to the senate that Piso should have chosen a form of death reflecting upon his sovereign . . .[1] and cross-examined him at length on the manner in which his father had spent his last day and night. Though there were one or two indiscretions, the answers were in general adroit enough, and he now read a note drawn up by Piso in nearly the following words:—" Broken by a confederacy of my enemies and the hatred inspired by their lying accusation, since the world has no room for my truth and innocence, I declare before Heaven, Caesar, that I have lived your loyal subject and your mother's no less dutiful servant. I beg you both to protect the interests of my children. Gnaeus has no connexion with my affairs, good or ill, since he spent the whole period in the capital; while Marcus advised me against returning to Syria. And I can only wish that I had given way to my youthful son, rather than he to his aged father! I pray, therefore, with added earnestness that the punishment of my perversity may not fall on his guiltless head. By my five-and-forty years[2] of obedience, by the consulate we held in common,[3] as the man who once earned the confidence of your father, the deified Augustus, as the friend who will never ask favour more, I appeal for the life of my unfortunate son." Of Plancina not a word.

XVII. Tiberius followed by absolving the younger Piso from the charge of civil war,—for " the orders came from a father, and a son could not have dis-

filium detrectare, simul nobilitatem domus, etiam ipsius quoquo modo meriti gravem casum miseratus. Pro Plancina cum pudore et flagitio disseruit, matris preces obtendens, in quam optimi cuiusque secreti questus magis ardescebant. Id ergo fas aviae interfectricem nepotis adspicere, adloqui, eripere senatui. Quod pro omnibus civibus leges obtineant, uni Germanico non contigisse. Vitellii et Veranii voce defletum Caesarem, ab imperatore et Augusta defensam Plancinam. Proinde venena et artes tam feliciter expertas verteret in Agrippinam, in liberos eius, egregiamque aviam ac patruum sanguine miserrimae domus exsatiaret. Biduum super hac imagine cognitionis absumptum, urgente Tiberio liberos Pisonis matrem uti tuerentur. Et cum accusatores ac testes certatim perorarent respondente nullo, miseratio quam invidia augebatur. Primus sententiam rogatus Aurelius Cotta consul (nam referente Caesare magistratus eo etiam munere fungebantur) nomen Pisonis radendum[1] fastis censuit, partem bonorum publicandam, pars ut Cn. Pisoni filio concederetur isque praenomen mutaret; Piso exuta dignitate et

---

[1] radendum] eradendum *Baiter* (*cf.* IV. 42 *fin.*).

---

[1] Had the emperor not been presiding, the *relatio* would normally have been made by a consul. In that case, the question would have been put in the first instance to the consuls-elect for the following year—the rule being that it was not put to the high magistrates present, though they possessed the right of speaking at any stage of the proceedings.

[2] He appears to have taken that of " Lucius," and to be rightly identified with L. Calpurnius Piso, consul in 27 A.D. (VI. 62). Stock examples of the penalty are the prohibition of the name " Marcus " among the Manlii (Liv. VI. 20) and that

obeyed,"—and at the same time expressed his sorrow
for a noble house and the tragic fate of its representative, whatever his merits or demerits. In
offering a shamefaced and ignominious apology for
Plancina, he pleaded the entreaties of his mother;
who in private was being more and more hotly
criticized by every person of decency:—" So it was
allowable in a grandmother to admit her grandson's
murderess to sight and speech, and to rescue her
from the senate! The redress which the laws
guaranteed to all citizens had been denied to Germanicus alone. The voice of Vitellius and Veranius
had bewailed the Caesar: the emperor and Augusta
had defended Plancina. It remained to turn those
drugs and arts, now tested with such happy results,
against Agrippina and her children, and so to satiate
this admirable grandmother and uncle with the
blood of the whole calamitous house!" Two days
were expended on this phantom of a trial, with
Tiberius pressing Piso's sons to defend their mother;
and as the accusers and witnesses delivered their
competing invectives, without a voice to answer,
pity rather than anger began to deepen. The question was put in the first instance to Aurelius Cotta,
the consul: for, if the reference came from the
sovereign, even the magistrates went through the
process of registering their opinion.[1] Cotta proposed
that the name of Piso should be erased from the
records, one half of his property confiscated, and the
other made over to his son Gnaeus, who should
change his first name;[2] that Marcus Piso should

of "Lucius" among the Claudii (Suet. *Tib.* 1): a more recent
case was the ban on Mark Antony's praenomen (Plut. *Cic.* fin.;
D. Cass. LI. 19).

THE ANNALS OF TACITUS

accepto quinquagies sestertio in decem annos relegaretur, concessa Plancinae incolumitate ob preces Augustae.

XVIII. Multa ex ea sententia mitigata sunt a principe : ne nomen Pisonis fastis eximeretur, quando M. Antonii qui bellum patriae fecisset, Iulli Antonii qui domum Augusti violasset, manerent. Et M. Pisonem ignominiae exemit concessitque ei paterna bona, satis firmus, ut saepe memoravi, adversum pecuniam et tum pudore absolutae Plancinae placabilior. Atque idem, cum Valerius Messalinus signum aureum in aede Martis Vltoris, Caecina Severus aram ultionis statuendam censuissent, prohibuit, ob externas ea victorias sacrari dictitans, domestica mala tristitia operienda. Addiderat Messalinus Tiberio et Augustae et Antoniae et Agrippinae Drusoque ob vindictam Germanici gratis agendas omiseratque Claudii mentionem. Et Messalinum quidem L. Asprenas senatu coram percontatus est an prudens praeterisset; ac tum demum nomen Claudii adscriptum est. Mihi quanto plura recentium seu veterum revolvo, tanto magis ludibria rerum mortalium cunctis in negotiis obversantur. Quippe fama, spe, veneratione potius omnes destinabantur imperio quam quem futurum principem fortuna in occulto tenebat.

---

[1] The milder form of banishment, the *relegatus*—unlike the *exul*—retaining his civic rights and property.

[2] In 44 B.C. and 32 B.C. His name was actually cancelled from the public monuments, but was restored, presumably in the later years of Augustus.

[3] I. 10.   [4] I. 75; II. 48.

[5] Probably not this year's consul, but his father (see chap. 2, note).

[6] The Caecina who commanded the Lower Army of Germany (I. 31, etc.).

be stripped of his senatorial rank, and relegated[1] for a period of ten years with a gratuity of five million sesterces: Plancina, in view of the empress's intercession, might be granted immunity.

XVIII. Much in these suggestions was mitigated by the emperor. He would not have Piso's name cancelled from the records, when the names of Mark Antony, who had levied war on his fatherland,[2] and of Iullus Antonius,[3] who had dishonoured the hearth of Augustus, still remained. He exempted Marcus Piso from official degradation, and granted him his patrimony: for, as I have often said,[4] he was firm enough against pecuniary temptations, and in the present case his shame at the acquittal of Plancina made him exceptionally lenient. So, again, when Valerius Messalinus[5] proposed to erect a golden statue in the temple of Mars the Avenger, and Caecina Severus[6] an altar of Vengeance, he vetoed the scheme, remarking that these memorials were consecrated after victories abroad; domestic calamities called for sorrow and concealment. Messalinus had added that Tiberius, Augusta, Antonia, Agrippina, and Drusus ought to be officially thanked for their services in avenging Germanicus: Claudius he had neglected to mention. Indeed, it was only when Lucius Asprenas[7] demanded point-blank in the senate if the omission was deliberate that the name was appended. For myself, the more I reflect on events recent or remote, the more am I haunted by the sense of a mockery in human affairs. For by repute, by expectancy, and by veneration, all men were sooner marked out for sovereignty than that future emperor whom destiny was holding in the background.

[7] I. 53.

XIX. Paucis post diebus Caesar auctor senatui fuit Vitellio atque Veranio et Servaeo sacerdotia tribuendi, Fulcinio suffragium ad honores pollicitus monuit ne facundiam violentia praecipitaret. Is finis fuit in ulciscenda Germanici morte, non modo apud illos homines qui tum agebant, etiam secutis temporibus vario rumore iactata. Adeo maxima quaeque ambigua sunt, dum alii quoquo modo audita pro compertis habent, alii vera in contrarium vertunt et gliscit utrumque posteritate. At Drusus urbe egressus repetendis auspiciis mox ovans introiit. Paucosque post dies Vipsania mater eius excessit, una omnium Agrippae liberorum miti obitu : nam ceteros manifestum ferro vel creditum est veneno aut fame extinctos.

XX. Eodem anno Tacfarinas, quem priore aestate[1] pulsum a Camillo memoravi, bellum in Africa renovat, vagis primum populationibus et ob pernicitatem inultis, dein vicos exscindere, trahere gravis praedas ; prostremo haud procul Pagyda flumine cohortem Romanam circumsedit. Praeerat castello Decrius impiger manu, exercitus militia et illam obsidionem flagitii ratus. Is, cohortatus milites, ut copiam

1 [priore aestate] *Nipperdey.*

---

1 The *imperium* was necessary to his ovation (see chap. 2), but had technically lapsed with his entry into Rome.
2 Daughter of Agrippa by his first wife Pomponia. For the fate of his children by Augustus' daughter Julia, see I. 3 (Gaius and Lucius Caesar); *ib.* 6 (Agrippa Postumus); IV. 71 (Julia); VI. 25 (Agrippina). The issue of his second marriage with Marcella (Suet. *Aug.* 63) are apparently ignored.
3 As in chap. 11, the words *priore aestate* are probably interpolated : at all events, Camillus' defeat of Tacfarinas took place in 17 A.D. (see II. 52).

XIX. A few days later, the Caesar recommended the senate to confer priesthoods on Vitellius, Veranius, and Servaeus. To Fulcinius he promised his support, should he become a candidate for preferment, but warned him not to let impetuosity become the downfall of eloquence.

This closed the punitive measures demanded by Germanicus' death: an affair which, not only to the generation which witnessed it, but in the succeeding years, was a battle-ground of opposing rumours. So true it is that the great event is an obscure event: one school admits all hearsay evidence, whatever its character, as indisputable; another perverts the truth into its contrary; and, in each case, posterity magnifies the error.

Drusus, who had left the capital, in order to regularize his command,[1] entered it shortly afterwards with an ovation. A few days later, his mother Vipsania[2] died—the only one of all Agrippa's children whose end was peace. The rest perished, part, it is known, by the sword; part, it was believed, by poison or starvation.

XX. In the same year, Tacfarinas—whose defeat by Camillus in the previous summer[3] I have already mentioned—resumed hostilities in Africa: at first, by desultory raids, too speedy for reprisals; then, by the destruction of villages and by plunder on a larger scale. Finally, he invested a Roman cohort not far from the river Pagyda.[4] The position was commanded by Decrius, who, quick in action and experienced in war, regarded the siege as a disgrace. After an address to the men, he drew up his lines in

---

[4] The stream is otherwise unknown.

pugnae in aperto faceret [1] aciem pro castris instruit. Primoque impetu pulsa cohorte promptus inter tela occursat fugientibus, increpat signiferos quod inconditis aut desertoribus miles Romanus terga daret; simul excepta [2] vulnera et, quamquam transfosso oculo, adversum os in hostem intendit neque proelium omisit donec desertus suis caderet.

XXI. Quae postquam L. Apronio (nam Camillo successerat) comperta, magis dedecore suorum quam gloria hostis anxius, raro ea tempestate et e vetere memoria facinore decumum quemque ignominiosae cohortis sorte ductos fusti necat. Tantumque severitate profectum ut vexillum veteranorum, non amplius quingenti numero, easdem Tacfarinatis copias praesidium cui Thala nomen adgressas fuderint. Quo proelio, Rufus Helvius gregarius miles servati civis decus rettulit donatusque est ab Apronio torquibus et hasta. Caesar addidit civicam coronam, quod non eam quoque Apronius iure proconsulis tribuisset questus magis quam offensus. Sed Tacfa-

---

[1] faceret *Probst*: facerent.   [2] excepta] exceptat *Held*.

---

[1] I. 56; 72; II. 32; III. 64; IV. 13; 22; 73; VI. 30; XI. 19.   The numismatic evidence fixes his proconsulate of Africa for the years 18–20 A.D.

[2] Sporadic cases of "decimation" crop up till a much later period. The practice dated traditionally from Appius Claudius (Liv. II. 59 *fin.*).

[3] In Tunis.

[4] The *torques* and "headless spear" (*hasta pura*) were usual military decorations: the "civic crown" of oak-leaves was, on the other hand, the most coveted and most sparingly awarded of all such distinctions. It was, in fact, a standing emblem of the imperial house, though declined by Tiberius (Suet. *Tib.* 26): The indispensable conditions were that the recipient should be a Roman citizen; that he should have saved the life of a Roman on the battle-field; that he should

front of the encampment so as to offer battle in the
open. As the cohort broke at the first onset, he
darted eagerly among the missiles, to intercept the
fugitives, cursing the standard-bearers who could
see Roman soldiers turn their backs to a horde of
undrilled men or deserters. At the same time, he
turned his wounded breast and his face—with one
eye pierced—to confront the enemy, and continued
to fight until he dropped forsaken by his troop.

XXI. When the news reached Lucius Apronius[1]
(the successor of Camillus), perturbed more by the
disgrace of his own troops than by the success of
the enemy, he resorted to a measure rare in that
period and reminiscent of an older world, drawing by
lot and flogging to death every tenth man in the dishonoured cohort.[2] And so effective was the severity
that, when the same forces of Tacfarinas assaulted a
stronghold named Thala,[3] they were routed by a
company of veterans not more than five hundred in
number. During the engagement a private soldier,
Helvius Rufus, earned the distinction of saving a
Roman life, and was presented by Apronius with the
collar and spear: the civic crown was added by the
emperor; who regretted, more in sorrow than in
anger, that the proconsul had not exercised his power
to award this further honour.[4] As the Numidians

have slain an enemy in so doing; and that he should not have
fallen back from the ground on which his exploit was performed
(Plin. *H.N.* XVI. 4; Gell. V. 6). Since Africa was unique
among senatorial provinces in that the proconsul had a legion
under him, Apronius would have been within his rights in
conferring the crown: otherwise, its bestowal would have
rested with the emperor (see XV. 12). From a still extant
inscription we gather that Helvius took the cognomen
"Civica," rose to be leading-centurion, and presented baths to
his fellow-townsmen of Varia (Vicovaro, near Tivoli).

rinas perculsis Numidis et obsidia aspernantibus
spargit bellum, ubi instaretur cedens ac rursum in
terga remeans. Et dum ea ratio barbaro fuit, inritum fessumque Romanum impune ludificabatur;
postquam deflexit ad maritimos locos, inligatus [1]
praeda stativis castris adhaerebat, missu patris Apronius Caesianus cum equite et cohortibus auxiliariis,
quis velocissimos legionum addiderat, prosperam
adversum Numidas pugnam facit pellitque in deserta.

XXII. At Romae Lepida, cui super Aemiliorum
decus L. Sulla et Cn. Pompeius proavi erant, defertur
simulavisse partum ex P. Quirinio divite atque orbo.
Adiciebantur adulteria, venena quaesitumque per
Chaldaeos in domum Caesaris, defendente ream
Manio Lepido fratre. Quirinius post dictum repu-
dium adhuc infensus quamvis infami ac nocenti
miserationem addiderat. Haud facile quis dispexerit
illa in cognitione mentem principis: adeo vertit ac
miscuit irae et clementiae signa. Deprecatus primo
senatum ne maiestatis crimina tractarentur, mox
M. Servilium e consularibus aliosque testis inlexit
ad proferenda quae velut reticeri [2] voluerat. Idem-
que servos Lepidae, cum militari custodia haberentur,
transtulit ad consules neque per tormenta interrogari

---

[1] inligatus] inligatusque *Walther.*
[2] reticeri *Acidalius* (reticere *Beroaldus*) : reicere.

---

[1] See the obituary notice in chap. 48.
[2] A treasonable offence : for other allusions to it see XII.
22 and 52; XVI. 14 and 30; and above II. 27.
[3] The malignity lay in the fact that the divorce had taken
place years ago.

had both lost heart and disdained sieges, Tacfarinas
fell back on guerilla warfare, yielding ground when
the enemy became pressing, and then returning to
harass the rear. Indeed, so long as the African
adhered to this strategy, he befooled with impunity
the ineffective and footsore Roman. But when he
deviated to the coastal district and encumbered himself with a train of booty which kept him near a
fixed encampment, Apronius Caesianus, marching at
his father's order with the cavalry and auxiliary
cohorts reinforced by the most mobile of the legionaries, fought a successful engagement and chased
the Numidians into the desert.

XXII. At Rome, in the meantime, Lepida, who,
over and above the distinction of the Aemilian family,
owned Sulla and Pompey for great-grandsires, was
accused of feigning to be a mother by Publius
Quirinius,[1] a rich man and childless. There were
complementary charges of adulteries, of poisonings,
and of inquiries made through the astrologers with
reference to the Caesarian house.[2] The defence was
in the hands of her brother, Manius Lepidus. Despite
her infamy and her guilt, Quirinius, by persisting
in his malignity after divorcing her,[3] had gained her
a measure of sympathy. It is not easy to penetrate
the emperor's sentiments during this trial: so adroitly
did he invert and confuse the symptoms of anger
and of mercy. He began by requesting the senate
not to deal with the charges of treason; then he
lured the former consul, Marcus Servilius, with a
number of other witnesses, into stating the very
facts he had apparently wished to have suppressed.
Lepida's slaves, again, were being held in military
custody; he transferred them to the consuls, and

557

passus est de iis quae ad domum suam pertinerent. Exemit etiam Drusum, consulem designatum, dicendae primo loco sententiae ; quod alii civile rebantur, ne ceteris adsentiendi necessitas fieret quidam ad saevitiam trahebant : neque enim cessurum nisi damnandi officio.

XXIII. Lepida ludorum diebus qui cognitionem intervenerant theatrum cum claris feminis ingressa, lamentatione flebili maiores suos ciens ipsumque Pompeium, cuius ea monimenta et adstantes imagines visebantur, tantum misericordiae permovit ut effusi in lacrimas saeva et detestanda Quirinio clamitarent, cuius senectae atque orbitati et obscurissimae domui destinata quondam uxor L. Caesari ac divo Augusto nurus dederetur. Dein tormentis servorum patefacta sunt flagitia itumque in sententiam Rubelli Blandi a quo aqua atque igni arcebatur. Huic Drusus adsensit quamquam alii mitius censuissent. Mox Scauro, qui filiam ex ea genuerat, datum ne bona publicarentur. Tum demum aperuit Tiberius compertum sibi etiam ex P. Quirinii servis veneno eum a Lepida petitum.

XXIV. Inlustrium domuum adversa (etenim haud

---

¹ See the note on chap. 17.

² They argued that Drusus was only the mouthpiece of his father : if, then, measures were taken to prevent his speaking first, the only possible inference was that Tiberius was bent upon a conviction and desired to escape the odium of proposing it through his son.

³ Probably the *Ludi Romani magni* (Sept. 4–19).

⁴ The great Theatre of Pompey in the Campus Martius; completed in 55 B.C.

⁵ See VI. 27.

⁶ She had presumably married Scaurus (*insignis nobilitate et orandis causis, vita probrosus,* VI. 29) after her divorce from

would not allow them to be questioned under torture upon the issues concerning his own family. Similarly, he exempted Drusus, who was consul designate, from speaking first to the question.[1] By some this was read as a concession relieving the rest of the members from the need of assenting: others took it to mark a sinister purpose on the ground that he would have ceded nothing save the duty of condemning.[2]

XXIII. In the course of the Games,[3] which had interrupted the trial, Lepida entered the theatre with a number of women of rank; and there, weeping, wailing, invoking her ancestors and Pompey himself, whom that edifice[4] commemorated, whose statues were standing before their eyes, she excited so much sympathy that the crowd burst into tears, with a fierce and ominous outcry against Quirinius, to whose doting years, barren bed, and petty family they were betraying a woman once destined for the bride of Lucius Caesar and the daughter-in-law of the deified Augustus. Then, with the torture of her slaves, came the revelation of her crimes; and the motion of Rubellius Blandus,[5] who pressed for her formal outlawry, was carried. Drusus sided with him, though others had proposed more lenient measures. Later, as a concession to Scaurus, who had a son by her, it was decided not to confiscate her property.[6] And now at last Tiberius disclosed that he had ascertained from Quirinius' own slaves that Lepida had attempted their master's life by poison.

XXIV. For the disasters of the great houses (for

Quirinius. Confiscation usually followed upon the "interdiction from fire and water"—exile, in the rigour of the term.

multum distanti tempore Calpurnii Pisonem, Aemilii Lepidam amiserant) solacio adfecit D. Silanus Iuniae familiae redditus. Casum eius paucis repetam. Vt valida divo Augusto in rem publicam fortuna, ita domi improspera fuit ob impudicitiam filiae ac neptis quas urbe depulit, adulterosque earum morte aut fuga punivit. Nam, culpam inter viros ac feminas vulgatam gravi nomine laesarum religionum ac violatae maiestatis appellando, clementiam maiorum suasque ipse leges egrediebatur. Sed aliorum exitus, simul cetera illius aetatis memorabo, si effectis in quae tetendi plures ad curas vitam produxero. D. Silanus in nepti Augusti adulter, quamquam non ultra foret saevitum quam ut amicitia Caesaris prohiberetur, exilium sibi demonstrari intellexit, nec nisi Tiberio imperitante deprecari senatum ac principem ausus est M. Silani fratris potentia, qui per insignem nobilitatem et eloquentiam praecellebat. Sed Tiberius gratis agenti Silano patribus coram respondit se quoque laetari quod frater eius e peregrinatione longinqua revertisset, idque iure licitum quia non senatus consulto, non lege pulsus foret; sibi tamen adversus eum integras parentis sui offensiones neque reditu Silani dissoluta quae Augustus

---

[1] For the elder Julia see I. 53, note: for her daughter, IV. 71.

[2] Death in the case of Iullus Antonius (I. 10); banishment in that of Silanus and Gracchus (I. 53).

[3] The lex *Iulia de adulteriis* (II. 50).

at no great distance of time Piso had been lost to
the Calpurnii and Lepida to the Aemilii) there was
some consolation in the return of Decimus Silanus
to the Junian family. His mischance deserves a
brief retrospect. Fortune, staunch to the deified
Augustus in his public life, was less propitious to
him at home, owing to the incontinence of his
daughter and granddaughter,[1] whom he expelled
from the capital while penalizing their adulterers
by death or banishment.[2] For designating as he did
the besetting sin of both the sexes by the harsh
appellations of sacrilege and treason, he overstepped
both the mild penalties of an earlier day and those
of his own laws.[3] But the fate of other delinquents
I shall record together with the general history of
that age, should I achieve the task I have set before
me and be spared for yet other themes. Decimus
Silanus, the lawless lover of Augustus' granddaughter,
though subjected to no harsher penalty than forfeiture of the imperial friendship, realized that the
implication was exile; nor was it until the accession
of Tiberius that he ventured to appeal to the senate
and sovereign through his influential brother, Marcus
Silanus,[4] whose high descent and eloquence gave him
a commanding position. Even so, while Silanus was
expressing his gratitude before the senate, Tiberius
replied that " he also was glad that his brother had
returned from his distant pilgrimage: he had an
indefeasible right to do so, as he had been exiled
neither by resolution of the senate nor by form of
law. At the same time, he retained his father's
objections to him intact; and the repatriation of
Silanus had not cancelled the wishes of Augustus."

---

[4] The future father-in-law of Caligula (VI. 20, note).

voluisset. Fuit posthac in urbe neque honores adeptus est.

XXV. Relatum dein[1] de moderanda Papia Poppaea, quam senior Augustus post Iulias rogationes incitandis caelibum poenis et augendo aerario sanxerat. Nec ideo coniugia et educationes liberum frequentabantur praevalida orbitate; ceterum multitudo periclitantium gliscebat, cum omnis domus delatorum interpretationibus subverteretur, utque antehac flagitiis, ita tunc legibus laborabatur. Ea res admonet ut de principiis iuris et quibus modis ad hanc multitudinem infinitam ac varietatem legum perventum sit altius disseram.

XXVI. Vetustissimi mortalium, nulla adhuc mala libidine, sine probro, scelere eoque sine poena aut coercitionibus agebant. Neque praemiis opus erat cum honesta suopte ingenio peterentur; et ubi nihil contra morem cuperent, nihil per metum vetabantur. At postquam exui aequalitas et pro modestia ac pudore ambitio et vis incedebat, provenere dominationes multosque apud populos aeternum mansere. Quidam, statim aut postquam regum pertaesum, leges maluerunt. Hae primo rudibus hominum animis simplices erant; maximeque fama celebravit Cretensium, quas Minos, Spartanorum, quas Lycurgus, ac mox Atheniensibus quaesitiores

----

[1] dein *Wölfflin* : deinde.

----

[1] Passed in 9 A.D. during the term of office of the *consules suffecti* M. Papius Mutilus and Q. Poppaeus Secundus—both childless and indeed unmarried (D. Cass. LVI. 10).

[2] The *lex Iulia de maritandis ordinibus* of 18 B.C., with regard to which the prayers of Horace were not answered (*Carm. saec.* 17–20).

[3] Torrentius on Suet. *Aug.* 34 cites Tertullian's description (*Apol.* 4):—*vanissimas Papias leges.*

Accordingly he resided for the future in Rome, but without holding office.

XXV. A motion was then introduced to qualify the terms of the *Lex Papia Poppaea*.[1] This law, complementary to the Julian rogations,[2] had been passed by Augustus in his later years, in order to sharpen the penalties of celibacy and to increase the resources of the exchequer. It failed, however, to make marriage and the family popular[3]—childlessness remained the vogue. On the other hand, there was an ever-increasing multitude of persons liable to prosecution, since every household was threatened with subversion by the arts of the informers; and where the country once suffered from its vices, it was now in peril from its laws. This circumstance suggests that I should discuss more deeply the origin of legislation and the processes which have resulted in the countless and complex statutes of to-day.

XXVI. Primeval man, untouched as yet by criminal passion, lived his life without reproach or guilt, and, consequently, without penalty or coercion: rewards were needless when good was sought instinctively, and he who coveted nothing unsanctioned by custom had to be withheld from nothing by a threat. But when equality began to be outworn, and ambition and violence gained ground in place of modesty and self-effacement, there came a crop of despotisms, which with many nations has remained perennial. A few communities, either from the outset or after a surfeit of kings, decided for government by laws. The earliest specimens were the artless creations of simple minds, the most famous being those drawn up in Crete by Minos, in Sparta by Lycurgus, and in Athens by Solon—the last already more recondite

iam et plures Solo perscripsit. Nobis Romulus ut
libitum imperitaverat: dein Numa religionibus et
divino iure populum devinxit, repertaque quaedam
a Tullo et Anco. Sed praecipuus Servius Tullius
sanctor legum fuit quis etiam reges obtemperarent.

XXVII. Pulso Tarquinio adversum patrum factiones multa populus paravit tuendae libertatis et
firmandae concordiae, creatique decemviri et accitis
quae usquam egregia compositae duodecim tabulae,
finis aequi iuris. Nam secutae leges etsi aliquando
in maleficos ex delicto, saepius tamen dissensione
ordinum et apiscendi inlicitos honores aut pellendi
claros viros aliaque ob prava per vim latae sunt.
Hinc Gracchi et Saturnini turbatores plebis nec
minor largitor nomine senatus Drusus; corrupti spe
aut inlusi per intercessionem socii. Ac ne bello
quidem Italico, mox civili omissum quin multa et

---

¹ The principal dates for this and the next chapter are the
following :—451 B.C. Patrician *decemviri legibus scribundis*,
superseding all magistrates, publish ten "Tables" (*fons omnis
publici privatique iuris*, Liv. III. 34). 450 B.C. Two tables
(*iniquissimae* according to Cicero) added by second body of
decemvirs, half plebeian in composition.—133 B.C. Tribunate,
agrarian law, and death of Tiberius Gracchus. 123 B.C.
Tribunate and legislation of C. Gracchus. 122 B.C. Second
tribunate and further legislation of C. Gracchus. The senate
employ M. Livius Drusus to outbid him for popular favour.
121 B.C. First *senatus consultum ultimum*. Massacre of
Gracchus and his adherents.—100 B.C. Sixth consulate of
Marius. Violent demagogic agitation of L. Apuleius Saturninus
and C. Servilius Glaucia. Second *senatus consultum ultimum* :
Marius suppresses Saturninus and Glaucia.—91 B.C. Far-
reaching and popular proposals of the tribune M. Livius
Drusus (son of the one mentioned above). His assassination
and failure to enfranchise the Italian allies precipitate the
Social War (91–88 B.C.). 88–82 B.C. Sulla and Marius.
Dictatorship of Sulla (82 B.C.). 81 B.C. "Cornelian Laws" of

and more numerous. In our own case, after the absolute sway of Romulus, Numa imposed on his people the bonds of religion and a code dictated by Heaven. Other discoveries were due to Tullus and Ancus. But, foremost of all, Servius Tullius became an ordainer of laws, to which kings themselves were to owe obedience.

XXVII.[1] Upon the expulsion of Tarquin, the commons, to check senatorial factions, framed a large number of regulations for the protection of their liberties or the establishment of concord ; the Decemvirs came into being ; and, by incorporating the best features of the foreign constitutions, the Twelve Tables were assembled, the final instance of equitable legislation. For succeeding laws, though occasionally suggested by a crime and aimed at the criminal, were more often carried by brute force in consequence of class-dissension—to open the way to an unconceded office, to banish a patriot, or to consummate some other perverted end. Hence our demagogues : our Gracchi and Saturnini, and on the other side a Drusus bidding as high in the senate's name ; while the provincials were alternately bribed with hopes and cheated with tribunician vetoes. Not even the Italian war, soon replaced by the Civil

Sulla. (The tribunes are left with little more than a restricted right of veto.) 79 B.C. Abdication of Sulla, who dies next year. 78 B.C. M. Aemilius Lepidus begins the attempt to overthrow the Sullan constitution. 70 B.C. The powers of the tribunate restored by Pompey and Crassus.—52 B.C. Chaos at Rome (Clodius, Milo, etc.). Pompey appointed consul for third time (without a colleague). 49 B.C. Outbreak of war between Caesar and Pompey. 48 B.C. Defeat and death of Pompey. 48–28 B.C. 'Continua per viginti annos discordia.' 27 B.C. Seventh consulate of Octavian, who receives the name Augustus. Formal establishment of the principate.

diversa sciscerentur, donec L. Sulla dictator abolitis vel conversis prioribus, cum plura addidisset, otium eius rei haud in longum paravit, statim turbidis Lepidi rogationibus neque multo post tribunis reddita licentia quoquo vellent populum agitandi. Iamque non modo in commune, sed in singulos homines latae quaestiones, et corruptissima re publica plurimae leges.

XXVIII. Tum Cn. Pompeius, tertium consul corrigendis moribus delectus et gravior remediis quam delicta erant suarumque legum auctor idem ac subversor, quae armis tuebatur armis amisit. Exim continua per viginti annos discordia, non mos, non ius; deterrima quaeque impune ac multa honesta exitio fuere. Sexto demum consulatu Caesar Augustus, potentiae securus, quae triumviratu iusserat abolevit deditque iura quis pace et principe uteremur. Acriora ex eo vincla, inditi custodes et lege Papia Poppaea praemiis inducti ut, si a privilegiis parentum cessaretur, velut parens omnium populus vacantia teneret. Sed altius penetrabant urbemque et Italiam et quod usquam civium corripuerant, multorumque excisi status. Et terror omnibus intentabatur, ni Tiberius statuendo remedio quinque consularium, quinque e praetoriis, totidem e cetero

---

[1] At this time more than a quarter of the property falling to the exchequer as a result of their activities (Suet. *Ner.* 10).

war, could interrupt the flow of self-contradictory legislation; until Sulla, in his dictatorship, by abolishing or inverting the older statutes and adding more of his own, brought the process to a standstill. But not for long. The calm was immediately broken by the Rogations of Lepidus, and shortly afterwards the tribunes were repossessed of their licence to disturb the nation as they pleased. And now bills began to pass, not only of national but of purely individual application, and when the state was most corrupt, laws were most abundant.

XXVIII. Then came Pompey's third consulate. But this chosen reformer of society, operating with remedies more disastrous than the abuses, this maker and breaker of his own enactments, lost by the sword what he was holding by the sword. There followed twenty crowded years of discord, during which law and custom ceased to exist: villainy was immune, decency not rarely a sentence of death. At last, in his sixth consulate, Augustus Caesar, feeling his power secure, cancelled the behests of his triumvirate, and presented us with laws to serve our needs in peace and under a prince. Thenceforward the fetters were tightened: sentries were set over us and, under the Papia-Poppaean law, lured on by rewards;[1] so that, if a man shirked the privileges of paternity, the state, as universal parent, might step into the vacant inheritance. But they pressed their activities too far: the capital, Italy, every corner of the Roman world, had suffered from their attacks, and the positions of many had been wholly ruined. Indeed, a reign of terror was threatened, when Tiberius, for the fixing of a remedy, chose by lot five former consuls, five former praetors, and an

senatu sorte duxisset, apud quos exsoluti plerique legis nexus modicum in praesens levamentum fuere.

XXIX. Per idem tempus Neronem e liberis Germanici iam ingressum iuventam commendavit patribus, utque munere capessendi vigintiviratus solveretur et quinquennio maturius quam per leges quaesturam peteret, non sine inrisu audientium, postulavit. Praetendebat sibi atque fratri decreta eadem, petente Augusto. Sed neque tum fuisse dubitaverim qui eius modi preces occulti inluderent; ac tamen initia fastigii Caesaribus erant magisque in oculis vetus mos et privignis cum vitrico levior necessitudo quam avo adversum nepotem. Additur pontificatus et, quo primum die forum ingressus est, congiarium plebi admodum laetae quod Germanici stirpem iam puberem aspiciebat. Auctum dehinc gaudium nup¹iis Neronis et Iuliae Drusi filiae. Vtque haec secundo rumore, ita adversis animis acceptum quod filio Claudii socer Seianus destinaretur. Polluisse nobilitatem familiae videbatur suspectumque iam nimiae spei Seianum ultro ¹ extulisse.

XXX. Fine anni concessere vita insignes viri

---

¹ ultro *Alciatus* : ultra.

---

¹ Still in 20 A.D.　　² He was probably born in 6 A.D.

³ A collective term for the four inferior magistracies (comprising in all 20 members), one of which must normally be held before the quaesto ship.

⁴ The twenty-fifth year.

⁵ It is shown by inscriptions that the pontificate was held, not by Nero, but by his brother Drusus.

⁶ Only an informal arrangement for the future, since Seianus' daughter must have been little more than an infant: see V. 9. The actual betrothal took place later, but was

equal number of ordinary senators: a body which, by untying many of the legal knots, gave for the time a measure of relief.

XXIX. About the same date,[1] he commended Germanicus' son Nero, who had now entered on man's estate,[2] to the good offices of the Fathers, and taxed the gravity of his audience by asking them to relieve him from the duty of serving on the Vigintivirate[3] and to allow his candidature for the quaestorship five years before the legal age.[4] His plea was that the same concessions had been voted to himself and his brother at the instance of Augustus. But even then, I should imagine, there must have been some who secretly scoffed at these princely petitions; and yet those were the early days of the Caesarian domination, early custom was more in the eyes of men, and the relationship of a stepfather and his stepsons is a slighter thing than that of a grandfather and a grandchild. Nero was granted a pontificate[5] in addition, and on the day of his first entry into the Forum, a largesse was distributed to the lower orders, who were overjoyed to see a scion of Germanicus arrived already at maturity. Their delight was soon increased by his marriage with Drusus' daughter, Julia; but the satisfaction expressed at these events was balanced by dislike for the choice of Sejanus as the future father-in-law of the son of Claudius.[6] The impression was that the emperor had sullied the dignity of his house, while needlessly exalting Sejanus, who even then was suspected of more than legitimate ambitions.

XXX. At the close of the year, two famous Romans

followed within a few days by the death of Claudius' son (Suet. *Claud.* 27).

L. Volusius et Sallustius Crispus. Volusio vetus familia neque tamen praeturam egressa : ipse consulatum intulit, censoria etiam potestate legendis equitum decuriis functus, opumque quis domus illa immensum viguit primus adcumulator. Crispum equestri ortum loco C. Sallustius, rerum Romanarum florentissimus auctor, sororis nepotem in nomen adscivit. Atque ille, quamquam prompto ad capessendos honores aditu, Maecenatem aemulatus, sine dignitate senatoria, multos triumphalium consulariumque potentia anteiit, diversus a veterum instituto per cultum et munditias copiaque et affluentia luxu propior. Suberat tamen vigor animi ingentibus negotiis par, eo acrior quo somnum et inertiam magis ostentabat. Igitur incolumi Maecenate proximus, mox praecipuus, cui secreta imperatorum inniterentur, et interficiendi Postumi Agrippae conscius, aetate provecta speciem magis in amicitia principis quam vim tenuit. Idque et Maecenati acciderat, fato potentiae raro sempiternae, an satias capit aut illos cum omnia tribuerunt aut hos cum iam nihil reliquum est quod cupiant.

XXXI. Sequitur Tiberi quartus, Drusi secundus consulatus, patris atque filii collegio insignis. Nam

---

[1] L. Volusius Saturninus, consul (*suffectus*) 12 B.C.; proconsul of Africa 6 B.C.; legate of Syria 5 A.D.

[2] His duty (probably as one of a commission of three appointed by Augustus) was to draw up and arrange the list of knights competent to serve as jurors.

[3] See Hor. *Carm.* II. 2.

[4] See I. 6.

gave up the ghost, Lucius Volusius [1] and Sallustius Crispus. Volusius belonged to an old family which, none the less, had never advanced beyond the praetorship. He himself enriched it with the consulate, and, besides discharging the duties of the censorship in the selection of the equestrian decuries,[2] became the first accumulator of the wealth which raised the family fortunes to such unmeasured heights. Crispus,[3] a knight by extraction, was the grandson of a sister of Gaius Sallustius, the brilliant Roman historian, who adopted him into his family and name. Thus for him the avenue to the great offices lay clear; but, choosing to emulate Maecenas, without holding senatorial rank he outstripped in influence many who had won a triumph or the consulate; while by his elegancy and refinements he was sundered from the old Roman school, and in the ample and generous scale of his establishment approached extravagance. Yet under it all lay a mental energy, equal to gigantic tasks, and all the more active from the display he made of somnolence and apathy. Hence, next to Maecenas, while Maecenas lived, and later next to none, he it was who sustained the burden of the secrets of emperors. He was privy to the killing of Agrippa Postumus;[4] but with advancing years he retained more the semblance than the reality of his sovereign's friendship. The same lot had fallen to Maecenas also,— whether influence, rarely perpetual, dies a natural death, or there comes a satiety, sometimes to the monarch who has no more to give, sometimes to the favourite with no more to crave.

XXXI. Now came the fourth consulate of Tiberius and the second of Drusus—a noticeable association A.V.C. 774 = A.U. 21

triennio[1] ante Germanici cum Tiberio idem honor
neque patruo laetus neque natura tam conexus
fuerat. Eius anni principio Tiberius quasi firmandae
valetudini in Campaniam concessit, longam et con-
tinuam absentiam paulatim meditans, sive ut amoto
patre Drusus munia consulatus solus impleret. Ac
forte parva res magnum ad certamen progressa prae-
buit iuveni materiem apiscendi favoris. Domitius
Corbulo, praetura functus, de L. Sulla nobili iuvene
questus est apud senatum quod sibi inter spectacula
gladiatorum loco non decessisset. Pro Corbulone
aetas, patrius mos, studia seniorum erant; contra
Mamercus Scaurus et L. Arruntius aliique Sullae
propinqui nitebantur. Certabantque orationibus et
memorabantur exempla maiorum qui iuventutis
inreverentiam gravibus decretis notavissent, donec
Drusus apta temperandis animis disseruit; et satis-
factum Corbuloni per Mamercum qui patruus simul
ac vitricus Sullae et oratorum ea aetate uberrimus
erat. Idem Corbulo, plurima per Italiam itinera
fraude mancipum et incuria magistratuum inter-
rupta et impervia clamitando, executionem eius
negotii libens suscepit; quod haud perinde publice
usui habitum quam exitiosum multis quorum in

---

[1] triennio *Nipperdey* : biennio.

---

[1] The association was ominous as well as remarkable. For
the list of Tiberius' colleagues in the consulate runs :—
Quintilius Varus (13 B.C.), Cn. Piso (7 B.C.), Germanicus
(18 A.D.), Drusus (21 A.D.), Sejanus (31 A.D.). See D. Cass.
LVII. 20.

[2] He must have been an older man than the celebrated
general of Claudius and Nero—possibly his father, though
the question is not free from difficulties.

[3] The magistrates in question were the *curatores viarum*,
a body reorganized, if not created, by Augustus.

of father and son.[1] For, three years earlier, the same
official partnership of Germanicus and Tiberius had
been neither grateful to the uncle nor knit so closely
by the ties of blood.

In the beginning of the year, Tiberius, with the
professed object of restoring his health, withdrew to
Campania; either to train himself step by step for
a protracted and continuous absence, or to cause
Drusus, through the retirement of his father, to fulfil
his consular duties alone. It chanced, indeed, that
a trivial affair which developed into a serious conflict
supplied the prince with the material of popularity.
Domitius Corbulo,[2] who had held the praetorship,
complained to the senate that the young aristocrat,
Lucius Sulla, had not given up his seat to him at a
gladiatorial exhibition. On Corbulo's side were his
age, national custom, and the partialities of the
older men: Mamercus Scaurus, Lucius Arruntius,
and other of Sulla's connections were active in the
opposite cause. There was a sharp exchange of
speeches, with references to the example of our
ancestors, who had censured youthful irreverence in
grave decrees; until Drusus made a speech calculated
to ease the tension, and Corbulo was accorded satisfaction by Mamercus, who was at once the uncle of
Sulla, his stepfather, and the most fluent orator of
that generation.

It was Corbulo, again, who raised the outcry that
numbers of roads throughout Italy were broken and
impracticable owing to the rascality of the contractors and the remissness of the magistrates.[3] He
readily undertook to carry out the prosecution; but
the results were considered to be less a benefit to
the community than a catastrophe to the many whose

pecuniam atque famam damnationibus et hasta saeviebat.

XXXII. Neque multo post, missis ad senatum litteris Tiberius motam rursum Africam incursu Tacfarinatis docuit iudicioque patrum deligendum pro consule gnarum militiae, corpore validum et bello suffecturum. Quod initium Sex. Pompeius agitandi adversus Marcum Lepidum odii nanctus, ut socordem, inopem et maioribus suis dedecorum eoque etiam Asiae sorte depellendum incusavit, adverso senatu qui Lepidum mitem magis quam ignavum, paternas ei angustias et nobilitatem sine probro actam honori quam ignominiae habendam ducebat. Igitur missus in Asiam et de Africa decretum ut Caesar legeret cui mandanda foret.

XXXIII. Inter quae Severus Caecina censuit ne quem magistratum cui provincia obvenisset uxor comitaretur, multum ante repetito concordem sibi coniugem et sex partus enixam, seque quae in publicum statueret domi servavisse, cohibita intra Italiam, quamquam ipse pluris per provincias quadraginta stipendia explevisset. Haud enim frustra

---

[1] The roads, it would seem, were put in order at the expense of the curators and contractors. If they were unable to meet the resultant demands for money, their property was auctioned. For the subsequent history of the obscure episode see D. Cass. LIX. 15 and LX. 17.

[2] The two great governorships still within the bestowal of the senate were those of Asia and Africa, which were normally assigned to the two doyens among the ex-consuls, the particular province to be held by each being determined by lot. But since, in this case, the destination of Africa is to be settled not by lot, but *iudicio patrum*, there remains only Asia; which should automatically fall to Lepidus as the senior ex-consul

property and repute suffered from the ruthless con-
demnations and forced sales.[1]

XXXII. Not long afterwards, a letter from Tiberius
apprized the senate that Africa had been disturbed
once more by an inroad of Tacfarinas, and that the
Fathers were to use their judgment in choosing a
proconsul, with military experience, and of a physique
adequate to the campaign. Sextus Pompeius improved the occasion by airing his hatred of Marcus
Lepidus, whom he attacked as a spiritless and
poverty-stricken degenerate, who should consequently be debarred from the Asiatic province as
well.[2] The senate disapproved: Lepidus, it held,
was gentle rather than cowardly; and, as his patrimony was embarrassed, an honoured name carried
without reproach was a title of honour, not of disgrace. To Asia accordingly he went; and, as for
Africa, it was decided to leave the emperor to choose
a man for the post.

XXXIII. In the course of the debate, Caecina
Severus moved that no magistrate, who had been
allotted a province, should be accompanied by his
wife. He explained beforehand at some length that
" he had a consort after his own heart, who had borne
him six children: yet he had conformed in private
to the rule he was proposing for the public; and,
although he had served his forty campaigns [3] in one
province or other, she had always been kept within
the boundaries of Italy. There was point in the old

(he had held office in 6 A.D. with L. Arruntius, and for one
reason or other had already been passed over five times).

[3] Either this is a round number for forty-one or *quadragesimum* (I. 64) for thirty-ninth: for the campaign of 16 A.D.
was now to be reckoned.

placitum olim ne feminae in socios aut gentis externas traherentur: inesse mulierum comitatui quae
pacem luxu, bellum formidine morentur et Romanum agmen ad similitudinem barbari incessus
convertant. Non imbecillum tantum et imparem
laboribus sexum, sed, si licentia adsit, saevum, am-
bitiosum, potestatis avidum; incedere inter milites,
habere ad manum centuriones; praesedisse nuper
feminam exercitio cohortium, decursu legionum.
Cogitarent ipsi quotiens repetundarum aliqui arguerentur plura uxoribus obiectari; his statim adhae-
rescere deterrimum quemque provincialium, ab his
negotia suscipi, transigi; duorum egressus coli, duo
esse praetoria, pervicacibus magis et impotentibus
mulierum iussis quae, Oppiis quondam aliisque legibus constrictae, nunc vinclis exsolutis, domos, fora,
iam et exercitus regerent.

XXXIV. Paucorum haec adsensu audita: plures
obturbabant neque relatum de negotio neque Caecinam dignum tantae rei censorem. Mox Valerius
Messalinus, cui parens Messala ineratque imago
paternae facundiae, respondit multa duritiae veterum in¹ melius et laetius mutata; neque enim, ut

---

¹ in melius *Muretus*: melius.

---

¹ The allusion, of course, is to Plancina (II. 55): later,
Caecina might have found a more scandalous example in the
wife of Calvisius Sabinus (*Hist.* I. 48).

² The statement would seem to be exaggerated: for a
similar view, compare Juv. VIII. 128–30.

³ The *lex Oppia*, directed mainly against extravagance in
dress, was passed as a measure of economy in the Hannibalian
War, but was rescinded twenty years later (see Liv. XXXIV.
init.).

⁴ I. 8, III. 18. His father was the famous orator, soldier,
littérateur and politician, M. Valerius Messala Corvinus, the

regulation which prohibited the dragging of women to the provinces or foreign countries: in a retinue of ladies there were elements apt, by luxury or by timidity, to retard the business of peace or war and to transmute a Roman march into something resembling an Eastern procession. Weakness and a lack of endurance were not the only failings of the sex: give them scope, and they turned hard, intriguing, ambitious. They paraded among the soldiers; they had the centurions at beck and call. Recently a woman had presided at the exercises of the cohorts and the manœuvres of the legions.[1]   Let his audience reflect that, whenever a magistrate was on his trial for malversation, the majority of the charges were levelled against his wife.[2]   It was to the wife that the basest of the provincials at once attached themselves; it was the wife who took in hand and transacted business. There were two potentates to salute in the streets; two government-houses; and the more headstrong and autocratic orders came from the women, who, once held in curb by the Oppian[3] and other laws, had now cast their chains and ruled supreme in the home, the courts, and by now the army itself."

XXXIV. A few members listened to the speech with approval: most interrupted with protests that neither was there a motion on the subject nor was Caecina a competent censor in a question of such importance. He was presently answered by Valerius Messalinus,[4] a son of Messala, in whom there resided some echo of his father's eloquence :—" Much of the old-world harshness had been improved and softened;

friend of Tibullus, of Horace, and, in his old age, of Tiberius, who took him as the model of his Latinity (Suet. *Tib.* 70).

olim, obsideri urbem bellis aut provincias hostilis
esse; et pauca feminarum necessitatibus concedi
quae ne coniugum quidem penatis, adeo socios non
onerent; cetera promisca cum marito nec ullum in
eo pacis impedimentum. Bella plane accinctis
obeunda; sed revertentibus post laborem quod
honestius quam uxorium levamentum? At quasdam
in ambitionem aut avaritiam prolapsas. Quid?
ipsorum magistratuum nonne plerosque variis libidinibus obnoxios? Non tamen ideo neminem in provinciam mitti. Corruptos saepe pravitatibus uxorum
maritos; num ergo omnis caelibes integros? Placuisse quondam Oppias leges, sic temporibus rei
publicae postulantibus; remissum aliquid postea et
mitigatum, quia expedierit. Frustra nostram ignaviam alia ad vocabula transferri: nam viri in eo
culpam si femina modum excedat. Porro ob unius
aut alterius imbecillum animum male eripi maritis
consortia rerum secundarum adversarumque. Simul
sexum natura invalidum deseri et exponi suo luxu,
cupidinibus alienis. Vix praesenti custodia manere
inlaesa coniugia: quid fore si per pluris annos in
modum discidii oblitterentur? Sic obviam irent iis
quae alibi peccarentur ut flagitiorum urbis meminissent. Addidit pauca Drusus de matrimonio suo;

for Rome was no longer environed with wars, nor
were the provinces hostile. A few allowances were
now made to the needs of women; but not such as to
embarrass even the establishment of their consorts,
far less our allies: everything else the wife shared
with her husband, and in peace the arrangement
created no difficulties. Certainly, he who set about
a war must gird up his loins; but, when he returned
after his labour, what consolations more legitimate
than those of his helpmeet?—But a few women had
lapsed into intrigue or avarice.—Well, were not too
many of the magistrates themselves vulnerable to
temptation in more shapes than one? Yet governors
still went out to governorships!—Husbands had often
been corrupted by the depravity of their wives.—
And was every single man, then, incorruptible? The
Oppian laws in an earlier day were sanctioned because
the circumstances of the commonwealth so demanded:
later remissions and mitigations were due to ex-
pediency. It was vain to label our own inertness
with another title: if the woman broke bounds, the
fault lay with the husband. Moreover, it was unjust
that, through the weakness of one or two, married
men in general should be torn from their partners in
weal and woe, while at the same time a sex frail by
nature was left alone, exposed to its own voluptuous-
ness and the appetites of others. Hardly by surveillance on the spot could the marriage-tie be kept
undamaged: what would be the case if, for a term
of years, it were dissolved as completely as by
divorce? While they were taking steps to meet
abuses elsewhere, it would be well to remember the
scandals of the capital!" Drusus added a few
sentences upon his own married life:—" Princes not

nam principibus adeunda saepius longinqua imperii. Quoties divum Augustum in Occidentem atque Orientem meavisse comite Livia! Se quoque in Illyricum profectum et, si ita conducat, alias ad gentis iturum, haud semper aequo animo si ab uxore carissima et tot communium liberorum parente divelleretur. Sic Caecinae sententia elusa est.

XXXV. Proximo[1] senatus die, Tiberius per litteras, castigatis oblique patribus quod cuncta curarum ad principem reicerent, M'.[2] Lepidum et Iunium Blaesum nominavit ex quis pro consule Africae legeretur. Tum audita amborum verba, intentius excusante se Lepido, cum valetudinem corporis, aetatem liberum, nubilem filiam obtenderet, intellegereturque etiam quod silebat, avunculum esse Seiani Blaesum atque eo praevalidum. Respondit Blaesus specie recusantis sed neque eadem adseveratione et consensu adulantium adiutus est.[3]

XXXVI. Exim promptum quod multorum intimis questibus tegebatur. Incedebat enim deterrimo cuique licentia impune probra et invidiam in bonos excitandi arrepta imagine Caesaris; libertique etiam ac servi, patrono vel domino cum voces, cum manus

[1] elusa est. Proximo *Freinsheim* : elusa. Et proximi.
[2] M'. *Lipsius* : M.
[3] adiutus *J. F. Gronovius* : haud iustus (auditus *margo*).

---

[1] It is doubtful, however, whether he would have allowed the precedent as valid : see Suet. *Aug.* 24.
[2] For the right of asylum attached to a statue of the emperor, compare the advice given to Agrippina (IV. 67 *fin.*). According to Suetonius—whatever the statement may be worth—matters went so far that it became a capital offence, *circa Augusti simulacrum servum cecidisse, vestimenta mutasse*

infrequently had to visit the remote parts of the empire. How often had the deified Augustus travelled to west and east with Livia for his companion![1] He had himself made an excursion to Illyricum; and, if there was a purpose to serve, he was prepared to go to other countries—but not always without a pang, if he were severed from the well-beloved wife who was the mother of their many common children." Caecina's motion was thus evaded.

XXXV. At the next meeting of the senate there was a letter from Tiberius; in which, after an indirect stricture upon the Fathers, " who transferred the whole of their responsibilities to the sovereign," he nominated Manius Lepidus and Junius Blaesus, either of whom was to be chosen for the proconsulate of Africa. The two were then heard. Lepidus, excusing himself with particular earnestness, pleaded the state of his health, the age of his children, and his now marriageable daughter; while it was also understood, though not said, that Blaesus was Sejanus' uncle, and therefore too powerful a competitor. The answer of Blaesus was in form a refusal; but it was a refusal less uncompromising, and unanimous flattery assisted him to change his mind.

XXXVI. Now came the disclosure of a practice whispered in the private complaints of many. There was a growing tendency of the rabble to cast insult and odium on citizens of repute, and to evade the penalty by grasping some object portraying the Caesar.[2] The freedmen and slaves, even, were genuinely feared by the patron or the owner against

(cf. D. Cass. LXVII. 12), *nummo vel anulo effigiem impressam* (cf. Philost. 18 Ol.) *latrinae aut lupanari intulisse* (*1 ib.* 58).

intentarent, ultro metuebantur. Igitur C. Cestius senator disseruit principes quidem instar deorum esse, sed neque a diis nisi iustas supplicum preces audiri neque quemquam in Capitolium aliave urbis templa perfugere ut eo subsidio ad flagitia utatur. Abolitas leges et funditus versas, ubi in foro, in limine curiae ab Annia Rufilla, quam fraudis sub iudice damnavisset, probra sibi et minae intendantur, neque ipse audeat ius experiri ob effigiem imperatoris oppositam. Haud dissimilia alii et quidam atrociora circumstrepebant precabanturque Drusum daret ultionis exemplum, donec accitam convictamque attineri publica custodia iussit.

XXXVII. Et Considius Aequus et Caelius Cursor equites Romani, quod fictis maiestatis criminibus Magium Caecilianum praetorem petivissent, auctore principe ac decreto senatus puniti. Vtrumque in laudem Drusi trahebatur: ab eo in urbe inter coetus et sermones hominum obversante secreta patris mitigari. Neque luxus in iuvene adeo displicebat: huc potius intenderet, diem aedificationibus,[1] noctem conviviis traheret, quam solus et nullis voluptatibus avocatus maestam vigilantiam et malas curas exerceret.

XXXVIII. Non enim Tiberius, non accusatores fatiscebant. Et Ancharius Priscus Caesium Cordum

---

[1] aedificationibus] editionibus *Lipsius*; *alii alia.*

---

[1] The mania for building was such as amply to justify the manuscript reading here. Literary references to it are very numerous : see for instance, Hor. *Carm.* II. 15; *Sat.* II. 3, 306; below, chap. 53. To a request for a loan an all-sufficient answer was " aedifico " (Mart. IX. 46).

whom they lifted their voices or their hands. Hence a speech of the senator, Gaius Cestius :—" Princes, he admitted, were equivalent to deities; but god-head itself listened only to the just petitions of the suppliant, and no man fled to the Capitol or other sanctuary of the city to make it a refuge subserving his crimes. The laws had been abolished—overturned from the foundations—when Annia Rufilla, whom he had proved guilty of fraud in a court of justice, could insult and threaten him in the Forum, upon the threshold of the curia; while he himself dared not try the legal remedy because of the portrait of the sovereign with which she confronted him." Similar and, in some cases, more serious experiences, were described by a din of voices around him ; and appeals to Drusus, to set the example of punishment, lasted till he gave orders for her to be summoned and imprisoned, after conviction, in the public cells.

XXXVII. In addition, Considius Aequus and Caelius Cursor, Roman knights, who had laid ficti-tious charges of treason against the praetor Magius Caecilianus, were at the emperor's instance punished by decree of the senate. Both incidents were laid to the credit of Drusus; for it was believed that, mov-ing in the capital among the gatherings and con-versations of his fellow-men, he had a softening influence on the inscrutable designs of his father. In view of his youth, not even his laxities were too unpopular : better he should follow the bent he did— play the architect[1] by day, the epicure by night—than live in solitude, deaf to the voice of pleasure, and immersed in sullen vigilance and sinister meditations.

XXXVIII. For Tiberius and the informers showed no fatigue. Ancharius Priscus had accused Caesius

pro consule Cretae postulaverat repetundis, addito maiestatis crimine, quod tum omnium accusationum complementum erat. Caesar Antistium Veterem e primoribus Macedoniae, absolutum adulterii, increpitis iudicibus ad dicendam maiestatis causam retraxit, ut turbidum et Rhescuporidis consiliis permixtum, qua tempestate Cotye [1] interfecto bellum adversus nos voluerat. Igitur aqua et igni interdictum reo adpositumque ut teneretur insula neque Macedoniae neque Thraeciae opportuna. Nam Thraecia diviso imperio in Rhoemetalcen et liberos Cotyis, quis ob infantiam tutor erat Trebellenus Rufus, insolentia nostri discors agebat neque minus Rhoemetalcen quam Trebellenum incusans popularium iniurias inultas sinere. Coelaletae Odrusaeque et Dii,[2] validae nationes, arma cepere, ducibus diversis et paribus inter se per ignobilitatem: quae causa fuit ne in bellum atrox coalescerent. Pars turbant praesentia, alii montem Haemum transgrediuntur ut remotos populos concirent; plurimi ac maxime compositi regem urbemque Philippopolim, a Macedone Philippo sitam, circumsidunt.

XXXIX. Quae ubi cognita P. Vellaeo (is proximum exercitum praesidebat), alarios equites ac levis cohortium mittit in eos qui praedabundi aut

---

[1] Cotye *Ernesti*: Cotye fratre.
[2] Dii *Lipsius*: alii.

---

[1] Strictly of Crete and Cyrene, the two having been combined by Augustus into a single senatorial province.
[2] See II. 64–67.
[3] The Balkans.
[4] In 342 B.C. The town, in the upper valley of the Maritza, has retained its importance and—at all events, till 1918—the name of its founder (Turk. *Filibé*).

Cordus, proconsul of Crete,[1] of malversation: a charge of treason, the complement now of all arraignments, was appended. Antistius Vetus, a grandee of Macedonia, had been acquitted of adultery: the Caesar reprimanded the judges and recalled him to stand his trial for treason, as a disaffected person, involved in the schemes of Rhescuporis during that period after the murder of Cotys when he had meditated war against ourselves.[2] The defendant was condemned accordingly to interdiction from fire and water, with a proviso that his place of detention should be an island not too conveniently situated either for Macedonia or for Thrace. For since the partition of the monarchy between Rhoemetalces and the children of Cotys, who during their minority were under the tutelage of Trebellenus Rufus, Thrace—unaccustomed to Roman methods—was divided against herself; and the accusations against Trebellenus were no more violent than those against Rhoemetalces for leaving the injuries of his countrymen unavenged. Three powerful tribes, the Coelaletae, Odrysae, and Dii, took up arms, but under separate leaders of precisely equal obscurity: a fact which saved us from a coalition involving a serious war. One division embroiled the districts at hand; another crossed the Haemus range [3] to bring out the remote clans; the most numerous, and least disorderly, besieged the king in Philippopolis, a city founded by Philip of Macedon.[4]

XXXIX. On receipt of the news, Publius Vellaeus, who was at the head of the nearest army,[5] sent the auxiliary horse and light cohorts to deal with the

[5] In Moesia—north of the Balkans. Vellaeus must have succeeded Pomponius Flaccus (II. 66).

adsumendis auxiliis vagabantur, ipse robur peditum
ad exsolvendum obsidium ducit. Simulque cuncta
prospere acta, caesis populatoribus et dissensione
orta apud obsidentis regisque opportuna eruptione
et adventu legionis. Neque aciem aut proelium
dici decuerit in quo semermi ac palantes trucidati
sunt sine nostro sanguine.

XL. Eodem anno Galliarum civitates ob magnitudinem aeris alieni rebellionem coeptavere, cuius
extimulator acerrimus inter Treviros Iulius Florus,
apud Aeduos Iulius Sacrovir. Nobilitas ambobus
et maiorum bona facta eoque Romana civitas olim
data, cum id rarum nec nisi virtuti pretium esset.
Ii secretis conloquiis, ferocissimo quoque adsumpto
aut quibus ob egestatem ac metum ex flagitiis maxima peccandi necessitudo, componunt Florus Belgas,
Sacrovir propiores Gallos concire. Igitur per con-
ciliabula et coetus seditiosa disserebant de con-
tinuatione tributorum, gravitate faenoris, saevitia
ac superbia praesidentium et discordare militem
audito Germanici exitio. Egregium resumendae
libertati tempus, si ipsi florentes quam inops Italia,
quam inbellis urbana plebes, nihil validum in exercitibus nisi quod externum, cogitarent.

XLI. Haud ferme ulla civitas intacta seminibus
eius motus fuit; sed erupere primi Andecavi ac

---

[1] Only two of the four " Galliae " were involved: the com-
pletely romanized Gallia Narbonensis (roughly equivalent to
Provence) stood aloof, and so also Aquitania in the south-west.
Of the remaining two, G. Lugdunensis (between the Loire,
Seine and Saône) included the Aedui, Andecavi and Turoni;
G. Belgica (bounded on the west by the Seine and Saône, on
the east by the Rhine from Lake Constance to the sea), was the
seat of the Treviri.

[2] The names survive in *Anjou* and *Touraine.*

roving bands who were in quest of plunder or recruits:
he himself led the flower of the infantry to raise the
siege. Success came everywhere at once: the
marauders were put to the sword; differences broke
out in the besieging force; the king made an oppor-
tune sally, and the legion arrived. Neither battle
nor engagement is a term applicable to an affair in
which half-armed men and fugitives were butchered
with no effusion of Roman blood.

XL. The same year saw an incipient rebellion
among the heavily indebted communities of the
Gallic provinces.[1] The most active promoters were
Julius Florus among the Treviri and Julius Sacrovir
among the Aedui. Each was a man of birth, with
ancestors whose services had been rewarded by
Roman citizenship in years when Roman citizenship
was rare and bestowed upon merit only. At secret
conferences, taking into their councils every desperado
or any wretch whose beggary and guilty fears made
crime a necessity, they arranged that Florus should
raise the Belgae and Sacrovir the less distant Gauls.
And so in assemblies and conventicles they made
their seditious pronouncements on the continuous
tributes, the grinding rates of interest, the cruelty
and pride of the governors:—" The legions were
mutinous since the news of Germanicus' murder, and
it was an unequalled opportunity for regaining their
independence: they had only to look from their own
resources to the poverty of Italy, the unwarlike city
population, the feebleness of the armies except for
the leavening of foreigners."

XLI. There was hardly a community into which
the seeds of the movement had not fallen; but the
first outbreak came from the Andecavi and Turoni.[2]

Turoni. Quorum Andecavos Acilius Aviola legatus excita cohorte quae Lugduni praesidium agitabat coercuit. Turoni legionario milite quem Visellius Varro inferioris Germaniae legatus miserat oppressi eodem Aviola duce et quibusdam Galliarum primoribus, qui tulere auxilium quo dissimularent defectionem magisque in tempore efferrent. Spectatus et Sacrovir intecto capite pugnam pro Romanis ciens ostentandae, ut ferebat, virtutis, sed captivi ne incesseretur telis adgnoscendum se praebuisse arguebant. Consultus super eo Tiberius aspernatus est indicium aluitque dubitatione bellum.

XLII. Interim Florus insistere destinatis, pellicere alam equitum, quae conscripta e Treviris militia disciplinaque nostra habebatur, ut caesis negotiatoribus Romanis bellum inciperet; paucique equitum corrupti, plures in officio mansere. Aliud vulgus obaeratorum aut clientium arma cepit; petebantque saltus quibus nomen Arduenna, cum legiones utroque ab exercitu, quas Visellius et C. Silius adversis itineribus obiecerant, arcuerunt. Praemissusque cum delecta manu Iulius Indus e civitate eadem, discors Floro et ob id navandae operae avidior, inconditam multitudinem adhuc disiecit.[1] Florus incertis latebris victores frustratus, postremo visis militibus, qui effugia insederant, sua manu cecidit. Isque Trevirici tumultus finis.

---

[1] multitudinem adhuc] adhuc multitudinem *Nipperdey*.

---

[1] Lyon.
[2] At that time much more extensive than now.
[3] Still legate of Upper Germany (1. 32): for his fall see IV. 18.

The former were quelled by the legate Acilius Aviola, who called out a cohort on garrison duty at Lugdunum:[1] the Turoni were crus.ed by a body of legionaries sent by Visellius Varro, the legate of Lower Germany. The commander was again Aviola, supported by several Gaulish chieftains, who brought up auxiliaries with the intention of screening their defection for the moment and unmasking it at a more favourable juncture. Sacrovir himself was there, a conspicuous figure, urging his men to strike for Rome, and bare-headed,—" to let his courage be seen," he explained. The prisoners, however, charged him with making his identity clear so as to avoid becoming a target for missiles. Tiberius, consulted on the point, rejected the information, and fostered the war by his indecision.

XLII. Meanwhile, Florus pressed on with his designs and endeavoured to induce a troop of horse, enrolled in the neighbourhood of Treves but kept in our service and under our discipline, to open hostilities by a massacre of Roman financiers. A few men were actually won over, but the greater number remained loyal. Apart from these, a rabble of debtors and dependants took up arms, and were making for the forest country known as the Ardennes,[2] when they were debarred by the legions which Visellius and Gaius Silius[3] had detached from their two armies, by opposite roads, to intercept their march. Julius Indus, a countryman of the insurgents, at feud with Florus and hence the more eager to be of service, was sent ahead with a body of picked men, and dispersed the still orderless multitude. Florus eluded the conquerors in unknown coverts, to fall at last by his own hand, on descrying the soldiers who had occupied every egress.

XLIII. Apud Aeduos maior moles exorta quanto civitas opulentior et comprimendi procul praesidium. Augustodunum caput gentis armatis cohortibus Sacrovir occupaverat, ut nobilissimam [1] Galliarum subolem, liberalibus studiis ibi operatam, et [2] eo pignore parentes propinquosque eorum adiungeret; simul arma occulte fabricata iuventuti dispertit. Quadraginta milia fuere, quinta sui parte legionariis armis, ceteri cum venabulis et cultris quaeque alia venantibus tela sunt. Adduntur e servitiis gladiaturae destinati quibus more gentico continuum ferri tegimen: cruppellarios vocant, inferendis ictibus inhabilis, accipiendis impenetrabilis. Augebantur eae copiae vicinarum civitatum ut nondum aperta consensione, ita viritim promptis studiis, et certamine ducum Romanorum, quos inter ambigebatur utroque bellum sibi poscente. Mox Varro, invalidus senecta, vigenti Silio concessit.

XLIV. At Romae non Treviros modo et Aeduos, sed quattuor et sexaginta Galliarum civitates descivisse, adsumptos in societatem Germanos, dubias

[1] ut *Bezzenberger*, nobilissimam *Lipsius* : nobilissimarum.
[2] et *Bezzenberger* : ut.

---

[1] The legions on the Rhine.
[2] Autun.—The college, founded by Augustus, long continued to flourish, and was even restored by Constantius Chlorus after the sack of the town by the Franks and Batavians in the reign of Claudius Gothicus (268–270 A.D).
[3] Since the Gauls despised body-armour, the phrase must refer only to the conventional equipment of the " Gallus " (*murmillo*)—like the Samnite and Thracian, one of the national types of the arena. In spite of this passage and Ammian XXIII. 6, 83, the monuments are said not to support the view that the *murmillones* were heavily armed. Caligula (who detested them as opponents of his favourite Thracians) would

XLIII. So ended the rising as far as the Treviri were concerned. Among the Aedui trouble came in the graver form to be expected from the superior wealth of the community and the remoteness of the suppressing force.[1] The tribal capital, Augustodunum,[2] had been seized by armed cohorts of Sacrovir, whose intention was to enlist those cadets of the great Gallic families who were receiving a liberal education at the city-schools, and to use them as pledges for the adhesion of their parents and relatives: simultaneously he distributed weapons, secretly manufactured, among the younger men. His followers amounted to forty thousand; one-fifth armed on the legionary model; the rest with boar-spears, hangers, and other implements of the hunting-field. To these he added a contingent of slaves, destined for the gladiatorial ring and encased in the continuous shell of iron usual in the country:[3] the so-called "cruppellarians"—who, if too weighty to inflict wounds, are impregnably fortified against receiving them. These forces were steadily increased: the neighbouring districts had not as yet openly committed themselves, but private enthusiasm ran high, and relations were strained between the Roman generals, then at issue over the conduct of the campaign, which was claimed by each as his own prerogative. Finally, Varro, now old and weakly, withdrew in favour of Silius, who was still in the prime of life.

XLIV. At Rome, however, the tale ran that not the Treviri and Aedui only were in revolt, but the four-and-sixty tribes of Gaul: the Germans had joined the league, the Spains were wavering, and, as

seem to have thought so, since he took the precaution of reducing their accoutrement (Suet. *Cal.* 55).

Hispanias, cuncta, ut mos famae, in maius credita. Optumus quisque rei publicae cura maerebat; multi odio praesentium et cupidine mutationis suis quoque periculis laetabantur increpabantque Tiberium quod in tanto rerum motu libellis accusatorum insumeret operam. An Sacrovirum maiestatis crimine reum in senatu fore? Extitisse tandem viros qui cruentas epistulas armis cohiberent. Miseram pacem vel bello bene mutari. Tanto impensius in securitatem compositus, neque loco neque vultu mutato, sed ut solitum per illos dies egit, altitudine animi, an comperat modica esse et vulgatis leviora.

XLV. Interim Silius cum legionibus duabus incedens praemissa auxiliari manu vastat Sequanorum pagos qui finium extremi et Aeduis contermini sociique in armis erant. Mox Augustodunum petit propero agmine, certantibus inter se signiferis, fremente etiam gregario milite, ne suetam requiem, ne spatia noctium opperiretur; viderent modo adversos et aspicerentur: id satis ad victoriam. Duodecimum apud lapidem Sacrovir copiaeque patentibus locis apparuere. In fronte statuerat ferratos, in cornibus cohortis, a tergo semermos. Ipse inter primores equo insigni adire, memorare veteres Gallo-

---

[1] To the senate, ordering the trial, and implicitly the condemnation of suspects. So far there has been little or nothing in the narrative of Tacitus to justify the phrase—apposite enough in Tiberius' later years, when *nullae in eos imperatoris litterae* (VI. 47) became an exception worth recording.

[2] They occupied roughly the Franche-Comté (Haute-Saône, Doubs, and Jura), and adjoined Upper Germany, where Silius was in command.

[3] From Autun.

in all rumours, every statement was amplified and
credited. The patriot, anxious for the commonwealth, grieved; but in many hatred of the
existing order and a craving for change were such
that they exulted even in their own perils, and
lavished reproaches on Tiberius, who, in this convul-
sion of affairs, could centre his attention on the
memoranda of the informers:—" Was Sacrovir also
to stand his trial for treason before the senate? At
last, *men* had arisen to check these murderous epistles[1]
by the sword! War itself was a welcome exchange
for the horrors of peace." All the more resolute was
his studied unconcern; he made no change of place,
none of looks, but maintained his wonted behaviour
through all those days, whether from deep reserve
or because he had information that the disturbances
were of moderate extent and slighter than reported.

XLV. In the meantime, Silius, marching with two
legions, had sent forward an auxiliary troop, and was
devastating the villages of the Sequani; who lay on
the extreme frontier,[2] adjoining the Aedui and
their allies under arms. Then he moved at full
speed upon Augustodunum. The march was a race
between the standard-bearers, and even the private
soldiers protested angrily against pausing for the
usual rest or the long nightly bivouac:—" Let them
only see the rebels in front, and be seen: it was
enough for victory!" At the twelfth milestone[3]
Sacrovir and his powers came into view on an open
piece of ground. He had stationed his iron-clad
men in the van, his cohorts on the wings, his half-
armed followers in the rear. He himself, splendidly
mounted, amid a group of chieftains, rode up to his
troops, reminding them of the ancient laurels of

rum glorias quaeque Romanis adversa intulissent:
quam decora victoribus libertas, quanto intolerantior
servitus iterum victis.

XLVI. Non diu haec nec apud laetos: etenim pro-
pinquabat legionum acies, inconditique ac militiae
nescii oppidani neque oculis neque auribus satis
competebant. Contra Silius, etsi praesumpta spes
hortandi causas exemerat, clamitabat tamen puden-
dum ipsis quod Germaniarum victores adversum
Gallos tamquam in hostem ducerentur. "Vna
nuper cohors rebellem Turonum, una ala Trevirum,
paucae huius ipsius exercitus turmae profligavere
Sequanos. Quanto pecunia dites et voluptatibus
opulentos, tanto magis imbellis Aeduos evincite et
fugientibus consulite." Ingens ad ea clamor et cir-
cumfudit eques frontemque pedites invasere, nec
cunctatum apud latera. Paulum morae attulere
ferrati, restantibus lamminis adversum pila et gladios; set miles correptis securibus et dolabris, ut
si murum perrumperet, caedere tegmina et corpora;
quidam trudibus aut furcis inertem molem proster-
nere iacentesque nullo ad resurgendum nisu quasi
exanimes linquebantur. Sacrovir primo Augustodunum, dein metu deditionis in villam propinquam cum
fidissimis pergit. Illic sua manu, reliqui mutuis ictibus occidere; incensa super villa omnis cremavit.

---

[1] In other words, "capture them alive." There seems,
however, no need to see in Silius' scornful rhetoric an allusion
to the fact that his victory was *per avaritiam foedata* (IV. 19).

the Gauls, and the reverses they had inflicted upon the Romans; how glorious their freedom, if they conquered; how much more insufferable their bondage, should they be vanquished once again.

XLVI. His words were few and to a cheerless audience: for the embattled legions were drawing on; and the undrilled townsmen, new to the trade of war, had little control over their eyes and ears. On the other side—though anticipated hope had removed the need for exhortation—Silius exclaimed that it was an insult to the conquerors of the Germanies to be led as though to meet an enemy and to be confronted with Gauls! " But recently one cohort shattered the rebel Turoni; one troop of horse, the Treviri; a few squadrons of this very army, the Sequani. The richer the Aedui, the more extravagant in their pleasures, the more unwarlike are they; put them to the rout, and have mercy on them when they flee." [1] The answer was returned in a great shout: the cavalry enveloped the flanks, and the infantry attacked the van. On the wings there was no delay; in front, the iron-clad men offered a brief impediment, as their plating was proof against javelin and sword. But the legionaries caught up their axes and picks and hacked at armour and flesh as if demolishing a wall: others overturned the inert masses with poles or forks, and left them lying like the dead without an effort to rise again. Sacrovir, with his staunchest adherents, made his way first to Augustodunum; then, apprehending his surrender, to an adjacent villa. Here he fell by his own hand, the rest by mutually inflicted wounds; the bodies were burnt by the house being fired over them.

XLVII. Tum demum Tiberius ortum patratumque bellum senatu scripsit; neque dempsit aut addidit vero, sed fide ac virtute legatos, se consiliis superfuisse. Simul causas cur non ipse, non Drusus profecti ad id bellum forent, adiunxit, magnitudinem imperii extollens, neque decorum principibus, si una alterave civitas turbet, . . . ¹ omissa urbe, unde in omnia regimen. Nunc quia non metu ducatur iturum ut praesentia spectaret componeretque. Decrevere patres vota pro reditu eius supplicationesque et alia decora. Solus Dolabella Cornelius, dum antire ceteros parat absurdam in adulationem progressus, censuit ut ovans e Campania urbem introiret. Igitur secutae Caesaris litterae quibus se non tam vacuum gloria praedicabat ut post ferocissimas gentis perdomitas, tot receptos in iuventa aut spretos triumphos, iam senior peregrinationis suburbanae inane praemium peteret.

XLVIII. Sub idem tempus ut mors Sulpicii Quirini publicis exequiis frequentaretur petivit a senatu. Nihil ad veterem et patriciam Sulpiciorum familiam Quirinius pertinuit, ortus apud municipium Lanuvium; sed impiger militiae et acribus

---

¹ . . . *Nipperdey. Supplendum velut* huc illuc meare: *cf.* IV. 5 *fin., supr.* 34.

---

¹ See below, chap. 69, IV. 66, XI. 22; and, for his termination of the war with Tacfarinas, IV. 23–26.

² He had received three (over the Dalmatians and Pannonians in 9 B.C., over the Germans in 7 B.C., over the Illyrian insurgents in 12 A.D.), and, according to his panegyrist Velleius Paterculus, had earned seven.

³ See II. 30 and, above, chap. 22. His consulate was in 12 B.C., and as governor of Syria, apparently for the second

XLVII. And now at last a letter from Tiberius informed the senate of the outbreak and completion of a war. He neither understated nor overstated the facts, but remarked that the fidelity and courage of his generals, and his own policy, had gained the day. At the same time, he added the reasons why neither Drusus nor himself had left for the campaign, insisting on the extent of the empire and on the loss of prestige to the sovereign if the disaffection of one or two communities could make him abandon the capital, which was the centre of government for the whole. However, now that fear was not the motive-force, he would go, view matters on the spot, and arrange a settlement. The Fathers decreed vows for his return, supplications, and other compliments: Cornelius Dolabella[1] alone, intent upon distancing his competitors, carried sycophancy to the absurd point of proposing that he should enter the city from Campania with an ovation. The sequel was a missive from the Caesar, who asserted, with a touch of pride, that " after subduing some of the fiercest of nations, and receiving or rejecting so many triumphs in his youth,[2] he was not so bankrupt in fame as to court in his age a futile honour conferred for an excursion in the suburbs."

XLVIII. About the same time, he asked the senate to allow the death of Sulpicius Quirinius[3] to be solemnized by a public funeral. With the old patrician family of the Sulpicii Quirinius—who sprang from the municipality of Lanuvium[4]—had no connection; but as an intrepid soldier and an active

time, he carried out the census referred to in Acts v. 37 and Luke ii. 2.

[4] In southern Latium, close to the Appian Way.

ministeriis consulatum sub divo Augusto, mox expugnatis super [1] Ciliciam Homonadensium castellis insignia triumphi adeptus, datusque rector C. Caesari Armeniam obtinenti. Tiberium quoque Rhodi agentem coluerat: quod tunc patefecit in senatu, laudatis in se officiis et incusato M. Lollio, quem auctorem Gaio Caesari pravitatis et discordiarum arguebat. Sed ceteris haud laeta memoria Quirini erat ob intenta, ut memoravi, Lepidae pericula sordidamque et praepotentem senectam.

XLIX. Fine anni Clutorium Priscum equitem Romanum, post celebre carmen quo Germanici suprema defleverat, pecunia donatum a Caesare, corripuit delator, obiectans aegro Druso composuisse quod, si extinctus foret, maiore praemio vulgaretur. Id Clutorius in domo P. Petronii socru eius Vitellia coram multisque inlustribus feminis per vaniloquentiam iecerat.[2] Vt delator exstitit, ceteris ad dicendum testimonium exterritis, sola Vitellia nihil

---

[1] super *Haupt* : per.   [2] iecerat *Weissbrodt* : legerat.

---

[1] . . . *gens Homonadum, quorum intus oppidum Homona : cetera castella X L I V inter asperas convalles latent,* Plin. *H.N.* V. 27. They had the reputation of being ἀληπτότατοι (Strab. 569).

[2] For Gaius Caesar in Armenia, see II. 4; for Tiberius at Rhodes, I. 4.

[3] Consul in 21 B.C.; defeated by the Germans in 16 B.C. with the loss of an eagle (*Lolliana clades,* I. 10); *rector* to C. Caesar in 1–2 A.D.; *abstinens Ducentis ad se cuncta pecuniae* according to Horace (*Carm.* IV. 9), but *infamatus regum muneribus in toto oriente* according to Pliny (*H.N.* IX. 35); disgraced and died (by suicide ?) in 2 A.D.

[4] Dio gives the name as C. Lutorius Priscus, and describes him as μέγα ἐπὶ ποιήσει φρονῶν (LVII. 20); Pliny (*H.N.* VII. 39) mentions him as paying a fabulous price for one of Sejanus' eunuchs.

servant he won a consulate under the deified Augustus, and, a little later, by capturing the Homonadensian strongholds beyond the Cilician frontier,[1] earned the insignia of triumph. After his appointment, again, as adviser to Gaius Caesar during his command in Armenia, he had shown himself no less attentive to Tiberius, who was then residing in Rhodes.[2] This circumstance the emperor now disclosed in the senate, coupling a panegyric on his good offices to himself with a condemnation of Marcus Lollius,[3] whom he accused of instigating the cross-grained and provocative attitude of Gaius Caesar. In the rest of men, however, the memory of Quirinius awoke no enthusiasm, in view of his attempt (already noticed) to ruin Lepida, and the combination of meanness with exorbitant power which had marked his later days.

XLIX. At the end of the year, Clutorius Priscus,[4] a Roman knight, who had been presented by the emperor with a sum of money in return for a widely circulated poem deploring the death of Germanicus, was attacked by an informer; the charge being that during an illness of Drusus he had composed another set of verses, to be published, in the event of his death, with a yet more lucrative result. Clutorius, with foolish loquacity, had boasted of his performance in the house of Publius Petronius,[5] before his host's mother-in-law, Vitellia, and many women of rank. When the informer appeared, the rest were terrified into giving evidence; Vitellia alone insisted

---

[5] Afterwards proconsul of Asia for six years and governor of Syria for three; τὴν φύσιν εὐμενὴς καὶ ἥμερος (Philo, t. II. 582 Mangey): an old friend of Claudius, and therefore ridiculed by Seneca (homo Claudiana lingua disertus, Apoc. 14).

THE ANNALS OF TACITUS

se audivisse adseveravit. Sed arguentibus ad perniciem plus fidei fuit, sententiaque Haterii Agrippae consulis designati indictum reo ultimum supplicium.

L. Contra M'.[1] Lepidus in hunc modum exorsus est: "Si, patres conscripti, unum id spectamus, quam nefaria voce Clutorius Priscus mentem suam et auris hominum polluerit, neque carcer neque laqueus, ne serviles quidem cruciatus in eum suffecerint. Sin flagitia et facinora sine modo sunt, suppliciis ac remediis principis moderatio maiorumque et vestra exempla temperant et vana a scelestis, dicta a maleficiis differunt, est locus sententiae per quam neque huic delictum impune sit et nos clementiae simul ac severitatis non paeniteat. Saepe audivi principem nostrum conquerentem si quis sumpta morte misericordiam eius praevenisset. Vita Clutorii in integro est, qui neque servatus in periculum rei publicae neque interfectus in exemplum ibit. Studia illi ut plena vaecordiae, ita inania et fluxa sunt; nec quicquam grave ac serium ex eo metuas qui suorum ipse flagitiorum proditor non virorum animis sed muliercularum adrepit. Cedat tamen urbe et bonis amissis aqua et igni arceatur: quod perinde censeo ac si lege maiestatis teneretur."

[1] M'. *Lipsius* : M.

---

[1] Chap. 14, note.
[2] Torture and crucifixion.
[3] Lepidus hints, first, that it may be doubted whether Clutorius' offence falls under the *lex maiestatis* ; second, that, even should that be the case, the legal penalty is not death but outlawry. The editors cite Paul. *Sent. rec.* V. 29, § 1, *antea in perpetuum aqua et igni interdicebatur ; nunc vero humiliores bestiis obiciuntur vel vivi exuruntur, honestiores capite puniuntur.*

that she had heard nothing. However, the witnesses who supported the fatal charge were considered the more credible; and, on the motion of the consul designate, Haterius Agrippa, the last penalty was invoked against the culprit.

L. Opposition came from Manius Lepidus, whose speech ran thus:—" If, Conscript Fathers, we regard one point only,—the enormity of the utterance by which Clutorius Priscus has defiled his own soul and the ears of men,—neither the cell, nor the noose,[1] nor even the torments reserved for slaves [2] are adequate to his punishment. But if, while vice and crime are limitless, the penalties and remedies of both are tempered by the sovereign's moderation and by the example of your ancestors and yourselves; if there is a difference between fatuity and villainy, between evil-speaking and evil-doing; then there is room for a proposal which neither leaves the defendant's guilt unpunished nor gives us cause to rue either our softness or our hardness of heart. Time and again I have heard our prince express his regret when anyone by taking his own life had forestalled his clemency. Clutorius' life is still intact: he is a man whom to spare can involve no public menace; whom to slay can create no public deterrent. His occupations are as futile and erratic as they are charged with folly; nor can any grave and considerable danger be expected from a person who by betraying his own infamy insinuates himself into the favour not of men but of silly women. Expel him, however, from Rome, confiscate his property, ban him from fire and water: this is my proposal, and I make it precisely as though he were guilty under the law of treason."[3]

LI. Solus Lepido Rubellius Blandus e consularibus
adsensit: ceteri sententiam Agrippae secuti, ductus-
que in carcerem Priscus ac statim exanimatus. Id
Tiberius solitis sibi ambagibus apud senatum incusavit, cum extolleret pietatem quamvis modicas
principis iniurias acriter ulciscentium, deprecaretur
tam praecipitis verborum poenas, laudaret Lepidum
neque Agrippam argueret. Igitur factum senatus
consultum ne decreta patrum ante diem decimum [1]
ad aerarium deferrentur idque vitae spatium damna-
tis prorogaretur. Sed non senatui libertas ad paeni-
tendum erat neque Tiberius interiectu temporis
mitigabatur.

LII. C. Sulpicius D. Haterius consules sequuntur,
inturbidus externis rebus annus, domi suspecta
severitate adversum luxum qui immensum pro-
ruperat ad cuncta quis pecunia prodigitur. Sed
alia sumptuum quamvis graviora dissimulatis plerumque pretiis occultabantur; ventris et ganeae
paratus adsiduis sermonibus vulgati fecerant curam
ne princeps antiquae parsimoniae durius adverteret.
Nam incipiente C. Bibulo ceteri quoque aediles disse-
ruerant, sperni sumptuariam legem vetitaque utensilium pretia augeri in dies nec mediocribus remediis

---

[1] diem decimum *Lipsius* : diem.

---

[1] Senatorial decrees only became operative when deposited
in the *aerarium*—the temple of Saturn on the Capitoline, close
by the temple of Concord. The period of grace was afterwards
extended to thirty days.

[2] C. Sulpicius Galba, elder brother of the future emperor.

[3] I. 77; II. 51; above, chap. 49; VI. 4.

[4] Probably the *lex Iulia* of 22 B.C. (D. Cass. LIV. 2); its
scale of expenditure for the *cena* may be found in Gell. II. 24.

LI. A single ex-consul, Rubellius Blandus, concurred with Lepidus: the remainder followed Agrippa's motion; and Priscus was led to the cells and immediately executed. This promptitude drew a typically ambiguous reprimand from Tiberius in the senate. He commended the loyalty of members, who avenged so sharply insults, however slight, to the head of the state, but deprecated such a hurried punishment of a verbal offence. Lepidus he praised; Agrippa he did not blame. It was therefore resolved that no senatorial decree should be entered in the Treasury before the lapse of nine full days,[1] all prisoners under sentence of death to be reprieved for that period. But the senate had not liberty to repent, nor was Tiberius usually softened by the interval.

LII. The consulate of Gaius Sulpicius[2] and Decimus Haterius[3] followed: a year of quiet abroad, though at home there was uneasiness at the prospect of stern measures against the luxury which had broken all bounds and extended to every object on which money can be squandered. But other extravagances, though actually more serious, could as a rule be kept private by concealing the prices paid: it was the apparatus of gluttony and intemperance which had become the eternal theme of gossip and had awakened anxiety lest a prince of old-world thriftiness might adopt too harsh measures. For, when the point was mooted by Gaius Bibulus, it had been maintained by his fellow-aediles also that the sumptuary law[4] was a dead letter; that the prohibited prices for articles of food were rising daily; and that the advance could not be checked by moderate methods. The senate, too, when consulted, had

sisti posse et consulti patres integrum id negotium ad principem distulerant. Sed Tiberius saepe apud se pensitato an coerceri tam profusae cupidines possent, num coercitio plus damni in rem publicam ferret, quam indecorum adtrectare quod non obtineret vel retentum ignominiam et infamiam virorum inlustrium posceret, postremo litteras ad senatum composuit quarum sententia in hunc modum fuit:

LIII. " Ceteris forsitan in rebus, patres conscripti, magis expediat me coram interrogari et dicere quid e re publica censeam; in hac relatione subtrahi oculos meos melius fuit, ne, denotantibus vobis ora ac metum singulorum qui pudendi luxus arguerentur, ipse etiam viderem eos ac velut deprenderem. Quod si mecum ante viri strenui, aediles, consilium habuissent, nescio an suasurus fuerim omittere potius praevalida et adulta vitia quam hoc adsequi, ut palam fieret quibus flagitiis impares essemus. Sed illi quidem officio functi sunt, ut ceteros quoque magistratus sua munia implere velim; mihi autem neque honestum silere neque proloqui expeditum, quia non aedilis aut praetoris aut consulis partis sustineo. Maius aliquid et excelsius a principe postulatur; et cum recte factorum sibi quisque gratiam trahant, unius invidia ab omnibus peccatur. Quid enim primum prohibere et pris-

referred the question without any discussion to the emperor. But Tiberius, after debating with himself repeatedly whether it was possible to arrest these uncurbed passions, whether such an arrest might not prove an even greater national evil, and what would be the loss of dignity should he attempt a reform which could not be enforced, or, if enforced, would demand the degradation and disgrace of his most illustrious subjects, finally composed a letter to the senate, the drift of which was as follows:—

LIII. " On other occasions, Conscript Fathers, it is perhaps preferable that, if my opinion is needed on a matter of public policy, the question should be put and answered when I am present; but in this debate it was better that my eyes should be withdrawn; otherwise, through your indicating the anxious features of members who might be charged with indecent luxury, I too might see and, so to speak, detect them. If our active aediles had taken me into their counsels beforehand, I am not sure but that I should have advised them to leave vigorous and full-blown vices alone, rather than force matters to an issue which might only inform the world with what abuses we were powerless to cope. Still, they have done their duty—and I could wish to see every other magistrate as thorough in the discharge of his office. But for myself it is neither honourable to be silent nor easy to be outspoken, because it is not the part of aedile or praetor or consul that I act. Something greater and more exalted is demanded from a prince; and, while the credit of his successes is arrogated by every man to himself, when all err it is one alone who bears the odium. For on what am I to make my first effort

cum ad morem recidere adgrediar? villarumne infinita spatia? familiarum numerum et nationes? argenti et auri pondus? aeris tabularumque miracula? promiscas viris et feminis vestis atque illa feminarum propria, quis lapidum causa pecuniae nostrae ad externas aut hostilis gentis transferuntur?

LIV. " Nec ignoro in conviviis et circulis incusari ista et modum posci; set si quis legem sanciat, poenas indicat, idem illi civitatem verti, splendidissimo cuique exitium parari, neminem criminis expertem clamitabunt. Atqui ne corporis quidem morbos veteres et diu auctos nisi per dura et aspera coerceas: corruptus simul et corruptor, aeger et flagrans animus haud levioribus remediis restinguendus est quam libidinibus ardescit. Tot a maioribus repertae leges, tot quas divus Augustus tulit, illae oblivione, hae, quod flagitiosius est, contemptu abolitae securiorem luxum fecere. Nam si velis quod nondum vetitum est, timeas ne vetere; at si prohibita impune transcenderis, neque metus ultra neque pudor est. Cur ergo olim parsimonia pollebat? quia sibi quisque moderabatur, quia[1] unius

---

¹ sibi quisque moderabatur, quia *Beroaldus* : sibique moderabatur qua.

---

[1] The subject is often touched, and usually in this strain of hyperbole. A fair example is Sen. *Ep.* 89:—*Omnibus licet locis tecta vestra splendeant, alicubi imposita montibus . . . alicubi ex plano in altitudinem montium educta e.q.s.*

[2] Cf. IV. 27, XIV. 43 and 44. The servile population was doubtless enormous; but modern attempts to estimate it have simply demonstrated that the data are inadequate for the task.

[3] "Corinthian" bronzes, the price of which had risen sharply under Tiberius (Suet. *Tib.* 34).

[4] See II. 33.

at prohibition and retrenchment to the ancient standard? On the infinite expanse of our villas?[1] The numbers—the nations—of our slaves?[2] The weight of our silver and gold? The miracles of bronze[3] and canvas? The promiscuous dress of male and female[4]—and the specially female extravagance by which, for the sake of jewels, our wealth is transported to alien or hostile countries?[5]

LIV. "I am aware that at dinner-parties and social gatherings these things are condemned, and the call is for restriction; but let any one pass a law and prescribe a penalty, and the same voices will be uplifted against ' this subversion of the state, this death-blow to all magnificence, this charge of which not a man is guiltless '! And yet even bodily ailments, if they are old and inveterate, can be checked only by severe and harsh remedies; and, corrupted alike and corrupting, a sick and fevered soul needs for its relief remedies not less sharp than the passions which inflame it. All the laws our ancestors discovered, all which the deified Augustus enacted, are now buried, those in oblivion, these— to our yet greater shame—in contempt. And this it is that has given luxury its greater boldness. For if you covet something which is not yet prohibited, there is always a fear that prohibition may come; but once you have crossed forbidden ground with impunity, you have left your tremors and blushes behind.—Then why was frugality once the rule?— Because every man controlled himself; because we

[5] A good many Roman coins have been found, for instance, on the pepper-coast of Malabar. Indeed, the constant efflux of the precious metals, combined with gradual exhaustion of the mines, was one of the causes which led ultimately to the debasement of the coinage.

urbis cives eramus; ne inritamenta quidem eadem
intra Italiam dominantibus. Externis victoriis aliena, civilibus etiam nostra consumere didicimus.
Quantulum istud est de quo aediles admonent!
Quam, si cetera respicias, in levi habendum! At
hercule nemo refert quod Italia externae opis indi-
get, quod vita populi Romani per incerta maris et
tempestatum cotidie volvitur. Ac nisi provinciarum copiae et dominis et servitiis et agris subve-
nerint, nostra nos scilicet nemora nostraeque villae
tuebuntur. Hanc, patres conscripti, curam sustinet
princeps; haec omissa funditus rem publicam trahet.
Reliquis intra animum medendum est: nos pudor,
pauperes necessitas, divites satias in melius mutet.
Aut si quis ex magistratibus tantam industriam ac
severitatem pollicetur ut ire obviam queat, hunc
ego et laudo et exonerari laborum meorum partem
fateor: sin accusare vitia volunt, dein, cum gloriam
eius rei adepti sunt, simultates faciunt ac mihi
relinquunt, credite, patres conscripti, me quoque
non esse offensionum avidum; quas cum gravis et
plerumque iniquas pro re publica suscipiam, inanis
et inritas neque mihi aut vobis usui futuras iure
deprecor."

LV. Auditis Caesaris litteris, remissa aedilibus
talis cura; luxusque mensae a fine Actiaci belli ad

---

¹ On the grain-fleet from Alexandria and the merchantmen
from the province of Africa: cf. XII. 43, *Africam potius et
Aegyptum exercemus, navibusque et casibus vita populi Romani
commissa est.*

were burghers of a single town; nor were there
even the same temptations while our empire was
confined to Italy. By victories abroad we learned to
waste the substance of others; by victories at home,
our own. How little a thing it is to which the aediles
call attention! How trivial, if you cast your eyes
around! But, Heaven knows, not a man points out
in a motion that Italy depends on external supplies,
and that the life of the Roman nation is tossed day
after day at the uncertain mercy of wave and wind.[1]
And if the harvests of the provinces ever fail to come
to the rescue of master and slave and farm, our
parks and villas will presumably have to support us!
That, Conscript Fathers, is a charge which rests upon
the shoulders of the prince; that charge neglected
will involve the state in utter ruin. For other ills
the remedy must be within our own breasts: let
improvement come to you and me from self-respect,
to the poor from necessity, to the rich from satiety.
Or, if there is a magistrate who can promise the
requisite energy and severity, I give him my praises
and confess my responsibilities lightened. But if it
is the way of reformers to be zealous in denouncing
corruption, and later, after reaping the credit of their
denunciation, to create enmities and bequeath them
to myself, then believe me, Conscript Fathers, I too
am not eager to incur animosities. True, while they
are serious—and often iniquitous—I face them for
the sake of the state; but when they are idle,
unmeaning, and unlikely to profit myself or you, I
beg with justice to be excused."

LV. When the Caesar's epistle had been read the
aediles were exempted from such a task; and spend-
thrift epicureanism, after being practised with ex-

ea arma quis Servius Galba rerum adeptus est, per annos centum profusis sumptibus exerciti, paulatim exolevere. Causas eius mutationis quaerere libet. Dites olim familiae nobilium aut claritudine insignes studio magnificentiae prolabebantur. Nam etiam tum plebem, socios, regna colere et coli licitum; ut quisque opibus, domo, paratu speciosus per nomen et clientelas inlustrior habebatur. Postquam caedibus saevitum et magnitudo famae exitio erat, ceteri ad sapientiora convertere. Simul novi homines e municipiis et coloniis atque etiam provinciis in senatum crebro adsumpti domesticam parsimoniam intulerunt, et, quamquam fortuna vel industria plerique pecuniosam ad senectam pervenirent, mansit tamen prior animus. Sed praecipuus adstricti moris auctor Vespasianus fuit, antiquo ipse cultu victuque. Obsequium inde in principem et aemulandi amor validior quam poena ex legibus et metus. Nisi forte rebus cunctis inest quidam velut orbis, ut quem ad modum temporum vices, ita morum vertantur; nec omnia apud priores meliora, sed nostra quoque aetas multa laudis et artium imitanda posteris tulit. Verum haec nobis in maiores [1] certamina ex honesto maneant.

[1] in maiores *Lipsius* (erga m. *Rhenanus*): maiores.

---

[1] 31 B.C.–68 A.D.
[2] Under Tiberius (in his later years), Caligula, Claudius (cf. Sen. *Apoc.* 14), and Nero.

travagant prodigality throughout the century between the close of the Actian War and the struggle which placed Servius Galba on the throne,[1] went gradually out of vogue. The causes of that change may well be investigated.

Formerly aristocratic families of wealth or outstanding distinction were apt to be led to their downfall by a passion for magnificence. For it was still legitimate to court or be courted by the populace, by the provincials, by dependent princes; and the more handsome the fortune, the palace, the establishment of a man, the more imposing his reputation and his clientèle. After the merciless executions,[2] when greatness of fame was death, the survivors turned to wiser paths. At the same time, the self-made men, repeatedly drafted into the senate from the municipalities and colonies, and even from the provinces, introduced the plain-living habits of their own hearths; and although by good fortune or industry very many arrived at an old age of affluence, yet their prepossessions persisted to the end. But the main promoter of the stricter code was Vespasian, himself of the old school in his person and table. Thenceforward, deference to the sovereign and the love of emulating him proved more powerful than legal sanctions and deterrents. Or should we rather say there is a kind of cycle in all things—moral as well as seasonal revolutions? Nor, indeed, were all things better in the old time before us; but our own age too has produced much in the sphere of true nobility and much in that of art which posterity well may imitate. In any case, may the honourable competition of our present with our past long remain!

LVI. Tiberius, fama moderationis parta quod ingruentis accusatores represserat, mittit litteras ad senatum quis potestatem tribuniciam Druso petebat. Id summi fastigii vocabulum Augustus repperit, ne regis aut dictatoris nomen adsumeret ac tamen appellatione aliqua cetera imperia praemineret. Marcum deinde Agrippam socium eius potestatis, quo defuncto Tiberium Neronem delegit ne successor in incerto foret. Sic cohiberi pravas aliorum spes rebatur; simul modestiae Neronis et suae magnitudini fidebat. Quo tunc exemplo Tiberius Drusum summae rei admovit,[1] cum incolumi Germanico integrum inter duos iudicium tenuisset. Sed principio litterarum veneratus deos ut consilia sua rei publicae prosperarent, modica de moribus adulescentis neque in falsum aucta rettulit. Esse illi coniugem et tres liberos eamque aetatem qua ipse quondam a divo Augusto ad capessendum hoc munus vocatus sit. Neque nunc propere, sed per octo annos capto experimento, compressis seditionibus, compositis bellis, triumphalem et bis consulem noti laboris participem sumi.

LVII. Praeceperant animis orationem patres; quo quaesitior adulatio fuit. Nec tamen repertum nisi ut effigies principum, aras deum, templa et arcus

---

¹ admovit *Halm* : admovet.

¹ They would have had an admirable field of activity if the proposed sumptuary legislation had been carried.

² He received the title for life in June, 23 B.C., and five years later conferred it on Agrippa, who held it till his death in 12 B.C.

³ The phrase is rather misleading, since it was not till 9 or 6 B.C. that he was given the title for five years; and only upon his adoption by Augustus after the death of Gaius Caesar in 4 A.D. was it renewed.

⁴ The thirty-fifth year.

LVI. Tiberius, now that his check to the onrush of informers [1] had earned him a character for moderation, sent a letter to the senate desiring the tribunician power for Drusus. This phrase for the supreme dignity was discovered by Augustus; who was reluctant to take the style of king or dictator, yet desirous of some title indicating his pre-eminence over all other authorities.[2] Later, he selected Marcus Agrippa as his partner in that power, then, on Agrippa's decease,[3] Tiberius Nero; his object being to leave the succession in no doubt. In this way, he considered, he would stifle the misconceived hopes of other aspirants; while, at the same time, he had faith in Nero's self-restraint and in his own greatness. In accordance with this precedent, Tiberius then placed Drusus on the threshold of the empire, although in Germanicus' lifetime he had held his judgment suspended between the pair.— Now, however, after opening his letter with a prayer that Heaven would prosper his counsels to the good of the realm, he devoted a few sentences, free from false embellishments, to the character of the youth:—" He had a wife and three children; and he had reached the age [4] at which, formerly, he himself had been called by the deified Augustus to undertake the same charge. Nor was it in haste, but only after eight years of trial, after mutinies repressed, wars composed, one triumph, and two consulates, that he was now admitted to share a task already familiar."

LVII. The members had foreseen this pronouncement, and their flatteries were therefore well prepared. Invention, however, went no further than to decree effigies of the princes, altars to the gods,

aliaque solita censerent, nisi quod M. Silanus ex
contumelia consulatus honorem principibus petivit
dixitque pro sententia ut publicis privatisve monimentis, ad memoriam temporum, non consulum
nomina praescriberentur, sed eorum qui tribuniciam
potestatem gererent. At Q.[1] Haterius cum eius diei
senatus consulta aureis litteris figenda in curia cen-
suisset deridiculo fuit senex foedissimae adulationis
tantum infam a usurus.

LVIII. Inter quae provincia Africa Iunio Blaeso
prorogata, Servius Maluginensis flamen Dialis ut
Asiam sorte haberet postulavit, frustra vulgatum
dictitans non licere Dialibus egredi Italia neque
aliud ius suum quam Martialium Quirinaliumque
flaminum: porro, si hi duxissent provincias, cur
Dialibus id vetitum? Nulla de eo populi scita, non
in libris caerimoniarum reperiri. Saepe pontifices
Dialia sacra fecisse, si flamen valetudine aut munere
publico impediretur. Quinque [2] et septuaginta annis
post Cornelii Merulae caedem, neminem suffectum
neque tamen cessavisse religiones. Quod si per tot
annos possit non creari nullo sacrorum damno, quanto
facilius afuturum ad unius anni proconsulare im-

---

[1] at Q. *Lipsius* : atque.
[2] quinque *Lachmann* : duobus.

---

[1] See above, chap. 24.   [2] IV. 61.
[3] See chap. 35.
[4] The fifteen Flamens ("kindlers"), a priesthood of im-
memorial antiquity, were devoted each to the service of a special
cult. Twelve were of secondary importance : of the remaining
three the chief was the Flamen of Jupiter (*Fl. Dialis*). The
extraordinary taboos, which must have embittered his
existence but have endeared him to the anthropologists, are
enumerated by Aulus Gellius (X. 15).

temples, arches, and other time-worn honours. An exception was when Marcus Silanus [1] sought a compliment to the principate in a slight to the consulship, and proposed that on public and private monuments the inscription recording the date should bear the names, not of the consuls for the year, but of the persons exercising the tribunician power. Quintus Haterius,[2] who moved that the day's resolutions should be set up in the senate-house in letters of gold, was derided as an old man who could reap nothing from his repulsive adulation save its infamy.

LVIII. Meanwhile, after the governorship of Junius Blaesus [3] in Africa had been extended, the Flamen Dialis,[4] Servius Maluginensis, demanded the allotment of Asia [5] to himself. "It was a common fallacy," he insisted, "that the flamens of Jove were not allowed to leave Italy; nor was his own legal status different from that of the flamens of Mars and Quirinus. If, then, they had had provinces allotted them, why was the right withheld from the priests of Jove? There was no national decree to be found on the point—nothing in the Books of Ceremonies. The pontiffs had often performed the rites of Jove, if the flamen was prevented by sickness or public business. For seventy-five years after the self-murder of Cornelius Merula [6] no one had been appointed in his room, yet the rites had not been interrupted. But if so many years could elapse without a new creation, and without detriment to the cult, how much more easily could he absent himself for twelve months of proconsular authority?

[5] The case is much the same as in the year before (see chap. 32, note), since Africa is again reserved for Blaesus.

[6] In 87 B.C. on the return of Cinna.

perium? Privatis olim simultatibus effectum ut a pontificibus maximis ire in provincias prohiberentur: nunc deum munere summum pontificum etiam summum hominum esse, non aemulationi, non odio aut privatis adfectionibus obnoxium.

LIX. Adversus quae cum augur Lentulus aliique varie dissererent, eo decursum est ut pontificis maximi sententiam opperirentur. Tiberius, dilata notione de iure flaminis, decretas ob tribuniciam Drusi potestatem caerimonias temperavit, nominatim arguens insolentiam sententiae aureasque litteras contra patrium morem. Recitatae et Drusi epistulae, quamquam ad modestiam flexae, pro superbissimis accipiuntur. Huc decidisse cuncta ut ne iuvenis quidem tanto honore accepto adiret urbis deos, ingrederetur senatum, auspicia saltem gentile apud solum inciperet. Bellum scilicet aut diverso terrarum distineri, litora et lacus Campaniae cum maxime peragrantem. Sic imbui rectorem generis humani, id primum e paternis consiliis discere. Sane gravaretur aspectum civium senex imperator fessamque aetatem et actos labores praetenderet: Druso quod nisi ex adrogantia impedimentum?

LX. Sed Tiberius, vim principatus sibi firmans,

---

¹ From 12 B.C. the title was invariably conferred on the emperor, until finally it passed to the bishops of Rome.

² Cn. Cornelius Lentulus. consul 14 B.C.; proconsul of Asia, 1 B.C.; famous for his wealth (estimated at 400,000,000 sesterc s), his stupidity and his slowness of speech (*tam pusilli oris quam animi : cum esset avarissimus, nummos citius emittebat quam verba*, Sen. *De ben.* II. 27); committed suicide under Tiberius (Suet. *Tib.* 49).

Personal rivalries had no doubt in former times led the pontiffs to prohibit his order from visiting the provinces: to-day, by the grace of Heaven, the chief pontiff was also the chief of men,[1] beyond the reach of jealousy, rancour, or private inclinations."

LIX. Since various objections to the argument were raised by the augur Lentulus [2] and others, it was determined, in the upshot, to wait for the verdict of the supreme pontiff himself.

Tiberius postponed his inquiry into the legal standing of the flamen, but modified the ceremonies with which it had been resolved to celebrate the tribunician power of Drusus; criticizing specifically the unprecedented motion of Haterius and the gold lettering so repugnant to Roman custom. A letter, too, from Drusus was read, which, though tuned to a modest key, left an impression of extreme arrogance. " So the world," men said, " had come to this, that even a mere boy, invested with such an honour, would not approach the divinities of Rome, set foot within the senate, or, at the least, take the auspices on his native soil. War, they must assume, or some remote quarter of the world detained him; though at that instant he was perambulating the lakes and beaches of Campania! Such was the initiation of the governor of the human race, these the first lessons derived from the paternal instruction! A grey-haired emperor might, if he pleased, recoil from the view of his fellow-citizens, and plead the fatigue of age and the labours he had accomplished: but, in the case of Drusus, what impediment could there be save pride ? "

LX. Tiberius, however, while tightening his grasp on the solid power of the principate, vouchsafed to the

imaginem antiquitatis senatui praebebat, postulata
provinciarum ad disquisitionem patrum mittendo.
Crebrescebat enim Graecas per urbes licentia atque
impunitas asyla statuendi; complebantur templa
pessimis servitiorum; eodem subsidio obaerati adversum creditores suspectique capitalium criminum
receptabantur, nec ullum satis validum imperium
erat coercendis seditionibus populi flagitia hominum
ut caerimonias deum protegentis. Igitur placitum
ut mitterent civitates iura atque legatos. Et quaedam quod falso usurpaverant sponte omisere; multae vetustis superstitionibus aut meritis in populum Romanum fidebant. Magnaque eius diei species fuit quo senatus maiorum beneficia, sociorum
pacta, regum etiam qui ante vim Romanam value-
rant decreta ipsorumque numinum religiones intro-
spexit, libero, ut quondam, quid firmaret mutaretve.

LXI. Primi omnium Ephesii adiere, memorantes
non, ut vulgus crederet, Dianam atque Apollinem
Delo genitos: esse apud se Cenchrium amnem,
lucum [1] Ortygiam, ubi Latonam partu gravidam et
oleae, quae tum etiam maneat, adnisam edidisse ea
numina, deorumque monitu sacratum nemus, atque
ipsum illic Apollinem post interfectos Cyclopas Iovis
iram vitavisse. Mox Liberum patrem, bello victorem, supplicibus Amazonum quae aram insiderant
ignovisse. Auctam hinc concessu Herculis, cum

---

[1] lucum *Lipsius* : locum.

---

[1] But only of the senatorial provinces.
[2] A common poetical name for Delos.

senate a shadow of the past by submitting the claims of the provinces [1] to the discussion of its members. For throughout the Greek cities there was a growing laxity, and impunity, in the creation of rights of asylum. The temples were filled with the dregs of the slave population; the same shelter was extended to the debtor against his creditor and to the man suspected of a capital offence; nor was any authority powerful enough to quell the factions of a race which protected human felony equally with divine worship. It was resolved, therefore, that the communities in question should send their charters and deputies to Rome. A few abandoned without a struggle the claims they had asserted without a title: many relied on hoary superstitions or on their services to the Roman nation. It was an impressive spectacle which that day afforded, when the senate scrutinized the benefactions of its predecessors, the constitutions of the provinces, even the decrees of kings whose power antedated the arms of Rome, and the rites of the deities themselves, with full liberty as of old to confirm or change.

LXI. The Ephesians were the first to appear. "Apollo and Diana," they stated, "were not, as commonly supposed, born at Delos. In Ephesus there was a river Cenchrius, with a grove Ortygia [2]; where Latona, heavy-wombed and supporting herself by an olive-tree which remained to that day, gave birth to the heavenly twins. The grove had been hallowed by divine injunction; and there Apollo himself, after slaying the Cyclopes, had evaded the anger of Jove. Afterwards Father Liber, victor in the war, had pardoned the suppliant Amazons who had seated themselves at the altar. Then the sanctity

Lydia poteretur, caerimoniam templo neque Persarum dicione deminutum ius; post Macedonas, dein nos servavisse.

LXII. Proximi hos Magnetes [1] L. Scipionis et L. Sullae constitutis nitebantur, quorum ille Antiocho, hic Mithridate pulsis fidem atque virtutem Magnetum decoravere, uti Dianae Leucophrynae [2] perfugium inviolabile foret. Aphrodisienses posthac et Stratonicenses dictatoris Caesaris ob vetusta in partis merita et recens divi Augusti decretum adtulere, laudati quod Parthorum inruptionem nihil mutata in populum Romanum constantia pertulissent. Sed Aphrodisiensium civitas Veneris, Stratonicensium Iovis et Triviae religionem tuebantur. Altius Hierocaesarienses exposuere, Persicam apud se Dianam, delubrum rege Cyro dicatum; et memorabantur Perpennae, Isaurici multaque alia imperatorum nomina qui non modo templo, sed duobus milibus passuum eandem sanctitatem tribuerant. Exim Cyprii tribus de delubris,[3] quorum vetustissimum

---

[1] proximi hos Magnetes *Wurm* (proximi Magnetes *Freinsheim*) : proximosnagnetes.

[2] Leucophrynae *Lipsius* (Leucophryenae *Beroaldus*) : leucophinae.

[3] de delubris *Bezzenberger* : delubris.

---

[1] Here, and at IV. 55, not the *Magnees a Sipylo* of II. 47, but those of Magnesia on the Maeander.

[2] In 190 B.C. and 88 B.C. : see Liv. XXXVII. 45 and *Epit.* LXXX.

[3] So named, apparently, from an older town, Leucophrys, on the site of which Magnesia stood.

[4] Stratonicea (named after the famous daughter of Demetrius Poliorcetes, wife of Seleucus and Antiochus Soter) lay in Caria : Aphrodisias is placed by Strabo on the Phrygian side of the frontier; by Pliny, on the Carian.

of the temple had been enhanced, with the permission of Hercules, while he held the crown of Lydia; its privileges had not been diminished under the Persian empire; later, they had been preserved by the Macedonians—last by ourselves."

LXII. The Magnesians,[1] who followed, rested their case on the rulings of Lucius Scipio and Lucius Sulla, who, after their defeats of Antiochus and Mithridates respectively,[2] had honoured the loyalty and courage of Magnesia by making the shrine of Leucophryne Diana[3] an inviolable refuge. Next, Aphrodisias and Stratonicea[4] adduced a decree of the dictator Julius in return for their early services to his cause, together with a modern rescript of the deified Augustus, who praised the unchanging fidelity to the Roman nation with which they had sustained the Parthian inroad.[5] Aphrodisias, however, was championing the cult of Venus; Stratonicea, that of Jove and Diana of the Crossways. The statement of Hierocaesarea[6] went deeper into the past: the community owned a Persian Diana[7] with a temple dedicated in the reign of Cyrus; and there were references to Perpenna,[8] Isauricus,[9] and many other commanders who had allowed the same sanctity not only to the temple but to the neighbourhood for two miles round. The Cypriotes followed with an appeal for three shrines—the oldest erected by their

[5] Under Q. Labienus and the Parthian prince Pacorus, in 40 B.C. Tacitus' sentence obscures the fact that the decree of Julius referred only to Aphrodisias; that of Augustus only to Stratonicea.

[6] In Lydia. [7] Anaïtis.

[8] Defeated and captured Aristonicus of Pergamum in 130 B.C.

[9] P. Servilius Vatia Isauricus, consul with Caesar in 48 B.C.; proconsul of Asia two years later.

Paphiae Veneri auctor Aërias, post filius eius Amathus Veneri Amathusiae et Iovi Salaminio Teucer, Telamonis patris ira profugus, posuissent. LXIII. Auditae aliarum quoque civitatium legationes. Quorum copia fessi patres, et quia studiis certabatur, consulibus permisere ut, perspecto iure et si qua iniquitas involveretur, rem integram rursum ad senatum referrent. Consules super eas civitates quas memoravi apud Pergamum Aesculapii compertum asylum rettulerunt, ceteros obscuris ob vetustatem initiis niti. Nam Zmyrnaeos oraculum Apollinis, cuius imperio Stratonicidi Veneri, templum dicaverint, Tenios eiusdem carmen referre quo sacrare Neptuni effigiem aedemque iussi sint. Propiora Sardianos: Alexandri victoris id donum. Neque minus Milesios Dareo rege niti; set [1] cultus numinum utrisque Dianam aut Apollinem venerandi. Petere et Cretenses simulacro divi Augusti. Factaque senatus consulta quis multo cum honore modus tamen praescribebatur, iussique ipsis in templis figere aera sacrandam ad memoriam, neu specie religionis in ambitionem delaberentur.

LXIV. Sub idem tempus Iuliae Augustae valetudo atrox necessitudinem principi fecit festinati in urbem reditus, sincera adhuc inter matrem filium-

---

[1] rege niti set *Lipsius* : regi utiset.

---

[1] See *Hist*. II. 3 (Titus' visit to the shrine). The image (ξυμβολικῶς ἱδρυμένον. Philostr. *V.A*. III. *fin*.) was apparently a conical stone (though see Max. Tyr. viii. 8 : ἡ δὲ ὕλη ἀγνοεῖται).

[2] In Mysia; the seat of the famous Hellenistic kingdom bequeathed to the Roman people by Attalus Philometor (133 B.C.). The name survives as Bergama.

[3] Tino[s] in the Cyclades, which were attached to the province of Asia.

[4] See above, chap. 31.

founder Aërias to the Paphian Venus;[1] the second by his son Amathus to the Amathusian Venus; and a third by Teucer, exiled by the anger of his father Telamon, to Jove of Salamis.

LXIII. Deputations from other states were heard as well; till the Fathers, weary of the details, and disliking the acrimony of the discussion, empowered the consuls to investigate the titles, in search of any latent flaw, and to refer the entire question back to the senate. Their report was that—apart from the communities I have already named—they were satisfied there was a genuine sanctuary of Aesculapius at Pergamum;[2] other claimants relied on pedigrees too ancient to be clear. " For Smyrna cited an oracle of Apollo, at whose command the town had dedicated a temple to Venus Stratonicis; Tenos,[3] a prophecy from the same source, ordering the consecration of a statue and shrine to Neptune. Sardis touched more familiar ground with a grant from the victorious Alexander; Miletus had equal confidence in King Darius. With these two, however, the divine object of adoration was Diana in the one case, Apollo in the other. The Cretans, again, were claiming for an effigy of the deified Augustus." The senate, accordingly, passed a number of resolutions, scrupulously complimentary, but still imposing a limit; and the applicants were ordered to fix the brass records actually inside the temples, both as a solemn memorial and as a warning not to lapse into secular intrigue under the cloak of religion.

LXIV. About the same time, a serious illness of Julia Augusta made it necessary for the emperor to hasten his return[4] to the capital, the harmony between mother and son being still genuine, or

que concordia sive occultis odiis. Neque enim multo
ante, cum haud procul theatro Marcelli effigiem divo
Augusto Iulia dicaret, Tiberi nomen suo postscrip-
serat idque ille credebatur ut inferius maiestate
principis gravi et dissimulata offensione abdidisse.
Set tum supplicia dis ludique magni ab senatu decernuntur, quos pontifices et augures et quindecimviri,
septemviris simul et sodalibus Augustalibus, ederent.
Censuerat L. Apronius ut fetiales quoque iis ludis
praesiderent. Contra dixit Caesar, distincto sacer-
dotiorum iure et repetitis exemplis: neque enim
umquam fetialibus hoc maiestatis fuisse. Ideo
Augustalis adiectos quia proprium eius domus
sacerdotium esset pro qua vota persolverentur.

LXV. Exequi sententias haud institui nisi insignis per honestum aut notabili dedecore, quod praecipuum munus annalium reor ne virtutes sileantur
utque pravis dictis factisque ex posteritate et infamia metus sit. Ceterum tempora illa adeo infecta
et adulatione sordida fuere ut non modo primores
civitatis, quibus claritudo sua obsequiis protegenda
erat, sed omnes consulares, magna pars eorum qui
praetura functi multique etiam pedarii senatores cer-

---

[1] Fast. Praenest. (VIII Kal. Mai.):—*Signum divo Augusto
patri ad theatrum Marcelli Iulia Augusta et Ti. Augustus
dedicarunt.*

[2] The *pontifices, augures,* and *quindecimviri* (entrusted with
the charge of the Sibylline books and a general supervision of
foreign cults), together with the *septemviri*—originally *tresviri*—
epulones (instituted in 196 B.C. to manage the sacred *epulae,*
and now ten in number) constituted the four great priestly
colleges. For the Augustales, see I. 54.

[3] Their functions (now largely obsolete) were concerned with
international formalities—declarations of war, conclusions of
treaties, etc. See, for instance, Livy, I. 24; *ib.* 32; XXX.
43; Gell. XVI. 4.

their hatred concealed: for a little earlier, Julia, in dedicating an effigy to the deified Augustus not far from the Theatre of Marcellus, had placed Tiberius' name after her own in the inscription;[1] and it was believed that, taking the act as a derogation from the imperial dignity, he had locked it in his breast with grave and veiled displeasure. Now, however, the senate gave orders for a solemn intercession and the celebration of the Great Games— the latter to be exhibited by the pontiffs, the augurs, and the Fifteen, assisted by the Seven and by the Augustal fraternities.[2] Lucius Apronius had moved that the Fetials[3] should also preside at the Games. The Caesar opposed, drawing a distinction between the prerogatives of the various priesthoods, adducing precedents, and pointing out that " the Fetials had never had that degree of dignity, while the Augustals had only been admitted among the others because theirs was a special priesthood of the house for which the intercession was being offered."

LXV. It is not my intention to dwell upon any senatorial motions save those either remarkable for their nobility or of memorable turpitude; in which case they fall within my conception of the first duty of history—to ensure that merit shall not lack its record and to hold before the vicious word and deed the terrors of posterity and infamy. But so tainted was that age, so mean its sycophancy, that not only the great personages of the state, who had to shield their magnificence by their servility, but all senators of consular rank, a large proportion of the ex-praetors, many ordinary members[4] even, vied with

[4] Probably senators who had not held a curule office: the term was obscure even to Varro (Gell. III. 18).

tatim exsurgerent foedaque et nimia censerent.
Memoriae proditur Tiberium, quoties curia egrederetur, Graecis verbis in hunc modum eloqui solitum:
" O homines ad servitutem paratos ! " Scilicet etiam
illum qui libertatem publicam nollet tam proiectae
servientium patientiae taedebat.

LXVI. Paulatim dehinc ab indecoris ad infesta
transgrediebantur. C. Silanum pro consule Asiae
repetundarum a sociis postulatum Mamercus Scaurus e consularibus, Iunius Otho praetor, Bruttedius
Niger aedilis simul corripiunt obiectantque violatum Augusti numen, spretam Tiberii maiestatem,
Mamercus antiqua exempla iaciens, L. Cottam a
Scipione Africano, Servium Galbam a Catone cen-
sorio, P. Rutilium a M. Scauro accusatos. Videlicet
Scipio et Cato talia ulciscebantur aut ille Scaurus,
quem proavum suum obprobrium maiorum Mamercus
infami opera dehonestabat. Iunio Othoni littera-
rium ludum exercere vetus ars fuit: mox Seiani
potentia senator obscura initia impudentibus ausis
prope polluebat.[1] Bruttedium artibus honestis
copiosum et, si rectum iter pergeret, ad clarissima
quaeque iturum festinatio exstimulabat, dum
aequalis, dein superiores, postremo suasmet ipse

---

1 prope polluebat *R. Seyffert* (*alii alia*): propolluebat.

---

1 I. 13; III. 23 and 31; VI. 9 and 29.
2 By perjury : see I. 73.
3 Between 132 and 129 B.C. (Cic. *pro. Mur.* 28).
4 149 B.C. (Cic. *Brut.* 23).
5 116 B.C. (Cic. *Brut.* 30)
6 It is difficult to believe in the compound *propolluebat*,
though the conjecture inserted in the text has no claim to
certainty: other suggestions are *occullebat* (Madvig), *porro
polluebat* (Lipsius), *ultro polluebat* (Ritter). As to Otho, it is

one another in rising to move the most repulsive and
extravagant resolutions. The tradition runs that
Tiberius, on leaving the curia, had a habit of ejaculat-
ing in Greek, " These men!—how ready they are
for slavery! " Even he, it was manifest, objecting
though he did to public liberty, was growing weary
of such grovelling patience in his slaves.

LXVI. Then, step by step, they passed from the
degrading to the brutal. Gaius Silanus, the proconsul of Asia, accused of extortion by the provincials, was attacked simultaneously by the ex-consul
Mamercus Scaurus,[1] the praetor Junius Otho, and
the aedile Bruttedius Niger, who flung at him the
charge of violating the godhead of Augustus [2] and
spurning the majesty of Tiberius, while Mamercus
made play with the precedents of antiquity—the
indictment of Lucius Cotta by Scipio Africanus,[3] of
Servius Galba by Cato the Censor,[4] of Publius Rutilius
by Marcus Scaurus.[5] Such, as all men know, were
the crimes avenged by Scipio and Cato or the famous
Scaurus, the great-grandsire of Mamercus, whom that
reproach to his ancestors dishonoured by his infamous
activity! Junius Otho's old profession had been to
keep a school: afterwards, created a senator by the
influence of Sejanus, by his effrontery and audacity
he brought further ignominy, if possible, upon the
meanness of his beginnings.[6] Bruttedius, amply provided with liberal accomplishments, and bound, if
he kept the straight road, to attain all distinctions,
was goaded by a spirit of haste, which impelled him
to outpace first his equals, then his superiors, and

known from the elder Seneca that he rose to be a rhetorician
of some eminence. The tribune, Junius Otho, of VI. 47, is
his son.

spes antire parat; quod multos etiam bonos pessum dedit, qui spretis quae tarda cum securitate, praematura vel cum exitio properant.

LXVII. Auxere numerum accusatorum Gellius Publicola et M. Paconius, ille quaestor Silani, hic legatus. Nec dubium habebatur saevitiae captarumque pecuniarum teneri reum; sed multa adgerebantur etiam insontibus periculosa, cum super tot senatores adversos facundissimis totius Asiae eoque ad accusandum delectis responderet solus et orandi nescius, proprio in metu qui exercitam quoque eloquentiam debilitat, non temperante Tiberio quin premeret voce, vultu, eo quod ipse creberrime interrogabat, neque refellere aut eludere dabatur, ac saepe etiam confitendum erat ne frustra quaesivisset. Servos quoque Silani, ut tormentis interrogarentur, actor publicus mancipio acceperat. Et ne quis necessariorum iuvaret periclitantem maiestatis crimina subdebantur, vinclum et necessitas silen.li. Igitur petito paucorum dierum interiectu defensionem sui deseruit, ausis ad Caesarem codicillis quibus invidiam et preces miscuerat.

LXVIII. Tiberius quae in Silanum parabat quo excusatius sub exemplo acciperentur, libellos divi

---

[1] Tt is inferred from Juv. X. 81 *sqq.* that he was one of those to whom the fall of Sejanus proved fatal.

[2] See II. 30.

finally his own ambitions: an infirmity fatal to many, even of the good, who, disdaining the sure and slow, force a premature success, though destruction may accompany the prize.[1]

LXVII. The number of the accusers was swelled by Gellius Publicola and Marcus Paconius, the former the quaestor of Silanus, the latter his legate. No doubt was felt that the defendant was guilty on the counts of cruelty and malversation; but there were many additional circumstances, which would have imperilled even the innocent. Over and above the array of hostile senators were the most fluent advocates of all Asia, selected, as such, to press the charge; and to these was replying a solitary man, devoid of forensic knowledge, and beset by that personal fear which enfeebles even professional eloquence: for Tiberius did not scruple to injure his case, by word, by look, by the fact that he himself was most assiduous in his questions, which it was permissible neither to refute nor to elude, while often an admission had to be made, lest the sovereign should have asked in vain. Further, to allow the examination of his slaves under torture, they had been formally sold to the treasury-agent[2]; and, lest a single friend should come to his help in the hour of peril, charges of treason were subjoined—a binding and inevitable argument for silence. He requested, therefore, an interval of a few days, and threw up his defence, first hazarding a note to the Caesar in which he had mingled reproaches with petitions.

LXVIII. Tiberius, in order that the measures he was preparing against Silanus might come with the better grace through being supported by a precedent, ordered the bill in which the deified Augustus had

Augusti de Voleso Messala eiusdem Asiae pro consule factumque in eum senatus consultum recitari
iubet. Tum L. Pisonem sententiam rogat. Ille
multum de clementia principis praefatus aqua atque
igni Silano interdicendum censuit ipsumque in insulam Gyarum relegandum. Eadem ceteri, nisi quod
Cn. Lentulus separanda Silani materna bona, quippe
Atia[1] parente geniti, reddendaque filio dixit,
adnuente Tiberio.

LXIX. At Cornelius Dolabella, dum adulationem
longius sequitur, increpitis C. Silani moribus addidit
ne quis vita probrosus et opertus infamia provinciam
sortiretur, idque princeps diiudicaret. Nam a legibus delicta puniri; quanto fore mitius in ipsos, melius in socios, provideri ne peccaretur? Adversum
quae disseruit Caesar: non quidem sibi ignara quae
de Silano vulgabantur, sed non ex rumore statuen-
dum. Multos in provinciis contra quam spes aut
metus de illis fuerit egisse: excitari quosdam ad
meliora magnitudine rerum, hebescere alios. Neque
posse principem sua scientia cuncta complecti neque
expedire ut ambitione aliena trahatur. Ideo leges
in facta constitui quia futura in incerto sint. Sic

---

[1] Atia *Madvig*: alia.

---

[1] L. Valerius Messala Volesus, proconsul of Asia *ca.* 12 A.D.
Seneca couples him with Phalaris and Hannibal as a type of
bloodthirstiness (*de ira* 5).

[2] A rock-bound islet in the Aegean, which served, with
others, as a Roman St. Helena (see Juv. I. 73, Mayor). The
modern name is Giura (Jura), and στὰ Γιοῦρα is, or was, a
Romaïc equivalent of βάλλ' ἐς κόρακας (Coraës on Isocr.
Aeginet. init.).

[3] The *gens* of Augustus' mother—daughter of M. Atius
Balbus and Caesar's sister Julia.

indicted Volesus Messala,[1] another proconsul of Asia, to be read aloud, together with the decree registered against him by the senate. He then asked Lucius Piso for his opinion. After a long preface devoted to the sovereign's clemency, he declared for the outlawry of Silanus from fire and water and his relegation to the isle of Gyarus.[2] So, too, the others; with the exception of Gnaeus Lentulus, who moved that, so far as the property of Silanus had been derived from his mother, it should, as she came of the Atian house,[3] be treated as distinct from the rest and restored to his son.

LXIX. Tiberius approved; but Cornelius Dolabella, to pursue the sycophancy further, proposed, after an attack on Silanus' character, that no man of scandalous life and bankrupt reputation should be eligible for a province, the decision in such cases to rest with the emperor. " For delinquencies were punished by the law; but how much more merciful to the delinquent, how much better for the provincial, to provide against all irregularities beforehand! " The Caesar spoke in opposition :—" True, the reports with regard to Silanus were not unknown to him; but judgments could not be based on rumour. Many a man by his conduct in his province had reversed the hopes or fears entertained concerning him : some natures were roused to better things by great position, others became sluggish. It was neither possible for a prince to comprehend everything within his own knowledge, nor desirable that he should be influenced by the intrigues of others. The reason why laws were made retrospective towards the thing done was that things to be were indeterminable. It was on this principle their fore-

a maioribus institutum ut, si antissent delicta, poenae
sequerentur: ne verterent sapienter reperta et
semper placita. Satis onerum principibus, satis etiam
potentiae: minui iura[1] quotiens gliscat potestas,
nec utendum imperio ubi legibus agi possit. Quanto
rarior apud Tiberium popularitas, tanto laetiori-
ribus animis accepta. Atque ille prudens moderandi,
si propria ira non impelleretur, addidit insulam
Gyarum immitem et sine cultu hominum esse:
darent Iuniae familiae et viro quondam ordinis
eiusdem ut Cythnum potius concederet. Id sororem quoque Silani Torquatam, priscae sanctimo-
niae virginem expetere. In hanc sententiam facta
discessio.

LXX. Post auditi Cyrenenses et accusante An-
chario Prisco Caesius Cordus repetundarum damnatur. L. Ennium equitem Romanum, maiestatis
postulatum quod effigiem principis promiscum ad
usum argenti vertisset, recipi Caesar inter reos
vetuit, palam aspernante Ateio Capitone quasi per
libertatem. Non enim debere eripi patribus vim
statuendi neque tantum maleficium impune habendum. Sane lentus in suo dolore esset: rei publicae
iniurias ne largiretur. Intellexit haec Tiberius, ut

---

[1] minui iura *Lipsius* : minutura.

[1] A larger island, south of Ceos (commonly Θερμιά, but now
again officially Κύθνος).

[2] Since no objection to the proposal could be expected, the
division (*discessio*) was taken without asking the opinion of
members in the usual rotation: see Gell. XIV. 7, § 9 and § 13
(after Varro and Ateius Capito).

[3] See chap. 38: the intervening year had been allowed
for the collection of evidence.—Cyrene (in conjunction with
Crete, a senatorial province) was the strip of territory between
Egypt and " Africa."

fathers had ruled that, if an offence had preceded, punishment should follow; and they must not now overturn a system wisely invented and always observed. Princes had enough of burdens—enough, even, of power: the rights of the subject shrank as autocracy grew; and, where it was possible to proceed by form of law, it was a mistake to employ the fiat of the sovereign." These democratic doctrines were hailed with a pleasure answering to their rarity on the lips of Tiberius. He himself, tactful and moderate when not swayed by personal anger, added that " Gyarus was a bleak and uninhabited island. Out of consideration for the Junian house and for a man once their peer, they might allow him to retire to Cythnus[1] instead. This was also the desire of Silanus' sister Torquata, a Vestal of old-world saintliness." The proposal was adopted without discussion.[2]

LXX. Later, an audience was given to the Cyrenaeans, and Caesius Cordus was convicted of extortion on the arraignment of Ancharius Priscus.[3] Lucius Ennius, a Roman knight, found himself indicted for treason on the ground that he had turned a statuette of the emperor to the promiscuous uses of household silver.[4] The Caesar forbade the entry of the case for trial, though Ateius Capito[5] protested openly and with a display of freedom: for " the right of decision ought not to be snatched from the senate, nor should so grave an offence pass without punishment. By all means let the sovereign be easy-tempered in a grievance of his own; but injuries to the state he must not condone!" Tiberius under-

---

[4] By melting it down into plate.
[5] See below, chap. 75.

erant magis quam ut dicebantur, perstititque inter-
cedere. Capito insignitior infamia fuit quod humani
divinique iuris sciens egregium publicum et bonas
domi artes dehonestavisset.

LXXI. Incessit dein religio quonam in templo
locandum foret donum quod pro valetudine Augustae equites Romani voverant equestri Fortunae:
nam etsi delubra eius deae multa in urbe, nullum
tamen tali cognomento erat. Repertum est aedem
esse apud Antium quae sic nuncuparetur cunctasque
caerimonias Italicis in oppidis templaque et numinum effigies iuris atque imperii Romani esse. Ita
donum apud Antium statuitur. Et quoniam de
religionibus tractabatur, dilatum nuper responsum
adversus Servium Maluginensem, flaminem Dialem,
prompsit [1] Caesar recitavitque decretum pontificum,
quotiens valetudo adversa flaminem Dialem inces-
sisset, ut pontificis maximi arbitrio plus quam binoc-
tium abesset, dum ne diebus publici sacrificii neu
saepius quam bis eundem in annum; quae principe
Augusto constituta satis ostendebant annuam absentiam et provinciarum administrationem Dialibus
non concedi. Memorabaturque L. Metelli pontificis
maximi exemplum qui Aulum Postumium flaminem attinuisset. Ita sors Asiae in eum qui consularium Maluginensi proximus erat conlata.

LXXII. Isdem diebus M.[2] Lepidus ab senatu

[1] prompsit *Lipsius*: promisit.
[2] M. Lepidus *Nipperdey*: Lepidus.

---

[1] One vowed in 180 B.C., to commemorate an exploit of the
Roman cavalry (Liv. XL. 40), and extant nearly 90 years later,
had presumably perished.
[2] Porto d'Anzio.   [3] See chap. 58.
[4] In 242 B.C.: he was, however, a flamen of Mars (Liv. *Epit.*
XIX.).

stood this for what it was, rather than for what it purported to be, and persisted in his veto. The degradation of Capito was unusually marked, since, authority as he was on secular and religious law, he was held to have dishonoured not only the fair fame of the state but his personal good qualities.

LXXI. A problem in religion now presented itself: in what temple were the knights to lodge the offering vowed, in connection with Augusta's illness, to Equestrian Fortune? For though shrines to Fortune were plentiful in the city, none carried the epithet in question.[1] It was found that there was a temple of the name at Antium,[2] and that all sacred rites in the country towns of Italy, with all places of worship and divine images, were subject to the jurisdiction and authority of Rome. At Antium, accordingly, the gift was placed.

And since points of religion were under consideration, the Caesar produced his recently deferred answer[3] to the Flamen Dialis, Servius Maluginensis; and read a pontifical decree, according to which the Flamen, whenever attacked by illness, might at the discretion of the supreme pontiff absent himself for more than two nights, so long as it was not on days of public sacrifice nor oftener than twice in one year. The ruling thus laid down in the principate of Augustus showed that a year's absence and a provincial governorship were not for the flamens of Jupiter. Attention was also called to a precedent set by the supreme pontiff, Lucius Metellus; who had vetoed the departure of the Flamen, Aulus Postumius.[4] Asia, therefore, was allotted to the consular next in seniority to Maluginensis.

LXXII. Nearly at the same time, Marcus Lepidus

petivit ut basilicam Pauli, Aemilia monimenta, propria pecunia firmaret ornaretque. Erat etiam tum in more publica munificentia; nec Augustus arcuerat Taurum, Philippum, Balbum hostilis exuvias aut exundantis opes ornatum ad urbis et posterum gloriam conferre. Quo tum exemplo Lepidus, quamquam pecuniae modicus, avitum decus recoluit. At Pompei theatrum igne fortuito haustum Caesar exstructurum pollicitus est, eo quod nemo e familia restaurando sufficeret, manente tamen nomine Pompei. Simul laudibus Seianum extulit tamquam labore vigilantiaque eius tanta vis unum intra damnum stetisset; et censuere patres effigiem Seiano quae apud theatrum Pompei locaretur. Neque multo post Caesar, cum Iunium Blaesum pro consule Africae triumphi insignibus attolleret, dare id se dixit honori Seiani, cuius ille avunculus erat. Ac tamen res Blaesi dignae decore tali fuere.

LXXIII. Nam Tacfarinas, quamquam saepius depulsus, reparatis per intima Africae auxiliis huc adrogantiae venerat ut legatos ad Tiberium mitteret sedemque ultro sibi atque exercitui suo postularet aut bellum inexplicabile minitaretur. Non alias magis sua populique Romani contumelia indo-

---

[1] Begun in 50 B.C. by the grandfather of Lepidus; completed and dedicated by his father; burnt down in 14 B.C., and restored by Augustus and friends of the family.

[2] Suet. *Aug.* 29:—With the encouragement of Augustus, *multa . . . a multis extructa sunt, sicut a Marcio Philippo aedes Herculis Musarum . . . a Cornelio Balbo theatrum, a Statilio Tauro amphitheatrum* (the first to be constructed of stone).

[3] Hence the epigram of Cremutius Cordus:—*Tunc vere theatrum perire* (Sen. *cons. ad Marc.* 22).

asked permission from the senate to strengthen and decorate the Basilica of Paulus,[1] a monument of the Aemilian house, at his own expense. Public munificence was a custom still; nor had Augustus debarred a Taurus, a Philippus, or a Balbus[2] from devoting the trophies of his arms or the overflow of his wealth to the greater splendour of the capital and the glory of posterity: and now Lepidus, a man of but moderate fortune, followed in their steps by renovating the famous edifice of his fathers. On the other hand, the rebuilding of the Theatre of Pompey, destroyed by a casual fire, was undertaken by the Caesar, on the ground that no member of the family was equal to the task of restoration: the name of Pompey was, however, to remain. At the same time, he gave high praise to Sejanus, "through whose energy and watchfulness so grave an outbreak had stopped at one catastrophe." The Fathers voted a statue to Sejanus, to be placed in the Theatre of Pompey.[3] Again, a short time afterwards, when he was honouring Junius Blaesus, proconsul of Africa, with the triumphal insignia, he explained that he did so as a compliment to Sejanus, of whom Blaesus was uncle.—None the less the exploits of Blaesus deserved such a distinction.

LXXIII. For Tacfarinas,[4] in spite of many repulses, having first recruited his forces in the heart of Africa, had reached such a pitch of insolence as to send an embassy to Tiberius, demanding nothing less than a territorial settlement for himself and his army, and threatening in the alternative a war from which there was no extrication. By all accounts, no insult to himself and the nation ever stung the emperor

[4] See chap. 32.

luisse Caesarem ferunt quam quod desertor et praedo hostium more ageret. Ne Spartaco quidem post tot consularium exercituum cladis inultam Italiam urenti, quamquam Sertorii atque Mithridatis ingentibus bellis labaret res publica, datum ut pacto in fidem acciperetur; nedum pulcherrimo populi Romani fastigio latro Tacfarinas pace et concessione agrorum redimeretur. Dat negotium Blaeso: ceteros quidem ad spem proliceret arma sine noxa ponendi, ipsius autem ducis quoquo modo poteretur. Et recepti ea venia plerique. Mox adversum artes Tacfarinatis haud dissimili modo belligeratum.

LXXIV. Nam, quia ille robore exercitus impar, furandi melior, pluris per globos incursaret eluderetque et insidias simul temptaret, tres incessus, totidem agmina parantur. Ex quis Cornelius Scipio legatus praefuit qua praedatio in Leptitanos et suffugia Garamantum; alio latere, ne Cirtensium pagi impune traherentur, propriam manum Blaesus filius duxit; medio cum delectis, castella et munitiones idoneis locis imponens, dux ipse arta et infensa hostibus cuncta fecerat, quia, quoquo inclinarent, pars aliqua militis Romani in ore, in latere et saepe

---

[1] Leader of the slaves and gladiators in the Servile War (73–71 B.C.). Of his half-dozen victories only two were, in strictness, over consular armies.

[2] Leptis Minor (*Lamta*)—Leptis Major (*Labda*) lying too far east to be reached by Tacfarinas, though it would be nearer the Garamantes (in Fezzan).

[3] See I. 19.

[4] The principal town in Numidia : later Constantina, now Constantine.

more than this spectacle of a deserter and bandit
aping the procedure of an unfriendly power. " Even
Spartacus,[1] after the annihilation of so many consular
armies, when his fires were blazing through an Italy
unavenged while the commonwealth reeled in the
gigantic conflicts with Sertorius and Mithridates,—
even Spartacus was not accorded a capitulation upon
terms. And now, at the glorious zenith of the
Roman nation, was this brigand Tacfarinas to be
bought off by a peace and a cession of lands? " He
handed over the affair to Blaesus; who, while induc-
ing the other rebels to believe they might sheathe
the sword with impunity, was to capture the leader
by any means whatsoever. Large numbers came in
under the amnesty. Then, the arts of Tacfarinas
were met by a mode of warfare akin to his own

LXXIV. Since it was noticed that the African,
overmatched in solid fighting strength but more
expert in the petty knaveries of war, operated with
a number of bands, first attacking, then vanishing,
and always manœuvring for an ambuscade, arrangements were made for three forward movements and
three columns to execute them. One, in charge of
the legate Cornelius Scipio, held the road by which
the enemy raided the Leptitanians [2] and then fell
back upon the Garamantians. On another side, the
younger Blaesus [3] marched with his own division to
prevent the hamlets of Cirta [4] from being ravaged
with impunity. In the centre, with the flower of
the troops, was the commander himself; who, by
securing the appropriate positions with fortresses or
entrenchments, had rendered the whole district
cramped and dangerous for his enemies. Turn where
they would, they found some part of the Roman

a tergo erat; multique eo modo caesi aut circumventi. Tunc tripertitum exercitum pluris in manus dispergit praeponitque centuriones virtutis expertae. Nec, ut mos fuerat, acta aestate retrahit copias aut in hibernaculis veteris provinciae componit, sed ut in limine belli dispositis castellis per expeditos et solitudinum gnaros mutantem mapalia Tacfarinatem proturbabat, donec fratre eius capto regressus est, properantius tamen quam ex utilitate sociorum, relictis per quos resurgeret bellum. Sed Tiberius pro confecto interpretatus id quoque Blaeso tribuit ut imperator a legionibus salutaretur, prisco erga duces honore qui bene gesta re publica gaudio et impetu victoris exercitus conclamabantur; erantque plures simul imperatores nec super ceterorum aequalitatem. Concessit quibusdam et Augustus id vocabulum ac tunc Tiberius Blaeso postremum.

LXXV. Obiere eo anno viri inlustres Asinius Saloninus, Marco Agrippa et Pollione Asinio avis, fratre Druso insignis Caesarique progener destinatus, et Capito Ateius, de quo memoravi, principem in civitate locum studiis civilibus adsecutus, sed avo

---

[1] The original province of Africa (annexed in 146 B.C.) had comprised merely the shrunken territories still held by Carthage immediately before her fall. Tripoli was a later accretion : then, after Thapsus (46 B.C.), the Cirta district, together with most of Numidia, became a separate command (" New Africa "), which in 25 B.C. was incorporated with the " Old Province."

[2] But not, apparently, after the formal institution of the principate in 27 B.C.

[3] He was the son of Asinius Gallus and Vipsania (daughter of Agrippa and first wife of Tiberius) and was to have married a daughter of Germanicus.

[4] I. 76 and 79; above, chap. 70.

forces—on the front, on the flank, often in the rear; and numbers were destroyed or entrapped by these methods. Next, he subdivided his tripartite army into yet more numerous detachments, headed by centurions of tested courage. Not even when summer was spent would he fall in with custom by withdrawing his men and quartering them for a winter's rest in the Old Province.[1] Precisely as though he stood on the threshold of a campaign, he arranged his chain of forts, and with flying columns of men familiar with the deserts kept hounding Tacfarinas from one desert camp to another; until at last, after capturing the renegade's brother, he returned; too hastily, however, for the interests of the province, since he left those behind him who were capable of resuscitating the war. Tiberius, however, chose to treat it as ended, and even conferred on Blaesus the privilege of being saluted *Imperator* by his legions: a time-honoured tribute to generals who, after a successful campaign, were acclaimed by the joyful and spontaneous voice of a conquering army. Several might hold the title simultaneously, nor did it raise them above an equality with their colleagues. It was awarded in a few cases even by Augustus[2]; and now for the last time Tiberius assigned it to Blaesus.

LXXV. This year saw the passing of two famous men: one, Asinius Saloninus, distinguished as the grandson of Marcus Agrippa and Asinius Pollio, as the brother of Drusus, and as the destined consort of the Caesar's grandchild[3]; the other, Ateius Capito, on whom I have touched already.[4] By his eminence as a jurist he had won the first position in the state; but his grandfather had been one of Sulla's cen-

centurione Sullano, patre praetorio. Consulatum ei adceleraverat Augustus ut Labeonem Antistium isdem artibus praecellentem dignatione eius magistratus anteiret. Namque illa aetas duo pacis decora simul tulit; sed Labeo incorrupta libertate et ob id fama celebratior, Capitonis obsequium dominantibus magis probabatur. Illi quod praeturam intra stetit commendatio ex iniuria, huic quod consulatum adeptus est odium ex invidia oriebatur.

LXXVI. Et Iunia, sexagesimo quarto post Philippensem aciem anno, supremum diem explevit, Catone avunculo genita, C. Cassii uxor, M. Bruti soror. Testamentum eius multo apud vulgum rumore fuit, quia in magnis opibus cum ferme cunctos proceres cum honore nominavisset Caesarem omisit. Quod civiliter acceptum; neque prohibuit quo minus laudatione pro rostris ceterisque sollemnibus funus cohonestaretur. Viginti clarissimarum familiarum imagines antelatae sunt, Manlii, Quinctii aliaque eiusdem nobilitatis nomina. Sed praefulgebant Cassius atque Brutus eo ipso quod effigies eorum non visebantur.

---

[1] Their names are famous in Roman jurisprudence as the founders of the two opposing schools of *Sabiniani* (followers of Capito) and *Proculiani* (followers of Labeo).

[2] Cato's sister, Servilia, was married first to M. Junius Brutus, then to D. Junius Silanus. Caesar's assassin, Brutus, sprang from the first union; Cassius' wife, Tertia (Tertulla), from the second.

turions, nor had his father risen above a praetorship. His consulate had been accelerated by Augustus, so that the prestige of that office should give him an advantage over Antistius Labeo, a commanding figure in the same profession. For that age produced together two of the glories of peace[1]; but, while Labeo's uncompromising independence assured him the higher reputation with the public, the pliancy of Capito was more to the taste of princes. The one, because he halted at the praetorship, won respect by his ill-treatment; the other, because he climbed to the consulate, reaped hatred from a begrudged success.

LXXVI. Junia, too, born niece to Cato, wife of Caius Cassius, sister of Marcus Brutus,[2] looked her last on life, sixty-three full years after the field of Philippi. Her will was busily discussed by the crowd; because in disposing of her great wealth she mentioned nearly every patrician of note in complimentary terms, but omitted the Caesar. The slur was taken in good part, and he offered no objection to the celebration of her funeral with a panegyric at the Rostra and the rest of the customary ceremonies. The effigies of twenty great houses preceded her to the tomb—members of the Manlian and Quinctian families, and names of equal splendour. But Brutus and Cassius shone brighter than all by the very fact that their portraits were unseen.

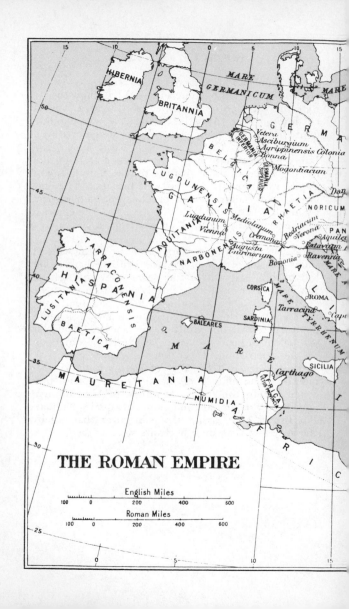

THE ROMAN EMPIRE

English Miles

100   0   200   400   600

Roman Miles

100   0   200   400   600

GERMANIA

English Miles

10 5 0   10   20   30   40   50   60

Angrivarii

Langobardi

Dümmer S.

Minden
Teutob.
Welch.Geb

Bückeburg

Steinhuder
Meer

Aller

Leine

SEMNONES

Elbe

CHERVSCI

Teutob.

Lippische.

DOREN
SCHLEUCHT

Externst.

Harz

Melibocus M.

Aliso

Paderborn

Weser

Cassel

Fritzlar

Adrana F.
(Eder)

Mattium

CHATTI

Hersfeld

Fulda

Fulda

Rhön
Geb

Taunus M.

Mattiaci

Frankfurt

Kinzig

Saale

HERMUNDURI

Kastellum
Mogontiacense

Worth

Spessart

Main

Main

Fichtel
Geb

Redniz

iones

Mo.

Heidelberg

Heilbronn

Naristi

Schwarzwald

Weissenburg

Altmühl

Castra Regina
Regensburg

Lorch

Rems

Donau

Donau

AGRIDECVMATES

Ulm

Danuvius F.

Augusta Vindelicum
Augsburg

RAETIA

Edward Stanford Ltd., London

Jerusalem

THIRD WALL

BEZETHA
(NEW CITY)

SECOND WALL

Damascus
Gate

Sheep's
Pools

Antonia
Fortress

Pool

St. Stephen's
Gate

New
Gate

Psephinus?

Amygdalon
Pool

Jaffa
Gate

Tower

FIRST WALL

Agrippa's
Palace

**TEMPLE
AREA**

Pool

**Herod's
Palace**

UPPER CITY

LOWER CITY

OPHLAS

Gihon
(Virgin's
Spring)

Serpent's
Pool

Valley of Hinnom

FIRST WALL

Essene Gate

Pool of
Siloam

Aqueduct
Water Gate

Valley of the Kedron

Tyropoeon

Valley

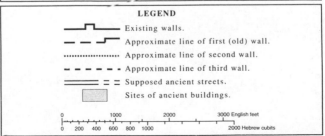

LEGEND

————	Existing walls.
– – – –	Approximate line of first (old) wall.
··············	Approximate line of second wall.
– · – · –	Approximate line of third wall.
═══ = =	Supposed ancient streets.
▨	Sites of ancient buildings.

0	1000	2000	3000 English feet
0	200 400 600 800 1000		2000 Hebrew cubits